FAT-FREE
LOW-FAT
COOKBOOK

200 RECIPES FOR DELICIOUSLY HEALTHY EATING, SHOWN IN
MORE THAN 850 STEP-BY-STEP PHOTOGRAPHS **ANNE SHEASBY**

southwater

This edition is published by Southwater, an imprint of Anness Publishing Ltd,
Blaby Road, Wigston, Leicestershire LE18 4SE; info@anness.com

www.southwaterbooks.com; www.annesspublishing.com

If you like the images in this book and would like to investigate using them for publishing, promotions
or advertising, please visit our website www.practicalpictures.com for more information.

Publisher: Joanna Lorenz
Senior Editor: Linda Fraser
Designer: Sara Kidd
Photographers: Karl Adamson, Steve Baxter, Amanda Heywood, Michael Michaels, Don Last, Edward Allwright,
Thomas Odulate, James Duncan, Peter Reilly, Patrick McLeavey
Recipes: Carla Capalbo and Laura Washburn, Stephen Wheeler, Christine France, Shirley Gill, Roz Denny, Annie Nichols
Linda Fraser, Catherine Atkinson, Maggie Pannell, Kit Chan, Sue Maggs, Christine Ingram
Home Economists: Wendy Lee, Jane Stevenson, Elizabeth Wolf Cohen, Kit Chan assisted by Lucy McKelvie, Kathryn Hawl
Stylists: Blake Minton and Kirsty Rawlings, Fiona Tillett, Hilary Guy, Thomas Odulate, Madeleine Brehaut, Jo Harris

© Anness Publishing Ltd 2012

NOTES
Bracketed terms are intended for American readers.
For all recipes, quantities are given in both metric and imperial measures and, where appropriate, in standard cups and spoo
Follow one set of measures, but not a mixture, because they are not interchangeable.
Standard spoon and cup measures are level. 1 tsp = 5ml, 1 tbsp = 15ml, 1 cup = 250ml/8fl oz.
Australian standard tablespoons are 20ml. Australian readers should use 3 tsp
in place of 1 tbsp for measuring small quantities.
American pints are 16fl oz/2 cups. American readers should use 20fl oz/2.5 cups in place of 1 pint when measuring liquid
Electric oven temperatures in this book are for conventional ovens. When using a fan oven, the temperature will probabl
need to be reduced by about 10–20°C/20–40°F. Since ovens vary, you should check with your manufacturer's
instruction book for guidance.
The nutritional analysis given for each recipe is calculated per portion (i.e. serving or item), unless otherwise stated.
If the recipe gives a range, such as Serves 4–6, then the nutritional analysis will be for the smaller portion size, i.e. 6 serving
The analysis does not include optional ingredients, such as salt added to taste.
Medium (US large) eggs are used unless otherwise stated.

CONTENTS

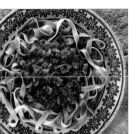

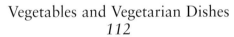

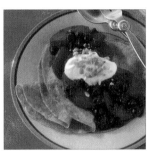

INTRODUCTION

Cooking and eating good food is one of life's greatest pleasures – and there's nothing wrong with enjoying good food, except that for too long good often meant fatty. Butter, oil, cheese and other fatty foods were considered essential for good cooking. We know now that all this fat – along with too much sugar and salt – has a huge impact on health.

Most of us eat fats in one form or another every day. In fact, we need to consume a small amount of fat to maintain a healthy and balanced diet, but almost everyone can afford to, and should, reduce their fat intake, particularly of saturated fats. Weight for weight, dietary fats supply far more energy than all the other nutrients in our diet. If you eat a diet that is high in fats and don't exercise enough to use up

that energy, you will put on weight. By cutting down on fat, you can easily reduce your energy intake without affecting the other essential nutrients. And by choosing the right types of fat, using low-fat and fat-free products whenever possible, and making small, simple changes to the way you cook and prepare food, you can reduce your overall fat intake quite dramatically and enjoy a much healthier diet without really noticing any difference.

As you will see, watching your fat intake doesn't have to mean dieting and deprivation. *The Ultimate Fat-Free Cookbook* opens with an informative introduction about basic healthy eating guidelines – you'll find out about the five main food groups, and how, by simply choosing a variety of food from these groups every day, you can

sure that you are eating all the nutrients
you need. One way to enjoy your favourite
foods without guilt is to substitute lower-fat
ingredients for higher-fat ones. This book
will introduce you to these lower-fat
ingredients and show you how to use them.
There are hints and tips on how to cook
with fat-free and low-fat ingredients;
techniques for using healthy, fat-free fruit
purée in place of butter or margarine in all
your favourite baking recipes; suggestions
for which foods to cut down on and what
to try instead; easy ways to reduce fat and
saturated fat in your foods; new no-fat and
low-fat cooking tech-niques and information
on the best cookware for fat-free cooking;
along with a delicious section on low-fat
and very low-fat snacks.

There are over 200 easy-to-follow recipes
for delicious dishes that your whole family
can enjoy. Every recipe has been developed
to fit into modern nutritional guidelines,
and each one has at-a-glance nutritional
information so you can instantly check the
calories and fat content. The recipes are
very low in fat – all contain less than five
grams of fat per serving and many contain
less than one. The selection of foods
included will surprise you: there are
barbecues and braises, pizza and pastas,
sautés and stews, vegetable dishes and
vegetarian main courses, fish and shellfish
dishes galore and delicious breads, cookies
and cakes. All without as much fat as
traditional recipes, of course, but packed
with flavour and vitality.

*Vegetables and beans, peas and lentils (far left), and fruit (left
and above) make ideal choices for fat-free and low-fat cooking.*

HEALTHY EATING GUIDELINES

A healthy diet is one that provides the body with all the nutrients it needs to be able to grow and repair properly. By eating the right types, balance and proportions of foods, we are more likely to feel healthy, have plenty of energy and a higher resistance to illness that will help protect our body against developing diseases such as heart disease, cancers, bowel disorders and obesity.

By choosing a variety of foods every day, you will ensure that you are supplying your body with all the essential nutrients, including vitamins and minerals, it needs. To get the balance right, it is important to know just how much of each type of food you should be eating.

There are five main food groups (see right), and it is recommended that we should eat plenty of fruit, vegetables (at least five portions a day, not including potatoes) and foods such as cereals,

pasta, rice and potatoes; moderate amounts of meat, fish, poultry and dairy products; and only small amounts of foods containing fat or sugar. By choosing a good balance of foods from these groups every day, and choosing lower-fat or lower-sugar alternatives wherever possible, we will be supplying our bodies with all the nutrients they need for optimum health.

THE ROLE AND IMPORTANCE OF FAT IN OUR DIET

Fats shouldn't be cut out of our diets completely. We need a small amount of fat for general health and well-being – fat is a valuable source of energy, and also helps to make foods more palatable to eat. However, if you lower the fats, especially saturated fats, in your diet, you will feel healthier; it will help you lose weight and reduce the risk of developing some diseases.

THE FIVE MAIN FOOD GROUPS

● Fruit and vegetables

● Rice, potatoes, bread, pasta and other cereals

● Meat, poultry, fish and alternative proteins

● Milk and other dairy foods

● Foods which contain fat and food which contain sugar

Aim to limit your daily intake of fats to no more than 30% of total calories. In real terms, this means tha for an average intake of 2,000 calori per day, 30% of energy would come from 600 calories. Since each gram o fat provides 9 calories, your total da intake should be no more than 66.6g fat. Your total intake of saturated fa should be no more than 10% of the total calories.

TYPES OF FAT

All fats in our foods are made up of building blocks of fatty acids and glycerol and their properties vary according to each combination.

There are two types of fat – saturated and unsaturated. The unsaturated group is divided into two types – polyunsaturated and monounsaturated fats.

There is always a combination of each of the three types of fat (satura polyunsaturated and monounsaturate fats) in any food, but the amount of each type varies greatly from one foo to another.

Left: By choosing a variety of foods from the five main food groups, you will ensure that you are supplying yo body with all the nutrients it needs.

SATURATED FATS

fatty acids are made up of chains of
ɔon atoms. Each atom has one or
·e free 'bonds' to link with other
ɪms and by doing so the fatty acids
ɪsport nutrients to cells throughout
body. Without these free 'bonds'
atom cannot form any links, that is
 say it is completely 'saturated'.
·ause of this, the body finds it hard
ɔrocess the fatty acid into energy, so
ɪmply stores it as fat.
Saturated fats are the fats which
ɪ should reduce, as they can increase
level of cholesterol in the blood,
ɪch in turn can increase the risk of
·eloping heart disease.
The main sources of saturated fats
animal products, such as meat, and
s, such as butter and lard (white
ɪking fat) that are solid at room
ɪperature. However, there are also
ɪrated fats of vegetable origin,
ɪably coconut and palm oils, and
ɪe margarines and oils, which are
ɪcessed by changing some of the
ɪaturated fatty acids to saturated
ɪs – they are labelled 'hydrogenated
ɪetable oil' and should be avoided.

POLYUNSATURATED FATS

ɪere are two types of polyunsaturated
s, those of vegetable or plant origin
ɪega 6), such as sunflower oil, soft
ɪrgarine and seeds, and those from
ɪ fish (omega 3), such as herring,
ɪckerel and sardines. Both fats are
ɪally liquid at room temperature.
ɪall quantities of polyunsaturated fats
essential for good health and are
ɪught to help reduce the level of
ɪlesterol in the blood.

MONOUNSATURATED FATS

ɪnounsaturated fats are also
ɪught to have the beneficial effect of
ɪucing the blood cholesterol level
ɪ this could explain why in some

Above: A selection of foods containing the three main types of fat found in foods.

Mediterranean countries there is such
a low incidence of heart disease.
Monounsaturated fats are found in
foods such as olive oil, rapeseed oil,
some nuts such as almonds and hazelnuts, oily fish and avocados.

CUTTING DOWN ON FATS AND
SATURATED FATS IN THE DIET

About one quarter of the fat we eat
comes from meat and meat products,
one-fifth from dairy products and
margarine and the rest from cakes,
cookies, pastries and other foods. It is
easy to cut down on obvious sources
of fat in the diet, such as butter, oils,
margarine, cream, full-fat (whole) milk
and full-fat cheese, but we also need to

know about – and watch out for –
'hidden' fats. Hidden fats can be found
in foods such as cakes, cookies and
nuts. Even lean, trimmed red meats
may contain as much as 10% fat.

By being aware of foods which
are high in fats and particularly
saturated fats, and by making simple
changes to your diet, you can reduce
the total fat content of your diet quite
considerably.

Whenever possible, choose
reduced-fat or low-fat alternatives to
foods such as milk, cheese and salad
dressings, and fill up on very low-fat
foods, such as fresh fruit and
vegetables, and foods that are high
in carbohydrate such as pasta, rice,
bread and potatoes.

EASY WAYS TO CUT DOWN FAT AND SATURATED FAT IN THE DAILY DIET

There are lots of simple no-fuss ways of reducing the fat in your diet. Just follow the simple 'eat less – try instead' suggestions below to discover how easy it is.

● EAT LESS – Butter, margarine and hard fats.

● TRY INSTEAD – low-fat spread, very low-fat spread or polyunsaturated margarine. If you must use butter or hard margarine, make sure they are softened at room temperature and spread them very thinly. Better still, use fat-free spreads such as low-fat soft cheese, reduced sugar jams or marmalades for sandwiches and toast.

● EAT LESS – Fatty meats and high-fat products such as meat pâtés, pies and sausages.

● TRY INSTEAD – low-fat meats, such as chicken, turkey and venison.

Use only the leanest cuts of such meats as lamb, beef and pork.

Always cut any visible fat and skin from meat before cooking.

Choose reduced-fat sausages and meat products and eat fish more often.

Try using low-fat protein products such as Quorn or tofu in place of meat in recipes.

Make gravies using vegetable water or fat-free stock rather than using meat juices.

● EAT LESS – Full-fat dairy products such as full-fat (whole) milk, cream, butter, hard margarine, crème fraîche, full-fat yogurts and hard cheese.

● TRY INSTEAD – Semi-skimmed (low-fat) or skimmed milk and milk products, low-fat yogurts and low-fat soft cheeses, reduced-fat hard cheeses such as Cheddar, and reduced-fat creams and crème fraîche.

● EAT LESS – Hard cooking fats, such as lard (white cooking fat) or margarine.

● TRY INSTEAD – Polyunsaturated or monounsaturated oils, such as olive, sunflower or corn oils for cooking.

● EAT LESS – Rich salad dressings such as full-fat mayonnaise, salad cream or French dressing.

● TRY INSTEAD – Reduced-fat or fat-free mayonnaise or dressings. Make salad dressings at home with low-fat yogurt.

● EAT LESS – Fried foods.

● TRY INSTEAD – Fat-free cooking methods such as grilling (broiling), microwaving, steaming or baking. Try cooking in a non-stick wok with only a very small amount of oil.

Always roast or grill (broil) meat or poultry on a rack.

● EAT LESS – Deep-fried chips (French fries) and sautéed potatoes.

● TRY INSTEAD – Fat-free starchy foods such as pasta, couscous and rice. Choose baked or boiled potatoes.

● EAT LESS – Added fat in cooking.

● TRY INSTEAD – To cook with little or no fat. Use heavy or good quality non-stick pans, so that the food doesn't stick.

Try using a small amount of spray oil in cooking to control exactly how much fat you are using.

Use fat-free or low-fat ingredients for cooking, such as fruit juice, low-fat or fat-free stock, wine or even beer.

● EAT LESS – High-fat snacks such as crisps (US potato chips), tortilla chips, fried snacks and pastries, cakes, muffins, doughnuts, sweet pastries and cookies – especially chocolate ones!

● TRY INSTEAD – low-fat and fat-free fresh or dried fruits, breadsticks or vegetable sticks.

Make your own home-baked low-fat cakes and cookies.

If you do buy ready-made cakes and cookies, always choose low-fat and reduced-fat versions.

FAT-FREE COOKING METHODS

t's very easy to cook without fat – whenever possible, grill (broil), bake, icrowave or steam foods without the ddition of fat, or try stir-frying with- ut fat – use a little low-fat or fat-free ock, wine or fruit juice instead.

Choosing heavy or good quality ookware, you'll find that the amount f fat needed for cooking foods can be ept to an absolute minimum. When aking casseroles or meat sauces such s bolognese, dry-fry the meat to rown it and then drain off all the xcess fat before adding the other ngredients. If you do need a little fat or cooking, choose an oil that is igh in unsaturates such as corn, unflower, olive or rapeseed oil and lways use as little as possible.

● When baking low-fat cakes and cookies, use good quality bakeware which doesn't need greasing before use, or use baking parchment and only lightly grease before lining.

● Look out for non-stick coated fabric sheet. This re-usable non-stick material is very versatile, it can be cut to size and used to line cake tins (pans), baking sheets or frying pans. Heat resistant up to 290°C/550°F and microwave safe, it will last for up to 5 years.

● When baking foods such as chicken or fish, rather than adding a knob (pat) of butter to the food, try baking the food in a loosely sealed parcel of foil or baking parchment and adding some wine or fruit juice and herbs or spices to the food before sealing the parcel.

● When grilling (broiling) foods, the addition of fat is often unnecessary. If the food shows signs of drying, lightly brush with a small amount of unsatu- rated oil such as sunflower or corn oil.

Above: Invest in a few of these useful items of cookware for easy fat-free cooking: non-stick cookware and accurate measuring equipment are essential.

● Microwaved foods rarely need the addition of fat, so add herbs or spices for extra flavour and colour.

● Steaming or boiling are easy, fat-free ways of cooking many foods, especially vegetables, fish and chicken.

● Try poaching foods, such as chicken, fish and fruit, in stock or syrup – it is another easy, fat-free cooking method.

● Try braising vegetables in the oven in low-fat or fat-free stock, wine or simply water with the addition of some herbs.

● Sauté vegetables in low-fat or fat-free stock, wine or fruit juice instead of fat or oil.

● Cook vegetables in a covered pan over a low heat with a little water so they cook in their own juices.

● Marinate food such as meat or poultry in mixtures of alcohol, herbs or spices, and vinegar or fruit juice. This will help to tenderize the meat and add flavour and colour and, in addition, the marinade can be used to baste the food while it is cooking.

● When serving vegetables such as boiled potatoes, carrots or peas, resist the temptation to add a knob of butter or margarine. Instead, sprinkle with chopped fresh herbs or ground spices, or squeeze over a little lemon juice to enhance the natural flavour.

COOKING WITH LOW-FAT OR NON-FAT INGREDIENTS

Nowadays many foods are available in full-fat and reduced-fat or very low-fat forms. In every supermarket you'll find a huge array of low-fat dairy products, such as milk, cream, yogurt, and hard and soft cheeses; reduced-fat sweets (candies) or chocolate biscuits (cookies); reduced-fat or fat-free salad dressings and mayonnaise; reduced-fat crisps (US potato chips) and snacks; low-fat, half-fat or very low-fat spreads; as well as such reduced-fat ready-made food products as desserts.

Other foods, such as fresh fruit and vegetables, pasta, rice, couscous potatoes and bread, contain very little fat. Some foods, such as soy sauce, wine, cider, sherry, sugar, honey, syrup and jam, contain no fat at all. By combining these and other low-fat foods you can create delicious dishes which contain very little fat.

Some low-fat or reduced-fat ingredients work better than others in cooking but often a simple substitution of one for another will work. The addition of low-fat or no-fat ingredients, such as herbs and spices, also adds plenty of extra flavour and colour to recipes.

LOW-FAT SPREADS IN COOKING

There is a huge variety of low-fat, reduced-fat and half-fat spreads available in supermarkets, along with some spreads that are very low in fat. Some are suitable for cooking, while others are only suitable for spreading.

Generally speaking, the very low-fat spreads with a fat content of around 20% or less have a high water content, which means that they are all unsuitable for cooking and are only suitable for spreading.

Low-fat or half-fat spreads with a fat content of around 40% are suitable for spreading and can be used for some cooking methods. They are suitable for recipes such as all-in-one cake and cookie recipes, all-in-one sauce recipes, sautéing vegetables over a low heat, choux pastry and some cake icings.

When using these low-fat spreads for cooking, the fat may behave slightly differently to full-fat products such as butter or margarine.

With some recipes, the cooked result may be slightly different, but will still be very acceptable. Other recipes will be just as tasty and successful. For example, choux pastry made using half- or low-fat spread is often slightly crisper and lighter in texture than traditional choux pastry, and a cheese-cake base made with melted half- or

low-fat spread combined with crushed cookie crumbs, may be slightly softer in texture and less crispy than a base made using melted butter.

When heating half- or low-fat spreads, never cook them over a high heat. Always use a heavy pan over a low heat to avoid the product burning, spitting or spoiling, and stir all the time. With all-in-one sauces, the mixture should be whisked continuously over low heat.

Half-fat or low-fat spreads are not suitable for shallow or deep-fat frying, pastry making, rich fruit cakes, some cookies, shortbread, clarified butter and preserves such as lemon curd.

Remember that the keeping quality of recipes made using half- or low-fat spreads may be reduced slightly, due the lower fat content.

Almost all dairy products now come in low-fat or reduced-fat versions.

other way to reduce the fat content recipes, particularly cake recipes is use a fruit purée in place of all or ne of the fat in a recipe. Many cake recipes work well using s method but others may not be so cessful. Pastry does not work well. ads work very well, perhaps because amount of fat is usually relatively all, as do some cookies and bars, h as brownies and flapjacks.

To make the dried fruit purée to use recipes, chop 115g/4oz/1 cup ready- to-eat dried fruit and place in a blender or food processor with 75ml/5 tbsp water and blend to a roughly smooth purée. Then, simply substitute the same weight of this dried fruit purée for all or just some of the amount of fat in the recipe. The purée will keep in the refrigerator for up to three days.

You can use prunes, dried apricots, dried peaches, or dried apples, or substitute mashed fresh fruit, such as ripe bananas or lightly cooked apples, without the added water.

LOW-FAT AND VERY LOW-FAT SNACKS

Instead of reaching for a packet of crisps (US potato chips), a cookie or a chocolate bar when hunger strikes, choose one of these tasty low-fat snacks to fill that hungry hole.

● A piece of fresh fruit or vegetable such as an apple, banana or carrot – keep chunks or sticks wrapped in a plastic bag in the refrigerator.

● Fresh fruit or vegetable chunks – skewer them on to cocktail sticks (toothpicks) or short bamboo skewers to make them into mini kebabs.

● A handful of dried fruit such as raisins, apricots or sultanas (golden raisins). These also make a perfect addition to children's packed lunches or to school break snacks.

● A portion of canned fruit in natural fruit juice – serve with a spoonful or two of fat-free yogurt.

● One or two crisp rice cakes – delicious on their own, or topped with honey, or reduced-fat cheese.

● Crackers, such as water biscuits or crisp breads, spread with reduced-sugar jam or marmalade.

● A bowl of wholewheat breakfast cereal or no-added-sugar muesli (granola) served with skimmed milk.

● A very low-fat plain (natural) or fruit yogurt.

● A toasted teacake spread with reduced-sugar jam or marmalade.

● Toasted crumpet spread with yeast extract or beef extract.

ove: A selection of cooking oils and low-fat spreads. Always check the packaging low-fat spreads – for cooking, they must have a fat content of about 40%.

THE FAT AND CALORIE CONTENTS OF FOOD

The following figures show the weight of fat (g) and the energy content per 100g/4oz of each food.

VEGETABLES

	FAT (g)	ENERGY		FAT (g)	ENERGY
Broccoli	0.9	33 Kcals/138 kJ	Onions	0.2	36 Kcals/151 kJ
Cabbage	0.4	26 Kcals/109 kJ	Peas	1.5	83 Kcals/344 kJ
Carrots	0.3	35 Kcals/146 kJ	Potatoes	0.2	75 Kcals/318 kJ
Cauliflower	0.9	34 Kcals/142 kJ	French fries, home-made	6.7	189 Kcals/796 kJ
Courgettes (zucchini)	0.4	18 Kcals/74 kJ	French fries, retail	12.4	239 Kcals/1001 k
Cucumber	0.1	10 Kcals/40 kJ	Oven-fries, frozen, baked	4.2	162 Kcals/687 kJ
Mushrooms	0.5	13 Kcals/55 kJ	Tomatoes	0.3	17 Kcals/73 kJ

BEANS, PEAS AND LENTILS

	FAT (g)	ENERGY		FAT (g)	ENERGY
Black-eyed beans, cooked	1.8	116 Kcals/494 kJ	Hummus	12.6	187 Kcals/781 kJ
Butter (lima) beans, canned	0.5	77 Kcals/327 kJ	Red kidney beans, canned	0.6	100 Kcals/424 kJ
Chickpeas, canned	2.9	115 Kcals/487 kJ	Red lentils, cooked	0.4	100 Kcals/424 kJ

FISH AND SHELLFISH

	FAT (g)	ENERGY		FAT (g)	ENERGY
Cod fillets, raw	0.7	80 Kcals/337 kJ	Prawns (shrimp)	0.9	99 Kcals/418 kJ
Crab, canned	0.5	77 Kcals/326 kJ	Trout, grilled (broiled)	5.4	135 Kcals/565 kJ
Haddock, raw	0.6	81 Kcals/345 kJ	Tuna, canned in brine	0.6	99 Kcals/422 kJ
Lemon sole, raw	1.5	83 Kcals/351 kJ	Tuna, canned in oil	9.0	189 Kcals/794 kJ

MEAT PRODUCTS

	FAT (g)	ENERGY		FAT (g)	ENERGY
Bacon, streaky (fatty)	39.5	414 Kcals/1710 kJ	Chicken fillet, raw	1.1	106 Kcals/449 kJ
Turkey rasher (strip)	1.0	99 Kcals/414 kJ	Chicken, roasted	12.5	218 Kcals/910 kJ
Minced (ground) beef, raw	16.2	225 Kcals/934 kJ	Duck, meat only, raw	6.5	137 Kcals/575 kJ
Minced beef, extra lean, raw	9.6	174 Kcals/728 kJ	Duck, roasted, meat,		
Rump steak, lean and fat	10.1	174 Kcals/726 kJ	fat and skin	38.1	423 Kcals/1750 k
Rump steak, lean only	4.1	125 Kcals/526 kJ	Turkey, meat only, raw	1.6	105 Kcals/443 kJ
Lamb chops, loin, lean and fat	23.0	277 Kcals/1150 kJ	Liver, lamb, raw	6.2	137 Kcals/575 kJ
Lamb, average, lean, raw	8.3	156 Kcals/651 kJ	Pork pie	27.0	376 Kcals/1564 k
Pork chops, loin, lean and fat	21.7	270 Kcals/1119 kJ	Salami	45.2	491 Kcals/2031 k
Pork, average, lean, raw	4.0	123 Kcals/519 kJ	Sausage roll, flaky pastry	36.4	477 Kcals/1985 k

Information from *The Composition of Foods* (5th Edition 1991) is reproduced with the permission of the Royal Society of Chemistry and the Controller of Her Majesty's Stationery Office.

DAIRY, FATS AND OILS

	FAT (g)	ENERGY		FAT (g)	ENERGY
am, double (heavy)	48.0	449 Kcals/1849 kJ	Low-fat yogurt, natural (plain)	0.8	56 Kcals/236 kJ
am, single (light)	19.1	198 Kcals/817 kJ	Greek (US strained		
am, whipping	39.3	373 Kcals/1539 kJ	plain) yogurt	9.1	115 Kcals/477 kJ
me fraîche	40.0	379 Kcals/156 kJ	Reduced-fat Greek yogurt	5.0	80 Kcals/335 kJ
luced-fat crème fraîche	15.0	165 Kcals/683 kJ	Butter	81.7	737 Kcals/3031 kJ
luced-fat double cream	24.0	243 Kcals/1002 kJ	Margarine	81.6	739 Kcals/3039 kJ
k, skimmed	0.1	33 Kcals/130 kJ	Low-fat spread	40.5	390 Kcals/1605 kJ
k, full-fat (whole)	3.9	66 Kcals/275 kJ	Very low-fat spread	25	273 Kcals/1128 kJ
e	26.9	319 Kcals/1323 kJ	Lard (white cooking fat)	99.0	891 Kcals/3663 kJ
eddar cheese	34.4	412 Kcals/1708 kJ	Corn oil	99.9	899 Kcals/3696 kJ
eddar-type, reduced-fat	15.0	261 Kcals/1091 kJ	Olive oil	99.9	899 Kcals/3696 kJ
am cheese	47.4	439 Kcals/1807 kJ	Eggs	10.8	147 Kcals/612 kJ
mage frais, plain	7.1	113 Kcals/469 kJ	Egg yolk	30.5	339 Kcals/1402 kJ
mage frais, very low-fat	0.2	58 Kcals/247 kJ	Egg white	Trace	36 Kcals/153 kJ
mmed milk soft cheese	Trace	74 Kcals/313 kJ	Fat-free dressing	1.2	67 Kcals/282 kJ
am cheese	25.4	333 Kcals/1382 kJ	French dressing	49.4	462 Kcals/1902 kJ
a cheese	20.2	250 Kcals/1037 kJ	Mayonnaise	75.6	691 Kcals/2843 kJ
mesan cheese	32.7	452 Kcals/1880 kJ	Mayonnaise, reduced-calorie	28.1	288 Kcals/1188 kJ

CEREALS, BAKING AND PRESERVES

	FAT (g)	ENERGY		FAT (g)	ENERGY
wn rice, uncooked	2.8	357 Kcals/1518 kJ	Digestive biscuit		
ite rice, uncooked	3.6	383 Kcals/1630 kJ	(graham cracker)	20.9	471 Kcals/1978 kJ
ta, white, uncooked	1.8	342 Kcals/1456 kJ	Shortbread	26.1	498 Kcals/2087 kJ
ta, wholemeal			Madeira cake	16.9	393 Kcals/1652 kJ
whole-wheat), uncooked	2.5	324 Kcal/1379 kJ	Fatless sponge cake	6.1	294 Kcals/1245 kJ
wn bread	2.0	218 Kcals/927 kJ	Doughnut, jam	14.5	336 Kcals/1414 kJ
ite bread	1.9	235 Kcals/1002 kJ	Sugar, white	0 3	94 Kcals/1680 kJ
olemeal bread	2.5	215 Kcals/914 kJ	Chocolate, milk	30.7	520 Kcals/2177 kJ
rnflakes	0.7	360 Kcals/1535 kJ	Chocolate, plain (semisweet)	28	510 Kcals/2157 kJ
iss-style muesli (granola)	5.9	363 Kcals/1540 kJ	Honey	0	288 Kcals/1229 kJ
pissant	20.3	360 Kcals/1505 kJ	Lemon curd	5.0	283 Kcals/1198 kJ
pjack	26.6	484 Kcals/2028 kJ	Fruit jam	0 26	268 Kcals/1114 kJ

FRUIT AND NUTS

	FAT (g)	ENERGY		FAT (g)	ENERGY
ples, eating	0.1	47 Kcals/199 kJ	Pears	0.1	40 Kcals/169 kJ
ocados	19.5	190 Kcals/784 kJ	Almonds	55.8	612 Kcals/2534 kJ
nanas	0.3	95 Kcals/403 kJ	Brazil nuts	68.2	682 Kcals/2813 kJ
ied mixed fruit	0.4	268 Kcals/1114 kJ	Hazelnuts	63.5	650 Kcals/2685 kJ
apefruit	0.1	30 Kcals/126 kJ	Pine nuts	68.6	688 Kcals/2840 kJ
anges	0.1	37 Kcals/158 kJ	Walnuts	68.5	688 Kcals/2837kJ
ches	0.1	33 Kcals/142 kJ	Peanut butter, smooth	53.7	623 Kcals/2581 kJ

SOUPS

Home-made soups are ideal served as an appetizer, a snack or for lunch. They are sustaining, nutritious and low in fat and are delicious served with a chunk of fresh crusty bread. The wide variety of fresh vegetables available ensures that the freshest ingredients can be used to create tempting and delicious home-made soups. We include a tasty selection, including vegetable soups, chowders and bean and pasta soups. Choose from temptations such as Italian Vegetable Soup, Spicy Tomato and Lentil Soup, and Creamy Cod Chowder.

Italian Vegetable Soup

The success of this clear soup depends on the quality of the stock, so for the best results, be sure you use home-made vegetable stock rather than stock (bouillon) cubes.

Ingredients

Serves 4

1 small carrot
1 baby leek
1 celery stick
50g/2oz green cabbage
900ml/1½ pints/3¾ cups vegetable stock
1 bay leaf
115g/4oz/1 cup cooked cannellini or
   haricot (navy) beans
25g/1oz/⅓ cup soup pasta, such as tiny
   shells, bows, stars or elbows
salt and black pepper
snipped fresh chives, to garnish

1 Cut the carrot, leek and celery into 5cm/2in long julienne strips. Slice the cabbage very finely.

Nutrition Notes

Per portion:	
Energy	69Kcals/288kJ
Protein	3.67g
Fat	0.71g
Saturated Fat	0.05g
Fibre	2.82g

2 Put the stock and bay leaf into a large pan and bring to the boil. Add the carrot, leek and celery, cover and simmer for 6 minutes.

3 Add the cabbage, beans and pasta shapes. Stir, then simmer uncovered for a further 4–5 minutes, or until the vegetables and pasta are tender.

4 Remove the bay leaf and season with salt and pepper to taste. Ladl[e] into four soup bowls and garnish with snipped chives. Serve immediately.

CHICKEN AND PASTA SOUP

INGREDIENTS

rves 4–6
0ml/1½ pints/3¾ cups chicken stock
ay leaf
spring onions (scallions), sliced
5g/8oz button (white)
mushrooms, sliced
5g/4oz cooked chicken breast
g/2oz soup pasta
0ml/¼ pint/⅔ cup dry
white wine
ml/1 tbsp chopped fresh parsley
t and black pepper

NUTRITION NOTES	
Per portion:	
Energy	126Kcals/529kJ
Fat	2.2g
Saturated Fat	0.6g
Cholesterol	19mg
Fibre	1.3g

Put the stock and bay leaf into a
pan and bring to the boil.

Add the sliced spring onions and
mushrooms to the stock.

3 Remove the skin from the chicken
and slice the meat thinly using a
sharp knife. Add to the soup and
season to taste. Heat through for about
2–3 minutes.

4 Add the pasta, cover and simmer
for 7–8 minutes. Just before serving,
add the wine and chopped parsley, heat
through for 2–3 minutes, then season
to taste.

BEETROOT SOUP WITH RAVIOLI

INGREDIENTS

Serves 4–6

1 quantity basic pasta dough (see page 68)
egg white, beaten, for brushing
flour, for dusting
1 small onion or shallot, finely chopped
2 garlic cloves, crushed
5ml/1 tsp fennel seeds
600ml/1 pint/2½ cups chicken stock
225g/8oz cooked beetroot (beet)
30ml/2 tbsp fresh orange juice
fennel or dill leaves, to garnish
crusty bread, to serve

For the filling

115g/4oz mushrooms, finely chopped
1 shallot or small onion, finely chopped
1–2 garlic cloves, crushed
5ml/1 tsp chopped fresh thyme
15ml/1 tbsp chopped fresh parsley
90ml/6 tbsp fresh white breadcrumbs
salt and black pepper
large pinch of ground nutmeg

1 Process all the filling ingredients and scoop into a bowl.

NUTRITION NOTES

Per portion:

Energy	358Kcals/1504kJ
Fat	4.9g
Saturated Fat	1.0g
Cholesterol	110mg
Fibre	4.3g

2 Roll the pasta dough into thin sheets. Lay one piece over a ravio tray and put a teaspoonful of the filli into each depression. Brush around t edges of each ravioli with egg white. Cover with another sheet of pasta, press the edges well together to seal and separate the individual shapes. Transfer to a floured dish towel and rest for 1 hour before cooking.

3 Cook the ravioli in a large pan of boiling, salted water for 2 minute in batches to stop them sticking togeth Remove and drop into a bowl of cold water for 5 seconds before placing on tray. (You can make these pasta shape a day in advance. Cover with clear fi (plastic wrap) and refrigerate.)

4 Put the onion, garlic and fennel seeds into a pan with 150ml/ ¼ pint/⅔ cup of the stock. Bring to the boil, cover and simmer for 5 minu until tender. Peel and dice the beetroc (reserve 60ml/4 tbsp for the garnish). Add the rest of the beetroot to the so with the remaining stock and bring to the boil.

5 Add the orange juice and cooked ravioli and simmer for 2 minutes. Pour into shallow soup bowls and garnish with the reserved diced beetroot and fennel or dill leaves.

Spicy Tomato and Lentil Soup

ves 4

nl/1 tbsp sunflower oil

nion, finely chopped

 garlic cloves, crushed

cm/1in piece fresh root ginger,
eeled and finely chopped

l/1 tsp cumin seeds, crushed

)g/1lb ripe tomatoes, peeled, seeded
nd chopped

g/4oz/½ cup red split lentils

litres/2 pints/5 cups vegetable or
hicken stock

nl/1 tbsp tomato purée (paste)

and black pepper

-fat natural (plain) yogurt and
hopped parsley, to garnish (optional)

Heat the sunflower oil in a large,
heavy pan and cook the chopped
on gently for about 5 minutes,
il softened.

Stir in the garlic, ginger and cumin,
followed by the tomatoes and
tils. Cook over a low heat for a
ther 3–4 minutes.

3 Stir in the stock and tomato purée.
Bring to the boil, then lower the
heat and simmer gently for about
30 minutes until the lentils are soft.
Season to taste with salt and pepper.

4 Purée the soup in a blender or food
processor. Return to the clean pan
and reheat gently. Serve in heated
bowls. If liked, garnish each portion
with a swirl of yogurt and a little
chopped parsley.

NUTRITION NOTES	
Per portion:	
Energy	165Kcals/695kJ
Fat	4g
Saturated Fat	0.5g
Cholesterol	0

CREAMY COD CHOWDER

A delicious light version of a classic, this chowder is a tasty combination of smoked fish, vegetables, fresh herbs and milk. To cut the calories and stock even more, use vegetable or fish stock in place of the milk. Serve as a substantial appetizer or snack, or as a light main meal accompanied by warm crusty wholemeal (whole-wheat) bread.

INGREDIENTS

Serves 4–6
350g/12oz smoked cod fillet
1 small onion, finely chopped
1 bay leaf
4 black peppercorns
900ml/1½ pints/3¾ cups skimmed milk
10ml/2 tsp cornflour (cornstarch)
200g/7oz canned corn kernels
15ml/1 tbsp chopped fresh parsley

1 Skin the fish and put it into a large pan with the onion, bay leaf and peppercorns. Pour over the milk.

2 Bring to the boil, then reduce the heat and simmer very gently for 12–15 minutes, or until the fish is just cooked. Do not overcook.

3 Using a slotted spoon, lift out the fish and flake into large chunks. Remove the bay leaf and peppercorns and discard.

4 Blend the cornflour with 10ml/2 tsp cold water and add to the pan. Bring to the boil and simmer for about 1 minute or until slightly thickened.

5 Drain the corn kernels and add t the pan together with the flaked fish and parsley. Reheat gently and serve hot.

COOK'S TIP
The flavour of the chowder improves if it is made a day in advance. Leave to cool, then chill in the refrigerator until required. Reheat gently over a low heat. D not allow the soup to boil, or the fish will disintegrate.

NUTRITION NOTES

Per portion:
Energy	200Kcals/840k
Protein	24.71
Fat	1.23
Saturated Fat	0.32

Spinach and Tofu Soup

This appetizing clear soup has an extremely delicate and mild flavour that can be used as a perfect counterbalance to the intense heat of a hot Thai curry.

Ingredients

Serves 6

30ml/2 tbsp dried shrimps
1 litre/1¾ pints/4 cups chicken stock
225g/8oz fresh tofu, drained and cut
  into 2cm/¾in cubes
30ml/2 tbsp fish sauce
350g/12oz fresh spinach, washed
black pepper
2 spring onions (scallions), finely sliced,
  to garnish

1 Rinse and drain the dried shrimps. Combine the shrimps with the chicken stock in a large pan and bring to the boil.

2 Add the tofu and simmer for about 5 minutes. Season with fish sauce and black pepper to taste.

3 Tear the spinach leaves into bites pieces and add to the soup. Cook for another 1–2 minutes.

4 Remove from the heat and sprink with the finely sliced spring onio to garnish.

Nutrition Notes

Per portion:

Energy	64Kcals/270k
Fat	225g
Saturated Fat	0.26g
Cholesterol	25mg
Fibre	1.28g

Cook's Tip
Home-made chicken stock makes the world of difference to clear soups. Accumulate enough bones to make a big batch of stock, use what you need and keep the rest in the freezer.

Put 1.5kg/3–3½lb meaty chicken bones and 450g/1lb pork bones (optional) into a large pan. Add 3 litres/5 pints/12 cups water and slowly bring to the boil. Occasionally skim off and discard any scum that rises to the surface. Add 2 slices fresh root ginger, 2 garlic cloves (optional), 2 celery sticks, 4 spring onions (scallions), 2 bruised lemon grass stalks, a few sprigs of coriander (cilantro) and 10 crushed black peppercorns Reduce the heat to low and simmer for about 2–2½ hours.

Remove from the heat and leave to cool, uncovered and undisturbed. Pour the liquid through a fine strainer, leaving the last dregs behind as they tend to cloud the soup. Leave to cool, then chill. Use as required, removing any fat that congeals on the surface.

VEGETABLE MINESTRONE

INGREDIENTS

ves 6–8
e pinch of saffron strands
nion, chopped
ek, sliced
lery stick, sliced
rrots, diced
garlic cloves, crushed
ml/1 pint/2½ cups chicken stock
400g/14oz cans chopped tomatoes
/2oz/½ cup frozen peas
/2oz soup pasta (anellini)
/1 tsp caster (superfine) sugar
l/1 tbsp chopped fresh parsley
l/1 tbsp chopped fresh basil
and black pepper

Soak the pinch of saffron strands in
15ml/1 tbsp boiling water. Leave to
d for 10 minutes.

Meanwhile, put the prepared onion,
leek, celery, carrots and garlic into a
ge pan. Add the chicken stock, bring
he boil, cover and simmer for about
minutes.

3 Add the canned tomatoes, the saffron
with its liquid and the frozen peas.
Bring back to the boil and add the
soup pasta. Simmer for 10 minutes
until tender.

COOK'S TIP
Saffron strands aren't essential
for this soup, but they give a
wonderful delicate flavour, with
the bonus of a lovely rich orange-
yellow colour.

4 Season with sugar, salt and pepper
to taste. Stir in the chopped herbs
just before serving.

NUTRITION NOTES

Per portion:
Energy	87Kcals/367kJ
Fat	0.7g
Saturated Fat	0.1g
Cholesterol	0
Fibre	3.3g

Corn Chowder with Pasta Shells

Smoked turkey rashers provide a tasty, low-fat alternative to bacon in this hearty dish. If you prefer, omit the meat altogether and serve the soup as is.

Ingredients

Serves 4

1 small green (bell) pepper
450g/1lb potatoes, peeled and diced
350g/12oz/2 cups canned or frozen
   corn kernels
1 onion, chopped
1 celery stick, chopped
a bouquet garni (bay leaf, parsley
   stalks and thyme)
600ml/1 pint/2½ cups chicken stock
300ml/½ pint/1¼ cups skimmed milk
50g/2oz small pasta shells
oil, for frying
150g/5oz smoked turkey rashers, diced
salt and black pepper
bread sticks, to serve

1 Halve the green pepper, then remove the stalk and seeds. Cut the flesh into small dice, cover with boiling water and stand for 2 minutes. Drain and rinse.

Nutrition Notes	
Per portion:	
Energy	215Kcals/904kJ
Fat	1.6g
Saturated Fat	0.3g
Cholesterol	13mg
Fibre	2.8g

2 Put the potatoes into a pan with corn, onion, celery, green pepper, bouquet garni and stock. Bring to the boil, cover and simmer for 20 minutes until tender.

3 Add the milk and season with salt and pepper. Process half of the soup in a food processor or blender and return to the pan with the pasta shells. Simmer for 10 minutes.

4 Fry the turkey rashers in a non-stick frying pan for 2–3 minutes. Stir into the soup. Season to taste and serve with bread sticks.

CARROT AND CORIANDER SOUP

arly all root vegetables make
ellent soups as they purée
l and have an earthy flavour
ich complements the sharper
ours of herbs and spices.
rrots are particularly versatile,
l this simple soup is elegant in
h flavour and appearance.

INGREDIENTS

es 6

l/2 tsp sunflower oil
ion, chopped
lery stick, sliced, plus 2–3 leafy
lery tops
nall potatoes, chopped
g/1lb carrots, preferably young and
nder, chopped
re/1¾ pints/4 cups chicken stock
15ml/2–3 tsp ground coriander
l/1 tbsp chopped fresh
riander (cilantro)
ml/7fl oz/1 cup semi-skimmed
ow-fat) milk
and black pepper

Heat the oil in a large flameproof
casserole or heavy pan and fry the
on over a gentle heat for 3–4 minutes
l slightly softened but not browned.
l the celery and potato, cook for a
minutes, then add the carrot. Fry
r a gentle heat for 3–4 minutes,
ing frequently, and then cover.
luce the heat even further and cook
about 10 minutes. Shake the pan or
occasionally so the vegetables do
stick to the base.

2 Add the stock, bring to the boil and
then partially cover and simmer for
a further 8–10 minutes until the carrot
and potato are tender.

3 Remove 6–8 tiny celery leaves for a
garnish and finely chop about
15ml/1 tbsp of the remaining celery
tops. In a small pan, dry-fry the ground
coriander for about 1 minute, stirring
constantly. Reduce the heat, add the
chopped celery and fresh coriander and
fry for about 1 minute. Set aside.

4 Process in a food processor or
blender and pour into a clean
pan. Stir in the milk, coriander
mixture and seasoning. Heat gently,
taste and adjust the seasoning. Serve
garnished with the reserved celery.

NUTRITION NOTES

Per portion:

Energy	76.5Kcals/320kJ
Fat	3.2g
Saturated fat	0.65g
Cholesterol	2.3mg
Fibre	2.2g

COOK'S TIPS

For a more piquant flavour, add
a little freshly squeezed lemon
juice just before serving. The
contrast between the orange-
coloured soup and the green
garnish is a feast for the eye as
well as the tastebuds.

Chicken and Coconut Soup

This aromatic soup is rich with coconut milk and intensely flavoured with galangal, lemon grass and kaffir lime leaves.

INGREDIENTS

Serves 4–6

750ml/1¼ pints/3 cups coconut milk
475ml/16fl oz/2 cups chicken stock
4 lemon grass stalks, bruised
* and chopped*
2.5cm/1in section galangal, thinly sliced
10 black peppercorns, crushed
10 kaffir lime leaves, torn
300g/11oz boneless chicken, cut into
* thin strips*
115g/4oz button (white) mushrooms
50g/2oz baby corn
60ml/4 tbsp lime juice
about 45ml/3 tbsp fish sauce
2 fresh chillies, seeded and chopped,
* chopped spring onions (scallions), and*
* coriander (cilantro) leaves, to garnish*

1 Bring the coconut milk and chicken stock to the boil. Add the lemon grass, galangal, peppercorns and half the kaffir lime leaves. Reduce the heat and simmer gently for 10 minutes.

2 Strain the stock into a clean pan. Return to the heat, then add the chicken, button mushrooms and baby corn. Simmer for 5–7 minutes or until the chicken is cooked.

3 Stir in the lime juice, fish sauce to taste and the rest of the lime leaves. Serve hot, garnished with chillies, spring onions and coriander.

NUTRITION NOTES	
Per portion:	
Energy	144Kcals/609kJ
Fat	2.5g
Saturated Fat	0.55g
Cholesterol	67.5mg
Fibre	0.6g

Hot and Sour Prawn Soup

This is a classic Thai shellfish soup and is probably the most popular and well-known soup from Thailand.

INGREDIENTS

Serves 4–6

450g/1lb king prawns (jumbo shrimp)
1 litre/1¾ pints/4 cups chicken stock
3 lemon grass stalks
10 kaffir lime leaves, torn in half
225g/8oz can straw mushrooms, drained
45ml/3 tbsp fish sauce
50ml/2fl oz/¼ cup lime juice
30ml/2 tbsp chopped spring
* onions (scallions)*
15ml/1 tbsp coriander (cilantro) leaves
4 fresh chillies, seeded and chopped
salt and black pepper

1 Shell and devein the prawns and set aside. Rinse the prawn shells, place them in a large pan with the stock and bring to the boil.

2 Bruise the lemon grass stalks with the blunt edge of a chopping knife and add them to the stock together with half the lime leaves. Simmer gently for 5–6 minutes, until the stalks change colour and the stock is fragrant.

NUTRITION NOTES	
Per portion:	
Energy	49Kcals/209kJ
Fat	0.45g
Saturated Fat	0.07g
Cholesterol	78.8mg
Fibre	0.09g

3 Strain the stock, return to the pan and reheat. Add the mushrooms and prawns, then cook until the prawns turn pink. Stir in the fish sauce, lime juice, spring onions, coriander, chillies and the rest of the lime leaves. Taste the soup and adjust the seasoning – it should be sour, salty, spicy and hot.

Red Onion and Beetroot Soup

This beautiful vivid ruby-red soup will look stunning at any dinner party.

Ingredients

Serves 6

10ml/2 tsp olive oil
350g/12oz red onions, sliced
2 garlic cloves, crushed
275g/10oz cooked beetroot (beet),
  cut into sticks
1.2 litres/2 pints/5 cups vegetable stock
  or water
50g/2oz/1 cup cooked soup pasta
30ml/2 tbsp raspberry vinegar
salt and black pepper
low-fat natural (plain) yogurt and
  snipped chives, to garnish

> VARIATION
> If you prefer, try substituting cooked barley for the pasta to give extra nuttiness.

1 Heat the olive oil and add the onions and garlic.

2 Cook gently for about 20 minutes or until soft and tender.

3 Add the beetroot, stock or water, cooked pasta shapes and vinegar and heat through.

4 Adjust the seasoning to taste. Ladl the soup into bowls. Top each on with a spoonful of yogurt and sprinkl with snipped chives. Serve piping hot.

NUTRITION NOTES

Per portion:

Energy	76Kcals/318kJ
Fat	2.01g
Saturated Fat	0.28g
Cholesterol	0.33mg
Fibre	1.83g

CAULIFLOWER AND BEAN SOUP

e sweet, liquorice flavour of
fennel seeds gives a delicious
e to this hearty soup.

INGREDIENTS

ves **6**

1/2 tsp olive oil
arlic clove, crushed
nion, chopped
1/2 tsp fennel seeds
uliflower, cut into small florets
400g/14oz cans flageolet (small
nnellini) beans, drained and rinsed
litres/2 pints/5 cups vegetable stock
water
and black pepper
pped fresh parsley, to garnish
ted slices of French bread, to serve

Heat the olive oil. Add the garlic,
nion and fennel seeds and cook
ly for 5 minutes or until the onion
ftened.

3 Bring to the boil. Reduce the heat
and simmer for 10 minutes or until
the cauliflower is tender.

4 Pour the soup into a blender and
blend until smooth. Stir in the
remaining beans and season to taste.
Reheat and pour into bowls. Sprinkle
with chopped parsley and serve with
toasted slices of French bread.

Add the cauliflower, half of the
beans and all the stock or water.

NUTRITION NOTES

Per portion:

Energy	194.3Kcals/822.5kJ
Fat	3.41g
Saturated Fat	0.53g
Cholesterol	0
Fibre	7.85g

MELON AND BASIL SOUP

A deliciously refreshing, chilled fruit soup, just right for a hot summer's day. It takes next to no time to prepare, leaving you free to enjoy the sunshine and, even better, it is almost totally fat-free.

INGREDIENTS

Serves 4–6
2 Charentais or rock melons
75g/3oz/6 tbsp caster (superfine) sugar
175ml/6fl oz/¾ cup water
finely grated rind and juice of 1 lime
45ml/3 tbsp shredded fresh basil
fresh basil leaves, to garnish

1 Cut the melons in half across the middle. Scrape out the seeds and discard. Using a melon baller, scoop out 20–24 balls and set aside for the garnish. Scoop out the remaining flesh and place in a blender or food processor. Set aside.

2 Place the sugar, water and lime ze in a small pan over a low heat. S until dissolved, bring to the boil and simmer for 2–3 minutes. Remove fro the heat and leave to cool slightly. P half the mixture into the blender or food processor with the melon flesh. Blend until smooth, adding the remaining syrup and lime juice to ta

3 Pour the mixture into a bowl, stir the basil and chill. Serve garnishe with basil leaves and melon balls.

NUTRITION NOTES

Per portion:

Energy	69Kcals/293.8k
Fat	0.14g
Saturated Fat	0
Cholesterol	0
Fibre	0.47g

COOK'S TIP
Add the syrup in two stages, as the amount of sugar needed will depend on the sweetness of the melon used.

CHILLED FRESH TOMATO SOUP

s effortless uncooked soup
be made in minutes.

INGREDIENTS

es 6
g/3–3½lb ripe tomatoes, peeled and
ughly chopped
rlic cloves, crushed
l/2 tbsp balsamic vinegar
ick slices wholemeal
hole-wheat) bread
k pepper
-fat natural (plain) yogurt,
garnish

Place the tomatoes in a blender with
he garlic. Blend until smooth.

Pass the mixture through a sieve
(strainer) to remove the seeds. Stir
alsamic vinegar and season to taste
n pepper. Chill in the refrigerator.

Toast the bread lightly on both
sides. While still hot, cut off the
ts and slice the toast in half
izontally. Place on a board with
uncooked sides facing down and,
g a circular motion, rub to remove
doughy pieces of bread.

COOK'S TIP
or the best flavour, it is
mportant to use only fully
ipened, flavourful tomatoes in
his soup.

4 Cut each slice into four triangles.
Place on a grill (broiler) pan and
toast the uncooked sides until lightly
golden. Garnish each bowl of soup
with a spoonful of yogurt and serve
with the Melba toast.

NUTRITION NOTES	
Per portion:	
Energy	111Kcals/475kJ
Fat	1.42g
Saturated Fat	0.39g
Cholesterol	0.16mg
Fibre	4.16g

APPETIZERS AND SNACKS

Healthy low fat appetizers provide a delicious start to a meal and are quick and easy to make. Appetizers should not be too filling as they are simply setting the scene for the main course to follow. Choose from a tempting selection of recipes, including light and refreshing fruit cocktails such as Minted Melon and Grapefruit and vegetable pâtés or dips such as Guacamole with Crudités. Quick and easy snacks and light dishes are ideal served with thick slices of warm, crusty bread for a low-fat, nutritious lunch or supper. We include a selection of tasty snacks, such as Pasta with Herby Scallops, Cheese and Chutney Toasties and Prosciutto and Pepper Pizzas.

MELON, PINEAPPLE AND GRAPE COCKTAI

A light, refreshing fruit salad, with no added sugar and almost no fat, perfect for breakfast or brunch – or any time.

INGREDIENTS

Serves 4
½ *melon*
225g/8oz fresh pineapple or 225g/8oz can pineapple chunks in own juice
225g/8oz seedless white grapes, halved
120ml/4fl oz/½ cup white grape juice
fresh mint leaves, to decorate (optional)

COOK'S TIP
A melon is ready to eat when it smells sweet even through its thick skin. Use a firm-fleshed fruit, such as a Galia or honey-dew melon.

1 Remove the seeds from the melon half and use a melon baller to scoop out even balls.

2 Using a sharp knife, cut the skin from the pineapple and discard. Cut the fruit into bitesize chunks.

3 Combine all the fruits in a glass serving dish and pour over the ju If you are using canned pineapple, measure the drained juice and make up to the required quantity with the grape juice.

4 If not serving immediately, cover and chill. Serve decorated with m leaves, if liked.

NUTRITION NOTES

Per portion:
Energy	95Kcals/395k
Fat	0.5g
Saturated Fat	0
Cholesterol	0

GRAPEFRUIT SALAD WITH ORANGE

e bitter-sweet flavour of
mpari combines especially
l with citrus fruit. Because of
alcohol content, this dish is
 suitable for young children.

INGREDIENTS

ves 4

l/3 tbsp caster (superfine) sugar
l/4 tbsp Campari
l/2 tbsp lemon juice
apefruit
ranges
rigs fresh mint

NUTRITION NOTES

er portion:	
nergy	196Kcals/822kJ
at	5.9g
aturated Fat	2.21g
holesterol	66.37mg
ibre	1.6g

Bring 150ml/5fl oz/²/₃ cup water to
the boil in a small pan, add the
ar and simmer until dissolved. Leave
cool, then add the Campari and
on juice. Chill until ready to serve.

COOK'S TIP
When buying citrus fruit, choose
rightly coloured specimens that
eel heavy for their size.

2 Cut the peel from the grapefruit
and oranges with a serrated knife.
Segment the fruit into a bowl by slipping
a small paring knife between the flesh
and the membranes. Combine the fruit
with the Campari syrup and chill.

3 Spoon the salad into four dishes
and garnish each dish with a sprig
of fresh mint.

Minted Melon and Grapefruit

Melon is always a popular appetizer. Here the succulent flavour of the Galia melon is complemented by the refreshing taste of citrus fruit and a simple mustard and vinegar dressing. Fresh mint, used in the cocktail and as a garnish, enhances both its flavour and appearance.

INGREDIENTS

Serves 4
1 small Galia melon, weighing about
*   1kg/2¼lb*
2 pink grapefruit
1 yellow grapefruit
5ml/1 tsp Dijon mustard
5ml/1 tsp raspberry or sherry vinegar
5ml/1 tsp clear honey
15ml/1 tbsp chopped fresh mint
sprigs of fresh mint,
*   to garnish*

1 Halve the melon and remove the seeds with a teaspoon. With a melon baller, carefully scoop the flesh into balls.

NUTRITION NOTES

Per portion:	
Energy	97Kcals/409kJ
Protein	2.22g
Fat	0.63g
Saturated Fat	0
Fibre	3.05g

2 With a small sharp knife, peel the grapefruit and remove all the white pith. Remove the segments by cutting between the membranes, holding the fruit over a small bowl to catch any juices.

3 Whisk the mustard, vinegar, honey chopped mint and grapefruit juice together in a mixing bowl. Add the melon balls together with the grapefr and mix well. Chill for 30 minutes.

4 Ladle the fruit into four glass dish and serve garnished with sprigs of fresh mint.

GUACAMOLE WITH CRUDITÉS

his fresh-tasting spicy dip is
ade using mashed peas instead
the avocados that are
aditionally associated with
is dish. This version saves on
oth fat and calories, without
ompromising on taste.

INGREDIENTS

rves 4–6
0g/12oz/2¼ cups frozen peas,
defrosted
garlic clove, crushed
spring onions (scallions), chopped
ol/1 tsp finely grated rind and
juice of 1 lime
5ml/½ tsp ground cumin
sh of Tabasco sauce
ml/1 tbsp reduced-fat mayonnaise
ml/2 tbsp chopped fresh coriander
(cilantro) or parsley
lt and black pepper
nch of paprika and lime slices,
to garnish

r the crudités
baby carrots
celery sticks
red-skinned eating apple
pear
5ml/1 tbsp lemon or lime juice
baby corn

Put the peas, garlic clove, spring
. onions, lime rind and juice, cumin,
basco sauce, mayonnaise and salt
d black pepper into a food processor
a blender for a few minutes and
ocess until smooth.

2 Add the chopped coriander or
parsley and process for a few more
seconds. Spoon into a serving bowl,
cover with clear film (plastic wrap) and
chill in the refrigerator for 30 minutes,
to let the flavours develop fully.

NUTRITION NOTES

Per portion:

Energy	110Kcals/460kJ
Protein	6.22g
Fat	2.29g
Saturated Fat	0.49g
Fibre	6.73g

COOK'S TIP
Serve the guacamole dip with
some warmed wholemeal (whole-
wheat) pitta bread for a more
sustaining light meal.

3 For the crudités, trim and peel the
carrots. Halve the celery sticks
lengthways and trim into sticks, the
same length as the carrots. Quarter,
core and thickly slice the apple and
pear, then dip into the lemon or lime
juice. Arrange with the baby corn on
a platter.

4 Sprinkle the paprika over the
guacamole and garnish with twisted
lime slices.

TZATZIKI

Tzatziki is a Greek cucumber salad dressed with yogurt, mint and garlic. It is typically served with grilled (broiled) lamb and chicken, but is also good served with crudités.

INGREDIENTS

Serves 4
1 cucumber
5ml/1 tsp salt
45ml/3 tbsp finely chopped fresh mint, plus a few sprigs to garnish
1 garlic clove, crushed
5ml/1 tsp caster (superfine) sugar
200ml/7fl oz reduced fat Greek-style (US strained plain) yogurt
cucumber flower, to garnish (optional)

COOK'S TIP
If you want to prepare Tzatziki in a hurry, then leave out the method for salting cucumber at the end of step 1. The cucumber will have a more crunchy texture, and will be slightly less sweet.

1 Peel the cucumber. Reserve a little of the cucumber to use as a garnish if you wish and cut the rest in half lengthways. Remove the seeds with a teaspoon and discard. Slice the cucumber thinly and combine with salt. Leave for about 15–20 minutes. The salt will soften the cucumber and draw out any bitter juices.

2 Combine the mint, garlic, sugar and yogurt in a bowl, reserving a few sprigs of mint as decoration.

3 Rinse the cucumber in a sieve (strainer) under water to flush away the salt. Drain well and combine with the yogurt. Decorate with cucumber flower and/or mint. Serve cold.

NUTRITION NOTES	
Per portion:	
Energy	41.5Kcals/174.5kJ
Fat	0.51g
Saturated Fat	0.25g
Cholesterol	2mg
Fibre	0.2g

CHILLI TOMATO SALSA

This universal dip is great served with absolutely anything and can be made up to 24 hours in advance, and then chilled.

INGREDIENTS

Serves 4

1 shallot, peeled and halved
2 garlic cloves, peeled
handful of fresh basil leaves
500g/1¼ lb ripe tomatoes
10ml/2 tsp olive oil
2 green chillies
salt and black pepper

1 Place the shallot and garlic in a food processor with the fresh basil. Process the shallot, garlic and basil until finely chopped.

2 Halve the tomatoes and add to the food processor. Pulse the machine until the mixture is well blended and coarsely chopped.

3 With the motor running, slowly pour in the olive oil. Add salt and pepper to taste.

NUTRITION NOTES	
Per portion:	
Energy	28Kcals/79kJ
Fat	0.47g
Saturated Fat	0.13g
Cholesterol	0
Fibre	1.45g

4 Halve the chillies lengthways and remove the seeds. Finely slice the chillies widthways into tiny strips and stir into the tomato salsa. Serve at room temperature.

COOK'S TIP
The salsa is best made in the summer when tomatoes are at their best. In winter, use a drained 400g/14oz can of plum tomatoes.

Melon with Wild Strawberries

This fragrant, colourful appetizer is the perfect way to begin a rich meal as both strawberries and melons are virtually fat-free. Here several varieties are combined with strongly flavoured wild strawberries. If wild ones are not available, use ordinary strawberries or raspberries instead.

Ingredients

Serves 4
1 cantaloupe or Charentais melon
1 Galia melon
900g/2lb watermelon
175g/6oz wild strawberries
4 sprigs fresh mint, to garnish

Nutrition Notes

Per portion:
Energy	42.5Kcals/178.6kJ
Fat	0.32g
Saturated Fat	0
Cholesterol	0
Fibre	1.09g

1 Using a large sharp knife, cut all three melons in half.

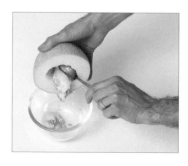

2 Scoop out the seeds from both the cantaloupe or Charentais and Galia melons with a spoon.

3 With a melon scoop, take out as many balls as you can from all three melons. Combine in a large bowl and chill for at least 1 hour.

4 Add the wild strawberries and mix together gently. Spoon out into four stemmed glass dishes.

5 Garnish each of the melon salads with a small sprig of mint and serv at once.

Cook's Tip
Ripe melons should give slightly when pressed at the base, and should give off a sweet scent. Buy carefully if you plan to use the fruit on the day. If one or more varieties of melon aren't available, then substitute another, or buy two or three of the same variety – the salad might not be quite so colourful, but it will taste equally refreshing.

MUSSELS WITH THAI HERBS

Another simple dish to prepare. The lemon grass adds a refreshing tang to the mussels.

INGREDIENTS

Serves 6

1kg/2¼ lb mussels, cleaned and
   beards removed
2 lemon grass stalks, finely chopped
4 shallots, chopped
4 kaffir lime leaves, roughly torn
2 red chillies, sliced
15ml/1 tbsp fish sauce
30ml/2 tbsp lime juice
2 spring onions (scallions), chopped, and
   coriander (cilantro) leaves, to garnish

1 Put all the ingredients, except the spring onions and coriander, in a large pan and stir thoroughly.

2 Cover and cook for 5–7 minutes, shaking the pan occasionally, until the mussels open. Discard any mussel that do not open.

3 Transfer the cooked mussels to a serving platter.

4 Garnish the mussels with chopped spring onions and coriander leaves. Serve immediately.

NUTRITION NOTES

Per portion:

Energy	56Kcals/238kJ
Fat	1.22g
Saturated Fat	0.16g
Cholesterol	0.32g
Fibre	27g

PASTA WITH HERBY SCALLOPS

w-fat fromage frais, flavoured
th mustard, garlic and herbs,
akes a deceptively creamy
ace for pasta.

INGREDIENTS

ves **4**

0ml/4fl oz/½ cup low-fat fromage
rais or cream cheese
ml/2 tsp wholegrain mustard
arlic cloves, crushed
–45ml/2–3 tbsp fresh lime juice
ml/4 tbsp chopped fresh parsley
ml/2 tbsp snipped chives
0g/12oz black tagliatelle
large scallops
ml/4 tbsp white wine
0ml/¼ pint/⅔ cup fish stock
t and black pepper
e wedges and parsley sprigs,
o garnish

To make the sauce, mix the fromage
frais, mustard, garlic, lime juice,
rsley, chives and seasoning together
a mixing bowl.

Cook the pasta in a large pan of
boiling salted water until *al dente*.
ain thoroughly.

3 Slice the scallops in half horizontally.
Keep any coral whole. Put the wine
and fish stock into a pan and heat to
simmering point. Add the scallops and
cook very gently for 3–4 minutes.
(Don't cook for any longer, or they
will toughen.)

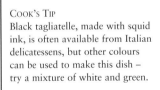

COOK'S TIP
Black tagliatelle, made with squid
ink, is often available from Italian
delicatessens, but other colours
can be used to make this dish –
try a mixture of white and green.

4 Remove the scallops. Boil the wine
and stock to reduce by half and add
the green sauce to the pan. Heat gently
to warm, then return the scallops to the
pan and cook for 1 minute. Spoon over
the pasta and garnish with lime wedges
and parsley.

NUTRITION NOTES	
Per portion:	
Energy	368Kcals/1561kJ
Fat	4.01g
Saturated Fat	0.98g
Cholesterol	99mg
Fibre	1.91g

FRESH FIG, APPLE AND DATE SALAD

Sweet Mediterranean figs and dates combine especially well with crisp eating apples. A hint of almond serves to unite the flavours, but if you'd prefer to reduce the fat even more, omit the marzipan and add another 30ml/2 tbsp low-fat yogurt or use low-fat fromage frais instead.

INGREDIENTS

Serves 4

6 large eating apples
juice of ½ lemon
175g/6oz fresh dates
25g/1oz white marzipan
5ml/1 tsp orange flower water
60ml/4 tbsp low-fat natural (plain) yogurt
4 green or purple figs
4 almonds, toasted

1 Core the apples. Slice thinly, then cut into fine matchsticks. Moisten with lemon juice to keep them white.

NUTRITION NOTES

Per portion:

Energy	255Kcals/876.5kJ
Fat	4.98g
Saturated Fat	1.05g
Cholesterol	2.25mg
Fibre	1.69g

2 Remove the stones (pits) from the dates and cut the flesh into strips, then combine with the apple slices.

3 Soften the marzipan with orange flower water and combine with the yogurt. Mix well.

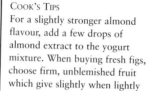

COOK'S TIPS
For a slightly stronger almond flavour, add a few drops of almond extract to the yogurt mixture. When buying fresh figs, choose firm, unblemished fruit which give slightly when lightly squeezed. Avoid damaged, bruised or very soft fruit.

4 Pile the apples and dates in the centre of four plates. Remove the stem from each of the figs and divide the fruit into quarters without cutting right through the base. Squeeze the base with the thumb and forefinger of each hand to open up the fruit.

5 Place a fig in the centre of each salad. Spoon the yogurt filling on to the figs and decorate each one with a toasted almond.

CHEESE AND CHUTNEY TOASTIES

Quick-and-easy cheese on toast can be made quite memorable with a few tasty additions. Serve these scrumptious toasties with a simple lettuce and cherry tomato salad.

INGREDIENTS

Serves 4
4 slices wholemeal (whole-wheat)
* bread, thickly sliced*
85g/3½oz Cheddar cheese, grated
5ml/1 tsp dried thyme
30ml/2 tbsp chutney or relish
black pepper
salad, to serve

1 Toast the bread slices lightly on each side.

2 Mix the cheese and thyme together and season to taste with pepper.

NUTRITION NOTES

Per portion:
Energy	157.25Kcals/664.25kJ
Fat	4.24g
Saturated Fat	1.99g
Cholesterol	9.25mg
Fibre	2.41g

3 Spread the chutney or relish on the toast and divide the cheese evenly between the four slices.

4 Return the toast to the grill (broile and cook until the cheese is browned and bubbling. Cut each slice into halves, diagonally, and serve immediately with salad.

VARIATION
If you prefer, use a reduced-fat hard cheese, such as mature (sharp) Cheddar or Red Leicester, in place of the full-fat Cheddar, to cut both calories and fat.

PROSCIUTTO AND PEPPER PIZZAS

he delicious flavours of these
asy pizzas are hard to beat.

INGREDIENTS

lakes 4

2 loaf ciabatta bread
red (bell) pepper, roasted and peeled
yellow (bell) pepper, roasted
and peeled
slices prosciutto, cut into thick strips
0g/2oz reduced-fat mozzarella cheese
lack pepper
ny basil leaves, to garnish

NUTRITION NOTES

Per portion:
Energy	93Kcals/395kJ
Fat	3.25g
Saturated Fat	1.49g
Cholesterol	14mg
Fibre	1g

Cut the bread into four thick slices
and toast until golden.

2 Cut the roasted peppers into thick
strips and arrange on the toasted
read with the strips of prosciutto.
reheat the grill (broiler).

3 Thinly slice the mozzarella and
arrange on top, then grind over
black pepper. Grill (broil) for 2–3
minutes, until the cheese is bubbling.

4 Sprinkle the basil leaves on top and
serve immediately.

PASTA, BEANS, PEAS LENTILS AND GRAINS

Pasta, beans, peas, lentils and grains on their own are low in fat and a good source of carbohydrate, but they are often prepared with high-fat ingredients and sauces. However, recipes do not need to be high in fat to be appetizing. There are delicious low-fat recipes for pasta, such as Fusilli with Smoked Trout and Spaghetti with Chilli Bean Sauce. Beans, peas, lentils and grains are a popular choice at mealtimes, and these recipes offer delicious and nutritious options, from Cracked Wheat and Mint Salad, to Spicy Bean Hot Pot.

TURKEY AND MACARONI CHEESE

A tasty low-fat alternative to macaroni cheese, the addition of turkey ensures this dish is a family favourite. Serve with warm ciabatta bread and a mixed leaf salad.

NUTRITION NOTES

Per portion:

Energy	152Kcals/637kJ
Fat	2.8g
Saturated Fat	0.7g
Cholesterol	12mg
Fibre	1.1g

INGREDIENTS

Serves 4

1 medium onion, chopped
150ml/¼ pint/⅔ cup vegetable or
  chicken stock
25g/1oz/2 tbsp low-fat margarine
45ml/3 tbsp plain (all-purpose) flour
300ml/½ pint/1¼ cup skimmed milk
50g/2oz reduced-fat Cheddar
  cheese, grated
5ml/1 tsp dry mustard
225g/8oz quick-cook macaroni
4 smoked turkey rashers (strips), halved
2–3 firm tomatoes, sliced
a few fresh basil leaves
15ml/1 tbsp grated Parmesan cheese
salt and black pepper

1 Put the chopped onion and stock into a non-stick frying pan. Bring to the boil, stirring occasionally and cook for 5–6 minutes or until the stock has reduced entirely and the onion is transparent.

2 Put the margarine, flour, milk and seasoning into a pan and whisk together over the heat until thickened and smooth. Draw aside and add the cheese, mustard and onion.

3 Cook the macaroni in a large pan of boiling, salted water according to the instructions on the packet. Preheat the grill (broiler). Drain thoroughly and stir into the sauce. Transfer to a shallow ovenproof dish.

4 Arrange the turkey rashers and tomatoes in neat overlapping rows on top of the macaroni cheese. Tuck in the basil leaves, then sprinkle with Parmesan and grill (broil) to lightly brown the top.

PASTA WITH TOMATO AND TUNA

INGREDIENTS

ves 6

medium onion, finely chopped
elery stick, finely chopped
ed (bell) pepper, seeded and diced
arlic clove, crushed
0ml/¼ pint/⅔ cup chicken stock
0g/14oz can chopped tomatoes
ml/1 tbsp tomato purée (paste)
ml/2 tsp caster (superfine) sugar
ml/1 tbsp chopped fresh basil
ml/1 tbsp chopped fresh parsley
0g/1lb pasta shells
0g/14oz canned tuna in
rine, drained
ml/2 tbsp capers in vinegar, drained
t and black pepper

Put the chopped onion, celery, red pepper and garlic into a pan. Add stock, bring to the boil and cook 5 minutes or until the stock has uced almost completely.

Add the tomatoes, tomato purée, sugar and herbs. Season to taste d bring to the boil. Simmer for about minutes until the sauce is thick, ring occasionally.

3 Meanwhile, cook the pasta in a large pan of boiling, salted water according to the packet instructions, until *al dente*. Drain thoroughly and transfer to a warm serving dish.

4 Flake the tuna fish into large chunks and add to the sauce with the capers. Heat gently for 1–2 minutes, pour over the pasta, toss gently and serve immediately.

VARIATION
If fresh herbs are not available, use a 400g/14oz can of chopped tomatoes with herbs and add 5–10ml/1–2 tsp mixed dried herbs, in place of the fresh herbs.

NUTRITION NOTES	
Per portion:	
Energy	369Kcals/1549kJ
Fat	2.1g
Saturated Fat	0.4g
Cholesterol	34mg
Fibre	4g

CRAB PASTA SALAD

Low-fat yogurt makes a piquant dressing for this salad.

INGREDIENTS

Serves 6

350g/12oz pasta twists
1 small red (bell) pepper, seeded and
  finely chopped
2 x 175g/6oz cans white crab
  meat, drained
115g/4oz cherry tomatoes, halved
¼ cucumber, halved, seeded and sliced
  into crescents
15ml/1 tbsp lemon juice
300ml/½ pint/1¼ cups low-fat yogurt
2 celery sticks, finely chopped
10ml/2 tsp horseradish cream
2.5ml/½ tsp paprika
2.5ml/½ tsp Dijon mustard
30ml/2 tbsp sweet tomato pickle
  or chutney
salt and black pepper
fresh basil, to garnish

1 Cook the pasta in a large pan of boiling, salted water, according to the instructions on the packet, until *al dente*. Drain and rinse thoroughly under cold water.

NUTRITION NOTES

Per portion:

Energy	305Kcals/1283kJ
Fat	2.5g
Saturated Fat	0.5g
Cholesterol	43mg
Fibre	2.9g

2 Cover the chopped red pepper wi boiling water and leave to stand f 1 minute. Drain and rinse under cold water. Pat dry on kitchen paper.

3 Drain the crab meat and pick ove carefully for pieces of shell. Put in a bowl with the halved tomatoes and sliced cucumber. Season and sprinkle with lemon juice.

4 To make the dressing, add the rec pepper to the yogurt, with the celery, horseradish cream, paprika, mustard and sweet tomato pickle or chutney. Mix the pasta with the dressing and transfer to a serving dis Spoon the crab mixture on top and garnish with fresh basil.

Fusilli with Smoked Trout

Ingredients

es 4–6

rots, *cut in julienne sticks*
k, *cut in julienne sticks*
ery sticks, *cut in julienne sticks*
·ml/¹⁄₄ pint/²⁄₃ cup vegetable or
·b stock
·/8oz smoked trout fillets, skinned
·d cut into strips
·/7oz low-fat cream cheese
·ml/¹⁄₄ pint/²⁄₃ cup medium sweet
·ite wine or fish stock
·l/1 tbsp chopped fresh dill
·fennel
·/8oz fusilli (long, corkscrew pasta)
·nd black pepper
·prigs, to garnish

ut the carrots, leek and celery into
pan with the vegetable or fish
·. Bring to the boil and cook
·kly for 4–5 minutes until the
·ables are tender and most of the
·· has evaporated. Remove from
·eat and add the smoked trout.

Nutrition Notes

r portion:

·ergy	339Kcals/1422kJ
·t	4.7g
·turated Fat	0.8g
·holesterol	57mg
·bre	4.1g

2 To make the sauce, put the cream cheese and wine or fish stock into a pan, heat and whisk until smooth. Season with salt and pepper. Add the chopped dill or fennel.

3 Cook the pasta according to the packet instructions in a large pan of boiling, salted water until *al dente*. Drain thoroughly.

4 Return the pasta to the pan with the sauce, toss lightly and transfer to a serving bowl. Top with the cooked vegetables and trout. Serve at once garnished with dill sprigs.

Cook's Tips
When making the sauce, it is important to whisk it continuously while heating, to ensure a smooth result. Smoked salmon may be used in place of the trout, for a tasty change.

Hot Spicy Prawns with Campanelle

This low-fat prawn sauce tossed with hot pasta is an ideal supper-time dish. Add less or more chilli depending on how hot you like your food.

Ingredients

Serves 4–6

225g/8oz tiger prawns (shrimp), cooked and peeled
1–2 garlic cloves, crushed
finely grated rind of 1 lemon
15ml/1 tbsp lemon juice
1.5ml/¼ tsp red chilli paste or 1 large pinch of chilli powder
15ml/1 tbsp light soy sauce
150g/5oz smoked turkey rashers (strips)
1 shallot or small onion, finely chopped
60ml/4 tbsp dry white wine
225g/8oz campanelle or other pasta shapes
60ml/4 tbsp fish stock
4 firm ripe tomatoes, peeled, seeded and chopped
30ml/2 tbsp chopped fresh parsley
salt and black pepper

Nutrition Notes

Per portion:

Energy	331Kcals/1388kJ
Fat	2.9g
Saturated Fat	0.6g
Cholesterol	64mg
Fibre	3.2g

Cook's Tip

To save time later, the prawns (shrimp) and marinade ingredients can be mixed together, covered and chilled in the refrigerator overnight, until ready to use.

1 In a glass bowl, mix the prawns with the garlic, lemon rind and juice, chilli paste or powder and soy sauce. Season with salt and pepper, cover and marinate for at least 1 hour.

2 Grill (broil) the turkey rashers, then cut them into 5mm/¼in dice.

3 Put the shallot or onion and white wine into a pan, bring to the boil, cover and cook for 2–3 minutes or until they are tender and the wine has reduced by half.

4 Cook the pasta according to the packet instructions in a large pan of boiling, salted water until al dente. Drain thoroughly.

5 Just before serving, put the prawns with their marinade into a large frying pan, bring to the boil quickly and add the smoked turkey and fish stock. Heat through for 1 minute.

6 Add to the pasta with the chopped tomatoes and parsley, toss quickly and serve at once.

TAGLIATELLE WITH MUSHROOMS

INGREDIENTS

Serves 4

1 small onion, finely chopped
2 garlic cloves, crushed
150ml/¼ pint/⅔ cup vegetable stock
225g/8oz mixed fresh mushrooms, such
*   as field (portobello), chestnut, oyster*
*   or chanterelles*
60ml/4 tbsp white or red wine
10ml/2 tsp tomato purée (paste)
15ml/1 tbsp soy sauce
5ml/1 tsp chopped fresh thyme
30ml/2 tbsp chopped fresh parsley,
*   plus extra to garnish*
225g/8oz fresh sun-dried tomato and
*   herb tagliatelle*
salt and black pepper
shavings of Parmesan cheese, to serve
*   (optional)*

1 Put the onion and garlic into a pan with the stock, then cover and cook for 5 minutes or until tender.

2 Add the mushrooms (quartered o sliced if large or left whole if sma wine, tomato purée and soy sauce. Cover and cook for 5 minutes.

NUTRITION NOTES

Per portion:
Energy	241Kcals/1010kJ
Fat	2.4g
Saturated Fat	0.7g
Carbohydrate	45g
Fibre	3g

3 Remove the lid from the pan and boil until the liquid has reduced half. Stir in the chopped fresh herbs and season to taste.

4 Cook the fresh pasta in a large pa of boiling, salted water for 2–5 minutes until *al dente*. Drain thoroug and toss lightly with the mushrooms Serve, garnished with parsley and shavings of Parmesan cheese, if liked.

PASTA PRIMAVERA

u can use any mixture of
sh, young spring vegetables to
ke this delicately flavoured
sta dish.

INGREDIENTS

ves 4

g/8oz thin asparagus spears,
hopped in half
g/4oz mangetouts (snow peas),
pped and tailed
g/4oz baby corn
g/8oz whole baby carrots, trimmed
nall red (bell) pepper, seeded
nd chopped
pring onions (scallions), sliced
g/8oz torchietti or other pasta shapes
)ml/¹/4 pint/²/₃ cup low-fat
ottage cheese
)ml/¹/4 pint/²/₃ cup low-fat yogurt
nl/1 tbsp lemon juice
nl/1 tbsp chopped parsley
nl/1 tbsp snipped chives
nmed milk (optional)
and black pepper
-dried tomato bread, to serve

Cook the asparagus spears in a pan
of boiling, salted water for 3–4
utes. Add the mangetouts halfway
ough the cooking time. Drain and
se both under cold water to stop
ther cooking.

2 Cook the baby corn, carrots, red
pepper and spring onions in the
same way until tender. Drain and rinse.

3 Cook the pasta in a large pan of
boiling, salted water according to
the packet instruction, until *al dente*.
Drain thoroughly.

4 Put the cottage cheese, yogurt,
lemon juice, parsley, chives and
seasoning into a food processor or
blender and process until smooth.
Thin the sauce with skimmed milk,
if necessary. Put into a large pan with
the pasta and vegetables, heat gently
and toss carefully. Serve at once with
sun-dried tomato bread.

NUTRITION NOTES	
Per portion:	
Energy	320Kcals/1344kJ
Fat	3.1g
Saturated Fat	0.4g
Cholesterol	3mg
Fibre	6.2g

Tagliatelle with Milanese Sauce

Ingredients

Serves 4

1 onion, finely chopped
1 celery stick, finely chopped
1 red (bell) pepper, seeded and diced
1–2 garlic cloves, crushed
150ml/¼ pint/⅔ cup vegetable or
    chicken stock
400g/14oz can tomatoes
15ml/1 tbsp tomato purée (paste)
10ml/2 tsp caster (superfine) sugar
5ml/1 tsp mixed dried herbs
350g/12oz tagliatelle
115g/4oz button (white)
    mushrooms, sliced
60ml/4 tbsp dry white wine
115g/4oz lean cooked ham, diced
salt and black pepper
15ml/1 tbsp chopped fresh parsley,
    to garnish

1 Put the chopped onion, celery, pepper and garlic into a pan. Add the stock, bring to the boil and cook for 5 minutes or until tender.

Variation

To reduce the calorie and fat content even more, omit the ham and use corn kernels or cooked broccoli florets instead.

2 Add the tomatoes, tomato purée, sugar and herbs. Season with salt and pepper. Bring to the boil and simmer for 30 minutes stirring occasionally, until the sauce is thick.

3 Cook the pasta in a large pan of boiling, salted water according to the packet instructions, until *al dente*. Drain thoroughly.

4 Put the mushrooms into a pan with the white wine, cover and cook for 3–4 minutes until the mushrooms are tender and all the wine has been absorbed.

5 Stir the mushrooms and ham into the tomato sauce and reheat gentl over a low heat.

6 Transfer the pasta to a warmed serving dish and spoon on the sauce. Garnish with parsley.

Nutrition Notes

Per portion:

Energy	405Kcals/1700kJ
Fat	3.5g
Saturated Fat	0.8g
Cholesterol	17mg
Fibre	4.5g

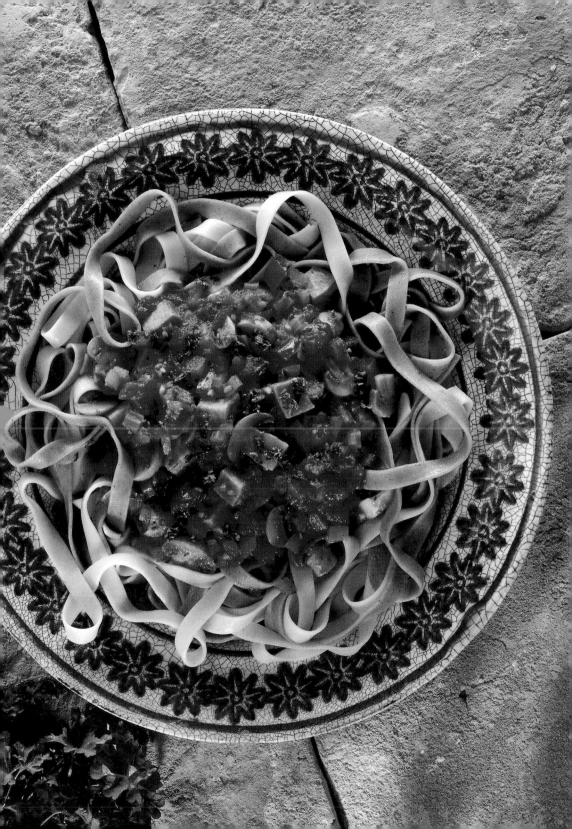

SPAGHETTI WITH CHILLI BEAN SAUCE

A nutritious vegetarian option,
ideal as a low-fat main course.

NUTRITION NOTES

Per portion:

Energy	431Kcals/1811kJ
Fat	3.6g
Saturated Fat	0.2g
Cholesterol	0
Fibre	9.9g

INGREDIENTS

Serves 6

1 onion, finely chopped
1–2 garlic cloves, crushed
1 large green chilli, seeded
  and chopped
150ml/¼ pint/⅔ cup vegetable stock
400g/14oz can chopped tomatoes
30ml/2 tbsp tomato purée (paste)
120ml/4fl oz/½ cup red wine
5ml/1 tsp dried oregano
200g/7oz French (green) beans, sliced
400g/14oz can red kidney
  beans, drained
400g/14oz can cannellini
  beans, drained
400g/14oz can chickpeas, drained
450g/1lb spaghetti
salt and black pepper

1 To make the sauce, put the chopped onion, garlic and chilli into a non-stick pan with the stock. Bring to the boil and cook for 5 minutes until tender.

2 Add the tomatoes, tomato purée, wine, seasoning and oregano. Bring to the boil, cover and simmer the sauce for 20 minutes.

3 Cook the French beans in boiling, salted water for about 5–6 minutes until tender. Drain thoroughly.

4 Add all the beans and the chickpeas to the sauce and simmer for a further 10 minutes. Meanwhile, cook the spaghetti in a large pan of boiling, salted water according to the individual packet instructions, until *al dente*. Drain thoroughly. Transfer the pasta to a serving dish or plates and top with the chilli bean sauce.

> **COOK'S TIP**
> Rinse canned beans thoroughly under cold, running water to remove as much salt as possible and drain well before use.

PINEAPPLE AND GINGER NOODLE SALAD

he tastes of the tropics are
rought together in this
ppetizing noodle salad, which
ideal served as a lunch or
ppertime dish.

INGREDIENTS

rves 4

5g/10oz dried udon noodles
pineapple, peeled, cored and sliced
 into 4cm/1½in rings
ml/3 tbsp soft light brown sugar
ml/4 tbsp fresh lime juice
ml/4 tbsp coconut milk
ml/2 tbsp fish sauce
ml/2 tbsp grated fresh root ginger
garlic cloves, finely chopped
ripe mango or 2 peaches, finely diced
ack pepper
spring onions (scallions), finely sliced,
2 red chillies, seeded and finely
shredded, plus mint leaves, to garnish

NUTRITION NOTES

Per portion:

Energy	350Kcals/1487kJ
Fat	4.49g
Saturated Fat	0.05g
Cholesterol	0
Fibre	3.13g

COOK'S TIPS

Use 4–6 canned pineapple rings in
fruit juice, if fresh pineapple is
not available. If you haven't any
fresh garlic, use 10ml/2 tsp ready-
minced garlic instead. Choose ripe
mangoes that have a smooth,
unblemished skin and give slightly
when you squeeze them gently.

1 Cook the noodles in a large pan of
boiling water until tender, following
the directions on the packet. Drain,
then refresh under cold water and
drain again.

3 Mix the lime juice, coconut milk
and fish sauce in a salad bowl. Add
the remaining brown sugar, with the
ginger and garlic, and whisk well. Add
the noodles and pineapple.

2 Place the pineapple rings in a
flameproof dish, sprinkle with
30ml/2 tbsp of the sugar and grill
(broil) for 5 minutes, or until golden.
Cool slightly and cut into small dice.

4 Add the mango or peaches to the
bowl and toss well. Scatter over
the spring onions, chillies and mint
leaves before serving.

SPAGHETTI BOLOGNESE

INGREDIENTS

Serves 8

1 onion, chopped
2–3 garlic cloves, crushed
300ml/¹/₂ pint/1¹/₄ cups beef or
* chicken stock*
450g/1lb extra-lean minced turkey
* or beef*
2 x 400g/14oz cans chopped tomatoes
5ml/1 tsp dried basil
5ml/1 tsp dried oregano
60ml/4 tbsp tomato purée (paste)
450g/1lb button (white) mushrooms,
* quartered and sliced*
150ml/¹/₄ pint/²/₃ cup red wine
450g/1lb spaghetti
salt and black pepper

NUTRITION NOTES

Per portion:

Energy	321Kcals/1350kJ
Fat	4.1g
Saturated Fat	1.3g
Cholesterol	33mg
Fibre	2.7g

1 Put the chopped onion and garlic into a non-stick pan with half of the stock. Bring to the boil and cook for about 5 minutes, or until the onion is tender and the stock has reduced and evaporated completely.

COOK'S TIP
Sautéing vegetables in fat-free stock rather than oil is an easy way of saving calories and fat. Choose fat-free stock to reduce even more.

2 Add the turkey or beef and cook 5 minutes, breaking up the meat with a fork. Add the tomatoes, herbs and tomato purée, bring to the boil, then cover and simmer for 1 hour.

3 Meanwhile, cook the mushrooms a non-stick pan with the wine for 5 minutes or until the wine has evaporated. Add the mushrooms to th meat with salt and pepper to taste.

4 Cook the pasta in a large pan of boiling salted water for 8–12 minutes until tender. Drain thorough Serve topped with the meat sauce.

RATATOUILLE PENNE BAKE

INGREDIENTS

rves 6

mall aubergine (eggplant)
courgettes (zucchini), thickly sliced
'0g/7oz firm tofu, cubed
ml/3 tbsp dark soy sauce
garlic clove, crushed
ml/2 tsp sesame seeds
small red (bell) pepper, seeded
ind sliced
onion, finely chopped
2 garlic cloves, crushed
0ml/¼ pint/⅔ cup vegetable stock
irm ripe tomatoes, skinned, seeded
ind quartered
ml/1 tbsp chopped mixed herbs
5g/8oz penne or other pasta shapes
lt and black pepper
isty bread, to serve

Wash the aubergine and cut into
2.5cm/1in cubes. Put into a colander
th the courgettes, sprinkle with salt
d leave to drain for 30 minutes.

Mix the tofu with the soy sauce,
garlic and sesame seeds. Cover and
arinate for 30 minutes.

3 Put the pepper, onion and garlic
into a pan with the stock. Bring to
the boil, cover and cook for 5 minutes
until tender. Remove the lid and boil
until all the stock has evaporated.
Add the tomatoes and herbs to the pan,
stir to combine and cook for a further
3 minutes, then add the rinsed
aubergine and courgettes and cook
until tender. Season to taste.

COOK'S TIP
Tofu is a low-fat protein, but it is
very bland. Marinating adds plenty
of flavour – make sure you leave it
for the full 30 minutes.

4 Meanwhile, cook the pasta in a
large pan of boiling, salted water
according to the packet instructions,
until al dente, then drain thoroughly.
Preheat the grill (broiler). Toss the pasta
with the vegetables and tofu. Transfer to
a shallow ovenproof dish and grill (broil)
until lightly toasted. Serve with bread.

NUTRITION NOTES	
Per portion:	
Energy	208Kcals/873kJ
Fat	3.7g
Saturated Fat	0.5g
Cholesterol	0
Fibre	3.9g

Sweet and Sour Peppers with Pasta

A tasty and colourful low-fat
dish – perfect for lunch
or supper.

Ingredients

Serves 4

1 each red, 1 yellow and 1 orange
  (bell) pepper
1 garlic clove, crushed
30ml/2 tbsp capers
30ml/2 tbsp raisins
5ml/1 tsp wholegrain mustard
rind and juice of 1 lime
5ml/1 tsp clear honey
30ml/2 tbsp chopped fresh
  coriander (cilantro)
225g/8oz pasta bows
salt and black pepper
shavings of Parmesan cheese,
  to serve (optional)

1 Quarter the peppers and remove the stalks, seeds and white membranes. Put the quarters into a pan of boiling water and cook for 10–15 minutes, until tender. Drain and rinse under cold water to prevent further cooking, then peel off the skin and cut the flesh into strips lengthways.

2 Put the garlic, capers, raisins, mustard, lime rind and juice, hone coriander and seasoning into a bowl and whisk together.

3 Cook the pasta in a pan of boiling salted water for 10–12 minutes, until *al dente*. Drain thoroughly.

4 Return the pasta to the pan and ad the pepper strips and dressing. Hea gently, tossing to mix. Transfer to a warm serving bowl and serve with a fe shavings of Parmesan cheese, if using.

Nutrition Notes	
Per portion:	
Energy	268Kcals/1125kJ
Fat	2.0g
Saturated Fat	0.5g
Cholesterol	1.3mg
Fibre	4.3g

PASTA WITH CHICKPEA SAUCE

is is a delicious, and very
eedy, low-fat dish. The quality
canned pulses and tomatoes is
good that it is possible to
nsform them into a very
sh-tasting pasta sauce in
nutes. Choose whatever pasta
apes you like, although hollow
apes, such as penne (quills) or
ells are particularly good with
s sauce.

INGREDIENTS

ves 6
)g/1lb penne or other pasta shapes
nl/2 tsp olive oil
nion, thinly sliced
ed (bell) pepper, seeded and sliced
)g/14oz can chopped tomatoes
5g/15oz can chickpeas
nl/2 tbsp dry vermouth (optional)
l/1 tsp dried oregano
arge bay leaf
nl/2 tbsp capers
 and black pepper
sh oregano, to garnish

COOK'S TIP
Choose fresh or dried unfilled
pasta for this dish. Whichever you
choose, cook it in a large pan of
salted water, so that the pasta
keeps separate and doesn't stick
together. Fresh pasta takes about
2–4 minutes to cook and dried
pasta about 8–10 minutes. Cook
pasta until it is al dente – firm
and neither too hard nor
too soft.

NUTRITION NOTES

Per portion:
Energy   268Kcals/1125kJ
Fat   2.0g
Saturated Fat   0.5g
Cholesterol   1.3mg
Fibre   4.3g

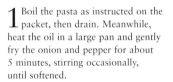

1 Boil the pasta as instructed on the
packet, then drain. Meanwhile,
heat the oil in a large pan and gently
fry the onion and pepper for about
5 minutes, stirring occasionally,
until softened.

2 Add the tomatoes, chickpeas with
their liquid, vermouth (if liked),
herbs and capers and stir well.

3 Season to taste and bring to the boil,
then simmer for about 10 minutes.
Remove the bay leaf and mix in the
pasta. Reheat and serve hot, garnished
with sprigs of oregano.

Pappardelle and Provençal Sauce

INGREDIENTS

Serves 4

2 small red onions
150ml/¼ pint/⅔ cup vegetable stock
1–2 garlic cloves, crushed
60ml/4 tbsp red wine
2 courgettes (zucchini), cut in fingers
1 yellow (bell) pepper, seeded and sliced
400g/14oz can tomatoes
10ml/2 tsp fresh thyme
5ml/1 tsp caster (superfine) sugar
350g/12oz pappardelle or other
 ribbon pasta
salt and black pepper
fresh thyme and 6 black olives, pitted
 and roughly chopped, to garnish

NUTRITION NOTES

Per portion:

Energy	369Kcals/1550kJ
Fat	2.5g
Saturated Fat	0.4g
Cholesterol	0
Fibre	4.3g

1 Cut each onion into eight wedges through the root end, to hold them together during cooking. Put into a pan with the stock and garlic. Bring to the boil, cover and simmer for 5 minutes until tender.

2 Add the red wine, courgettes, yellow pepper, tomatoes, thyme, sugar and seasoning. Bring to the boil and cook gently for 5–7 minutes, shaking the pan occasionally to coat the vegetables with the sauce. (Do not overcook the vegetables as they are much nicer if they remain slightly crunchy.)

3 Cook the pasta in a large pan of boiling, salted water according to the packet instructions, until *al dente*. Drain thoroughly.

4 Transfer the pasta to warmed serving plates and top with the vegetables. Garnish with fresh thyme and chopped black olives.

BASIC PASTA DOUGH
To make fresh pasta, sift 200g/7oz/1¾ cups plain (all-purpose) flour and a pinch of salt on to a work surface and make a well in the centre. Break two eggs into the well, together with 10ml/2 tsp cold water. Using a fork, beat the eggs gently, then gradually draw in the flour from the sides to make a thick paste. When the mixture becomes too stiff to use a fork, use your hands to mix to a firm dough. Knead for 5 minutes until smooth. Wrap and leave to rest for 20–30 minutes before rolling out and cutting.

SPAGHETTI ALLA CARBONARA

s is a variation on the classic
rcoal burner's spaghetti,
ng turkey rashers and low-fat
am cheese instead of the
ditional bacon and egg.

INGREDIENTS

es **4**

g/5oz smoked turkey rashers (strips)
for frying
edium onion, chopped
garlic cloves, crushed
ml/¼ pint/⅔ cup chicken stock
ml/¼ pint/⅔ cup dry white wine
g/7oz low-fat cream cheese
g/1lb chilli and garlic-flavoured
aghetti
ul/2 tbsp chopped fresh parsley
and black pepper
vings of Parmesan cheese,
serve

Cut the turkey rashers into 1cm/½in
strips. Fry quickly in a non-stick
for 2–3 minutes. Add the onion,
ic and stock to the pan. Bring
he boil, cover and simmer for about
inutes until tender.

2 Add the wine and boil rapidly until
reduced by half. Whisk in the cream
cheese and season to taste.

4 Return the spaghetti to the pan
with the sauce and parsley, toss well
and serve immediately with a few thin
shavings of Parmesan cheese.

ARIATION
f you can't find chilli and garlic-
lavoured spaghetti, use plain
paghetti and add a small amount
f raw chilli and garlic in step 4
r use the pasta of your choice.

3 Meanwhile, cook the spaghetti in a
large pan of boiling, salted water
for 10–12 minutes until *al dente*. Drain
thoroughly.

NUTRITION NOTES	
Per portion:	
Energy	500Kcals/2102kJ
Fat	3.3g
Saturated Fat	0.5g
Cholesterol	21mg
Fibre	4g

FRUITY HAM AND FRENCH BREAD PIZZA

French bread makes a great pizza base. For a really speedy recipe, use ready-prepared pizza topping instead of the tomato sauce and cook the pizzas under a hot grill (broiler) for a few minutes instead of baking them in the oven.

INGREDIENTS

Serves 4

2 small baguettes
300ml/½ pint/1¼ cups tomato sauce
75g/3oz lean sliced cooked ham
4 canned pineapple rings, drained
and chopped
½ small green (bell) pepper, seeded
and cut into thin strips
50g/2oz reduced-fat mature (sharp)
Cheddar cheese
salt and black pepper

1 Preheat the oven to 200°C/400°F/ Gas 6. Cut the baguettes in half lengthways and toast the cut sides until crisp and golden.

VARIATION
If you prefer, omit the ham and substitute cooked chicken, peeled prawns (shrimp) or tuna fish.

2 Spread the tomato sauce over the toasted baguettes.

3 Cut the ham into strips and lay on the baguettes with the pineapple and green pepper. Season to taste with salt and pepper.

4 Grate the cheese and sprinkle on top of the other toppings. Bake in the preheated oven for 15–20 minutes until crisp and golden.

NUTRITION NOTES
Per portion:

Energy	111Kcals/468.7kJ
Fat	3.31g
Saturated Fat	1.63g
Cholesterol	18.25mg
Fibre	0.79g

CRACKED WHEAT AND MINT SALAD

INGREDIENTS

ves 4

)g/9oz/1⅔ cups cracked wheat
omatoes
mall courgettes (zucchini), thinly
iced lengthways
pring onions (scallions), sliced on
he diagonal
eady-to-eat dried apricots, chopped
g/1½oz/¼ cup raisins
ce of 1 lemon
ml/2 tbsp tomato juice
ml/3 tbsp chopped fresh mint
arlic clove, crushed
t and black pepper
ig of fresh mint, to garnish

Put the cracked wheat into a large
bowl. Add enough boiling water to
ne 2.5cm/1in above the level of the
eat. Leave to soak for 30 minutes,
n drain well and squeeze out any
cess water in a clean dish towel.

Meanwhile, plunge the tomatoes
into boiling water for 1 minute and
en into cold water. Slip off the skins.
.lve, remove the seeds and cores and
ighly chop the flesh.

3 Stir the tomatoes, courgettes, spring
onions, apricots and raisins into the
cracked wheat.

NUTRITION NOTES	
Per portion:	
Energy	293Kcals/1231.7kJ
Fat	1.69g
Saturated Fat	0.28g
Fibre	2.25g

4 Put the lemon and tomato juice,
mint, garlic clove and seasoning
into a small bowl and whisk together
with a fork. Pour over the salad and
mix well. Chill for at least 1 hour.
Serve garnished with a sprig of mint.

CHILLI BEAN BAKE

The contrasting textures of sauce, beans, vegetables and a crunchy cornbread topping make this a memorable meal.

INGREDIENTS

Serves 4

225g/8oz/1¼ cups red kidney beans
1 bay leaf
1 large onion, finely chopped
1 garlic clove, crushed
2 celery sticks, sliced
5ml/1 tsp ground cumin
5ml/1 tsp chilli powder
400g/14oz can chopped tomatoes
15ml/1 tbsp tomato purée (paste)
5ml/1 tsp dried mixed herbs
15ml/1 tbsp lemon juice
1 yellow (bell) pepper, seeded and diced
salt and black pepper
mixed salad, to serve

For the cornbread topping

175g/6oz/1½ cups cornmeal
15ml/1 tbsp wholemeal
 (whole-wheat) flour
5ml/1 tsp baking powder
1 egg, beaten
175ml/6fl oz/¾ cup skimmed milk

1 Soak the beans overnight in cold water. Drain and rinse well. Pour 1 litre/1¾ pints/4 cups water into a large, heavy pan, add the beans and bay leaf and boil rapidly for 10 minutes. Lower the heat, cover the pan and simmer for 35–40 minutes or until the beans are tender.

NUTRITION NOTES

Per portion:

Energy	399Kcals/1675kJ
Protein	22.86g
Fat	4.65g
Saturated Fat	0.86g
Fibre	11.59g

2 Add the onion, garlic, celery, cumin chilli powder, chopped tomatoes, tomato purée and dried mixed herbs. Half cover the pan with a lid and simmer for a further 10 minutes.

3 Stir in the lemon juice, yellow pepper and seasoning. Simmer for a further 8–10 minutes, stirring occasionally, until the vegetables are tender. Discard the bay leaf and spoo the mixture into a large casserole.

4 Preheat the oven to 220°C/425°F/ Gas 7. To make the topping, put t cornmeal, flour, baking powder and a pinch of salt into a bowl and mix together. Make a well in the centre an add the egg and milk. Mix and pour over the bean mixture. Bake in the ov for 20 minutes or until brown. Serve hot with mixed salad.

SPICY BEAN HOT POT

INGREDIENTS

~ves 4

~5g/8oz/3 cups button
~white) mushrooms
~ml/1 tbsp sunflower oil
~nions, sliced
~arlic clove, crushed
~ml/1 tbsp red wine vinegar
~0g/14oz can chopped tomatoes
~ml/1 tbsp tomato purée (paste)
~ml/1 tbsp Worcestershire sauce
~ml/1 tbsp wholegrain mustard
~ml/1 tbsp soft dark brown sugar
~0ml/8fl oz/1 cup vegetable stock
~0g/14oz can red kidney
~eans, drained
~0g/14oz can haricot (navy) or
~annellini beans, drained
~ay leaf
~g/3oz/¹/2 cup raisins
~t and black pepper
~opped fresh parsley, to garnish

Wipe the mushrooms, then cut them
into small pieces. Set aside.

Heat the oil in a large pan, add the
onions and garlic and cook over a
~ntle heat for 10 minutes until soft.

3 Add all the remaining ingredients
except the mushrooms and seasoning.
Bring to the boil, lower the heat and
simmer for 10 minutes.

4 Add the mushrooms and simmer
for 5 minutes more. Stir in salt and
pepper to taste. Transfer to warm
plates and sprinkle with parsley.

NUTRITION NOTES

Per portion:	
Energy	280Kcals/1175kJ
Fat	4.5g
Saturated Fat	0.5g
Cholesterol	0

Bean Purée with Chicory

The slightly bitter flavours of the radicchio and chicory make a wonderful marriage with the creamy bean purée. Walnut oil adds a nutty taste, but olive oil could also be used.

Ingredients

Serves 4

400g/14oz can cannellini beans
45ml/3 tbsp low-fat fromage frais or
  cream cheese
finely grated rind and juice of
  1 large orange
15ml/1 tbsp finely chopped rosemary
4 heads of chicory
2 medium heads of radicchio
10ml/2 tbsp walnut oil
shreds of orange rind,
  to garnish (optional)

1 Drain the beans, rinse, and drain again. Purée the beans in a blender or food processor with the fromage frais or cream cheese, orange rind, orange juice and rosemary. Set aside.

2 Cut the heads of chicory in half lengthwise.

3 Cut each radicchio head into eight wedges. Preheat the grill (broiler).

4 Lay out the chicory and radicchio on a baking tray and brush with the walnut oil. Grill (broil) for 2–3 minutes. Serve with the purée and sprinkle over the orange shreds, if using.

Nutrition Notes

Per portion:

Energy	103Kcals/432kJ
Protein	6.22g
Fat	1.54g
Saturated Fat	0.4g
Fibre	6.73g

LENTIL BOLOGNESE

 really useful sauce to serve
th pasta, as a pancake stuffing
 even as a protein-packed
uce for vegetables.

INGREDIENTS

rves 6

ml/3 tbsp olive oil
onion, chopped
garlic cloves, crushed
carrots, coarsely grated
celery sticks, chopped
5g/4oz/²/³ cup red lentils
0g/14oz can chopped tomatoes
ml/2 tbsp tomato purée (paste)
0ml/³/4 pint/2 cups stock
ml/1 tbsp fresh marjoram, chopped,
or 5ml/1 tsp dried marjoram
lt and black pepper

 Heat the oil in a large pan and
 gently fry the onion, garlic, carrots
d celery for about 5 minutes, until
ey are soft.

NUTRITION NOTES

Per portion:
Energy	103Kcals/432kJ
Fat	2.19g
Saturated Fat	0.85g
Fibre	2.15g

2 Add the lentils, tomatoes, tomato
purée, stock, marjoram and
seasoning to the pan.

3 Bring the mixture to the boil, then
partially cover with a lid and
simmer for 20 minutes until thick and
soft. Use the sauce as required.

COOK'S TIP
You can easily reduce the fat in
this recipe by using less olive oil,
or substituting a little of the stock
and cooking the vegetables over a
low heat in a non-stick frying pan
until they are soft.

Vegetable Biryani

This exotic dish made from everyday ingredients will be appreciated by vegetarians and meat-eaters alike. It is extremely low in fat, but packed full of exciting flavours.

Nutrition Notes

Per portion:

Energy	175Kcals/737kJ
Protein	3.66g
Fat	0.78g
Saturated Fat	0.12g
Fibre	0.58g

Ingredients

Serves 4–6

175g/6oz/1 cup long grain rice
2 whole cloves
seeds of 2 cardamom pods
450ml/¾ pint/scant 2 cups vegetable
    stock
2 garlic cloves
1 small onion, roughly chopped
5ml/1 tsp cumin seeds
5ml/1 tsp ground coriander
2.5ml/½ tsp ground turmeric
2.5ml/½ tsp chilli powder
1 large potato, peeled and cut into
    2.5cm/1in cubes
2 carrots, sliced
½ cauliflower, broken into florets
50g/2oz French (green) beans, cut into
    2.5cm/1in lengths
30ml/2 tbsp chopped fresh
    coriander (cilantro)
30ml/2 tbsp lime juice
salt and black pepper
sprig of fresh coriander,
    to garnish

Variations
Substitute other vegetables, if you like. Courgettes (zucchini), broccoli, parsnip and sweet potatoes would all be excellent choices.

4 Preheat the oven to 180°C/350°F/ Gas 4. Spoon the spicy paste into a flameproof casserole and cook over a low heat for 2 minutes, stirring occasionally to prevent sticking.

5 Add the potato, carrots, cauliflower florets, beans and 90ml/6 tbsp water. Cover and cook over a low heat for a further 12 minutes, stirring occasionally. Add the chopped coriander.

2 Reduce the heat, cover and simmer for 20 minutes, or until all the stock has been absorbed.

3 Meanwhile put the garlic cloves, onion, cumin seeds, coriander, turmeric, chilli powder and seasoning into a blender or coffee grinder together with 30ml/2 tbsp water. Blend to a smooth paste.

6 Remove the cloves and spoon the rice over the vegetables. Sprinkle over the lime juice. Cover and cook in the oven for 25 minutes, or until the vegetables are tender. Fluff up the rice with a fork before serving and garnish with a sprig of fresh coriander.

1 Put the rice, cloves and cardamom seeds into a large, heavy pan. Pour over the stock and bring to the boil.

COCONUT RICE

A delicious alternative to plain boiled rice, brown or white rice will both work well.

INGREDIENTS

Serves 6
450g/1lb/2 cups long grain rice
250ml/8fl oz/1 cup water
475ml/16fl oz/2 cups coconut milk
2.5ml/½ tsp salt
30ml/2 tbsp sugar
fresh shredded coconut, to garnish

COOK'S TIP
Coconut milk is available in cans, but if you cannot find it, use creamed coconut mixed with water according to the packet instructions, or coconut cream.

1 Wash the rice in cold water until it runs clear. Place the water, coconut milk, salt and sugar in a heavy pan or flameproof casserole.

2 Add the rice, cover and bring to the boil. Reduce the heat to low and simmer for about 15–20 minutes or until the rice is tender to the bite and cooked through.

3 Turn off the heat and allow the rice to rest in the pan for a further 5–10 minutes.

4 Fluff up the rice with chopsticks or a fork before serving garnished with shredded coconut.

NUTRITION NOTES	
Per portion:	
Energy	322.5Kcals/1371kJ
Fat	2.49g
Saturated Fat	1.45g
Cholesterol	0
Fibre	0.68g

JASMINE RICE

Perfectly cooked rice makes an ideal, low-fat accompaniment to many delicious low-fat dishes such as vegetable chilli and vegetable bolognese.

INGREDIENTS

Serves 6

450g/1lb/2 cups long grain rice
750ml/1¼ pints/3 cups cold water
2.5ml/½ tsp salt

NUTRITION NOTES

Per portion:

Energy	270.8Kcals/1152kJ
Fat	0.75g
Saturated Fat	0
Cholesterol	0
Fibre	0.37g

COOK'S TIP

An electric rice cooker both cooks the rice and keeps it warm. Different sizes and models are available. The top of the range is a non-stick version, which is expensive, but well worth the money if you eat rice a lot.

1 Rinse the rice in several changes of cold water until the water stays clear.

2 Put the rice in a heavy pan or flameproof casserole and add the water and salt. Bring the rice to a vigorous boil, uncovered, over a high heat.

3 Stir and reduce the heat to low. Cover and simmer for up to 20 minutes, or until all the water has been absorbed. Remove from the heat and leave to stand for 10 minutes.

4 Remove the lid and stir the rice gently with chopsticks or a fork to fluff up and separate the grains.

MEAT AND POULTRY

Make the most of the wide range of leaner cuts of meat available to make delicious, low-fat dishes. Included here are tempting, light and nutritious main courses, which are packed with flavour, try spicy Thai Beef Salad or Tandoori Chicken Kebabs for an al fresco summer lunch, Ragoût of Veal, Chicken, Carrot and Leek Parcels or Venison with Cranberry Sauce for a special occasion dinner. If you are feeding a family, there are plenty of recipes here that will please, from Turkey and Tomato Hot Pot to Barbecued Chicken.

THAI BEEF SALAD

A hearty salad of beef, laced with a chilli and lime dressing.

INGREDIENTS

Serves 6

75g/3oz lean sirloin steaks
1 red onion, finely sliced
1/2 cucumber, sliced into matchsticks
1 lemon grass stalk, finely chopped
30ml/2 tbsp chopped spring
    onions (scallions)
juice of 2 limes
15–30ml/1–2 tbsp fish sauce
2–4 red chillies, finely sliced, to garnish
fresh coriander (cilantro), Chinese
    mustard cress and mint leaves,
    to garnish

NUTRITION NOTES

Per portion:

Energy	101Kcals/424kJ
Fat	3.8g
Saturated Fat	1.7g
Cholesterol	33.4mg
Fibre	0.28g

VARIATION
Rump or fillet steaks would work just as well in this recipe and are considerably cheaper than sirloin steaks. Choose good-quality lean steaks and remove and discard any visible fat.

1 Grill (broil) the sirloin steaks until they are medium-rare, then allow t rest for 10–15 minutes.

2 When cool, thinly slice the beef an put the slices in a large bowl.

3 Add the sliced onion, cucumber matchsticks and lemon grass.

4 Add the spring onions. Toss and season with lime juice and fish sauce. Serve at room temperature or chilled, garnished with the chillies, coriander, mustard cress and mint.

RAGOÛT OF VEAL

you are looking for a low-
lorie dish to treat yourself – or
me guests – then this is perfect,
d quick, too.

INGREDIENTS

rves 4
5g/12oz veal fillet or loin
ml/2 tsp olive oil
–12 tiny onions, kept whole
yellow (bell) pepper, seeded and cut
into eighths
orange or red (bell) pepper, seeded
and cut into eighths
tomatoes, peeled and quartered
fresh basil sprigs
ml/2 tbsp dry martini or sherry
t and black pepper

NUTRITION NOTES

Per portion:
Energy	158Kcals/665.5kJ
Fat	4.97g
Saturated Fat	1.14g
Cholesterol	63mg
Fibre	2.5g

Trim off any fat and cut the veal
into cubes. Heat the oil in a frying
n and gently stir-fry the veal and
ions until browned.

2 After a couple of minutes, add the
peppers and tomatoes. Continue
stir-frying for another 4–5 minutes.

VARIATIONS
Lean beef or pork fillet may be
used instead of veal, if you prefer.
Shallots can replace the onions.

3 Add half the basil leaves, roughly
chopped (keep some for garnish),
the martini or sherry and seasoning.
Cook, stirring frequently, for another
10 minutes, or until the meat is tender.

4 Sprinkle with the remaining basil
leaves and serve hot.

VENISON WITH CRANBERRY SAUCE

Venison steaks are now readily available. Lean and low in fat, they make a healthy choice for a special occasion. Served with a sauce of fresh cranberries, port and ginger, they make a dish with a wonderful combination of flavours.

INGREDIENTS

Serves 4
1 orange
1 lemon
75g/3oz/1 cup fresh or
    frozen cranberries
5ml/1 tsp grated fresh root ginger
1 thyme sprig, plus extra to garnish
5ml/1 tsp Dijon mustard
60ml/4 tbsp redcurrant jelly
150ml/¼ pint/⅔ cup ruby port
10ml/2 tsp sunflower oil
4 x 90g/3½oz venison steaks
2 shallots, finely chopped
salt and black pepper
mashed potato and broccoli, to serve

NUTRITION NOTES

Per portion:

Energy	250Kcals/1055.5kJ
Fat	4.39g
Saturated Fat	1.13g
Cholesterol	50mg
Fibre	1.59g

COOK'S TIP
When frying venison, always remember: the briefer the better. Venison will turn to leather if subjected to fierce heat after it has reached the medium-rare stage. If you dislike any hint of pink, cook it to this stage, then let it rest in a low oven for a few minutes.

1 Pare the rind from half the orange and half the lemon using a vegetable peeler, then cut into very fine strips.

2 Blanch the strips in a small pan of boiling water for about 5 minutes until tender. Drain the strips and refresh under cold water.

3 Squeeze the juice from the orange and lemon, then pour into a small pan. Add the cranberries, ginger, thyme sprig, mustard, redcurrant jelly and port. Cook over a low heat until the jelly melts.

4 Bring the sauce to the boil, stirring occasionally, then cover and reduce the heat. Cook for about 15 minutes, until the cranberries are just tender.

VARIATION
When fresh cranberries are unavailable, use redcurrants instead. Stir them into the sauce towards the end of the cooking with the orange and lemon rinds.

5 Heat the oil in a heavy frying pan, add the venison steaks and cook over a high heat for 2–3 minutes.

6 Turn over the steaks and add the shallots to the pan. Cook the steak on the other side for 2–3 minutes, depending on whether you like rare or medium-cooked meat.

7 Just before the end of cooking, pour in the sauce and add the strips of orange and lemon rind.

8 Leave the sauce to bubble for a few seconds to thicken slightly, then remove the thyme sprig and adjust the seasoning to taste.

9 Transfer the venison steaks to warmed plates and spoon over the sauce. Garnish with thyme sprigs and serve accompanied by mashed potato and broccoli.

BARBECUED CHICKEN

INGREDIENTS

Serves 4 or 8

8 small chicken pieces
2 limes, cut into wedges, 2 red chillies,
    finely sliced, and 2 lemon grass
    stalks, to garnish
rice, to serve

For the marinade

2 lemon grass stalks, chopped
2.5cm/1in piece fresh root ginger
6 garlic cloves
4 shallots
1/2 bunch coriander (cilantro) roots
15ml/1 tbsp palm sugar (jaggery)
120ml/4fl oz/1/2 cup coconut milk
30ml/2 tbsp fish sauce
30ml/2 tbsp soy sauce

COOK'S TIPS
Don't eat the skin of the chicken –
it's only left on to keep the flesh
moist during cooking. Coconut
milk makes a good base for a
marinade or sauce, as it is low in
calories and fat.

NUTRITION NOTES

Per portion (for 8):

Energy	106Kcals/449kJ
Fat	2.05g
Saturated Fat	1.10g
Cholesterol	1.10mg
Fibre	109g

1 To make the marinade, put all the ingredients into a food processor and process until smooth.

2 Put the chicken pieces in a dish and pour over the marinade. Leave in a cool place to marinate for at least 4 hours or overnight.

3 Preheat the oven to 200°C/400°F/ Gas 6. Put the chicken pieces on a rack on a baking tray. Brush with marinade and bake in the oven for about 20–30 minutes or until the chicken is cooked and golden brown. Turn the pieces over halfway through and brush with more marinade.

4 Garnish with lime wedges, finely sliced red chillies and lemon grass stalks. Serve with rice.

TANDOORI CHICKEN KEBABS

This dish originates from the plains of the Punjab at the foot of the Himalayas, where food is traditionally cooked in clay ovens known as *tandoors* – hence the name.

INGREDIENTS

Serves 4

4 skinless chicken breast fillets
  (about 130g/3¹/₂oz each)
15ml/1 tbsp lemon juice
45ml/3 tbsp tandoori paste
45ml/3 tbsp low-fat natural
  (plain) yogurt
1 garlic clove, crushed
30ml/2 tbsp chopped fresh
  coriander (cilantro)
1 small onion, cut into wedges and
  separated into layers
10ml/1 tsp oil, for brushing
salt and black pepper
fresh coriander sprigs, to garnish
pilau rice and naan bread, to serve

1 Chop the chicken breasts into 2.5cm/1in cubes, put in a bowl and add the lemon juice, tandoori paste, yogurt, garlic, coriander and seasoning. Cover and leave to marinate in the refrigerator for 2–3 hours.

2 Preheat the grill (broiler) to high. Thread alternate pieces of chicken and onion on to four skewers.

VARIATION
Use chopped, boned and skinned chicken thighs, or strips of turkey breasts, for a cheaper and equally low-fat alternative.

3 Brush the onions with a little oil, lay the skewers on a grill rack and cook for 10–12 minutes, turning once.

4 Garnish the kebabs with coriander and serve at once with pilau rice and naan bread.

NUTRITION NOTES	
Per portion:	
Energy	215.7Kcals/911.2kJ
Fat	4.2g
Saturated Fat	0.27g
Cholesterol	122mg
Fibre	0.22g

CHICKEN, CARROT AND LEEK PARCELS

These intriguing parcels may sound a bit fiddly for everyday eating, but actually they take very little time, and you can freeze them ready to cook from frozen when needed.

INGREDIENTS

Serves 4
4 skinless chicken breast fillets
2 small leeks, sliced
2 carrots, grated
2 pitted black olives, chopped
1 garlic clove, crushed
4 anchovy fillets, halved lengthways
salt and black pepper
black olives and herb sprigs,
   to garnish

1 Preheat the oven to 200°C/400°F/ Gas 6. Season the chicken well.

2 Cut out four sheets of lightly greased baking parchment about 23cm/9in square. Divide the leeks equally among them. Put a piece of chicken on top of each.

3 Mix the carrots, olives and garlic together. Season lightly and place on top of the chicken portions. Top each with two of the anchovy fillets.

4 Carefully wrap up each parcel, making sure the paper folds are sealed. Bake the parcels for 20 minutes and serve hot, in the paper, garnished with black olives and herb sprigs.

NUTRITION NOTES

Per portion:
Energy	154Kcals/651kJ
Fat	2.37g
Saturated Fat	0.45g
Cholesterol	78.75mg
Fibre	2.1g

COOK'S TIP
Skinless chicken breast fillets are low in fat and an excellent source of protein. Small, skinless turkey breast fillets also work well in this recipe and make a tasty change if you fancy something different.

THAI CHICKEN AND VEGETABLE STIR-FRY

INGREDIENTS

Serves 4

1 piece lemon grass (or the rind of
  ½ lemon)
1 cm/½in piece fresh root ginger
1 large garlic clove
30ml/2 tbsp sunflower oil
275g/10oz lean chicken,
  thinly sliced
½ red (bell) pepper, seeded and sliced
½ green (bell) pepper, seeded and sliced
4 spring onions (scallions), chopped
2 medium carrots, cut into matchsticks
115g/4oz fine green beans
25g/1oz peanuts, lightly crushed
30 ml/2 tbsp oyster sauce
pinch of sugar
salt and black pepper
coriander (cilantro) leaves, to garnish
boiled rice, to serve

NUTRITION NOTES

Per portion:

Energy	106Kcals/449kJ
Fat	2.05g
Saturated Fat	1.10g
Cholesterol	1.10mg
Fibre	109g

1 Thinly slice the lemon grass or lemon rind. Peel and chop the ginger and garlic. Heat the oil in a frying pan over a high heat. Add the lemon grass or lemon rind, ginger and garlic, and stir-fry for 30 seconds until brown.

2 Add the chicken and stir-fry for about 2 minutes. Then add all the vegetables and stir-fry for 4–5 minutes, until the chicken is cooked and the vegetables are almost cooked.

3 Finally, stir in the peanuts, oyster sauce, sugar and seasoning to taste. Stir-fry for another minute to blend the flavours. Serve at once, sprinkled with the coriander leaves and accompanied by rice.

> VARIATION
> Make this quick supper dish a little hotter by adding more fresh root ginger, if liked.

DUCK BREAST SALAD

Tender slices of succulent cooked duck breasts served with a salad of mixed pasta, fruit and vegetables, tossed together in a light dressing, ensure that this gourmet dish will impress friends and family alike.

INGREDIENTS

Serves 6

2 small duck breasts, boned
5ml/1 tsp coriander seeds, crushed
350g/12oz rigatoni or penne pasta
150ml/¼ pint/⅔ cup fresh orange juice
15ml/1 tbsp lemon juice
10ml/2 tsp clear honey
1 shallot, finely chopped
1 garlic clove, crushed
1 celery stick, chopped
75g/3oz dried cherries
45ml/3 tbsp port
15ml/1 tbsp chopped fresh mint,
   plus extra to garnish
30ml/2 tbsp chopped fresh coriander
   (cilantro), plus extra to garnish
1 eating apple, diced
2 oranges, segmented
salt and black pepper

> **COOK'S TIPS**
> Choose skinless duck breast fillets to reduce fat and calories.
> Crush your own spices, such as coriander seeds, to create fresh, aromatic, spicy flavours. Ready-ground spices lose their flavour more quickly than whole spices, which are best freshly ground just before use.

1 Remove the skin and fat from the duck breasts and season with salt and pepper. Rub with coriander seeds. Preheat the grill (broiler), then grill (broil) the duck for 10 minutes on each side. Wrap in foil and leave for 20 minutes.

2 Cook the pasta in a large pan of boiling, salted water according to the packet instructions, until *al dente*. Drain thoroughly and rinse under cold running water. Leave to cool.

3 To make the dressing, put the orange juice, lemon juice, honey, shallot, garlic, celery, cherries, port, mint and fresh coriander into a bowl, whisk together and leave to marinate for 30 minutes.

4 Slice the duck breasts very thinly. (They should be pink in the centre.)

5 Put the pasta into a large bowl, then add the dressing, diced apple and segments of orange. Toss well to coat the pasta. Transfer the salad to a serving plate with the duck slices and garnish with the extra chopped mint and coriander.

NUTRITION NOTES	
Per portion:	
Energy	348Kcals/1460kJ
Fat	3.8g
Saturated Fat	0.9g
Cholesterol	55mg
Fibre	3g

FRAGRANT CHICKEN CURRY

In this dish, the mildly spiced sauce is thickened using lentils rather than the traditional onions fried in ghee.

INGREDIENTS

Serves 4–6

75g/3oz/¹/₂ cup red lentils
30ml/2 tbsp mild curry powder
10ml/2 tsp ground coriander
5ml/1 tsp cumin seeds
475ml/16fl oz/2 cups vegetable stock
8 chicken thighs, skinned
225g/8oz fresh shredded spinach, or
    frozen, thawed and well drained
15ml/1 tbsp chopped fresh
    coriander (cilantro)
salt and black pepper
sprigs of fresh coriander, to garnish
white or brown basmati rice and grilled
    (broiled) poppadums, to serve

1 Rinse the lentils in a sieve (strainer) under cold running water. Transfer to a large, heavy pan with the curry powder, ground coriander, cumin seeds and stock.

2 Bring to the boil, then lower the heat. Cover the pan and simmer the lentils gently for 10 minutes.

NUTRITION NOTES

Per portion:

Energy	152Kcals/640kJ
Fat	4.9g
Saturated Fat	1.3g
Added Sugar	0
Fibre	2.6g

COOK'S TIP
Lentils are an excellent source of fibre, and add colour and texture.

3 Add the chicken and spinach. Replace the cover and simmer gently for a further 40 minutes, or until the chicken has cooked.

4 Stir in the chopped coriander and season to taste. Serve garnished with fresh coriander and accompanied by the rice and grilled poppadums.

TURKEY AND PASTA BAKE

INGREDIENTS

Serves 4

275g/10oz minced (ground) turkey
150g/5oz smoked turkey rashers
(strips), chopped
2 garlic cloves, crushed
1 onion, finely chopped
2 carrots, diced
30ml/2 tbsp tomato purée (paste)
300ml/¹/₂ pint/1¹/₄ cups chicken stock
225g/8oz rigatoni or penne pasta
30ml/2 tbsp grated Parmesan cheese
salt and black pepper

1 Brown the minced turkey in a non-stick pan, breaking up any large pieces with a wooden spoon, until well browned all over.

2 Add the chopped turkey rashers, garlic, onion, carrots, purée, stock and seasoning. Bring to the boil, cover and simmer for 1 hour until tender.

3 Preheat the oven to 180°C/350°F/ Gas 4. Cook the pasta in a large pan of boiling, salted water according to the packet instructions, until *al dente*. Drain thoroughly and mix with the turkey sauce.

VARIATIONS
Minced (ground) chicken or extra lean minced beef work just as well in this tasty recipe.

4 Transfer to a shallow ovenproof dish and sprinkle with grated Parmesan cheese. Bake for 20–30 minutes until lightly browned on top.

NUTRITION NOTES

Per portion:

Energy	391Kcals/1641kJ
Fat	4.9g
Saturated Fat	2.2g
Cholesterol	60mg
Fibre	3.5g

TURKEY AND TOMATO HOT POT

Here, turkey is turned into tasty meatballs in a rich tomato sauce.

INGREDIENTS

Serves 4

25g/1oz white bread, crusts removed
30ml/2 tbsp skimmed milk
1 garlic clove, crushed
2.5ml/¹/₂ tsp caraway seeds
225g/8oz minced (ground) turkey
1 egg white
350ml/12fl oz/1¹/₂ cups chicken stock
400g/14oz can tomatoes
15ml/1 tbsp tomato purée (paste)
90g/3¹/₂oz/¹/₂ cup easy-cook rice
salt and black pepper
fresh basil, to garnish
carrot and courgette (zucchini) ribbons,
    to serve

3 Whisk the egg white until stiff, then fold, half at a time, into the turkey mixture. Chill for 10 minutes.

4 While the turkey mixture is chilling, put the stock, tomatoes and tomato purée into a large pan and bring to the boil.

1 Cut the bread into small cubes and put into a mixing bowl. Sprinkle over the milk and leave to soak for 5 minutes.

2 Add the garlic clove, caraway seeds, turkey and seasoning to the bread. Mix together well.

5 Add the rice, stir and cook briskly for about 5 minutes. Turn the heat down to a gentle simmer.

6 Meanwhile, shape the turkey mixture into 16 small balls. Carefully drop them into the tomato stock and simmer for a further 8–10 minutes, or until both the turkey balls and rice are cooked. Garnish with basil, and serve with carrot and courgette ribbons.

COOK'S TIPS

To make carrot and courgette (zucchini) ribbons, cut them lengthways into thin strips using a vegetable peeler, and blanch or steam until lightly cooked.
Lean minced (ground) turkey is low in fat and is a good source of protein. It makes an ideal base for this tasty low fat supper dish. Use minced chicken in place of turkey for an appetizing alternative.

NUTRITION NOTES

Per portion:

Energy	190Kcals/798kJ
Protein	18.04g
Fat	1.88g
Saturated Fat	0.24g
Fibre	10.4g

FISH AND SHELLFISH

The range of fresh fish available in our supermarkets is impressive, and fish is always a good choice for a healthy low-fat diet. Most fish, particularly white fish, is low in fat and is a good source of protein. Oily fish contains more fat than white fish, but contains high levels of essential fatty acids which are vital for good health. Fish is quick and easy to prepare and cook and is ideal for serving with fresh seasonal vegetables as part of a healthy low-fat meal. Try Cajun-style Cod, Herby Fishcakes with Lemon Sauce, Mediterranean Fish Cutlets or Curried Prawns in Coconut Milk – just some of the delicious, low-fat recipes included in this chapter.

CAJUN-STYLE COD

This recipe works equally well with any firm-fleshed fish – choose low-fat fish, such as haddock or monkfish.

NUTRITION NOTES

Per portion:

Energy	137Kcals/577kJ
Protein	28.42g
Fat	1.75g
Saturated Fat	0.26g
Fibre	0.06g

INGREDIENTS

Serves 4

4 cod steaks, each weighing about
   175g/6oz
30ml/2 tbsp low-fat natural
   (plain) yogurt
15ml/1 tbsp lime or lemon juice
1 garlic clove, crushed
5ml/1 tsp ground cumin
5ml/1 tsp paprika
5ml/1 tsp mustard powder
2.5ml/¹/₂ tsp cayenne pepper
2.5ml/¹/₂ tsp dried thyme
2.5ml/¹/₂ tsp dried oregano
non-stick cooking spray
lemon slices, to garnish
new potatoes and a mixed salad,
   to serve

1 Pat the fish dry on kitchen paper. Mix together the yogurt and lime or lemon juice in a small bowl and brush lightly over both sides of the fish with a pastry brush.

2 Mix together the crushed garlic, spices and herbs. Coat both sides of the fish with the seasoning mix, rubbing in well.

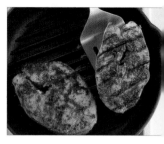

3 Spray a ridged grill (broiler) pan o heavy frying pan with non-stick cooking spray. Heat until very hot. Add the fish and cook over a high he for 4 minutes, or until the undersides are well browned.

4 Turn the steaks over and cook for further 4 minutes, or until cooked through. Serve immediately, garnishec with lemon and accompanied by new potatoes and a mixed salad.

PLAICE PROVENÇAL

INGREDIENTS

ves 4
rge plaice fillets
nall red onions
ml/4fl oz/½ cup vegetable stock
nl/4 tbsp dry red wine
arlic clove, crushed
ourgettes (zucchini), sliced
ellow (bell) pepper, seeded and sliced
)g/14oz can chopped tomatoes
nl/1 tbsp chopped fresh thyme
and black pepper
ato gratin, to serve

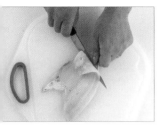

Preheat the oven to 180°C/350°F/
Gas 4. Lay the plaice skin-side
vn and, holding the tail end, push a
rp knife between the skin and flesh
a sawing movement. Hold the knife
a slight angle with the blade towards
skin.

Cut each onion into eight wedges.
Put into a heavy pan with the stock.
ver and simmer for 5 minutes.
cover and continue to cook, stirring
asionally, until the stock has
uced entirely. Add the wine and
lic clove to the pan and continue to
k until the onions are soft.

3 Add the courgettes, yellow pepper,
tomatoes and thyme and season to
taste. Simmer for 3 minutes. Spoon the
sauce into a large casserole.

COOK'S TIP
Skinless white fish fillets such as
plaice are low in fat and make
an ideal tasty and nutritious basis
for many low-fat recipes such as
this one.

4 Fold each fillet in half and put on
top of the sauce. Cover and cook in
the oven for 15–20 minutes, until the
fish is opaque and flakes easily. Serve
with a potato gratin.

NUTRITION NOTES	
Per portion:	
Energy	191Kcals/802kJ
Protein	29.46g
Fat	3.77g
Saturated Fat	0.61g
Fibre	1.97g

Monkfish and Mussel Skewers

Skinless white fish such as monkfish is a good source of protein whilst also being low in calories and fat. These attractive shellfish kebabs, flavoured with a light marinade, are excellent grilled (broiled) or barbecued and served with herby boiled rice and a mixed leaf salad.

Ingredients

Serves 4

450g/1lb monkfish, skinned and boned
5ml/1 tsp olive oil
30ml/2 tbsp lemon juice
5ml/1 tsp paprika
1 garlic clove, crushed
4 turkey rashers (strips)
8 cooked mussels
8 raw prawns (shrimp)
15ml/1 tbsp chopped fresh dill
salt and black pepper
lemon wedges, to garnish
salad leaves and long grain and wild
* rice, to serve*

1 Cut the monkfish into 2.5cm/1in cubes and place in a shallow glass dish. Mix together the oil, lemon juice, paprika and garlic clove and season.

2 Pour the marinade over the fish and toss to coat evenly. Cover and leave in a cool place for 30 minutes.

3 Cut the turkey rashers in half and wrap each strip around a mussel. Thread on to skewers, alternating with the fish cubes and raw prawns. Preheat the grill (broiler) to high.

4 Grill (broil) the kebabs for 7–8 minutes, turning once and basting with the marinade. Sprinkle with chopped dill and salt. Garnish with lemon wedges and serve with salad and rice.

NUTRITION NOTES	
Per portion:	
Energy	133Kcals/560kJ
Protein	25.46g
Fat	3.23g
Saturated Fat	0.77g
Fibre	0.12g

LEMON SOLE BAKED IN A PAPER CASE

INGREDIENTS

rves 4
emon sole fillets, each weighing
 bout 150g/5oz
 small cucumber, sliced
 emon slices
 ml/4 tbsp dry white wine
 rigs of fresh dill, to garnish
 tatoes and braised celery, to serve

r the yogurt hollandaise
 0ml/¼ pint low-fat natural
 plain) yogurt
 al/1 tsp lemon juice
 gg yolks
 al/1 tsp Dijon mustard
 t and black pepper

Preheat the oven to 180°C/350°F/
. Gas 4. Cut out four heart shapes
 om baking parchment, each about 20
 15cm/8 x 6in.

Place a sole fillet on one side of
 each heart. Arrange the cucumber
 d lemon slices on top of each fillet.
 rinkle with the wine and close the
 rcels by turning the edges of the paper
 d twisting to secure. Put on a baking
 ay and cook for 15 minutes.

3 Meanwhile make the hollandaise. Beat together the yogurt, lemon juice and egg yolks in a double boiler or bowl placed over a pan. Cook over simmering water, stirring for about 15 minutes, or until thickened. (The sauce will become thinner after 10 minutes, but will thicken again.)

COOK'S TIP
Make sure that the paper parcels are well sealed, so that none of the delicious juices can escape.

4 Remove from the heat and stir in the mustard. Season to taste with salt and pepper. Open the fish parcels, garnish with a sprig of dill and serve accompanied with the sauce, new potatoes and braised celery.

NUTRITION NOTES

Per portion:	
Energy	185Kcals/779kJ
Protein	29.27g
Fat	4.99g
Saturated Fat	1.58g
Fibre	0.27g

Herby Fishcakes with Lemon Sauce

The wonderful flavour of fresh herbs makes these fishcakes the catch of the day.

Ingredients

Serves 4
350g/12oz potatoes, roughly chopped
75ml/5 tbsp skimmed milk
350g/12oz haddock or hoki
   fillets, skinned
15ml/1 tbsp lemon juice
15ml/1 tbsp creamed horseradish sauce
30ml/2 tbsp chopped fresh parsley
flour, for dusting
115g/4oz/2 cups fresh wholemeal
   (whole-wheat) breadcrumbs
salt and black pepper
flat leaf parsley sprigs, to garnish
sugar snap peas or mangetouts (snow
   peas) and a sliced tomato and onion
   salad, to serve

For the lemon and chive sauce
thinly pared rind and juice of
   ½ small lemon
120ml/4fl oz/½ cup dry white wine
2 thin slices of fresh root ginger
10ml/2 tsp cornflour (cornstarch)
30ml/2 tbsp snipped fresh chives

Nutrition Notes

Per portion:
Energy	232Kcals/975kJ
Protein	19.99g
Fat	1.99g
Saturated Fat	0.26g
Fibre	3.11g

Variation
Dry white wine is a tasty fat-free basis for this herby sauce. Try using cider as an alternative to wine, for a change.

1 Cook the potatoes in a large pan of boiling water for 15–20 minutes. Drain and mash with the milk and season to taste.

2 Purée the fish together with the lemon juice and horseradish sauce in a blender or food processor. Mix with the potatoes and parsley.

3 With floured hands, shape the mixture into eight fishcakes and coat with the breadcrumbs. Chill in the refrigerator for 30 minutes.

4 Preheat the grill (broiler) to mediur and cook the fishcakes for 5 minute on each side, until browned.

5 To make the sauce, cut the lemon rind into julienne strips and put int a large pan together with the lemon juice, wine and ginger. Season to taste with salt and pepper.

6 Simmer, uncovered, for about 6 minutes. Blend the cornflour with 15ml/1 tbsp of cold water, add to the pan and simmer until clear. Stir in the chives immediately before serving.

7 Serve the sauce hot with the fishcakes, garnished with parsley sprigs and accompanied by mangetouts and a tomato and onion salad.

STEAMED FISH WITH CHILLI SAUCE

Steaming is one of the best – and lowest fat – methods of cooking fish. By leaving the fish whole and on the bone, you'll find that all the delicious flavour and moistness is retained.

INGREDIENTS

Serves 6
1 large or 2 medium, firm fish like bass
  or grouper, scaled and cleaned
a fresh banana leaf or large piece
  of foil
30ml/2 tbsp rice wine
3 red chillies, seeded and finely sliced
2 garlic cloves, finely chopped
2cm/³⁄₄in piece of fresh root ginger,
  finely shredded
2 lemon grass stalks, crushed and
  finely chopped
2 spring onions (scallions), chopped
30ml/2 tbsp fish sauce
juice of 1 lime

For the chilli sauce
10 red chillies, seeded and chopped
4 garlic cloves, chopped
60ml/4 tbsp fish sauce
15ml/1 tbsp sugar
75ml/5 tbsp lime juice

1 Rinse the fish under cold running water. Pat dry with kitchen paper. With a sharp knife, slash the skin of the fish a few times on both sides.

2 Place the fish on the banana leaf or foil. Mix together the remaining ingredients and spread over the fish.

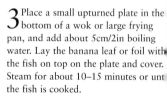

3 Place a small upturned plate in the bottom of a wok or large frying pan, and add about 5cm/2in boiling water. Lay the banana leaf or foil with the fish on top on the plate and cover. Steam for about 10–15 minutes or until the fish is cooked.

4 Meanwhile, put all the chilli sauce ingredients in a food processor and process until smooth. You may need to add a little cold water.

5 Serve the fish hot, on the banana leaf if liked, with the sweet chilli sauce to spoon over the top.

NUTRITION NOTES

Per portion:

Energy	170Kcals/721kJ
Fat	3.46g
Saturated Fat	0.54g
Cholesterol	106mg
Fibre	0.35g

BAKED COD WITH TOMATOES

or the very best flavour, use
rm sun-ripened tomatoes for
e sauce and make sure it is
irly thick before spooning it
ver the cod.

rves 4
)ml/2 tsp olive oil
onion, chopped
garlic cloves, finely chopped
0g/1lb tomatoes, peeled, seeded
and chopped
nl/1 tsp tomato purée (paste)
)ml/4 tbsp dry white wine
)ml/4 tbsp chopped flat leaf parsley
cod cutlets
)ml/2 tbsp dried breadcrumbs
lt and black pepper
2w potatoes and green salad, to serve

NUTRITION NOTES

Per portion:

Energy	151Kcals/647kJ
Fat	1.5g
Saturated Fat	0.2g
Cholesterol	55.2mg
Fibre	2.42g

VARIATION
For extra speed, use a 400g/14oz
can of chopped tomatoes in place
of the fresh tomatoes and 5–10ml/
1–2 tsp ready-minced garlic in
place of the garlic cloves.

1 Preheat the oven to 190°C/375°F/
Gas 5. Heat the oil in a pan and fry
the onion for about 5 minutes. Add the
garlic, tomatoes, tomato purée, wine
and seasoning.

2 Bring the sauce just to the boil, then
reduce the heat slightly and cook,
uncovered, for 15–20 minutes until
thick. Stir in the parsley.

3 Grease an ovenproof dish, put in
the cod cutlets and spoon an equal
quantity of the tomato sauce on to
each. Sprinkle the dried breadcrumbs
over the top.

4 Bake for 20–30 minutes, basting the
fish occasionally with the sauce,
until the fish is tender and cooked
through, and the breadcrumbs are
golden and crisp. Serve hot with new
potatoes and a green salad.

MEDITERRANEAN FISH CUTLETS

These low-fat fish cutlets are well complemented by boiled potatoes, broccoli and carrots.

INGREDIENTS

Serves 4

*4 white fish cutlets, about
  150g/5oz each
about 150ml/¹/4 pint/²/3 cup fish stock
  or dry white wine (or a mixture of
  the two), for poaching
1 bay leaf, a few black peppercorns
  and a strip of pared lemon rind
chopped fresh parsley, to garnish*

For the tomato sauce

*400g/14oz can chopped tomatoes
1 garlic clove, crushed
15ml/1 tbsp pastis or other aniseed-
  flavoured liqueur
15ml/1 tbsp drained capers
12–16 pitted black olives
salt and black pepper*

1 To make the sauce, place the chopped tomatoes, garlic, pastis or liqueur, capers and olives in a pan. Season to taste with salt and pepper and cook over a low heat for about 15 minutes, stirring occasionally.

2 Place the fish in a frying pan, pour over the stock and/or wine and add the bay leaf, peppercorns and lemon rind. Cover and simmer for 10 minutes or until it flakes easily.

3 Using a slotted spoon, transfer the fish into a heated dish. Strain the stock into the tomato sauce and boil to reduce slightly. Season the sauce, pour it over the fish and serve immediately, sprinkled with the chopped parsley.

> ### VARIATIONS
> Remove skin from cutlets and reduce the quantity of olives to reduce calories and fat. Use 450g/1lb fresh tomatoes, skinned and chopped, in place of the canned tomatoes.

NUTRITION NOTES

Per portion:

Energy	165Kcals/685kJ
Fat	3.55g
Saturated Fat	0.5g
Cholesterol	69mg

BAKED FISH IN BANANA LEAVES

Fish that is prepared in this way is particularly succulent and flavourful. Fillets are used here, rather than whole fish, which is easier for those who don't like to mess about with bones. It is a great dish for a barbecue.

INGREDIENTS

Serves 4

250ml/8fl oz/1 cup coconut milk
30ml/2 tbsp red curry paste
45ml/3 tbsp fish sauce
30ml/2 tbsp sugar
5 kaffir lime leaves, torn
4 x 175g/6oz fish fillets, such
    as snapper
175g/6oz mixed vegetables, such as
    carrots or leeks, finely shredded
4 banana leaves or pieces of foil
30ml/2 tbsp shredded spring onions
    (scallions), to garnish
2 red chillies, finely sliced, to garnish

NUTRITION NOTES

Per portion:

Energy	258Kcals/1094kJ
Fat	4.31g
Saturated Fat	0.7g
Cholesterol	64.75mg
Fibre	1.23g

COOK'S TIPS
Coconut milk is low in calories and fat and so makes an ideal basis for a low-fat marinade or sauce. Choose colourful mixed vegetables such as carrots, leeks and red (bell) pepper, to make the dish more attractive.

1 Combine the coconut milk, curry paste, fish sauce, sugar and kaffir lime leaves in a shallow dish.

2 Marinate the fish in this mixture for about 15–30 minutes. Preheat the oven to 200°C/400°F/Gas 6.

3 Mix the vegetables together and lay a portion on top of a banana leaf or piece of foil. Place a piece of fish on top with a little of its marinade.

4 Wrap the fish up by turning in the sides and ends of the leaf and secure with cocktail sticks (toothpicks). (With foil, just crumple the edges together.) Repeat with the rest of the fish.

5 Bake for 20–25 minutes or until the fish is cooked. Alternatively, cook under the grill (broiler) or on a barbecue. Just before serving, garnish the fish with a sprinkling of spring onions and sliced red chillies.

PINEAPPLE CURRY WITH SHELLFISH

The delicate sweet and sour flavour of this curry comes from the pineapple, and although it seems an odd combination, it is delicious.

INGREDIENTS

Serves 4

600ml/1 pint/2½ cups coconut milk
30ml/2 tbsp red curry paste
30ml/2 tbsp fish sauce
15ml/1 tbsp sugar
225g/8oz king prawns (jumbo shrimp), shelled and deveined
450g/1lb mussels, cleaned and beards removed
175g/6oz fresh pineapple, finely crushed or chopped
5 kaffir lime leaves, torn
2 red chillies, chopped, and fresh coriander (cilantro) leaves, to garnish

1 In a large pan, bring half the coconut milk to the boil and heat, stirring, until it separates.

2 Add the red curry paste and cook until fragrant. Add the fish sauce and sugar and continue to cook for a few moments.

3 Stir in the rest of the coconut milk and bring back to the boil. Add the king prawns, mussels, pineapple and kaffir lime leaves.

4 Reheat until boiling and then simmer for 3–5 minutes, until the prawns are cooked and the mussels have opened. Remove any mussels that have not opened and discard. Serve garnished with chillies and coriander.

NUTRITION NOTES

Per portion:

Energy	187Kcals/793kJ
Fat	3.5g
Saturated Fat	0.53g
Cholesterol	175.5mg
Fibre	0.59g

CURRIED PRAWNS IN COCONUT MILK

A curry-like dish where the prawns are cooked in a spicy coconut gravy with sweet and sour flavours from the tomatoes.

INGREDIENTS

Serves 4

600ml/1 pint/2½ cups coconut milk
30ml/2 tbsp Thai curry paste
15ml/1 tbsp fish sauce
2.5ml/½ tsp salt
5ml/1 tsp sugar
450g/1lb shelled king prawns (jumbo shrimp), tails left intact and deveined
225g/8oz cherry tomatoes
1 chilli, seeded and chopped
juice of ½ lime, to serve
chilli and coriander (cilantro), to garnish

1 Put half the coconut milk into a pan or wok and bring to the boil.

2 Add the curry paste to the coconut milk, stir until it disperses, then simmer for about 10 minutes.

3 Add the fish sauce, salt, sugar and remaining coconut milk. Simmer for another 5 minutes.

4 Add the prawns, cherry tomatoes and chilli. Simmer gently for about 5 minutes until the prawns are pink and tender.

5 Serve sprinkled with lime juice and garnish with sliced chilli and chopped coriander leaves.

NUTRITION NOTES

Per portion:

Energy	184Kcals/778kJ
Fat	3.26g
Saturated Fat	0.58g
Cholesterol	315mg
Fibre	0.6g

TUNA AND MIXED VEGETABLE PASTA

INGREDIENTS

Serves 4

10ml/2 tsp olive oil
115g/4oz/1½ cups button (white)
 mushrooms, sliced
1 garlic clove, crushed
½ red (bell) pepper, seeded
 and chopped
15ml/1 tbsp tomato purée (paste)
300ml/½ pint/1¼ cups tomato juice
115g/4oz/1 cup frozen peas
15–30ml/1–2 tbsp drained pickled
 green peppercorns, crushed
350g/12oz whole-wheat pasta shapes
200g/7oz can tuna chunks in
 water, drained
6 spring onions (scallions),
 diagonally sliced

1 Heat the oil in a pan and gently sauté the mushrooms, garlic and pepper until softened. Stir in the tomato paste, then add the tomato juice, peas and some or all of the crushed peppercorns, depending on how spicy you like the sauce. Bring to the boil, lower the heat and simmer.

2 Bring a large pan of lightly salted water to the boil and cook the pasta for about 12 minutes (or according to the instructions on the packet), until just tender. When the pasta is almost ready, add the tuna to the sauce and heat through gently. Stir in the spring onions. Drain the pasta, turn it into a heated bowl and pour over the sauce. Toss to mix. Serve immediately.

NUTRITION NOTES

Per portion:

Energy	354Kcals/1514kJ
Fat	4.5g
Saturated Fat	0.67g
Cholesterol	22.95mg
Fibre	10.35g

SWEET AND SOUR FISH

White fish is high in protein, vitamins and minerals, but low in fat. Serve this tasty, nutritious dish with brown rice and stir-fried cabbage or spinach for a delicious lunch.

INGREDIENTS

Serves 4

60ml/4 tbsp cider vinegar
45ml/3 tbsp light soy sauce
50g/2oz/¼ cup sugar
15ml/1 tbsp tomato purée (paste)
25ml/1½ tbsp cornflour (cornstarch)
250ml/8fl oz/1 cup water
1 green (bell) pepper, seeded and sliced
225g/8oz can pineapple pieces in
 fruit juice
225g/8oz tomatoes, peeled
 and chopped
225g/8oz/2 cups button (white)
 mushrooms, sliced
675g/1½lb chunky haddock
 fillets, skinned
salt and black pepper

1 Preheat the oven to 180°C/350°F/ Gas 4. Mix together the vinegar, soy sauce, sugar and tomato purée in a pan. Put the cornflour in a jug (pitcher), stir in the water, then add the mixture to the pan, stirring well. Bring to the boil, stirring constantly until thickened. Lower the heat and simmer the sauce for 5 minutes.

2 Add the green pepper, canned pineapple pieces (with juice) and tomatoes to the pan and stir well. Mix in the mushrooms and heat through. Season to taste with salt and pepper.

3 Place the fish in a single layer in a shallow ovenproof dish, spoon over the sauce and cover with foil. Bake for 15–20 minutes until the fish is tender. Serve immediately.

NUTRITION NOTES

Per portion:

Energy	255Kcals/1070kJ
Fat	2g
Saturated Fat	0.5g
Cholesterol	61mg

VEGETABLES AND VEGETARIAN DISHES

Vegetarian food provides a tasty and nutritious choice at mealtimes for everyone and is especially tempting when it is low in fat too. Choose from delicious vegetable dishes such as Mixed Mushroom Ragoût, Devilled Onions en Croûte and Courgettes in Citrus Sauce or tempting low-fat vegetarian meals such as Autumn Glory, Ratatouille Pancakes, and Tofu and Green Bean Curry.

Herby Baked Tomatoes

Ingredients

Serves 4–6

675g/1½ lb large red and
yellow tomatoes
10ml/2 tsp red wine vinegar
2.5ml/½ tsp wholegrain mustard
1 garlic clove, crushed
10ml/2 tsp chopped fresh parsley
10ml/2 tsp snipped fresh chives
25g/1oz/½ cup fresh fine white
breadcrumbs, for topping
salt and black pepper

Nutrition Notes

Per portion:	
Energy	37Kcals/156kJ
Fat	0.49g
Saturated Fat	0.16g
Cholesterol	0
Fibre	1.36g

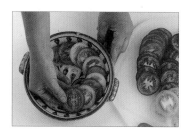

1 Preheat the oven to 200°C/400°F/ Gas 6. Thickly slice the tomatoes and arrange half of them in a 900ml/ 1½ pint/3¾ cup ovenproof dish.

Variations

Use wholemeal (whole-wheat) breadcrumbs in place of white, for added colour, flavour and fibre. Use 5–10ml/1–2 tsp mixed dried herbs, if fresh ones are not available.

2 Mix the vinegar, mustard, garlic and seasoning together in a small bowl. Stir in 10ml/2 tsp cold water. Sprinkle the tomatoes with half the parsley and chives, then drizzle over half the dressing.

3 Lay the remaining tomato slices on top, overlapping them slightly. Drizzle with the remaining dressing.

4 Sprinkle over the breadcrumbs. Bake for 25 minutes or until the topping is golden. Sprinkle with the remaining parsley and chives. Serve immediately, garnished with sprigs of parsley.

POTATO GRATIN

The flavour of Parmesan is wonderfully strong, so a little goes a long way. Leave the cheese out altogether for an almost fat-free dish.

INGREDIENTS

Serves 4
1 garlic clove
5 large baking potatoes, peeled
45ml/3tbsp freshly grated
    Parmesan cheese
600ml/1 pint/2½ cups vegetable or
    chicken stock
pinch of grated nutmeg
salt and black pepper

1 Preheat the oven to 200°C/400°F/ Gas 6. Halve the garlic clove and rub over the base and sides of a large shallow gratin dish.

2 Slice the potatoes very thinly and arrange a third of them in the dish. Sprinkle with a little grated Parmesan cheese, and season with salt and pepper. Pour over some of the stock to prevent the potatoes from discolouring.

3 Continue layering the potatoes and cheese as before, then pour over the rest of the stock. Sprinkle with the grated nutmeg.

VARIATION
For a potato and onion gratin, thinly slice one medium onion and layer with the potato.

4 Bake in the preheated oven for about 1¼–1½ hours or until the potatoes are tender and the tops well browned.

NUTRITION NOTES	
Per portion:	
Energy	178Kcals/749kJ
Protein	9.42g
Fat	1.57g
Saturated Fat	0.30g
Fibre	1.82g

MIXED MUSHROOM RAGOÛT

These mushrooms are delicious served hot or cold and can be prepared up to two days in advance.

INGREDIENTS

Serves 4

1 small onion, finely chopped
1 garlic clove, crushed
5ml/1 tsp coriander seeds, crushed
30ml/2 tbsp red wine vinegar
15ml/1 tbsp soy sauce
15ml/1 tbsp dry sherry
10ml/2 tsp tomato purée (paste)
10ml/2 tsp soft light brown sugar
150ml/¼ pint/⅔ cup vegetable stock
115g/4oz button (white) mushrooms
115g/4oz chestnut mushrooms,
  quartered
115g/4oz oyster mushrooms, sliced
salt and black pepper
coriander (cilantro) sprig, to garnish

NUTRITION NOTES

Per portion:
Energy	41Kcals/172kJ
Protein	2.51g
Fat	0.66g
Saturated Fat	0.08g
Fibre	1.02g

COOK'S TIP

There are many types of fresh mushrooms available and all are low in calories and fat. They add flavour and colour to many low-fat dishes such as this tasty ragoût.

1 Put the first nine ingredients into a large pan. Bring to the boil and reduce the heat. Cover and simmer for 5 minutes.

2 Uncover the pan and simmer for 5 more minutes, or until the liquid has reduced by half.

3 Add the button and chestnut mushrooms and simmer for 3 minutes. Stir in the oyster mushrooms and cook for a further 2 minutes.

4 Remove the mushrooms from the pan with a slotted spoon and transfer them to a serving dish. Keep warm, if serving hot.

5 Boil the juices for about 5 minutes, or until reduced to about 75ml/ 5 tbsp. Season to taste.

6 Allow to cool for 2–3 minutes, then pour over the mushrooms. Serve hot or well chilled, garnished with a sprig of coriander.

DEVILLED ONIONS EN CROÛTE

Fill crisp bread cups with tender
button onions tossed in a
mustardy glaze. Try other low-fat
mixtures of vegetables, such as
ratatouille, for a delicious change.

INGREDIENTS

Serves 4
12 thin slices of white or wholemeal
  (whole-wheat) bread
225g/8oz button (pearl) onions
  or shallots
150ml/¼ pint/⅔ cup vegetable stock
15ml/1 tbsp dry white wine or sherry
2 turkey rashers (strips), cut into strips
10ml/2 tsp Worcestershire sauce
5ml/1 tsp tomato purée (paste)
1.5ml/¼ tsp prepared English mustard
salt and black pepper
sprigs of flat leaf parsley, to garnish

1 Preheat the oven to 200°C/400°F/
Gas 6. Stamp out the bread into
rounds with a 7.5cm/3in fluted cookie
cutter and use to line a 12–cup tin (pan).

2 Cover each bread case with baking
parchment and fill with baking
beans. Bake blind for 5 minutes.
Remove the paper and beans and bake
for a further 5 minutes, until lightly
browned and crisp.

3 Meanwhile, put the button onions
or shallots in a bowl and cover with
boiling water. Leave for 3 minutes, then
drain and rinse under cold water. Trim
off their top and root ends and slip
them out of their skins.

4 Simmer the onions and stock in a
covered pan for 5 minutes. Uncover
and cook, stirring occasionally until
the stock has reduced entirely. Add
all the remaining ingredients, except
the flat leaf parsley, and cook for
2–3 minutes.

5 Fill the toast cups with the devilled
onions. Serve hot, garnished with
sprigs of flat leaf parsley.

NUTRITION NOTES

Per portion:
Energy	178Kcals/749kJ
Protein	9.42g
Fat	1.57g
Saturated Fat	0.30g
Fibre	1.82g

KOHLRABI STUFFED WITH PEPPERS

f you haven't sampled kohlrabi,
r have only eaten it in stews
where its flavour is lost, this dish
s recommended. The slightly
harp flavour of the peppers are
n excellent foil to the more
arthy flavour of the kohlrabi.

INGREDIENTS

erves 4
small kohlrabies, about 175g–225g/
  6–8oz each
bout 400ml/14fl oz/²⁄₃ cup hot
  vegetable stock
5ml/1 tbsp sunflower oil
onion, chopped
red (bell) pepper, seeded and sliced
green (bell) pepper, seeded and sliced
alt and black pepper
lat leaf parsley, to garnish (optional)

NUTRITION NOTES

Per portion:

Energy	112Kcals/470kJ
Fat	4.63g
Saturated Fat	0.55g
Cholesterol	0
Fibre	5.8g

1 Preheat the oven to 180°C/350°F/
Gas 4. Trim and top and tail the
ohlrabies and arrange in the base of a
medium ovenproof dish.

2 Pour over the stock to come about
halfway up the vegetables. Cover and
raise in the oven for about 30 minutes,
ntil tender. Transfer to a plate and
llow to cool, reserving the stock.

3 Heat the oil in a frying pan and
fry the onion for 3–4 minutes over
a gentle heat, stirring occasionally.
Add the peppers and cook for a
further 2–3 minutes, until the onion is
lightly browned.

4 Add the reserved vegetable stock
and a little seasoning and simmer,
uncovered, over a moderate heat until
the stock has almost evaporated.

5 Scoop out the insides of the kohlrabies and chop roughly. Stir into
the onion and pepper mixture, taste
and adjust the seasoning. Arrange the
shells in a shallow ovenproof dish.

6 Spoon the filling into the kohlrabi
shells. Put in the oven for 5–10
minutes to heat through and then
serve, garnished with a sprig of flat
leaf parsley, if liked.

Courgettes in Citrus Sauce

If baby courgettes are unavailable, you can use larger ones, but they should be cooked whole so that they don't absorb too much water. After cooking, halve them lengthways and cut into 10cm/4in lengths. These tender, baby courgettes served in a very low-fat sauce make this a tasty and low-fat accompaniment to grilled (broiled) fish fillets.

Nutrition Notes

Per portion:

Energy	33Kcals/138kJ
Protein	2.18g
Fat	0.42g
Saturated Fat	0.09g
Fibre	0.92g

Ingredients

Serves 4

350g/12oz baby courgettes (zucchini)
4 spring onions (scallions), finely sliced
2.5cm/1in fresh root ginger, grated
30ml/2 tbsp cider vinegar
15ml/1 tbsp light soy sauce
5ml/1 tsp soft light brown sugar
45ml/3 tbsp vegetable stock
finely grated rind and juice of ½ lemon
    and ½ orange
5ml/1 tsp cornflour (cornstarch)

1 Cook the courgettes in lightly salted boiling water for 3–4 minutes, or until just tender. Drain well.

2 Meanwhile, put all the remaining ingredients, except the cornflour, into a small pan and bring to the boil. Simmer for 3 minutes.

3 Blend the cornflour with 10ml/2 tsp cold water and add to the sauce. Bring to the boil, stirring continuously, until the sauce has thickened.

4 Pour the sauce over the courgettes and heat gently, shaking the pan to coat them evenly. Transfer to a warmed serving dish and serve.

Variation
Use baby corn or aubergines (eggplants) in place of the courgettes (zucchini) for a change.

COURGETTE AND ASPARAGUS PARCELS

To appreciate the aroma, these
paper parcels should be broken
open at the table.

INGREDIENTS

Serves 4

2 medium courgettes (zucchini)
1 medium leek
225g/8oz young asparagus, trimmed
4 tarragon sprigs
4 whole garlic cloves, unpeeled
1 egg, beaten, to glaze
salt and black pepper

NUTRITION NOTES

Per portion:

Energy	110 Kcals/460kJ
Protein	6.22g
Fat	2.29g
Saturated Fat	0.49g
Fibre	6.73g

1 Preheat the oven to 200°C/400°F/
Gas 6. Using a potato peeler,
carefully slice the courgettes lengthways
into thin strips.

2 Cut the leek into very fine julienne
strips and cut the asparagus evenly
into 5cm/2in lengths.

3 Cut out four sheets of baking
parchment measuring 30 x 38cm/
12 x 15in and fold in half. Draw a
large curve to make a heart shape when
unfolded. Cut along the inside of the
line and open out.

4 Divide the courgettes, asparagus
and leek evenly between each paper
heart, positioning the filling on one side
of the fold line, and topping each with
a sprig of tarragon and an unpeeled
garlic clove. Season to taste.

5 Brush the edges lightly with the
beaten egg and fold over.

6 Twist the edges together so that
each parcel is completely sealed.
Lay the parcels on a baking sheet and
cook for 10 minutes. Serve immediately.

> **VARIATION**
> Experiment with other vegetable
> combinations, if you like.

AUTUMN GLORY

Glorious pumpkin shells summon up the delights of autumn and look too good to throw away, so use one as a serving pot. Pumpkin and pasta make marvellous partners, especially as a main course served from the baked shell.

INGREDIENTS

Serves 4–6
1 pumpkin, about 2kg/4–4½lb
1 onion, sliced
2.5cm/1in fresh root ginger
15ml/1 tbsp extra virgin olive oil
1 courgette (zucchini), sliced
115g/4oz sliced mushrooms
400g/14oz can chopped tomatoes
75g/3oz/1 cup pasta shells
450ml/¾ pint/2 cups stock
60ml/4 tbsp fromage frais or low-fat
   cream cheese
30ml/2 tbsp chopped fresh basil
salt and black pepper

NUTRITION NOTES

Per portion (6 servings):
Energy	140Kcals/588kJ
Fat	4.29g
Saturated Fat	1.17g
Cholesterol	2.5mg
Fibre	4.45g

VARIATIONS
Use reduced-fat or very low-fat fromage frais to cut the calories and fat. Cook the onion, ginger and pumpkin flesh in 30–45ml/ 2–3 tbsp vegetable stock in place of the oil, to cut the calories and fat more.

1 Preheat the oven to 180°C/350°F/ Gas 4. Cut the top off the pumpkin with a large sharp knife, then scoop out and discard the seeds.

2 Using a small sharp knife and a sturdy tablespoon, extract as much of the pumpkin flesh as possible, then chop it into chunks.

3 Bake the pumpkin shell with its lid on for 45 minutes to 1 hour until the inside begins to soften.

4 Meanwhile make the filling. Gently fry the onion, ginger and pumpkin chunks in the olive oil for about 10 minutes, stirring occasionally.

5 Add the courgette and mushrooms and cook for a further 3 minutes, then stir in the tomatoes, pasta shells and stock. Season well, bring to the boil, then cover and simmer gently for another 10 minutes.

6 Stir the fromage frais and basil into the pasta and spoon the mixture into the pumpkin. (It may not be possible to fit all the filling into the pumpkin shell; serve the rest separately if this is the case.)

Vegetables à la Grecque

This simple side salad is made with winter vegetables, but you can vary it according to the season. This combination of vegetables makes an ideal, low-fat side salad to serve with grilled (broiled) lean meat or poultry, or with slices of fresh, crusty bread.

INGREDIENTS

Serves 4

175ml/6fl oz/³⁄₄ cup white wine
5ml/1 tsp olive oil
30ml/2 tbsp lemon juice
2 bay leaves
sprig of fresh thyme
4 juniper berries
450g/1lb leeks, trimmed and cut into
   2.5cm/1in lengths
1 small cauliflower, broken into florets
4 celery sticks, sliced on the diagonal
30ml/2 tbsp chopped fresh parsley
salt and black pepper

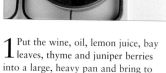

1 Put the wine, oil, lemon juice, bay leaves, thyme and juniper berries into a large, heavy pan and bring to the boil. Cover and let simmer for 20 minutes.

NUTRITION NOTES	
Per portion:	
Energy	88Kcals/368kJ
Protein	4.53g
Fat	2.05g
Saturated Fat	0.11g
Fibre	4.42g

2 Add the leeks, cauliflower and celery. Simmer very gently for 5–6 minutes or until just tender.

3 Remove the vegetables with a slotted spoon and transfer them to a serving dish. Briskly boil the cooking liquid for 15–20 minutes, or until reduced by half. Strain.

4 Stir the parsley into the liquid and season with salt and pepper to taste. Pour over the vegetables and leave to cool. Chill in the refrigerator for at least 1 hour before serving.

COOK'S TIP
Choose a dry or medium-dry white wine for best results.

ROASTED MEDITERRANEAN VEGETABLES

or a really colourful dish, try
ese vegetables roasted in olive
l with garlic and rosemary. The
avour is wonderfully intense.

INGREDIENTS

rves 6
each red and yellow (bell) pepper
Spanish (Bermuda) onions
large courgettes (zucchini)
large aubergine (eggplant) or
4 baby aubergines, trimmed
fennel bulb, thickly sliced
beefsteak tomatoes
fat garlic cloves
ml/2 tbsp olive oil
esh rosemary sprigs
ack pepper
non wedges and black olives
(optional), to garnish

Halve and seed the peppers, then
cut them into large chunks. Peel the
ions and cut into thick wedges.

NUTRITION NOTES

Per portion:	
Energy	120Kcals/504kJ
Fat	5.2g
Saturated Fat	0.68g
Cholesterol	0

2 Cut the courgettes and aubergines into large chunks.

3 Preheat the oven to 220°C/425°F/ Gas 7. Spread the peppers, onions, courgettes, aubergines and fennel in a lightly oiled, shallow ovenproof dish or roasting pan, or, if liked, arrange in rows to make a colourful design.

4 Cut each tomato in half and place, cut-side up, with the vegetables.

5 Tuck the garlic cloves among the vegetables, then brush them with the olive oil. Place some sprigs of rosemary among the vegetables and grind over some black pepper, particularly on the tomatoes.

6 Roast for 20–25 minutes, turning the vegetables halfway through the cooking time. Serve from the dish or on a flat platter, garnished with lemon wedges. Scatter some black olives over the top, if you like.

RATATOUILLE PANCAKES

These pancakes are made slightly thicker than usual to hold the juicy vegetable filling. By using cooking spray, you can control the amount of fat you are using and keep it to a minimum.

INGREDIENTS

Serves 4
75g/3oz/²⁄₃ cup plain (all-purpose) flour
pinch of salt
25g/1oz/¹⁄₄ cup medium oatmeal
1 egg
300ml/¹⁄₂ pint/1¹⁄₄ cups skimmed milk
non-stick cooking spray
mixed salad, to serve

For the filling
1 large aubergine (eggplant), cut into
*   2.5cm/1in cubes*
1 garlic clove, crushed
2 medium courgettes (zucchini), sliced
1 each green and red (bell) pepper,
*   seeded and sliced*
75ml/5 tbsp vegetable stock
200g/7oz can chopped tomatoes
5ml/1 tsp cornflour (cornstarch)
salt and black pepper

NUTRITION NOTES	
Per portion:	
Energy	182Kcals/767kJ
Protein	9.36g
Fat	3.07g
Saturated Fat	0.62g
Fibre	4.73g

VARIATION
Adding oatmeal to the batter mixture adds flavour, colour and texture to the cooked pancakes. If you like, wholemeal (whole-wheat) flour may be used in place of white flour to add extra fibre.

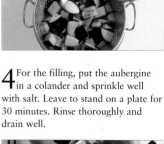

1 Sift the flour and a pinch of salt into a bowl. Stir in the oatmeal. Make a well in the centre, add the egg and half the milk and mix to a smooth batter. Gradually beat in the remaining milk. Cover the bowl and leave to stand for 30 minutes.

2 Spray an 18cm/7in heavy frying pan with cooking spray. Heat the pan, then pour in just enough batter to cover the base of the pan thinly. Cook for 2–3 minutes, until the underside is golden brown. Flip over and cook for a further 1–2 minutes.

3 Slide the pancake out on to a plate lined with baking parchment. Stack the other pancakes on top as they are made, interleaving each with baking parchment. Keep warm.

4 For the filling, put the aubergine in a colander and sprinkle well with salt. Leave to stand on a plate for 30 minutes. Rinse thoroughly and drain well.

5 Put the garlic clove, courgettes, peppers, stock and tomatoes into a large pan. Simmer uncovered, stirring occasionally, for 10 minutes. Add the aubergine and cook for a further 15 minutes. Blend the cornflour with 10ml/2 tsp water to form a smooth paste and stir into the pan. Simmer for 2 minutes. Season to taste.

6 Spoon some of the ratatouille mixture into the middle of each pancake. Fold each one in half, then in half again to make a cone shape. Serve hot with a mixed salad.

CONCERTINA GARLIC POTATOES

With a low-fat topping these would make a superb meal in themselves or could be enjoyed as a nutritious accompaniment to grilled (broiled) fish or meat.

—— INGREDIENTS ——

Serves 4

4 baking potatoes
2 garlic cloves, cut into slivers
60ml/4 tbsp low-fat cream cheese
60ml/4 tbsp low-fat natural (plain) yogurt
30ml/2 tbsp snipped chives
6–8 watercress sprigs, finely chopped
  (optional)

—— NUTRITION NOTES ——

Per portion:

Energy	195Kcals/815kJ
Fat	3.5g
Saturated Fat	2g
Cholesterol	10mg

1 Preheat the oven to 200°C/400°F/ Gas 6. Slice each potato at about 5mm/¼in intervals, cutting not quite to the base, so that they retain their shape. Slip the slivers of the garlic between the cuts in the potatoes.

COOK'S TIP
The most suitable potatoes for baking are of the floury variety. Some of the best include Estima, Cara and Kerr's Pink.

2 Place the garlic-filled potatoes in a roasting pan and bake for 1–1¼ hours or until soft when tested with a knife. Meanwhile, mix the cream cheese and yogurt in a bowl, then stir in the snipped chives, along with the watercress, if using.

3 Serve the baked potatoes on individual plates, with a dollop of the yogurt and cream cheese mixture on top of each.

POTATO, LEEK AND TOMATO BAKE

—— INGREDIENTS ——

Serves 4

675g/1½lb potatoes
2 leeks, sliced
3 large tomatoes, sliced
a few fresh rosemary sprigs, crushed
1 garlic clove, crushed
300ml/½ pint/1¼ cups vegetable stock
15ml/1 tbsp olive oil
salt and black pepper

—— NUTRITION NOTES ——

Per portion:

Energy	180Kcals/740kJ
Fat	3.5g
Saturated Fat	0.5g
Cholesterol	0

1 Preheat the oven to 180°C/350°F/ Gas 4 and grease a 1.2 litre/2 pint/ 5 cup shallow ovenproof dish. Scrub and thinly slice the potatoes. Layer them with the leeks and tomatoes in the dish, scattering some rosemary between the layers and ending with a layer of potatoes.

2 Add the garlic to the stock, stir in salt if needed and pepper to taste, then pour over the vegetables. Brush the top layer of potatoes with olive oil

3 Bake for 1¼–1½ hours until the potatoes are tender and the topping is golden and slightly crisp.

MUSHROOM AND OKRA CURRY

This simple but delicious curry with its fresh gingery mango relish is best served with plain basmati rice.

INGREDIENTS

Serves 4

4 garlic cloves, roughly chopped
2.5cm/1in piece fresh root ginger,
    peeled and roughly chopped
1–2 red chillies, seeded and chopped
175ml/6fl oz/¾ cup water
15ml/1 tbsp sunflower oil
5ml/1 tsp coriander seeds
5ml/1 tsp cumin seeds
5ml/1 tsp ground cumin
2 cardamom pods, seeds removed
    and crushed
pinch of ground turmeric
400g/14oz can chopped tomatoes
450g/1lb mushrooms, quartered if large
225g/8oz okra, trimmed and cut into
    1cm/½in slices
30ml/2 tbsp chopped fresh
    coriander (cilantro)
basmati rice, to serve

For the mango relish
1 large ripe mango, about 500g/1¼lb
1 small garlic clove, crushed
1 onion, finely chopped
10ml/2 tsp grated fresh root ginger
1 fresh red chilli, seeded and
    finely chopped
pinch of salt and sugar

1 For the mango relish, peel the mango and then cut off the fruit from the stone (pit). Put the mango into a bowl and mash with a fork, or use a food processor.

2 Add the rest of the mango relish ingredients to the mango, mix well and set aside.

3 Place the garlic, ginger, chillies and 45ml/3 tbsp of the water into a blender and blend until smooth. Heat the oil in a large pan. Add the coriander and cumin seeds and allow them to sizzle for a few seconds, then add the ground cumin, cardamom seeds and turmeric and cook for 1 minute more.

4 Add the paste from the blender, the tomatoes, remaining water, mushrooms and okra. Stir and bring to the boil. Reduce the heat, cover and simmer for 5 minutes. Uncover, turn up the heat slightly and cook for another 5–10 minutes until the okra is tender. Stir in the fresh coriander and serve with rice and the mango relish.

NUTRITION NOTES	
Per portion:	
Energy	139Kcals/586kJ
Fat	4.6g
Saturated Fat	0.63g
Cholesterol	0
Fibre	6.96g

TOFU AND GREEN BEAN CURRY

his exotic curry is simple and
ick to make. This recipe uses
ans and mushrooms, but you
n use almost any kind of
getable such as bamboo shoots
broccoli.

INGREDIENTS

rves 4

0ml/12fl oz/1½ cups coconut milk
ml/1 tbsp red curry paste
ml/3 tbsp fish sauce
ml/2 tsp sugar
5g/8oz button (white) mushrooms
5g/4oz French (green) beans, trimmed
5g/6oz tofu, rinsed and cut into
2cm/¾in cubes
kaffir lime leaves, torn
ed chillies, seeded and sliced
riander (cilantro) leaves, to garnish

NUTRITION NOTES

Per portion:
Energy	100Kcals/420kJ
Fat	3.36g
Saturated Fat	0.48g
Cholesterol	0
Fibre	1.35g

Put about one third of the coconut
milk in a wok or pan. Cook until it
arts to separate and an oily sheen
pears on the surface.

Add the red curry paste, fish sauce
and sugar to the coconut milk. Mix
gether thoroughly.

3 Add the mushrooms. Stir and cook
for 1 minute.

4 Stir in the rest of the coconut milk
and bring back to the boil.

> **COOK'S TIP**
> Use 5–10ml/1–2 tsp hot chilli
> powder, if fresh red chillies aren't
> available. When preparing fresh
> chillies, wear rubber gloves and
> wash hands, work surfaces and
> utensils thoroughly afterwards.
> Chillies contain volatile oils which
> can irritate and burn sensitive
> areas, especially eyes.

5 Add the French beans and cubes of
tofu and simmer gently for another
4–5 minutes.

6 Stir in the kaffir lime leaves and
chillies. Serve garnished with the
coriander leaves.

VEGETARIAN CASSOULET

Every town in south-west France has its own version of this popular classic. Warm French bread is all that you need to accompany this hearty low-fat vegetable version.

INGREDIENTS

Serves 4–6

400g/14oz/2 cups dried haricot
  (navy) beans
1 bay leaf
2 onions
3 whole cloves
2 garlic cloves, crushed
5ml/1 tsp olive oil
2 leeks, thickly sliced
12 baby carrots
115g/4oz button (white) mushrooms
400g/14oz can chopped tomatoes
15ml/1 tbsp tomato purée (paste)
5ml/1 tsp paprika
15ml/1 tbsp chopped fresh thyme
30ml/2 tbsp chopped fresh parsley
115g/4oz/2 cups fresh white
  breadcrumbs
salt and black pepper

NUTRITION NOTES

Per portion:
Energy	325Kcals/1378kJ
Fat	3.08g
Saturated Fat	0.46g
Cholesterol	0
Fibre	15.68g

VARIATION

If you're short of time, use canned haricot (navy) beans – you'll need two 400g/14oz cans. Drain, reserving the bean juices and make up to 400ml/14fl oz/1²/₃ cups with vegetable stock.

1 Soak the beans overnight in a large bowl with plenty of cold water. Drain and rinse under cold running water. Put them in a pan with 1.75 litres/3 pints/7½ cups of cold water and the bay leaf. Bring to the boil and cook rapidly for 10 minutes.

2 Peel one of the onions and spike with the cloves. Add to the beans, then reduce the heat. Cover and simmer gently for 1 hour, until the beans are almost tender. Drain, reserving the stock but discarding the bay leaf and onion.

3 Chop the remaining onion and put it into a large flameproof casserole together with the crushed garlic and olive oil. Cook gently for 5 minutes, or until softened.

4 Preheat the oven to 160°C/325°F/ Gas 3. Add the leeks, carrots, mushrooms, chopped tomatoes, tomato purée, paprika and thyme to the casserole, then pour in about 400ml/14fl oz/1²/₃ cups of the reserved stock.

5 Bring to the boil, cover and simmer gently for 10 minutes. Stir in the cooked beans and parsley. Season to taste with salt and pepper.

6 Sprinkle the breadcrumbs over the top and bake, uncovered, for 35 minutes or until the topping is golden brown and crisp.

SALADS

Salads are healthy and refreshing and can be served either as accompaniments to other dishes or as perfect low-fat meals in themselves. Presented here is a wonderful selection of recipes: vegetarian delights include Marinated Cucumber Salad and a fresh, fast and sustaining Fruit and Fibre Salad; there are fish and shellfish dishes, such as Prawn Noodle Salad and a tasty Thai-style Seafood Salad with Fragrant Herbs; and healthy salads made with grains and rice, such as Bulgur Wheat Salad with Oranges and Brown Rice Salad with Fruit, which can be served as a meal on their own.

MARINATED CUCUMBER SALAD

Sprinkling cucumbers with salt draws out some of the water and makes them softer and sweeter.

INGREDIENTS

Serves 6

2 medium cucumbers
15ml/1 tbsp salt
90g/3½oz/½ cup sugar
175ml/6fl oz/¾ cup dry cider
15ml/1 tbsp cider vinegar
45ml/3 tbsp chopped fresh dill
pinch of pepper

NUTRITION NOTES

Per portion:
Energy	111Kcals/465kJ
Fat	0.14g
Saturated Fat	0.01g
Fibre	0.62g

1 Slice the cucumbers thinly and place them in a colander, sprinkling salt between each layer. Put the colander over a bowl and leave to drain for 1 hour.

COOK'S TIP

As a shortcut, leave out the method for salting cucumber described in step 1.

2 Thoroughly rinse the cucumber under cold running water to remove excess salt, then pat dry on absorbent kitchen paper.

3 Gently heat the sugar, cider and vinegar in a pan, until the sugar has dissolved. Remove from the heat and leave to cool. Put the cucumber slices in a bowl, pour over the cider mixture and leave to marinate for about 2 hours.

4 Drain the cucumber and sprinkle with the dill and pepper to taste. Mix well and transfer to a serving dish. Chill until ready to serve.

TURNIP SALAD WITH HORSERADISH

The robust-flavoured turnip
partners well with the taste of
horseradish and caraway seeds.
This salad is delicious with cold
roast beef or smoked trout.

INGREDIENTS

Serves 4
350g/12oz medium turnips
4 spring onions (scallions), white part
  only, chopped
15ml/1 tbsp caster (superfine) sugar
salt
30ml/2 tbsp horseradish cream
10ml/2 tsp caraway seeds

NUTRITION NOTES

Per portion:

Energy	48.25Kcals/204kJ
Fat	1.26g
Saturated Fat	0.09g
Cholesterol	1mg
Fibre	2.37g

1 Peel, slice and shred the turnips – or
grate them if you wish.

VARIATIONS
If turnips are not available, mooli
(daikon) can be used as a
substitute. For extra sweetness,
try using red onion instead of
spring onions (scallions).

2 Add the spring onions, sugar and
salt, then rub together with your
hands to soften the turnip.

3 Fold in the horseradish cream
and caraway seeds to combine
thoroughly and serve immediately.

FRUIT AND FIBRE SALAD

Fast and sustaining, this salad makes a great supper or snack.

Serves 6
225g/8oz red or white cabbage, or a
  mixture of both
3 medium carrots
1 pear
1 red-skinned eating apple
200g/7oz can green flageolet or
  cannellini beans, drained
50g/2oz/¼ cup chopped dates

For the dressing
2.5ml/½ tsp dry English mustard
10ml/2 tsp clear honey
30ml/2 tbsp orange juice
5ml/1 tsp white wine vinegar
2.5ml/½ tsp paprika
salt and black pepper

1 Shred the cabbage very finely, discarding the core and tough ribs.

2 Cut the carrots into very thin strips, about 5cm/2in long.

3 Quarter, core and slice the pear and the apple, leaving the peel on.

4 Put the fruit and vegetables in a bowl with the beans and dates. Mix well.

5 To make the dressing, blend the mustard with the honey until smooth. Add the orange juice, vinegar, paprika and seasoning and mix well.

6 Pour the dressing over the salad and toss to coat. Chill in the refrigerator for 30 minutes before serving.

NUTRITION NOTES

Per portion:
Energy	137Kcals/574kJ
Fat	0.87g
Saturated Fat	0.03g
Fibre	6.28g

VARIATIONS
Use other canned beans, such as red kidney beans or chickpeas, in place of the flageolet or cannellini beans. Add 2.5ml/½ tsp ground spice, such as chilli powder, cumin or coriander, for extra flavour. Add 5ml/1 tsp finely grated orange or lemon rind to the dressing, for extra flavour.

AUBERGINE SALAD

An appetizing and unusual salad that you will find yourself making over and over again.

INGREDIENTS

Serves 6

2 aubergines (eggplants)
15ml/1 tbsp oil
30ml/2 tbsp dried shrimps, soaked
    and drained
15ml/1 tbsp coarsely chopped garlic
30ml/2 tbsp freshly squeezed lime juice
5ml/1 tsp palm sugar (jaggery)
30ml/2 tbsp fish sauce
1 hard-boiled egg, chopped
4 shallots, thinly sliced into rings
coriander (cilantro) leaves, to garnish
2 red chillies, seeded and sliced,
    to garnish

VARIATION
For an interesting variation, try using salted duck's or quail's eggs, cut in half, instead of chopped hen's eggs.

1 Grill (broil) or roast the aubergines until charred and tender.

2 When cool enough to handle, peel away the skin and slice the aubergine into thick pieces.

3 Heat the oil in a small frying pan, add the drained shrimps and the garlic and fry until golden. Remove from the pan and set aside.

4 To make the dressing, put the lime juice, palm sugar and fish sauce in a small bowl and whisk together.

5 To serve, arrange the aubergine on a serving dish. Top with the chopped egg, shallot rings and dried shrimp mixture. Drizzle over the dressing and garnish with coriander and red chillies.

NUTRITION NOTES

Per portion:

Energy	70.5Kcals/295kJ
Fat	3.76g
Saturated Fat	0.68g
Cholesterol	57mg
Fibre	1.20g

BAMBOO SHOOT SALAD

This salad, which has a hot and sharp flavour, originated in north-east Thailand. Use fresh young bamboo shoots if you can find them, otherwise substitute canned bamboo shoots.

INGREDIENTS

Serves 4

400g/14oz can whole bamboo shoots
25g/1oz glutinous rice
30ml/2 tbsp chopped shallots
15ml/1 tbsp chopped garlic
45ml/3 tbsp chopped spring
  onions (scallions)
30ml/2 tbsp fish sauce
30ml/2 tbsp lime juice
5ml/1 tsp sugar
2.5ml/½ tsp dried flaked chillies
20–25 small mint leaves
15ml/1 tbsp toasted sesame seeds

1 Rinse and drain the bamboo shoots, then slice and set aside.

2 Dry-roast the rice in a frying pan until it is golden brown. Remove and grind to fine crumbs with a mortar and pestle.

3 Tip the rice into a bowl, add the shallots, garlic, spring onions, fish sauce, lime juice, sugar, chillies and half the mint leaves.

VARIATIONS
Omit the sesame seeds to reduce calories and fat. Use ready-minced or 'lazy' garlic instead of crushing your own.

4 Mix thoroughly, then pour over the bamboo shoots and toss together. Serve sprinkled with sesame seeds and the remaining mint leaves.

NUTRITION NOTES

Per portion:
Energy	73.5Kcals/308kJ
Fat	2.8g
Saturated Fat	0.41g
Cholesterol	0
Fibre	2.45g

BULGUR WHEAT SALAD WITH ORANGES

Bulgur wheat makes an excellent alternative to rice or pasta.

INGREDIENTS

Serves 6

1 small green (bell) pepper
150g/5oz/1 cup bulgur wheat
600ml/1 pint/2½ cups water
½ cucumber, diced
15g/½oz/½ cup chopped fresh mint
40g/1½oz/⅓ cup flaked (sliced)
  almonds, toasted
grated rind and juice of 1 lemon
2 seedless oranges
salt and black pepper
mint sprigs, to garnish

1 Using a sharp vegetable knife, carefully halve and seed the green pepper. Cut it on a board into small cubes and put to one side.

2 Place the bulgur wheat in a pan and add the water. Bring to the boil, lower the heat, cover and simmer for 10–15 minutes until tender. Alternatively, place the bulgur wheat in a heatproof bowl, pour over boiling water and leave to soak for 30 minutes. Most, if not all, of the water should be absorbed; drain off any excess.

3 Toss the bulgur wheat with the cucumber, green pepper, mint and toasted almonds in a serving bowl. Add the grated lemon rind and juice.

4 Cut the rind from the oranges, then working over the bowl to catch the juice, cut the oranges into neat segments. Add to the bulgur mixture, then season and toss lightly. Garnish with the mint sprigs.

NUTRITION NOTES

Per portion:
Energy	160Kcals/672kJ
Fat	4.3g
Saturated Fat	0.33g
Cholesterol	0

BROWN RICE SALAD WITH FRUIT

n Oriental-style dressing gives
his colourful rice salad extra
iquancy. Whole grains like
rown rice are unrefined, so
hey retain their natural fibre,
itamins and minerals.

INGREDIENTS

erves 4–6
15g/4oz/²⁄₃ cup brown rice
 small red (bell) pepper, seeded
 and diced
00g/7oz can corn niblets, drained
5ml/3 tbsp sultanas (golden raisins)
25g/8oz can pineapple pieces in
 fruit juice
5ml/1 tbsp light soy sauce
ml/1 tsp sunflower oil
0ml/2 tsp hazelnut oil
 garlic clove, crushed
ml/1 tsp finely chopped fresh
 root ginger
round black pepper
 spring onions (scallions), sliced,
 to garnish

> **COOK'S TIP**
> Hazelnut oil contains mainly
> monounsaturated fats.

1 Cook the brown rice in a large pan
of lightly salted boiling water for
bout 30 minutes, or until it is tender.
Drain thoroughly and leave to cool.
Meanwhile, prepare the garnish by
icing the spring onions at an angle
nd setting aside.

2 Tip the rice into a bowl and add
the red pepper, corn and sultanas.
Drain the pineapple pieces, reserving
the juice, add them to the rice mixture
and toss lightly.

3 Pour the reserved pineapple juice
into a clean screw-top jar. Add the
soy sauce, sunflower and hazelnut oils,
garlic and root ginger. Add some salt
and pepper to taste, then close the jar
tightly and shake well to combine.

4 Pour the dressing over the salad
and toss well. Scatter the spring
onions over the top.

NUTRITION NOTES

Per portion:
Energy	245Kcals/1029kJ
Fat	4.25g
Saturated Fat	0.6g
Cholesterol	0

SEAFOOD SALAD WITH FRAGRANT HERBS

INGREDIENTS

Serves 6

250ml/8fl oz/1 cup fish stock or water
250g/12oz squid, cleaned and cut
  into rings
12 uncooked king prawns (jumbo
  shrimp), shelled
12 scallops
50g/2oz bean thread noodles, soaked in
  warm water for 30 minutes
½ cucumber, cut into thin sticks
1 lemon grass stalk, finely chopped
2 kaffir lime leaves, finely shredded
2 shallots, finely sliced
juice of 1–2 limes
30ml/2 tbsp fish sauce
30ml/2 tbsp chopped spring
  onions (scallions)
30ml/2 tbsp chopped coriander
  (cilantro) leaves
12–15 mint leaves, roughly torn
4 red chillies, seeded and sliced
coriander sprigs, to garnish

1 Pour the stock or water into a medium pan, set over a high heat and bring to the boil.

2 Cook each type of shellfish separately in the stock. Don't overcook – it takes only a few minutes for each type of shellfish to cook. Remove and set aside.

3 Drain the bean thread noodles and cut them into short lengths, about 5cm/2in long. Combine the noodles with the cooked seafood.

4 Add all the remaining ingredients, mix together well and serve garnished with coriander sprigs.

NUTRITION NOTES

Per portion:

Energy	78Kcals/332kJ
Fat	1.12g
Saturated Fat	0.26g
Cholesterol	123mg
Fibre	0.37g

VARIATIONS
Use other prepared shellfish, such as mussels and cockles, in place of the prawns (shrimp) or scallops. If fresh chillies are not available, use 10–15ml/2–3 tsp of hot chilli powder or, alternatively, use ready-chopped chillies.

GREEN PAPAYA SALAD

There are many variations of this salad in South-east Asia. As green papaya is not easy to get hold of, shredded carrots, cucumber or green apple may be substituted. Serve this salad with raw white cabbage and rice.

INGREDIENTS

Serves 4
1 medium green papaya
4 garlic cloves
15ml/1 tbsp chopped shallots
3–4 red chillies, seeded and sliced
2.5ml/½ tsp salt
2–3 French (green) or runner beans,
    cut into 2cm/¾in lengths
2 tomatoes, cut into wedges
45ml/3 tbsp fish sauce
15ml/1 tbsp caster (superfine) sugar
juice of 1 lime
30ml/2 tbsp crushed roasted peanuts
sliced red chillies, to garnish

1 Peel the papaya and cut in half lengthways, scrape out the seeds with a spoon and finely shred the flesh.

2 Grind the garlic, shallots, chillies and salt together in a large mortar with a pestle.

3 Add the shredded papaya a little at a time and pound until it becomes slightly limp and soft.

4 Add the sliced beans and tomatoes and lightly crush. Season with fish sauce, sugar and lime juice.

5 Transfer the salad to a serving dish, sprinkle with crushed peanuts and garnish with chillies.

NUTRITION NOTES

Per portion:
Energy	96Kcals/402kJ
Fat	4.2g
Saturated Fat	0.77g
Cholesterol	0

COOK'S TIP
If you do not have a large mortar and pestle, use a bowl and crush the shredded papaya with a wooden meat tenderizer or the end of a rolling pin.

THAI-STYLE CHICKEN SALAD

This salad comes from Chiang Mai, a city in the north-east of Thailand. It's hot and spicy, and wonderfully aromatic. Choose strong-flavoured leaves, such as curly endive or rocket, for the salad.

INGREDIENTS

Serves 6

450g/1lb minced (ground) chicken
    breast fillet
1 lemon grass stalk, finely chopped
3 kaffir lime leaves, finely chopped
4 red chillies, seeded and chopped
60ml/4 tbsp lime juice
30ml/2 tbsp fish sauce
15ml/1 tbsp roasted ground rice
2 spring onions (scallions), chopped
30ml/2 tbsp coriander (cilantro) leaves
mixed salad leaves, cucumber and
    tomato slices, to serve
mint sprigs, to garnish

1 Heat a large non-stick frying pan. Add the minced chicken and cook in a little water. Stir constantly until the chicken is cooked, which will take about 7–10 minutes.

COOK'S TIP
Use sticky (glutinous) rice to make roasted ground rice. Put the rice in a frying pan and dry-roast until golden brown. Remove and grind to a powder with a mortar and pestle or in a food processor. Keep in a glass jar in a cool dry place and use as required.

2 Transfer the cooked chicken to a large bowl and add the rest of the ingredients. Mix thoroughly.

3 Serve on a bed of mixed salad leaves, cucumber and tomato slices, garnished with mint sprigs.

NUTRITION NOTES

Per portion:

Energy	106Kcals/446kJ
Fat	1.13g
Saturated Fat	0.28g
Cholesterol	52.5mg
Fibre	0.7g

FRUITY PASTA AND PRAWN SALAD

Orange cantaloupe or
Charentais melon look
spectacular in this salad. Or
try a mixture of ogen,
cantaloupe and water melon.

INGREDIENTS

Serves 6

175g/6oz pasta shapes
225g/8oz/2 cups frozen prawns
    (shrimp), thawed and drained
1 large or 2 small melons
30ml/2 tbsp olive oil
15ml/1 tbsp tarragon vinegar
30ml/2 tbsp snipped fresh chives or
    chopped parsley
herb sprigs, to garnish
shredded Chinese leaves
    (Chinese cabbage), to serve

NUTRITION NOTES

Per portion:

Energy	167Kcals/705kJ
Fat	4.72g
Saturated Fat	0.68g
Cholesterol	105mg
Fibre	2.08g

1 Cook the pasta in boiling salted
water according to the packet
instructions. Drain well and cool.

VARIATIONS
Use whole-wheat pasta instead of
white pasta, and mussels or scallops
in place of prawns (shrimp).

2 Peel the thawed prawns and discard
the shells.

3 Halve the melon(s) and remove the
seeds with a teaspoon. Scoop the
flesh into balls with a melon baller and
mix with the prawns and pasta.

4 Whisk the oil, vinegar and chopped
herbs together. Pour on to the
prawn mixture and turn to coat. Cover
and chill for at least 30 minutes.

5 Meanwhile, shred the Chinese
leaves and use to line a shallow
bowl or the empty melon shells. Pile
the prawn mixture on to the Chinese
leaves and garnish with herb sprigs.

PRAWN NOODLE SALAD

A light, refreshing salad with all the tangy flavour of the sea. Instead of prawns, try squid, scallops, mussels or crab.

INGREDIENTS

Serves 4

115g/4oz cellophane noodles, soaked in
    hot water until soft
16 cooked prawns (shrimp), peeled
1 small red (bell) pepper, seeded and
    cut into strips
½ cucumber, cut into strips
1 tomato, cut into strips
2 shallots, finely sliced
salt and black pepper
coriander (cilantro) leaves, to garnish

For the dressing
15ml/1 tbsp rice vinegar
30ml/2 tbsp fish sauce
30ml/2 tbsp fresh lime juice
pinch of salt
2.5ml/½ tsp grated fresh root ginger
1 lemon grass stalk, finely chopped
1 red chilli, seeded and finely sliced
30ml/2 tbsp roughly chopped mint
a few sprigs of tarragon, roughly chopped
15ml/1 tbsp snipped chives

1 Make the dressing by combining all the ingredients in a small bowl or jug (pitcher); whisk well.

2 Drain the softened noodles, then plunge them in a pan of boiling water for 1 minute. Drain, rinse under cold running water and drain again well.

3 In a large bowl, combine the noodles with the prawns, red pepper, cucumber, tomato and shallots. Lightly season with salt and pepper, then toss with the dressing.

4 Spoon the noodles on to individual plates. Garnish with a few coriander leaves and serve immediately.

NUTRITION NOTES

Per portion:

Energy	164.5Kcals/697kJ
Fat	2.9g
Saturated Fat	0.79g
Cholesterol	121mg
Fibre	1.86g

COOK'S TIP
Prawns (shrimp) are available ready-cooked and often shelled. To cook prawns, boil them for 5 minutes. Leave them to cool in the cooking liquid, then gently pull off the tail shell and twist off the head.

CACHUMBAR

Cachumbar is a salad relish most commonly served with Indian curries. There are many versions; this one will leave your mouth feeling cool and fresh after a spicy meal.

INGREDIENTS

Serves 4

3 ripe tomatoes
2 spring onions (scallions), chopped
1.5ml/¼ tsp caster (superfine) sugar
salt
45ml/3 tbsp chopped fresh
   coriander (cilantro)

NUTRITION NOTES

Per portion:	
Energy	9.5Kcals/73.5kJ
Fat	0.23g
Saturated Fat	0.07g
Cholesterol	0
Fibre	0.87g

1 Remove the tough cores from the bottom of the tomatoes with a small sharp-pointed knife.

> COOK'S TIP
> Cachumbar also makes a fine accompaniment to fresh crab, lobster and shellfish.

2 Halve the tomatoes, remove the seeds and dice the flesh.

3 Combine the tomatoes with the chopped spring onions, sugar, salt and chopped coriander. Serve at room temperature.

HOT DESSERTS

When we talk of desserts we tend to imagine deliciously rich, creamy, calorie-laden treats which are well out of reach if you are following a low-fat diet. However, it is very easy to create delicious, low-fat desserts, full of flavour, colour and appeal that will satisfy a sweet tooth any day. We include a tasty selection of hot treats, including temptations such as Sultana and Couscous Pudding, Baked Apples in Honey and Lemon, Cinnamon and Apricot Soufflés, Blueberry and Orange Crêpe Baskets, and Blushing Pears.

Strawberry and Apple Crumble

This is a high-fibre, healthier version of the classic apple crumble. Raspberries can be used instead of strawberries, either fresh or frozen.

Ingredients

Serves 4
450g/1lb cooking apples
150g/5oz/1¼ cups strawberries
30ml/2 tbsp granulated (white) sugar
2.5ml/½ tsp ground cinnamon
30ml/2 tbsp orange juice
custard or yogurt, to serve

For the crumble
45ml/3 tbsp plain wholemeal
  (all-purpose whole-wheat) flour
50g/2oz/⅔ cup rolled oats
25g/1oz/⅛ cup low-fat spread

1 Preheat the oven to 180°C/350°F/ Gas 4. Peel, core and slice the apples. Halve the strawberries.

Nutrition Notes

Per portion:

Energy	182.3Kcals/785kJ
Fat	4g
Saturated Fat	0.73g
Cholesterol	0.5mg
Fibre	3.87g

2 In a bowl, toss together the apples, strawberries, sugar, cinnamon and orange juice. Tip into a 1.2 litre/ 2 pint/5 cup ovenproof dish, or four individual dishes.

3 Combine the flour and oats in a bowl and mix in the low-fat spread with a fork.

4 Sprinkle the crumble evenly over the fruit. Bake for 40–45 minutes (20–25 minutes for individual dishes), until golden brown and bubbling. Serve warm with custard or yogurt.

SULTANA AND COUSCOUS PUDDING

Most couscous on the market now is the pre-cooked variety, which needs only the minimum of cooking, but check the packet instructions first to make sure. Serve hot, with yogurt or skimmed-milk custard.

INGREDIENTS

Serves 4

50g/2oz/⅓ cup sultanas (golden raisins)
475ml/16fl oz/2 cups apple juice
90g/3½oz/1 cup couscous
2.5ml/½ tsp mixed (apple pie) spice

Lightly grease four 250ml/8fl oz/ 1 cup heatproof bowls or one litre/1¾ pint/4 cup heatproof bowl. Put the sultanas and apple juice in a pan.

Bring the apple juice to the boil, then cover the pan and leave to simmer gently for 2–3 minutes to plump up the fruit. Using a slotted spoon, lift out about half the fruit and put it in the bottom of the bowl(s).

3 Add the couscous and mixed spice to the pan and bring back to the boil, stirring. Cover and leave over a low heat for 8–10 minutes, or until the liquid has been absorbed.

NUTRITION NOTES

Per portion:

Energy	130.5Kcals/555kJ
Fat	0.40g
Saturated Fat	0
Cholesterol	0
Fibre	0.25g

4 Spoon the couscous into the bowl(s), spread it level, then cover the bowl(s) tightly with foil. Put the bowl(s) in a steamer over boiling water, cover and steam for about 30 minutes. Run a knife around the edges, turn the puddings out carefully and serve.

VARIATIONS

You could use chopped ready-to-eat dried apricots or pears, in place of the sultanas (golden raisins). Use unsweetened pineapple or orange juice in place of the apple juice.

CHUNKY APPLE BAKE

This sustaining, economical family dessert is a good way to use up slightly stale bread – any type of bread will do, but whole-wheat is richer in fibre.

INGREDIENTS

Serves 4

450g/1lb cooking apples
75g/3oz wholemeal (whole-wheat) bread
115g/4oz/½ cup cottage cheese
45ml/3 tbsp light muscovado (brown) sugar
200ml/7fl oz/scant 1 cup semi-skimmed (low-fat) milk
5ml/1 tsp demerara (raw) sugar

NUTRITION NOTES

Per portion:	
Energy	172.5Kcals/734.7kJ
Fat	2.5g
Saturated Fat	1.19g
Cholesterol	7.25mg
Fibre	2.69g

1 Preheat the oven to 220°C/425°F/ Gas 7. Peel the apples, cut them into quarters and remove the cores.

2 Roughly chop the apples into even pieces, about 1cm/½in across.

3 Trim the crusts from the bread, then cut into 1cm/½in dice.

4 Toss together the apples, bread, cottage cheese and muscovado sugar.

5 Stir in the milk, then transfer the mixture to a wide ovenproof dish. Sprinkle with the demerara sugar.

6 Bake the pudding for about 30–35 minutes, or until golden brown and bubbling. Serve hot.

COOK'S TIP
You may need to adjust the amount of milk used, depending on the dryness of the bread; the more stale the bread, the more milk it will absorb.

Baked Apples in Honey and Lemon

A classic mix of flavours in a healthy, traditional family dessert. Serve warm, with skimmed-milk custard or low-fat frozen yogurt.

Ingredients

Serves 4

4 medium cooking apples
15ml/1 tbsp clear honey
grated rind and juice of 1 lemon
15ml/1 tbsp low-fat spread
skimmed-milk custard, to serve

Nutrition Notes

Per portion:

Energy	61Kcals/259.5kJ
Fat	1.62g
Saturated Fat	0.42g
Cholesterol	0.25mg

1 Preheat the oven to 180°C/350°F/ Gas 4. Remove the cores from the apples, leaving them whole and with their skins intact.

2 With a cannelle or sharp knife, cut lines through the apple skin at intervals. Put the apples in an oven-proof dish.

3 Mix together the honey, lemon rind, juice and low-fat spread.

4 Spoon the mixture into the apples and cover the dish with foil or a lid. Bake for 40–45 minutes, or until the apples are tender. Serve with skimmed-milk custard.

APPLE AND BLACKCURRANT PANCAKES

These pancakes are made with a whole-wheat batter and are filled with a delicious fruit mixture.

INGREDIENTS

Makes 10

115g/4oz/1 cup plain wholemeal
(all-purpose whole-wheat) flour
300ml/½ pint/1¼ cups skimmed milk
1 egg, beaten
15ml/1 tbsp sunflower oil, plus extra
for greasing
half-fat crème fraîche, to serve
(optional)
toasted nuts or sesame seeds, for
sprinkling (optional)

For the filling
450g/1lb cooking apples
225g/8oz blackcurrants
30–45ml/2–3 tbsp water
30ml/2 tbsp demerara (raw) sugar

1 To make the batter, put the flour in a bowl and make a well in the centre.

2 Add a little of the milk with the egg and the oil. Beat the flour into the liquid, then gradually beat in the rest of the milk, keeping the batter smooth and free from lumps. Cover the batter and chill while you prepare the filling.

VARIATION
If you wish, substitute other combinations of fruit for apples and blackcurrants.

3 Quarter, peel and core the apples. Slice them into a pan and add the blackcurrants and water. Cook over a gentle heat for 10–15 minutes until the fruit is soft. Stir in enough demerara sugar to sweeten.

NUTRITION NOTES	
Per portion:	
Energy	120Kcals/505kJ
Fat	3g
Saturated Fat	0.5g
Cholesterol	25mg

4 Lightly grease a non-stick pan with just a smear of oil. Heat the pan, pour in about 30ml/2 tbsp of the batter, swirl it around and cook for about 1 minute. Flip the pancake over with a spatula and cook the other side. Put on a sheet of kitchen paper, cover with foil and keep hot while cooking the remaining pancakes.

5 Fill the pancakes with the apple and blackcurrant mixture and roll them up. Serve with a dollop of crème fraîche, if using, and sprinkle with nuts or sesame seeds, if liked.

CINNAMON AND APRICOT SOUFFLÉS

Don't expect these to be difficult simply because they're soufflés – they really couldn't be easier, and, best of all, they're very low in calories.

INGREDIENTS

Serves 4

3 eggs
115g/4oz/¹⁄₂ cup apricot fruit spread
finely grated rind of ¹⁄₂ lemon
5ml/1 tsp ground cinnamon
extra cinnamon, to decorate

NUTRITION NOTES

Per portion:	
Energy	102Kcals/429kJ
Fat	4.97g
Saturated Fat	1.42g
Cholesterol	176.25mg
Fibre	0

1 Preheat the oven to 190°C/375°F/ Gas 5. Lightly grease four individual soufflé dishes and dust them lightly with flour.

2 Separate the eggs and put the yolks in a bowl with the fruit spread, lemon rind and cinnamon.

3 Whisk for 7–10 minutes, until the mixture is thick and pale in colour.

4 Place the egg whites in a clean bowl and whisk them until they are stiff enough to hold soft peaks.

5 Using a large metal spoon or spatula, fold the egg whites evenly into the yolk mixture.

6 Divide the soufflé mixture between the prepared dishes and bake for 10–15 minutes, until well risen and golden brown. Serve immediately, dusted with a little extra cinnamon.

VARIATION
Puréed fresh or well-drained canned fruit can be used instead of the apricot spread, but make sure the mixture is not too wet, or the soufflés will not rise properly.

BLUEBERRY AND ORANGE CRÊPE BASKETS

Impress your guests with these pretty, fruit-filled crêpes. When blueberries are out of season, replace them with other soft fruit, such as raspberries.

INGREDIENTS

Serves 6

150g/5oz/1¼ cups plain
  (all-purpose) flour
pinch of salt
2 egg whites
200ml/7fl oz/⅞ cup skimmed milk
150ml/¼ pint/⅔ cup orange juice
oil, for frying
yogurt or light crème fraîche, to serve

For the filling
4 medium oranges
225g/8oz/2 cups blueberries

1 Preheat the oven to 200°C/400°F/ Gas 6. To make the pancakes, sift the flour and salt into a bowl. Make a well in the centre and add the egg whites, milk and orange juice. Whisk hard, until all the liquid has been incorporated and the batter is smooth and bubbly.

2 Lightly grease a heavy or non-stick pancake pan and heat it until it is very hot. Pour in just enough batter to cover the base of the pan, swirling it to cover the pan evenly.

3 Cook until the pancake has set and is golden, then turn it to cook the other side. Remove the pancake to a sheet of kitchen paper and keep warm. Cook the remaining batter to make 6–8 pancakes.

4 Place six small ovenproof bowls or moulds on a baking sheet and lay the pancakes over these. Bake them in the oven for about 10 minutes, until they are crisp and set into shape. Lift the 'baskets' off the moulds.

5 Pare a thin piece of orange rind from one orange and cut it into fine strips. Blanch the strips in boiling water for 30 seconds, rinse them in cold water and set them aside. Cut all the peel and white pith from the oranges.

6 Divide the oranges into segments, catching the juice, combine with the blueberries and warm them gently. Spoon the fruit into the baskets and scatter the rind over the top. Serve with yogurt or light crème fraîche.

> **COOK'S TIP**
> Don't fill the pancake baskets until you're ready to serve them, because they will absorb the fruit juice and begin to soften.

NUTRITION NOTES

Per portion:

Energy	157.3Kcals/668.3kJ
Fat	2.20g
Saturated Fat	0.23g
Cholesterol	0.66mg
Fibre	2.87g

FILO CHIFFON PIE

ilo pastry is low in fat and is
ery easy to use. Keep a packet
1 the freezer, ready to make
npressive desserts like this one.

INGREDIENTS

erves 6
00g/1¼lb rhubarb
ml/1 tsp mixed (apple pie) spice
nely grated rind and juice of 1 orange
5ml/1 tbsp granulated (white) sugar
5g/½oz/1 tbsp butter
filo pastry sheets

1 Preheat the oven to 200°C/400°F/
Gas 6. Chop the rhubarb into
.5cm/1in pieces and put them in
bowl.

2 Add the mixed spice, orange rind
and juice and sugar. Tip the rhubarb
nto a 1 litre/1¾ pint/4 cup pie dish.

3 Melt the butter and brush it over
the pastry. Lift the pastry on to the
pie dish, butter-side up, and crumple it
up decoratively to cover the pie.

4 Put the dish on a baking sheet and
bake for 20 minutes, until golden
brown. Reduce the heat to 180°C/350°F/
Gas 4 and bake for a further 10–15
minutes, until the rhubarb is tender.

NUTRITION NOTES

Per portion:
Energy	71Kcals/299kJ
Fat	2.5g
Saturated Fat	1.41g
Cholesterol	5.74mg
Fibre	1.48g

VARIATION
Other fruit can be used in this pie –
just prepare depending on type.

Blushing Pears

Pears poached in rosé wine and sweet spices absorb all the subtle flavours and turn a delightful soft pink colour.

Ingredients

Serves 6

6 firm eating pears
300ml/½ pint/1¼ cups rosé wine
150ml/¼ pint/⅔ cup cranberry or
    clear apple juice
strip of thinly pared orange rind
1 cinnamon stick
4 whole cloves
1 bay leaf
75ml/5 tbsp caster (superfine) sugar
small bay leaves, to decorate

3 Heat gently, stirring all the time, until the sugar has dissolved. Add the pears and stand them upright in the pan. Pour in enough cold water to barely cover them. Cover and cook gently for 20–30 minutes, or until just tender, turning and basting occasionally.

6 Strain the syrup and pour over the pears. Serve hot or well-chilled, decorated with small bay leaves.

Nutrition Notes

Per portion:

Energy	148Kcals/620kJ
Fat	0.16g
Saturated Fat	0
Fibre	2.93g

1 Thinly peel the pears with a sharp knife or vegetable peeler, leaving the stalks attached.

4 Using a slotted spoon, gently lift the pears out of the syrup and transfer to a serving dish.

Cook's Tip

Check the pears by piercing with a skewer or sharp knife towards the end of the poaching time, because some may cook more quickly than others. Serve immediately, or leave to cool in the syrup and then chill.

2 Pour the wine and cranberry or apple juice into a large heavy pan. Add the orange rind, cinnamon stick, cloves, bay leaf and sugar.

5 Bring the syrup to the boil and boil rapidly for 10–15 minutes, or until it has reduced by half.

COLD DESSERTS

There is such a vast range of ready-made desserts available
today that it may hardly seem worth making your own,
but it is definitely well worth the effort. In no time at all,
you can make and enjoy a wide variety of nutritious low-fat
delicious cold desserts, such as Rhubarb and Orange
Water-ice, Apple and Blackberry Terrine, Mandarins in
Syrup and Raspberry Vacherin.

APRICOT DELICE

A fluffy mousse base with a layer of fruit jelly on top makes this dessert doubly delicious.

INGREDIENTS

Serves 8

2 x 400g/14oz cans apricots in
   natural juice
60ml/4 tbsp sugar
25ml/5 tbsp lemon juice
25ml/5 tsp powdered gelatine
425g/15oz low-fat ready-to-serve
   custard
150ml/¼ pint/⅔ cup Greek
   (US strained plain) yogurt
1 apricot, sliced, and fresh mint sprig,
   to decorate
whipped cream, to decorate (optional)

NUTRITION NOTES

Per portion:
Energy	155Kcals/649kJ
Fat	0.63g
Saturated Fat	0.33g
Fibre	0.9g

VARIATIONS

Use reduced-fat Greek (US strained plain) yogurt to cut calories and fat. Add the finely grated rind of 1 lemon to the mixture, for extra flavour. Peaches or pears are good alternatives to apricots.

1 Line the base of a 1.2 litre/2 pint/ 5 cup heart-shaped or round cake tin (pan) with baking parchment.

2 Drain the apricots, reserving the juice. Put the apricots in a food processor or blender fitted with a metal blade, together with the sugar and 60ml/4 tbsp of the apricot juice. Blend to a smooth purée.

3 Measure 30ml/2 tbsp of the apricot juice into a small bowl. Add the lemon juice, then sprinkle over 10ml/ 2 tsp of the gelatine. Leave for about 5 minutes, until spongy.

4 Stir the gelatine into half of the purée and pour into the prepared tin. Chill in the refrigerator for about 1½ hours, or until firm.

5 Sprinkle the remaining 15ml/3 tsp of gelatine over 60ml/4 tbsp of the apricot juice. Leave for about 5 minute until spongy. Mix the remaining apric purée with the custard, yogurt and gelatine. Pour on to the layer of set fruit purée and chill for 3 hours.

6 Dip the cake tin into hot water for few seconds and unmould the delic on to a serving plate and peel off the lining paper. Decorate with the sliced apricot and mint sprig; for a special occasion, pipe whipped cream round the edge.

MELON, GINGER AND GRAPEFRUIT

This pretty fruit combination is very light and refreshing for any summer meal.

INGREDIENTS

Serves 4

500g/1¼ lbs diced watermelon flesh
2 ruby or pink grapefruit
2 pieces stem ginger in syrup
30ml/2 tbsp stem ginger syrup

NUTRITION NOTES

Per portion:

Energy	76Kcals/324.5kJ
Fat	0.42g
Saturated Fat	0.125g
Cholesterol	0
Fibre	0.77g

1 Remove any seeds from the watermelon and discard. Cut the fruit into bitesize chunks. Set aside.

2 Using a small sharp knife, cut away all the peel and white pith from the grapefruits and carefully lift out the segments, catching any juice in a bowl

3 Finely chop the stem ginger and put in a serving bowl with the melon cubes and grapefruit segments, also adding the juice.

4 Spoon over the ginger syrup and toss the fruits lightly to mix evenly. Chill before serving.

COOK'S TIP
Take care to toss the fruits gently – grapefruit segments will break up easily, which would spoil the appearance of the dish.

MANGO AND GINGER CLOUDS

The sweet, perfumed flavour of ripe mango combines beautifully with ginger, and this low-fat dessert makes the very most of them both.

INGREDIENTS

Serves 6

2 ripe mangoes
2 pieces stem ginger
45ml/3 tbsp stem ginger syrup
75g/3oz/¹/2 cup silken tofu
2 egg whites
pistachio nuts, chopped

1 Cut the mangoes in half, remove the stones (pits) and peel. Roughly chop the mango flesh.

2 Put the chopped mango in a food processor bowl, with the ginger, syrup and tofu. Process the mixture until it is smooth and spoon into a mixing bowl.

3 Put the egg whites in a bowl and whisk them until they form soft peaks. Fold them lightly into the mango mixture.

4 Spoon the mixture into wide dishes or glasses and chill before serving, sprinkled with the chopped pistachios.

NUTRITION NOTES	
Per portion:	
Energy	112Kcals/472kJ
Fat	3.5g
Saturated Fat	0.52g
Cholesterol	0
Fibre	2.25g

VARIATION
This dessert can be served lightly frozen. If you prefer not to use ginger, omit the ginger pieces and syrup and use 45ml/3 tbsp clear honey instead.

GOOSEBERRY CHEESE COOLER

INGREDIENTS

Serves 4

500g/1¼lb/4 cups fresh or frozen
  gooseberries
1 small orange
15ml/1 tbsp clear honey
250g/9oz/1 cup half-fat cottage cheese

NUTRITION NOTES

Per portion:
Energy	123Kcals/525kJ
Fat	1.29g
Saturated Fat	0.69g
Cholesterol	3.25mg
Fibre	3.64g

1 Top and tail the gooseberries and place them in a pan. Finely grate the rind from the orange and squeeze out the juice, then add them both to the pan. Cover the pan and cook gently, stirring occasionally, until the fruit is tender.

2 Remove from the heat and stir in the honey. Purée the gooseberries with their juice in a blender or food processor until almost smooth. Cool.

3 Press the cottage cheese through a sieve (strainer) until smooth. Stir half the cooled gooseberry purée into the cheese.

4 Spoon the cheese mixture into four serving glasses. Top each with gooseberry purée. Serve chilled.

VARIATION
If fresh or frozen gooseberries are not available, canned ones are often packed in heavy syrup, so substitute a different fresh fruit.

MANGO AND LIME SORBET IN LIME SHELLS

This richly flavoured sorbet looks pretty served in the lime shells, but is also good served in scoops in a bowl for a more traditional presentation.

INGREDIENTS

Serves 4
4 large limes
1 medium-size ripe mango
7.5ml/1½ tsp powdered gelatine
2 egg whites
15ml/1 tbsp granulated (white) sugar
lime rind strips, to decorate

1 Cut a thick slice from the top of each of the limes, and then cut a thin slice from the bottom end so that the limes will stand upright. Squeeze out the juice, then use a small knife to remove all the white membrane from the centre.

3 Whisk the egg whites until they hold soft peaks. Whisk in the sugar, then quickly fold the egg-white mixture into the mango mixture. Spoon the sorbet into the lime shells. (Any leftover sorbet that will not fit in can be frozen in small ramekins.)

4 Wrap the shells in clear film (plastic wrap) and put in the freezer until the sorbet is firm. Before serving, allow the shells to stand at room temperature for about 10 minutes; decorate them with strips of lime rind.

2 Halve, stone (pit), peel and chop the mango, then purée the flesh in a blender or food processor with 30ml/2 tbsp of the lime juice. Dissolve the gelatine in 45ml/3 tbsp lime juice and stir it into the mango mixture.

COOK'S TIP
If you have any lime juice left over, it will freeze well for future use. Pour into a freezer container, seal and freeze for up to six months.

NUTRITION NOTES	
Per portion:	
Energy	50.5Kcals/215kJ
Fat	0.09g
Saturated Fat	0.3g
Cholesterol	0
Fibre	1g

RHUBARB AND ORANGE WATER-ICE

Pretty pink rhubarb, with sweet
oranges and honey – the perfect
sweet ice.

INGREDIENTS

Serves 4
350g/12oz rhubarb
1 medium orange
15ml/1 tbsp clear honey
5ml/1 tsp/1 sachet powdered gelatine
orange slices, to decorate

COOK'S TIP
Most pink, forced rhubarb is
naturally quite sweet, but if yours
is not, you could add a little
more honey, sugar or artificial
sweetener to taste.

1 Trim the rhubarb and slice into
2.5cm/1in lengths. Put the pieces in
a pan without adding water.

NUTRITION NOTES	
Per portion:	
Energy	36Kcals/155kJ
Fat	0.12g
Saturated Fat	0
Cholesterol	0
Fibre	1.9g

2 Finely grate the rind from the
orange and squeeze out the juice.
Add about half the orange juice and a
the grated rind to the rhubarb in the
pan and allow to simmer until the
rhubarb is just tender. Stir in the honey

3 Heat the remaining orange juice an
sprinkle in the gelatine to dissolve
it. Stir into the rhubarb. Turn the
whole mixture into a rigid freezer
container and freeze it for about
2 hours until slushy.

4 Remove the mixture from the
freezer and beat it well to break up
the ice crystals. Return the container to
the freezer and freeze the mixture again
until it is firm. Allow the water-ice to
soften slightly at room temperature
before serving.

ICED ORANGES

The ultimate fat-free treat –
these delectable orange sorbets
served in fruit shells were
originally sold in the beach cafés
in the south of France.

INGREDIENTS

Serves 8

150g/5oz/⅔ cup granulated (white) sugar
juice of 1 lemon
14 medium oranges
8 fresh bay leaves, to decorate

NUTRITION NOTES

Per portion:

Energy	139Kcals/593kJ
Fat	0.17g
Saturated Fat	0
Cholesterol	0
Fibre	3g

COOK'S TIP
Use crumpled kitchen paper to
keep the shells upright.

1 Put the sugar in a heavy pan. Add
half the lemon juice, then add 120ml/
4fl oz/½ cup water. Cook over a low
heat until the sugar has dissolved. Bring
to the boil and boil for 2–3 minutes
until the syrup is clear.

2 Slice the tops off eight of the
oranges to make 'hats'. Scoop out
the flesh of the oranges and reserve.
Freeze the empty orange shells and
'hats' until needed.

3 Grate the rind of the remaining
oranges and add to the syrup.
Squeeze the juice from the oranges, and
from the reserved flesh. There should
be 750ml/1¼ pints/3 cups. Squeeze
another orange or add bought orange
juice, if necessary.

4 Stir the orange juice and remaining
lemon juice, with 90ml/6 tbsp water
into the syrup. Taste, adding more
lemon juice or sugar as desired. Pour
the mixture into a shallow freezer
container and freeze for 3 hours.

5 Turn the orange sorbet mixture into
a bowl and whisk thoroughly to
break up the ice crystals. Freeze for
4 hours more, until firm, but not solid.

6 Pack the mixture into the hollowed-
out orange shells, mounding it up,
and set the 'hats' on top. Freeze the
sorbet shells until ready to serve. Just
before serving, push a skewer into the
tops of the 'hats' and push in a bay
leaf, to decorate.

APPLE AND BLACKBERRY TERRINE

Apples and blackberries are a classic autumn combination; they really complement each other. This pretty, three-layered terrine can be frozen, so you can enjoy it at any time of year.

INGREDIENTS

Serves 6

500g/1½lb cooking or eating apples
300ml/½ pint/1¼ cups sweet cider
15ml/1 tbsp clear honey
5ml/1 tsp vanilla extract
200g/7oz fresh or frozen and
  thawed blackberries
15ml/1 tbsp/1 sachet powdered gelatine
2 egg whites
apple slices and blackberries,
  to decorate

NUTRITION NOTES

Per portion:

Energy	72Kcals/306kJ
Fat	0.13g
Saturated Fat	0
Cholesterol	0
Fibre	2.1g

VARIATION

For a quicker version, the mixture can be set without layering. Purée the apples and blackberries together, stir the dissolved gelatine and whisked egg whites into the mixture, turn the whole thing into the tin (pan) and leave the mixture to set.

1 Peel, core and chop the apples and place them in a pan with half the cider. Bring the cider to the boil, and then cover the pan and let the apples simmer gently on a medium heat until they are tender.

2 Tip the apples into a blender or food processor and process them to a smooth purée. Stir in the honey and vanilla. Add half the blackberries to half the purée, then process again until smooth. Push through a sieve (strainer).

3 Heat the remaining cider until it is almost boiling, then sprinkle the powdered gelatine over and stir until the gelatine has completely dissolved. Add half the gelatine and cider liquid to the apple purée and half to the blackberry purée.

4 Leave the purées to cool until almost set. Whisk the egg whites until they are stiff, then quickly fold them into the apple purée. Remove half the purée to another bowl. Stir the remaining whole blackberries into half the apple purée, and then turn this into a 1.75 litre/3 pint/7½ cup loaf tin (pan).

5 Top with the blackberry purée and spread it evenly. Finally, add a layer of the apple purée and smooth it evenly. To make sure the layers remain clearly separated, you can freeze each one until firm before adding the next.

6 Freeze until firm. To serve, allow to stand at room temperature for about 20 minutes to soften, then serve in thick slices, decorated with apples and blackberries.

QUICK APRICOT WHIP

INGREDIENTS

Serves 4

400g/14oz can apricot halves in juice
15ml/1 tbsp Grand Marnier or brandy
175g/6oz/¾ cup low-fat yogurt
30ml/2 tsp flaked (sliced) almonds

NUTRITION NOTES

Per portion:

Energy	114Kcals/480kJ
Fat	4.6g
Saturated Fat	0.57g
Cholesterol	0
Fibre	1.45g

1 Drain the juice from the apricots and place the fruit and liqueur in a blender or food processor.

2 Process the apricots until they are completely smooth.

3 Put alternate spoonfuls of the fruit purée and yogurt into four tall glasses or glass dishes, swirling them together slightly to give a marbled effect.

4 Lightly toast the almonds until they are golden-brown. Let them cool slightly and then sprinkle them on top of the desserts.

VARIATION

If you prefer to omit the liqueur, add a little of the fruit juice from the can.

MANDARINS IN SYRUP

Mandarins, tangerines, clementines, mineolas; any of these lovely citrus fruits are suitable for this recipe.

INGREDIENTS

Serves 4

10 mandarin oranges
15ml/1 tbsp icing (confectioners') sugar
10ml/2 tsp orange-flower water
15ml/1 tbsp chopped pistachio nuts

1 Thinly pare a little of the rind from one mandarin and cut it into fine shreds for decoration. Squeeze the juice from two mandarins and set aside.

2 Peel the remaining fruit, removing as much of the white pith as possible. Arrange the peeled fruit whole in a wide dish.

3 Mix the mandarin juice, sugar and orange-flower water and pour it over the fruit. Cover the dish and chill for at least an hour.

4 Blanch the shreds of mandarin rind in boiling water for 30 seconds. Drain, leave to cool and then sprinkle them over the mandarins, with the pistachio nuts, to serve.

NUTRITION NOTES

Per portion:

Energy	53.25Kcals/223.5kJ
Fat	2.07g
Saturated Fat	0.28g
Cholesterol	0
Fibre	0.38g

COOK'S TIP
Mandarin oranges look very attractive if you leave them whole, but you may prefer to separate the segments.

CRUNCHY FRUIT LAYER

Serves 2

1 peach or nectarine

75g/3oz/1 cup crunchy toasted
    oat cereal

150ml/¼ pint/⅔ cup low-fat
    natural (plain) yogurt

15ml/1 tbsp jam

15ml/1 tbsp fruit juice

NUTRITION NOTES	
Per portion:	
Energy	240Kcals/1005kJ
Fat	3g
Saturated Fat	1g
Cholesterol	3mg

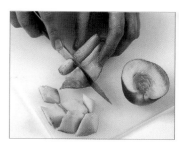

1 Remove the stone (pit) from the peach or nectarine and cut the fruit into bitesize pieces with a sharp knife.

2 Divide the chopped fruit between two tall glasses, reserving a few pieces for decoration.

3 Sprinkle the oat cereal over the fruit in an even layer, then top with the low-fat yogurt.

4 Stir the jam and the fruit juice together in a jug (pitcher), then drizzle the mixture over the yogurt. Decorate the top with the reserved peach or nectarine pieces and serve the desserts immediately.

RASPBERRY MUESLI LAYER

As well as being a delicious, low-fat, high-fibre dessert, this recipe can also be served for a quick, healthy breakfast.

INGREDIENTS

Serves 4

225g/8oz/2¼ cups fresh or frozen and thawed raspberries
225g/8oz/1 cup low-fat natural (plain) yogurt
75g/3oz/½ cup Swiss-style muesli (granola)

1 Reserve four raspberries for decoration, then spoon a few raspberries into each of four stemmed glasses or glass dishes.

2 Top the raspberries with a spoonful of yogurt in each glass.

3 Sprinkle a layer of muesli mixture over the yogurt.

4 Repeat the layers with the remaining ingredients, finishing with muesli. Top each dish with a whole raspberry.

COOK'S TIP
This recipe can be made in advance and stored in the refrigerator for several hours, or overnight if you plan to serve it for breakfast.

NUTRITION NOTES	
Per portion:	
Energy	114Kcals/483kJ
Fat	1.7g
Saturated Fat	0.48g
Cholesterol	2.25mg
Fibre	2.6g

Yogurt Sundaes with Passion Fruit

Here is a sundae you can enjoy every day! The frozen yogurt has less fat and fewer calories than traditional ice cream, and the fruits provide vitamins A and C.

Ingredients

Serves 4

350g/12oz strawberries, hulled and halved
2 passion fruit, halved
10ml/2 tsp icing (confectioners') sugar (optional)
2 peaches, stoned (pitted) and chopped
8 scoops vanilla or strawberry frozen yogurt

Cook's Tip
Choose reduced-fat or virtually fat-free frozen yogurt or ice cream, to cut the calories and fat.

1 Purée half the strawberries. Scoop out the passion fruit pulp and add it to the coulis. Sweeten, if necessary.

Nutrition Notes	
Per portion:	
Energy	135Kcals/560kJ
Fat	1g
Saturated Fat	0.5g
Cholesterol	3.5mg

2 Spoon half of the remaining strawberries and half the chopped peaches into four tall sundae glasses. Top each dessert with a scoop of frozen yogurt. Set aside a few choice pieces of fruit for decoration, and use the rest to make a further layer on the top of each sundae. Top each sundae with a final scoop of frozen yogurt.

3 Pour over the passion fruit coulis and decorate the sundaes with the remaining strawberries and pieces of peach. Serve immediately.

Fruit Fondue with Hazelnut Dip

Ingredients

Serves 2

selection of fresh fruit for dipping, such as satsumas, kiwi fruit, grapes and physalis
50g/2oz/½ cup reduced-fat soft cheese
150ml/5fl oz/1¼ cup low-fat hazelnut yogurt
5ml/1 tsp vanilla extract
5ml/1 tsp caster (superfine) sugar

Nutrition Notes	
Per portion (dip only):	
Energy	170Kcals/714kJ
Fat	4g
Saturated Fat	2.5g
Cholesterol	6.5mg

1 First prepare the fruit. Peel and segment the satsumas, removing as much of the white pith as possible. Quarter the kiwi fruit, wash the grapes and peel back the papery casing on the physalis.

2 Beat the soft cheese with the yogurt, vanilla extract and sugar in a bowl. Spoon the mixture into a glass serving dish set on a platter or into small pots on individual plates.

3 Arrange the prepared fruits around the dip and serve immediately.

PINEAPPLE, ALLSPICE AND LIME

Fresh pineapple is easy to prepare and always looks very festive, so this dish is perfect for easy entertaining.

INGREDIENTS

Serves 4

1 ripe medium pineapple
1 lime
15ml/1 tbsp dark muscovado
  (molasses) sugar
5ml/1 tsp ground allspice

1 Cut the pineapple lengthways into quarters and remove the core.

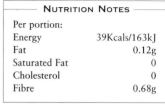

2 Loosen the fruit by sliding a knife between it and the skin. Cut the pineapple flesh into thick slices.

3 Remove a few shreds of rind from the lime and set aside, then squeeze out the juice.

4 Sprinkle the pineapple with the lime juice and rind, muscovado sugar and allspice. Serve immediately, or chill for up to 1 hour.

PAPAYA SKEWERS WITH PASSION FRUIT

Tropical fruits, full of natural
sweetness, make a simple dessert.

INGREDIENTS

Serves 6

3 ripe papayas
10 small passion fruit or kiwi fruit
30ml/2 tbsp lime juice
30ml/2 tbsp icing (confectioners') sugar
30ml/2 tbsp white rum
lime slices, to decorate (optional)

NUTRITION NOTES

Per portion:	
Energy	83Kcals/351kJ
Fat	0.27g
Saturated Fat	0
Cholesterol	0
Fibre	2.8g

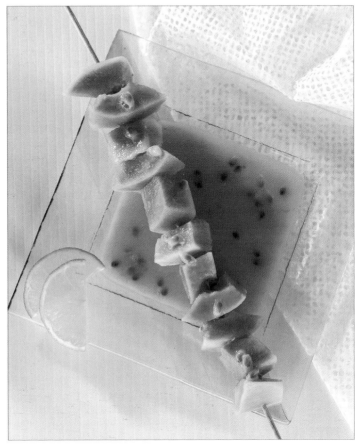

1 Cut the papayas in half and scoop
out the seeds. Peel and cut the flesh
into even chunks. Thread the chunks
on to six bamboo skewers.

2 Halve eight of the passion fruit or
kiwi fruit and scoop out the insides.
Purée for a few seconds in a blender or
food processor.

3 Press the passion fruit or kiwi fruit
pulp through a sieve (strainer) set
over a bowl and discard the seeds. Add
the lime juice, icing sugar and white
rum, then stir the coulis well until the
sugar has dissolved.

4 Spoon a little of the coulis on to
six serving plates. Place the fruit
skewers on top. Scoop the flesh from
the remaining passion fruit or kiwi
fruit and spoon it over. Decorate with
lime slices.

RASPBERRY VACHERIN

Meringue rounds filled with orange-flavoured low-fat fromage frais or yogurt and fresh raspberries make this a perfect dinner party dessert.

INGREDIENTS

Serves 6
3 egg whites
175g/6oz/³/4 cup caster (superfine) sugar
5ml/1 tsp chopped almonds
icing (confectioners') sugar, for dusting
raspberry leaves, to decorate (optional)

For the filling
175g/6oz/³/4 cup low-fat soft cheese
15–30ml/1–2 tbsp clear honey
15–30ml/1–2 tbsp Cointreau
120ml/4fl oz/¹/2 cup low-fat
*   fromage frais or natural*
*   (plain) yogurt*
225g/8oz raspberries

NUTRITION NOTES

Per portion:
Energy	197Kcals/837.5kJ
Fat	1.02g
Saturated Fat	0.36g
Cholesterol	1.67mg
Fibre	1g

COOK'S TIP
When making the meringue, whisk the egg whites until they are so stiff that you can turn the bowl upside-down without them falling out.

1 Preheat the oven to 140°C/275°F/ Gas 1. Draw a 20cm/8in circle on two pieces of baking parchment. Turn the paper over so the marking is on the underside and use it to line two heavy baking sheets.

2 Whisk the egg whites in a clean bowl until very stiff, then gradually whisk in the caster sugar to make a stiff meringue mixture.

3 Spoon the mixture on to the circles on the prepared baking sheets, spreading the meringue evenly to the edges. Sprinkle one meringue round with the chopped almonds.

4 Bake for 1¹/2–2 hours until crisp and dry, and then carefully lift the meringue rounds off the baking sheets. Peel away the paper and cool the meringues on a wire rack.

5 To make the filling, cream the soft cheese with the honey and liqueur in a bowl. Fold in the fromage frais or yogurt and the raspberries, reserving three berries for decoration.

6 Place the plain meringue round on a board, spread with the filling and top with the nut-covered round. Dust with the icing sugar, transfer to a serving plate and decorate with the reserved raspberries and a sprig of raspberry leaves, if you like.

COOL GREEN FRUIT SALAD

A sophisticated, simple fruit salad for any time of year.

INGREDIENTS

Serves 6

3 Ogen or Galia melons
115g/4oz green seedless grapes
2 kiwi fruit
1 star fruit (carambola)
1 green-skinned eating apple
1 lime
175ml/6fl oz/³/₄ cup sparkling
    grape juice

NUTRITION NOTES

Per portion:	
Energy	67Kcals/285kJ
Fat	0.27g
Saturated Fat	0
Cholesterol	0
Fibre	1.22g

1 Cut the melons in half and scoop out the seeds. Keeping the shells intact, scoop out the fruit with a melon baller, or scoop it out with a spoon and cut into bitesize cubes. Set aside the melon shells.

2 Remove any stems from the grapes, and, if they are large, cut them in half. Peel and chop the kiwi fruit. Thinly slice the star fruit. Core and thinly slice the apple and place the slices in a bowl, with the melon, grapes, kiwi fruit and star fruit.

> **COOK'S TIP**
> If you're serving this dessert on a hot summer day, serve the filled melon shells nestling on a platter of crushed ice to keep them beautifully cool.

3 Thinly pare the rind from the lime and cut it into fine strips. Blanch the strips in boiling water for 30 seconds, then drain them and rinse in cold water. Squeeze the juice from the lime and toss it into the fruit. Mix gently.

4 Spoon the fruit into the melon shells and chill in the refrigerator until required. Just before serving, spoon the sparkling grape juice over the fruit and scatter it with the blanched lime rind.

THREE FRUIT COMPÔTES

INGREDIENTS

Each Compôte Serves 1
ORANGE AND PRUNE COMPÔTE
1 orange
50g/2oz ready-to-eat prunes
75ml/5 tbsp orange juice

PEAR AND KIWI FRUIT COMPÔTE
1 ripe eating pear
1 kiwi fruit
60ml/4 tbsp apple or pineapple juice

GRAPEFRUIT AND STRAWBERRY COMPÔTE
1 ruby grapefruit
115g/4oz strawberries
60ml/4 tbsp orange juice

To serve
low-fat natural (plain) yogurt and
  toasted hazelnuts

NUTRITION NOTES

Per portion (minus topping):

Orange and Prune

Energy	155Kcals/650kJ
Fat	0.5g
Saturated Fat	0
Cholesterol	0

Pear and Kiwi Fruit

Energy	100Kcals/405kJ
Fat	0.5g
Saturated Fat	0
Cholesterol	0

Grapefruit and Strawberry

Energy	110Kcals/465kJ
Fat	0.5g
Saturated Fat	0
Cholesterol	0

COOK'S TIP
Choose fresh-pressed fruit juices
or squeeze your own fruit juice
using a blender or food processor.

1 For the orange and prune compôte,
segment the orange and place in a
bowl with the prunes.

2 For the pear and kiwi fruit compôte,
peel the pear and cut it into wedges,
and peel and slice the kiwi fruit.

3 For the grapefruit and strawberry
compôte, segment the grapefruit
and halve the strawberries.

4 Put your selected fruits together in a
bowl and pour over the fruit juice.

5 Serve the chosen fruit compôte
topped with a spoonful of low-fat
natural yogurt and a sprinkling of
chopped toasted hazelnuts, to decorate.

PRUNE AND ORANGE POTS

This simple, store cupboard (pantry) dessert can be made in minutes. Serve immediately or, for the best result, chill it for half an hour before serving.

INGREDIENTS

Serves 4

225g/8oz/1½ cups ready-to-eat dried prunes
150ml/¼ pint/⅔ cup orange juice
225g/8oz/1 cup low-fat natural (plain) yogurt
shreds of orange rind, to decorate

NUTRITION NOTES

Per portion:	
Energy	112Kcals/474kJ
Fat	0.62g
Saturated Fat	0.34g
Cholesterol	2.25mg
Fibre	2.8g

2 Bring the juice to the boil, stirring. Reduce the heat, cover and leave to simmer for 5 minutes, until the prunes are tender and the liquid has reduced by half.

4 Transfer the purée mixture to a bowl. Stir in the low-fat yogurt, swirling the yogurt and fruit purée together lightly to give an attractive marbled effect.

3 Remove from the heat, allow to cool slightly and then beat well with a wooden spoon, until the fruit breaks down to a rough purée.

5 Spoon the mixture into individual dishes or stemmed glasses, using a spoon to smooth the tops.

1 Remove the pits from the prunes and roughly chop them. Place them in a pan with the orange juice.

VARIATIONS
This dessert can also be made with other ready-to-eat dried fruit, such as apricots or peaches. For a special occasion, add a dash of brandy or Cointreau with the yogurt.

6 Top each pot with a few shreds of orange rind, to decorate. Chill before serving.

TROPICAL FOAMY YOGURT RING

An impressive, light and
colourful tropical dessert with a
truly fruity flavour.

Serves 6
For the yogurt ring
175ml/6fl oz/³/4 cup tropical fruit juice
15ml/1 tbsp/1 sachet powdered gelatine
3 egg whites
150g/5oz low-fat natural (plain) yogurt
finely grated rind of 1 lime

For the filling
1 mango
2 kiwi fruit
10–12 physalis
juice of 1 lime

1 Place the tropical fruit juice in
a small pan and sprinkle the
powdered gelatine over. Heat gently
until the gelatine has dissolved.

2 Whisk the egg whites in a clean, dry
bowl until they hold soft peaks.
Continue whisking, while gradually
adding the yogurt and lime rind.

3 Continue whisking hard and pour in
the hot gelatine and the egg white and
yogurt mixture in a steady stream, until
everything is smooth and evenly mixed.

4 Quickly pour the mixture into a
1.5 litre/2½ pint/6¼ cup ring mould.
Chill the mould in the refrigerator until
set. The mixture will separate into
two layers.

5 Halve, stone (pit), peel and dice the
mango. Peel and slice the kiwi fruit.
Remove the outer leaves from the
physalis and cut in half. Toss all the
fruits together and stir in the lime juice.

6 Run a knife around the edge of the
ring to loosen the mixture. Dip
the ring quickly into cold water and
then turn the chilled yogurt mould
out on to a serving plate. Spoon all
the prepared fruit into the centre of the
ring and serve immediately.

NUTRITION NOTES	
Per portion:	
Energy	83.5Kcals/355kJ
Fat	0.67g
Saturated Fat	0.27g
Cholesterol	2.16mg
Fibre	1.77g

VARIATIONS
Any mixture of fruit works in this
recipe, depending on the season.
In summer try using apple juice in
the ring mixture and fill it with
luscious, red summer fruits.

STRAWBERRY ROSE-PETAL PASHKA

This light version of a traditional
Russian dessert is ideal for dinner
parties – make it a day or two in
advance for best results.

INGREDIENTS

Serves 4

350g/12oz/1½ cups cottage cheese
175g/6oz/¾ cup low-fat natural
 (plain) yogurt
30ml/2 tbsp clear honey
2.5ml/½ tsp rose water
275g/10oz strawberries
handful of scented pink rose petals,
 to decorate

NUTRITION NOTES

Per portion:

Energy	150.5Kcals/634kJ
Fat	3.83g
Saturated Fat	2.32g
Cholesterol	0.13mg
Fibre	0.75g

VARIATION

The flowerpot shape is traditional
for pashka, but you could make it
in any shape – the small porcelain
heart-shaped moulds with draining
holes usually reserved for *coeurs
à la crème* would make a very
pretty alternative.

1 Drain any liquid from the cottage
cheese and tip the cheese into a
sieve (strainer). Use a wooden spoon to
rub it through the sieve into a bowl.

2 Stir the yogurt, honey and rose
water into the cheese.

3 Roughly chop about half of the
strawberries and stir them into
the cheese mixture.

4 Line a clean flowerpot or a sieve
with muslin (cheesecloth) and put
the mixture in it. Leave it to drain over
a bowl for several hours, or overnight.

5 Invert the flowerpot or sieve on to a
serving plate, turn out the pashka
and remove the muslin.

6 Decorate with strawberries and rose
petals. Serve chilled.

CAKES, BARS AND BROWNIES

We tend to think of cakes, bars and brownies as being
out of bounds for those following a low-fat diet, but
you will be pleased to learn that this is not the case at all.
There are many ways of creating delicious treats without the
need for high-fat mixtures, and all the recipes in this chapter,
both sweet and savoury, are low in fat. Choose from tempting
delights such as Tia Maria Gâteau, Coffee Sponge Drops,
Muscovado Meringues, and Chocolate and Banana Brownies.

IRISH WHISKEY CAKE

This moist rich fruit cake is drizzled with whiskey as soon as it comes out of the oven.

INGREDIENTS

Serves 12
115g/4oz/²⁄₃ cup glacé (candied) cherries
175g/6oz/1 cup dark muscovado (molasses) sugar
115g/4oz/²⁄₃ cup sultanas (golden raisins)
115g/4oz/²⁄₃ cup raisins
115g/4oz/¹⁄₂ cup currants
300ml/¹⁄₂ pint/1¹⁄₄ cups cold tea
300g/10oz/2¹⁄₂ cups self-raising (self-rising) flour, sifted
1 egg
45ml/3 tbsp Irish whiskey

> COOK'S TIP
> If time is short, use hot tea and soak the fruit for just 2 hours.

1 Mix the cherries, sugar, dried fruit and tea together in a large bowl. Cover and leave to soak overnight until all the tea has all been absorbed into the fruit.

NUTRITION NOTES

Per portion:	
Energy	265Kcals/1115kJ
Fat	0.88g
Saturated Fat	0.25g
Cholesterol	16mg
Fibre	1.48g

2 Preheat the oven to 180°C/350°F/ Gas 4. Grease and line a 1kg/2¹⁄₄lb loaf tin (pan). Add the flour, then the egg to the fruit mixture and beat thoroughly until well mixed.

3 Pour the mixture into the prepared tin and bake for 1¹⁄₂ hours or until a skewer inserted into the centre of the cake comes out clean.

4 Prick the top of the cake with a skewer and drizzle over the whiskey while the cake is still hot. Allow to stand for about 5 minutes, then remove from the tin and cool on a wire rack.

ANGEL CAKE

A delicious light cake to serve as a dessert for a special occasion.

INGREDIENTS

Serves 10

50g/1½oz/⅓ cup cornflour (cornstarch)
40g/1½oz/⅓ cup plain (all-purpose) flour
7 egg whites
225g/8oz/1 cup caster (superfine) sugar, plus extra for sprinkling
5ml/1 tsp vanilla extract
90ml/6 tbsp orange-flavoured glacé icing, 4–6 physalis and a little icing (confectioners') sugar, to decorate

1 Preheat the oven to 180°C/350°F/ Gas 4. Sift both flours on to a sheet of baking parchment.

2 Whisk the egg whites in a large, clean, dry bowl until very stiff, then gradually add the sugar and vanilla extract, whisking until the mixture is thick and glossy.

3 Gently fold in the flour mixture with a large metal spoon. Spoon into an ungreased 25cm/10in angel cake tin (pan), smooth the surface and bake for 45–50 minutes, until the cake springs back when lightly pressed.

VARIATION
If you prefer, omit the glacé icing and physalis and simply dust cake a little icing (confectioners') sugar – it is delicious to serve as a coffee-time treat, and also makes the perfect accompaniment to vanilla yogurt ice cream for a dessert.

4 Sprinkle a piece of baking parchment with caster sugar and set an egg cup in the centre. Invert the cake tin over the paper, balancing it carefully on the egg cup. When cold, the cake will drop out of the tin. Transfer it to a plate, spoon over the glacé icing, arrange the physalis on top and then dust with icing sugar and serve.

NUTRITION NOTES	
Per portion:	
Energy	139Kcals/582kJ
Fat	0.08g
Saturated Fat	0.01g
Cholesterol	0
Fibre	0.13g

TIA MARIA GÂTEAU

This is a feather-light coffee sponge with a creamy liqueur-flavoured filling.

INGREDIENTS

Serves 8
75g/3oz/¾ cup plain (all-purpose) flour
30ml/2 tbsp instant coffee powder
3 eggs
115g/4oz/½ cup caster (superfine) sugar
coffee beans, to decorate (optional)

For the filling
175g/6oz/¾ cup low-fat soft cheese
15ml/1 tbsp clear honey
15ml/1 tbsp Tia Maria liqueur
50g/2oz/¼ cup stem ginger,
    roughly chopped

For the icing
225g/8oz/1¾ cups icing (confectioners')
    sugar, sifted
10ml/2 tsp coffee extract
15ml/1 tbsp water
5ml/1 tsp reduced-fat unsweetened
    cocoa powder

NUTRITION NOTES

Per portion:
Energy	226Kcals/951kJ
Fat	3.14g
Saturated Fat	1.17g
Cholesterol	75.03mg
Fibre	0.64g

COOK'S TIP
When folding in the flour mixture in step 3, be careful not to remove the air, as it helps the cake to rise.

1 Preheat the oven to 190°C/375°F/ Gas 5. Grease and line a 20cm/8in deep round cake tin (pan). Sift the flour and coffee powder together on to a sheet of baking parchment.

2 Whisk the eggs and sugar in a bowl with a hand-held electric whisk until thick and mousse-like. (When the whisk is lifted, a trail should remain on the surface of the mixture for at least 15 seconds.)

3 Gently fold in the flour mixture with a metal spoon. Turn the mixture into the prepared tin. Bake the sponge for 30–35 minutes or until it springs back when lightly pressed. Turn on to a wire rack to cool completely.

4 To make the filling, mix the soft cheese with the honey in a bowl. Beat until smooth, then stir in the Tia Maria and chopped stem ginger.

5 Split the cake in half horizontally and sandwich the two halves together with the Tia Maria filling.

6 Make the icing. In a bowl, mix the icing sugar and coffee extract with enough water to make a consistency that will coat the back of a wooden spoon. Pour three-quarters of the icing over the cake, spreading it evenly to the edges.

7 Stir the cocoa into the remaining icing until smooth. Spoon into a piping bag fitted with a writing nozzle and pipe the mocha icing over the coffee icing. Decorate with coffee beans, if liked.

CHOCOLATE AND ORANGE ANGEL CAKE

This light-as-air sponge with its fluffy icing is virtually fat-free, yet tastes heavenly.

INGREDIENTS

Serves 10

25g/1oz/¼ cup plain (all-purpose) flour
15g/½oz/2 tbsp reduced-fat
  unsweetened cocoa powder
15g/½oz/2 tbsp cornflour (cornstarch)
pinch of salt
5 egg whites
2.5ml/½ tsp cream of tartar
115g/4oz/scant ½ cup caster
  (superfine) sugar
blanched and shredded rind of
  1 orange, to decorate

For the icing
200g/7oz/1 cup caster (superfine) sugar
1 egg white

NUTRITION NOTES

Per portion:

Energy	53Kcals/644kJ
Fat	0.27g
Saturated Fat	0.13g
Fibre	0.25g

COOK'S TIP
Make sure you do not over-beat the egg whites. They should not be stiff but should form soft peaks, so that the air bubbles can expand further during cooking and help the cake to rise.

1 Preheat the oven to 180°C/350°F/ Gas 4. Sift the flour, cocoa powder, cornflour and salt together three times. Beat the egg whites in a large clean, dry bowl until foamy. Add the cream of tartar, then whisk until soft peaks form.

2 Add the caster sugar to the egg whites a spoonful at a time, whisking after each addition. Sift a third of the flour and cocoa mixture over the meringue and gently fold in. Repeat, sifting and folding in the flour and cocoa mixture two more times.

3 Spoon the mixture into a non-stick 20cm/8in ring mould and level the top. Bake for 35 minutes or until springy to the touch. Turn upside-down on to a wire rack and leave to cool in the mould. Carefully ease out of the mould.

4 For the icing, put the sugar in a pan with 75ml/5 tbsp cold water. Stir over a low heat until dissolved. Boil until the syrup reaches a temperature of 120°C/240°F on a sugar thermometer, or when a drop of the syrup makes a soft ball when dropped into a cup of cold water. Remove from the heat.

5 Whisk the egg white until stiff. Add the syrup in a thin stream, whisking all the time. Continue to whisk until the mixture is very thick and fluffy.

6 Spread the icing over the top and sides of the cooled cake. Sprinkle the orange rind over the top of the cake and serve.

CINNAMON APPLE GÂTEAU

Make this lovely cake for an autumn celebration.

INGREDIENTS

Serves 8
3 eggs
115g/4oz/¹/₂ cup caster (superfine) sugar
75g/3oz/³/₄ cup plain (all-purpose) flour
5ml/1 tsp ground cinnamon

For the filling and topping
4 large eating apples
60ml/4 tbsp clear honey
15ml/ 1 tbsp water
75g/3oz/¹/₂ cup sultanas (golden raisins)
2.5ml/¹/₂ tsp ground cinnamon
350g/12oz/1¹/₂ cups low-fat soft cheese
60ml/4 tbsp reduced-fat fromage frais
*   or natural (plain) yogurt*
10ml/2 tsp lemon juice
45ml/3 tbsp apricot glaze
mint sprig, to decorate

1 Preheat the oven to 190°C/375°F/ Gas 5. Grease and line a 23cm/9in shallow round cake tin (pan). Place the eggs and sugar in a bowl and beat with a hand-held electric whisk until thick and mousse-like. (When the whisk is lifted, a trail should remain on the surface of the mixture for at least 15 seconds.)

NUTRITION NOTES

Per portion:
Energy	244 Kcals/1023kJ
Fat	4.05g
Saturated Fat	1.71g
Cholesterol	77.95mg
Fibre	1.50g

2 Sift the flour and cinnamon over the egg mixture and fold in with a large spoon. Pour into the prepared tin and bake for 25–30 minutes or until the cake springs back when lightly pressed. Turn the cake on to a wire rack to cool.

3 To make the filling, peel, core and slice three of the apples and put them in a pan. Add 30ml/2 tbsp of the honey and the water. Cover and cook over a gentle heat for about 10 minutes. Add the sultanas and cinnamon, stir well, replace the lid and leave to cool.

4 Put the soft cheese in a bowl with the remaining honey, the fromage frais and half the lemon juice. Beat until the mixture is smooth.

5 Halve the cake horizontally, place the bottom half on a board and drizzle over any liquid from the apples. Spread with two-thirds of the cheese mixture, then top with the apple filling. Fit the top of the cake in place.

6 Swirl the remaining cheese mixture over the top of the sponge. Core and slice the remaining apple, sprinkle with lemon juice and use to decorate the edge of the cake. Brush the apple with the apricot glaze and place mint sprigs on top, to decorate.

COOK'S TIP
Apricot glaze is useful for brushing over any kind of fresh fruit topping or filling. Place a few spoonfuls of apricot jam in a small pan along with a squeeze of lemon juice. Heat the jam, stirring until it is melted and runny. Pour the melted jam into a wire sieve (strainer) set over a bowl. Stir the jam with a wooden spoon to help it go through. Return the strained jam to the pan. Keep the glaze warm until needed.

SNOWBALLS

These light and airy little mouthfuls make an excellent accompaniment to low-fat yogurt ice cream.

INGREDIENTS

Makes about 20
2 egg whites
115g/4oz/¹/₂ cup caster
  (superfine) sugar
15ml/1 tbsp cornflour
  (cornstarch), sifted
5ml/1 tsp white wine vinegar
1.5ml/¹/₄ tsp vanilla extract

1 Preheat the oven to 150C°/300°F/ Gas 2. Line two baking sheets with baking parchment. Whisk the egg whites in a large grease-free bowl until very stiff, using an electric whisk.

2 Add the sugar, whisking until the meringue is very stiff. Whisk in the cornflour, vinegar and vanilla extract.

3 Drop teaspoonfuls of the mixture on to the baking sheets, shaping them into mounds, and bake for 30 minutes until crisp.

4 Remove from the oven and leave to cool on the baking sheet. When the snowballs are cold, remove them from the baking parchment.

NUTRITION NOTES	
Per portion:	
Energy	29Kcals/24kJ
Fat	0.01g
Saturated Fat	0
Cholesterol	0

MUSCOVADO MERINGUES

These light brown meringues are extremely low in fat and are delicious served on their own or sandwiched together with a fresh fruit and soft cheese filling.

INGREDIENTS

Makes about 20

115g/4oz/⅔ cup light muscovado
  (brown) sugar
2 egg whites
5ml/1 tsp finely chopped walnuts

NUTRITION NOTES

Per portion:

Energy	30Kcals/124kJ
Fat	0.34g
Saturated Fat	0.04g
Cholesterol	0
Fibre	0.02g

1 Preheat the oven to 160°C/325°F/ Gas 3. Line two baking sheets with baking parchment. Press the sugar through a metal sieve (strainer) into a bowl.

2 Whisk the egg whites in a clean, dry bowl until very stiff and dry, then whisk in the sugar, about 15ml/1 tbsp at a time, until the meringue is very thick and glossy.

3 Spoon small mounds of the mixture on to the prepared baking sheets.

4 Sprinkle the meringues with the chopped walnuts. Bake for about 30 minutes. Cool for 5 minutes on the baking sheets, then leave to cool on a wire rack.

COOK'S TIP
For a sophisticated filling, mix 115g/4oz/½ cup low-fat soft cheese with 15ml/1 tbsp icing (confectioners') sugar. Chop 2 slices of fresh pineapple and add to the mixture. Use to sandwich the meringues together in pairs.

LEMON SPONGE FINGERS

These tangy, light sponge fingers are virtually fat-free and are perfect to serve either as an accompaniment to low-fat desserts, or to serve with coffee.

INGREDIENTS

Makes about 20
2 eggs
75g/3oz/¹/₂ cup caster (superfine) sugar
grated rind of 1 lemon
50g/2oz/¹/₂ cup plain
   (all-purpose) flour, sifted
caster sugar, for sprinkling

1 Preheat the oven to 190°C/375°F/ Gas 5. Line two baking sheets with baking parchment.

2 Whisk the eggs, sugar and lemon rind together with an electric whisk until the mixture is thick and mousse-like and leaves a thick trail on the surface for at least 15 seconds.

3 Carefully fold in the flour with a large metal spoon. Place the mixture in a large piping bag fitted with a 1cm/¹/₂in plain nozzle and pipe into finger lengths on the baking sheets.

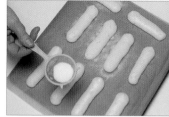

4 Dust the fingers with sugar and bake for 6–8 minutes until golden brown.

VARIATION
To make Spice Fingers, omit the lemon rind and fold in 5ml/1 tsp mixed (apple pie) spice with the flour.

APRICOT SPONGE BARS

These fingers are delicious at tea time – the apricots keep them moist for several days.

INGREDIENTS

Makes 18
225g/8oz/2 cups self-raising
   (self-rising) flour
115g/4oz/¹/₂ cup soft light brown sugar
50g/2oz/¹/₂ cup semolina
175g/6oz/1 cup ready-to-eat dried
   apricots, chopped
30ml/2 tbsp clear honey
30ml/2 tbsp malt extract
2 eggs
60ml/4 tbsp skimmed milk
60ml/4 tbsp sunflower oil
a few drops of almond extract
30ml/2 tbsp flaked (sliced) almonds

1 Preheat the oven to 160°C/325°F/
Gas 3. Lightly grease and then line
an 18 x 28cm/7 x 11in baking tin (pan).

2 Sift the flour into a bowl and mix
in the sugar, semolina and apricots.
Make a well in the centre and add the
honey, malt extract, eggs, milk, oil and
almond essence. Mix the ingredients
together thoroughly until smooth.

3 Spoon the mixture into the tin,
spreading it to the edges, then
sprinkle over the flaked almonds.

4 Bake for 30–35 minutes, or until
the centre springs back when lightly
pressed. Remove from the tin and turn
on to a wire rack to cool. Cut into
18 slices using a sharp knife.

VARIATION
If you can't find pre-soaked
apricots, just chop ready-to-eat
dried apricots soak them in
boiling water for 1 hour, then
drain and add to the mixture.

NUTRITION NOTES

Per portion:	
Energy	153Kcals/641kJ
Fat	4.56g
Saturated Fat	0.61g
Cholesterol	21.5mg
Fibre	1.27g

COFFEE SPONGE DROPS

These are delicious on their own, but taste even better with a filling made by mixing low-fat soft cheese with drained and chopped stem ginger.

INGREDIENTS

Makes 12

50g/2oz/½ cup plain (all-purpose) flour
15ml/1 tbsp instant coffee powder
2 eggs
75g/3oz/6 tbsp caster (superfine) sugar

For the filling
115g/4oz/½ cup low-fat soft cheese
40g/1½oz/¼ cup chopped
    stem ginger

VARIATION

As an alternative to stem ginger in the filling, try walnuts.

1 Preheat the oven to 190°C/375°F/ Gas 5. Line two baking sheets with baking parchment. Make the filling by beating together the soft cheese and stem ginger. Chill until required. Sift the flour and instant coffee powder together onto a piece of parchment.

NUTRITION NOTES

Per portion:

Energy	69Kcals/290kJ
Fat	1.36g
Saturated Fat	0.50g
Cholesterol	33.33mg
Fibre	0.29g

2 Combine the eggs and caster sugar in a bowl. Beat with a hand-held electric whisk until thick and mousse-like. (When the whisk is lifted, a trail should remain on the surface of the mixture for at least 15 seconds.)

3 Carefully add the sifted flour and coffee mixture and gently fold in with a metal spoon, being careful not to knock out any air.

4 Spoon the mixture into a piping bag fitted with a 1cm/½in plain nozzle. Pipe 4cm/1½in rounds on the baking sheets. Bake for 12 minutes. Cool on a wire rack, then sandwich together with the filling.

CHOCOLATE AND BANANA BROWNIES

Nuts traditionally give brownies their chewy texture. Here oat bran is used instead, creating a low-fat, moist, moreish, yet healthy alternative.

INGREDIENTS

Serves 9

75ml/5 tbsp reduced-fat unsweetened
  cocoa powder
15ml/1 tbsp caster (superfine) sugar
75ml/5 tbsp skimmed milk
3 large bananas, mashed
215g/7½oz/1 cup soft light brown sugar
5ml/1 tsp vanilla extract
5 egg whites
75g/3oz/¾ cup self-raising
  (self-rising) flour
75g/3oz/¾ cup oat bran
15ml/1 tbsp icing (confectioners') sugar,
  for dusting

NUTRITION NOTES

Per portion:

Energy	230Kcals/968kJ
Fat	2.15g
Saturated Fat	0.91g
Fibre	1.89g

COOK'S TIPS

Store these brownies in an airtight tin for a day before eating – they improve with keeping. You'll find reduced-fat unsweetened cocoa powder in health food stores. If you can't find it, standard unsweetened cocoa powder will work just as well, but the fat content will be much higher.

1 Preheat the oven to 180°C/350°F/ Gas 4. Line a 20cm/8in square tin (pan) with baking parchment.

2 Blend the reduced-fat cocoa powder and caster sugar with the skimmed milk. Add the bananas, soft light brown sugar and vanilla extract.

3 Lightly beat the egg whites with a fork. Add the chocolate mixture and continue to beat well. Sift the flour over the mixture and fold in with the oat bran. Pour into the prepared tin.

4 Cook in the preheated oven for 40 minutes or until firm. Cool in the tin for 10 minutes, then turn out on to a wire rack. Cut into squares and lightly dust with icing sugar before serving.

Peach Swiss Roll

A feather-light sponge enclosing peach jam – delicious at tea time.

Ingredients

Serves 6–8
3 eggs
115g/4oz/^{1}/2 cup caster (superfine) sugar
75g/3oz/^{3}/4 cup plain (all-purpose)
   flour, sifted
15ml/1 tbsp boiling water
90ml/6 tbsp peach jam
icing (confectioners') sugar,
   for dusting (optional)

Nutrition Notes

Per portion:
Energy	178Kcals/746kJ
Fat	2.45g
Saturated Fat	0.67g
Cholesterol	82.50mg
Fibre	0.33g

COOK'S TIP
To decorate the Swiss roll (jelly roll), put 115g/4oz glacé icing in a piping bag fitted with a small writing nozzle and pipe lines over the top.

2 Carefully fold in the flour with a large metal spoon, then add the boiling water in the same way.

5 Neatly trim the edges of the cake. Make a neat cut two-thirds of the way through the cake, about 1cm/^{1}/2in from the short edge nearest you.

3 Spoon into the prepared tin, spread evenly to the edges and bake for about 10–12 minutes until the cake springs back when lightly pressed.

6 Spread the cake with the peach jam and roll up quickly from the partially cut end. Hold in position for a minute, making sure the join is underneath. Cool on a wire rack. Decorate with glacé icing (see Cook's Tip) or dust with a little icing sugar before serving, if you like.

1 Preheat the oven to 200°C/400°F/ Gas 6. Grease and line a 30 x 20cm/ 12 x 8in Swiss roll tin (jelly roll pan). Combine the eggs and sugar in a bowl. Beat with a hand-held electric whisk until thick and mousse-like. (When the whisk is lifted, a trail should remain on the surface of the mixture for at least 15 seconds.)

4 Spread a sheet of greaseproof (waxed) paper on a flat surface, sprinkle it with caster sugar, then invert the cake on top. Peel off the lining paper.

LEMON CHIFFON CAKE

Lemon mousse provides a
tangy filling for this light-as-air
lemon sponge.

INGREDIENTS

Serves 8
2 eggs
75g/3oz/6 tbsp caster (superfine) sugar
grated rind of 1 lemon
50g/2oz/¹/² cup plain (all-purpose)
 flour, sifted
lemon shreds, to decorate

For the filling
2 eggs, separated
75g/3oz/6 tbsp caster (superfine) sugar
grated rind and juice of 1 lemon
30ml/2 tbsp water
15ml/1 tbsp gelatine
125ml/4fl oz/¹/² cup low-fat fromage
 frais or natural (plain) yogurt

For the icing
15ml/1 tbsp lemon juice
115g/4oz/scant 1 cup icing
 (confectioners') sugar, sifted

1 Preheat the oven to 180°C/350°F/
Gas 4. Grease and line a 20cm/8in
loose-bottomed cake tin (pan). Whisk
the eggs, sugar and lemon rind together
with a hand-held electric whisk until
thick and mousse-like. Gently fold in
the flour, then turn the mixture into the
prepared tin.

2 Bake for 20–25 minutes until the
cake springs back when lightly
pressed in the centre. Turn on to a wire
rack to cool. Once cold, split the cake
in half horizontally and return the
lower half to the clean cake tin.

3 Make the filling. Put the egg yolks,
sugar, lemon rind and juice in a
bowl. Beat with a hand-held electric
whisk until thick, pale and creamy.

4 Pour the water into a heatproof
bowl and sprinkle the gelatine on
top. Leave until spongy, then stir over
simmering water until dissolved. Cool,
then whisk into the yolk mixture. Fold
in the fromage frais or yogurt. When
the mixture begins to set, whisk the
egg whites to soft peaks. Fold the egg
whites into the mousse mixture.

5 Pour the lemon mousse over the
sponge in the cake tin, spreading it
to the edges. Set the second layer of
sponge on top and chill until set.

6 Slide a metal spatula dipped in hot
water between the tin and the cake
to loosen it, then carefully transfer the
cake to a serving plate. Make the icing
by adding enough lemon juice to the
icing sugar to make a mixture thick
enough to coat the back of a wooden
spoon. Pour over the cake and spread
evenly to the edges. Decorate with the
lemon shreds.

NUTRITION NOTES

Per portion:
Energy	202Kcals/849kJ
Fat	2.81g
Saturated Fat	0.79g
Cholesterol	96.41mg
Fibre	0.20g

COOK'S TIP
The mousse should be just setting
when the egg whites are added.
Speed up this process by placing
the bowl of mousse in iced water.

Banana and Gingerbread Slices

Very quick to make and deliciously moist due to the addition of bananas.

INGREDIENTS

Makes 20

275g/10oz/2 cups plain
  (all-purpose) flour
20ml/4 tsp ground ginger
10ml/2 tsp mixed (apple pie) spice
5ml/1 tsp bicarbonate of soda
  (baking soda)
115g/4oz/½ cup soft light brown sugar
60ml/4 tbsp sunflower oil
30ml/2 tbsp molasses or black treacle
30ml/2 tbsp malt extract
2 eggs
60ml/4 tbsp orange juice
3 bananas
115g/4oz/⅔ cup raisins

NUTRITION NOTES

Per portion:
Energy	148Kcals/621kJ
Fat	3.07g
Saturated Fat	0.53g
Cholesterol	19.30mg
Fibre	0.79g

VARIATION
To make Spiced Honey and Banana Cake: omit the ground ginger and add another 5ml/1 tsp mixed (apple pie) spice; omit the malt extract and the molasses or treacle and add 60ml/4 tbsp strong-flavoured clear honey instead; and replace the raisins with either sultanas (golden raisins), or coarsely chopped ready-to-eat dried apricots, or semi-dried pineapple. If you choose to use the pineapple, then you could also replace the orange juice with fresh pineapple juice.

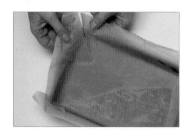

1 Preheat the oven to 180°C/350°F/ Gas 4. Lightly grease and line an 18 x 28cm/7 x 11in baking tin (pan).

2 Sift the flour into a bowl with the spices and bicarbonate of soda. Mix in the sugar with some of the flour and sift it all into the bowl.

3 Make a well in the centre, add the oil, molasses or black treacle, malt extract, eggs and orange juice and mix together thoroughly.

4 Mash the bananas, add them to the bowl with the raisins and mix well together.

5 Pour the mixture into the prepared tin and bake for about 35–40 minutes, until the centre springs back when lightly pressed.

6 Leave the cake in the tin to cool for 5 minutes, then turn out on to a wire rack and leave to cool completely. Cut into 20 slices.

COOK'S TIP
The flavour of this cake develops as it keeps, so if you can, store it for a few days before eating.

SCONES, MUFFINS, BUNS AND COOKIES

Many scones, muffins, buns and cookies are low in fat and make ideal snacks or treats at any time of day. Try serving them on their own or with a little low-fat spread, honey or jam. They are delicious served warm for breakfast or brunch, cold for afternoon tea or packed up and taken away, to enjoy at your leisure. We include a selection of tempting scones, muffins, buns and cookies, including Pineapple and Cinnamon Drop Scones, Date and Apple Muffins, Banana and Apricot Chelsea Buns and Oaty Crisps.

PINEAPPLE AND CINNAMON DROP SCONES

Making the batter with pineapple juice instead of milk cuts down on fat and adds to the taste.

INGREDIENTS

Makes 24

115g/4oz/1 cup self-raising wholemeal (self-rising whole-wheat) flour
115g/4oz/1 cup self-raising (self-rising) white flour
5ml/1 tsp ground cinnamon
15ml/1 tbsp caster (superfine) sugar
1 egg
300ml/½ pint/1¼ cups pineapple juice
75g/3oz/½ cup semi-dried pineapple, chopped

NUTRITION NOTES

Per portion:
Energy	15Kcals/215kJ
Fat	0.81g
Saturated Fat	0.14g
Cholesterol	8.02mg
Fibre	0.76g

1 Preheat a griddle, heavy frying pan or an electric frying pan. Put the wholemeal flour in a mixing bowl. Sift in the white flour, add the ground cinnamon and sugar and make a well in the centre.

> COOK'S TIPS
> Drop scones do not keep well and are best eaten freshly cooked. Other semi-dried fruit, such as apricots or pears, can be used in place of the pineapple.

2 Add the egg with half the pineapple juice and gradually incorporate the surrounding flour to make a smooth batter. Beat in the remaining juice with the chopped pineapple.

3 Lightly grease the griddle or pan. Drop tablespoons of the batter on to the surface, leaving them until they bubble and the bubbles begin to burst.

4 Turn the drop scones with a palette knife or metal spatula and cook until the underside is brown. Keep the cooked scones warm and moist by wrapping them in a clean napkin while continuing to cook successive batches.

DROP SCONES

These little scones are delicious spread with jam.

INGREDIENTS

Makes 18

225g/8oz/2 cups self-raising
   (self-rising) flour
2.5ml/½ tsp salt
15ml/1 tbsp caster (superfine) sugar
1 egg, beaten
300ml/½ pint/1¼ cups skimmed milk
oil, for frying

1 Preheat a griddle, heavy frying pan or an electric frying pan. Sift the flour and salt into a mixing bowl. Stir in the sugar and make a well in the centre.

2 Add the egg and half the milk, then gradually incorporate the surrounding flour to make a smooth batter. Beat in the remaining milk.

3 Lightly oil the griddle or pan. Drop tablespoons of the batter on to the surface, leaving them until they bubble and the bubbles begin to burst.

NUTRITION NOTES	
Per portion:	
Energy	64Kcals/270kJ
Fat	1.09g
Saturated Fat	0.2g
Cholesterol	11.03mg
Fibre	0.43g

4 Turn the scones over with a palette knife or metal spatula and cook until the underside is golden brown. Keep the cooked scones warm and moist by wrapping them in a clean napkin while cooking successive batches.

VARIATION
For savoury scones, add 2 chopped spring onions (scallions) and 15ml/ 1 tbsp freshly grated Parmesan cheese. Serve with cottage cheese.

CHIVE AND POTATO SCONES

These little scones should be fairly thin, soft and crisp on the outside. They're extremely quick to make, so serve them for breakfast or lunch.

INGREDIENTS

Makes 20
450g/1lb potatoes
115g/4oz/1 cup plain (all-purpose) flour, sifted
30ml/2 tbsp olive oil
30ml/2 tbsp snipped chives
salt and black pepper
low-fat spread, for topping (optional)

NUTRITION NOTES

Per portion:
Energy	50Kcals/211kJ
Fat	1.24g
Saturated Fat	0.17g
Cholesterol	0
Fibre	0.54g

1 Cook the potatoes in a pan of boiling salted water for 20 minutes, then drain thoroughly. Return the potatoes to the clean pan and mash them. Preheat a griddle or heavy frying pan over a low heat.

COOK'S TIP
Cook the scones over a low heat so that the outsides do not burn before the insides are cooked through.

2 Add the flour, olive oil and snipped chives with a little salt and pepper to the hot mashed potato in the pan. Mix to a soft dough.

3 Roll out the dough on a well-floured surface to a thickness of 5mm/¼in and stamp out rounds with a 5cm/2in plain pastry cutter.

4 Cook the scones, in batches, on the hot griddle or frying pan for about 10 minutes until they are golden brown on both sides. Keep the heat low. Top with a little low-fat spread, if you like, and serve immediately.

CHEESE AND CHIVE SCONES

INGREDIENTS

Makes 9

115g/4oz/1 cup self-raising (self-rising) white flour
150g/5oz/1 cup self-raising wholemeal (self-rising whole-wheat) flour
2.5ml/½ tsp salt
75g/3oz feta cheese
15ml/1 tbsp snipped fresh chives
150ml/¼ pint/⅔ cup skimmed milk, plus extra for glazing
1.25ml/¼ tsp cayenne pepper

1 Preheat the oven to 200°C/400°F/ Gas 6. Sift the flours and salt into a mixing bowl, adding any bran left over from the flour in the sieve (strainer).

2 Crumble the feta cheese and rub into the dry ingredients. Stir in the chives, then add the milk and mix to a soft dough.

NUTRITION NOTES

Per portion:

Energy	121Kcals/507kJ
Fat	2.24g
Saturated Fat	1.13g
Fibre	1.92g

3 Turn out on to a floured surface and knead lightly until smooth. Roll out to 2cm/¾in thick and stamp out nine scones with a 6cm/2½in pastry cutter.

4 Transfer the scones to a non-stick baking sheet. Brush with skimmed milk, then sprinkle over the cayenne pepper. Bake in the oven for about 15 minutes, or until golden brown.

HAM AND TOMATO SCONES

These scones make an ideal accompaniment for soup. Choose a strongly flavoured ham, trimmed of fat, and chop it finely, so that a little goes a long way. Use wholemeal (whole-wheat) flour or a mixture of wholemeal and white flour for extra flavour, texture and fibre.

INGREDIENTS

Makes 12

225g/8oz/2 cups self-raising
  (self-rising) flour
5ml/1 tsp dry mustard
5ml/1 tsp paprika, plus extra
  for sprinkling
2.5ml/½ tsp salt
25g/1oz/2 tbsp soft margarine
15ml/1 tbsp snipped fresh basil
50g/2oz/1 cup drained sun-dried
  tomatoes in oil, chopped
50g/2oz cooked ham, chopped
90–120ml/3–4fl oz/6 tbsp–½ cup
  skimmed milk, plus extra for brushing

1 Preheat the oven to 200°C/
400°F/Gas 6. Flour a large baking sheet. Sift the flour, mustard, paprika and salt into a bowl. Rub in the margarine until the mixture resembles breadcrumbs.

NUTRITION NOTES

Per portion:

Energy	113Kcals/474kJ
Fat	4.23g
Saturated Fat	0.65g
Cholesterol	2.98mg
Fibre	0.65g

2 Stir in the basil, sun-dried tomatoes and ham, and mix lightly. Pour in enough milk to mix to a soft dough.

3 Turn the dough out on to a lightly floured surface, knead briefly and roll out to a 20 x 15cm/8 x 6in rectangle. Cut into 5cm/2in squares and arrange on the baking sheet.

4 Brush lightly with milk, sprinkle with paprika and bake for about 12–15 minutes. Transfer to a wire rack to cool.

> **COOK'S TIP**
> To cut calories and fat, choose dry-packed sun-dried tomatoes and soak them in warm water.

DATE AND APPLE MUFFINS

You will only need one or two of these wholesome muffins per person, as they are substantial.

INGREDIENTS

Makes 12

*150g/5oz/1¼ cups self-raising wholemeal
 (self-rising whole-wheat) flour*
*150g/5oz/1¼ cups self-raising
 (self-rising) white flour*
5ml/1 tsp ground cinnamon
5ml/1 tsp baking powder
25g/1 oz/2 tbsp soft margarine
*75g/3oz/½ cup light muscovado
 (brown) sugar*
1 eating apple
250ml/8fl oz/1 cup apple juice
30ml/2 tbsp pear and apple spread
1 egg, lightly beaten
75g/3oz/½ cup chopped dates
15ml/1 tbsp chopped pecan nuts

1 Preheat the oven to 200°C/400°F/
Gas 6. Put 12 paper cake cases in a deep muffin tin (pan). Put the wholemeal flour in a mixing bowl. Sift in the white flour with the cinnamon and baking powder. Rub in the margarine until the mixture resembles breadcrumbs, then stir in the muscovado sugar.

2 Quarter and core the apple, chop the flesh finely and set aside. Stir a little of the apple juice with the pear and apple spread until smooth. Mix in the remaining juice, then add to the rubbed-in mixture with the egg. Add the chopped apple to the bowl with the dates. Mix quickly until just combined.

3 Divide the mixture among the muffin cases.

4 Sprinkle with the chopped pecan nuts. Bake the muffins for 20–25 minutes until golden brown and firm in the middle. Remove to a wire rack and serve while still warm.

NUTRITION NOTES

Per muffin:

Energy	163Kcals/686kJ
Fat	2.98g
Saturated Fat	0.47g
Cholesterol	16.04mg
Fibre	1.97g

VARIATIONS
Use a pear in place of the eating apple and chopped ready-to-eat dried apricots in place of the dates. Mixed (apple pie) spice is a good alternative to cinnamon.

RASPBERRY MUFFINS

These American muffins are made using baking powder and low-fat buttermilk, giving them a light and spongy texture. They are delicious to eat at any time of the day.

Ingredients

Makes 10–12
275g/10oz/2½ cups plain
   (all-purpose) flour
15ml/1 tbsp baking powder
115g/4oz/½ cup caster (superfine) sugar
1 egg
250ml/8fl oz/1 cup buttermilk
60ml/4 tbsp sunflower oil
150g/5oz raspberries

1 Preheat the oven to 200°C/400°F/ Gas 6. Arrange 12 paper cake cases in a deep muffin tin (pan). Sift the flour and baking powder into a mixing bowl, stir in the sugar, then make a well in the centre.

NUTRITION NOTES	
Per muffin:	
Energy	171Kcals/719kJ
Fat	4.55g
Saturated Fat	0.71g
Cholesterol	16.5mg
Fibre	1.02g

2 Mix the egg, buttermilk and oil together in a bowl, pour into the flour mixture and mix quickly.

3 Add the raspberries and lightly fold in with a metal spoon. Spoon the mixture into the paper cases.

4 Bake the muffins for 20–25 minutes until golden brown and firm in the middle. Transfer to a wire rack and serve warm or cold.

SPICED BANANA MUFFINS

These light and nutritious muffins include banana for added fibre, and make a tasty tea-time treat. If liked, slice off the tops and fill with jam.

INGREDIENTS

Makes 12

75g/3oz/²⁄₃ cup plain wholemeal
  (all-purpose whole-wheat) flour
50g/2oz/¹⁄₂ cup plain (all-purpose)
  white flour
10ml/2 tsp baking powder
pinch of salt
5ml/1 tsp mixed (apple pie) spice
40g/1¹⁄₂oz/¹⁄₄ cup soft light brown sugar
50g/2oz/¹⁄₄ cup polyunsaturated
  margarine
1 egg, beaten
150ml/¹⁄₄ pint/²⁄₃ cup semi-skimmed
  (low-fat) milk
grated rind of 1 orange
1 ripe banana
20g/³⁄₄oz/¹⁄₄ cup rolled oats
15ml/1 tbsp chopped hazelnuts

1 Preheat the oven to 200°C/400°F/ Gas 6. Line a muffin tin (pan) with 12 paper cases. Sift together both flours, the baking powder, salt and mixed spice into a bowl, then add any bran remaining in the sieve. Stir in the sugar.

NUTRITION NOTES

Per muffin:

Energy	110Kcals/465kJ
Fat	5g
Saturated Fat	1g
Cholesterol	17.5mg

2 Melt the margarine and pour it into a mixing bowl. Cool slightly, then beat in the egg, milk and grated orange rind.

3 Add the dry ingredients to the wet ones and gently fold in. Mash the banana with a fork, then stir it gently into the mixture, being careful not to overmix or the muffins will be tough.

4 Spoon the mixture into the paper cases. Combine the oats and hazelnuts and sprinkle a little of the mixture over each muffin.

5 Bake for 20 minutes until the muffins are well risen and golden, and a skewer inserted in the centre comes out clean. Transfer to a wire rack and serve warm or cold.

BANANA AND APRICOT CHELSEA BUNS

These buns are old favourites given a low-fat twist with a delectable fruit filling.

INGREDIENTS

Serves 9
90ml/6 tbsp warm skimmed milk
5ml/1 tsp active dried yeast
pinch of sugar
225g/8oz/2 cups strong white
  bread flour
10ml/2 tsp mixed (apple pie) spice
2.5ml/¹/₂ tsp salt
50g/2oz/¹/₄ cup caster (superfine) sugar
25g/1oz/2 tbsp soft margarine
1 egg

For the filling
1 large ripe banana
175g/6oz/1 cup ready-to-eat dried
  apricots
30ml/2 tbsp light muscovado
  (brown) sugar

For the glaze
30ml/2 tbsp caster (superfine) sugar
30ml/2 tbsp water

COOK'S TIP
Do not leave the buns in the tins (pans) for too long, or the glaze will stick to the sides, making them very difficult to remove.

NUTRITION NOTES

Per bun:

Energy	214Kcals/901kJ
Fat	3.18g
Saturated Fat	0.63g
Cholesterol	21.59mg
Fibre	2.18g

1 Lightly grease an 18cm/7in square tin (pan). Put the warm milk in a jug (pitcher) and sprinkle the yeast on top. Add a pinch of sugar to help activate the yeast, mix well and leave for 30 minutes.

2 Sift the flour, spice and salt into a mixing bowl. Stir in the caster sugar, rub in the margarine, then stir in the yeast mixture and the egg. Gradually mix in the flour to make a soft dough, adding extra milk if needed.

3 Turn out the dough on to a floured surface and knead for 5 minutes until smooth and elastic. Return the dough to the clean bowl, cover with a damp dish towel and leave in a warm place for about 2 hours, until doubled in bulk.

4 To prepare the filling, mash the banana in a bowl. Using scissors, snip the apricots into pieces, then stir into the banana with the sugar.

5 Knead the dough on a floured surface for 2 minutes, then roll out to a 30 x 23cm/12 x 9in rectangle. Spread the filling over the dough and roll up lengthways like a Swiss (jelly) roll, with the join underneath.

6 Cut the roll into nine buns. Place, cut side down, in the tin, cover and leave to rise for 30 minutes. Preheat the oven to 200°C/400°F/Gas 6 and bake for 20–25 minutes. Meanwhile, mix the caster sugar and water in a small pan. Heat, stirring, until dissolved, then boil for 2 minutes. Brush the glaze over the buns while still hot.

OATY CRISPS

These cookies are very crisp and crunchy – ideal to serve with morning coffee.

INGREDIENTS

Makes 18
175g/6oz/1¾ cups rolled oats
75g/3oz/½ cup light muscovado (brown) sugar
1 egg
60ml/4 tbsp sunflower oil
30ml/2 tbsp malt extract

NUTRITION NOTES

Per portion:
Energy	86Kcals/360kJ
Fat	3.59g
Saturated Fat	0.57g
Cholesterol	10.7mg
Fibre	0.66g

1 Preheat the oven to 190°C/375°F/ Gas 5. Lightly grease two baking sheets. Mix the rolled oats and sugar in a bowl, breaking up any lumps in the sugar. Add the egg, sunflower oil and malt extract, mix well, then leave to soak for 15 minutes.

2 Using a teaspoon, place small heaps of the mixture well apart on the prepared baking sheets. Press the heaps into 7.5cm/3in rounds with the back of a dampened fork.

3 Bake the cookies for 10–15 minutes until golden brown. Leave them to cool for 1 minute, then remove to a wire rack to cool.

COOK'S TIPS
To give these cookies a coarser texture, substitute jumbo oats for some or all of the rolled oats. Once cool, store the cookies in an airtight container to keep them as crisp and fresh as possible.

OATCAKES

Try serving these oatcakes with reduced-fat hard cheeses. They are delicious topped with thick honey for breakfast.

INGREDIENTS

Makes 8

175g/6oz/1 cup medium oatmeal,
  plus extra for sprinkling
2.5ml/½ tsp salt
a pinch of bicarbonate of soda
  (baking soda)
15g/½oz/1 tbsp butter
75ml/5 tbsp water

1 Preheat the oven to 150°C/300°F/ Gas 2. Mix the oatmeal with the salt and bicarbonate of soda in a bowl.

2 Melt the butter with the water in a pan. Bring to the boil, then add to the oatmeal mixture and mix to a dough.

3 Turn the dough on to a surface sprinkled with oatmeal and knead to a smooth ball. Turn a large baking sheet upside-down, grease it, sprinkle it lightly with oatmeal and place the ball of dough on top. Sprinkle the dough with oatmeal, then roll out to a 25cm/10in round.

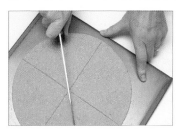

4 Cut the round into eight sections, ease them apart slightly and bake for about 50–60 minutes until crisp. Leave to cool on the baking sheet, then remove the oatcakes with a metal spatula.

COOK'S TIP
To achieve a neat round, place a 25cm/10in cake board or plate on top of the oatcake. Cut away any excess dough with a knife.

NUTRITION NOTES

Per portion:

Energy	102Kcals/427kJ
Fat	3.43g
Saturated Fat	0.66g
Cholesterol	0.13mg
Fibre	1.49g

BREADS AND TEABREADS

Breads and teabreads can be ideal low-fat snacks at any time of day. Bread is the perfect accompaniment to many meals, and moist, flavourful teabread, served with a warm beverage, is a delightful treat. Among the appetizing selection of recipes presented here are Rosemary and Sea Salt Focaccia, Prosciutto and Parmesan Bread, Pear and Sultana Teabread and Banana and Cardamom Bread.

ROSEMARY AND SEA SALT FOCACCIA

Focaccia is an Italian flat bread
made with olive oil. Here it is
given added flavour with
rosemary and coarse sea salt.

INGREDIENTS

Serves 8
350g/12oz/3 cups plain
(all-purpose) flour
2.5ml/¹/₂ tsp salt
10ml/2 tsp easy-blend (rapid-rise)
dried yeast
250ml/8fl oz/1 cup lukewarm water
45ml/3 tbsp olive oil
1 small red onion
leaves from 1 large rosemary sprig
5ml/1 tsp coarse sea salt
oil, for greasing

1 Sift the flour and salt into a large
mixing bowl. Stir in the yeast, then
make a well in the middle of the dry
ingredients. Pour in the water and
30ml/2 tbsp of the oil. Mix well,
adding a little more water if the
mixture seems too dry.

VARIATIONS
Use flavoured olive oil, such as
chilli or herb oil, for extra flavour.
Wholemeal (whole-wheat) flour or
a mixture of wholemeal and white
flour works well with this recipe.

2 Turn the dough on to a lightly
floured surface and knead for about
10 minutes until smooth and elastic.

3 Place the dough in a greased bowl,
cover and leave in a warm place
for about 1 hour until doubled in size.
Knock back and knead the dough for
2–3 minutes.

4 Meanwhile, preheat the oven to
220°C/425°F/Gas 7. Roll out the
dough to a large circle about 1cm/¹/₂in
thick, and transfer to a greased baking
sheet. Brush with the remaining oil.

5 Halve the onion and slice it into
thin wedges. Sprinkle over the
dough, with the rosemary and sea salt,
pressing lightly.

6 Using a finger, make indentations in
the dough. Cover the surface with
greased clear film (plastic wrap), then
leave to rise in a warm place for
30 minutes. Remove the clear film and
bake for 25–30 minutes until golden.

NUTRITION NOTES

Per portion:

Energy	191Kcals/807kJ
Fat	4.72g
Saturated Fat	0.68g
Cholesterol	0
Fibre	1.46g

OLIVE AND OREGANO BREAD

This bread is an excellent accompaniment to all salads and is especially good served warm.

INGREDIENTS

Serves 8–10
300ml/10fl oz/1¼ cups warm water
5ml/1 tsp active dried yeast
pinch of sugar
15ml/1 tbsp olive oil
1 onion, chopped
450g/1lb/4 cups strong white bread flour
5ml/1 tsp salt
1.5ml/¼ tsp black pepper
50g/2oz/⅓ cup pitted black olives,
    roughly chopped
15ml/1 tbsp black olive paste
15ml/1 tbsp chopped fresh oregano
15ml/1 tbsp chopped fresh parsley

NUTRITION NOTES

Per portion:
Energy	202Kcals/847kJ
Fat	3.28g
Saturated Fat	0.46g
Cholesterol	0
Fibre	22.13g

1 Put half the warm water in a jug (pitcher). Sprinkle the yeast on top. Add the sugar, mix well and leave to stand for 10 minutes.

2 Heat the olive oil in a small frying pan and fry the onion gently until golden brown.

3 Sift the flour into a mixing bowl with the salt and pepper. Make a well in the centre. Add the yeast mixture, the fried onion (with the oil), the olives, olive paste, herbs and remaining water. Gradually incorporate the flour and mix to a soft dough, adding a little extra water if necessary.

4 Turn the dough on to a floured surface and knead for 5 minutes until smooth and elastic. Place in a mixing bowl, cover with a damp dish towel and leave in a warm place to rise for about 2 hours until the dough has doubled in bulk. Lightly grease a baking sheet.

5 Turn the dough on to a floured surface and knead again for a few minutes. Shape into a 20cm/8in round and place on the prepared baking sheet. Using a large sharp knife, make criss-cross cuts over the top. Cover and leave in a warm place for 30 minutes until well risen. Preheat the oven to 220°C/425°F/Gas 7.

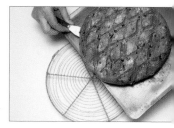

6 Dust the loaf with a little flour. Bake for 10 minutes, then lower the oven temperature to 200°C/400°F/ Gas 6. Bake for 20 minutes more, or until the loaf sounds hollow when tapped underneath. Transfer to a wire rack and allow to cool slightly before serving.

VARIATIONS

If fresh herbs are not available, use 5–10 ml/1–2 tsp dried herbs instead. Omit the olives and olive paste and use chopped sun-dried tomatoes and sun-dried tomato paste, for a tasty change.

RYE BREAD

Rye bread is popular in northern Europe and makes an excellent base for open sandwiches – add a low-fat topping of your choice.

INGREDIENTS

Serves 16

350g/12oz/3 cups wholemeal (whole-wheat) flour
225g/8oz/2 cups rye flour
115g/4oz/1 cup strong white bread flour
7.5ml/1½ tsp salt
30ml/2 tbsp caraway seeds
475ml/16fl oz/2 cups warm water
10ml/2 tsp active dried yeast
pinch of sugar
30ml/2 tbsp black treacle (molasses)

1 Put the flours and salt in a bowl. Set aside 5ml/1 tsp of the caraway seeds and add the rest to the bowl.

2 Put half the water in a jug (pitcher). Sprinkle the yeast on top. Add the sugar, mix and leave for 10 minutes.

3 Make a well in the flour mixture, then add the yeast mixture with the treacle and the remaining water. Gradually incorporate the flour and mix to a soft dough, adding a little water if necessary.

4 Turn the dough on to a floured surface and knead for 5 minutes until smooth and elastic. Return to the clean bowl, cover with a damp dish towel and leave in a warm place for about 2 hours until doubled in bulk. Grease a baking sheet.

5 Turn the dough on to a floured surface and knead for 2 minutes. Divide the dough in half, then shape into two 23cm/9in long oval loaves. Flatten the loaves slightly and place them on a baking sheet.

6 Brush the loaves with water and sprinkle with the remaining caraway seeds. Cover and leave in a warm place for about 40 minutes until well risen.

7 Preheat the oven to 200°C/400°F/ Gas 6. Bake the loaves for 30 minutes or until they sound hollow when tapped underneath. Cool on a wire rack. Serve the bread plain, or slice and add a low-fat topping.

NUTRITION NOTES

Per portion:

Energy	156Kcals/655kJ
Fat	1.2g
Saturated Fat	0.05g
Cholesterol	0
Fibre	4.53g

SODA BREAD

Finding the bread bin empty need never be a problem again when your repertoire includes a recipe for soda bread. It takes only a few minutes to make and needs no rising or proving. If possible, eat soda bread while still warm from the oven as it does not keep well.

INGREDIENTS

Serves 8

450g/1lb/4 cups plain (all-purpose) flour
5ml/1 tsp salt
5ml/1 tsp bicarbonate of soda (baking soda)
5ml/1 tsp cream of tartar
350ml/12fl oz/1½ cups buttermilk

1 Preheat the oven to 220°C/425°F/ Gas 7. Flour a baking sheet. Sift all the dry ingredients into a mixing bowl and make a small well in the centre.

2 Add the buttermilk and mix quickly to a soft dough. Turn on to a floured surface and knead lightly. Shape into a round about 18cm/7in across and put on the baking sheet.

3 Cut a deep cross on top of the loaf and sprinkle with a little flour. Bake for 25–30 minutes, then transfer the soda bread to a wire rack to cool.

COOK'S TIP
Soda bread needs a light hand. The ingredients should be bound together quickly in the bowl and kneaded very briefly. The aim is to get rid of the largest cracks, as the dough will become tough if it is handled for too long.

NUTRITION NOTES	
Per portion:	
Energy	230Kcals/967kJ
Fat	1.03g
Saturated Fat	0.24g
Cholesterol	0.88mg
Fibre	1.94g

PEAR AND SULTANA TEABREAD

This is an ideal teabread to make when pears are plentiful – an excellent use for windfalls.

INGREDIENTS

Serves 6–8

25g/1oz/¼ cup rolled oats
50g/2oz/¼ cup light muscovado
  (brown) sugar
30ml/2 tbsp pear or apple juice
30ml/2 tbsp sunflower oil
1 large or 2 small pears
115g/4oz/1 cup self-raising
  (self-rising) flour
115g/4oz/¾ cup sultanas (golden raisins)
2.5ml/½ tsp baking powder
10ml/2 tsp mixed (apple pie) spice
1 egg

1 Preheat the oven to 180°C/350°F/ Gas 4. Grease and line a 450g/1lb loaf tin (pan). Mix the oats and sugar, then mix in the pear or apple juice and oil, and leave to stand for 15 minutes.

2 Quarter, core and coarsely grate the pear(s). Add to the oat mixture with the flour, sultanas, baking powder, mixed spice and egg, then mix together thoroughly to combine.

3 Spoon the mixture into the prepared loaf tin and level the top. Bake in the preheated oven for 50–60 minutes or until a skewer inserted into the centre comes out clean.

COOK'S TIP
Health food stores sell concentrated pear and apple juice, ready for diluting as required.

4 Transfer the teabread on to a wire rack and peel off the lining paper. Leave to cool completely.

NUTRITION NOTES

Per portion:

Energy	200Kcals/814kJ
Fat	4.61g
Saturated Fat	0.79g
Cholesterol	27.50mg
Fibre	1.39g

PROSCIUTTO AND PARMESAN BREAD

This nourishing bread is almost a meal in itself.

INGREDIENTS

Serves 8

225g/8oz/2 cups self-raising wholemeal (self-rising whole-wheat) flour
225g/8oz/2 cups self-raising (self-rising) white flour
5ml/1 tsp baking powder
5ml/1 tsp salt
5ml/1 tsp black pepper
75g/3oz prosciutto
25g/1oz/2 tbsp grated Parmesan cheese
30ml/2 tbsp chopped fresh parsley
45ml/3 tbsp Meaux mustard
350ml/12fl oz/1½ cups buttermilk
skimmed milk, to glaze

NUTRITION NOTES

Per portion:

Energy	250Kcals/1053kJ
Fat	3.65g
Saturated Fat	1.30g
Cholesterol	7.09mg
Fibre	3.81g

1 Preheat the oven to 200°C/400°F/ Gas 6. Flour a baking sheet. Place the wholemeal flour in a bowl and sift in the white flour, baking powder and salt. Add the pepper and the prosciutto. Set aside about 15ml/1 tbsp of the Parmesan and stir the rest into the flour mixture with the parsley. Make a well in the centre.

2 Mix the mustard and buttermilk, pour into the flour and quickly mix to a soft dough.

3 Turn the dough on to a floured surface and knead briefly. Shape into an oval loaf, brush with milk and sprinkle with the Parmesan cheese. Put the loaf on the prepared baking sheet.

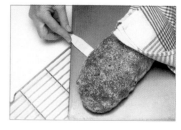

4 Bake the loaf for 25–30 minutes. Allow to cool before serving.

CARAWAY BREAD STICKS

Ideal to nibble with drinks, these can be made with all sorts of other seeds – try cumin seeds, poppy seeds or celery seeds.

INGREDIENTS

Makes about 20
150ml/¹/4 pint/²/3 cup warm water
2.5ml/¹/2 tsp active dried yeast
pinch of sugar
225g/8oz/2 cups plain (all-purpose) flour
2.5ml/¹/2 tsp salt
10ml/2 tsp caraway seeds

1 Grease two baking sheets. Put the warm water in a jug (pitcher). Sprinkle the yeast on top. Add the sugar, mix and leave for 10 minutes.

2 Sift the flour and salt into a mixing bowl, stir in the caraway seeds and make a well in the centre. Add the yeast mixture and gradually incorporate the flour to make a soft dough, adding a little water if necessary.

3 Preheat the oven to 200°C/425°F/ Gas 7. Turn the dough on to a lightly floured surface and knead for 5 minutes until smooth. Divide the mixture into 20 pieces and roll each into a 30cm/12in stick.

4 Arrange the sticks on the baking sheets, leaving room to allow for rising.

5 Bake the bread sticks for about 10–12 minutes until golden brown. Cool on the baking sheets.

NUTRITION NOTES	
Per portion:	
Energy	45Kcals/189kJ
Fat	0.24g
Saturated Fat	0.02g
Cholesterol	0
Fibre	0.3g

CHEESE AND ONION HERB STICKS

An extremely tasty bread which is very good with soups or salads. Use an extra-strong cheese to give plenty of flavour without piling on the fat.

INGREDIENTS

Makes 2 sticks, each serving 4–6
300ml/½ pint/1¼ cups warm water
5ml/1 tsp active dried yeast
pinch of sugar
15ml/1 tbsp sunflower oil
1 red onion, finely chopped
450g/1lb/4 cups strong white bread flour
5ml/1 tsp salt
5ml/1 tsp dry mustard
45ml/3 tbsp chopped fresh herbs, such as thyme, parsley, marjoram or sage
75g/3oz/¾ cup grated reduced-fat Cheddar cheese

NUTRITION NOTES

Per portion:
Energy	210Kcals/882kJ
Fat	3.16g
Saturated Fat	0.25g
Cholesterol	3.22mg
Fibre	1.79g

VARIATION
To make Onion and Coriander Sticks, omit the cheese, herbs and mustard. Add 15ml/1 tbsp ground coriander and 45ml/3 tbsp finely chopped fresh coriander (cilantro).

1 Put the water in a jug (pitcher). Sprinkle the yeast on top. Add the sugar, mix and leave for 10 minutes.

2 Heat the oil in a small frying pan and fry the onion until it is well coloured.

3 Stir the flour, salt and mustard into a mixing bowl, then add the herbs. Set aside 30ml/2 tbsp of the cheese. Stir the rest into the flour mixture and make a well in the centre. Add the yeast mixture with the fried onions and oil, then gradually incorporate the flour and mix to a soft dough, adding extra water if necessary.

4 Turn the dough on to a floured surface and knead for 5 minutes until smooth and elastic. Return to the clean bowl, cover with a damp dish towel and leave in a warm place to rise for about 2 hours until doubled in bulk. Lightly grease two baking sheets.

5 Turn the dough on to a floured surface, knead briefly, then divide the mixture in half and roll each piece into a 30cm/12in long stick. Place each stick on a baking sheet and make diagonal cuts along the top.

6 Sprinkle with the reserved cheese. Cover and leave for 30 minutes until well risen. Preheat the oven to 220°C/425°F/Gas 7. Bake the sticks for 25 minutes or until they sound hollow when tapped underneath.

Granary Baps

These make excellent picnic fare, filled with cottage cheese, tuna, salad and low-fat mayonnaise. They are also very good served warm with soup.

Ingredients

Makes 8
300ml/¹/₂ pint/1¹/₄ cups warm water
5ml/1 tsp active dried yeast
pinch of sugar
450g/1lb/4 cups malted brown
  bread flour
5ml/1 tsp salt
15ml/1 tbsp malt extract
15ml/1 tbsp rolled oats

Nutrition Notes

Per portion:

Energy	223Kcals/939kJ
Fat	1.14g
Saturated Fat	0.16g
Cholesterol	0
Fibre	3.10g

Cook's Tip
To make a large loaf, shape the dough into a round, flatten slightly and bake for 30–40 minutes. Test by tapping the base of the loaf – if it sounds hollow, it is cooked.

1 Put half the warm water in a jug (pitcher). Sprinkle in the yeast. Add the sugar, mix and leave for 10 minutes.

2 Put the malted brown flour and salt in a mixing bowl and make a well in the centre. Add the yeast mixture with the malt extract and the remaining water. Gradually incorporate the flour and mix to a soft dough.

3 Turn the dough on to a floured surface and knead for 5 minutes until smooth and elastic. Return to the clean bowl, cover with a damp dish towel and leave in a warm place to rise for about 2 hours until doubled in bulk.

4 Lightly grease a large baking sheet. Turn the dough on to a floured surface, knead for 2 minutes, then divide into eight pieces. Shape the pieces into balls and flatten them with the palm of your hand to make neat 10cm/4in rounds.

5 Place the rounds on the prepared baking sheet, cover loosely with a large plastic bag (ballooning it to trap the air inside), and leave to stand in a warm place until the baps are well risen. Preheat the oven to 220°C/425°F/Gas 7.

6 Brush the baps with water, sprinkle with the oats and bake for about 20–25 minutes or until they sound hollow when tapped underneath. Cool on a wire rack, then serve with the low-fat filling of your choice.

Poppy Seed Rolls

Pile these soft rolls in a basket
and serve them for breakfast or
with dinner.

Ingredients

Makes 12
*300ml/¹/₂ pint/1¹/₄ cups warm
    skimmed milk*
5ml/1 tsp active dried yeast
pinch of sugar
450g/1lb/4 cups strong white bread flour
5ml/1 tsp salt
1 egg, lightly beaten

For the topping
1 egg, beaten
poppy seeds

Nutrition Notes

Per portion:

Energy	160Kcals/674kJ
Fat	2.42g
Saturated Fat	0.46g
Cholesterol	32.58mg
Fibre	1.16g

2 Sift the flour and salt into a mixing
bowl. Make a well in the centre and
pour in the yeast mixture and the egg.
Gradually incorporate the flour, adding
enough of the remaining milk to mix to
a soft dough.

3 Turn the dough on to a floured
surface and knead for 5 minutes
until smooth and elastic. Return to the
clean bowl, cover with a damp dish
towel and leave in a warm place to rise
for about 1 hour until doubled in bulk.

4 Lightly grease two baking sheets.
Turn the dough on to a floured
surface. Knead for 2 minutes, then cut
into 12 pieces and shape into rolls.

5 Place the rolls on the prepared
baking sheets, cover loosely with a
large plastic bag (ballooning it to trap
the air inside) and leave to stand in a
warm place until the rolls have risen
well. Preheat the oven to 220°C/425°F/
Gas 7.

6 Glaze the rolls with beaten egg,
sprinkle with poppy seeds and bake
for 12–15 minutes until golden brown.
Transfer to a wire rack to cool.

Variations
Use easy-blend (rapid-rise) dried
yeast if you prefer. Add it directly
to the dry ingredients and mix
with hand-hot milk. The rolls will
only require one rising (see packet
instructions). Vary the toppings.
Linseed, sesame seeds and caraway seeds are all good; try
adding caraway seeds to the
dough, too, for extra flavour.

1 Put half the warm milk in a small
bowl. Sprinkle the yeast on top.
Add the sugar, mix well and leave for
30 minutes.

BANANA AND CARDAMOM BREAD

The combination of banana and cardamom is delicious in this soft-textured moist loaf. It is perfect for tea time, served with low-fat spread and jam. No fat is used or needed to make this delicious loaf, creating a healthy low-fat bread for all to enjoy.

INGREDIENTS

Serves 6

150ml/¼ pint/⅔ cup warm water
5ml/1 tsp active dried yeast
pinch of sugar
10 cardamom pods
400g/14oz/3½ cups strong white
   bread flour
5ml/1 tsp salt
30ml/2 tbsp malt extract
2 ripe bananas, mashed
5ml/1 tsp sesame seeds

1 Put the warm water in a bowl. Sprinkle the yeast on top. Add the sugar, mix and leave for 10 minutes.

2 Split the cardamom pods. Remove the seeds and chop them finely.

3 Sift the flour and salt into a mixing bowl and make a well in the centre. Add the yeast mixture with the malt extract, chopped cardamom seeds and bananas.

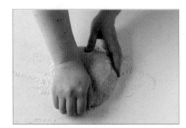

4 Gradually incorporate the flour and mix to a soft dough, adding a little extra water if necessary. Turn the dough on to a floured surface and knead for about 5 minutes until smooth and elastic. Return to the clean bowl, cover with a damp dish towel and leave to rise for about 2 hours until doubled in bulk.

NUTRITION NOTES

Per portion:
Energy	299Kcals/1254kJ
Fat	1.55g
Saturated Fat	0.23g
Cholesterol	0
Fibre	2.65g

5 Grease a baking sheet. Turn the dough on to a floured surface, knead briefly, then divide into three and shape into a plait (braid). Place the plait on the baking sheet and cover loosely with a plastic bag (ballooning it to trap the air). Leave until well risen. Preheat the oven to 220°C/425°F/Gas 7.

6 Brush the plait lightly with water and sprinkle with the sesame seeds. Bake for 10 minutes, then lower the oven temperature to 200°C/400°F/ Gas 6. Cook for 15 minutes more, or until the loaf sounds hollow when it is tapped underneath. Cool on a wire rack.

COOK'S TIPS
Make sure the bananas are really ripe, so that they impart maximum flavour to the bread. As well as being low in fat, bananas are a good source of potassium, therefore making an ideal nutritious, low-fat snack. If you prefer, place the dough in one piece in a 450g/1lb loaf tin (pan) and bake for an extra 5 minutes.

SWEDISH SULTANA BREAD

A lightly sweetened fruit bread that is delicious served warm. It is also excellent toasted and topped with low-fat spread.

INGREDIENTS

Serves 8–10

150ml/¼ pint/⅔ cup warm water
5ml/1 tsp active dried yeast
15ml/1 tbsp clear honey
225g/8oz/2 cups wholemeal (whole-wheat) flour
225g/8oz/2 cups strong white bread flour
5ml/1 tsp salt
115g/4oz/⅔ cup sultanas (golden raisins)
50g/2oz/½ cup walnuts, finely chopped
175ml/6fl oz/¾ cup warm skimmed milk, plus extra for glazing

NUTRITION NOTES

Per portion:

Energy	273Kcals/1145kJ
Fat	4.86g
Saturated Fat	0.57g
Cholesterol	0.39mg
Fibre	3.83g

1 Put the water in a small jug (pitcher). Sprinkle the yeast on top. Add a few drops of the honey to help activate the yeast, mix well and leave to stand for 10 minutes.

2 Put the flours in a mixing bowl with the salt and sultanas. Set aside 15ml/1 tbsp of the walnuts and add the rest to the bowl. Mix together lightly and make a well in the centre.

3 Add the yeast mixture to the flour mixture with the milk and remaining honey. Gradually incorporate the flour, mixing to a soft dough; add a little extra water if you need to.

4 Turn the dough on to a floured surface and knead for 5 minutes until smooth and elastic. Return to the clean bowl, cover with a damp dish towel and leave in a warm place to rise for about 2 hours until doubled in bulk. Grease a baking sheet.

5 Turn the dough on to a floured surface and form into a 28cm/11in long sausage shape. Place on the baking sheet. Make some diagonal cuts down the whole length of the loaf.

6 Brush the loaf with milk to glaze, sprinkle with the reserved walnuts and leave to rise for about 40 minutes.

7 Preheat the oven to 220°C/425°F/ Gas 7. Bake the loaf for 10 minutes. Lower the oven temperature to 200°C/ 400°F/Gas 6 and bake for about 20 minutes more, or until the loaf sounds hollow when tapped underneath.

VARIATION

To make Apple and Hazelnut Bread, replace the sultanas with two chopped eating apples and use chopped toasted hazelnuts instead of the walnuts. Add 5ml/1 tsp ground cinnamon with the flour.

Index

NOTES

NOTES

NOTES

NOTES

NOTES

NOTES

NOTES

NOTES

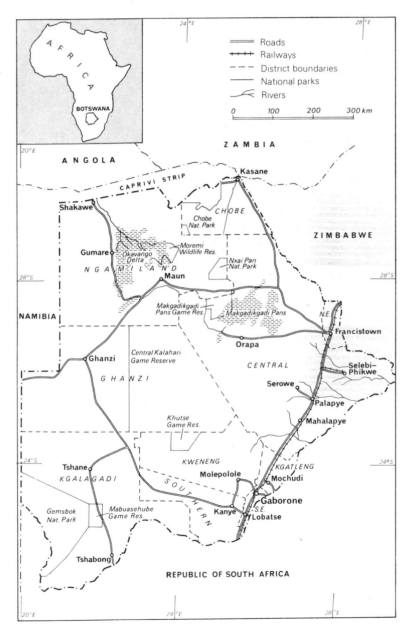

Frontispiece   *Republic of Botswana*

Contents

List of Tables

List of Figures

List of Appendixes

Introduction

There has been very little published on the economy of Botswana, no doubt partly because of the country's very small population, and partly because the country only became politically independent quite recently. What little published work there is tends to be in the form of official reports, not always easily available to the general public. There is no financial press in Botswana and no local academic journal devoted to economics.

A book such as this, therefore, should satisfy an important need. Clearly many people in Botswana – planners, students, businessmen, government officials and many others – have much to gain from the publication of informed analysis of Botswana's economic problems and achievements. Many people outside the country should also find here something of interest, both those who have a direct interest in the country and those who are generally interested in economic development and feel they can learn from particular cases.

Botswana's economic development, and the economic decisions it faces in the future, contain much that should perhaps be of wider interest: the country's extraordinarily rapid economic growth, the costs of being landlocked and dependent on difficult neighbours, the constraints imposed by soil and climate, and much else. There is much to learn, from both the successes and mistakes, fortunes and misfortunes, of the country.

The book also takes advantage of some of the transient expertise in Botswana. Shortage of skilled manpower, common to many developing countries but a particularly chronic problem in Botswana, has forced the country to rely heavily on expatriates to fill many key positions. One of the great disadvantages of this situation is that although many people learn a great deal about the country while working here, much of this knowledge leaves with them when they go. Some of their accumulated experience may remain among the files – but few have access to those files, and even fewer read them. This book tries to make some of the experience more widely available, in the pleasant tradition of open debate about difficult issues which Botswana is happy to cultivate.

It gives me great pleasure, then, to introduce this book. It will, I believe, be extremely useful. I would also like to thank the United States Agency for International Development for providing a subsidy to enable the book to be published more cheaply, and so to be available to a wider audience, than would otherwise have been possible.

the Rt. Hon. Quett Masire,
President of the Republic of Botswana.

Disclaimer

All of the contributors to this book have written in their personal capacities: the views expressed are their own and do not necessarily reflect the views of the institutions for which they have worked in the past, or for which they are now working.

The people of Botswana are called Batswana in the plural; one person is called a Motswana. The language is Setswana.

1 Economic and Social Development in Botswana 1966–78[1]

HANS-ERIK DAHL

Background

On 30 September 1966, Bechuanaland Protectorate became an independent republic – Botswana – after having been under British sovereignty since 1885. The nation's three main resources were:

1　a large but arid landlocked table land, approximately 1000m (3280 ft) above sea level, the size of Kenya or France;
2　a small (526 000 *de facto*), relatively young population (about 44 per cent below the age of 15) with only 74 000 attending any type of school; and
3　a large national herd of cattle (916 000).

Independence came at the end of a most severe drought cycle, which had lasted for more than five years. In Botswana's *Transitional Plan of Social and Economic Development* (p. 5), dated 30 September 1966 – the country's Independence Day – the situation was described as follows:

> Botswana is now experiencing the most calamitous drought in living memory. Its end is not in sight. No one yet knows how many cattle have died, but it is reliably estimated that the national herd has been reduced by over one-third and that the losses in some areas have exceeded 50 per cent. More particularly, a whole year's crop of calves has been lost, and it is calculated that it will need some five years for full recovery to take place. It is possible that the rains will fail again in 1966–67, but even if the cycle of drought years has ended, another cycle will start within a few years. The present drought has brought with it famine, making one-fifth of the population dependent on international famine relief assistance. Furthermore, in numerous areas the vegetation has been entirely grazed away; permanent destruction to the veld due to soil erosion is occurring in many places. The immediate financial implications of the drought are considerable. Heavy expenditure totalling over R2 million – or some 20 per cent of the total recurrent budget and over 40 per cent of the internally generated Government revenue – is being spent on drought and famine relief and rehabilitation measures.

In hard statistical terms, the national herd had declined by about 244 000 during the 1965–6 season alone, and by about 400 000 in all, through deaths from starvation and thirst, and consequently also from necessary slaughtering of the nation's most important capital asset.

The social and economic outlook was discouraging. To generate domestic resources for development was unthinkable – even the most modest recurrent central government budget would have to be substantially supplemented by the UK, the former Protector – perhaps for as long as 10–12 years. Few Independence ceremonies can have taken place under dustier, bleaker economic circumstances. But also, it must be added, *expectations* were consequently not excessive. Thus the combination of more abundant resources available for development than originally envisaged and an extremely cautious government spending behaviour may explain some of the development success in later years.

The new government was nevertheless determined to build an independent, financially viable and peaceful multiracial society in the very heart of Southern Africa.

In the following paragraphs and tables we shall point out a few of the changes that have taken place – some man-made, some through the discovery of the country's hidden mineral wealth, and some through most favourable co-operation from nature itself.

It is convenient to start the survey by giving the main geographical, meteorological, demographic and national cattle herd characteristics, and then to move on to the institutional and economic development which has taken place during the last twelve years.

Physical features of special relevance to the economy

Botswana is situated at the centre of the Southern African Plateau and is completely landlocked. The area is about 582 000 sq km (231 660 sq mi) with a *de jure* population of about 576 000 at independence in 1966.[2] The density of population is very low, about $\frac{1}{20}$ of Kenya's for example, whose territory is of about the same size.

Rainfall is erratic, unevenly distributed and extremely low. The high mean temperature leads to substantial evapo-transpiration. The soils are poor. Botswana consequently is marginal and large areas are even sub-marginal where agricultural activities are concerned. Hence the population carrying capacity of the land is much smaller than Kenya's.

Grasslands, though poor, are abundant. Perennial surface water is, however, not available in most areas. Consequently the Batswana have adopted a semi-sedentary economic way of life based on extensive cattle ranching.[3] This was the basis of the economy in 1966; and still is, in 1979, the most important economic activity, when one takes into account the relatively wide distribution of cattle ownership and of earnings from livestock ranching.

Finally, it should be noted that mining with its ups and downs is an old industry in the area: twelfth–thirteenth-century iron and copper mines and sixteenth–seventeenth-century workings of gold bearing ore have been identified. A gold rush took place at Francistown in the second half of the last century. Modern mining operations lasting right into the 1960s have included asbestos and manganese, while alluvial diamonds were known in the north-east.

From a geological point of view, Botswana at the time of independence had definitely proved its mining potential but was almost virgin from a systematic geological surveying point of view.

Population

Botswana's population is small compared to the size of the country; its *de jure* population density being only 1 per sq km (0.38 sq mi) in 1966. The relative smallness of its population may be explained in economic terms. Likewise the unprecedentedly high population *growth rate* of more than 3 per cent, calculated in about 1971, may be an indicator of rapidly increasing basic welfare. The population consequently is young – with about 53 per cent of the *de jure* population below the age of twenty.

Table 1.1   De jure *population of Botswana 1964, 1971 and 1978*

1964	550 000
1971	636 000
1978	766 000

Sources
Report of the Census of the Bechuanaland Protectorate 1964, Bechuanaland Government 1965; *Report on the Population Census 1971*, CSO 1972; 1978 figure CSO estimate.

Not only is the Botswana population growing fast and faster probably than ever before, but there is a noticeable tendency towards increasing concentration of the population in townships,[4] some of which are of recent origin due to new economic developments. About half the 1964–78 population increase has been drawn into these townships.

Table 1.2   De jure *population living in townships 1964, 1971 and 1978 (percentage)*

1964	2·2
1971	7·6
1978	15·4

Sources
As for Table 1.1.

A further population characteristic, partly explained by economic factors, should be noted: there is a longstanding Botswana tradition of migrating temporarily to South Africa in order to obtain cash incomes, mainly to work in the Transvaal mines. This tradition has been upheld at the same level as before right through to about 1975. Due to the recent recession in the South African economy, to higher wages for African miners and perhaps also to internal South African political considerations, the labour intake from Botswana has fallen off in later years. It is too early yet to know whether this is a new tendency.

Table 1.3   *Absentees 1964, 1971 and 1976*

1964	35 132
1971	45 735
1976	46 000

Sources
As for Table 1.1.

The absentees constituted 7·2 per cent of the *de jure* population during 1971, a figure which might meaningfully be compared to unemployment levels in other countries. The absentee labour system, however, not only helps towards solving a substantial labour surplus problem;[5] it is also a way of draining the economy of its most able young men. About 35 per cent of men in the 20–34 age bracket were thus absent according to the 1971 Population Census. The *de facto* population age–sex pyramid has the truncated look of a nation just emerging from a major war – with sex ratios as low as 37·7 men per 100 women in the 25–29 age bracket.[6]

There must be substantial opportunity costs involved in maintaining this labour drain, in the form of lower agricultural production. There must also be negative habit formation effects towards agricultural work among young miners, after being away from rural Botswana and their families for about one year at a time. The standard TEBA (The Employment Bureau of Africa – formerly known as NRC/MLO/WENELA, etc.) contracts are for nine months but state a specific number of shifts to be completed during the life of the contract. The effective contract period is about eleven months. A large proportion of the labour recruited from Botswana would normally be so-called 'novices', while the remainder would be returnees. TEBA offers a bonus to returnees coming back within a stipulated period of time. During the most recent years, when lesser numbers have been recruited in Botswana, the supply and demand forces in this temporary labour market have substantially increased the share of returnees, and have reduced the negative effects on agriculture mentioned above.

Rainfall and cattle ranching

When good rains occur there is ample grazing and surface water. This is the natural foundation upon which the national herd of cattle grows in numbers, improves in condition and increases in weight.

The years preceding 1966 were extremely dry, with adverse effects on the condition, weight and size of the cattle herds. Drought eventually not only leads to increasing death rates and reduction in birth rates and calves' survival rates, but also to an increased supply – after a time lag – of cattle for slaughter, at the only export abattoir, Botswana Meat Commission (BMC), in Lobatse. The prices fetched would then fall, partly due to increased supply but mainly due to reduced condition of animals. Thus during a drought period the national herd is depleted, growing again in years with good rainfall.

In Table 1.4 is set out an estimate of the size of the national cattle herd by mid-year against average rainfall in major cattle areas (+ above average, − below

Table 1.4 *Size of national cattle herd, rainfall and BMC offtake*

	Head of cattle ('000)	Rainfall +/− norm	BMC[b] offtake ('000)
1966	1237	−	138
1967	1492	+	136
1968	1688	−	122
1969	1945	−	99
1970	2017	−	110
1971	2092	n[a]	147
1972	2177	+	162
1973	2117	−	183
1974	2316	+	198
1975	2564	+	187
1976	2832	+	212
1977	3124	+	221
1978	3454	+	145

Notes
[a] At the long-term seasonal norm.
[b] BMC's capacity has doubled over the period.
Figures are for BMC accounting years.

average) during the previous season. In the last column is given the BMC offtake.

The size of the national cattle herd has increased dramatically, having almost trebled during the period, while total exports during the same period amount to more than 150 per cent of the initial herd. A second feature to notice is the unprecedented sequence of good rainfall years 1973–4 to 1977–8. While the long term weighted seasonal rainfall norm for cattle areas is slightly above 400 mm (15·75 in) per season, each of the five seasons mentioned above exceeded the norm by at least 25 per cent.

Gains in income and in wealth from cattle are more widely distributed than cattle ownership because of the *mafisa* system (a traditional Botswana 'cattle loan' system whereby non-cattle owners may obtain access to draught animals, milk and some meat, etc., through looking after other people's cattle) and other traditional systems of redistribution. Cattle prices during most of this period have also been high due to very favourable marketing arrangements abroad. As a result, wealth both in cash and on hooves has spread across the countryside as never before. The period, however, concluded with three setbacks. First, a limited foot and mouth epidemic broke out in Ngamiland during late 1977 reducing abattoir throughput by 30 per cent during 1977–8 and causing lower prices as access to the EEC market was blocked; secondly, the 1978–9 season was very dry, causing cattle herd reduction processes as described earlier; thirdly, another foot and mouth outbreak occurred in 1979.

Drought years tend to cluster. This is the lesson to be learnt from Botswana's meteorological statistics. The closing years of the 1976–81 National Development Plan could therefore bring back rural poverty and famine conditions such as were known during the first half of the 1960s. The conditions, if they occurred, would, however, constitute a national disaster on a vaster scale than before, as the cattle herds are now almost three times their size in 1966, while the BMC abattoir capacity has only doubled. Thus the size of the 'bet' is much larger than before, while the risk of not being able to have one's cattle slaughtered by BMC has increased as well. So the expected loss from a drought period has increased considerably. From this consideration flows the following conclusion: a substantial BMC extension, 50 per cent at least, is required even to re-establish the same riskiness of operations as in 1966. Adding in elements of regional economical considerations, and weight loss calculations due to long distance transport of cattle which could be avoided, a second abattoir would seem an attractive way of reducing the overall risk in the cattle industry.[7]

The expansion has taxed the environment – grass is becoming more scarce in central areas, even when good rains occur. It is unlikely that the cattle sector will expand much longer in this uncontrolled fashion. Some regulation of cattle numbers, grazing and water needs to be instituted, in order to maximize the longer term return to scarce resources like grass and water. *This will imply a reduced national herd and a much larger current offtake than at present.* This is clearly an important goal to strive for during the 1980s – attempting to strike a proper balance between the goals of economic efficiency on the one hand and the personal distribution of land, cattle and income on the other.

This section has dealt with the cattle industry and its reliance on favourable natural conditions and on man-made arrangements like slaughtering capacity, prices and marketing. The latter are required, both as a way of converting the annual cattle surplus into commodities not produced in Botswana (for example, machinery and equipment, but also consumer goods) for the promotion of welfare and development and as a way of intertemporal transfers of income during periods of drought.

In the following section we shall deal more closely with the man-made arrangements which took place during the Independence period. This we shall do under two broad headings: development of the economy and more briefly the development of institutions necessary to complement the development of an economic structure.

Development of the economy

The drought-cycle came to an end during 1966 and farming, especially of cattle, expanded. This helped to start moving the economy out of its extremely depressed state. A further impetus came from moving the central government from Mafeking (in South Africa) to the newly built capital of Gaborone (the Capital Project). More government spending now took place *inside* Botswana. Imports grew, and so did customs revenues. Demand injections from central government during 1966–7 and 1967–8 led to an increase in government employment and contribution to value added. These two factors helped to lift the economy up to a new, higher level of spending and production. After this initial economic 'break-out', only a slow economic progress was expected. Even as late as March 1969 (in the Budget Speech) it was officially expected that budgetary grants-in-aid from UK would have to continue for another 7–10 years.

Three major events took place during the last few years of the 1960s, gradually changing the economic perspective in a most profound way: first, De Beers announced its rich diamond discovery at Orapa; secondly, Bamangwato Concessions Ltd (an Anglo-American and Amax subsidiary) decided to develop the Selebi and Phikwe copper–nickel deposits; and thirdly, renegotiations of the 1910 Customs Union Agreement with South Africa were successfully concluded. These three events led to a phenomenal increase in government revenue and of exports (which increased by almost 700 per cent or by P91 million during 1969–70 to 1975). The first two events resulted in vastly increased imports, while the third greatly increased the revenue from a given level of imports.

Table 1.5 *Imports, customs revenues, government consumption, expenditure and Gross Domestic Product (GDP) – selected years 1965–77 (P million)*

	GDP	Imports[a]	Customs and excise	Government consumption
1965	32·8	16·6	—[b]	7·9
1966	36·8	18·8	1·1[c]	9.3
1967–8	43·8	27·8	1·7	11.6
1968–9	51·2	32·0	1·4	11·3
1971–2	103·6	50·7	8·3	16·0
1973–4	197·5	104·0	20·9	28·3
1974–5	213·1	119·6	30·4	39·2
1975–6	276·2	152·4	24·6	50·6
1976–7	299·2	174·2	15·4	70·5

Notes
[a] Excluding customs duties.
[b] Not available.
[c] 1966–7.

The upswing was further strengthened by a fourth event – the unprecedentedly strong export demand for Botswana beef. The BMC throughput of cattle increased from 127 000 during the calendar year 1970 to a peak of 209 000 during 1974, while the effective price more than doubled. Thus BMC's total payments to farmers were P9·2 million in 1970 and P28·0 million in 1974, the increase coming entirely from export demand. A substantial increase in rural earnings – of freehold and of traditional farmers – took place.

These four events set in motion a vast expansion of the overall demand in the economy – and of imports especially. Imports rose by more than 375 per cent during the 1968–9 to 1975–6 period, from P32 million to about P152 million (see Table 1.5). The two mining companies started developing the Orapa (diamonds) and Selebi/Phikwe (copper–nickel) mining infrastructure, while central government shouldered the considerable Shashe Complex (P55 million) for the Selebi/Phikwe physical and social infrastructure.

From late 1969 to early 1970 and onwards the economy entered a phase of expansion led by construction and other fixed capital formation. Building and construction output increased from P5·7 million during 1968–9 to P23·8 million during 1971–2 and to P49·6 million during 1973–4 (see Table 1.6). Following this came a substantial expansion of service sectors; trade, transport, business and household services and utilities (see Table 1.7). Value added from these sectors increased from P13·6 million during 1968–9, to P31·4 million during 1971–2 and P64·4 million during 1973–4 according to CSO calculations.

Table 1.6 *Gross capital formation at current prices by kind of asset 1966 to 1975–6 (P million)*

Kind of asset	1966	1967–8	1968–9	1971–2	1973–4	1974–5	1975–6
Raw materials and goods for re-sale	2·4	−1·5	1·2	1·9	8·4	25·3	15·9
Work-in-progress	..	..	..	..	0·2	5·8	6·7
Increase in cattle herd	−3·8	3·6	6·1	−0·7	17·4	13·7	12·5
Residential buildings	} 4·2	} 4·0	3·0	6·4	10·8	10·7	12·8
Non-residential buildings			1·1	5·8	7·9	9·5	10·7
Other construction			1·6	11·6	30·9	21·2	29·2
Transport equipment, other machinery and equipment	5·7	5·9	4·2	30·7	27·9	15·6	26·4
TOTAL	8·5	12·0	17·2	55·7	103·5	101·6	114·2

Table 1.7 *Industrial origin of GDP at current market prices: 1966 to 1975–6 (P million)*

	1966	1967–8	1968–9	1971–2	1973–4	1974–5	1975–6
Agriculture, forestry, hunting and fishing	14·5	18·3	23·2	33.1	69.2	61·2	64·2
Mining, quarrying and prospecting	0·0	0·7	0·2	11·2	15·9	15·2	33·9
Manufacturing	2·9	3·6	2·8	5·1	10·1	15·5	20·9
Water and electricity	0·3	0·3	0·3	1·3	3·3	6·9	11·1
Building and construction	2·1	2·0	1·9	10·0	21·1	21·2	20·3
Wholesale and retail trade, restaurants and hotels	6·8	5·0	5·1	17·5	35·1	43·0	53·9
Transport, storage and communication	3·0	2·4	3·4	3·8	5·3	5·5	7·6
Other services	2·4	3·9	4·8	8·8	19·3	19·7	28·2
General government	4·9	7·7	9·5	11·8	18·2	24·9	36·1
TOTAL	36·8	43·8	51·2	102·6	197·5	213·1	276·2

Although the value added contribution of general government increased by between 20–50 per cent per annum from 1967–8 to 1973–4, its relative contribution to GDP was actually halved on account of the fast overall expansion of the economy. Government was no longer the leading sector – as it briefly had been around Independence. While construction value added at current prices peaked in 1973–4 (Table 1.7), setting in motion a slight downward cycle in real economic terms, followed by a levelling off of imports and declining customs duties, this has been offset by the increasing mineral output. Growth in mineral output during the beginning of the second decade of Independence thus leads the economy (see Table 1.8). Once more the economy is being lifted to a higher level of incomes and demand, but growth rates are no longer high.

Table 1.8 *Production of coal, copper–nickel (CuNi) matte and diamonds*

	Coal (tonnes)	CuNi matte (tonnes)	Diamonds, export value (P million)
1968	—	—	0·1
1969	—	—	0·2
1970	—	—	2·7
1971	—	—	5·3
1972	—	—	19·5
1973	—	—	23·2
1974	25 498	6663	30·1
1975	68 639	16 513	29·6
1976	224 175	32 506	33·8
1977	294 039	30 772	48·6

The reason for the simultaneous upsurge in coal and copper–nickel matte production as from 1975 was due to the coming on stream of the Selebi–Phikwe plant after years of teething problems.

Diamond exports continued their expansion after 1975 due to increased production at the Orapa/Lethlakane Mine and to increased diamond prices. A substantial increase in diamond production, perhaps by 100 per cent, is expected around 1982 when the new Jwaneng Mine starts commercial operations.

Formal sector employment (excluding self-employment) has grown considerably, by about 36 per cent, during the four years (1972–6) for which data are available (see Table 1.9). The employment growth is, however, moderate when compared to the increase in value added, cf. Table 1.7. The exclusion of (the high) employment growth in traditional agriculture (including self-employment) due to high cattle prices and offtake, is one explanation. Another is the expansion of capital-intensive industries like mining, still employing less people than, say, education. One should note the importance of government employment, the expansion of which is subject to manpower and financial constraints. Finally, one should take note of the mid-decennial stagnation of the building and construction sector, pausing before the commencement of the large Jwaneng diamond mine and township development during the second half of the 1970s.

Table 1.9   *Formal sector employment 1972–6*

	1972	1974	1976[a]
Freehold agriculture	5058	5108	5300
Mining and quarrying	1680	4140	4530
Manufacturing incl. water and electricity	2639	3022	3470
Construction	6468	6787	7000
Trade, hotels, and other services[b]	8143	9539	10 430
Community and personal services, incl. domestic servants	10 759	12 965	14 525
Central and local government incl. education	13 452	17 729	20 510
TOTAL	48 199[c]	59 290[c]	65 765

Notes
[a] Estimated.
[b] Trade, hotels, restaurants, transport, communications, finance, insurance, real estate and business services.
[c] Of which non-citizens: 3708 (1972), 3962 (1974), 4320 (1977).

The picture of employment given in Table 1.9 is incomplete. Both Batswana working abroad (about 45 000) and informal sector employment are excluded. The number of expatriates in relation to formal sector employment has not grown, but due to the continued emphasis on mineral-led expansion their number continues to increase.

One of the major national targets at Independence was to build an economically viable sovereign state. Among other things this meant freedom from reliance on recurrent budgetary grants-in-aid from the United Kingdom. The history of government finance in Bechuanaland Protectorate[8] shows the perennial necessity for such recurrent grants-in-aid, which meant that government budgets were not for the National Assembly alone to pass.

In Tables 1.10 and 1.11 recurrent government revenue is given by major sources. A vast growth has taken place: from P6·2 million during 1966–7 to P72·7 million during 1975–6, tailing off slightly in the following year before increasing quite rapidly during 1977–8. Recurrent budgets have increased from P10·3 million during 1966–7 to P72·3 million during 1977–8; while development budgets have grown from P3·7 million to P44·4 million.

The money spent has been accounted for, been subject to audit and before that to a conscientious husbandry of resources and constitutes proof of a substantially expanded administrative capacity.

The phasing out of British budgetary grants-in-aid coincided with a period of recurrent budgetary surpluses, sometimes quite substantial as in 1975–6 and 1977–8 (see Table 1.11). These surpluses introduced new dimensions in

Table 1.10 *Central government recurrent revenues – selected years 1966–7 to 1977–8 (P million)*

	1966–7	1969–70	1971–2	1973–4	1975–6	1977–8
Customs and excise	1·1	5·1	8·3	20·9	24·6	37·8
Other taxes	2·2	2·4	3·8	8·9	22·8	29·0
Mineral royalties and dividends	—	—	0·9	2·8	15·2	13·6
Other	2·9	3·1	4·1	8·1	10·1	24·1
TOTAL	6·2	10·6	17·1	40·7	72·7	104·5

Sources
As before.

Table 1.11 *Central government development expenditure and recurrent budget surplus – selected years 1966–7 to 1977–8 (P million)*

	1966–7	1969–70	1971–2	1973–4	1975–6	1977–8
Recurrent budget surplus/deficit	−4·2	−1·8	−1·0	14·2	26·1	32·2
Development expenditure	3·7	4·9	12·3	30·3	33·1	44·4
Per cent of development expenditure financed from recurrent surplus	0	0	0	47·0	79·0	73·0

Sources
As before.

government finance and planning: a surplus meant an improved future debt servicing capacity and a domestic source of finance for development expenditure in the present. It meant being able to finance some projects which could not find external funding, and it meant that local costs could be met by local resources where external funding was only available for foreign exchange costs. Finally, it enabled the government to accrue reserves, at first with the commercial banking system and, in later years, increased foreign exchange reserves at the Bank of Botswana (Table 1.12).

The considerable improvement in Botswana's financial affairs may in the future imply reduced development assistance from abroad, especially as the Bank of Botswana's foreign exchange reserves have continued to increase. However, Botswana's economy remains extremely vulnerable, so that high reserves are a crucial protection against the many possible crises that can occur.

Table 1.12   *Central government reserves, foreign exchange reserves of Bank of Botswana, foreign developmental finance to central government – selected years 1967–77 (P million)*

	1967[a]	1969	1971	1973	1976	1977
Government cash in hand and on deposit	− 2·9	0·1	2·5	8·1	43·9	47·9
Bank of Botswana foreign exchange reserves	..	..	..	..	65·1[b]	82·8[b]
Estimated inflow of foreign developmental finance to central government[c]	3·7	3·8	7·5	29·7	19·2	50·5

Notes
[a] As at end of financial year unless otherwise stated.
[b] As at end of calendar year.
[c] During the preceding financial year.
Sources
As before.

Development of institutions

Botswana, and previously the Bechuanaland Protectorate, had since 1895 availed itself on an informal basis of the use of various Southern African currencies as legal tender; and from 1960 of the South African Reserve Bank's Rand. Botswana's informal membership in the Rand Monetary Area did not carry any influence over the management of the Rand currency, while the area's monetary and foreign exchange regime had to be followed.

During 1974, after lengthy deliberations and analyses of the monetary options available, the Botswana government decided to establish its own national currency and to withdraw from the Rand Monetary Area. A Monetary Preparatory Commission was appointed, necessary legislation drafted and passed during the first half of 1975. The Bank of Botswana, scheduled to be a fully fledged central bank, came into existence on 1 July 1975, commenced financial operations on its own account in January 1976, and introduced the Pula on 23 August 1976.

The establishment of a central bank was the latest in a long series of new institutions created during the first ten years of independence. At the start the ministries had very broadly defined portfolios of responsibility, but a more clear-cut functional structure developed over time, especially after 1970. It is also around this point in time that the major utilities corporations were launched, Water Utilities Corporation and Botswana Power Corporation, coinciding with the Shashe Project getting off the ground. Following from the activity generated here, a Department of Customs and Excise was established. A major institution of national importance was created with the building of the national campus of the regional university as from 1972–3, gaining momentum after the 1976 secession of Lesotho. Following from the increased awareness of Botswana's responsibilities in international politics, a ministry of External Affairs was created; and the regional security situation resulted in the formation of the Botswana Defence Force.

The Gaborone Capital Project (1963) and the subsequent move from Mafeking around 1965 was thus the start of a long search for economic and institutional independence, which still continues. The social organization which constitutes present-day Botswana, when coming of age in 1984 before the closing year of the Fifth National Development Plan, may indeed look back with contentment to its formative years.

Notes

1. An earlier version of the text has appeared as Chapter 1, 'The Independence Decade 1966–1976' of (Botswana's) *National Development Plan 1976–81*, Government Printer, Gaborone, May 1977, pp. 1–13. An extensive collection of tables has previously been published as *Botswana National Accounts and Selected Indicators 1966–1976*, Government Printer, Gaborone, September 1976. These tables represent the maximum amount of time-series information which could be collated on the Independence decade and formed the analytical skeleton for the present and earlier paper; they are the source for all the tables unless otherwise stated.
2. The concept of *de jure* population includes absentees, for example, temporary mine workers in the Republic of South Africa.
3. Migrating seasonally between village, cattle post and lands.
4. Lobatse, Gaborone, Selebi-Phikwe, Francistown and Orapa.
5. cf. Lipton, M., *Botswana: Employment and Labour Use in Botswana*, Government Printer, Gaborone, Vol. I, 1979, p. 20.
6. *Report on the Population Census 1971*, CSO, Gaborone, 1972, Table 9.
7. See Chapter 4 by Hubbard in this volume, pp. 44–65.
8. Hermans, Q., 'A review of Botswana's financial history 1900 to 1973', *Botswana Notes and Records*, vol. 6, 1974, pp. 89–115.

Hans-Erik Dahl is the Director of the Institute of Economics, University of Bergen, Norway; formerly National Income Statistician, Central Statistics Office, Botswana.

2 The Potential Problems of Diamond-Dependent Development

STEPHEN R. LEWIS, Jr

Introduction

Botswana is exceedingly fortunate to have what appear to be major reserves of diamonds. The revenues generated by the encashment of these natural resources can provide a source of financing for the diversification of the economy and the achievement of Botswana's 'basic objectives of national planning': rapid economic growth, social justice, economic independence and sustained production. As argued below, the presence of large reserves of diamonds is almost equivalent to having a succession of gifts in the form of completely untied foreign exchange. However, the process by which diamonds are encashed and some of the resulting pressures that arise 'automatically' generate problems that work against the effective use of resources and the balanced spreading of the development effort. Botswana has so far been able to resist many aspects of these pressures and to take measures to offset the forces at work. A great deal of resolve is needed in the future, especially with the prospect of another major diamond development at Jwaneng, in order to avoid a pattern of diamond-dependent development that *could* lead to general stagnation with rising income inequalities.

The nature of the 'diamond dividend'

Deposits of natural resources such as diamonds have no economic value unless they are mined and sold, either in raw or finished form. The value of the deposits depends on the costs associated with extraction and marketing of the resources. The excess of the value of the product over the full costs (including the cost of capital employed) of extraction can be referred to as the economic rents that accrue to the deposit. Negotiations between the owners of the rights to the natural resources (often, and in the case of Botswana's diamonds always, the state) and the individuals or companies wishing to undertake the exploitation of the resource (so far in Botswana, De Beers Consolidated Mines) often involve the issue of who will share, and how much, in the rents that occur because of a difference between the market value of the resource and the costs of the mining. While there are many other aspects to the negotiation process, they will not concern us here.

The economic rents accruing to the owners of the mineral rights are, in effect, a gift from nature. To the extent that these rents arise because of the sale of the resources in international markets, the gift comes in the form of freely convertible foreign exchange, which can be used for any purpose. Thus, the rents accruing from diamonds to the government of Botswana have the same economic effect as a unilateral transfer of funds (*not* a loan) from a bilateral or multilateral agency, with no strings attached as to use – no specified projects, no division between recurrent or development budget, no limitation on the source of the imports of goods or services, etc.

In addition to these attributes of economic rents, the presence of sizeable rents, especially when combined with some form of restriction on the quantity mined, means that the total quantity of output and variations of output at the margin (where everything important in economic analysis happens) will not vary with changes either in the prices of the natural resource or in the costs of operating the mine. Only when the cost or price changes have been so large as to eliminate economic rents at the margin will variations in mining rate and quantity produced take place. This is particularly true for a commodity like diamonds where various producers have agreements with the Central Selling Organization regarding their shares of the overall market. While the nature of arrangements with producers is kept confidential, De Beers makes it quite clear that production management is important to maintain the 'stability of the diamond trade'.

The reason for emphasizing this last point is that variations in costs or output prices that might come from *exchange rate* changes, or *wage rate* changes, are not likely to have any significant effect on the quantity of the resource extracted and sold. This, as will be seen, raises major issues with respect to wage and exchange rate policies for balanced development in other sectors of the economy. Further, when some form of production agreement exist, there is the danger that in soft markets for the mineral production may be cut back irrespective of the price/cost relationships then existing (that is, in order to maintain the international price, producers may jointly agree to reduce output even if production costs are well below existing market prices). This, too, raises issues for the management of a mineral-dependent economy.

The question naturally arises, are these problems worth worrying about in Botswana? The answer to this question is a clear 'yes', both with respect to developments to date and even more emphatically with respect to the developments that will be associated with the economy following the expansion of Orapa and the large increases in production expected when Jwaneng comes on stream in 1982.

Due to the relationships between the government and De Beers over the economics of the diamond mining industry in Botswana, it is not possible to estimate accurately the rents, or the revenues, that accrue to government from the diamond mines. However, some orders of magnitude can be found by examining De Beers' own *Annual Reports* and the data on exports of diamonds from Botswana for recent years. Until 1978 De Beers annually published the processing costs per tonne of ore at the various mines associated with the De Beers group. It is not clear whether these include or exclude any capital costs;

so, the costs may underestimate the opportunity cost of mining. However, costs per tonne times the number of tonnes mined give the costs, as reported by De Beers, for working the mines at Orapa and Letlhakane. In 1975, 1976 and 1977 these came to P6·9, P8·5 and P13·1 million, respectively (Letlhakane came on stream in 1977).

Total diamond exports as reported by the Botswana Central Statistical Office for those years were P32·1, P37·5, and P48·4 million, respectively. The calendar year periods for costs will probably not match the calendar year period for exports; there will be accumulations or run-downs of stocks; the switchover from sorting and valuing abroad to sorting and valuing locally during this period may affect both the costs and the timing of exports relative to production, etc. However, the order of magnitude figures (e.g. for 1975, P6·9 million in costs divided by P32·1 million reported exports) suggest costs of extraction in the range of 25 per cent of total value of exports. Even if these costs do not include something for the cost of capital employed, they would be the relevant variable costs on the basis of which one might make short-run decisions about increasing or decreasing production in response to changes in production costs or output prices for an existing mine. The figures suggest both that rents relative to market prices have been quite high; and that production decisions might not be particularly sensitive to cost/price changes, even in the absence of any agreements on production levels.

The amounts involved are quite sizeable. Botswana's total GDP at market prices in 1975–6 and 1976–7 is presently estimated at P276 and P299 million, respectively. The operating surpluses for 1975, 1976, and 1977 calculated by deducting the operating costs reported by De Beers from the export values reported by the Botswana government come to P25·2, P29·0, and P35·3 million, respectively, indicating levels approximating 10 per cent of GDP. Press releases from De Beers and the government of Botswana when settlements in negotiations have been announced indicate the government share of 'profits' is in the 65–70 per cent range. If the profits referred to in the agreements are of the same order of magnitude as the operating surpluses estimated in this paragraph it may be plausible to conclude that the economic rents accruing to government from diamonds represent 6–7 per cent of GDP. Since it accrues in the form of convertible foreign exchange, this is a sizeable boon to the government's development efforts; and it is a magnitude that is worth further consideration due to its other side effects. Further, since the output of the Orapa mine was doubled in late 1978, and the Jwaneng mine now under construction will be larger than the expanded Orapa production, the size of the problem, if such it is, will be much larger than the 6–7 per cent of GDP estimated above.

Several other aspects of the mineral rents are important to a consideration of their role in the government's development plans and strategy. First, the flows of revenue from mining rents are quite different from other taxes on economic activity. Mining projects tend to come on stream in discontinuous 'lumps'. Shortly after a mine is opened, the full design capacity of the mine is reached. Government revenue rises from zero to the amount determined by the agreement, based on the full production level. These break-in periods in Botswana's diamond mines (Orapa stage 1, Letlhakane and Orapa expansion) have each lasted less than a calendar year. So, one sees a series of three lumpy increases in the government revenue stream from mining revenues. After the achievement of full production levels, government revenue will not grow in real terms, *unless* the price of the mineral rises more rapidly than other prices abroad and at home. Therefore, as the rest of the economy grows, and as the levels of government expenditures expand, the percentage contribution of revenues from existing mines would be expected to fall. Plans for the use of the mineral revenues must take account of this fact.

Secondly, not only will mining revenues from any given deposit level off once full production is reached, but also at some point the revenues may cease. There is little published information on the likelihood of this or its timing in the case of Botswana's diamonds, but the policy related to spending of mineral rents and of making other policy adjustments is obviously dependent on the length of life of the flow of such rents to government.

Thirdly, the flow of rents raises some problems different from GDP growth in other sectors of the economy. This is particularly true when the company operating the mine is externally owned. In such cases, there is less assurance that the increments in GDP will be re-invested in productive assets in the economy than if the income in the first instance flowed to farmers, businessmen and entrepreneurs who were seeking productive outlets for their savings. As will be discussed further, governments are not particularly effective at finding productive investments in the enterprise sectors of an economy; and foreign mining companies have a world-wide view, not a national view, of where to invest their earnings. In Botswana, De Beers in fact has increased its investment and its prospecting activities constantly since Orapa was first opened, which is a happy occurrence. But, since De Beers is exclusively interested in diamonds, this activity has not contributed directly to the *diversification* of Botswana's economic structure.

Finally, there is a special situation in Botswana with respect to the impact of mineral revenues and projects on other government revenues. As indicated in Chapter 9 (pp. 132–159), the customs union arrangements of which Botswana is a part provide revenue to Botswana based on the level of imports into Botswana from all sources (with certain timing adjustments). Thus, during the construction phase of a mining project, Botswana accrues revenue based on the capital goods and related imports associated with the project. During the operating phases of the project, revenue will accrue from the direct and indirect imports of the intermediate products needed in the mine. In addition, as government spends the revenues from the project, and as those expenditures flow directly and indirectly for the purchase of imports, revenues will accrue to government from the common customs pool. In these circumstances, a reduction in the real flow of diamond revenues (say, due to stagnation of diamond prices or cutbacks in production during world recessions) could result in a multiplied pressure on government budgets (if the initial decline in revenue flow leads to any reduction in spending, resulting imports, and thus, accruals of revenue from the customs pool). This is, in a way, a special case of a familiar multiplier effect on total GDP that would come from a fall in the export earnings of any sector of the economy. But, since it affects the government budget, adjustments may be more difficult politically than if they took place elsewhere.

In summary, the large size and the nature of the economic rents, or the 'diamond dividend', to the government of Botswana raise some special issues related to economic management. These rents are in many ways like a transfer to government of convertible foreign exchange; the relatively high ratio of rents to costs of mining means that the cost and revenue structure of the mines, and their desired levels of output, may not be affected by changes in external prices, internal wage rates, or the foreign exchange rate; the flow of revenues tends to come in discontinuous jumps, not in continuous increases; government revenue is vulnerable to changes in the terms of trade for diamonds abroad; the limited life of mining deposits (less clear in the case of Botswana's two largest finds at Orapa and Jwaneng, but in general a problem) means that the flow of revenues cannot be assumed to exist in perpetuity, as would be the case in an investment in a sector other than one exploiting a non-renewable resource; the flow of mining GDP mainly to government and to an externally owned mining company may adversely affect the chances for re-investment in productive enterprise sectors of the economy, and, therefore, the effort to diversify; and, finally, the interrelationship between government expenditures and the other sources of government revenue, particularly the customs revenue in the case of Botswana, may give a multiplied effect, up or down, that accompanies changes in the real price of diamonds abroad.

Diversification and reduction of dependence

The basic task for developing economies is to raise productivity over a wide range of economic activities, principally in agriculture, but also in other sectors. This increase in productivity will be accompanied by a series of other structural changes familiar to all students of economic development: a lowered share of agriculture's contribution to GDP and to employment; increased shares of manufacturing, construction, and a wide range of modern services; increased shares of personal and corporate saving in GDP; reductions of the disparities of productivity per worker among the various sectors of the economy (principally reflected in a rise in the relative productivity of labour engaged in agriculture); increased urbanization, etc. In general, the transition from lower to higher levels of real income per head of population may come more readily if some external capital can supplement domestic savings at earlier stages of development and lead to higher rates of capital formation, faster real growth and a more rapid transition than would be possible if the economy had to depend on its own capacities for increasing saving and for earning the foreign exchange necessary to carry out an accelerated development programme.

The presence of significant flows of rents from mineral deposits should make life easier for the people and the government of a developing country. But the allocation of investment and the structure of incentives needed to have a successful transition to a more rapidly developing economy over a broad range of sectors are not random occurrences.

The main requirement is that there be a diversification of the productive sectors of the economy – that is, those that sell output domestically or internationally, and do not depend on involuntary transfers of income for their survival. This means sectors other than general government, *not* because the government does only unproductive things but because there is no market in government services; they must be paid for by taxes. Also, since the private demand for goods (either produced domestically or imported) increases as incomes generated domestically rise, there will be a need to meet the increased demand for such goods by producing either import substitutes or exports to pay for the imports. This will require expanded productive investments in the exporting and the import substituting sectors. Further, sectors such as mining have very little direct employment creation per Pula of investment or even per Pula of GDP generated. The same is true of the government sectors – largely because government is the most education- and skill-intensive sector of the economy, and employs relatively few semi-skilled and unskilled workers. Thus, if employment opportunities are to be expanded over a wide range of the population, investment must take place in a variety of productive sectors outside government and the mines.

Naturally, the investment in other sectors will have to be profitable (if it is to attract private investors) or at least cost-covering (if it is to provide opportunities for parastatal investments). The key factor in determining such profitability will be related to the wage rate/exchange rate relationship. Especially in an economy such as Botswana's, local production must be thought of in relation to the relative costs of production in Botswana as compared with abroad, both for import substitutes and for exports. Therefore, special attention needs to be paid to the incentive structure facing the productive sectors, including agriculture, manufacturing and modern services.

Finally, all developing countries have found special problems in some lagging sectors of the economy, especially in the rural areas. If a government has a commitment to social justice and the broad spread of the benefits of development to all parts of the population, special attention must be paid to rural development. And, it is quite clear that this is a problem area for almost all countries: projects effective in assisting the rural poor are notoriously difficult to design and even more difficult to implement. Yet, they must be pushed, otherwise the fruits of development are unlikely to be widely spread.

An 'automatic adjustment' mechanism for mineral rents

While the presence of mineral rents should make it easier for governments to undertake the investments needed to diversify the economy, and to finance the projects needed to spread the benefits of development widely, it seems clear that in practice this is not the case. The lessons of the oil-rich countries provide particularly striking examples of the problems. Closer to Botswana, Zambia's experience with copper dependence seems to bear out the same lessons. Botswana has avoided some of the worst problems thus far. But, with the effects of the Orapa expansion just beginning, and with the Jwaneng development yet to come, an understanding is needed of some of the forces at work when large mineral rents are present, if problems are to be avoided. Thus, this section briefly lays out a political-social-economic 'adjustment mechanism' operating in the 'mineral-led' countries.

First, it will be remembered that the mining rents can be equated with a large transfer of freely convertible currency to the country – for the most part to the government. Depending on where the government *initially* places its bank deposits, and what happens to its pattern of spending, one may observe a rapid increase in the credit base and the money supply. If the spending of the revenues were to flow entirely abroad, of course, there would be an equivalent drop in foreign exchange reserves and the domestic monetary base. But the spending is not all devoted to imports and as a result there will generally be a substantial increase in the domestic money supply and an incentive for banks to increase their lending – for all purposes, including consumption loans as well as business investments and inventory accumulation.

Secondly, governments are under political pressure to spend as rapidly as possible for development purposes – and sometimes to spend for any purpose. Unless there is a large list of projects 'on the shelf' when mining revenues increase, there may simply be an increase in government spending on less well-prepared projects and on general 'waste'. Whereas a Ministry of Finance could use the 'we-don't-have-any-money' excuse for not taking on a less deserving project before it had mining rents to spend, it no longer has that reason. It must be very tough and say 'no' to less deserving projects, and be willing to see foreign exchange reserves and government bank balances rise until more productive projects come along. If it is not willing to do so, the mix of projects will become skewed away from those more consistent with government's development objectives. This is not a necessary, or an inevitable, outcome. It is just more likely.

Rural development projects will fare worst in this sort of scramble for the allocation of public funds. And, remember, the increase in mineral rentals is generally a once-for-all increase in the level; they will not continue to grow in real terms unless there is a succession of new mining ventures. Once pushed out of the allocation process by fast-spending ministries, usually those purchasing hardware or undertaking large contracts, the rural development ministries may have a difficult time ever getting another turn at the tap.

Thirdly, both in the mines themselves and in the government sector, there will be pressure for increased wages. In both cases it will be demonstrable that the employers 'have the money' and can 'afford' to pay higher wages. But in general, and certainly in Botswana, those already employed in such sectors are already well compensated by comparison with the average citizen – usually several times over. However, the more concentrated political power of the miners and civil servants, whether formally organized or not, will almost certainly lead to increases in wages. Thus, part of the *nation's* economic rents from national resources will be spent in financing higher standards of living for a relatively small and fortunate minority already employed. Note, again, the dissimilarities of the growth *rates* of income and expenditure for the government. The mining rents rise once and stay at that level (in the absence of a new project that will generate a new flow of rents). The increase in wage levels paid to the civil service, however, applies to all new entrants. Thus, there is a continuing erosion of the government's resources for non-salary expenditures, and even of its resources for hiring of more individuals, due to the increase in wage levels brought about by the one-time increase in mining rents.

Fourthly, while the mining rents should be channelled into real capital formation in the enterprise sectors of the economy (private or parastatal) to spread employment opportunities, governments generally are not set up to perform such an intermediation function. Indeed, the intermediation function generally has seen governments tap the saving of the private sectors through the direct or indirect issuance of government debt to the public. The danger is twofold. First, governments will not transfer as much of the rents as would be optimal to capital formation in the enterprise sectors (partly due to the wage pressure discussed immediately above). Secondly, such transfers of funds as do take place will go into large, capital intensive projects that create little direct or indirect employment. This latter pressure in turn arises for two quite separate reasons. One, such projects can be 'managed' more easily and the money can be disposed of more rapidly than would be the case with a project that provided assistance to small rural farmers and businessmen. In many countries with new increments of mining rents, turn-key projects of a large-scale capital intensive nature are the order of the day, in order to speed up the 'rate of implementation'. Two, as wages rise in the modern sector, under pressure from government and mining company settlements, the less labour intensive projects will look relatively more attractive to private or parastatal investors seeking projects.

Fifthly, and a phenomenon common to almost all the mineral-rich countries, the expansion of government and mining activities in response to the mining rents results in an increased flow of expatriate workers – highly skilled and highly paid in some countries, less so in others. At least two consequences follow. First, as a result of the influx of expatriates, the measured increases in the GDP exceed the increases in income going to citizens. This is a simple point, but often overlooked: maximizing GDP growth may not maximize the growth of citizen incomes (never mind the distribution problems that may arise among citizens). Secondly, the presence of large numbers of visible, highly paid expatriates will add significant pressures to those already felt by governments and mining companies to raise the wages of citizens. Despite these dangers, too restrictive a policy on expatriate labour in the face of severe skill shortages could well slow down the growth of citizen incomes. As is often the case, the optimum flow is unlikely to be either the maximum or the minimum number.

Sixthly, whenever one tries to do things in a great rush, 'waste' is likely to occur. This comes from a variety of sources, including the desire to spend money quickly, strains at key points in the management and implementation systems for projects and programmes as the task rises faster than the capacity to handle it, shortages of key materials or services that may arise from time to time. The result is similar in all cases: the real costs of undertaking a project or programme turn out to be greater than had been anticipated. Unless benefits are somehow increased the net productivity of the projects will decrease. For any given project, of course, starting the flow of benefits sooner rather than later would generally improve the benefit/cost ratio, properly discounted. But the same will not be true when there is an attempt to *accelerate* projects in the face of real bottlenecks in the management and delivery systems.

Finally, while the difficulties encountered in rapid implementation of a broad development thrust financed by mining rents may push up costs domestically, both in terms of labour and other goods, the fact that the mining rents came in the form of foreign exchange means that the balance of payments will be relatively healthy; there will be no need to contemplate any adjustment downward in the value of the local currency. Indeed, there may be pressures to revalue the currency upward, in order to lower import costs in local currency terms and alleviate the effects of 'inflation' (which in the above scenario is domestically induced, not imported; doing something about imported inflation is a quite separate problem). Further, as explained in an earlier section, this pressure of increased costs at a constant price of foreign exchange has no effect on the production levels of the mining sector itself. Even as the balance of payments moves back towards equilibrium, or even to deficit (in the face of rapidly rising domestic spending by government, and, through the expansion of the monetary base, the private sector as well), there will be little apparent need to devalue the currency. There will be few 'obvious' benefits, either, as the devaluation would not have any effect on the level of mining exports, which are the principal export earner.

This last aspect of the 'automatic adjustment' that operates in countries receiving significant mining rents is probably the single most serious part of the problem of achieving diversification of the economy. The combination of rising money wages without corresponding increases in productivity, and a constant price of foreign exchange, will make it less and less likely that investment opportunities in the productive enterprise sectors of the economy will be profitable, or even cost-covering. Further, an exchange rate dominated by the effects of a mining export produced at low average and marginal costs may make it possible to support a price of foreign exchange, or a value of the domestic currency, that makes it virtually impossible for other domestic activities to compete, either with imports or in export markets. In some cases there has been a decline in the diversification of the economy and an absolute decline in the level of non-mineral exports following a large flow of mining rents. The rents support a value of the domestic currency that, in combination with the increases in wages and other costs associated with the domestic spending of those mining rents, has made once-profitable activities no longer profitable. Not only have such countries failed in part of their diversification efforts; they have even undiversified! This has further concentrated the benefits of mining development into the hands of relatively few people.

In summary, there are a variety of pressures at work both politically and economically in the presence of mining rents of any significant size. Pressures that work 'automatically' to adjust the initial surplus in the balance of payments back to balance or even to deficit; to reduce employment opportunities and the level of real government services below what would otherwise take place at the same real levels of revenue from other sources; to discourage the investments in productive activity that would diversify the economy; to reduce the net benefits from individual projects; to lower the share of citizens in GDP increases; and, overall, to move the economy in the direction of greater dualism between traditional and modern sectors and greater dependence on mining activities for both exports and government revenue. It would require a determined government to fully compensate for the pressures in these directions: one that both understood the pressures and had the will and the public support to take a longer view – rather than to yield to the easier route in the short run.

Performance and prospects in Botswana

Since Botswana has been a mineral-led economy for about a decade, it is possible to give an interim assessment of performance in 'leaning against the wind' – as compared with the 'automatic adjustment' mechanism just outlined. This section presents some evidence, some personal judgments based on several years of observation, of the situation in Botswana. The points are taken up in the order of the last section.

First, how has the government done in controlling the monetary expansion that might have come from sharply increased net export earnings? Botswana's own currency, the Pula, was not introduced until August 1976, so the early years of mineral-led growth cannot be examined from that point of view. Since August 1976, however, the Bank of Botswana made two things clear regarding management of money and credit in the economy. First, the location of government balances, as between the commercial banks and the Bank of Botswana, is a tool of monetary management. In the first year of an independent Pula, the government shifted most of its deposits to the Bank of Botswana in order to soak up excess liquidity in the banking system and avoid excessive monetary growth and credit expansion. Then, during 1978, a further problem arose (apparently associated with increased diamond revenues combined with a domestic recession associated with foot and mouth disease), with a considerable increase in banking system liquidity. As reported in the September 1978 *Statistical Bulletin*, the Bank arranged for a special deposit facility for a 'large company' at the Bank of Botswana. This had the effect of shifting the excess liquidity out of the banking system, and reducing the surplus of liquid assets held by the commercial banks that could have been converted to short-term commercial credits in excess of those the Bank of Botswana and the government felt were prudent and productive. In fact, on this particular occasion, the government and the Bank of Botswana were probably less concerned with increases in bank lending than with the unwillingness of the commercial banks to accept further deposits – a phenomenon that could have led to disintermediation and problems for the commercial banking system generally. While the record is short, the government and the Bank of Botswana have been creative in their responses, and have shown no inclination to allow the monetary base, that is, currency and commercial bank deposits with the Bank of Botswana, to expand automatically as reserves expand.

Secondly, what has been the record on government spending? Before the mineral growth began, government was still dependent on British grant-in-aid in support of its recurrent budget, and was able to make no direct contribution to financing the development budget. In his 'Introduction' to the *National Development Plan 1970–5*, the Vice-President, Dr Masire, listed as his second goal for the Plan, 'to achieve budgetary self-sufficiency in the shortest possible time consistent with rapid economic growth'. The government moved into budgetary self-sufficiency in 1972–3. In addition to the normal Development Fund for government projects, it created two special funds to channel the mineral revenues into sources other than immediate recurrent spending. The Public Debt Service Fund (PDSF) was intended to provide long-term capital to local authorities and parastatal bodies, and, through their repayment of such debt, PDSF would provide the government with a flow of resources in the future to service the external debt it was contracting for development purposes. The Revenue Stabilization Fund (RSF) was created to absorb temporary increases in revenues above the levels that could be spent productively, and to assure a more steady growth of both recurrent and development spending than would occur if there were pressures to increase spending to match increased revenues whenever they occurred. Both funds have been actively used in the years since 1972–3 when they received their first appropriations.

The creation of these special funds has not meant that government has neglected its efforts at development. On the contrary, recurrent expenditures have grown very rapidly both in current prices and in real terms. For example, total recurrent expenditures in 1971–2 were P18 million, while in 1978–9 they are estimated to be around P90 million – a five-fold increase during a time when the price level had not even doubled. Employment in the public sector (including education) rose by nearly 12 per cent per year from 1972 to 1977 (the last year for which data are available). Increases in expenditures were particularly rapid in areas such as education and health services. Development expenditures (other than those for the Shashe Copper–Nickel Project) rose from around P6 million in 1971–2 to around P60 million in 1978–9. Despite increases in construction and other costs, this must represent at least a quadrupling of real efforts. And a glance at the composition indicates that the investment has taken place in basic infrastructure, education, health services, water supply systems, etc. Thus, while one can always make a case that the allocations of resources could be improved, the government of Botswana has thus far restrained its spending rate to one in which reasonably productive projects and services for the population could be undertaken; and, at the same time, it has made provision in the RSF and the PDSF for putting some funds away for less fortunate times. Even spending for the Botswana Defence Force, created in 1977, has been moderate by the standards of other developing countries with mineral wealth.

Thirdly, how has the government done on wage policies? Here, the record is mixed, with more success at the skilled levels through Government Incomes Policy and less success at the unskilled levels. Professor Michael Lipton, in the course of producing his comprehensive report on the employment problem in Botswana, has indicated the pattern of increases in minimum wages paid both in government and in the private sectors covered by minimum wage regulations over approximately the past decade. The data he presented are converted in Table 2.1 to US cents per hour, using the exchange rate between the US dollar and the Pula (formerly the Rand) prevailing in each year. The pattern is quite clear: there was a four- or five-fold increase in the wage rate relative to the price of foreign exchange in the past decade, most of it coming after the beginning of the mineral-led phase of Botswana's growth. The Salaries Commission of 1974 provided the largest jump, and increases in the past four or five years have been

Table 2.1   *Minimum wages in Botswana – US cents per hour*[a]

	Government	Private sector[b]
1969	9·8	6·3
1970	12·5	6·3
1973	16·4	6·5
1974	32·5	19·3
1976	30·9	15·3
1977	30·9	23·0
1978 (April)	38·5	24·2
1978 (October)	43·7	29·0

Notes
[a] Converted at the prevailing exchange rate.
[b] The 'private sector' excludes agriculture, personal services, and also such sectors as trades, hotels and restaurants.

Source
M. Lipton, *Employment and Labour Use in Botswana*, Vol. I, p. 42, Table 5.

considerably more moderate in the public sector. The decline in 1974–6 reflects the devaluation of the rand, in September 1975. The private sectors have been 'catching up' with government, and since these are the sectors which must maintain competitive costs and prices in external markets (whether producing import substitutes or exports) the problem may be worsening. While it is difficult to say much with certainty about the skill situation and its effects on wage and salary levels, in the case of unskilled labour there is an abundance of supply, and not enough jobs. In these circumstances, the rise in the unskilled wage rate relative to the exchange rate, as indicated above, is a major difficulty for the future, as an abundant resource is being priced as if it were scarce.

The government adopted an Incomes Policy in 1972 (Government Paper No. 2 of 1972, *National Policy on Incomes, Employment, Prices and Profits*). The policy recognized that government was to be the wage/salary leader in the economy, and that private and parastatal sectors should follow government in both the level and structure of wages. A fundamental objective was to prevent the extreme short-term scarcity of skilled manpower from leading to the creation of a wage-salary élite. This could be a severe problem, especially with expatriate managements bargaining with local labour unions. While the implementation of the policy has produced considerable strain, government has been able to exercise considerable restraint on the practices of the private sector and of parastatal bodies.

Fourthly, has government been able to perform a role as financial intermediary, transferring resources to the productive sectors of the economy and away from those that must be tax-supported? As indicated above, the establishment of the PDSF was a major step in the direction of providing long-term finance for sectors of the economy that were meant to be cost-covering: parastatals producing housing, water, and electricity, the Botswana Development Corporation, etc. The PDSF has made substantial loans over the seven years since it was established. In the case of the Botswana Power Corporation (BPC), the financial structure was clearly unsupportable by the small equity base initially provided, given the government's decision not to depend on imported power and the substantial diseconomies of small-scale power generation. A major refinancing, substituting equity for PDSF loans, was undertaken in 1978. Apart from the BPC, the loans have been for productive purposes in enterprises that would not otherwise have been able to find long-term capital.

Another aspect of government's intermediation efforts has come recently through the commercial banks. In the nature of a mining-led economy is the likelihood of a build-up of revenue ahead of the capacity of government to spend. This is due partly to planning capacity, partly to implementation capacity. The government realized after the establishment of the Pula that during mining-led growth, the banking system was likely to be quite liquid, but it would not have enough longer-term liabilities to assure growth of longer-term lending. Further, Botswana is not yet a large enough economy to support a fully developed long-term capital market. As a result, the Finance and Audit Act was amended in 1977 to allow the government to place deposits in commercial banks for up to five years. Arrangements were made with the banks to make such deposits available to them as their longer-term lending demand increased. The programme is new, and it cannot be evaluated yet. But it is indicative of an effort on the part of government to perform the intermediation role that *must* take place if the mining rents are to be invested in productive assets for the longer run.

The net results on intermediation are modest but in the right direction. The failure to get one major parastatal, the Power Corporation, functioning properly from the beginning is not a good sign. There have been temporary problems, now solved, with some major BDC subsidiaries, notably the brewery. However, the effort is being made, and the mechanisms have been established. On the other hand there is still a very large allocation of total capital by the government to the expansion of investment in sectors that will not be cost-covering: roads, schools, health services, etc. That these things are demanded by the population cannot be denied. Whether the balance achieved so far (which, apart from mining, places the vast majority of investment in infrastructure and government services) is consistent with the diversification and independence of the economy must still be questioned. Fortunately, the 1979 Budget Speech indicated that during the next development plan 'the share of government resources allocated to directly productive activities' would be increased.

Fifthly, how is localization going; and what is happening to the flow of expatriates and their wage/salary levels? Given the extremely rapid growth of the mining, government and modern-services sectors of the economy in this decade, the demand for skilled and trained personnel has exceeded the output capacity of the education system. As a result, the number of expatriates employed has continued to rise, both in government and in the private sector. Between the 1974 and 1977 employment surveys, for example, the numbers of expatriates rose from 950 to 1770 in government service and teaching, and from 2250 to 2460 in the rest of the economy. At the same time, 2000 expatriates and 1200 citizens earned more than P200 per month in the 1974 survey; while in 1976 2400 expatriates and only 1100 citizens earned more than P300 per month. Data for 1977, only for private and parastatal sectors, show 2010 expatriates and 850 citizens earning more than P300 per month. The problem of increasing numbers of expatriates at the higher income levels required to recruit them to Botswana is likely to continue. Government is sufficiently concerned to have had two Presidential Commissions on Localization and Training. While they have focused exclusively on the public service, the issue is a broader one. The combined effect of larger numbers and of high incomes is bound to have its impact on the ability of government to deal with wage demands from citizens, both skilled and unskilled. Thus, the difficult area of wage rates in relation to productivity and to foreign markets is likely to be made even more difficult.

Having pointed to a problem area, however, as a personal aside I must express admiration for the extent to which the government has been able to discourage conspicuous consumption on the part of expatriates in Botswana. While the contrasts between expatriate living standards and those of Batswana, even skilled senior Batswana, are certainly evident, the gap is a small fraction of the one that exists in most countries of Africa and Asia.

Sixthly, can one make any sort of judgment about 'waste' in Botswana? One would require detailed studies to do a proper evaluation, but the long lists of demonstrably bad projects and corrupt practices that one can point to in many mining countries are notably absent in Botswana. There are numerous anecdotal items in connection, for example, with the Accelerated Rural Development Programme, to the effect that a large push in construction substantially raised prices, and a Pula spent in that programme built less than had been the case before ARDP. And the 1979 experience with the insolvency of Botoka Construction Company is indicative of some of the problems of overheating the economy and a waste of resources. But by and large economic and financial control has been good, the Central Tender Board has been effective, and the police have been vigorous in pursuing cases of suspected misappropriation of funds, regardless of the level or status of alleged miscreants. As indicated earlier, the most substantial question one can raise is whether the expenditure on large infrastructure projects (each well justified and reasonably well executed) has been overextended at the expense of productive projects that would be less dependent on the public purse and would employ more individuals.

Finally, how has the government managed in dealing with the adverse effects of the wage/exchange rate relationship stressed earlier? On the positive side, the Central Tender Board now gives modest local preference for purchase of its manufactured items. The provision in the Customs Union Agreement providing for the temporary protection of a local industry has been used in the case of the brewery (though many aspects of that project have been less than optimal). Diversification of product line by the Botswana Meat Commission into manufactured beef and the tanning of hides has begun. But, on the negative side, the provisions of the Customs Union have not been pushed aggressively, manufacturing output has not advanced much (either for local production or for export), and production of arable agriculture has been on a downward trend (partly, no doubt, due to the increased profitability of cattle farming in recent years, but also due to wage increases relative to the price of foreign exchange).

In connection with the wage rate/exchange rate relationship, the Pula revaluation of April 1977 bears mention. In the Vice-President's address explaining the rationale for the revaluation (which was to mitigate the inflationary effects of the 1977 budget measures in South Africa, Botswana's principal source of imports), he mentioned that there would be a small penalty for exporters as a result of the revaluation. Naturally, there would also be a similar penalty for producers of import competing goods, as imports would become cheaper in Pula terms while domestic costs, particularly wages, would remain unchanged. The key question in assessing the longer-run effects of the Pula revaluation is what *would* have happened in the absence of the revaluation during the 1978 review of salaries by the government, and subsequently by the private sector. It seems clear from the evidence presented in the Bank of Botswana's *Annual Report* for 1977 that the 5 per cent revaluation of the Pula did have the effect of slowing the rate of price increases in Botswana to a level below that for similar goods in South Africa. To the extent that this lower rate of increase in the price level led to lower rates of increases in money wages during 1978 (something that can only be the subject of conjecture to outsiders), the revaluation of the Pula would not have adversely affected the longer run wage/exchange rate relationship. A key issue for the future is to assure that the entire package of government policies is consistent with sufficient incentives to producers (both of import-competing goods and of non-mineral exports) to overcome the adverse effects on their profitability arising in a situation of sizeable mining rents accruing to government.

Conclusion

I believe the evidence is clear from other countries that have gone through periods of substantial mineral-led growth that a variety of pressures are inherent in such situations, tending to frustrate efforts both to diversify the productive base of the economy and to spread the benefits of development more widely. These pressures are focused in a small nexus of activities related to the mining companies, the central government, and the financial system; and within this nexus, to the relationships that evolve between the exchange rate and the wage rates in the economy. Unless a government is committed to a longer view of the development process, is willing and able to resist the temptation to spend everything in the bank the moment it arrives, has the capacity to analyse and choose projects consistent with long-run and broad-based development, and is able to deal successfully with the delicate issues of wage and incomes policy in the presence of sizeable numbers of highly compensated expatriates on temporary contract; it is likely to drift into a situation where the economic rents from nature's 'gift' to the economy are shared by a small number of well-paid citizens, employed in mining, government and their immediate service industries and enjoying good infrastructure and basic services financed by the same source. Goals such as those of Botswana's National Development Plans of rapid growth, social justice, economic independence and sustained production will simply not be met.

To date, with nearly a decade of mining-led development already behind her, Botswana must be graded well above average in the capacity to manage this unusual set of problems. However, the dangers *are* present, and will become more serious as the Jwaneng diamond revenues appear on the horizon. Now that much of the basic infrastructure lacking at Independence has been put in place, and the educational system and other aspects of social services have been established on a fairly wide basis, the question for the next decade of development must be one of whether the revenues from mining can successfully be re-invested *outside* the government sector. This will require attention to all the points mentioned above, but most particularly the need for government to be an effective financial intermediary, moving mining revenues into productive investment, and the need to keep the wage/productivity/exchange rate relationship under sufficient control so that the enterprises with access to financing from the mineral revenues also have the needed incentives to invest productively.

Stephen R. Lewis, Jr is Professor of Economics, Williams College, USA and Economic Consultant, Ministry of Finance and Development Planning, Botswana, and formerly Economic Consultant Ministry of Finance and Economic Planning, Kenya.

3 Arable Agriculture in Botswana: a Case for Subsidies

DAVID JONES

Introduction: economic distortions

The thesis of this paper is that there are 'distortions' in Botswana's economy that depress arable agriculture, and that the situation might be improved by use of subsidies, or by other manipulation of the price mechanism.

The value-loaded word 'distortion' is often loosely used to support special pleading by interest groups wanting assistance. Many such 'distortions' are fraudulent: for example, high-cost producers of labour-intensive products in developed countries insist that their markets are being distorted by lower-priced imports from developing countries. Other 'distortions' are so permanent a feature of the economic landscape that it is better policy to exploit them than to try and reverse their effects; for example, the world price of sugar is chronically depressed by the protectionist activities of many consuming countries. This is a distortion that makes exports unprofitable for potential exporting countries, but it would not be in the latters' interests to 'correct' this distortion by subsidies – unless they believed that the distortion was temporary.'

I shall argue that in the case of Botswana's arable sector, the distortions are such that they are either likely to be temporary, thus putting Botswana's economic security at risk, or such that it is *currently* in Botswana's interest to take countervailing measures.

The situation of arable agriculture in Botswana

Botswana is not an ideal country for arable farming. Most of the soils are of poor to very poor fertility and rainfall is low – generally less than 500 mm (20 in) per year – and highly variable from year to year. The brief rainy season from October to March is followed by very cold nights, and even frosts, in May and June, giving a short growing season for most crops. Despite this, there is a tradition of extensive low input arable farming, in the relatively more fertile hardveld soils where most people live – with sorghum, maize, millet, beans and melons as the main crops. It is technically possible in these areas to obtain yields

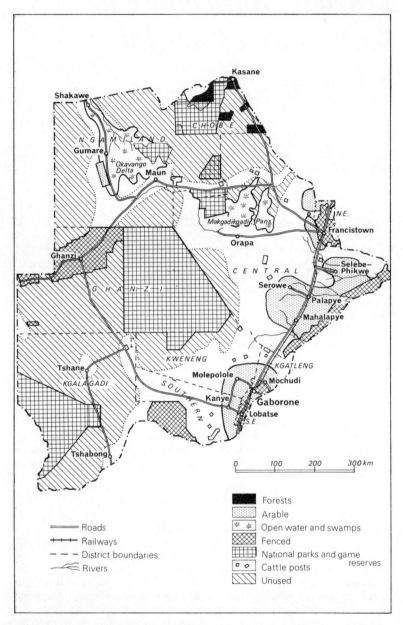

Figure 3.1 *Present land use in Botswana*

of two tonnes per hectare (2.47 acres) for the cereal crops in most years.[1] Actual yields, however, average around 200 kg (440 lb).

. Much grain is sold or exchanged in informal local markets, but the price structure is increasingly influenced by the prices of the Botswana Agricultural Marketing Board (BAMB) – a government parastatal company. The BAMB would necessarily be the main instrument in any deliberate grain price policy. Up to now, BAMB prices have been set only a few percentage points above South African Maize Board prices, because of fears about smuggling. There might also be legal complications arising from the South African Customs Union Agreement if Botswana raised domestic prices and tried to deny access to South African produce, although such problems would certainly not pose an insuperable barrier.[2] In 1979, BAMB raised the gap between internal and South African release prices to about 20 per cent, but still kept within the margin of natural protection afforded by the transport costs between South African producing areas and Botswana consuming/processing centres.

Although land is free for most potential users, arable farming as a preferred occupation comes after local wage employment and self-employment with cattle and, for many people, after migrant labour. About 16 per cent of the potential labour-force prefers work in the Republic of South Africa – some 20 000 in the mines, and 40–50 000 in other employment (mainly farming). Out of 70 000 households involved in crop production,[3] probably only a few thousand regard themselves as arable farmers by choice or vocation.

What is somewhat more surprising is that some households appear to prefer non-employment to arable agriculture – or else have unutilized labour time which they either cannot, or will not, sell to the arable sector. Many households appear to depend almost wholly on transfers and remittances.[4]

Lipton has estimated that as much as 45 per cent of potential labour time in Botswana is unused.[5] This may well be an overestimate,[6] but there almost certainly is unused labour time that could theoretically have been employed in agriculture, and this is not because of lack of land or lack of demand for food. Domestic cereal production has rarely exceeded 100 000 tonnes, while cereal consumption, including processed products (mainly maize meal) exceeds 200 000 tonnes a year.[7]

To tackle this situation, the government of Botswana has announced that it will set up an Arable Lands Development Programme (ALDEP), whose twin goals will be employment creation and self-sufficiency in basic foodstuffs. An ALDEP preparation team was established in the Ministry of Agriculture in mid-1978, and was given a two-year planning period to come up with a package of measures. Frequent reference will be made here to two discussion papers produced by the ALDEP team: 'Technology Packages', and a subsequent paper 'Pricing and Subsidies' which updates some of the data in the earlier paper. The Technology Package paper proposes a step-by-step advancement of small farmers from their present technology.

At the rural householder's level, there are some fairly simple reasons why agriculture is at the bottom of the pile. The returns to arable activity are poor. The Rural Income Distribution Survey (RIDS) reported an annual value of arable output per household of P126 in 1974–5 – P114 after deducting production expenses.[8] While the methodology behind this calculation is open to questions,[9] the magnitudes were probably about right. The ALDEP team's calculations indicate that a household, using 'traditional' methods of broadcasting seed before the plough and minimizing other cultivation activities, cultivating two and a half hectares (6 acres) each of maize and sorghum and one (2½ acres) of beans, would have earned a net return to labour (including subsistence) of P206·83 for 96 man-days' work,[10] or P2·15 per man-day, using the BAMB buying price as a basis for valuation. Since the yield from this area only narrowly exceeds the subsistence needs of an average household, it is arguable that the real value to the household is higher than this. If the returns from crop farming are to be compared with the returns from (mainly urban) wage employment, the BAMB release price would be a better basis for valuation. On this basis, the net income would rise to P245·22, or P2·55 per man-day (valuing excess over subsistence at BAMB purchase price).[11]

This is not a bad rate of pay – if it is correct. There is, however, much uncertainty about the labour coefficients and yields. Lipton[12] estimated labour inputs 23 per cent higher than those of the ALDEP team, and preliminary farm management statistics for 1977–8 indicate lower average yields and higher average labour inputs, which would mean that even at the higher BAMB release price valuation, total net return to labour would be only P129·7 for 176 man-days on the crop hectarages outlined – P0·74 per man-day. This, incidentally, tallies with the reported wage rate of P0·66 per man-day in traditional arable agriculture,[13] and the RIDS data.

The presumption must be that the net returns given in the ALDEP paper are more likely to be too high than too low. Even if they are right, however, this six-hectare model represents about the maximum that can be cultivated by one household using traditional techniques. To increase labour and cash inputs per hectare (cultivating, weeding, manuring) would actually have led to a reduction in the return per man-day. For example, the 'highest' ALDEP 'package' (involving 2 ha. (5 acres) each of maize and sorghum, and 1 each of beans and sunflower using row planting, fertilizer, planter and cultivator) would raise total net income to P380,[14] but it would raise man-days of labour input to 230 (using ALDEP coefficients), so that the net return to labour per man-day would be only P1·65. Arable farming on this scale does not, therefore, compare favourably with the minimum wage in government employment of P2·30 a day – P672 for a 48-week working year – or with the non-farm private-sector minimum wage of P2·16 a day, or with mine employment in South Africa at over P100 a month plus – however unsatisfactory – food and lodging.

Resource-poor households also face serious practical obstacles to successful involvement in arable agriculture. Arable farming requires access to capital assets, in the form of a plough and a source of draught-power. The very poor lack such assets and the wherewithal to rent them. There are traditional means by which they obtain access: provision of labour in plough-planting fields of wealthier people in exchange for subsequent loan of plough and/or oxen (*majako*), and simple borrowing from relatives. However, the non-owner is last in the queue, and may well have to plough at an unfavourable time. There may also be a labour availability problem, even in a household with unemployed labour-time. Arable farming involves heavy tasks that are normally considered to be men's work; plough-planting requires a minimum of two people. A poor household is likely to have a single resident adult member – often a woman – who cannot easily do the heavy work of ploughing and de-stumping the land.

It must, however, be doubted whether these handicaps are enough to explain why a substantial amount of labour-time remains unused and why about two-thirds of cleared land appears to remain unploughed even in the more densely populated parts of the country. There are established mechanisms for the pooling and/or exchange of labour.[15] There is no shortage of draught animals, and a simple ox-plough costs only P70. If the factors, labour and land, are in excess supply and have been so for a long time, their rentals should be low and entrepreneurs should have developed arrangements to employ them profitably in crop production.

To some extent, this has happened. Arable land in tribal areas is, in principle, free, and is allocated according to need. Those with the ability to cultivate large areas may be allocated far more land than is necessary to feed a single household, sometimes running to more than 100 ha. (240 acres), but there are limits to the area that a Land Board will allocate to a single household; and entrepreneurs with ploughs and draught-power (often tractors) do operate on a limited scale, share-cropping unused land and giving the person who has lent the land a share of the harvest. This, however, makes the situation more puzzling. The mechanism exists and works; the constraint is not, therefore, one of absolute social or structural rigidity. And yet, unemployed labour-time exists side by side with potential productive employment.

Why does this situation exist? There are several answers apart from low productivity.

Exchange rate, minerals and meat

The exchange rate is unfavourable to arable agricultural production. For arable crop farmers, the Pula is overvalued.[16] This statement does not require a great deal of empirical verification. The situation is that there is unemployment of resources, there are opportunities to produce a good which is in internal demand, and the exchange rate is such that the good in question is imported instead of being produced domestically. It follows that the domestic currency is overvalued. One has to ask how this situation can continue. Normally (or neo-classically) in such a situation one would expect unemployment to bring down the price of labour and thus correct the over-valuation of the currency. Further, if the situation of trade deficit plus uncompetitiveness that clearly characterizes the crop sector was general to the whole economy, pressures on the balance of payments would tend to lead to a corrective devaluation.

The basic reason why the latter does not happen is that Botswana's overall payments position is healthy, despite a productive economy that in most sectors is high cost, underdeveloped and actually non-existent for most manufactures.[17] The situation is outlined in Table 3.1. A substantial negative balance on visible and invisible trade has been offset by positive net grants and transfers (aid and Customs Union receipts), and capital inflows. Official reserves and unofficial holdings of currencies have both tended to increase. This has even caused some embarrassment. The Bank of Botswana revalued the Pula by 5 per cent in 1977, and again in September 1979, to spread the benefit of Botswana's prosperity by making imports cheaper.[18] Commercial banks have several times dropped their rate on time deposits, for example from 7·5 per cent to 4 per cent on three month deposits over a three year period, reflecting the rates paid by the Bank of Botswana on the deposits that the banks have to hold, and the surplus of liquidity in the banking system. Botswana must be one of the easiest developing countries to transfer money out of, as the Bank of Botswana has progressively eased even paper restrictions.

Table 3.1   *Balance of payments 1975–8 (P million)*

Item	1975	1976	1977	1978
Balance of visible trade	−55	−39	−49	−72
Services (net)	+8	−10	−7	−33
Transfers	+16	+50	+79	+84
Current account	−32	+1	+23	−21
Capital	+57	+25	+2	+50
Overall balance	+25	+26	+25	+29

Note
In 1977 P33 million of loans to Botswana was converted into grants: this is shown as a transfer into Botswana and an outward capital flow of P33 million.
Source
Bank of Botswana Annual Reports (1976 and 1977 figures were adjusted in the 1978 Report from the figures shown in the 1977 Report).

In bankers' terms, the prognosis for the Pula is excellent. Diamonds are now the largest export item, and receipts from existing mines are rising, while the new mine at Jwaneng is preparing to come into production. Diamonds are not Botswana's only mineral. Copper–nickel matte is the third largest export item, and there are huge known deposits of coal, and of low-grade copper, while evidence of other minerals has been provided by a recent geomagnetic survey. At present, prospects for copper and nickel are uncertain, while other minerals have yet to be developed. Based on diamonds alone, however, it is likely that mineral export revenues will rise for some years. To some extent, high imports represent investment in mineral production, and are automatically offset by simultaneous capital inflows. A large proportion of the transfer item is Customs Union revenue on the same goods.

Apart from minerals, beef and associated livestock products – the traditional mainstay of the economy – remain a strong export area. The 'cream' on beef exports is provided by an arrangement whereby Botswana exports 17 360 tonnes of deboned beef a year to the EEC duty-free, and pays only 10 per cent of the levy normally charged on third country imports. Over the life of the first Lomé Convention this gave Botswana a price some 60 per cent higher than exports to alternative markets, and approximately doubles the price which the Botswana Meat Commission can pay to farmers.

The going rate for labour

Little is known of the details of rates of pay for labour involved in the traditional arable sector. It clearly varies according to category of labour and type of work (male more than female; ploughing more than bird-scaring). It often involves payments in kind that are hard to measure. Lipton speaks of 25 thebe (100 thebe = 1 pula) a day being a common wage for a female bird-scarer.[19] The draft farm management statistics for 1977–8 quote an average actual rate of 66 thebe a day.[20] This is meant to include payments in kind, although in such a difficult area one can have little confidence in statistics which have been collected 'incidentally' – that is, in the absence of an enquiry directed specifically at this particular problem. One can, however, be fairly certain that normal rates of remuneration of labour in this sector are well below formal sector wage rates, because farmers could not conceivably afford to pay such wage rates. Despite the existence of unemployed labour, one of the commonest complaints of arable farmers is that there is a shortage of labour. The construction one must put on this complaint is that, for many of those with unused labour time, the rate of pay at which they will work exceeds the amount arable farmers are willing to pay.

If the exchange rate will not be forced down to make arable production competitive, why does not the pressure of unemployment force down the going rate for labour (including own labour)? The answer is four-fold: first, most modern-sector employers in Botswana have been under no pressure to lower wages in order to be competitive. Rather they have put pressure on government to let them raise wages. Secondly, the South African mines have, until recently, provided a source of relatively lucrative employment for unemployed able-bodied males. Thirdly, the livestock sector is artificially made more profitable by the beef arrangement with the European Economic Community. And fourthly, transfers and remittances, from these sectors, have created a safety net of incomes that has permitted the unemployed in Botswana to spurn poorly remunerated arable agriculture.

To elaborate, the largest productive activity in Botswana in economic terms is producing diamonds. This is essentially a matter of digging a large amount of foreign exchange out of the ground. It is highly profitable, and uses little labour; Orapa and Letlhakane provide 1500 citizen jobs and Jwaneng will provide a further 1100.[21]

It is in the employer's interest to pay this small labour force high wages, because high wages both attract better labour and buy industrial peace (which allows the capital equipment to go on working); given the small size of the labour force, it would be a false economy to try and let wages sink to their 'natural' level.

One might have expected more downward pressure on wages in the copper–nickel mine and smelter, because this has been unprofitable. However, this again is a very capital intensive enterprise with a small labour force – only 3000 – and the same considerations apply as for diamonds. In the beef export sector, the main formal sector employer is the Botswana Meat Commission, which is also in a similar position to the diamond sector in that a small, highly trained labour force is working with a lot of sophisticated capital in a highly profitable operation.

Apart from mining and meat processing, there are few industrial or commercial enterprises in Botswana apart from those that enjoy a high degree of natural protection. Construction and services in Botswana cannot be wholly imported. Some people actually do go to the Republic of South Africa to do their shopping, or get their cars repaired, but most service enterprises can rely on the natural protection of transport costs, or the simple need to have services here and now, to make up for their inefficiency and high prices. It is a fair approximation to say that there is no commercial modern-sector enterprise in Botswana which is not able to support high real wage costs.

Government, the largest wage employer, has felt little pressure to resist normal demands for higher wages. Its rapidly increasing revenues have permitted it to pay ever higher wages, and its acceptance of the role of pacemaker for the private sector has increased the upward pressures.

Mine labour in South Africa has an even more long-standing role as a counter-attraction to potential agricultural labour. It has long constituted an apparently inexhaustible supply of employment for healthy able-bodied Batswana. The mines, and the government of the Republic of South Africa, preferred to recruit foreign labour on contract rather than employ black South Africans. This kept down the price of labour, and created a labour force which was internally divided, unstable, had few claims to permanency and was difficult to unionize.[22]

Already in the 1930s Schapera[23] speaks of mine labour as an established – almost traditional – institution. In the early 1970s recruiting reached a peak. External pressures on South Africa to increase black wages coincided with a rising gold price, and an expansion in mining. Cash wages rose to about R100 a month, matched by income in kind of the same order of magnitude, and in 1976 recruitment peaked at 40 000,[24] but has since gone into rapid decline.

The reason for this is that government policy in South Africa now favours a stable, local (including Bantustan) *élite* black labour force, and this harmonizes with the mining companies' wish to mechanize and transform their black labour force to one that is more highly skilled as well as smaller. Mine recruiting has almost ceased in some parts of Botswana, for example Ngamiland, and recruitment is limited to those who have already served at least one contract period (9 months) in the mines. Total recruiting in 1979 was expected to be less than 20 000.[25] The indications are that this decline will continue.

Outside the formal sector, the EEC beef arrangement has greatly increased returns from livestock relative to arable farming. It has, for example, been possible to organize beef production on an export basis even in the northern areas of Botswana which are furthest from the BMC's single export abattoir at Lobatse. Without the EEC arrangement to hold up prices (and without a northern abattoir)[26] beef production in these areas would have remained very largely on a subsistence basis, and the economics of even such traditional commercial producing areas as Ghanzi would have been thrown into question.[27]

Further, the increased commercial value of cattle is probably a disincentive to ploughing – even for people who own no cattle. This is because cattle owners are aware that use for ploughing reduces the sale value of their cattle. Not only are they more reluctant to use their cattle for ploughing their own lands (the reasoning behind a noticeable shift to use of donkeys for ploughing) but also, they no longer see loan of cattle to poorer relatives as a piece of costless charity.

Transfers

The factors discussed above explain why those who have the option of working in the mines, in government, in Botswana's modern sector, or with their own cattle herds have a going wage rate higher than the returns from employment or self-employment in arable agriculture, but it does not explain why those without this option should also be in a position to reject arable agricultural employment. The answer lies in the network of transfers and remittances.[28]

This network operates at a number of levels. At the village level there is a network of kinship: Solway says in the *Report on Dutlwe Village* 'as long as some people have food, no one will starve'.[29] This may be an extreme case, since the whole village is descended from common ancestors, but a similar situation of inter-household transfers appears to be common.

The network of remittances from migrant labour accounts for substantial flows of cash. 'Deferred pay' (pay drawn at end of contract) of mine labourers amounted to P10·5 million in 1977, and a further P2·5 million in remittances passed through official channels.[30] There must also be substantial remittances from the even greater number of Batswana in non-mine employment in the Republic of South Africa, as well as from household members in wage employment in Botswana. The line between remittances, and cash income from household members is, of course, blurred, but Sheppard reported that 30 per cent of household members in his Kweneng drought survey received remittances, and 32 per cent had at least one member earning a wage (the two categories of income not overlapping).[31] In the same survey, half of the households involved in *majako* – work for payment in kind – had either a resident or an absent household member earning a wage.[32] Lastly, one should mention that the Institutional Feeding Programme, supplied via the World Food Programme, provides one meal a day for almost a third of the population – school children, TB patients, pregnant and nursing mothers.

The outcome of these mechanisms – all highly desirable in limiting real rural poverty – is a thick cushion of transfers into rural households. The RIDS estimated that in 1974–5 almost all rural households had substantial transfers in. The lowest 0·5–10 per cent of households received an average of 21 per cent of all their disposable income in this way: P34 per household. For these households (many of which were elderly single people) transfers were the largest source of incomes. Households from the 15th–50th percentiles received an average of P60, or 14 per cent of all incomes, and even households from the 60th–95th percentiles received an average of P70 – 4 per cent of disposable incomes.

The impact on output

The conclusion is a simple one: although only a quarter of the potential citizen labour force is in wage employment, and another 10 per cent have enough cattle to be able to afford to make significant transfers to other households,[33] the network of transfers and remittances from these sources is sufficient to permit many people who have no other source of profitable employment to reject the low and risky returns of employment or self-employment in arable agriculture – or to indulge in arable agriculture only on a minimum-effort-maximum-return-to-labour basis. Is this a bad thing?

Clearly, sharing of what would otherwise be very unequally distributed income is not, in itself, objectionable. Nor is it necessarily a bad thing that people prefer to have idle time rather than indulge in arable agriculture for low returns. Certainly this leads to a loss of potential National Product, but National Product does not measure the disutility of work, and since people are freely acting out their preferences, they are better off than if they did work harder at arable agriculture, given the present set of prices. If we are concerned with maximizing national *welfare*, the question that has to be asked is whether the set of prices can be altered so that people can produce more *and* consider themselves better off without equivalent losses of 'welfare' or production elsewhere. If they could, it would, of course, reduce the degree of income inequality which leads to the network of transfers. *Transfers to potential arable producers are the consequence of poor returns to arable agriculture, not the cause.*

Three other cogent arguments can be advanced for government intervention to change the present situation:

1   It increases the rate of rural-urban migration, which is socially disruptive and costly, since it leads to urban unemployment. Again, this is a consequence of the poor returns to arable agriculture.
2   Botswana has become dangerously dependent on cereal production in the Republic of South Africa. Supplies could easily be curtailed, either deliberately, to exert pressure on Botswana, or incidentally, as a result of the explosion of racial/social unrest that can fairly reliably be predicted.
3   The factors which make the network of income transfers possible are all temporary or subject to uncertainty. Migrant labour in the Republic of South Africa is almost certain to fall rapidly for reasons already stated. Mineral deposits all have finite lives, and the diamond market could conceivably collapse. Presently it is in a speculative boom, partly because of fear of holding money, but speculative booms can be spectacularly reversed. It is even conceivable that the diamond market could be undermined by synthetic diamonds if the present cartel is broken. The EEC beef arrangement is at the grace and favour of the EEC, and there are strong internal EEC pressures working against it. It is probably safe for the five years of the next Lomé Convention, but is not wholly secure for even that long, as veterinary considerations, like foot and mouth disease, can halt exports.

Arguments 1, 2 and 3 are all reasons why it might be in the national interest to devote more resources to arable agriculture, even at the expense of production or 'welfare' lost in other sectors. I would argue strongly, however, that it is possible to meet the more stringent condition that incomes in arable agriculture can be increased without countervailing losses of income or welfare elsewhere.

At present, Botswana's increasing income is in very large measure soaked up by a minority of wage earners, predominantly urban, predominantly in non-productive sectors. Lipton has amply demonstrated that formal sector wage-earners are an 'aristocracy'. In particular, there is no apparent limit to the ability of the public service to absorb revenues. Government is the largest wage employment sector, and since Independence its payroll has grown by 10 per cent a year, while minimum wages have grown in real terms by about 9 per cent a year.[34] The impact of this process is to worsen income distribution, increase rural-urban migration and weaken competitiveness in productive sectors. Few people would dispute that an extra Pula used to remunerate arable producers would lead to a greater increment in real output and real employment than the same Pula spent on public sector employment.

The political 'pull' of the public sector, is however, such that it will continue to soak up resources, unless strong countervailing pressure groups can be created that contribute to production and wider income distribution. At present, there is such a pressure group in the beef sector, which government neglects at its peril. Arable producers are presently too weak and insignificant to constitute an equivalent pressure group, but if arable farming was made highly profitable for only five years, it would be difficult ever to withdraw the assistance given. And, paradoxically, the economy would benefit. It would produce more, it would provide more employment, and it would be protected to some extent against disasters in other sectors.

How can resources be channelled to arable agriculture?

It has been suggested that Botswana uses a special exchange rate for the mineral sector – essentially as a cure for the same disease. I am by no means convinced that such a system can be made to work in a sufficiently watertight way to achieve its ends, without being so bureaucratic as to constitute a real obstacle to both trade and development of the minerals sector.

A general devaluation of the Pula would have the effect of stimulating all domestic producing sectors, including mining, but the cost would be borne by all consumers, including the poor, thus worsening income distribution and there is no reason to suppose that the objectives of transferring resources from minerals to arable agriculture, or of limiting the resource flow to the public service, would be achieved.

The ALDEP paper on Pricing and Subsidies comes out strongly in favour of government subsidizing arable farming, but argues that it should subsidize infrastructure rather than pay higher BAMB prices for crops and subsidize consumers. The benefits of this approach are:

1   that aid can be directed towards specific technical improvements;
2   it is possible to give disproportionately greater amounts of aid to smaller farmers;
3   it is possible to subsidize households' production for their own consumption;
4   it creates a flow of benefits over many years;
5   it limits problems of cross-border smuggling and complications arising from the Southern African Customs Union Agreement.

These are all good arguments. However, two questions must be raised. First, whether we really wish to tie most subsidies to arable agriculture to the adoption of specific technologies; secondly, whether this approach alone can increase profitability enough to effect the radical change in attitudes that appears to be needed.

On the first point, two presumptions are being made: that the 'experts' are better than the farmers in choosing production techniques, and are thus justified in 'rigging' relative prices to get their prescriptions adopted; and that farmers will in fact respond as required to the new relative prices. Now, no doubt there are quite a few areas where officials of the Ministry of Agriculture do know best, but their record is far from perfect. Some would argue that the most remarkable aspect of established official wisdom on agriculture in many countries is that it is continually being reversed. Peasant farmers, however, have a fairly consistent record of adapting new technologies *within their financial and technological capacities* when these are made available. There is quite a lot to be said for making production more profitable, putting new technologies – or products – on offer, and letting farmers adopt those they find profitable without making increased profitability conditional on adoption of predetermined packages.

This argument is stronger where, as in the ALDEP case, the new packages are not, in fact, radically new. Most farmers know about them and most have not adopted them. Certainly, when they are made cheaper, more farmers will adopt them, but are we really so sure that we have the right packages for all farmers? For this is where the Ministry of Agriculture almost certainly does not know best. The package which is most profitable for a particular farmer depends on *his* labour resources, *his* cash resources, *his* source of draught power, the amount of land *he* has available and its quality. While there will be common factors, there has also be be a package for every individual farmer, which in the end only he can work out.

By directing assistance to adoption of certain inputs we not only limit the choice of packages open to a farmer, but we also limit the number of farmers able to create their own technology packages, because only 'adopters' will benefit fully, and it is common ground that the number of adopters will at first be quite small. Increased profitability through higher crop prices is likely to influence many farmers who have no interest in adopting anything, but see that it is now worth ploughing another hectare, or weeding better, or being more serious about getting onto the lands within twenty-four hours of rain. This is a good thing because such farmers may be right, given their circumstances, in taking this approach; but even if they are wrong, improved profitability (= decreased household risk) will make them more disposed to try new methods. There is at least a strong case for mixing input and infrastructure subsidies with producer price subsidies – that is, measures that raise prices to farmers without raising them to consumers.

On the second point concerning the adequacy of the subsidy, it turns out to be quite difficult to give enough subsidies on implements and inputs to raise returns on labour to levels comparable with current minimum wages. For instance the ALDEP team suggests a 30 per cent subsidy on planters and cultivators as the highest priority. However, even if the team's labour input coefficients were right, this would raise returns per man-day by only P0·11 to P1·76. On the coefficients given, it would require both a 50 per cent planter and cultivator subsidy, and a 15 per cent output price increase to produce a return of P2·20 on the highest ALDEP package.

Because of the uncertainty that exists on labour inputs and yields, little significance can be attached to such figures. It would, however, appear that equipment subsidies alone are unlikely to make the higher ALDEP packages attractive to many farmers, let alone produce a major change of attitude towards crop production, and one should work on the premise that producer price subsidies will be needed.

Would such measures be worth the costs? Without specifying the package, we cannot detail the costs. However, to give an idea of orders of magnitude, we can roughly cost the package cited as an example – a 50 per cent subsidy on planters and cultivators, plus a 15 per cent crop price subsidy. The ALDEP team put the cost of a 30 per cent subsidy on planters and cultivators at P875 000 over five years – an average of P175 000 a year. A higher subsidy would lead to a higher adoption rate, say 50 per cent higher, leading to an average annual cost of P440 000 for this element of subsidy. At present the cost of a BAMB price subsidy would be quite low, because of the small amounts of produce marketed – 30 000 tonnes in a good year like 1978. The cost of 15 per cent subsidy on this would be about P540 000. If in five years production had risen to 200 000 tonnes, probably about 120 000 tonnes would be marketed, and the subsidy (at present day prices) would rise to P2·16 million. In this example therefore (which is rather optimistic about production), the total subsidy bill would rise from about P1 million to about P2·7 million over five years. This is a laughably small bill for obtaining extra rural incomes of at least P13·6 million (first round only), plus a sound start for rural economic transformation.

Notes

1. The Dryland Farming Research Team at the Department of Agriculture Research managed to obtain this yield even in the drought season 1978–9.
2. See Eakes, M. D., *Crop Pricing and Protection in Botswana: 1978*, Ministry of Agriculture, Gaborone (August 1978), pp. 9–14.
3. *Rural Income Distribution Survey in Botswana, 1974–5*, Government Printer, Gaborone (1977) (henceforth referred to as RIDS), p. 30.
4. RIDS, pp. 97 and 101, shows that the largest source of income for the bottom 10 per cent of households is transfers into the households.
5. Lipton, M., *Employment and Labour Use in Botswana*, Government Printer, 1978 (henceforth referred to as ELUB), Vol. I, para. 3.32.
6. Lipton has estimated unused labour time by deducting amounts of time accountable to various types of employment from a theoretical total of labour time in the economy based on an eight-hour day for 240 days a year. However, the amounts of time actually needed for these activities is somewhat uncertain, as is the amount needed for the other activities involved in staying reasonably comfortably alive in rural Botswana – such as collecting firewood and water, pounding grain, maintaining and building houses, etc. The Activities Survey conducted by Lipton, but completed after the main text of the ELUB, showed that reported 'social and recreational' activities took up 34 per cent of the time of men and 27 per cent of that of women (unweighted averages), but as the survey covered a seven-day week with a thirteen-hour day, the basic forty-hour week of a developed country wage-worker would, presumably, leave around 30 per cent of the same time period for such activities, even after making some allowance for necessary non-leisure activities, for example, household chores, child care, travel to work, outside those eight hours. Also there is necessarily a degree of seasonality in agricultural work, so that all theoretically available hours cannot easily be used up. See Duggan, W. R., *Informal Markets, Technology and Employment on Arable Lands in Botswana*, Ministry of Agriculture (1979) for a full discussion of this survey.
7. Output data from Ministry of Agriculture Planning and Statistics Unit; consumption data from Purcell, R., 'ALDEP Targets Paper' (mimeo, 1979).
8. RIDS, pp. 30, 31.
9. Data on inputs and outputs relate to two different crop years.
10. ALDEP Discussion Papers: 'Technology Packages' and 'Pricing and Subsidies' (mimeo, Ministry of Agriculture, 1979). No allowance made for costs of draught power, or amortization of plough and tackle. P15 have been allowed here for the latter item and seed, bags, etc.

11. Possibly too low a value, since many local sales take place at prices higher than those offered by the BAMB.

12. ELUB, Vol. I, para. 3.3.

13. Draft 1977–8, Farm Management Statistics, Ministry of Agriculture.

14. ALDEP papers referred to above. This figure involves an upward adjustment of the estimate in these papers for value of subsistence consumption, but nets out the amortization of planter and cultivator over a six-year life.

15. See Duggan, op. cit., for an explanation of the labour constraints and exchange mechanisms.

16. This section was written before the 5 per cent revaluation of the pula on 14 September 1979, which adds to the arguments stated here.

17. Selwyn, P., *Industries in the Southern Africa Periphery*, London, Croom Helm (1975).

18. Rees, D., 'Botswana's revaluation', *New African Development* (June 1977). The Pula subsequently dropped somewhat against most currencies, as it is tied to the dollar, but it remained at slightly more than parity with the South African Rand, which is the only currency that matters for most trade because of proximity and the preference implicit in the Customs Union Agreement.

19. ELUB, Vol. I, para. 5.9, p. 42.

20. op. cit.

21. Lipton, M., ELUB, Vol. I, p. 119.

22. Wilson, F., *Labour in the South African Gold Mines, 1911–1969*, Cambridge, Cambridge University Press (1972).

23. Schapera, I., *Migrant Labour and Tribal Life: A Study of Conditions in the Bechuanaland Protectorate*, Oxford, Oxford University Press (1947).

24. *Statistical Bulletin*, Vol. 3, no. 4 (Central Statistics Office, Gaborone, December 1978, p. 7).

25. Labour Department, Gaborone, personal communication.

26. See M. Hubbard, Chapter 4 in this book, pp. 44–65.

27. Ghanzi farmers tend to attribute the development of their area, which had been a settlement of cattle posts owned by poor whites, to the formal demarcation and fencing of the farms in the 1960s. It is arguable that the real cause was a combination of high beef prices and low fuel costs for road transport.

28. It is possible to draw a vague distinction between 'transfers' between households living close to one another, and remittances from household members living and working elsewhere, for example, in South Africa or Gaborone. However, this is not a very useful distinction, since many remittances really are transfers (unrequited gifts) from people who are effectively outside the local economy.

29. Solway, J. S., *Report on Dutlwe Village* (Rural Sociology Unit, Ministry of Agriculture, Gaborone, April 1979).

30. Central Statistics Office, Gaborone, *Statistical Bulletin*, Vol. 4, no. 1 (March 1979). There would also be remittances made through unofficial channels but total transfers to households in Botswana are probably less than the total of deferred pay plus official remittances, because returning miners often spend some or all of their deferred pay without returning home.

31. Sheppard, C., *Coping with Drought in Botswana* (Interim Report, Rural Sociology Unit, Ministry of Agriculture, Gaborone, August 1979), pp. 28, 30. On page 28 it is reported that 28 per cent of households receive wage income, but on page 30, Table 14, a figure of 32 per cent is given.

32. op. cit., p. 24.

33. According to RIDS, p. 111, 8 per cent of households own more than 45 head of cattle. At 9 per cent offtake rate, 45 cattle provide a cash income of P650 if the owner can sell cattle direct to BMC without going through an agent or incurring rail or motor transport charges – but the majority of small owners do sell through agents and do incur such charges. 10 per cent is therefore a generous estimate of the proportion of households able to make significant transfers out of their cattle enterprises.

34. Lipton, ELUB.

David Jones is with the Ford Foundation, Nairobi; formerly Consultant, Ministry of Agriculture, Botswana.

4 Botswana's Beef Export Industry: the Issue of the Proposed Northern Abattoir

MICHAEL HUBBARD

Introduction[1]

The period since Independence in 1966 has been one of unprecedented expansion in Botswana's beef cattle industry, despite the recent setback caused by the epidemic of foot and mouth disease since October 1977. From 1966 to 1977, net sales of the Botswana Meat Commission (BMC), which processes all of Botswana's meat exports at the Lobatse abattoir, rose from P7 million to P42 million (sixfold), the number of cattle slaughtered rose from 132 000 to 197 000 (up 49 per cent), the average price paid to producers rose from P52 to P156 (threefold), while the net sales value per beast rose from P51 to P214 (fourfold). During the same period the country's cattle population approximately doubled in size, from 1·5–3 million (see Table 4.1).

Two observations suggested by this basic information are: first, the percentage increase in cattle slaughtered was only about half the increase in the cattle population. Secondly, increased export prices have contributed almost twice as much as increases in number of cattle slaughtered to the rise in net sales (66 per cent against 34 per cent). Most of the rise in export prices occurred 1972–4.

It follows, first, that percentage offtake for export has possibly fallen ('possibly', because the herd-size figures are only estimates); secondly, it might appear that the boom in the industry, particularly since 1972, has been to a large extent a monetary one. But the rising price, together with rising incomes caused by rapidly increasing state employment and generally favourable rainfall during the period, have called forth the most frenetic expansion of cattle production in the country's history, through herd building and borehole drilling. In turn this has brought large tracts of land in the drier parts of the country into regular grazing use for the first time. The expansion of cattle production has raised the question of the adequacy and location of processing facilities.

The purpose of the present paper is threefold:

1   to tell the story of the Northern Abattoir Proposal and throw some light on how the main actors in the post-independence beef industry (government,

Table 4.1 *Basic data on BMC's throughput, sales, payments and offtake*

Year	(1) BMC throughput	(2) Net sales (P'000)	(3) Payments to owners (P'000)	(4) Payments to owners / net sales	(5) Payments to owners / throughput (Pula)	(6) Net sales / throughput (Pula)	(7) Cattle population ('000)	(8) % BMC offtake
1966	132 232	6805	6915	1·02	52·30	51·46	1237	11
1967	88 535	11 120	6370	0·57	71·95	125·60	1492	6
1968	103 776	10 593	8059	0·76	77·66	102·08	1688	6
1969	93 074	9334	7426	0·80	79·78	100·28	1945	5
1970	127 317	11 915	9248	0·78	72·64	93·59	2017	6
1971	167 180	14 962	12 143	0·81	72·64	89·50	2092	8
1972	156 510	19 547	15 096	0·77	96·45	124·89	2177	7
1973	209 443	31 297	26 496	0·85	126·51	149·43	2117	10
1974	186 041	34 711	27 986	0·81	150·43	186·58	2316	8
1975	188 440	33 889	27 386	0·81	145·33	179·84	2564	7
1976	211 987	44 814	31 832	0·71	150·16	211·40	2989	7
1977	196 850	42 042	30 782	0·73	156·37	213·57	3124	6
1978	149 346	31 133	21 714	0·69	145·39	209·76	3454	4

Sources

BMC Annual Reports and Accounts, Columns (1), (2) and (3).
Ministry of Agriculture, 'A Handbook of Livestock Statistics', 1978, Column (7).

BMC, the EEC, breeders and fatteners–speculators) have perceived the proposal in relation to their interests at different times.

2   to show how the Northern Abattoir Proposal relates to the central issues under discussion in the industry today: grazing land tenure reform and contingency planning against drought.

3   to set up a broad framework within which the micro-economic planning problems of the northern abattoir might be discussed.

Central issues: grazing lands and drought

During the period of boom a debate has taken place within Botswana over the course which the expansion of cattle raising is taking and how this course should be altered. That it should be altered is generally agreed: the expansion of the national herd has caused extensive overgrazing in the areas of greatest cattle density, particularly around watering points. *How* it should be altered is the most hotly discussed issue in the industry at present, with proposed solutions focusing on changes in herd and range management. The main thrust of the government's solution is the Tribal Grazing Land Policy (TGLP)[2] under which 'commercial zones' have been defined within the communal Tribal Lands. The commercial zones are being sub-divided into private ranches (mostly of 64 sq km/25 sq mi) to be leased to private individuals or partnerships. The idea is that private landowners will ensure that their own grazing land is not degraded by poor grazing management and that grazing pressure in the remaining communal areas will be relieved by larger owners moving their herds into the commercial zones. Encouragement is also to be given to the formation of groups of small cattle owners (based in the communal areas) for co-operation to improve their herd management.

The state's research efforts for the industry have been directed towards developing a 'minimum package' of improvements in herd and range management which will ensure increased productivity and offtake and be economically attractive.[3] While the Tribal Grazing Land Policy has been much criticized, the point here is that government policy towards cattle raising is an expansionary one.

Another issue, less hotly debated but of increasing prominence in discussion, is that of government strategy in the event of a major drought. The last severe drought was in 1965–6 and each succeeding year increases the risk of another. With cattle numbers higher than ever before the losses resulting from a drought stand to be even greater than those in the mid-1960s. Two recent consultancies and a conference[4] have focused the discussion onto 'sell' and 'keep' policies. 'Keep' policies refer to those designed to maintain herds through the drought, and 'sell' policies to those designed to increase offtake quickly and efficiently. The issue hinges on the relative emphasis to be given to the two policies, their administration and their impact on small and large cattle owners.

Integral to both these debates (herd management and drought strategy) is the question of the adequacy and location of slaughtering and processing capacity in the industry, since the vast bulk of the extra offtake (generated either by herd expansion or by increased sales during a drought) will be slaughtered and processed for export. Thus the relatively less well-known discussion over whether and where a second abattoir should be constructed turns out to be rather central. After being 'on' and 'off' for several years, and a subject of some controversy among BMC, the government, northern cattle owners and the EEC, the second abattoir is now scheduled to become a reality during the next planning period (1981–5).

The northern abattoir proposal

Background

Botswana's beef industry is very small by world standards[5] and geared very highly to the export market (only about 6 per cent of marketed offtake was sold on the local market in 1976). This means that Botswana's exports have minimal effect upon the markets she sells in, while fluctuations in these markets are magnified in their effect on the domestic industry – since there is effectively no local market to which supplies can be diverted in the event of loss of export markets. Therefore, many of the historical developments in Botswana's beef industry have been in the nature of adjustments and accommodations to changes in her export markets.

Export of live cattle from Botswana began in the 1880s to the Witwatersrand, but did not regularly extend beyond neighbouring countries until the 1960s. The first successful export abattoir in Botswana was opened by the Commonwealth Development Corporation in 1954 at Lobatse. In the early 1960s, with the further expansion of demand for beef in the industrialized countries, Botswana (along with several other small beef-exporting countries of the periphery[6]) had her first extended experience of selling in larger and more distant markets: in Botswana's case, to the UK, at that time the largest single importer of beef. By the late 1960s, the UK was fast becoming Botswana's best market and the BMC's investments in processing and product innovations at the Lobatse abattoir have since then been geared more and more to the requirements and standards of that market: an increasing proportion of the kill has been deboned, chilled and vacuum-packed,[7] while the recommendations of UK veterinarians regarding the maximum veterinarily-acceptable level of throughput and alterations to equipment have been adhered to religiously.

The issue of a second export abattoir (often mooted previously) arose seriously in 1971. A decision was needed regarding improvements to the Lobatse plant to upgrade it, eliminate bottlenecks and raise its throughput capacity in order to process the increasing offtake. The question emerged as to whether enlarged capacity would not better be provided by an additional abattoir. Consultants recommended in 1972 that the Lobatse plant be stabilized at a capacity of 800 head per day and that a new 300-head-per-day plant be set up at Motopi, near Maun in the northwest. They concluded: 'The world-wide trend in beef processing is to phase out the upgrading of older, inefficient high maintenance plants in favour of building new automated operations nearer to the livestock producers.'[8] In 1973 the rains were poor and late and the Lobatse plant was overstretched to process a record kill of 209 000 head, as a result of which the abattoir's condition was reported to have deteriorated.[9] In 1974, the visiting UK veterinarian laid down a number of improvements (including a completely new by-products plant) which had to be made in order to comply with EEC veterinary measures. He also fixed the maximum daily throughput at 750 head per day.[10] This was a severe setback since the Lobatse plant had slaughtered over 1200 head per day in 1973. An emergency programme of improvements to the plant was begun, aiming for a veterinarily-acceptable capacity of 1200 head per day,[11] in order to cope with short-term increases in offtake. At the same time, the government resolved that a second abattoir (300-head-per-day capacity)[12] be constructed at Dukwe in the northeast in order to process longer-term expansion in offtake. A feasibility study[13] reported favourably on the project and the abattoir was scheduled to come into operation in 1978. Dukwe had been selected in order to share external economies (water, housing, services) with the proposed soda ash mine at Sua Pan. Despite the lack of interest by mining companies in taking on the Sua Pan venture, planning for the abattoir continued.

Although BMC had apparently been unenthusiastic from the start about the northern abattoir, they nonetheless were publicly committed to the project[14] and by early 1976 the protracted negotiations were nearly ended, with only the final formalities relating to financing remaining.[15] However, at this time, the government was involved in delicate and difficult negotiations with the EEC. When the UK joined the EEC in 1975, there were two immediate consequences for Botswana's beef exports. First, tariff and quota barriers now stood between her and her most valuable export market. Secondly, the EEC Veterinary Commission replaced the UK Ministry of Agriculture as the licensing authority for meat imports. Botswana was thus negotiating both for favourable access and acceptance of her 'veterinary credentials'. Suddenly in April 1976, the government announced that the Dukwe abattoir project would be shelved in order not to jeopardize the negotiations with the EEC. Apparently it had been impressed upon Botswana that the siting of a new abattoir producing meat intended for Europe in or adjacent to a region where foot and mouth disease was thought to be endemic, could be detrimental to a favourable outcome. Even though the Dukwe abattoir was not being planned with the European market primarily in mind, the Botswana government clearly felt it judicious to withdraw the project. BMC's negative attitude may have provided additional incentive. The rumoured European objection is difficult to comprehend in the light of the fact that neither the UK independently nor the EEC, thereafter or beforehand, proposed any special regulation[16] on the slaughter of Ngamiland cattle at Lobatse for export to Europe. It is thus open to the speculation that, in the circumstances of 1976, when the European markets were oversupplied, veterinary objections may have been voiced by some or other party as a means of discouraging increased export production in a country which had a strong case for gaining privileged access to EEC markets. Botswana has suffered from such abuse of veterinary regulations in the past in relation to the South African market, as Ettinger (1972) has documented.

The costs of the shelving of the Dukwe abattoir would later be borne by the northern population who, since the foot and mouth disease outbreaks in the north, beginning in October 1977, have been cut off from the Lobatse abattoir and therefore from export markets.[17] EEC veterinary regulations do not permit the import of any meat from an abattoir which is also slaughtering cattle from a zone[18] in which there has been a foot and mouth disease outbreak within the previous twelve months.[19] Thus in late 1977, Botswana was faced with the choice of being excluded altogether from EEC markets or isolating the northern zones and chose the latter. Had the Dukwe abattoir gone ahead as scheduled, beginning to slaughter in mid-1978, a market for northern cattle would have been provided by the time restrictions on cattle movement were lifted.

Returning to the negotiations of 1976, Botswana did manage to secure reasonably favourable access for her beef to the protected EEC markets in a special concession appended to the Lomé Convention Agreement.[20] As a result, 1976 was a record year for BMC net sales and producer prices – at a time when beef prices in the major producing countries were plummeting.

At that stage, the northern abattoir seemed to have been postponed indefinitely. But it re-entered discussion shortly thereafter in the context of contingency planning against another major drought. Sandford (1977) concluded that, given the size of the cattle population in the mid-1970s, a drought of the severity of that of the mid-1960s could result in 750 000 cattle being offered for slaughter in a single year; attention was also drawn to the inadequacy of current abattoir capacity to handle such an offtake, or even the extra offtake levels which might be expected in the event of a milder, statistically more probable drought. Since then, the case for a northern abattoir has gathered momentum under the drought banner. Most important of all has been the 1978–9 drought in the south of the country. Offtake increased sharply and the Lobatse plant operated beyond capacity in early 1979 to slaughter 1400 head per day, while almost 20 per cent of the national herd was and is still cut off from the abattoir by quarantine regulations. The result has been that BMC, an opponent of the northern abattoir proposal in the past, is now reportedly advocating it in order to cope with further increases in offtake. With the EEC rumoured to be prepared now to accept meat from a northern abattoir and with the scheduling of the project in the next development plan, all major parties involved (government, BMC and EEC) seem for the first time to be in agreement – if not about its desirability, then at least about its inevitability.

Arguments in favour

The need for additional processing capacity

1 Projections of offtake from the growing national herd indicate that the current capacity of the Lobatse abattoir will shortly be inadequate to process offtake even in years of normal rains. Estimates differ: the most conservative suggest the mid-1980s. Increased abattoir capacity has been viewed as the only long-term solution since live exports are 'counter to the government's policy of the development of meat exports'.[21] A live export strategy would in any case limit the export market possibilities for the increased offtake to Botswana's immediate neighbours.

2 The most conservative projections of the size of offtake which would occur now in the event of a major drought (400 000 head per annum)[22] exceed the most optimistic estimates of the Lobatse abattoir's maximum capacity (320 000 head per annum).[23]

3 Increased processing capacity is a logical extension of the government's policies with regard to the rest of the livestock sector, which are geared towards increasing offtake by investing in raising the productivity of herds.

The case for a second abattoir

1   Further substantial capacity cannot easily be added at the Lobatse plant. It
     was noted in 1974[24] that the outmoded double-storeyed design of the original
     1954 building made economical modification and expansion difficult. Since
     then, both the slaughtering and deboning capacity have been extended and
     a cannery has been set up on an adjacent site. Space limitations also make it
     unlikely that the abattoir could be much further extended in the locality.[25]
2   The Lobatse plant may already be suffering from diseconomies of scale,
     that is, the extensions of its capacity since 1973 may have resulted in sharply
     rising costs per head slaughtered, if the data in Figure 4.1 can be trusted.[26]
     The costs per head slaughtered (at constant 1973 prices) have risen rapidly
     since 1974. The data should only be regarded as approximations,
     nevertheless they suggest that a smaller plant slaughtering 100 000 to
     130 000 head per annum should be able to run at substantially lower
     production costs per head than the Lobatse abattoir,[27] especially if some
     costs, for example, marketing, are shared.

The case for a northern abattoir

1   The location of the only export abattoir at the southern tip of the country
     places northern cattle owners (particularly those in Ngamiland, far from
     the railway line) at a disadvantage with respect to marketing costs and ease

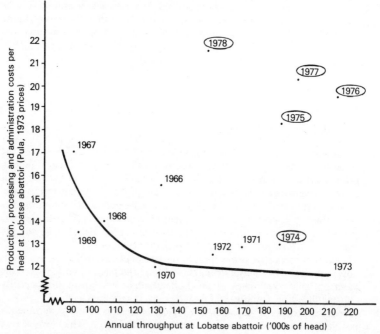

Figure 4.1   *Average costs of production at Lobatse*

of direct sale to BMC. Higher trekking and trucking costs, loss of weight and condition, danger of contraction of heartwater disease, higher risks of death during transport, higher risks of the animal being 'condemned' on arrival at Lobatse, longer periods to wait for payment – these are the extra costs that must now be paid for raising cattle in the north rather than the south. In addition, the smaller northern producer, who has inadequate finance or knowledge of how to organize direct sale of his few beasts to BMC, often has little option but to sell to middlemen at much lower net prices than would have been received at Lobatse.[28]

2 The ultimate cost is that currently experienced – being totally cut off from outside markets in the event of an outbreak of foot and mouth disease. Thus the most powerful single argument for a northern abattoir is the raw deal which the northern producer (especially the smaller one) receives during a foot and mouth outbreak in the north, by comparison with others.

3 A northern abattoir would be better situated than Lobatse to supply African markets to the north of Botswana.

4 Even for exports to the south, transport costs would be reduced because of the lower rail and road charges applicable to dead meat per unit weight than to live meat.[29] Rail freight for the deboned carcase of a 400 kg (881·85 lb) liveweight steer for Francistown to Cape Town is at present P13. The charge for the same beast railed live Francistown–Lobatse and in carcase form Lobatse–Cape Town exceeds P21.[30] This should more than offset increased freight costs on abattoir supplies from the south. Although no figures are available for the relative transport costs of livestock and meat by road in Botswana, the results of a recent study in South Africa[31] indicate that the relative savings on road motor transport of meat are so substantial that there can be little doubt that meat is cheaper to transport than livestock in Botswana by road per unit weight (on tar or good gravel roads).

5 Additional savings will result for some producers if the abattoir is located some distance west of Francistown, since it is the transport of live cattle from Ngamiland to the railhead at Francistown which is the most difficult and expensive component of transport costs.

6 A northern abattoir would increase the local level of offtake and thereby relieve the growing pressure on northern grazing lands.[32]

7 Bonemeal for supplementary feeding is in short supply in the country. The subsidization of the price of bonemeal and the present system of its distribution has aggravated its shortage for northern cattle raisers and others far from Lobatse. Supplies are quickly bought up privately at Lobatse and only a fraction is obtained by the Ministry of Agriculture for distribution across the country through its Livestock Advisory Centres. Since the subsidized price is P1·50 per bag, while the price in South Africa is P10 to P12 per bag, there is little doubt that much is taken across the border, thus subsidizing South African ranchers and depriving Batswana.[33] A northern abattoir (producing at least some boneless beef) would increase bonemeal supplies and enable northern producers to have a closer source of supply.

8 If located northwest of Francistown, the northern abattoir would provide industry and employment in an area which has had little industrial stimulus to date.

9 The major bottlenecks in cattle marketing in Botswana are assembly

facilities at loading points and the shortage of road and rail trucks. These bottlenecks are in large part the result of having to transport all the country's export slaughter-stock to Lobatse on the southern border. During a drought, these bottlenecks would be an impediment to a successful 'sell' policy. A northern abattoir would reduce the pressure on long-distance transport facilities and thus facilitate an effective 'sell' policy during a drought; a 'keep' policy would thereby also stand a better chance of success. The 'keep' policy is dependent on the 'sell' policy to relieve pressure on grazing and water and to provide farmers with funds to buy supplementary feed for their remaining stock.

10 A northern abattoir could make fattening and finishing of cattle in the north a worthwhile activity. At present, fattening and finishing is effectively confined to southern farmers and those along the railway line in the east, because of the loss of condition by animals on the long journey to Lobatse.

Arguments against

Additional processing capacity

1 It has been argued that additional processing capacity may not be needed, at least in the short term, to cope with current and expected levels of offtake. Thus McGowan (1979) concluded that unless active buying efforts were made to increase offtake, the investment in a second abattoir might not pay, since the second abattoir would then subtract from the Lobatse plant's throughput, creating expensive excess capacity at Lobatse.

2 Assuming enough offtake to make use of the expanded capacity, the additional production will result in a lower average price to producers than would otherwise be the case – as long as EEC prices are above world market levels. Botswana is forced to sell additional production on lower-priced markets. This cost would be borne by those who at present sell to the Lobatse abattoir, who might therefore be expected to create political difficulties.

3 Although increased slaughtering and processing capacity may be needed *during* a drought, decreased capacity is needed *after* a drought when, with herds severely depleted, offtake is at a minimum for two or three years at least (see Table 4.1 for BMC throughput 1967–9 following 1965–6 drought).

A second abattoir

The only argument against a second abattoir specifically would be that there are still savings to be had in the expansion of the Lobatse plant by comparison with a second abattoir. This argument carried some weight in the early 1970s when it was decided to expand Lobatse rather than stabilize it at 800 head per day capacity. With space limitations on the site and rapidly increasing production costs per head, there now seems little question of further overall expansion at Lobatse. The extension of the boneless beef department (presently 1200 head per day capacity) to bring it more into line with slaughter hall capacity (1800 head per day) is the only expansion recommended recently.

A northern abattoir

1 Remoteness–creating difficulties for administration maintenance, and transport.
2 Disease–proximity to Ngamiland where foot and mouth disease is sometimes regarded as endemic.

Location of a northern abattoir

Since the second objection to a northern abattoir has turned out to be rather specious (p. 48), only the problems associated with remoteness remain. Here the issue is less that of a northern location as such that of how far west or northwest of the railhead at Francistown the abattoir should be situated. To minimize the problems of remoteness a site near Francistown is preferable; but such a location would reduce severely the benefits of the abattoir for northwestern herders, whose major problem under the present marketing system is precisely the transport of cattle to the rail head.

The matter seems to boil down to who should pay for the remoteness from the railhead of Ngami, North Central and Chobe herds. A northwesterly location would shift some of the cost burden onto the northern abattoir, that is, onto the BMC and therefore onto cattle owners in the country as a whole. The discrimination by the existing system against cattle raisers in the northwest constitutes a strong case for sharing of the burden. But locating the abattoir in the northwest may not necessarily be the best means of sharing the burden. Abattoir development costs and running costs and cattle supplies, at various locations, need to be taken into account in deciding the location, in conjunction with alternative possible means of relieving the financial plight of northwestern herders, for example, marketing subsidies, improved trucking and trekking facilities.

Notwithstanding the above, other grounds for a northwesterly location are: (1) Northeastern producers are already close to the railhead and could therefore continue to send cattle to Lobatse should they find transport to the northern abattoir difficult. (2) Should the mooted east–west extension to the railway become a reality in the future, the remoteness of a more northwesterly location would probably be reduced. (3) Most importantly, given the greater frequency of foot and mouth disease in the northwest, if the northern abattoir is to dispose of cattle from the diseased area during an outbreak (or during the quarantine period after an outbreak), it should be located west of the Dukwe quarantine fence. Otherwise cattle from the diseased area would have to cross the fence (defeating its purpose) or be denied access to the abattoir. (4) The relative cheapness of road transport of meat by comparison with live cattle (see p. 51).

The results of feasibility studies

The benefits of a northern abattoir are largely social and political, as well as being of a long-term nature. Quantification of such benefits, except in a very

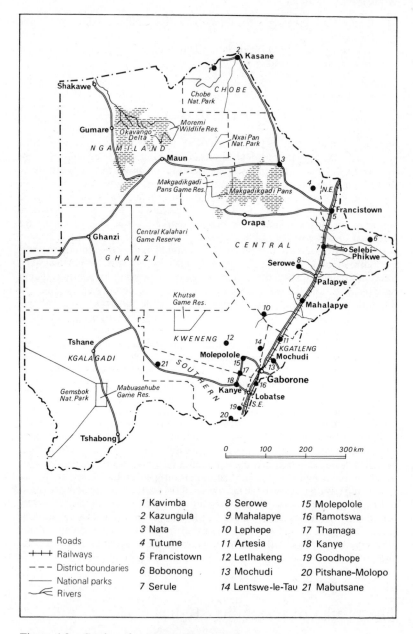

Figure 4.2   *Cattle trek routes in Botswana*

arbitrary way, is impossible. Thus the attempts in the existing feasibility studies to quantify the net benefit of the investment tend to include only the more easily quantifiable benefits and costs. Given the importance of the non-quantifiable benefits, the figures probably tend to underestimate the net benefit.

The estimates of the internal rate of return[34] on the investment have been 34 per cent (150 head per day capacity),[35] 29 per cent (300 head per day)[36] and 34 per cent to 11 per cent (500 head per day).[37] The current opportunity cost of capital in Botswana is usually estimated at 12 per cent. Of course, in each feasibility study the rate of return varies with alteration of the critical assumptions underlying the cost and benefit estimates. Even with adverse assumptions, the two earlier studies arrive at satisfactory rates of return (18 and 16 per cent).

In the latest study, however, the rate of return with 'adverse' assumptions (11 per cent) appears to put the investment at risk. The 11 per cent figure is based on the assumption that the 'value of stock if not sold' is P150 per head (whereas the 34 per cent assumes only P100 per head). There are indications that northern cattle raisers would be prepared to accept the gross price of less than P150 per head in order to assure the benefits of selling to a northern abattoir. Thus in 1977 (the last year in which Ngamiland sold to BMC), the average price paid by BLDC (see p. 58 below) in Ngamiland was P80–5 per head; and the BLDC plus traders and buyers (whose prices are roughly in line with BLDC's) accounted for 75 per cent of all cattle exports from Ngamiland. Thus the vast majority of Ngamiland producers sell to middlemen for cash, because of the difficulties of marketing directly to BMC – despite the much lower returns. (The average gross price received by those selling directly to BMC through livestock marketing co-operatives in Ngamiland was P164 in 1977.)[38]

The overall conclusion drawn by looking at the results of the existing feasibility studies is therefore favourable to the investment; especially when it is allowed for that significant non-quantifiable benefits are not included in the calculations. The next section examines the crucial issues about which assumptions have had to be made in the feasibility studies in order to arrive at this conclusion.

The crucial variables: markets, offtake and policy

The crucial variables determining the micro-economic success of an enterprise are those which have most effect on its costs and revenues. Figure 4.3 tries to schematize the main factors which determine the costs and revenues of expanded abattoir facilities in Botswana.

Drawing on the relations indicated in Figure 4.3, in planning the northern abattoir, what values should be assumed for the immediate determinants of costs and revenues – price, throughput and the size and type of a northern abattoir?

Price: the state of the export markets

World beef prices are crucial, because BMC exports 90 per cent of its production, and because the gap between world prices and EEC prices, while

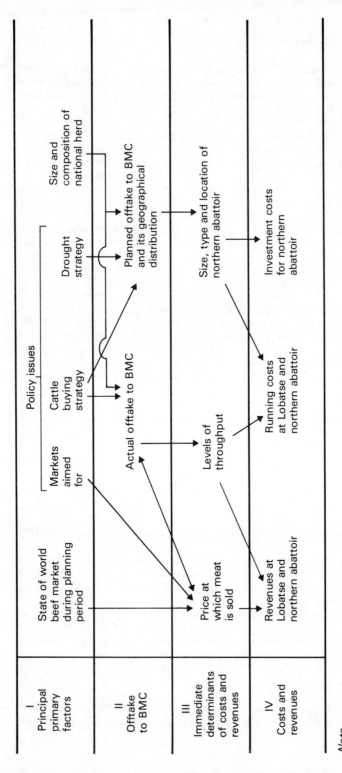

Note

The direction of causation is indicated by the arrows. Other factors and links between factors have been omitted in order to emphasize what seem to be the principal ones in the issue of the northern abattoir.

Figure 4.3 *Main factors determining the costs and revenues of expanded abattoir facilities in Botswana*

EEC imposes a quota, is crucial to the viability of a second abattoir. World beef prices collapsed in 1974, in defiance of all market predictions. The market remained poor for three years, but improved significantly in 1978–9. The 1978 FAO projections[39] predict cautiously that the market will remain buoyant to 1985.

In the longer term, the outlook for exports from Third World countries is regarded as bright;[40] meat has a high income elasticity of demand; the demand for manufacturing-type beef (for canning, etc.,) is strong and the fat, grain-fed beef raised in the major importing regions is not well-suited for manufacturing purposes;[41] the price of grain for animal feed is likely to continue rising making range-fed beef from Third World countries more competitive. Import demand is reported to be shifting away from such restricted markets as the EEC to countries with more liberal trade policies – oil-exporting countries, rapidly growing economies such as South Korea and some West African countries. Botswana is well-placed to share in the benefits of these longer-term trends.

The existing feasibility studies for a northern abattoir have all based their projections of revenue on the average BMC price at the time and not allowed for any inflation of meat prices or production and selling costs. At the present time, this may be a fair procedure, provided that beef prices do indeed rise during the planning period. Were the market likely to be slacker, it would be better to project price on the basis of current world market prices rather than the average BMC price, which reflects strongly the gap between EEC and world prices.

Throughput

Throughput will depend on herd size and offtake, buying policy and prices offered to producers.

Herd size and offtake

Given the uncertainties in the basic data concerning offtake and the national herd, it is not possible to predict with any accuracy what the offtake available to a northern abattoir would be. Estimates of current herd size range from 2·5 to 3·5 million. Annual average percentage offtake is thought to be about 11 per cent, making for a range of total annual offtake of 275–385 000 head. With private slaughter and slaughter at local abattoirs absorbing some 120 000 head per year,[42] and the Lobatse plant requiring about 200 000, the availability of adequate offtake for a 500-head per day (about 100 000 per year) northern abattoir seems likely to depend upon the diversion of animals from private slaughter and upon increased offtake. How many cattle are presently slaughtered privately, or left to age in the herds because of transport problems or BMC quotas, therefore becomes crucial for the short-term operations of the northern abattoir. A recent guess is that annual offtake available to BMC would increase by 20 000 because of the convenience of the northern abattoir or by up to 50 000 if buying activities were also stepped up.[43] In the longer term, availability of offtake should be no problem if offtake continues to grow by some 13 000 head per annum.[44] But in the short term an abattoir with a capacity of 100 000 head per year might either create unused capacity at Lobatse or run below capacity itself.

Buying policy

If marketing difficulties, especially from remoter areas, are a reason for low offtake, then increased cattle buying might be necessary to ensure adequate throughput at a northern abattoir. If so, who should do the increased buying? BMC might seem the obvious candidate, but BMC has been unwilling in the past to increase its involvement 'before the factory gate' beyond its grazier scheme – a scheme whereby BMC loans money to fatteners and breeders for purchase of approved stock. The BMC also divested itself in 1977 of the Botswana Livestock Development Corporation (BLDC), which was set up to buy and fatten cattle, especially in the north. The BLDC succeeded in raising prices in Ngamiland – but ran large losses.

By tending to maximize producer prices rather than total payments to producers or throughput, the BMC lowers the demand for slaughter-stock, and thereby lowers the up-country price of cattle bought for fattening or speculative purposes.[45] The winners in the system are those cattle owners who secure direct access to BMC and its higher prices. Of these, the ones who stand to gain most are those who also buy cattle for speculation and fattening so that they benefit both from lower up-country prices and from higher BMC prices. The losers are those, predominantly small, herders, with insufficient means or knowledge, or who are too remote, to organize direct sale to BMC, and who therefore sell at a much lower price or not at all. The fact that the winners are well-represented on the BMC's board may help to explain BMC's prior coolness to a northern abattoir – an attitude altered, apparently, only because of the Lobatse plant's inability to slaughter the cattle offered (from southern and central parts alone) during the moderate drought of 1979.

Leaving aside the question of whether BMC should or should not be the body charged with operating a more active livestock supply system, the present reality seems to be that BMC would not operate such a system (buyers, transport, holding grounds) energetically. Other agencies, such as BLDC, the livestock marketing co-operatives or private dealers might therefore prove better suited to the task. Notwithstanding the above, it also remains possible that any present failure of potential offtake to be marketed may be more a result of the lack of conveniently situated slaughter facilities than of any weakness in the marketing system which can only be remedied by stepping-up cattle buying. Should this be so, a well-situated northern abattoir could result in a larger than expected increase in cattle deliveries and so make increased buying unnecessary.

Producer price

While both large and small-scale cattle owners may respond to a price increase, expected to be permanent, by building up herds rather than increasing sales, this reaction is short term. In the long run sales will increase. Furthermore, the cattle industry in northern Botswana is in a highly abnormal condition following exclusion from the export market for two years, high expenses and risks in sending cattle to Lobatse, a series of good rainfall years before 1978–9, rising incomes from employment and lack of alternative investment opportunities other than cattle accumulation. In these circumstances, supply to a northern abattoir might be high even in the short term.

It seems probable, therefore, that the level of producer prices will not (in the next few years at least) be a major factor determining offtake availability to BMC (both at Lobatse and at a northern abattoir). Furthermore the extensive and low-cost nature of cattle raising in Botswana ensures that offtake

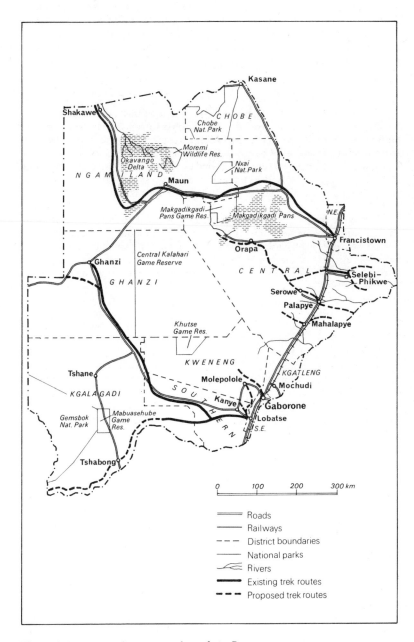

Figure 4.4   *Livestock auction saleyards in Botswana*

availability will not fluctuate sharply in response to a reduction in price[46] caused by additional production having to be sold on lower priced markets (owing to Botswana's limited quota on the high-priced EEC market). Drought it seems, not producer price, remains the principal determinant of short-term variations in offtake availability.

Size and type of northern abattoir

The northern abattoir should be able to make a substantial contribution to absorbing offtake during a drought. To do so its capacity needs to be at least 100 000 head per annum – since the lowest estimate of offtake during a major drought with present herd size is 400 000 head while the Lobatse plant can handle some 300 000 head, running beyond capacity. At the same time it should create as little excess capacity as possible in the processing sector during normal times when its throughput will probably be less than half that ocurring during a drought.

Therefore the plant must be able to run economically over a wide range of throughput, for example, 40 000–100 000 head per annum, but carry low fixed costs. Fixed costs can be minimized by keeping the plant small but designing it, and selecting the machinery, with the goal of intensive operation in mind, that is, so that it can when necessary be run on two or three shifts per day for fairly extended periods.

The costs of carrying excess capacity during normal times, and especially in the wake of a drought, have been emphasized in the arguments against a northern abattoir. But these costs have to be weighed against the costs of inadequate and inconveniently situated capacity which (as discussed above) are at present substantial. Furthermore, the costs of present inadequate capacity fall only on those with poorest access to Lobatse whereas the costs of excess capacity would be shared by all farmers (assuming there is a single producer price at both abattoirs).

As regards the type of processing facilities, all the feasibility studies have recommended that the northern abattoir should be 'a completely modern meat processing plant and include all facilities necessary for the production of quality meat and meat products',[47] – in order to ensure veterinary acceptability, lower production costs and production which is reasonably autonomous of the Lobatse plant.

Conclusions

Botswana's beef industry has altered considerably since the 1950s. The main forces for change have been the expansion of demand for beef in Europe and decolonization. Higher producer prices and salaries from newly-created civil service posts provided the incentive and funds for increased borehole drilling and purchase of breeding stock – resulting in a rapidly growing national herd and the attendant problems of overgrazing and increased drought risk. The dominance of traders, speculators and fatteners is being undermined increasingly by direct marketing (encouraged by the state) to the BMC, and by the loss of much of the influence they had in colonial times.

The story to date of the northern abattoir proposal reflects some of the strains which have been developing during this process of transformation and growth.

1 The problem of ensuring sufficient offtake in a situation where many livestock owners find access to the export abattoir difficult or expensive but private buying has not grown proportionately to the national herd, and the export abattoir is a monopsony (whose goal is not the maximizing of throughput).

2 The need to relieve northern herders (particularly the smaller ones) from their disadvantaged position in the industry, but the opposition from parties whose interests stand to be affected adversely by the northern abattoir.

3 The need to increase abattoir capacity, but the problems of selling additional meat on high-priced markets because of domestic overproduction in those markets.

4 The need to maintain a high average producer price in order to make long-term investments in improved productivity viable (the TGLP Programme), but at the same time the need to expand into lower-priced markets in order to sell the increased production.

5 The primary dependence on a market (the EEC) which does not need Botswana's beef (only giving it privileged access for political or 'aid' reasons), but the risks of alienating this favour by further increasing export production.

With all the main parties now agreed to the implementation of the northern abattoir, perhaps the major risk is that, as a compromise, it will unquestioningly be located on the railway line near Francistown – too far east to be of significant benefit for the herders in northwest Central District, Ngamiland, and Chobe, as far as their marketing risks and expenses are concerned. A Francistown location is made the more likely by the tendency of feasibility studies to concentrate on the micro-economic issues affecting the viability of the specific project, rather than the broader costs and benefits – many of then nonquantifiable. In this instance, the broader issues seem particularly important and call for a more northwesterly location.

As regards other planning issues, undoubtedly the main problem in planning the project adequately will be the present lack of reliable cattle census figures. Although more livestock statistics have been compiled recently,[48] interpretation of them is hampered at every turn by the lack of sound information on the size, composition and rate of growth of the cattle population.

Finally, attention should be drawn to the absence of considerations regarding small stock (goats, sheep, pigs) from the existing planning studies for the northern abattoir. Each study has provided for some small stock slaughtering facility as a sideline, but otherwise ignored the matter. If small stock are to continue to be overlooked, a much fuller justification for doing so is needed than has appeared up to now.

Postscript

Since this paper was written two major developments have occurred. First, there has been a further outbreak of foot and mouth disease in the north (August 1979), thus prolonging the north's isolation from all external markets and extending the resulting hardship. The urgency of setting-up processing facilities in the north has been thereby reinforced and planning is now proceeding quickly. Secondly, a new EEC–ACP convention has recently been agreed upon which includes an increased beef quota. This will help to maintain buoyant producer prices in Botswana during the next few years and could increase the viability of the northern abattoir (provided its meat is admitted to the EEC).

Notes

1. The research on which this paper is based, part of a larger project on the history of Botswana's beef industry, has been assisted by a grant from the University College of Botswana. Iain McDonald, Ministry of Agriculture, Botswana, Manfred Bienefeld and Charles Harvey, IDS, Sussex, provided valuable criticisms. Opinions and mistakes are, of course, the sole responsibility of the author.

2. Government Paper no. 2 (1975).

3. 'Livestock and Range Research in Botswana 1978', Animal Production Research Unit, Ministry of Agriculture.

4. Sandford (1977); McGowan (1979); The Botswana Society (1978).

5. For example, in 1977 the BMC slaughtered 197 000 cattle, equivalent to about 30 000 tonnes of beef and veal. In 1970, exports alone of Argentina, Australia and Ireland were respectively 650 000, 320 000, and 290 000 tonnes. Source: Jasiorowski (1972).

6. Documented in Roux (1975), p. 356.

7. BMC Annual Reports and Accounts.

8. Experience, Incorporated (1973), p. 38.

9. The finding of a 1973 study reported in USAID (1975), p. 16.

10. 'Some considerations concerning the establishment of an abattoir in northern Botswana', Ministry of Agriculture (1974), section III, p. 1.

11. Achieved in 1975. BMC Report and Accounts (1975), p. 4.

12. National Development Plan 1976–81, p. 363.

13. USAID (1975).

14. BMC Annual Report (1974), p. 9.

15. USAID (1975), p. 35.

16. Over and above the normal veterinary regulations which apply in the event of disease outbreaks.

17. Not only do the cattle owners bear the costs. Studies of the impact of the veterinary measures imposed to isolate the foot and mouth outbreaks reveal that the lack of a market and the restrictions on cattle movement resulted in various hardships, including loss of employment, failure to pay wages, inability to plough fields and restriction of traders' credit. See Merafe (1978), Ntseane (1978) and Hitchcock (1978).

18. Botswana has a network of veterinary cordon fences, dividing the country into veterinary zones, for the purpose of isolating animal diseases.

19. The regulations stress that the period can be altered at the discretion of the EEC.

20. A 90 per cent rebate on the variable levy on up to 17 000 tonnes per annum. Exemption from the 20 per cent Common External Tariff for up to 23 000 tonnes per annum increasing by 7·5 per cent each year. Renegotiable every six months, later changed to every 12 months. See Hubbard (1978) for further details.

21. Ministry of Agriculture (1974), p. 1.

22. Sandford (1977), p. 24.

23. McGowan (1979), p. 24.

24. Ministry of Agriculture (1974), p. 2.

25. McGowan, op. cit., annex 6, p. 11.

26. From Ministry of Agriculture (1974), section 2, p. 10. The encircled figures for 1974–8 have been added to the diagram. 1966 was omitted as unrepresentative in the original. Since the data indicate cost increases for each of the years 1974–8, despite throughput variations, the price index used to deflate costs (SA industrial: food processing) is probably inappropriate. This, together with product changes, leaves the figures as no more than approximations.

27. McGowan (1979), p. 37, argues that economies of scale in abattoir operation persist up to a level of 100 000 to 120 000 head per annum.

28. No study is available of how much of the difference between the price to producers in Lobatse and in the northwest represents cost which would have to be met under any marketing system, and how much represents profit which exceeds a competitive return on capital employed.

29. This is the principal reason why abattoirs in industrialized countries are generally being moved away from consuming areas towards producing areas. See Mittendorf (1978), p. 13.

30. McGowan (1979), p. 38.

31. Kennington Incorporated 'National Abattoirs Planning Study' (1978).

32. In order for the ratio of cattle/grazing land (a measure of grazing pressure) to remain constant when grazing land is fixed in quantity, it is not sufficient that percentage offtake remains constant – the entire absolute increase in cattle number needs to be taken off. In Botswana during the 1970s percentage offtake seems to have remained constant at about 10–11 per cent (McDonald, 1979) leading to the conclusion that grazing pressure has increased.

33. It is pleasing to note that the Livestock Advisory Centres will soon become sole distributors of BMC bonemeal output.

34. The rate of discount of the net cash flow of the investment which reduces the present value of the net cash flow to zero.

35. Experience, Incorporated (1973).

36. USAID (1975).

37. McGowan (1979).

38. All of this information from McDonald (1979), section III, pp. 6, 7.

39. FAO (1978).

40. Jasiorowski (1976), p. 11.

41. Spray (1977), p. 57.

42. Ministry of Agriculture (1978), Table 6.20. Figures for private slaughter are based on the number of hides sold.

43. McGowan (1979), p. 57.

44. Assuming annual offtake to be 320 000 head and 4 per cent growth.

45. Factors which have caused BMC to tend towards maximization of producer prices rather than total payments to producers or total throughput include the following:

a.   The orientation of abattoir management towards efficient processing and sale in the highest-priced market of a given amount of meat determined by abattoir capacity;

b.   The existence of only a single export abattoir, restrictions on live exports and a very limited local market, meaning that the Lobatse plant has not had to compete at all for offtake and therefore has not needed to concern itself with livestock supply issues.

46. In intensive livestock production, for example, in the US, which requires costly inputs (particularly of animal feeds) offtake and herd size are particularly sensitive to producer price changes, leading to the widely documented 'beef cycle'. See, for example, Connolly (1976).

47. USAID (1975), p. 30.

48. For example, Ministry of Agriculture (1978), which supplies details of inter-regional cattle movements, slaughterings at local abattoirs, etc.

References

Botswana Meat Commission (BMC), *Accounts and Report* (Annual).

Connolly, L., *Beef and Veal: World Situation and Outlook*, Republic of Ireland, Agricultural Institute: Economics and Rural Welfare Research Centre (1976).

Ettinger, S., 'South Africa's weight restrictions on cattle exports from Bechuanaland 1924–41', *Botswana Notes and Records* (1972), pp. 21–30.

Experience, Incorporated, *Technical/Economic Feasibility of Establishing Additional Meat Processing Facilities in Botswana* (1973).

FAO, *Meat: Supply, Demand and Trade Projections 1985*, Commodities and Trade Division, Economic and Social Planning Department, Rome (June 1978).

Hinchey, M. (ed.), *Proceedings of the Symposium on Drought in Botswana*, Botswana Society and Clark University (June 1978).

Hitchcock, R., *The Impact of Foot and Mouth Disease on the Poorer Sectors of Botswana's Population, with Special Reference to the Western Sandveld Region of Central District*, Consultancy Report no. 9, Ministry of Local Government and Lands, Botswana (1978).

Hubbard, M., 'Notes on beef in the Lomé Convention', in Jeske, J. (ed.), *Botswana's External Trade in the Light of the Lomé Convention*, National Institute of Research, Gaborone (1978).

International Livestock Centre for Africa, 'Livestock and meat exports after the drought in the Sahel', *ILCA Bulletin* (March 1979).

Jasiorowski, H., 'The developing world as a source of meat for world markets', in Smith, A. (ed.), *Beef Cattle Production in Developing Countries*, University of Edinburgh (1976).

McDonald, I., *A Report on Cattle Marketing in Botswana* (draft), Animal Production Division, Ministry of Agriculture, Botswana (1979).

McGowan, G. and Associates Pty Ltd, *Botswana: A Study of Drought Relief and Contingency Measures Relating to the Livestock Sector*, Albury, Australia (1979).

Meat and Livestock Commission (UK), *International Market Survey. Economic Information Service* (1979, no. 1).

Merafe, Y., *A Social Investigation into the Effects of Foot and Mouth Disease in Nokaneng, Tsau, Gweta and Nata*, Rural Sociology Unit, Ministry of Agriculture, Botswana (1978).

Mittendorf, H., 'Factors affecting the location of slaughter houses in developing countries', *World Animal Review* 25 (FAO Rome, 1978), pp. 13–17.

Ntseane, P., *Report on Foot and Mouth Social Investigations in Ngamiland and Central Districts*, Rural Sociology Unit, Ministry of Agriculture, Botswana (1978).

Republic of Botswana, *Botswana Meat Commission* in *Laws of Botswana* CAP. 74:04 (1965).

Republic of Botswana, *National Development Plan 1976–81*, Ministry of Finance and Development Planning (1977).

Republic of Botswana, *National Policy on Tribal Grazing Land*, Government Paper no. 2 (1975).

Republic of Botswana, *The Rural Income Distribution Survey in Botswana 1974–5*, Central Statistics Office, Ministry of Finance and Development Planning (1976).

Republic of Botswana: Ministry of Agriculture, *An Application by the Government of Botswana for a Loan to Finance a Second Livestock Development Project (Livestock II)*, Division of Planning and Statistics (1976).

Republic of Botswana: Ministry of Agriculture, *A Handbook of Livestock Statistics,* Animal Production Division (1978).

Republic of Botswana: Ministry of Agriculture, *Livestock and Range Research in Botswana 1978*, Animal Production Research Unit (1978).

Republic of Botswana: Ministry of Agriculture, *Some Considerations Concerning the Establishment of an Abattoir in Northern Botswana*, Division of Planning and Statistics (1974).

Roux, B., 'Expansion du capitalisme et développement du sous-développement: L'intégration de l'Amérique centrale au marché mondial de la viande bovine', *Revue Tiers Monde* XVI 62 (April–June 1975), pp. 355–80.

Sandford, S., *Dealing with Drought and Livestock in Botswana*, Overseas Development Institute, London (1977).

Spray, P., 'The integration of Botswana into the world beef market', M. Phil. thesis, University of Sussex (1977, unpublished).

USAID, *Botswana Northern Abattoir (Phase I)* (1975).

Von Kaufmann, R., 'The second Livestock Development Project as an integral part of national policy on tribal grazing land', in Weimer, B. (ed.), *A Policy for Rural Development: the Case of Botswana's National Policy on Tribal Grazing Land*, National Institute of Research, Botswana, Discussion Paper no. 6 (1977).

Weimer, B., 'The tribal grazing land policy – some critical aspects', in Weimer, B. (ed.), ibid.

Michael Hubbard was formerly Lecturer in Economics, University of Botswana and Swaziland.

5 The Taxation of Income from Cattle Farming

DEREK J. HUDSON

An overview of government revenue

The Botswana government is fortunate to have two sources of income which are both large and growing. These are Botswana's share of the revenue pool in the Southern African customs union, and the government's share of revenue from the diamond mining industry. Furthermore, the collection of these two huge contributions is highly efficient; the amount of revenue actually collected is very nearly 100 per cent of the revenue due. Only a small amount of customs revenue escapes the tax collection net. The cost of collection is relatively small.

The government's revenue from all sources in the fiscal year 1979–80 may be estimated as shown in Table 5.1.

Collection of income tax

In sharp contrast to the relative ease with which customs revenue and mineral revenues are brought in, the collection of income tax is much more difficult. The Department of Taxes has to assess and then collect many small amounts of tax from the smaller companies and from self-employed individuals.

Taxable employees of government and the larger private employers have their tax deducted from their paycheques on a Pay As You Earn (PAYE) basis, so the collection of employees' income tax is not difficult. The Department of Taxes, however, has to see whether the employee will either be sent a notice of assessment for a small balance owed, or else he will receive a cheque for a small balance in his favour. It is thus necessary for the Department of Taxes to devote some of its scarce manpower to the collection of negligible amounts of revenue. This can reduce the amount of time left over for the more complicated tax cases, including some which may have a considerable revenue potential.

The contribution of agriculture to the national economy

For purposes of this paragraph, it is convenient to combine agriculture proper with its 'vertically integrated' partner, the Botswana Meat Commission (which is strictly a manufacturing industry). Agriculture plus the BMC account for 23–9 per cent of the gross domestic product of Botswana. (See Dahl, Table 1.7. Value added by BMC was P6 million in 1974–5.) The bulk of this contribution is derived from cattle farming.

Table 5.1 *Approximate estimates of government revenue April 1979–March 1980*

		(P million)
Customs Union revenue pool[a]		78
Mineral revenues[b]		49
Grants		25
Tax on BMC's turnover in 1978[c]		3·2 ⎫
Income tax, farming companies	Farming 4·4	0·5 ⎬
Income tax, farming individuals		0.7 ⎭
Income tax, other companies (excluding mining and farming)		2·6
Income tax, other self-employed		1
Income tax, employees		9
Fees, charges and reimbursements		8
Other income, net[d]		9
TOTAL		186

Notes

[a] First instalment of customs and excise revenue accrued in 1979–80, plus second instalment of revenue accrued in 1977–8. See Chapter 9 in this book (pp. 131–58).

[b] Royalties on minerals produced, plus income tax on mining companies, plus dividends from government's shareholdings in mining companies, plus withholding tax on dividends to other shareholders.

[c] See 1978 annual report of Botswana Meat Commission for estimate of tax payable in 1979–80. It is convenient to treat the BMC's tax as tax on farming income.

[d] Including net interest earned by government.

Sources

Financial Statements, Tables and Estimates of Consolidated and Development Fund Revenues, 1979–80, published by the Ministry of Finance and Development Planning. *Sixth Annual Report of Commissioner of Taxes*, published by the Department of Taxes.

Typical incomes

The total national income from cattle farming varies considerably from year to year, because of drought, foot and mouth disease and fluctuations in the price received by the BMC on its overseas sales. For present purposes, we may use P70 million as a rough estimate of total income from cattle farming in an average year. This is spread out over some 50 000 households (HHs) which *own* one or more cattle, plus their employees, plus additional households of cattle holders, plus farming companies and their employees. A rough average of P1250 average annual income among the cattle owners is probably not too far off.

Taxable incomes

In the tax year July 1979–June 1980, a married farmer needed to have chargeable income of P3600 before he was liable to income tax. An unmarried farmer was taxable on an income in excess of P1800. The previous paragraph makes it clear that most cattle owners are not subject to income tax unless they have other sources of income. It is unlikely that a farmer with less than 100 cattle would reach the taxable level, if his income were derived mainly from cattle farming. This suggests that something like 5 per cent of cattle owners might have taxable incomes, and that 95 per cent of cattle owners are probably not taxable. See also Table 5.7.

The contribution of cattle farming to the *fiscus*

The net tax collection from the cattle industry as a whole, including the BMC, is quite small. The number of taxable cattle farmers is small, the Department of Taxes does not know all of them and even the BMC's tax only partially compensates the government for the government's subsidies to the cattle industry. These subsidies include free vaccinations against foot and mouth disease and against anthrax; construction and maintenance of veterinary cordon fences and quarantine camps; and government meat inspectors stationed at the BMC. More recently, a new foot and mouth vaccine factory in Gaborone has been financed by the EEC. This represents a further subsidy to the cattle industry in Botswana (see Table 5.2).

Table 5.2   *Estimated government expenditure on animal health and agricultural field services, April 1979–March 1980*

Item	Expenditure	Revenue	Net
	(P million)		
Animal health, recurrent[a]	5·3	1·2	4·0
Field services, recurrent[b]	3·3	0·2	3·0
Animal health, development[c]	2·0	..	2·0
Field services, development[d]	1·7	..	1·7
TOTAL	12·2	1·5	10·7

Notes

[a] Veterinary staff; running costs of vaccine production factory; foot and mouth vaccination campaigns; etc.
[b] Agricultural demonstrators; artificial insemination service; demonstration ranches; etc.
[c] Construction of vaccine production factory; cordon fences; new veterinary diagnostic laboratory; new trek routes; etc.
[d] Livestock development project I; sheep and goat development project; rural training centres; development of crop production; etc.

Source
'Details to support 1979–80 estimates of expenditure from the consolidated and development funds', published by the Ministry of Finance and Development Planning.

We may summarize the first part of this paper by saying that the incidence of taxation of income from cattle farming is small, the method of collection is inadequate (see page 76 below), and the net tax collected (after allowing for subsidies) is nearly zero. Yet the subject is of considerable importance. The handful of large, taxable farmers make a significant contribution to the national economy. They often wield political influence. The National Assembly, the Cabinet, the Ministry of Finance and Development Planning, and the Ministry of Agriculture all treat the taxation of farming as a subject of major importance. A detailed study of the complicated sets of rules for taxing farmers is certainly justified.

Criteria for an ideal system

An ideal system for taxing the income of cattle farmers might include the following principles.

1   All taxable farmers should be taxed (referred to here as the principle of *horizontal equity*).
2   It is possible for cattle farmers to receive nearly all their income as income in kind, several years running. This can be followed by a year of high cash income. The tax payable by a farmer should if possible be higher in those years when he has cash income, and lower in those years when he has the same total income but his income is primarily in kind (the *cash flow* principle).
3   The tax payable in a year of high cash income should, however, not be at an abnormally high rate, just because the farmer happened to receive his income in cash, rather than in kind, in that year (the *cash income averaging* principle).
4   Rates of tax should be higher for those farmers who have bigger incomes, taking one year with another (the *progressivity* principle).
5   Rates of tax on income from cattle farming should be similar to rates of tax on income from similar activities, such as crop farming, but need not be similar to rates of tax on income from completely different sources such as employment, trading or mining (the *similarity* principle). If taxation of farming income is lower than taxation of other forms of income, then the extent of the difference should be measured.
6   Rates of tax should not be so high as to either discourage entrepreneurship or to create other harmful disincentives (the principle of *worthwhileness*).
7   Rates of tax should not be so low, in comparison to rates of tax on other sources of income, that there is a strong disincentive for successful cattle farmers to expand into non-farming forms of entrepreneurial activity (the *anti-concentration* principle).
8   Taxable deductions and other allowances should be in line with publicly declared national objectives (the *social objectives* principle). Prevention of overstocking and preservation of the veld, for example, should be encouraged.

It is the object of this paper to examine how well Botswana's tax system meets the above criteria. The author's personal impression is that the tax system in Botswana has successfully met most of the above criteria, but has failed to satisfy the principle of horizontal equity mentioned in (1). Yet it is perhaps the most basic of all tax principles that although nobody actually likes paying tax, most people are reasonably willing to do so if, as an absolute minimum, others in like circumstances are also paying their share.

Definition of 'taxation'

There are a large number of taxes related to cattle farming. For purposes of this article, taxation of income from cattle farming consists of the following taxes only.

1   Personal income tax on the farming income of unincorporated farmers, including farmers who are members of a partnership, and also including trusts engaged in cattle farming.
2   Company tax on the income of farming companies.
3   Personal income tax on dividends received by shareholders in farming companies.
4   So-called 'income tax' paid by the BMC on its annual turnover.
5   Government subsidies to the cattle industry, including the cost of veterinary cordon fences, quarantine camps, free vaccinations of cattle, and meat inspectors at the BMC.

For the sake of simplicity, I have excluded various taxes on the export of beef (which are insignificant), taxes paid on the sale of beef in other countries, for example, 10 per cent of the regular EEC levy on beef is charged on Botswana beef exported to the EEC, the local government tax (maximum rate of tax is P84 per year) and any customs and excise duties payable on intermediate products and capital goods used in the cattle industry.

We may now proceed to compute the tax paid on income from cattle farming, but first we need to solve a semantic problem. The word 'income', as used in the tax rules, has a different meaning from the commonly accepted meaning of the word. For tax purposes, 'income' means exactly what the Income Tax Act defines to be income, no more and no less. This 'income' for tax purposes could, under some circumstances, be only a fraction of what an economist would understand by the word 'income'. In order to make progress, I will refer to 'real income' and 'chargeable income', it being understood that one has to convert 'real income' into 'chargeable income' before the tax on the income can be computed. The conversion rules are spelled out in the Income Tax Act.

It should also be emphasized that the rates of tax are the same for income from any source, once a taxpayer's chargeable income has been computed. It follows that, if any one sector such as agriculture is to have a lower effective tax rate, it has to be the rules that convert real income into chargeable income that favour one sector over another.

Definition of 'real income'

It is convenient to proceed in stages. First, let us define 'trading receipts' as:

Trading receipts = sales of cattle – purchase of cattle
+ value of closing inventory at the end of the tax year
– value of opening inventory at the beginning of the tax year
= sales – purchases + stock adjustment   (1)

Secondly,
Total receipts = trading receipts
+ value of goods produced for own use   (2)

Thirdly,
Real income = total receipts
– running expenses and depreciation   (3)

Formula (1) is a standard formula for measuring gross receipts, whenever an entrepreneur can choose whether to sell his 'production' (cattle) or to 'reinvest' his production in the 'business', that is, keep the cattle in the herd. The stock adjustment, closing inventory minus opening inventory, measures the extent to which he may have liquidated his opening stocks, that is, sold his production from previous years, or 'saved' his current production in the form of an increase in stocks. the inventories should be valued at current cattle post prices (see Appendix 5. A). Goods produced for own use are listed in Table 5.3, together with a suggested valuation for them.

Table 5.3   *Suggested valuation of goods produced for own use*

Type of goods	Method of valuation
Cattle slaughtered for home consumption	Current cattle post value (see Appendix 5. A)
Meat of cattle that died and were eaten	Use half the above value
Milk for human consumption	15 thebe per litre[a]

Note
[a] 100 thebe = 1 Pula

Definition of 'chargeable income'

The disadvantage of formula (1) above is that a farmer who has no cash sales can still have a large real income, but he has put his entire year's production into his closing inventory so his income is almost entirely income in kind. If he were then charged tax on his real income he might not have any cash with which to pay the tax. This would undermine the cash flow principle explained above.

The Income Tax Act recognizes this problem by giving the farmer several options as to the method of valuation of the stock adjustment. The Department of Taxes permits some discretion in reporting production for own use. The Act allows certain kinds of depreciation to be measured on an accelerated basis. Finally, the Act permits a farmer to replace his current year's income by the average of this year's income and the income he earned in the previous two years. We may write:

$$
\begin{aligned}
\text{Chargeable income} \quad &= \quad a \times (\text{sales} - \text{purchases}) \\
&+ \quad b \times (\text{stock adjustment}) \\
&+ \quad c \times (\text{own production}) \\
&- \quad d \times (\text{running expenses}) \\
&- \quad e \times (\text{depreciation}),
\end{aligned}
$$

where the permitted values of the parameters a, b, c, d and e are laid down in the Act. The parameter a may, in the most extreme case, be as low as one third; the parameter b may be zero in certain circumstances, but if b is zero then a may have to be unity; own production is not always reported; and the parameter e may be a large number, for example, $e = 10$, if a new borehole with a lifetime of ten years is 'written off' in one year, that is, treated as a deductible expense incurred in the year of its completion, rather than depreciated over ten years. The more sophisticated farmers have to hire tax accountants to choose the combination of parameters that will minimize their tax liability.

As an illustration of the options available, Table 5.4 shows some of the methods of valuing a cattle inventory.

Table 5.4   *Various methods of valuing a cattle inventory for tax purposes* (*Pula*)

Type of animal	Age (years)	Valuation method[f]				
		Omit[a]	75%[b]	SV[c]	125%[d]	Market[e]
Calves	0–1	0	5	7	9	40
Heifers	1–2	0	12	16	20	70
Tollies	1–2	0	12	16	20	85
Heifers	2–3	0	19	25	31	95
Tollies	2–3	0	19	25	31	120
Cows	3+	0	25	34	43	110
Oxen	3–4	0	34	45	56	150
Oxen	4+	0	39	55	71	165
Bulls	3+	0	38	50	62	170

Notes

[a] Omission of stock adjustment, i.e., b = 0 is equivalent to putting a zero value on each animal.

[b] '75%' means 75 per cent of 'standard values'.

[c] 'SV' means 'standard values', as defined in section 7 of Part II of the First Schedule of the Income Tax Act.

[d] '125%' means 125 per cent of 'standard values'.

[e] Author's estimate of current market prices at cattle posts. See also Appendix 5.A.

[f] Stock that have been purchased specifically for breeding purposes must be valued at purchase price. These prices can be much higher than the market prices at cattle posts.

The effect of various valuation options on chargeable income

If a farmer chooses a lower scale of valuation of his cattle inventory, then it can be seen from formula (1) that;

1   chargeable income per cow is reduced during the years when the cow is growing,
2   chargeable income per cow is substantially increased in the year in which the cow is sold.

If the farmer chooses to make significantly more sales of cattle every third year, then he can mitigate the effect of the 'burst' of income in the third year by use of the income averaging rule. This permits him to average down the third year's income, without having to make any adjustment to the incomes in the first two years.

Example

Suppose a new farmer has been given 30 male calves to start his herd. The thirty calves are to be reared for $3\frac{1}{2}$ years and then sold. All calculations in Table 5.5 are at constant 1979 Pula. For simplicity, it is assumed that running expenses plus depreciation come to P12 per beast per year. (The figure of P12 in 1979 is based on a rough national accounts estimate of P10·6 in 1977–8.)

Table 5.5   *Income from thirty male calves*

	Chargeable income[a]		Real income[a]
	Method (1)	Method (3)	Method (5)
		(Pula)	
Year 1	− 360	− 150	840
Year 2	− 360	− 90	990
Year 3	− 360	− 90	690
Year 4 (unadjusted)	4380	3630	780
TOTAL (unadjusted)	3300	3300	3300
Year 4 (adjusted)[b]	1460	1210	780
TOTAL (adjusted)[b]	380	880	3300

Notes
[a] 'Method 1' refers to omission of stock adjustment. 'Method 3' refers to the use of 'Standard Values'. 'Method 5' refers to the use of market related values. See Table 5.4.
[b] 'Adjusted' income is obtained by using the average of the incomes in years 2, 3 and 4 in place of the actual income for year 4, if the average is smaller. In calculating the average, however, negative incomes are treated as zero incomes.

The example in Table 5.5 was chosen to illustrate how significant use can be made of the income averaging provision. Provided the farmer uses zero or low valuations, and provided he eventually sells all his cattle in the same tax year, he will reduce his chargeable income in the peak fourth year to about P49 per beast per year (method 1) or P40 (method 3). A chargeable income only becomes taxable when it exceeds P3600 per year, provided that the farmer is married. This suggests that he would need to have started with a herd of 70–90 beasts, in order to have a taxable income in the fourth year, if he had followed the pattern set out in the example.

The example also illustrates the kind of problem faced by the national accounts statisticians in the Central Statistics Office in Gaborone. The farm's contribution to the gross domestic product, which is based on the farmer's real income, bears no resemblance to the chargeable income reported by the farmer for tax purposes. The statisticians have to convert the income tax statistics in one of the first two columns into the real economic statistics in the third column, in order to calculate the GDP. (See Chapter 14 by Weedon and Ystgaard, pp. 220–51.)

Transfer of farming losses to profits from other activities

It is a general principle of income tax law in Botswana that a loss from one kind of activity may not be set against a profit from another kind of activity. For example, if a trader runs a trucking business, he might make a profit of P5000 on his trading business and a loss of P1000 on his trucking business. The trader has to pay tax on his P5000 trading business; he may not deduct the trucking loss and pay tax only on P4000. He should instead carry his P1000 trucking loss forward and use it to reduce the profit (hopefully) from his trucking business in the following year.

A special exception is made for those farmers who do not use the zero valuation option (no stock adjustment) and who have not incorporated their farms into farming companies. Thus if an eligible trader makes a trading profit of P5000, and a farming loss of P1000, the trader/farmer may choose to bring his taxable income down to P4000 in that year, by deducting the farming loss from the trading profit. In this case, the farming loss may not be carried over to the following year.

This provision could be of particular benefit to an employee whose main income is from employment, but who wants to build up a cattle herd as a retirement activity. It is common for an employee to incur tax losses while he is an absentee farmer, especially if he elects to use a low stock valuation. The special transfer provision permits him to reduce his tax liability on his employment income, and this in turn helps him to carry the loss from the farming operation until such time as he becomes a full time farmer.

Farming companies

The tax rules for companies are somewhat different from the tax rules for unincorporated farmers. The main differences are:

1   There is no personal allowance for a company, that is, tax is payable on the company's entire chargeable income, not just the portion which exceeds P3600 per year.
2   The rate of company tax is a flat 35 per cent, whereas the tax rate for individuals increases in stages from 10–75 per cent, depending on the level of income.
3   If a company pays a dividend out of its post-tax profits to a shareholder, the shareholder has to add the dividend to his taxable income. This could amount to a double taxation of the company's original income. The double taxation effect is offset, however, in that dividends paid to resident shareholders are deductible expenses for the company. The double taxation effect only applies to non-resident shareholders.
4   If a company retains some of its post-tax profits in a reserve fund, the claim that each shareholder has on the retained profits is tax free for the shareholder, that is, there is no tax on undistributed earnings. This remains true even if the company is subsequently sold, since there is no capital gains tax in Botswana.
5   A farming company is restricted in its choice of valuation options for valuing its cattle inventory.

From the above set of rules, it would appear that a farmer might pay either more or less tax if he turns his farm into a farming company, depending on the circumstances. It is in general only worthwhile to incorporate if a farm is quite large.

Special deductions for farmers

All businesses in Botswana are allowed to reduce their chargeable income by deducting certain expenses of a capital nature. In some instances, the capital expense must be depreciated over a number of years. This could apply to a truck or a tractor, which might for example be depreciated over five years. On the other hand, businesses are from time to time allowed accelerated depreciation. For example, a business may deduct up to P5000 per dwelling house which was constructed during the tax year, for housing its employees.

In the case of farming, there is a special list of capital expenses that may be written off completely in the year in which the expenses were incurred. These expenses are those on:

1 eradication of noxious plants, that is, plants which could poison cattle,
2 the prevention of soil erosion,
3 dipping tanks,
4 boreholes, wells, dams, tanks, reservoirs, irrigation channels, water furrows, piping and pumping,
5 fencing, stock yards and cattle crushes,
6 farm buildings,
7 the establishment of trees, plantations, orchards and vineyards,
8 roads, bridges or airstrips used in farming operations,
9 supply of electric power,
10 making firebreaks.

These special deductions for farmers have two distinct results. If a farmer is having a good year and anticipates a larger than normal income, he can reduce his income for tax purposes by incurring capital expenses of the kind outlined above, provided that the money is spent before the end of the tax year on 30 June. The farmer's capital expenses will then in effect be subsidised to the extent of his personal marginal tax rate. For example, if he is in a 45 per cent tax bracket, the government will in effect bear 45 per cent of the cost of his optional additional capital expenses, because his tax bill will be reduced by that amount. The second effect is obviously to encourage farmers to improve their farms along the lines that government would like to see.

Tax principles which do not favour farming

There are two tax principles which work to the disadvantage of cattle farming. The first concerns the cost of travel to a place of work. The second concerns the cost of land.

It is a firmly established principle that a taxpayer should not be permitted to deduct the cost of travelling to work. An employee who drives to work to an office in his home town is not allowed to deduct his commuting expenses. In the case of cattle farming where the owner does not live at the cattle post, he may not claim as a farming expense the cost of driving his truck to the cattle post. Such expenses may be very heavy indeed, and the fact that they are not deductible tends to reduce the number of visits that an absentee cattle owner will make to his cattle post. This in turn tends to reduce the efficiency with which the farm is managed.

Similarly, it is an established principle that the cost of land may not normally be deducted from chargeable income, not even on a depreciation basis. This clearly affects the purchaser of a freehold farm more than it affects businessmen who wish to purchase a plot of land on an industrial site. The would-be farmer has to face a much larger capital outlay, with only partial assistance from the tax man, as follows.

An unincorporated citizen farmer or a partnership of citizens may deduct the cost of a farm from chargeable income, up to a maximum of P75 000. A pro rata share of this tax deduction will have to be recouped if the farmer sells the farm within ten years. The deduction appears to be applicable once only to each farm, that is, it is only the first citizen purchaser of the farm who is entitled to utilize the tax deduction. The effect is to make it easier for a citizen farmer to buy a freehold farm from a non-citizen. Thereafter, there will probably not be any tax relief to a second and subsequent citizen buyer.

How many taxable farmers are in fact taxed?

Latest figures indicate that about 335 taxable unincorporated farmers are assessed by the Department of Taxes. There are also about 78 taxable farming companies (see Appendix 5.C).

From the Rural Income Distribution Survey (RIDS), which estimated rural incomes between March 1974 and February 1975, one may estimate the number of farmers whose incomes probably reached a taxable level in 1974–5. For this purpose, I have assumed that the households (HHs) with a 'gross available income' from all sources of P3000 or more in 1974–5 would have been taxable in 1974–5. (The personal allowances in 1974–5 were P2400 for a married man and P1200 for a working wife or an unmarried individual.)

Table 5.6   *Estimates of the number of taxable cattle farmers in 1974–5*

No. of cattle owned by HH	Estimated proportion of HHs with taxable income (percentage)	Estimated number of taxable HHs
50–80	15	520
81–100	30	430
101–150	65	720
151–200	95	290
201–250	98	360
251 +	100	660
TOTAL		2980

Source
Appendix 29 of RIDS, 1974–5.

This could be a conservative estimate, since subsequent analysis of RIDS has indicated that RIDS may have underestimated the number of HHs with large numbers of cattle. Be that as it may, the available evidence suggests that something like only one out of every eight taxable farmers is taxed. The other seven taxable farmers do not file tax returns with the Department of Taxes. The

Department has been trying to track down more of the taxable farmers, and the number increases slowly each year. But it is still likely that the number of untaxed farmers will continue to exceed by a large margin those who are taxed.

Taxation of the Botswana Meat Commission

The BMC is a kind of non-profit co-operative. It tries to keep the prices paid to cattle producers high enough so that it barely makes any profit.[1]

The tax paid by the BMC on its sales, however, has to be taken into account when the BMC sets its producer prices. The BMC would be able to pay the farmers about 15 per cent more for their cattle if the BMC did not have to pay its so-called income tax. This explains why it is appropriate to include the tax paid by the BMC as part of the overall tax on the cattle industry.

Of some theoretical interest is the question of whether or not there is any progressivity built into the BMC's tax. In other words, does the passing back of the BMC's tax to the farmers (by way of lower producer prices) have a proportionately larger impact on the farmers with larger incomes? There is some evidence that this is in fact so.

Large farmers in Botswana tend to purchase more inputs, including immature cattle, relative to their sales than do small farmers. Large farmers tend to develop bigger incomes for themselves on large turnovers, not on large profit margins. A reduction in the prices at which cattle can be sold tends to affect large farmers proportionately more than small farmers. Thus the BMC tax, viewed as a tax on cattle farmers, is slightly progressive in nature. This idea is illustrated in Table 5.7 with data from the 1974–5 Rural Income Distribution Survey. If we think of the hypothetical livestock income without the BMC tax as the 'tax-free' income, and the actual income as the 'taxed' income (after the BMC tax has been passed back to the farmer), then we can summarize the results in Table 5.7 as shown in Table 5.8

Table 5.7 *Comparison of actual farming income in 1974–5 with a hypothetical income without BMC income tax (Pula per farmer per year)*

Locality of farmer	Livestock receipts		Expenses		Livestock income	
	Actual	Hypothetical	A.	H.	A.	H.
Small villages	598	(688) (increase of 15%)	187	(187)	411	(501) (increase of 22%)
Large villages	982	(1129) (increase of 15%)	336	(336)	616	(763) (increase of 24%)
Barolong farms	1067	(1228) (increase of 15%)	506	(506)	562	(722) (increase of 28%)
Freehold farms	49 155	(56 529) (increase of 15%)	34 275	(36 846)[a]	14 880	(19 683) (increase of 32%)

Note
[a] Large farmers' expenses would increase because their expenses include the purchase of immature cattle, which would also be more costly.
Source
RIDS, 1974–5.

Table 5.8   *Summary of effect of BMC's income tax on farmers' incomes, in 1974–5*

	'Tax-free'	Income after BMC tax	'Tax rate'
Small farmers	501	411	18
Medium farmers	742	589	21
Freehold farmers	19 683	14 880	24

The last column in Table 5.8 shows very roughly how much the government would have had to tax the livestock income of *all* cattle farmers, if the government had wanted to recover the BMC's tax from the individual farmers instead of from the BMC. This tax would have had to be additional to ordinary income tax.

The BMC tax has a lot to recommend it. It applies nearly equally, through the mechanism of passing the BMC tax back to producers, to *all* farmers with equal income (the principle of horizontal equity). It has a slightly higher proportional effect on the farmers with higher incomes (the progressivity principle). It also goes some way towards reimbursing the government for its subsidies to agriculture. (Compare Table 5.3 above.)

Analysis of the original objectives

We now return to the criteria in Section 7 for an ideal tax system.

1   *Horizontal equity* is satisfied in the way that the BMC's tax is passed back to cattle producers. Conversely, the taxation of taxable unincorporated farmers is manifestly unfair when so many taxable farmers escape the tax net.
2   *Cash flow* problems are catered for by the use of low valuations of cattle inventories.
3   *Income averaging* is generously provided for by the so-called income averaging procedure for farming income.
4   *Progressivity* applies to most farmers, whether through the progressivity of the personal income tax rates, or whether through the effect of the BMC's tax.
5   *Similarity* between the taxation of incomes from crop farming and cattle farming does exist, but the availability of lower than market valuations of livestock gives the cattle farmer an advantage over crop farmers.
6   *Worthwhileness* derives from the high profitability (over the long run) and low taxation for most of the cattle farming industry. Exceptions arise, however, when an unincorporated farmer has to pay the 75 per cent rate of tax on the top slice of his personal income.
7   *Concentration* of farmers' energies on, and financial backing for, their cattle businesses is bound to continue, as long as the post-tax returns to cattle farming are high in relation to other entrepreneurial activities
        It has been of particular interest to the present author to see how little use has been made by the farmers of the new Hypothecation Act. This Act permits the farmers to pledge some of their P500 million worth of cattle as collateral if they want to borrow from a bank, but the new facility has

hardly been used. Where it *has* been used, the borrower has tended to plough his borrowed funds back into cattle farming, not into some other kind of activity.

8   *Social objectives* are satisfied by the nature of the special tax deductions for farmers. On the other hand, the potential for high profits has led many farmers to take risks by overstocking. The tax system, especially the use of low valuations of cattle inventories, has failed to discourage this highly undesirable practice. A slightly higher set of Standard Values would put pressure on farmers to sell more of their cattle, in order to keep up the cash flow needed to pay the increased income tax.

Some suggestions for the future

The present system of taxing farming income includes many praiseworthy characteristics. It is therefore unfortunate that it suffers from the gross inequity of the hit and miss nature of its application. Furthermore, the basic inability to tax all, or nearly all, of the taxable farmers is going to persist. At the level of local government, the problems of taxation are compounded by the excessively high cost of collecting local government tax. One cannot help wondering whether the time is now ripe for a radical change in the method of taxing farming income, so that it becomes a much fairer system.

The logical alternative to trying to tax farming income by means of income tax is to increase the tax charged on the slaughter of cattle, both at the BMC and at all other abattoirs in Botswana. At the same time, one may not wish to throw away all the aids to farming that are contained in the present tax legislation. A possible compromise is suggested below.

1   Income from farming should not be included at all in the calculation of local government tax.
2   There should be a new slaughter tax, between 5 per cent and 10 per cent *ad valorem*, on the value of any beast which is slaughtered at an abattoir. It should be explained to the public that this tax is in payment for the free vaccinations given to their cattle. Alternatively, a portion of this slaughter tax could be set aside to compensate local government authorities for the revenue lost because of proposal 1 above.
3   Income tax on farming income should be reduced as follows:
     a   A portion, say 50 per cent, of an absentee farmer's expenses in travelling to his cattle post should be deductible. This would encourage absentee farmers to pay more attention to their cattle.
     b   Farmers should receive either a tax credit or a taxable deduction for the slaughter tax they have paid.
4   Standard Values should be indexed to producer prices. (They have not been changed since July 1974.) This would provide some disincentive against overstocking.

Finally, it is not clear to the writer whether the various authorities in Botswana have publicly spelled out their broad policies with respect to the taxation of farming income. If it is desired to tax cattle farming income less than income from other sources, and if it is desired to have the government continue to subsidize the cattle industry as heavily as at present, these are perfectly legitimate objectives. But would it not be more in line with the national characteristic of open public debate on important issues, for these tax objectives to be spelled out more clearly? This would give all concerned, not least the Department of Taxes, a well defined goal towards which all could work.

The present situation is most undesirable, in that the Department of Taxes and the revenue collectors in local government have been set tasks which are impossible to achieve. The suggestions outlined above could move the taxation system in the direction where the well intentioned and hard working civil servants who try to make the system work will have a better chance of achieving their goals. At the same time, the small amount of tax collected from farming will be seen to be a deliberately stated objective, not an embarrassing statistic.

Note

1. This is a tricky operation. The BMC sets its producer prices in advance of each calendar quarter. The farmer is paid immediately his cattle have been slaughtered, whereas the BMC has to wait up to six months to sell the resulting beef. The BMC has to try to forecast future beef prices abroad with considerable accuracy, in order to determine current cattle prices in Botswana.

References

Botswana Government, *Income Taxation in Botswana with Special Reference to the Income Tax Bill, 1973*. Government white paper no. 1 (1973).

Botswana Government, Income Tax Act (Cap. 52:01), as amended (1973).

Botswana Meat Commission, Annual Report for 1978 (1979).

Central Statistics Office, *The Rural Income Distribution Survey in Botswana, 1974–5* (1976).

Central Statistics Office, *National Accounts of Botswana, 1977–8* (1979).

Department of Taxes, *Sixth Annual Report of Commissioner of Taxes, for the Tax Year Ended 30th June, 1977* (1979).

Department of Taxes, *Notes on Provisions of Income Tax (Amendment) Act, 1979 in Relation to Farmers* (1979).

Ministry of Finance and Development Planning, *Financial Statements, Tables and Estimates of Consolidated and Development Fund Revenues, 1979–80* (1979).

Ministry of Finance and Development Planning, *Details to Support 1979–80 Estimates of Expenditure from the Consolidated and Development Funds* (1979).

Appendix 5.A
Estimated average value of cattle at traditional cattle posts as at July 1979

Age	Female	Male	Age	Female	Male
(months)	(Pula)		(months)	(Pula)	
	Calves	Calves		Cows	Oxen
2	10	10	38	103	138
4	25	25	40	105	145
6	39	41	42	108	152
8	48	55	44	110	156
10	49	57	46	110	156
12	49	57	48	110	156
			50	112	158
	Heifers	Tollies	52	113	161
14	50	58	54	115	166
16	59	71	56	116	170
18	72	89	58	116	170
20	82	101	60	116	170
22	84	104	62	117	171
24	84	104	64	120	175
26	86	106	66	122	183
28	94	120	68	124	187
30	98	129	70	124	187
32	102	136	72	124	187
34	102	136	74	124	188
36	102	136	76 +	125	190

Notes

Cattle post prices above are BMC prices paid to producers, *less* average rail, truck, trek and other selling expenses.

Immature cattle, such as those up to 36 months old, are traditionally traded among the farmers themselves at lower prices than the prices indicated above.

Mature cattle are traditionally traded between the farmer and a cattle buyer at lower prices than the prices indicated above, if the farmer is unable to sell the cattle directly to the BMC himself.

Appendix 5.B
Selected income tax statistics (July 1978–June 1979)

A. Unincorporated farmers

		Taxable income (after allowances)[a]								
From	Loss	1	1501	3001	6001	10001	25001	50001	
to	0	1500	3000	6000	10000	25000	50000	+	TOTAL
No. of assessments	71	101	87	77	34	28	3	5	406
Taxable income (P'000)	—	76	183	329	274	411	108	420	1801
Tax due (P'000)[c]	0	11	28	64	77	157	78	287	702
Average tax rate (percentage)	—	15	15	19	28	38	72	68	39

B. Farming companies

			Taxable income							
From	Loss	Nil[b]	1	1501	3001	6001	10001	25001	50001	
to	Loss		1500	3000	6000	10000	25000	50000	+	TOTAL
No. of assessments	71	23	29	13	12	8	7	5	4	172
Taxable income (P'000)	—	0	19	30	52	69	122	194	901	1388
Tax due (P'000)[c]	0	0	7	11	19	25	42	68	315	489
Average tax rate (percentage)	—	—	38	37	37	36	34	35	35	35

Notes

[a] Taxable income = chargeable income *minus* allowances, where personal allowance = P3600 p.a. for a married man, education allowance = up to P600 p.a., etc.

[b] A nil return for a company indicates that the company had not yet commenced operation, or else was dormant.

[c] Delays in collecting revenue are reported each year by the Commissioner of Taxes. An arrear arises if a taxpayer does not pay his tax within one month of receiving his assessment. Collectible arrears of tax due will probably be about 7–8% of tax due in 1980.

Appendix 5.C
The Effects of 1979 Amendment to the Income Tax Act

1   Farmers may now be classified in four ways. The following is a layman's
    guide to the system of classification.

Incorporated		Unincorporated	
A Farming companies (they must keep full records)	B Full records of purchases, sales and inventory	C Full records of purchases and sales only	D Adequate records not kept

2   Farmers of types A, B and C may substitute a three-year average for their
    chargeable farming income in the third year. In calculating the average, a
    loss is treated as if the chargeable income in that year were zero.
3   Farmers of type D will be deemed to have a chargeable income of 60 per
    cent of the value of cattle sold during the year, if such value is known. In any
    case, the Commissioner of Taxes may determine the chargeable income.
4   Farmers of type B only may deduct farming losses from income arising
    from some other kind of business.
5   Farmers of types A and B must make an irrevocable choice of their method
    of valuing their cattle inventories. Basically, they can choose either the
    current market price (method 5 in Table 5.5 in the text), or any value between
    75 and 125 per cent of the Standard Values (methods 2, 3 and 4, or
    valuations based on some other permitted percentage of the Standard
    Values).

Derek J. Hudson is Director of Research Bank of Botswana; formerly Research
Statistician and Government Statistician, Central Statistics Office, Botswana.

6 Mining Development: Environment, Social Costs, Retained Value and Shadow Wage Rates

BALEDZI GAOLATHE

Introduction

The second section of this contribution considers, with particular reference to Botswana's experience, the environmental protection problems that arise in the course of mineral development and makes some suggestions as to how they should be handled. The section on 'Social costs of mining development' briefly discusses social problems and associated social costs of mineral development, especially in relation to settlements at the existing mines and those planned to serve future mineral projects in Botswana. The following section calculates the retained values of the Selebi-Phikwe, Orapa and Morupule mining projects for selected years, to obtain an appreciation of the net benefits, to Botswana, of those projects. *Retained value* is defined so as to show how much of the gross income of mineral projects actually accrues to Botswana (government and people) as opposed to that part which accrues to foreigners. The fifth section, using the Morupule Colliery project as an example, discusses how shadow wage rates can be applied in project appraisal to aid decision making, especially in the countries like Botswana, where the authorities are anxious to promote labour-intensive projects, as one of the major ways of spreading the benefits of economic growth. It is beyond the scope of this contribution to discuss fully the theory and estimation of shadow wages. It suffices to regard a *shadow wage rate* as a measure of the opportunity cost of labour, that is, the output forgone elsewhere in the economy had it not been employed in a particular project, suitably adjusted to take into account national objectives favouring equitable income distribution.

Environmental protection in the mining sector

Background

In recent years environmental pollution problems have become a major area of

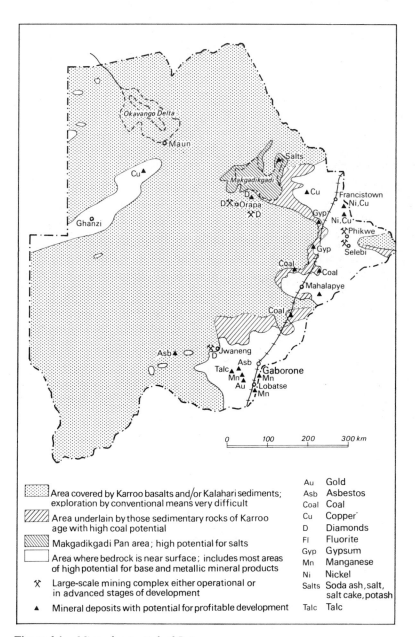

Figure 6.1   *Mineral potential of Botswana*

international attention. Among the several reasons for this concern are the:

1   Increased degree of international co-operation in many spheres including
     economic and cultural.
2   Increased realization that common property resources such as air, water
     and other ecological systems are finite and need co-ordinated management
     at both national and international level.
3   Realization that economic activities which are not subject to environmental
     rules in one country cause spillovers into other countries, for example
     through sea, or river pollution.
4   Fear that global pollution such as that of the atmosphere might cause major
     changes, for example, climatic, to the detriment of all.
5   Desire and nostalgia for the undegraded natural environment especially on
     the part of crowded urban dwellers.

The need to take measures, in the development process, aimed at protecting
the environment, was recognized in the international strategy for the second UN
Development Decade adopted in 1970, which declared that 'Governments will
intensify national and international efforts to arrest the deterioration of the
human environment and to take measures towards its improvement and
promote activities that will help to maintain the ecological balance on which
human survival depends'.[1] These environmental concerns culminated in the
holding, in 1972, of the first UN Conference on Human Environment in
Stockholm, Sweden.[2] The Conference adopted an Action Plan and
recommended the establishment of the UN Environmental Fund to be used for
financing environmental programmes envisaged in the plan. Such a fund has
since been established with offices located in Nairobi, Kenya.
    The need to take appropriate action to deal with the environmental
problems facing the world has brought about new concerns in the relationship
and interdependence between developed and developing countries.
Governments and industries of developed countries have been engaged in
research aimed at increasing the efficiency with which materials are used. Less
developed countries are concerned that this would decrease the demand for these
commodities, thereby depressing further their already relatively low prices.
There have also been fears on the part of developing countries that the tightening
up of environmental standards in the developed world would adversely affect
their trade positions, international assistance and transfer of technology. It is
expected that some developed countries will increase tariff protection for their
home industries under the guise that products from developing countries are
inferior and detrimental to the environment. Also, subsidies for pollution
control might reduce the resources available for foreign aid while whatever aid
remains would be disbursed only if developing countries adopted higher, even
though costly, environmental protection standards, irrespective of their
appropriateness to local circumstances.
    The controls referred to above may also prove advantageous to developing
countries. First, the concern for global pollution engenders a spirit of
international co-operation. Secondly, the disposal problems, for example, of
synthetics might once more foster an increased demand for natural fibres to the
advantage of primary producing countries. It is, however, very important that
developing countries should begin now to tighten their environmental

protection standards as the costs of reconstruction later would be higher. These countries ought to learn from the mistakes of those which were earlier in the process of development.

The mining sector

Mineral exploration, mining and processing constitute activities that may degrade or destroy the environment. They do not only scar the land but also create vast quantities of effluent, rich in various wastes including chemicals, and also generate waste dust fumes and toxic gases which are emitted into the air.

In mineral development planning, the objective should be the conservation of not only the minerals themselves but also the environmental resources. Since as a general rule mines are eventually exhausted there is need to plan mining as one of a series of land uses. At exploration stage, restrictions should be very stringent since at this stage viable mineral discoveries are not assured and since the costs of environmental protection are relatively low. The approach to costing should be the determination of the alternatives of not undertaking mineral exploration or mining.

Once a decision has been taken to allow mineral development in an area, operational restrictions should be invoked, as a general rule, with costs being met by the developers themselves (that is, internalized), to reduce adverse side effects to the maximum extent possible for each unit of output.

There are certain costs which cannot be added to production costs but have to be met by national agencies. These costs arise from the need to measure and monitor changes in existing and potential mining areas so that the impact of mining can be fully appreciated and predicted, and from the need to embark on research to develop mining and processing methods that will reduce or eliminate adverse impacts from mining on the environment and to determine the best ways of dealing with waste disposal. Costs also are incurred in the diagnosis and control of occupational diseases.

It should be appreciated that by internalizing many of the environmental costs, the net effect is to increase the unit cost of the product. The additional cost will be borne by either the investor (the most likely in the circumstances of mining in developing countries), shared between the investor and the consumer or entirely borne by the latter by way of increased price. Generally a mineral project ought not to be allowed to go ahead unless it can meet all its direct and indirect economic and social costs, including associated environmental ones.

Botswana's experience

There are three Acts of post-Independence origin which provide a legal framework for the control of mineral development activities including their impact on the environment. The Mines, Quarries, Works and Machinery Act of 1973, in addition to providing for the supervision of prospecting, mining, quarrying and ancillary operations, mainly on matters affecting the safety, health and welfare of employees, gives extensive powers to the Minister to make regulations for protecting the land (including from undermining), water resources and other aspects of the environment of a mine or quarry.

The Mines and Minerals Act, while allowing a prospector to sink shafts or dig holes or trenches, requires him to fence them while in use and fill them in after use. It also makes provision for advance deposits by developers to defray restoration expenses in the event of the government having to do it rather than the developer. The Act imposes further restrictions, in conjunction with the National Parks Act, on operations within a national park. Such restrictions were in fact imposed on a company which was given a licence to prospect in the Chobe National Park and Maikaelelo Game Reserve.

The Atmospheric Pollution Prevention Act makes provision for the prevention of pollution of the atmosphere resulting from the carrying on of mining and other industrial operations. The Act also makes provisions for studies of the levels of concentration of matter polluting the air anywhere in Botswana.

All the major industrial and mining townships have since been declared controlled areas for the purpose of the Atmospheric Pollution Prevention Act. These are:

1   Selebi-Phikwe Township and Mining area
2   Lobatse Township
3   Francistown Township
4   Orapa Township and Mining Area
5   Gaborone Township

Furthermore, all the mining leases issued and agreements made since Independence contain clauses on the environment to supplement or emphasize the provisions of the law. For example, the Master Agreement between the government and the copper-nickel mining company contained a clause (no. 19) imposing extensive obligations on the company to protect the environment – but also allowing 'good mining practice' and the 'economic consequences for the Company' to be considered.

Selebi-Phikwe

The Selebe-Phikwe mining, smelting and power station complex constituted a particularly serious threat to the environment from the sulphur dioxide gases that were to be emitted and from other wastes. In the planning process various steps were taken to counteract the potential hazards to human and animal population as well as the general ecology of the area. The township, though relatively near the complex, was located away from the direction of prevailing winds from the complex. The smelter complex incorporated a sulphur reduction facility to reduce the amount of sulphur dioxide emitted into the atmosphere and in the process produce elemental sulphur, which, though not profitable, could be sold at some return, although this eventually proved unsuccessful. To reduce the atmospheric pollution incidence further, the smelter and power station stacks were to attain heights of 160m and 76m (525 and 250 ft) respectively. These were considered, by experts, to be the minimum heights which could afford dilution and dispersion of toxic gases to acceptable levels before meeting tree-line and ground levels. With these precautions being fully implemented it was anticipated the sulphur dioxide (SO_2) daily average ground level concentration would be below a maximum acceptable level of 0·1 mg/cu m.

In addition the government set up a monitoring system. Two automatic sulphur dioxide analysers, Beckman Model 906A, were in operation in 1976 to monitor changes in sulphur dioxide concentration emitted by both the smelter and the coal-fired 65 MW power station. Earlier seven primary air pollution monitoring units had been set up at Selebi-Phikwe. Dust fallout has also been under measurement. In 1974, air pollution primary monitoring stations were also set up at Orapa, Morupule where a small coal mine is in operation, Sua Spit (the future location of brine works), and at Gaborone, the major non-mining industrial centre.

The sulphur dioxide emissions at Selebi-Phikwe are of particular concern because the company's original plans to produce sulphur did not succeed, greatly increasing the amount of sulphur dioxide emitted; as a result the government negotiated greatly increased expenditure by the company on pollution control. (See Chapter 7 by Lewis in this volume on 'The impact of the Shashe Project on Botswana's economy' (especially pp. 107–8). Sulphur dioxide emissions cause acute damage to vegetation, including certain types of leaf injury at concentrations above 0·4 parts per million (PPM), while chlorosis and excessive leaf drop is known to occur at long exposures even where the concentration is as low as 0·25 PPM. In America large areas of land were denuded of vegetation by sulphur dioxide and other pollutants emitted from smelters in the early part of this century before control measures there became stringent. Vegetation has now re-entered some of the areas due to pollution control. Laboratory studies indicate that some people will experience mild chronic respiratory irritation at 5 PPM, while sensitive people will react at 1–2 PPM and have severe bronchiospasms at 5–10 PPM.

Table 6.1   *Air quality standards for sulphur dioxide in selected countries*

Country	Single exposure 20 minutes averaging time		24 hours averaging time	
	mg/cu m	PPM	mg/cu m	PPM
USSR	0·5	0·19	0·15	0·058
Poland	0·25	0·1	0·075	0·03
Sweden	0·22	0·08	0·09	0·03
Switzerland (March–October)	0·25	0·1	0·17	0·07
Canada (Ontario–Industrial)	0·26	0·1	0·52	0·2
Federal Republic of Germany (Long-term exposure)	0·13	0·05	—	—

Source
Compiled by the writer, the main source of information being World Bank, *Environmental, Health and Human Ecologic Considerations in Economic Development Projects* (1974).

Air quality standards are also attained indirectly by controlling the sources of emissions. For this purpose various countries have established emission standards alongside air quality standards. Emission standards establish maximum amounts of pollutants permitted to be emitted from specific sources. Table 6.2 gives examples of emission standards for sulphur dioxide in various countries.

Table 6.2   *Emission standards for sulphur dioxide in various countries*

Country	Source of emission	mg/cu m	PPM
Britain	Contact sulphuric acid plants other than sulphur burning	9200	—
USA (New York)	—	5200	2000
Australia (Queensland)	Metallic plant SO$_2$ recovery	9200	3540

Source
Compiled by the writer, the main source of information being World Bank, *Environmental, Health and Human Ecologic Considerations in Economic Development Projects* (1974).

Botswana benefits considerably by keeping abreast of air quality control developments in other countries. Being a late-comer to mining and industrial development generally Botswana is well placed to avoid the mistakes of other countries which were in the business earlier.

The original plan of operation at Selebi-Phikwe envisaged that all the mining would be underground. Waste dumps would be an insignificant element because 55 per cent of the tailings would be used underground as backfill material, and the remainder would be the ore material eventually to be discarded after treatment as slime. Later it was decided to work a section of the mine for a time as an opencast operation. As a result an area of 527×10^3 sq m (630×10^3 sq yd) will be required for tailings for the life of the mine. Some of the rock being dumped is good construction material which a few firms are already using. On the other hand the slime dams will eventually cover an area of 225×10^4 sq m (269×10^4 sq yd).

The effluent water from the slime is treated and chemically analysed regularly. The results in 1977 showed that the water led to neighbouring streams posed no danger to human or animal life. It contained traces of copper (0·2 PPM), nickel and xanthate understood to be much below WHO maximum levels though it had a sulphate smell. The future plans envisage a complete recycling of the water, a move very much consistent with the needs of a water thirsty country such as Botswana. The alternative use of the area to be covered by dumps and tailings would have been subsistence agriculture and cattle ranching; at the most this would have been worth P7000 per annum since, without detriment to the environment, one livestock unit can be grazed per 4 hectares. (9·9 acres). This is a small sum bearing in mind the use being made of the dump material which is believed to have an even higher net turnover.

The waterborne sewerage from the mine complex and the town is inter-connected and treated through a series of dams. By 1977 the water finally discharged to the neighbouring streams did not appear to be sufficiently pure as to pose no health hazard. The chemical analysis results were not available. Plans were, however, underway to develop irrigation based on the final effluent water and this would obviate further disposal to neighbouring streams. With regard to the refuse, burning and deep-burying of the remains are the methods being adopted. These methods allow for rehabilitation of the land for other uses.

The noise element from the opencast operations poses a serious nuisance to the township inhabitants and there is no evidence that any steps were taken to try to control it. However, this section of the mine will be shortlived. With regard to the welfare of the miners themselves, safety equipment and training were to be provided. The miners were to be periodically examined and other health and safety problems including dust control were to be dealt with seriously, and the government as provided for in the Acts would undertake regular inspections. Up to 1977 there had been no industrial disease cases.

It is worth noting that the costs of most of these control measures – erection of sulphur reduction plant and tall stacks and liquid effluent treatment works, other than the township ones, and their maintenance – are being met by the operating company. The government, of course, spends money on monitoring and inspections.

Other mining areas

The opencast Orapa diamond mine poses no serious hazard to the atmosphere since the power station is presently liquid-fuel fired and the rest of the processing plant electrically driven. Up to 1984 the mine tailings will take up an area of 46×10^4 sq m (55×10^4 sq yd) and since the life of the mine is indeterminate the ultimate size cannot be determined. The tailings are diamondiferous and it is envisaged that with the advance of technology and development of markets, they will ultimately be reprocessed. Whereas the opportunity cost of the land is known the value of the tailings cannot be accurately determined. The slime disposal area will have covered an area of 72×10^4 sq m (86×10^4 sq yd) by 1982 and the ultimate size will also depend on the economic life of the diamond pipe.

The waterborne effluent treatment at the mine is one of the most advanced. The treatment system includes equipment which artificially activates bacteria to act fast on organic matter as the effluents circulate in concentric cement channels. The net effect is that the system as a whole covers a very small area and virtually all the treated effluent water is re-used for irrigating dairy cattle feed. The decomposed liquid is used for soil fertilization. The non-waterborne refuse is buried and the top soil turned to cultivation afterwards. The mine also has an incinerator where some of the undesirables, e.g. wastes from the abattoir, are burnt.

With regard to Morupule, the small size of the mine and the fact that there is little treatment of coal on site have meant that the environmental impact is still insignificant. In the mine process the coal dust is controlled by a wetting system.

The government and the private sector have for some time been considering the development of brines in the Sua Pan, part of a huge depression in northeastern Botswana, which contain a variety of salts including sodium chloride, soda ash, sodium sulphate, potash and bromine. The processing of the brine for the commercially viable salts such as soda ash would require disposal of vast quantities of effluent potentially damaging to the environment. After studies covering various alternatives it was eventually decided to locate the brine processing works 22 km (14 mi) from the Pan, near a township planned to serve the project but to be established far away for reasons to be explained later; two pipes had to be constructed, one to the brine refinery, the other to take effluent back to the Pan area.[3] The returned brine effluent would contain other salts for potential extraction in the future and because of the size of the brine pans the dilution possibility would be remote. Other factors taken into account in the planning were air pollution, smell and noise. The brine works township was chosen as a potential site for a big abattoir. The siting of it was to have regard to prevailing winds to minimize smell in the direction of the township. The same applied to the power station where the smoke stack also had to be high. The main road and the airport would be far enough from the populated areas to minimize the noise incidence.

As far as can be ascertained Botswana appears to be among the forefront of countries which have made considerable progress in codifying environmental control legislation. There are other Botswana laws which have not been mentioned dealing with environmental protection such as the Water Act, the Agricultural Resource Act and the Fauna Conservation Proclamation. In the Mineral Section, although a series of regulations is still to be promulgated, the major problem in Botswana is that of recruiting and retaining officers with expertise to help implement the laws and enforce standards.

Concluding remarks on environmental protection

A co-ordinated approach, at international, national and project levels, in deriving and implementing measures for the protection of the environment is essential, since the main transporters of waste (namely air and water) have no respect for international borders. There may be a temptation in sparsely populated developing countries, such as Botswana, to pay less attention to the environment, on the grounds that the waste disposal media within their borders still have excessive absorptive capacity, and to pursue the growth objective without taking into account the environmental degradation trade-offs. This temptation must be resisted, since environmental rehabilitation measures taken after the event or too late are likely to be more costly and moreover such costs would unfairly fall on future generations.

Generally a policy of controlling pollution at source using the best available technology and fully internalizing all the environmental costs is preferable. Apart from encouraging project promoters to seek out and adopt less damaging processes, internalization facilitates more comprehensive appreciation of the costs and benefits of projects before they are implemented. In any event it is easier to monitor and control pollution at source than to identify, monitor and control its effects.

Social costs of mining development

Mining disrupts the old or existing sociological set-up; and after a period of time the mine may be exhausted. The new society cannot easily adapt to the old ways when its livelihood derived from mining is displaced, while the new skills gained may prove to be irrelevant. If disaster is to be avoided planning must be geared to provide long-term alternative outlets for skills gained once mining is finished.

When a new mine is developed, local people are disturbed or displaced.

Adequate compensation for such people for disturbance, and to help them resettle in other areas, must be given. Also infrastructure must be designed not only to meet the requirements of the mine but also of the region, to facilitate its orderly development and the integration of the mining community into the local community. Such infrastructure should include adequate facilities for health, safety and material well-being of all local persons employed and living in the vicinity. There are also costs associated with the preservation of harmony in the area of operations, such as additional police, social welfare workers' salaries, and so on.

On the periphery of modern mining towns, especially in developing countries, squatter townships have always developed to which authorities have given little, if any, attention, as they have regarded these settlements as unauthorized and transitional. To the surprise of all concerned these townships have perpetuated themselves. Their inmates have largely been the unemployed, the lowly-paid or rural people who have come in search of jobs and better prospects or those who have merely heard of the glamour of town life. Their dreams having not been fulfilled they have continued to live in these settlements at the barest subsistence level and have not been provided with adequate, if any, basic facilities such as potable water and sewerage, nor with health, education and recreation amenities at convenient distances, or indeed at all. In some cases squatter settlements in population terms have exceeded the main adjoining towns. Clearly, planning for a new project or expansion of an old project should take these problems into account. On the cost side adequate provision should be made for basic amenities and resettlement expenses; and the potential influx of the unemployed should be planned for and costed.

Rights to mine in Botswana are conferred on the mining company by a mining lease issued in terms of the Mines and Minerals Act. The Act obliges the mining company to compensate those occupants of the area to be covered by a mining lease who have to be removed or whose other rights are affected by mining operations. The level of compensation is a matter for negotiations between the mining company and the owners of the land. The Minister is, however, empowered to intervene if the two parties cannot agree. The owners or occupiers of land under a mining lease are further allowed to retain rights to grazing their stock or growing crops on such land, provided these activities do not interfere with mining operations. In addition to these provisions, annual rentals are payable to the owner of the land and to the central government. Even at the prospecting stage, provision exists for compensating, within reason, people whose rights are disturbed. These arrangements go a long way to internalizing the opportunity costs of land. Grazing and cultivation can, and to some degree do, take place within the present mining lease areas, other than the two pertaining to diamonds. The diamond lease areas are fenced off for security reasons, but to compensate for the total alienation of the land much higher rentals are payable. The mining company has also turned part of the area to cattle ranching and cultivation and at the same time the area has become a haven for wildlife.

Botswana has not been immune from the sociological problems, especially those of squatter townships, brought by mining. Selebi-Phikwe copper–nickel project was the first major mineral project to be embarked on after Independence. The project, though it directly employs a labour force of 3500, has brought into being nearby a town of 25 000 people. Of this number 12 000 people live in the squatter sector of the town which was not anticipated and for which no plans were made. For the anticipated and planned part of the township, the financial aspects were gone into thoroughly and among other things the company had to contribute 75 per cent of the cost of common services, the balance being met by other anticipated users of the township including the government. Estimates showed that the maintenance of the townships would be fully met from the anticipated local revenues and would not require a government subsidy. The squatter settlement, however, took everybody by surprise by becoming a permanent reality. The authorities have since been forced to do something about the situation. At the time of writing 36 water taps had been installed throughout the settlement, some access roads had been constructed, a clinic and local school had been provided and plans were under way to develop residential plots and a local shopping area and to provide other common facilities. More than P40 000 had already been spent by the township authority and in the short term an unforeseen recurrent budget of at least P30 000 was anticipated. The name of the settlement is Botshabelo, which in the local language means place of refuge.

This whole problem of mining settlements has since been under study to avoid Botshabelo experience in future mining projects. At the diamond township, Orapa, the squatter problems did not arise because of the township location within a diamond security fenced area and because of the diamond protection controls. These measures, of course, do interfere with other freedoms including that of mobility and choice to live where one likes within Botswana, whether employed or not. However, for the new diamond mine at Letlhakane it was decided to house the miners at an existing village 12 km ($7\frac{1}{2}$ mi) away where their housing would be completely integrated within that of the existing society. The company undertook to provide the initial housing and to contribute towards the development of common services in the village. An unforeseen problem has been reluctance on the part of the new settlers to fully integrate and respect the traditional authority in the village

The coal mine at Morupule happened to be some 14 km (9 mi) from a large village, Palapye, which had come into existence for different socio-economic reasons. Here again the local miners, who number about 130, were given plots within the village and assisted to build for themselves or to rent houses or huts. The squatter problem was avoided. In both cases extra costs are incurred in transporting the workers to and from the mine.

The Sua Project infrastructure studies provide another interesting example of how the mine township problems are being tackled in Botswana with the aim of meeting the national economic and social objectives.[4] The Sua mineral project is yet to reach maturity. It has already been explained that it will be based on the brines of a large depression in the northeastern part of the country, known to contain a variety of salts including sodium chloride, soda ash, sodium sulphate, potash and bromine. Pending the attraction of companies with the necessary expertise and finance for the project the government undertook infrastructure feasibility studies, covering township, roads, railways, water supplies, power and other services. With regard to the township, the potential squatter problem was anticipated and a deliberate effort made to plan the township in such a way that the squatter problem would be greatly minimized, if not eliminated. The planning took into account the results of sociological and housing studies carried out at Selebi-Phikwe and at other modern townships.

Attention was first given to the location of the town. A location 22 km (13½ mi) away from the Sua brine pan was chosen for several reasons including availability of favourable agricultural soils, pollution problems and nearness to a potential source of water. It was hoped the relatively good agricultural conditions could be taken advantage of by some of the unemployed. This would be in line with the traditional pattern of large villages which have been carefully located as economic and social centres from which people disperse to the lands, cattle posts and other areas of economic activity and to which they come for social interaction and services during slack periods.

The town planning aimed at a simple town pattern to facilitate quick demarcation of plots, cheap construction of roads and other infrastructure facilities. The town could be developed on the basis of an environmental area of, say, 700 households containing different social groups, and with basic common facilities such as a school, social centre and open space or park. The town would be expanded by adding units of this kind rather than be allowed to grow in a haphazard manner. These town units would be located with a view to facilitating ease of access to the industrial and commercial areas. Among the freedoms to be enjoyed by newcomers to the township would be to choose a plot of an appropriate size for the family and suitably located to satisfy individual desires, to design their own houses or to choose among the various drawings, to select construction materials according to taste and financial resources, to extend the houses with the passage of time and to use their plots for informal small industrial and commercial undertakings. The freedom to build would, of course, be restricted to comply with minimum hygienic standards and safety requirements. On arrival the newcomers would find receptionist workers ready to receive and settle them. Construction materials would also be made conveniently available. The self-help process shown to prevail in other centres would be encouraged. This approach derives from other towns where experience and studies have shown that people, allocated properly serviced plots and helped to find materials and allowed to build themselves over time, come up with durable structures at low cost.

The above discussion touched upon the social costs arising in particular from the squatter settlements that have usually not been planned for, but which do emerge as soon as the implementation of a mining project commences. In a free society facing unemployment, people are bound to congregate at project sites hoping to find jobs. The important point is that the planning of a mineral project or any other major project must take this problem into account and, subject to the manner in which authorities wish to deal with it, allocate the resultant costs to the particular project. The planning and appraisal must also address the problem of what becomes of the mining township and its satellites after exhaustion of the mine.

The net contribution, or retained value, of the mining sector

At the time Botswana attained its Independence in 1966 there was virtually no mining activity. Since then, a copper–nickel mine has been opened at Selebi-Phikwe, diamond mines are in production at Orapa and Letlhakane, a new diamond mine will come into production in 1982 at Jwaneng, while a coal mine is also producing at Morupule. There are prospects for future mineral development projects based on the following minerals:[5] brines, coal, diamonds, copper, nickel, asbestos, gypsum and semi-precious stones.

Mineral development has been the major factor in the growth of Botswana's economy which will continue to be mineral-led into the future. The sales of the mineral industry increased from P3·4 million in 1970–1 to nearly P95 million in 1976–7. During the same period its share of total exports increased from 17–63 per cent. In terms of direct and indirect revenue it is estimated that the mining industry accounted for about 41 per cent of total recurrent revenue to the government in 1975–6. It is estimated that over P350 million had been spent in mineral projects and related infrastructure from independence to 1979. According to the National Development Plan 1976–81, the mining industry should be the largest contributor to the GDP by 1980–1.

However, in a developing country such as Botswana, which has to recruit expatriate skilled manpower and is dependent on imported industrial and consumer goods, the gross estimation of benefits very often overestimates the real benefits to the country. In the following pages an attempt will be made, using Mikesell's approach,[6] to estimate the retained value to Botswana in selected years for the ongoing copper–nickel, diamond, and coal projects mentioned above.

We shall first consider the Selebi-Phikwe Project (BCL) for the years 1974–5. The BCL retained value (RV) can be represented by the following equation:

$$RV = W - SE + DP - Md + RO + L + DD + CT + WT + CU + OT$$

where

W = total wages, salaries, and salary supplements
SE = salaries of expatriates accruing abroad
DP = domestic purchases of goods and services
Md = import content of DP
RO = royalty payments to Botswana
L = payments to landowners
DD = dividends paid to Botswana government and to Botswana resident equity shareholders
CT = corporate income tax
WT = withholding tax on dividends to non-residents
CU = customs duties
OT = other taxes

The results of the above equation with figures substituted for 1974 and 1975 are summarized in Table 6.3.

In 1974 the retained value of copper–nickel production exceeded export value by over P5 million. The reason for the high proportion of retained value was that the mine had not yet reached full production and to a large extent both capital and working costs were being financed from imported investment finance. In 1975 the recorded export value was P22 million whereas the retained value was about P15 million. The retained value still appears large in relation to the export value. The structure was expected to change for the worse when the mine begins to repay accumulated loans and to declare dividends in the long-run. The figures in Table 6.3 can rightly be reduced further by P2 million and P3

Table 6.3   *BCL mining project retained value 1974–5 (P'000)*

	1974	1975
W	5707	6893
−SE	−710	−969
DP	18 774	22 568
−Md	−17 303	−20 589
RO	750	750
L	22	22
DD	—	—
CT	—	—
WT	—	—
CU	5975	6553
OT	121	144
Retained value	13 336	15 372
Copper-nickel exports	8200	22 000

Source
BCL and Central Statistics Office.

million respectively for 1974 and 1975 since expatriates spend some 40 per cent of their income on imported goods. The retained value figures given in the table are also an estimate of the foreign exchange contribution of BCL in the years in question. Table 6.4 gives the results of the retained value analysis for the diamond project for 1973–5.

Table 6.4   *Debswana diamond project retained value 1973–5 (P'000)*

	1973	1974	1975
W	758	1025	1313
−SE	−50	−63	−72
DP	206	531	1557
−Md	−185	−478	−1401
RO	1105	1470	1411
L	37	37	37
DD	1872	1094	8449
CT	3372	7314	5792
CU	359	658	753
OT	26	30	41
Retained value	7500	11 618	17 880
Total diamond exports	20 000	30 100	32 100

Sources
Debswana, Central Statistics Office and Ministry of Finance and Development Planning.

The following results emerge. Retained value increases from 38 per cent in 1973 to 39 per cent in 1974 and 56 per cent in 1975. The sharp increase in the retained value in 1975 was the result of the renegotiation of the diamond deal, which led to increased revenues to the government. For the Debswana project the total wages paid to expatriate employees did not constitute significant figures. The low retained values were mainly due to high dividend income to the foreign shareholders and the high import content of inputs to the mine.

We now turn to Morupule Colliery, the retained value of which is shown in Table 6.5. In 1974 Morupule Colliery achieved retained value of P150 000 or 62 per cent of value of production because output was below capacity. The following year it had decreased to 29 per cent of value of production as output increased much faster than the labour force and local purchases. The leakages go to transport costs, imported goods and expatriate wages remitted abroad.

Table 6.5   *Morupule Colliery retained value 1974–5 (P'000)*

	1974	1975
W	135	174
− SE	−20	−29
DP	87	110
− Md	−78	−99
RO	1	2
L	3	3
DD	—	—
CT	—	—
CU	22	28
Retained value	150	189
Total coal production	242	641

Source
Table computed on the basis of information provided by Morupule Colliery.

From the above retained value analysis for the three projects some conclusions can be drawn for Botswana. A substantial portion of the wages went to the skilled expatriate manpower employed at the mines. Most of the income which expatriates earned left the country either as home remittances or to pay for imported goods which Botswana itself did not produce. Concerted training and localization programmes designed to produce local skilled manpower would go some way to solving the problem. It is clear from the tables that the greater portion of the purchases of the mines involve imported goods. In other words backward linkages were insignificant at the time. The reason is that the hardware material inputs of the mines are products of sophisticated modern industry not yet established in developing countries such as Botswana. With forward planning, simple inputs such as miners' overalls and helmets can be manufactured locally right from the start and as more mines are opened industries for producing hardware can be embarked upon to increase retained value.

Also, in the case of Botswana, at that time no serious effort had been made to promote agricultural production to serve not only the needs of the miners but also of the many other people who have congregated in mining townships. In this connection it is encouraging to note that timely action is being taken to maximize retained value at Jwaneng. Maximization of retained value by localization and promotion of backward linkages has positive impact on the balance of payments through increase of the net foreign exchange earnings of the projects concerned. Other ways to increase retained value include negotiating mineral deals, which while leaving a reasonable return to the foreign investor, obtain a greater part of the mineral rent for the national income, in the form of taxes, royalties and dividends.

Shadow wage rates in the determination of mining method at Morupule Colliery

Morupule Colliery is operated by Morupule Colliery (Pty) Ltd, a company owned in the majority by Anglo American Corporation of South Africa Ltd. The coal mine was developed mainly to serve the needs of the Selebi-Phikwe project by providing coal to the power station and the smelter.

The colliery is located 12 km (7½ mi) west of Palapye village and railway station in eastern Botswana. The mining lease area is covered by 20–50m (65–165 ft) of Kalahari beds consisting of sand, unconsolidated and semi-consolidated pebbles, gravels, calcrete and ferricrete. Below the Kalahari beds are strata of the ecca and Dwyka series consisting mainly of shale, mudstone, siltstone, coal, sandstone and tillite. Coal occurs in two seams in the mining lease area. The lower seam which has an average thickness of 8·6m (28 ft) has better quality coal, while the upper seam, apart from being extensively weathered, contains interbedded shale which renders mining uneconomic. As at 1976 the mining lease area contained mineable reserves in situ of 53·8 million tonnes. Table 6.6 summarizes the quality characteristics of the coal being mined from seam No. 1, and from the information in Table 6.6 it is evident that Morupule

Table 6.6 *Quality characteristics of Morupule coal on air-dry basis*

Moisture	4·0–6·0%
Ash	17·7–23·7%
Volatiles	21·1–24·6%
Fixed carbon	49·7–54·3%
Calorific value	22·75–24·86% MJ/kg
Sulphur content	1·3–2·1%
Phosphorus content	0·017–0·06%
Ash fusion temperature °C—	
	Def: 1250–1300
	Hem: 1300–1350
	Flow: 1350–1400 +
Abrasive index	94–244
Hardgrove index	64–73

Source
Morupule Colliery (Pty) Ltd.

coal is of relatively low grade in quality, though suitable for thermal power stations and comparable purposes.

The colliery came into production in 1973 with a production capacity of 17 500 tonnes per month. However, the colliery operated below capacity till 1975 when it produced 13 000 tonnes per month owing to technical problems at the Selebi-Phikwe smelter and power station. By 1977 the rate of production approximated 30 000 tonnes per month or 360 000 tonnes per annum. The original plan anticipated production of 78 000 tonnes for the first delivery year increasing to 173 000 tonnes per year by 1977. Later there would be phase II involving the expansion of the mine to produce 640 000 tonnes per annum, some of which would be exported to neighbouring countries if markets were available. Phase III in the planning envisaged, in the long-run, a further expansion of the mine to a capacity of 1 million tonnes per year, provided the cost of a washing plant and transport would permit viable coal export.

The mining method adopted at Morupule Colliery was the underground mechanized method, working on the board and pillar system of mining. Before this decision was taken, opencast and underground handgot methods were also considered. The opencast method had to be considered since, though usually capital intensive, it is less wasteful and at high production levels has relatively low unit costs arising from economies of sale. In the context of Botswana, owing to unemployment problems, the handgot method which is relatively more labour intensive, had also to be examined.

The opencast method was rejected for several reasons. At the relatively low production levels for phases I and II indicated above, the capital costs were going to be higher and the benefits of economies of scale would not arise. Though the area had a favourable overburden to coal ratio of 2·9:1 to start with, the softness of the overburden, which required maintenance of flat slope angles, increased potential stripping costs. With the application of opencast methods 90–100 per cent of the coal would be removed whereas with underground methods up to 50 per cent of the coal would not be extracted, for safety and technical reasons. In the case of Morupule Colliery the wastage factor could be ignored for two reasons. First, the coal left behind would be recoverable if the scale of operation warranted opencast methods in the future. Secondly, at the low rate of production the wastage would be negligible overall when one takes into account the large size of the deposit.

The underground handgot method, despite its labour intensity, was not adopted because of higher capital and operating costs as compared with the

Table 6.7   *Comparison of capital and working cost of handgot and mechanized mining methods at Morupule – 1972 prices*

Method	Annual sales tonnes	Number of employees	Capital expenditure P million	Working cost thebe
Handgot	210 000	308	2·8	252
Mechanized	210 000	49	2·3	152

Source
Morupule Colliery (Pty) Ltd.

Table 6.8   *Morupule Colliery working cost comparison at 220 500 ROM tonnes per annum*

Item	Mechanized thebe per ROM tonne	Total (P per month)	Handgot thebe per ROM tonne	Total (P per month)
Labour	51	9400	158	29 000
Power	26	4800	30	5500
Miscellaneous stores	15	2800	8	1500
Explosives and accessories	7	1300	7	1300
Loader costs	18	3300	—	—
Crushing and screening	7	1300	7	1300
Administration and overheads (including township costs)	15	2700	16	3000
Water	1	200	2	300
Head office charges	3	500	3	500
Contingencies	9	1700	9	1700
SUBTOTAL	152	28 000	240	44 100
5% discard	8		12	
Working costs per metric tonne sales	160		252	
Capital charges	164		178	
Selling price at mine	324 t		430 t	

Source
Morupule Colliery (Pty) Ltd.

mechanized method. Table 6.7 shows the comparison of the two methods at the anticipated annual production level of 210 000 tonnes in the early years.

Table 6.8 gives a breakdown of the estimated operating costs at the run of mine (ROM) production of 220 500 tonnes per annum, which is equivalent to sales tonnage shown in Table 6.7. Table 6.8 provides additional arguments against the adoption of the handgot method, it being assumed wages could not be reduced below 20 per cent of those prevailing at the Orapa Mine. The price for handgot coal would be more than 30 per cent higher than the mechanized method. P4·30 per tonne for handgot would yield the same profit as P3·24 per tonne using the mechanized method. Because of the cost-plus arrangement which Morupule Colliery had with the major consumers, adoption of the handgot method could have meant an extra annual cost to the consumers and some loss of revenue to the government. For the handgot method capital costs were higher because 37 houses for priority personnel on the mine property, costing P463 000, would be required while for the mechanized method 12 houses for essential personnel costing only P231 000 were needed. In both cases the rest of the labour force was to be assisted to fend for itself for housing in the neighbouring village of Palapye, and transport to and from the mine would be provided.

The various elements of Table 6.8 were costed at market prices. Virtually all the inputs, other than labour, came from the Southern African customs area duty free into Botswana and it is unlikely that any of these could have been obtained any more cheaply from outside the area. So for the rest of the inputs, exclusive of local labour, we can accept the market prices as reflecting the true opportunity costs. For local labour, a shadow wage rate could have been used in order to reflect employment objectives which favours income distribution through job creation. For the handgot method, of the P29 000 for labour P8600 went to expatriates, leaving P20 400 for locals. Elsewhere, it has been argued that the shadow wages for Botswana unskilled labour, which is largely drawn from rural areas, can for practical purposes be equated to zero.[7] Most of these people were to be employed initially as unskilled, and to be trained on the job. For the mechanized method the estimated expatriate labour cost was P6175, and by similar reasoning the local labour cost should have been zero. If we apply shadow wage rates to Table 6.8 we obtain Table 6.9 and it will be seen that adoption of shadow wages has reduced the working costs per sales tonne for the handgot method to 135 t, whereas those of the mechanized method are now higher at 142 t. Taking the capital charges into account the selling price for handgot method remains slightly higher, but by only 2·2 per cent as compared to more than 30 per cent before shadow wage rates were applied. The two methods almost balance, leaving a final choice to be made on intuitive judgement or other

Table 6.9   *Morupule Colliery working cost comparison at 220 500 ROM tonnes at shadow prices*

Item	Mechanized thebe per ROM tonne	Total (per month)	Handgot thebe per ROM tonne	Total (per month)
Labour	34	6175	47	8600
Power	26	4800	30	5500
Miscellaneous stores	15	2800	8	1500
Explosives and accessories	7	1300	7	1300
Coal loader operating costs	18	3300	—	—
Crushing and screening	7	1300	7	1300
Administration and overheads	15	2700	16	3000
Water	1	200	2	300
Head office charges	3	500	3	500
Contingencies	9	1700	9	1700
SUBTOTAL	135	24 775	129	23 700
5% discard	7		6	
Working costs per tonne sales	142		135	
Capital charges	164		178	
Selling price at mine	306 t		313 t	

considerations. If cash flow figures, showing phasing of capital expenditure, were available, then calculating the net present value might have revealed a different picture. The most expensive capital item for the handgot method as compared with the corresponding item for the mechanized method is housing. Housing cost P232 000 more for the handgot method. Breaking down the housing figure into labour and other costs, and shadow pricing, the former would further reduce the selling price per tonne produced by the handgot method.

The above analysis was intended to illustrate how shadow wage rates, which are part of shadow prices, can be applied in project appraisal to reflect the national employment creation objective, where there is more than one option of implementing a given project. The same principles apply where selection has to be made from several projects with different cost structures and labour intensities. The use of shadow prices on an *ad hoc* basis would, however, be inappropriate since it may lead to inconsistency in project choice and would make comparison of projects difficult. Therefore a move towards the use of shadow prices should be preceded by formulation of a comprehensive set of national economic parameters, reflecting a balance of the various national objectives, to be applied in the appraisal of all development projects.

Notes

1. United Nations, *International Strategy for the Second Development Decade*, New York (1970).
2. United Nations, *United Nations Conference on Human Environment Proceedings*, Stockholm (1972).
3. Ministry of Mineral Resources and Water Affairs, *Sua Project–Dukwe New Township*, prepared by SWECO Consulting Group (1975).
4. ibid.
5. See *National Development Plan 1976–81* and Geological Survey Department, *Resources Inventory of Botswana Metallic Minerals, Fuels and Diamonds, Mineral Resources Report No. 4* compiled by J. W. Baldock with contributions by J. V. Hepworth and B. S. I. Marengwa, Gaborone, Government Printer (1977).
6. R. F. Mikesell, *Foreign Investment in Copper Mining: Case Studies of mines in Peru and Papua New Guinea*, Baltimore and London, Johns Hopkins University Press (1975).
7. B. Gaolathe, 'The costs and benefits of mineral development, a cost benefit approach to mineral investment with special reference to mineral projects in Botswana', draft thesis, University of Bradford.

Baledzi Gaolathe is Permanent Secretary, Ministry of Finance and Development Planning; formerly Permanent Secretary, Ministry of Mineral Resources and Water Affairs, Botswana.

7 The Impact of the Shashe Project on Botswana's Economy

STEPHEN R. LEWIS, Jr

Introduction

The Shashe Project, a copper–nickel mine and related infrastructure in northeastern Botswana, is the largest single investment made in the country thus far. Despite great hopes for its contribution to the success of Botswana's development objectives, as well as to the profits of the private shareholders in the mining company, the project has been a severe disappointment, plagued by technical and financial difficulties every year since its operations were supposed to commence in 1973. The entire financial arrangements of the project (covered by five volumes of legal documents, some 3700 pages) were restructured in 1978, following two years of negotiations among all parties. While 1978 saw considerable improvement in the physical results of mining operations, continued low metal prices led the mining company to state in February 1979 that they had again 'initiated negotiations with various lenders and the Government to attempt to obtain financial assistance'. This paper aims first to clarify how the Shashe project fits into the economy of Botswana; secondly, to explain the significance of the financial restructuring, and thirdly, to indicate some of the unusual analytical problems that arise in interpreting the statistical performance of Botswana's economy in light of the peculiar nature of this very large project.

The Shashe Project bulks large in all of Botswana's statistics. The initial projection of capital investment required for the project as reported in the 1968–73 National Development Plan was about P122 million; the total estimated GDP in 1968–9 was P51 million. By 1977, the total capital invested in the project through both the mining company and the government (for infrastructure) was around P350 million, due to cost over-runs and operating losses met through increased borrowing by the mining company; estimated GDP in 1976–7 was only P299 million. If any project could be described as 'lumpy', the Shashe Project qualified. At the end of 1977, the direct employment by the mining company was 3424 persons including 366 expatriates. Total formal sector wage employment in Botswana, apart from the government, was estimated to be 38 200 in mid-1977. The project supports an entirely new town of Selebi-Phikwe, with a population estimated to be in excess of 25 000 in 1978, third largest in the country. And, as discussed further below, the project accounts for about 30 per cent of total commodity exports, and a very large share of the government's external debt. An understanding of the project, therefore, is essential if one is to fully comprehend the performance of Botswana's economy.

The original project

Prospecting activity in northeastern Botswana led to the initial discovery of the Selebi-Phikwe ore bodies in 1964, and by 1969 an estimated 45 million tonnes of proven and probable reserves had been established with an average nickel content of 1·2 per cent and an average copper content of 1·3 per cent. Since nickel has varied between three and four times the value per tonne of copper, the nickel content of the reserves is most important in determining their value. The project was designed, (1) to mine the ore (first at Phikwe, a larger ore body with a higher nickel content, and later in Phase 2 at Selebi, which is about 15 km (9 mi) from the Phikwe shaft); (2) to smelt it to form a copper–nickel matte; and (3) to produce elemental sulphur as a by-product, since the ore is high in sulphur content. The matte produced at the project was refined at AMAX Nickel's refinery in Port Nickel, Louisiana, USA and AMAX Nickel received a 'toll' refining charge. The metals from the final refining were then sold in the Federal Republic of Germany by Metallgesellschaft (MG), for which MG received sales commissions. Sale in Germany was a condition of a substantial portion of the financing.

Proceeds from the sale of metals were paid by MG into a trust account at Barclays Bank in Jersey. Amounts due to the major lenders to the project (see below) and to government and parastatal organizations providing infrastructure services to the mining project were accumulated in the trust, and were paid over to payees as specified in the various loan and tax agreements.

As one can see, working capital needs were substantial. The mining company and its sales subsidiary had to finance: initial extraction expenses, initial smelting, transport to the USA, transport to Germany, and accumulation of the required amounts in the trust accounts owing to other parties to the agreements, plus any stock-holding at any point in the pipeline from initial mining to final sale.

Financing of the project was, and is, complex. Infrastructure provided by government and its principal parastatals, the Botswana Power Corporation (BPC) and Water Utilities Corporation (WUC), was financed by loans from the World Bank (US $37·5 million), Canadian assistance (Can. $30 million), and US assistance (US $6·5 million).

The operating company for the mine and smelter is BCL Ltd (formerly Bamangwato Concessions Ltd), whose equity is owned 15 per cent by the government of Botswana (issued free of consideration as part of the original financial agreement) and 85 per cent by Botswana RST Ltd (BRST, or, in the financial press, Botrest). BRST is a publicly quoted company with shares trading in New York, Johannesburg, and London. AMAX Inc. of the United States and Anglo American Corporation of South Africa, Ltd (including certain associate companies) each own approximately 30 per cent of BRST's shares, with the remainder held by the general public. Botrest was at one point a 'hot stock' on the strength of the richness of the Selebi-Phikwe ore body and hopes for the Shashe project among the private investors.

In addition to P33 million of shareholder capital, BCL's investment in the mine and smelter also was supported by long-term loans from a consortium of German banks, led by Kreditanstalt für Wiederaufbau (KFW – DM222 million) and from the Industrial Development Corporation of South Africa (IDC – R13·5 million), as well as certain subordinate loans from AMAX/AAC. Assured delivery in Germany was important for the KFW participation – which also brought the interests of the Bonn government. The 'major lenders' (IBRD, KFW, and IDC) obtained various guarantees from AMAX/AAC, including a very important provision for the financial support of the project by the major shareholders until completion of Phase I (the mine at Phikwe and the smelting facilities; the mine at Selebi is in Phase II). The loans were secured by a first mortgage over mining rights and assets of the project. MG provided some guarantees for the principal value of the major loans, but was not involved in the commitment to 'complete' the project. The trust deed governing the Barclays trust arrangement referred to above contained detailed restrictions on the ability of BCL to borrow funds other than subordinated shareholder loans without the prior consent of the major lenders.

Compensation to the government for the lease of the mining rights was in three parts: (1) a royalty of 7·5 per cent of profits, subject to a minimum of P750 000 per year; (2) income tax on the profits of BCL, and (3) dividends on the 15 per cent of equity in BCL owned by government. In addition. income taxes on employees and customs duties arising from the importation of both capital goods and intermediate goods were expected from the project, but were not part of the mining lease.

Problems with the project

Shortly after the initial agreements were signed in 1972, it became obvious that the BCL portion of the project would involve substantial cost over-runs. By the terms of the agreements, these over-runs were met by AMAX/AAC through loans to BRST, which in turn lent to BCL. BCL was to pay no more than 1 per cent above the prime rate (in the relevant borrowing centre) for such 'completion loans'. Interest and principal on the loans were subordinated to payments to the major lenders, and could not be paid unless BCL first had net income from which to make such payments, and secondly, met a current assets/liabilities test. BRST was a conduit for the funds, and BRST paid the major shareholders 4 per cent above prime for its funds. The interest spread was intended to be covered by BRST dividend income from BCL: such income has never materialized, and is unlikely to do so. The technical problems and cost over-runs involved a continuing inflow of completion loans from the major shareholders, plus the accumulation of interest on such loans because BCL never had net income to pay even the interest on its loans. A financing facility was arranged by which Barclays Bank (both International and Botswana) provided added funds to support the project, both through BRST and direct to BCL, most of the latter secured through a charge on the 'pipeline' of matte and metals.

As engineering and operating problems continued, losses due both to operating deficits and interest charges mounted and increased debt to cover them continued to accumulate. At the end of 1973, BRST (which has few other interests now other than BCL, and which, therefore can be used to approximate what has happened in BCL, which does not publish accounts) had approximately P36 million in paid-up share capital and P75 million of debt. By the end of 1977 BRST had the same P36 million equity, and approximately P280 million in debt, including commercial bank loans. Around P100 million of the debt is attributed to accumulated operating losses.

Among the most important technical problems in terms of the financing arrangements was that the project could not produce sulphur as a by-product, as had originally been envisaged. This led to (1) inability to meet contracts with Triomf Fertilizer for delivery of sulphur, (2) emission of sulphur dioxide into the atmosphere at much higher concentrations than planned, and (3) the inability of the project to 'complete' Phase I. As a result, the obligations of the major shareholders to finance the project through subordinated completion loans could not be terminated and AMAX and AAC were effectively locked into a losing project with quite open-ended commitments. Further, the SO_2 emission created serious pollution problems that eventually required an additional and quite specific agreement by BCL, BRST and the major shareholders to undertake and finance a programme of anti-pollution works.

Finance restructuring

By 1976 all parties to the transaction agreed that some financial restructuring was needed, and negotiations began. They were finalized by signature of agreements on 16 March 1978, which added another volume to the project documentation. The final twelve months of negotiations took place in the atmosphere of the worst metal markets since the 1930s, and the continued appreciation of the Deutschmark, which added significantly to the 'senior' indebtedness obligations of BCL. The restructuring arrangements were significant for all parties, in varying degrees, and were also significant for Botswana as a whole.

Under the new arrangements, BCL sells copper-nickel matte to AMAX Nickel once it is shipped from Southern African ports. This substantially shortens the 'pipeline' of matte and metals, which saves an interest burden by reducing stocks needing financing. The arrangements also eliminate the MG sales commissions, which were large. Further, the trust deed has been amended to allow BCL to withdraw the amounts held in trust, in exchange for a guarantee from the principal shareholders for the same amounts. The net effect of these changes is to decrease BCL's working capital needs and increase its current assets, with a net benefit to its financial position.

The two major lenders to BCL (IDC and KFW) were each pre-paid a portion of their loans – and in the case of the KFW loan this reduced BCL's DM exchange risk considerably. The partial pre-payment without premium was funded by a US $25 million loan provided by Chase Manhattan Bank on Eurodollar terms. Barclays Bank (International and Botswana) arranged longer repayment terms for their loans both to BCL (P25 million) and BRST (P6·5 million). Both the Chase loan and the Barclays loan (excluding any portion secured by the 'pipeline' of matte) to BCL are guaranteed by the major shareholders. The Barclays loans stretch the maturities of the bank credit to BCL farther than had the previous arrangements.

While these changes in the debt position have not had great impact on BCL's balance sheet or income statement, P75 million of 'completion loans' from the major shareholders were cancelled and an equivalent amount of 10 per cent cumulative preference shares were issued to replace them. Dividends on, and redemption of, the preference shares may not be paid unless BCL has net income. However, the substitution of the 10 per cent dividend for *compounding* interest on subordinated loans will improve both the reported operating position of BCL and its balance sheet. Preference dividends payable will not show as an expense, whereas interest payments do – raising reported net losses; and the substitution of P75 million preference share capital for loans will lower the debt/equity ratio. The reduced interest will reduce measured interest losses on Botswana's balance of payments as well. Whether these changes have major significance in real terms for BCL, or for BRST, remains to be seen.

The previous royalty based on profits of BCL has been cancelled, and a royalty of 3 per cent on the gross value of the recoverable metals (principally nickel and copper but also cobalt) in the matte sold by BCL will be effective from 1 January 1977. This should triple or quadruple government's revenue from the project, and reflects a consensus among the parties that government is entitled to more significant compensation for removal of a depletable resource than was the case under the old arrangements, given that the project has turned out to be unprofitable.

The changes in the project 'description' led to a deletion of the requirement that BCL produce sulphur. This change made it possible to 'complete' Phase I of the project. Two very significant results emerge. First, in recognition of the removal of the sulphur facilities and consequent increased SO_2 emissions, BCL, BRST and the major shareholders have agreed to a programme of pollution abatement, with the major shareholders agreeing to provide up to P10 million in support of such a programme. Secondly, with the completion of Phase I, the shareholders are no longer required by their agreements with the major lenders to provide essentially unlimited financial support for BCL. Their financial obligations now are to assist BCL to (1) complete Phase II (the Selebi mine and related works estimated at P22 million), (2) undertake the pollution programme (assured shareholder finance is committed to P10 million), (3) provide funds or guarantees for the payment of royalty to government for the first three years (if such royalty is paid by a special guaranteed note of BCL), and (4) in addition to the previous items, provide a fund of approximately P41·8 million to meet BCL's other cash requirements, up to 31 December 1981. Thus, instead of an open-ended commitment to support the project, the major shareholders have a defined and limited commitment, as to both amounts and timing of funds. At the same time, the restrictions in the trust deed were amended to allow BCL much more flexibility in borrowing from sources other than the shareholders without the specific permission of the lenders. The poor metal prices in the 12 months following the signing of the restructuring agreements led in February 1979 to the shareholder proposals (already mentioned) for additional assistance to the project, that is, the P41·8 million commitment was nearing exhaustion.

The Shashe Project and the economy

The significance for Botswana of the original arrangements, as well as the restructuring, is substantial, and some examples of the project's impact may be instructive.

It is common to examine the trade position of developing countries and draw conclusions about their vulnerability to international trade with reference to dependence on certain primary exports. However, Botswana as a nation has been relatively isolated from the fluctuations of metal prices in the Shashe Project for two reasons. In the first place, the project never made profits. In the second place, the shareholders were committed to support the project financially. As the project has always run at a loss, improved metal prices simply reduce the need for new shareholder funds; weak metal prices increase the need for new shareholder funds. Operating losses have reduced GDP estimates; overall losses have reduced estimates of GNP, because payments of interest to persons abroad are subtracted from GDP in arriving at GNP. But these losses have not really affected Botswana citizens, because there has been an inflow of loans to cover the losses. The only losses to Botswana, and they are in some sense only national ones, have been of income tax not payable up to now because the mine has made no profits, and of income tax not payable if and when the mine does make profits until accumulated losses have been offset. In these circumstances, improved or worsened performance by the BCL project has had little effect on Botswana's foreign exchange reserve position. In such a situation one may wonder whether one should look at the prices of copper and nickel as guides to the fortunes of Botswana's economy.

As a related problem, consider the construction of a terms of trade index for Botswana. If one were choosing weights for the external terms of trade, one would normally use the relative value of the major commodities in the export basket for a base year – which would give copper–nickel matte a weight of nearly one-third for 1977. However, increases and decreases in the prices of copper and nickel have had no net effect on Botswana incomes, nor on Botswana's import capacity, since the Shashe Project began operations, because of the two factors mentioned above. Should copper and nickel prices even be included in the terms of trade index for that period, under these circumstances? One might argue they should not.

The operations of BCL/BRST have a major impact on the balance of payments *statement* of Botswana, if not on the overall balance as reflected in reserves. For the years 1975–8, the Bank of Botswana indicates that net investment income has flowed *to* Botswana in three years out of four, despite the large amounts of private foreign investment in Botswana. As explained in the bank's annual report this is the result of 'certain large non-resident controlled establishments' which made losses in those years – and the only establishment large enough to affect the figures in such a way is BCL/BRST. As indicated, no changes in reserves have occurred due to the peculiar financing arrangements of the losses.

Prior to restructuring and the completion of Phase I, fluctuations of BCL's position were met mainly by increased or decreased flows of shareholder funds. With the new arrangements, the shareholders' *obligations* stop when the various funds referred to have been exhausted. However, the shareholders may support the project if it still needs financing in order to protect the investment they have made. However, the removal of both the shareholder obligation and the limitations on other borrowing by BCL make the financing of any cash needs of BCL less straightforward. The improvement or deterioration of BCL's position will potentially have a greater impact on Botswana's foreign exchange reserve position. Botswana is no longer so isolated from the fortunes of the markets for copper and nickel.

Of the P125 million of external government debt outstanding on 31 March 1977, nearly P60 million was debt for the Shashe infrastructure. The Canadian dollar loans were converted to grants during 1977, so the total exposure has fallen considerably. The World Bank Loan is covered by a direct cash guarantee from the major shareholders in certain circumstances; and it is secured by an agreement of hypothecation over the mining lease and a first mortgage over certain of the real properties of BCL. In addition, the agreements covering the infrastructure involve 'take-or-pay' arrangements with BCL and the major shareholders which assure that service payments will be made on government's debt. Thus a substantial part of the debt exposure of the government of Botswana is highly qualified by various aspects of the Shashe project agreements.

From a 'country risk' point of view, commercial lenders are concerned not only with government external debt but also with the external debt of major private and parastatal bodies. BCL/BRST external debt at 31 December 1977 was in the range of P260 million. Of that amount, P168 million was 'completion loans' (including accumulated interest) due to the major shareholders, which cannot be paid except out of net income, nor can it be paid unless BCL meets a target ratio of current assets to liabilities. Some of the balance of the debt, for example, the Chase loan and part of the Barclays loans, is guaranteed by the major shareholders. Most of the remainder is secured either by the matte in transit or by an agreement of hypothecation over the mining lease of BCL and a mortgage bond over some properties in Selebi-Phikwe township. The external debt of BCL/BRST is, therefore, largely payable on a contingent basis, and much of the rest is guaranteed or is secured by stocks or by real income-earning properties. Also, before Phase I was completed, the major shareholders were obligated to supply funds to pay the external lenders to BCL. They are also obligated to the extent of the standby funds under the restructuring agreements as well. Only that portion of the P260 million debt which is secured by stocks and real property represents an unambiguous claim on Botswana's national income and foreign exchange.

The size of the Shashe Project relative to Botswana's economy has already been mentioned, and some indications of its relative importance are given in Table 7.1. In 1972, when the project documents were originally signed, the estimated capital cost of the project was P150 million for both the mine and the infrastructure. GDP in 1971–2 was only P103 million; imports in 1971 were only P57 million, and in 1972 (reflecting in part the beginning of project construction) were P84 million. Gross fixed capital formation figures were not estimated for 1972–3, but in 1973–4 the national estimate was P78 million; 'mining assets' as reported in the BRST annual reports increased P45 million during 1973 and P55 million in 1974. (Company figures exclude the government-provided infrastructure.) The project accounted for the majority of gross domestic investment in those years.

On the government side, Shashe Project expenditures were projected to be

Table 7.1   *Selected data on Botswana and the Shashe Project (P million—at current prices)*

Botswana	1971–2	1972–3	1973–4	1974–5	1975–6	1976–7		
GDP at market price	103	n.a.	198	213	276	299		
GDP in mining	11	n.a.	16	13	34	43		
Operating surplus, modern sectors	26	n.a.	44	32	58	54		
Gross fixed capital formation	53	n.a.	78	57	79	77		
Changes in stocks (excluding cattle)	2	n.a.	9	31	28	3		

Botswana	1971	1972	1973	1974	1975	1976	1977	1978
Imports	57	84	115	125	159	181	240	291
Exports	28	45	59	82	105	153	157	183
Copper–nickel exports	0	0	0	8	22	52	42	50
Commercial bank advances at 31 Dec.	12	16	23	38	56	71	74	77

BRST		1972	1973	1974	1975	1976	1977	1978
Mining assets and rights (31 Dec.)		79	124	179	196	204	203	226
Total debt (31 Dec.)		n.a.	75	140	223	254	282	230[a]
Commercial bank loans (31 Dec.)		0	0	9	20	27	29	53
Stocks (31 Dec.)		n.a.	3	10	25	27	17	7
Operating profit (loss)		con.	con.	con.	(15)	0	(4)	2
Interest charges		—	6	13	20	26	28	27
Total profit (loss)		con.	con.	con.	(39)	(26)	(32)	(25)

Notes

n.a. = not available.

con.: construction period, profit and loss not relevant.

[a] This drop reflects reduction of BRST loans from major shareholders, on-lent to BCL, in exchange for P75 million of redeemable cumulative preference shares as part of restructuring agreements.

Sources

Data on Botswana are from various issues of *Statistical Bulletin*, published quarterly by the Central Statistics Office (CSO), Ministry of Finance and Development Planning; and from various issues of the annual National Accounts, also published by the CSO.

Data on BRST and BCL are taken from the published *Annual Reports* of BRST, which are usually available in March of the year following the year covered by the report.

37 per cent of the total estimated public sector development expenditures in the 1970–5 Development Plan, and exceeded half in some years. Projections in the 1970–5 Plan anticipated that the revenue from the Shashe Project (tax, royalty and dividends on the mining project, plus customs revenue arising from the construction and operating phases, plus income tax on employees) would

provide 26 per cent of government's internal revenue during the Plan. Further, it would account for P14 million of the projected P33 million *increase* in government revenue between 1970–1 and 1974–5 – an important 42 per cent of the expected rise in revenues. No wonder that the Plan stated that:

> the very rapid development of the economy projected in this Plan is almost entirely dependent on the successful creation of a mining sector . . . The main factor determining the allocation of funds is the need to provide basic infrastructure for mining development. (pp. 17, 19)

The reader will also wish to look at Chapter 9 on the Customs Agreement to see how the Shashe Project was important in generating additional customs revenue for the government through the operation of the customs formula (pp. 131–58).

Even with the unfortunate results of the project's delay and financial difficulties, the very high rates of growth experienced in Botswana in the early to mid-1970s were closely related to the development of the Shashe Project. The impact on construction has already been alluded to. In electric power, the Shashe division of the Botswana Power Corporation began operations in 1973 and now produces for the use of the project about 70 per cent of the total electricity generated in Botswana.

In the transport sector, rail traffic carried to and from Botswana stations between 1972 and 1977 increased by 78 million tonne–kilometres. Of this, around 50 million, or nearly two thirds, can be accounted for by (1) transport of coal to the Shashe power station from the Morupule Colliery and (2) transport of the copper–nickel matte for export. Inclusion of the movement of raw materials and capital goods for the project would result in an even larger share of the increase.

In banking, advances by the commercial banks to borrowers in Botswana increased by about P62 million in 1971–7 (P12–74 million). The increase in advances to the mining sector accounted for over P20 million of the increase – about one-third of the total. An amount of approximately P20 million can be identified in the BRST annual reports as the debt by BCL or BRST to the banking system in Botswana. (It might be noted here that this increase in domestic bank credit may have come at the expense of building foreign exchange reserves, as domestic borrowing substituted for foreign borrowing.)

Export earnings of Botswana increased by P98 million in 1973–7. Copper–nickel matte exports grew from zero to P42 million, accounting for more than 40 per cent of the increase. Of course, in light of the comments earlier on BCL's operating losses, the contribution of the project to *net* foreign exchange earnings, and to GDP, was not as great as might be implied at first from the gross export figures.

With respect to GDP, individual enterprises are not broken out of the accounts, but some comments can be made on the basis of the information in the public BRST annual report. Unfortunately, operations in practice are less important than the hopes in the 1973–8 National Development Plan, where it was stated that the GDP contribution from the project 'may be as high as P40 million' (p. 220). (In 1973–4, total GDP was only P198 million, indicating the relative positive contribution that was anticipated from the project.)

Because of the size of the Shashe Project, variations in the BCL/BRST profit and loss position have significant effects on measured GDP, especially in year to year changes. For example, from 1973–4 to 1974–5, GDP at market price only increased by P7 million – considerably less than the rate of inflation. But GDP in mining and quarrying fell by P2·7 million. BRST reported in 1975 an operating loss, before interest charges of P15 million. Since BCL had not been operating in 1973, the huge loss contributed to negative growth in GDP originating in that subsector over the period, pulling down both mining GDP and overall GDP growth. On the other hand, GDP rose by about P60 million between 1974–5 and 1975–6, partly on the strength of a P21 million increase in mining GDP. This increase was related to the fact that BRST's operating position changed from P15 million loss in 1975 to break-even in 1976. This would have given measured GDP a boost of P15 million on a calendar year basis. However, as already noted, the import capacity of Botswana's economy, or the value of foreign exchange reserves were hardly affected by the large changes since (1) almost the entire loss was financed by external lending to BRST/BCL, and (2) the improved loss position in 1976 simply meant fewer new shareholder funds.

There are some interesting aspects of the inventory or stocks position of BCL/BRST as well. In 1973–5, BCL increased its stocks by P22 million (while total increase in national, non-cattle, stocks in 1973–4 and 1974–5 combined was estimated to be about P40 million). In 1977 BCL/BRST stock fell by P10 million; the 1976–7 GDP estimates indicate non-cattle stocks nationally only rose by P3 million, down from a P28 million increase the previous year.

The terms of restructuring provided for BCL/BRST to sell P14 million of its remaining stocks to AMAX Nickel during the first half of 1978. Normally one would expect an increase in stocks of exportables to be associated with a decrease in foreign exchange reserves, and a decrease in stocks to be associated with an increase in reserves. The peculiar financing situation of BCL, however, renders these generalizations inaccurate. It would be convenient to explain a sizeable portion of the increase in Botswana's foreign exchange reserve building in the first half of 1978 by an equivalent run-down of stocks, thus indicating little overall change in the national position on real and financial external assets. However, the lack of significant change in the BRST/BCL borrowing from the domestic banking system indicates that the cash flow from the liquidation of stocks simply enabled BCL/BRST to incur fewer new debts abroad to finance its operating deficit during that same period, rather than adding to the foreign reserves of Botswana.

Conclusion

The Shashe Project was originally expected to be a striking success, both for the shareholders in BRST and for Botswana. In the event, the early technical difficulties, the inflation in Southern Africa and cost over-runs, the disastrous state of the metals market in recent years, the peculiar nature of the financing of 'completion' capital, the debt burden of DM222 million, among other factors, all contributed to a project with which no one is happy: shareholders, lenders or Botswana. The fact stressed earlier, that the losses on the Shashe Project to date have not directly harmed Botswana, is related to the fact that Botswana had never received the benefits that *should* have flowed from a profitable and well-run project. Many lessons might be learned from the experience; they are not the subject of this article. Here the intention has simply been to point out some salient features of the original and restructured agreements from the point of view of how they, and the project, affect the measured performance of Botswana's economy.

Stephen R. Lewis, Jr is Professor of Economics at Williams College, USA and Economic Consultant, Ministry of Finance and Development Planning, Botswana; formerly Economic Consultant, Ministry of Finance and Economic Planning, Kenya.

8 Botswana's Trade Structure Compared with Those of Other Small Countries

E. O. OCHIENG

Introduction

Like most colonized countries, Botswana's economy was and still is closely integrated in the economic structure of industrialized countries, especially that of the colonizing power, and in the case of Botswana the economies of the Republic of South Africa and Britain. Independence in September 1966 only removed a facet of domination, the political one, but those of foreign trade and investment remained more or less intact. The international trade arena has developed in such a way that the less developed countries have become exporters of a few primary products whose demand and price are externally controlled and can fluctuate violently. This has frustrated many attempts by poor countries to develop via production of primary products; and the historical experience of dependence on the industrialized countries' markets for exports and imports gives little grounds for confidence that the existing structures will satisfy the developmental aspirations of these countries.[1] More recently the entire Third World has been engulfed by a steep upward movement of inflation, world-wide food shortages, sharp increases in petroleum oil prices and serious upheavals and instability in the international monetary system leading to devaluation and revaluation of major world currencies.

Botswana has not been excluded from these predicaments. In this paper we intend to look at aspects of her dependence on international trade and finance and to make comparisons with other similarly small countries. Consequently we shall briefly outline the economic structure of Botswana, then proceed to have a closer look at her foreign trade structure. Finally we shall have a brief evaluation of data on 14 small countries with populations less than 1·5 million for comparison purposes.

Structure of the economy

Botswana is a landlocked country with an area of 570 000 sq km (220 077 sq mi) of which more than two-thirds is covered by the Kgalagadi (Kalahari) desert.

The climate is continental and semi-arid with an erratic average annual rainfall of 475 mm (20·5 in), and recurrent droughts. The population is 766 000 (mid-1978 estimate) which is growing at about 3 per cent per annum. The numbers of people in paid employment are 60 400 (1976) within the country and over 60 000 (1977) mostly in mines in the Republic of South Africa.

Starting from a very weak and dependent economy, because historically the colonial powers meant eventually to amalgamate Botswana, Lesotho and Swaziland into the Republic of South Africa and therefore did not take any interest in developing these countries as viable economic units, Botswana has made tremendous efforts to achieve self-reliance. From a country which was regarded merely as a place where unskilled labour could be got for the flourishing extractive and manufacturing industries in South Africa; and from an economy which had to depend largely on grants-in-aid to balance its recurrent budget, major events and initiatives have helped to create a less dependent economy:

1   The movement of the central government from Mafeking in South Africa to Gaborone created new impetus, especially in the construction industry and more importantly, government expenditure now took place within Botswana.
2   The discovery and exploitation of a rich diamond mine at Orapa by De Beers, and the development of the copper–nickel mine at Selebi-Phikwe by Bamangwato Concessions Ltd. relieved the economy from its overwhelming dependence on beef exports as a source of foreign exchange. (In 1966–8 beef exports contributed 96 per cent of total export earnings.)
3   The renegotiation of the 1910 Customs Union Agreement with South Africa in 1969 gave the government a substantial boost in revenue and made it independent from grants-in-aid to support its recurrent expenditure by 1972–3.
4   The continued strong demand for Botswana beef ensured stable foreign exchange earnings.
5   The creation of the Bank of Botswana and the subsequent issue of the new national currency, the Pula, promoted monetary independence and encouraged more rational and nationalistic use of monetary and fiscal policies.
6   Stable and continuous government committed to development.

The interactions of these events and many others culminated in an economic structure depicted by Table 8.1, which shows the industrial origin of GDP at current market prices for the years 1965, 1971–2 and 1976–7. In 1965 just before Independence we see a very minute economy with GDP = P32·8 million and very much dependent on agricultural production (34 per cent), mainly livestock agriculture. Notably the mining sector formed a tiny 0·6 per cent of GDP, and most of the rest of the GDP was derived from commerce, services and construction.

The interim period of 1971–2 shows increases in all sectors and changes in the structure of the economy. The agricultural sector shows a decline in relative importance and the mining and commerce sectors show a big increase in relative importance. GDP has increased by more than three times. The construction and government sectors were also prominent. Manufacturing was still relatively

Table 8.1   *Industrial origin of the GDP at current market prices (P million)*

	1965		1971–2		1976–7		Index
	P (million)	% of Total	P (million)	% of Total	P (million)	% of Total	1976–7 / 1965
Agriculture	11·1	33·8	33·1	30·3	70·8	23·7	638
Mining and quarrying	0·2	0·6	11·2	10·9	43·4	14·5	21 700
Manufacturing	3·8	11·6	5·1	5·0	21·0	7·0	553
Water and electricity	0·2	0·6	1·3	1·2	10·9	3·6	545
Construction	4·8	14.6	13·8	13·4	19·2	6·4	400
Commerce	8·3	25·3	23·6	23·0	81·3	27·2	980
General government	⎫		11·8	11·5	47·3	15·8 ⎫	
Other services	⎬ 4·5	13·7	3·5	3·7	12·1	4·0 ⎬	1169
Dummy sector	⎭		−0·8	−0·8	−6·8	−2·3 ⎭	
TOTAL	32·8	100	102·6	100	299·2	100	912

Source
National Accounts of Botswana, 1976–7, Government Printer, Gaborone (p. 7).

unimportant (5·0 per cent of GDP), and consisted anyway mostly of the value added by the abattoir in converting live cattle to chilled, deboned beef.

The final period 1976–7 showed further increases in all sectors and changes in the structure of the economy. There were very big increases in the mining, commerce and government sectors. Agricultural and manufacturing sectors also showed marked increases. Structurally commerce became the most important sector followed by the agricultural sector. The government and mining sector were now also prominent. The great prominence of the commerce sector clearly reflects the role of distribution: nearly all goods for use in Botswana are imported with local production for domestic consumption still relatively unimportant. This is a serious structural imbalance; and when coupled with the fact that imports are a very large percentage of GDP (Table 8.9), shows a lack of 'real' growth, although the figures give an average annual growth rate of GDP of 28 per cent in recent years.

Foreign trade structure

Trends in trade

The trend in trade in Botswana is in conformity with historical studies which suggest a high probability that a country's import requirements will grow faster than its export expansion as the economy accelerates its growth.[2] Table 8.2 shows an ever widening gap between imports and exports, although this has not yet manifested itself in balance of payments difficulties. Before the introduction of the new national currency, in 1976, Botswana was just a province of South Africa in monetary terms, so that it was not possible for the country to have a balance of payments problem as such (although either public or private sector could, of course, have financial problems).

Table 8.2   *Annual trade statistics for selected years 1946–77 (P million)*

Year	Imports	Exports	Balance
1946	2·6	1·4	− 1·2
1951	3·5	4·3	+ 0·8
1956	6·1	5·8	− 0·3
1961	5·8	6·3	+ 0·5
1966	18·9	10·8	− 8·1
1970	40·9	18·3	−22·6
1971	59·1	30·3	−28·8
1972	84·2	44·8	−39·4
1973	115·0	59·2	−55·8
1974	125·4	82·0	−43·4
1975	159·3	105·0	−54·3
1976	181·4	153·2	−28·2
1977	239·6	156·7	−82·9

Source

Department of Customs and Excise: External Trade Statistics, 1977, Government Printer, Gaborone (p. 23).

Secondly, as Table 8.3 indicates, there have been huge inflows of foreign private capital, loans and grants which have more than offset the visible trade account deficit, and actually increased Botswana's external reserves. This could represent a future problem: when the full effects of loan repayment, repatriation of profits, dividends and interest come into play, or if political problems were to endanger foreign grants, this seemingly healthy situation could be eroded away, plunging Botswana into balance of payments difficulties – unless exports are dynamically increased or Botswana continues to obtain loans to repay previous loans. Already in 1975 the repatriation of profits, dividends and interest alone

Table 8.3   *Balance of payments (P million)*

Item	1975	1976	1977
Current items			
1.1 Balance of visible trade	−55	−39	−49
1.2 Balance on services	+ 8	−10	− 7
1.3 Transfer payments	+16	+50	+79
Balance on current a/c	−32	+ 1	+23
Capital items			
Balance on capital a/c	+57	+ 1	+ 2.
Overall balance	+25	+26	+25

Note

Current surplus 1977 includes a notional transfer to Botswana of P33 million and a notional capital payment of the same amount as a result of the cancellation of certain loans by donors.

Source

Bank of Botswana Annual Reports.

amounted to about 19 per cent of GDP.[3] Botswana's position is strengthened, for the time being, by the development of the large new diamond mine at Jwaneng which will indeed yield a large increase in exports, and by the fact that nearly all the country's external public debt is on concessionary terms, thus greatly alleviating debt service. Only one large government loan in commercial terms has been negotiated, although not yet drawn down, and that is for Jwaneng.

Botswana's economy is extremely open. The total of imports and exports almost equals GDP. Imports alone are nearly 60 per cent of GDP. The figure for exports is about 40 per cent. This openness in the economy makes it very vulnerable to the vagaries of unstable international market demand and prices for exports. The prevailing low prices for copper and nickel have plunged the Shashe Copper–Nickel Project, which is Botswana's largest single investment, into financial difficulties.[4] As a result, although the huge debts of the mining company are the private liabilities of the foreign shareholders and not of the government, there has been a major loss of public revenue as compared to what had been expected from the profits of the mine; and if copper and nickel prices should rise in the future, the proceeds will have to be appropriated for a long time to paying off the debts. Botswana is also highly vulnerable, in different ways, because of the risks involved in being dependent on exports of beef: the continuing need to renegotiate access to the EEC on the marketing side and the continuing risks of drought and disease on the production side. Relatively speaking, the international marketing of diamonds seems stable and secure; but Botswana is entirely in the hands of the De Beers Central Selling Organization over which it has no control.

The direction of trade

Botswana has very few trading partners. Her trade is dominated by three countries, South Africa, UK and USA, which together accounted for 85·9 per cent of total trade in 1973 and 84·5 per cent in 1977 (Table 8.4). South Africa takes the largest share – over 50 per cent – and its domination on the import side is on the increase – from 69·2 per cent in 1973 to 85·2 per cent in 1977. The export side was dominated by UK which still takes 40 per cent; the share taken by USA has dynamically increased from 0·6 per cent in 1973 to 26·8 per cent in 1978 because of purchases of copper–nickel. The share of 'Rest of Europe' is also becoming significant.

Figures for the Common Customs Area (CCA) indicate serious implications for Botswana: while the other countries in the CCA, overwhelmingly South Africa, have increased their exports to Botswana from UA 79·5 million in 1973 to UA 205·5 million (UA = 1 rand) in 1977 – an increase of 158 per cent – their imports from Botswana have increased from 11·1 million to only 18·1 over the same period – an increase of 64 per cent. This is an indication that Botswana has attracted less economic activity and especially less industrialization than South Africa in relative terms. The situation is made worse for Botswana because sales to South Africa of beef which has been her biggest export commodity is *subject to a small weekly quota*.[5] Why should Botswana's main export commodity suffer from restricted entry into the Common Customs Area? This means that Botswana will find it extremely difficult to increase her exports to the CCA because *her main exports have no*

Table 8.4   *The direction of trade 1973 and 1977 (UA million; UA = 1 rand)*

Area	1973 M	1973 X	1977 M	1977 X	Index 1977/1973 M	Index 1977/1973 X	% of total trade 1973	% of total trade 1977
CCA	79·5	11·1	205·5	18·1	258	164	52·0	56·4
% of total	69·2	18·7	85·8	11·6				
Other								
Africa	12·4	4·3	23·8	13·1	191	302	9·6	9·3
% of total	10·8	7·3	9·9	8·4				
UK	6·4	40·2	3·9	61·5	62	153	26·7	16·5
% of total	5·5	67·9	1·6	39·3				
Other								
Europe	2·2	3·0	1·4	21·3	62	708	3·0	5·7
% of total	1·9	5·1	0·6	13·6				
USA	12·6	0·03	4·1	42·0	32	127 315	7·2	11·6
% of total	10·9	0·0	1·7	26·8				
Rest of								
world	1·9	0·6	0·9	0·5	51	92	1·4	0·4
% of total	1·6	1·0	0·4	0·3				
TOTAL	115·0	59·2	239·6	156·7	208	265	100	100

Notes
M = Imports.
X = Exports.
M + X = Total Trade.
CCA = Common Customs Area.
Source
Department of Customs and Excise, External Trade Statistics 1975, 1977, Government Printer, Gaborone.

market there: the export of beef is restricted, copper–nickel by agreement is sold to USA,[6] the other partner states are also exporters of diamonds, and Botswana's manufacturing base is still in its infancy.

Botswana is clearly at a disadvantage in its trade relations with South Africa in being so dependent on South African imports. If Botswana were able to supply any significant exports to South Africa, it would at least create a degree of interdependence. There is nevertheless a minor advantage in the present structure of trade, namely that Botswana's earnings from exports are mainly in the form of freely convertible currencies. In due course the greater part of these foreign currencies are converted to rand in order to pay for imports, but in the interim the Bank of Botswana can invest these earnings in currencies of its own choice. Rand earned from exports to South Africa are not normally convertible into other currencies, certainly not without application to the South African authorities, so that they have to be held in South Africa until they are spent. Botswana, therefore, has greater freedom in its foreign exchange reserve investment policy than it would have if exports to South Africa were greater. This situation contrasts sharply with that of Lesotho, for example, since if

Lesotho were to withdraw from the Rand Monetary Area, a large part of Lesotho's foreign earnings would then be in Rand.

Exports to 'other Africa' and 'Rest of World' decreased in relative terms: the percentage of total trade for the two together decreased from 11 per cent in 1973 to 9·7 per cent in 1977 thereby making Botswana even more dependent on a few countries for external trade.

Commodity composition of trade: imports

The structure of imports by commodities did not change very much between 1973 and 1977 (Table 8.5). In 1973 the import of vehicles, machinery and

Table 8.5 *External trade – principal commodities imports 1973–7 (P million)*

	1973		1977		Index
	P (m)	% of T	P (m)	% of T	1977 / 1973
Food, live animals, beverages and tobacco	17·8	15·5	47·5	19·8	267
Mineral fuels and chemicals	11·3	9·8	44·1	18·4	390
Vehicles, machinery and equipment	39·9	34·8	55·5	23·2	139
Metals and metal products	11·4	10·0	22·8	9·5	200
Paper and paper products	2·4	2·1	8·1	3·4	338
Textiles	8·4	7·3	25·6	10·7	305
Other goods	23·7	20·6	35·9	15·0	152
TOTAL	115·0	100	239·6	100	208

Source
Department of Customs and Excise – External trade statistics 1975, 1977.

equipment took the greatest share of total imports followed by 'other goods' and food and drinks. In 1977 machinery still looked the biggest share but that of fuels increased fastest – by 290 per cent, reflecting the phenomenal rises in petroleum oil prices. The import of food also increased absolutely and in relative terms to become the second biggest category of imports. Textiles is the third fastest growing import in Botswana.

Looking at imports more closely[7] in 1973 the major imports were machinery and equipment (P23·8 million), transport equipment (16·5), metal products (11·4), special items (10·2), prepared food, drink and tobacco (8·7), textiles (8·4), mineral products (8·1) and vegetable products (7·6). In 1977 the major imports were machinery and equipment (31·3), mineral products (28·9), transport equipment (24·2), food (23·5), metal products (17·5).

Botswana's import structure seems normal for a developing country but what should cause concern is the amount of the food import bill. This is part of the colonial history trend: for through the redirection of effort away from food production the colonizers created the greatest dependence of all on international capitalism – inadequacy of food.[8] In Botswana, as in all the other Southern and

Central African countries, able-bodied young men were lured to work in mines in South Africa and only old men and women were left to till the land.

Another area we should look at seriously is the textile bill. Botswana has a climate in which it is possible to grow cotton; and based on this an integrated ginning-spinning-textile-garment industrial complex could be set up to reduce the textile import bill and probably promote exports.

Commodity composition of trade: exports

Until recently Botswana depended wholly on beef exports; however, recent developments already mentioned have increased this to three major exports: beef, diamonds and copper–nickel which together formed 87·1 per cent of total exports in 1977 (Table 8.6).

Table 8.6　*External trade – principal commodities exports 1973–7 (P million)*

| | 1973 | | 1977 | | Index |
	P (m)	% of T	P (m)	% of T	1977 / 1973
Animal products	23·5	54·9	46·9	29·9	200
Diamonds	20·0	33·9	48·4	30·9	241
Copper–nickel	—	—	41·2	26·3	—
Textiles	1·5	2·5	6·3	4·0	418
All other	5·2	8·7	14·0	8·9	271
TOTAL	59·2	100	156·7	100	265

Source
Same as Table 8.5.

Beef production is very much affected by weather and disease conditions. The incidence of droughts in Botswana is regular and at their worst the effects on the livestock industry are: no calves are born, there is a 50–75 per cent cattle population decrease, loans in the livestock sector are written off, there is a permanent damage to range, and there is panic sale of cattle.[9]

The other two major exports are minerals, and the crucial point to note here is that they are exhaustible resources. We should, therefore, be careful about the *rate at which we exploit exhaustible natural resources*, since if we exhaust them now, what will the future generations have? They have as equal a right to them as we have. As a minimum, that part of mineral production representing the value of natural resources should be invested in productive assets and not consumed.

An international comparison

We have had a close look at Botswana's economic structure, and several features clearly stand out:

1　Botswana has a growing deficit on the visible balance although this is offset at present by the inflow of loans, grants and private foreign investment.

2   Botswana has an extremely open and dependent economy:
    (a) her exports and imports form a large percentage of GDP,
    (b) she trades with few countries,
    (c) she depends on few primary exports,
    (d) her main exports are restricted by quotas, tariff and non-tariff
        arrangements and other international agreements,
    (e) she is landlocked – a significant proportion of the world's smaller
        countries are landlocked or are islands.[10]

The purpose of this section is to compare and contrast Botswana's trade
structure with those of 13 countries as defined by population only, that is,
countries with populations of less than 1·5 million. The purpose of this
comparison is to see whether Botswana's economic structure and international
dependency are in some sense typical of small countries in general, or whether
they are features peculiar to Botswana's own particular circumstances.

A type of stratified sampling technique was used to select countries for
comparison from most regions of the world. The availability of time series data
was crucial, so we considered those countries which had attained independence
by 1970. The countries finally selected were: Cyprus population 0·65 million; Fiji
0·56; Gambia 0·51; Gabon 0·53; Barbados, 0·24; The People's Republic of the
Congo 1·3; Guyana 0·81; Iceland 0·22, Mauritania 1·29, Mauritius 0·87,
Trinidad and Tobago 1·07, Swaziland 0·48 and Lesotho 1·19. At the outset I
must emphasize that comparative published data is notoriously out of date and
so in some cases less recent data has been used in the analysis.

The only common denominator about the countries selected is that they
have populations less than 1·5 million and nothing else (Table 8.7), but even so
their populations range from 0·22 million (Iceland), to 1·3 million (Congo); they
have average annual population growth rates 1965–73 of between 0·3 per cent
(Barbados) and 3 per cent (Swaziland). Their 1974 GDP ranges from US $90
million (Gambia) to US $1810 million (Trinidad and Tobago); and the GDP
average annual growth rates 1965–73 ranging from 1·8 per cent (Lesotho) to 12·3
per cent (Botswana). GDP per capita (1974) ranges from US $29 (Mauritania) to
US $5430 (Iceland); and growth rates of GDP per capita range from minus 0·2
per cent (Lesotho) to 10·2 per cent (Botswana).

The structure of the GDP by industrial origin also varies considerably
(Table 8.7). Nevertheless, all except four have services as the most important
sector, and manufacturing still forms a small share of GDP: ranging from 3 per
cent in Gambia to 19 per cent in Iceland. Of the four countries whose services
sectors were not the largest, three have important mining sectors, as shown in the
share of 'other industry': Gabon (50 per cent), Mauritania (42 per cent),
Botswana (32 per cent). A large percentage share for mining necessarily reduces
the share of other sectors, but even when this is the case, the large share of
services in GDP remains very striking, as it is for all 14 countries.

Table 8.8 shows that like Botswana, 9 out of the 13 other countries had
growing deficits on their visible balance of trade. Of the remaining four which
had surplus visible balances of trade, three were oil producers. Table 8.8 also
shows that over the seven years 1971–7 the cumulative deficit has, in most cases,
reached enormous proportions of a year's exports. Clearly this is not the whole
picture, nor is it necessarily a function of smallness. Indeed, small countries are
sometimes forced into correcting their balance of payments because of their

Table 8.7 *Basic economic indicators for 14 small countries*

Country	Population '000 mid-1974	GDP 1974 $ million	GDP per capita 1974 $	Annual growth rates 1965–73			% of GDP derived from each of the sectors			
				Population	GDP	GDP per capita	Agri-culture	Manu-facturing	Other industry	Services
Iceland	220	1200	5430	1·0	3·4	2·4	7	19	14	60
Barbados	241	290	1200	0·3	6·1	5·8	11	13	8	68
Swaziland	478	190	390	3·0	7·3	4·2	33	13	13	41
Gambia	506	90	170	2·2	3·3	1·1	56	3	1	40
Gabon	528	1030	1960	1·5	8·6	7·0	12	8	50	30
Fiji	564	470	840	2·2	7·5	5·2	23	11	9	57
Cyprus	645	850	1320	1·2	7·4	6·2	14	12	15	59
Botswana	654	190	290	1·9	12·3	10·2	28	9	32	31
Guyana	810	413	510	2·4	2·6	0·2	18	11	25	46
Mauritius	871	510	580	1·5	2·7	1·2	29	16	10	45
Trinidad and Tobago	1070	1810	1700	0·9	3·8	2·9	5	13	23	59
Lesotho	1191	170	140	2·0	1·8	−0·2	45	3	4	48
Mauritania	1290	380	29	2·5	3·7	1·2	29	4	42	25
Congo	1300	610	470	2·8	5·4	2·6	17	11	22	50

Note

For Guyana population, GDP and GDP per capita figures are for 1975 (Source: Notes on the Commonwealth, February 1979).

Source

World Bank, *World Tables 1976*, Johns Hopkins University Press, Baltimore.

Table 8.8 *Annual trade balance for selected countries (1971–7, selected years)*

Country	1971	1973	1975	1977	Cumulative deficit 1971–7	Cumulative deficit as % of 1977 exports
Cyprus (million Cyprus £)	−59·6	−97·0	−57·9	−107·6	−557	419
Fiji (million Fiji $)	−49·9	−100·3	−79·5	−118·2	−625	383
Gambia (million dalasis)	−17·6	−18·3	−23·6	−67·5	−225	205
Gabon (billion CFA francs)	+22·5	+49·2	+106·5	+151·5[a]	+459[b]	(161)
Barbados (million Barbados $)	−163·3	−224·9	−219·3	−358·5	−1692	886
People's Republic of the Congo (billion CFA francs)	−11·6	−0·8	+12·3	+6·3	+54	(95)
Guyana (million Guyana $)	+35·4	−84·6	+47·5	−137·9	−312	47
Iceland (million kroner)	−5·4	−5·8	−27·7	−19·1	−106	104
Mauritania (million ougniya)	+1·9	+1·2	+0·6	−2·4	+6	(86)
Mauritius (million rupees)	−101·0	−168·0	−156·0	−876·0	−1966	96
Trinidad and Tobago (million Trinidad and Tobago $)	−287·0	−189·0	+635·0	+717·0	+1351	(26)
Swaziland (million rand)	+7·9	+7·6	+14·1	−5·7[a]	+62[b]	(37)
Lesotho (million rand)	−25·0	−51·8	−69·3[c]		−183[d]	1867
Botswana (million pula)	−28·8	−55·8	−54·2	−82·9	−333	199

Notes
[a] 1976.
[b] 1971–6.
[c] 1974.
[d] 1971–4.

Sources
IMF, *International Financial Statistics*, Vol. XXXII, no. 2, February, 1979; Department of Customs and Excise, External Trade Statistics, 1977, Government Printer, Gabarone (p. 23); Kingdom of Lesotho, *Second Five Year Plan*, Vol. One, 1975/76–79/80.

inability to obtain finance. Special factors also play a part: for example Lesotho has quite large earnings from the remittances of migrant workers in South Africa as a partial offset to the country's very low level of commodity exports. Nevertheless, the figures in Table 8.8 do demonstrate the general tendency towards increasing deficits and their huge absolute size. This situation tends to lead to increasing dependency, whether it be on aid donors, access to jobs for migrant workers, or access to international credit.

The countries in the sample are all very open. Exports and imports expressed as a percentage of GDP ranged from 81–137 per cent in 1973 (Table 8.9). Furthermore, these percentages have been increasing in every case except that of Iceland. In most cases the increase in openness 1960–73 is far from being marginal but amounts to a major structural increase in dependence on international trade over what, in historical terms, is quite a short period of time (the average of the last column of Table 8.10, that is, the average amount by which openness on this measure had increased was no less than 26 percentage points).

The countries in the sample also tend to trade with relatively few countries, with large and in some cases dominant, shares for one trading partner (Table 8.10). The three small countries of Southern Africa – Botswana, Lesotho and Swaziland – are extreme cases on the import side because of their nearness to South Africa and because of the Southern African Customs Union. Geographical situation also plays a part in the cases of Fiji, which imports heavily from Australia, and Barbados, Guyana and Trinidad and Tobago, which import heavily from the USA – in the cases of Barbados and Guyana, switching from the former colonial power (UK). Geography is not all, however, as is shown by the continuing large share, and in some cases increasing share, of trade with France of the former French colonies in the sample (Gabon, Congo, Mauritania).

On the export side, the former colonial power is the dominant trading partner in most cases, suggesting possibly that ex-colonies were and are valued more for their importance as sources of raw materials than for their value as markets for metropolitan country exports.

Only Trinidad and Tobago, which sells most of its oil to the USA, and Iceland, which has not been a colony since 1918 and which is more a part of Europe (although of the periphery) than of the Third World, were exceptions to this rule in 1970; and only Barbados had changed categories by 1977. What is more, the figures in the last column of Table 8.10 (for changes in share) do not show any marked or consistent trend for the countries to diversify away from dominant trading partners.

The countries also depend on a few mining and agricultural products, or even on a single product, for over 80 per cent of their exports and only four have had a proportion of less than 45 per cent for their principal export in 1977 (Table 8.11). There was a slight tendency for the importance of the main export to· diminish over the years 1971–7, with the exception of oil exporters.

Finally, the countries are part of a growing and disconcerting trend for developing countries as a whole, and with few exceptions, to be increasingly dependent on imports of staple food. 'While the developing countries as a group were virtually self-sufficient in food in the 1950s, they were already importing 15 million to 20 million tons of major staple foods by 1970', and this deficit was expected to be more than twice as large by 1985.[11]

Table 8.9 *Exports and imports and total trade as percentages of GDP (1960, 1973)*

Country	1960			1973			Increase in trade dependence 1960–73
	Exports %	Imports %	Total trade %	Exports %	Imports %	Total trade %	% points
Barbados	42	71	113	56	81	137	+20
Gabon	38	36	74	69	63	132	+58
Congo	29	74	103	51	74	125	+22
Mauritania	17	56	83	56	64	120	+37
Fiji	38	40	78	50	68	118	+40
Swaziland	47	31	78	64	53	117	+39
Guyana	49	58	107	51	65	116	+9
Mauritius	32	55	87	53	56	109	+22
Gambia	43	46	89	48	60	108	+19
Botswana	23	34	57	39	59	98	+41
Cyprus	28	38	66	43	54	97	+31
Iceland	44	48	92	40	44	84	−8
Trinidad & Tobago	36	36	72	39	42	81	+9
Lesotho	12	39	51	11	70	81	+30

Source
World Bank, *World Tables 1976,* Johns Hopkins University Press, Baltimore.

Table 8.10 *Direction of trade: main trading partners' share of exports and imports, selected years 1970–7 (percentage of total)*

Country[b]	1970	1973	1977	1970–7 Change % points[a]
Botswana				
Exports (UK)		68	39	−29
Imports (South Africa)		69	86	+17
Trinidad and Tobago				
Exports (USA)		57	72	+27
Imports (USA 71–2, Saudi Arabia 74–7)		24	24	+6
Gabon				
Exports (France)	42	38	27	−15
Imports (France)	56	59	68	+12

(see over)

Table 8.10   (*continued*)

Country	1970	1973	1977	1970–7 Change % points
Mauritius				
Exports (UK)	65	45	61	−4
Imports (UK)	22	22	18	−4
Congo				
Exports (France)	13	29	26	+13
Imports (France)	54	56	49	−5
Fiji				
Exports (UK)	—	29	42	+14
Imports (Australia)	—	31	28	+1
Mauritania				
Exports (France)	—	12	24	+3
Imports (France)	—	55	45	+8
Barbados				
Exports (UK 70–3, USA 74–7)	39	33	33	−6
Imports (UK 70–5, USA 76–7)	30	25	26	−4
Gambia				
Exports (UK)	43	20	28	−15
Imports (UK)	30	28	25	−5
Guyana				
Exports (UK)	—	30	26	+1
Imports (UK 71–3, USA 74–7)	—	26	25	−6
Cyprus				
Exports (UK)	39	40	31	−8
Imports (UK)	29	25	19	−10
Iceland				
Exports (USA)	—	27	30	−7
Imports (Germany)	—	11	10	−6
Swaziland				
Exports	—	—	—	—
Imports (South Africa)	91	91	90	−1

Notes

[a] Changes in last column taken from nearest available year where exact comparison not available. No figures available for Lesotho, but trade is thought to be overwhelmingly with South Africa for both exports and imports.

[b] Countries ranked by sum of shares of trade with leading partners in exports and imports.

Source

IMF, 'Direction of Trade', *Annual Report 1971–7*.

Table 8.11 *Main export as percentage of total exports for selected small countries (selected years 1971–7)*

Country	1971	1974	1977
Trinidad and Tobago (petroleum)	76	85	92
Gambia (groundnuts)	94	86	89
Mauritania (iron ore)	84	72	80
Gabon (crude oil)	44	85	79
Mauritius (sugar)	89	88	72
Lesotho (animal products)	67	67	—
Congo (crude petroleum)	1	62	59
Fiji (sugar)	54	55	57
Iceland (fish)	54	45	45
Swaziland (sugar)	21	38	34[a]
Botswana (animal products)	42[b]	41	30
Guyana (sugar)	31	47	28
Barbados (sugar)	33	30	25
Cyprus (citrus fruits 1971–4, potatoes 1975–7)	28	20	18

Notes
[a] 1976.
[b] 1972.
Source
IMF: *International Financial Statistics*, Vol. XXXII, no. 2, February 1979; Kingdom of Lesotho: *Second Five Year Development Plan*, Vol. 1, 1975/6–1979/80, (p. 261); The Monetary Authority of Swaziland: *Annual Report for the Financial Year 1976–7*.

Conclusion

Comparing Botswana with a sample of countries of roughly similar size, as measured by population, has shown that Botswana fits into a fairly typical pattern – in her dependence on a few trading partners, on increasing inflows of capital to offset a growing trade deficit, on a few commodities for export and on increasing imports of staple foods. There are other crucial forms of dependence – on foreign skills and technology, and on international transit and transport rights, to give just two examples. This is to be expected. The wave of colonialism which created these small countries also brought with it several other evils:[12]

1 It redirected these economies away from the self-sufficiency they once had to that of permanent dependency on international capitalism because the colonialists wanted other things, for example, mineral and agricultural raw materials for their industry.
2 It destroyed indigenous development processes and altered patterns of demand towards goods which required such technology, capital and human skills which these countries did not have and so had to import.
3 It proliferated the people's needs, thereby greatly increasing their dependence on outside forces over which they had, and have, no control.

The situation of permanent dependence on international capitalism is bound to persist and even worsen for a long time to come, unless the small countries pursue certain policies which, with a little bit of luck, will reduce or at least halt this increasing rate of peonage. Here I can only mention a few of these policies, not because they are altogether new, but for the sake of emphasis only:

1   Policies aimed at self-sufficiency in food.
2   Fight for liberalization of trade especially for processed and manufactured goods from less developed countries.
3   In order to satisfy the day-to-day needs of the people, the development of indigenous technology that is cheap enough to produce goods that are accessible to virtually everyone, that is suitable for small scale applications, which encourages production by the masses rather than mass production, and that takes account of resource endowments and factor proportions of the country.
4   Production from local resources for local needs, because dependence on imports from afar and the consequent need to produce for exports to unknown distant peoples is very uneconomic and risky and signifies failure.

Notes

1. Ochieng, E. O., 'Alternative industrial strategies for Botswana', *National Workshop on African Industrial Policies and Strategies*, IDM (16–18 August 1978).
2. Vinnai, V., *Kenya's External Trade 1964–71*, Discussion Paper No. 165, IDS, University of Nairobi (April 1973) p. 3.
3. Bank of Botswana, *Annual Report, 1976*, p. 30. Nearly three-quarters of this figure consists of interest on the debt of the Shashe Project which is shown as an interest payment outflow on current account and an inflow on capital account since it is simply added to shareholder loans. See Lewis' Chapter 7 on the Shashe Project in this book, pp. 109–13.
4. Ministry of Finance and Development Planning, *Statistical Bulletin* (June 1978) Vol. 3, no. 2, pp. 1–7.
5. Bank of Botswana, *Annual Report, 1977*, pp. 6 and 13. Exports of beef to the EEC are also subject to a quota.
6. See note 5 above. See Chapter 9, footnote 5, p. 147.
7. Department of Customs and Excise, *External Trade Statistics 1975 and 1977*, Government Printer, Gaborone.
8. Ochieng, E. O., 'Impediments to sustained peasant participation in the development process', *Eastern African Social Science Consultative Workshop on Popular Participation and Rural Development*, IDS, University of Nairobi (26–9 March 1978), pp. 7–17.
George, S., *How the Other Half Lives*, Pelican Books (1976), p. 16. See also note 11.
9. Sandford, S., 'Dealing with drought and livestock in Botswana', London, ODI (May 1977), p. 21.
10. See Selwyn, P. (ed.), *Development Policy in Small Countries*, London (1975) and Selwyn, P., *Small, Poor and Remote: Islands at a Geographical Disadvantage*, IDS Discussion Paper (1978).
11. World Bank, *World Development Report 1978*, Washington DC (1978) p. 22.
12. Ochieng, E. O., 'Industrial strategies and rural industrialization in Africa', *Eastern African Social Science Research Consultative Workshop on Industrialization and Rural Development*, E. African Management Institute, Arusha, Tanzania (4–6 April 1979), p. 12.

E. O. Ochieng is Lecturer in Economics, Makerere University, Uganda; formerly Lecturer in Economics, University of Botswana and Swaziland.

9 Botswana's Membership of the Southern African Customs Union

DEREK J. HUDSON

Historical background

The Bechuanaland Protectorate[1] adopted its first customs tariff[2] in 1892. At that time, goods entering Bechuanaland from overseas had to pay both the Cape Colony and the Bechuanaland import duties. Then in 1893, Bechuanaland Protectorate joined in a customs union with Basutoland, Cape Colony and the Orange Free State. The Tati Concession in the northeast of what is now Botswana was initially excluded, but joined the customs union nearly six years later. Bechuanaland received three-quarters of the duties charged on its overseas imports, the remaining quarter being treated as administration expenses of the customs union.

At the conclusion of the Anglo-Boer war in South Africa, the entire customs union was reshaped to take account of the changed status of the Transvaal and the Orange Free State. A new customs union was formed in 1903 by Cape Colony, Natal, Orange Free State, Southern Rhodesia and Transvaal. Basutoland and Bechuanaland were not consulted but were nevertheless included in the union. Swaziland and Barotseland joined later on. The common external tariff for most categories of imports was set at 7·5 per cent on British goods and 10 per cent on goods from other countries. In 1906, these rates were increased to 12 and 15 per cent, respectively.

The first agreement with South Africa

In 1910 the four provinces of Cape Colony, Natal, Orange Free State and Transvaal were combined into the Union of South Africa. In that year, South Africa signed a customs agreement with Bechuanaland Protectorate, Basutoland and Swaziland. The three smaller countries agreed with South Africa on the following points:

Customs and excise duties

1   There would be no customs duties on goods moving from one country within the customs union to any other member country, except that Basutoland, Bechuanaland and Swaziland collected the duties themselves on South African beer, spirits and certain wines.

2   All four countries would charge the same rate of customs duty on goods entering a member country from outside the common customs area, and the same rate of excise duty on dutiable goods produced anywhere within the common customs area.

3   Any member could in principle initiate a change in the rate of duty, but in practice these would be set by South Africa.

Financial arrangements

4   South Africa would act as the custodian of the duty collected, including duty paid at South African ports on goods destined for Basutoland, Bechuanaland and Swaziland; all duties collected would go into a revenue 'pool'.

5   Each member country would annually receive a fixed percentage of the total amount of duty collected; payments would be made out of the common revenue pool referred to in (4) above.

6   The percentages were to be based on estimates of duty on the goods consumed in each country during the period April 1907–March 1910.

Furthermore, because there was no statement in the 1910 agreement to the contrary:

7   The fixed percentages apparently could not be changed, even if the patterns of consumption of dutiable goods among the member countries changed significantly.

The percentages that were agreed in 1910 are given in Table 9.1, together with an amendment in 1965 which took place in spite of item (7) above. The amended percentages were based on the estimated patterns of consumption of dutiable goods in 1962 and 1963 in Basutoland, Bechuanaland and Swaziland.

Table 9.1   *Shares of common revenue pool of customs and excise duty under the 1910 agreement*

	Percentage shares	
Country	1910	1965
Basutoland	0·88	0·47
Bechuanaland	0·28	0·31
South Africa	98·69	98·69
Swaziland	0·15	0·53
TOTAL	100·00	100·00

The main effect of the 1965 amendment was to increase Swaziland's share at the expense of Basutoland. No account was taken of the possibility that South Africa's share might need to be reduced.

By 1968, imports into Botswana, Lesotho and Swaziland (the BLS countries) amounted to about 4·1 per cent of imports into South Africa, but the BLS countries continued to receive only 1·3 per cent of the pool of customs duty.

At that time, therefore, the formula for sharing the revenue appeared to be working in South Africa's favour.

The 1910 agreement did not prevent South Africa from applying non-tariff barriers to BLS products. When a beef surplus developed in Johannesburg, South Africa banned imports of Botswana beef, imposed unnecessarily severe veterinary restrictions on Botswana cattle when there was an outbreak of foot and mouth disease in Rhodesia, and set a minimum weight requirement on live Botswana cattle sent to South Africa for slaughter. Between 1926 and 1941, typical requirements were that oxen had to weigh 1000 lb (455 kg) on arrival at a Johannesburg abattoir, and cows had to weigh 750 lb (341 kg). These weight limits were apparently chosen at a level that most white farmers in Bechuanaland could meet, so the weight limits did not discriminate against them nearly as much as against the traditional black farmers.

The agreement with the Federation of Rhodesia and Nyasaland

In 1956, the Bechuanaland Protectorate joined in a customs agreement with Basutoland, Swaziland and the Federation of Rhodesia and Nyasaland. This agreement included the following provisions:

1   Goods produced or manufactured in Bechuanaland and those from the Federation (Northern Rhodesia, Nyasaland or Southern Rhodesia) could be moved from one area to another without payment of customs duty.
2   Goods imported into the Federation from overseas and subsequently re-exported to Bechuanaland would be liable for the *difference* in customs duty, if the Bechuanaland rate of customs on the goods, that is, the rate set by South Africa, was higher than the Federation's rate of duty.
3   Any such differential duty would be collected inside the Federation and sent directly to South Africa.

When the Federation broke up in 1963, Rhodesia (previously Southern Rhodesia, now Zimbabwe) and Malawi (previously Nyasaland) made it clear that they wanted the customs agreement with Bechuanaland to remain in force. Zambia (previously Northern Rhodesia) initially made no statement but subsequently made it clear that it considered its agreement with Bechuanaland to have fallen away.

Many years later, Botswana and Zambia expressed the wish to enter into a trade agreement. It might have been desirable for both countries to lower the rates of customs duty on imports from each other. By then it was too late, however, since the 1969 Customs Union Agreement *inter alia* gives South Africa (and Lesotho and Swaziland) the right to veto any tariff concessions that might have been granted to Zambia by Botswana. The 1971 trade agreement between Botswana and Zambia is thus limited to pledges of mutual friendship and a statement of intent to increase mutual trade. The sad outcome is that Zambia, which gave up its duty free access to Botswana in 1964, now has to overcome the high tariff barriers which effectively protect South Africa's exports to Botswana.

The second agreement with South Africa

As Botswana approached Independence in 1966, a careful review of the 1910 customs union agreement with South Africa was undertaken. It was noted by the Botswana government that:

1   The revenue accruing to Botswana was not related to the growth of economic activity in Botswana (because of the fixed percentage share of revenue from the common revenue pool).
2   The tariffs paid by residents of Botswana on goods they imported from outside the customs union were determined by South African interests.
3   Where a high external protective tariff 'forces' residents of Botswana to buy South African goods, in preference to overseas goods,
     (a)   the common revenue pool was reduced (because the overseas goods would have attracted customs duty).
     (b)   At the same time Botswana usually paid more for the South African goods than the duty free price of overseas goods (because the South African manufacturer was sheltering behind the protective tariff). The tariff-induced pressure to buy more expensive South African goods had the effect of a subsidy from Botswana to South Africa.
4   It is common for there to be a continuing polarization of development between two countries in a customs union, whenever one country's economy is very much more powerful than the other. There was thus a need to reshape the customs union agreement in an attempt to redistribute economic growth from the powerful, attractive central growth point towards peripheral areas.

The above factors affected Lesotho and Swaziland as much as they did Botswana, but Botswana was probably the first country to recognize the urgency of the situation and state the case for renegotiation to the South African government. The negotiations between the four countries lasted two years. During that period, South Africa announced its intention to charge a new kind of sales duty[3] on manufactures or imports of certain classes of goods, as a way of raising more revenue for the South African government. Taxable items included paint, furniture, toothpaste, motor vehicles, etc. Tax rates could vary between 5–35 per cent.

The BLS countries were concerned that such a major fiscal measure could have been planned by South Africa without prior consultation with their partners in the Customs Union Agreement. In the event, the introduction of the new sales duty[4] was brought into the negotiations and included in the final Agreement.

The main changes that were negotiated in 1969

The most important changes were:

1   The revenue-sharing formula was made to depend on the *current* patterns of consumption of imports plus locally produced dutiable goods. (Dutiable goods were those which incurred either excise duty or sales duty, or both.)
2   The revenue-sharing formula was changed from being asymmetrical in South Africa's favour (the BLS percentages had been too small) to being asymmetrical in favour of the BLS countries (each now receives more than a pro rata share).

3   The BLS countries agreed to charge sales duty on those goods which South
    Africa determined should be dutiable, and to charge the same rates of duty
    on those goods as South Africa charged. This meant that the BLS countries
    would at all times adhere to the full tariff of customs, excise and sales duties
    in force in South Africa.

4   In principle, South African non-tariff barriers on BLS products would no
    longer be permitted.[5] Thus the BLS producers and manufacturers in
    principle have guaranteed access to the huge South African market.

5   Each country (and South Africa in particular) could maintain its own
    separate import quotas on goods from outside the Common Customs Area
    (CCA). For example, when South Africa had a balance of payments
    problem in 1977, they set low quotas on imports of luxury goods such as
    Mozambique prawns. In principle Botswana or more likely, Swaziland,
    could import as many prawns as they wished, because the South African
    quota did not apply to them, but they could not re-export the prawns to
    South Africa.

6   South Africa agreed to an asymmetrical protection clause for infant
    industries. The BLS countries may impose a temporary (up to eight years)
    additional duty against South African imports which compete with BLS
    infant industries, but South Africa may not impose a similar tariff against
    imports from the BLS countries.

7   The four contracting parties agreed to set up a Customs Union
    Commission, for purposes of mutual consultation on the working of the
    Agreement.

As part and parcel of the new Agreement, the BLS countries agreed that
each would establish a Department of Customs and Excise. An immediate
burden on the new Department in Botswana was the collection from Botswana
importers of sales duty charged on imports from Rhodesia and Malawi.

Similarly, each of the BLS countries agreed to introduce and maintain
customs legislation which is similar to that in force in South Africa. For
example, the administrative rules in Botswana concerning removal of petrol
from a bonded warehouse in Botswana and the charging of duty thereon are
similar to the rules in force in South Africa.

There were a number of minor changes, any one of which could at some
future time become of increased significance.

1   For purposes of demarcating the common customs area to which the
    Agreement applied, it was agreed that the term 'South Africa' included the
    territory of South West Africa. Thus there is no customs duty on imports
    into Botswana from Namibia, and vice versa.

2   South Africa should consult the other members before changing the tariff;
    and should give sympathetic consideration to the maintenance of suitably
    high customs duties required to protect any specified industries which could
    be of major importance to any one of the BLS countries. For example, if the
    huge soda ash deposits at Sua Pan (west of Francistown) were ever mined,
    Botswana would probably be able to supply a significant portion of the
    soda ash requirements of South Africa. Botswana could then reasonably
    ask for an external tariff against imports of soda ash from outside the
    Customs Union.

3   Member states could make their own, unilateral decisions to waive customs duty on imported goods related to famine relief, other national disasters, a technical assistance programme or a multilateral international agreement; but any such privileged imports would not enter the revenue sharing formula. Botswana has imported food for famine relief under this dispensation.

4   Each member country has the right to prohibit or restrict the importation of goods for social or cultural reasons, for example, prohibitions on pornographic literature; Botswana might not allow importation of a particular magazine but Lesotho and Swaziland could if they so wished.

5   The BLS countries shall have access to South African marketing arrangements for agricultural products. For example, Bokspits karakul farmers participate in the karakul marketing co-operative in Upington.

6   Rail and road tariffs within a given country must be applied without discrimination as to country of origin or destination. For example, a packet of cement railed from Pretoria to Ramatlabama (on the South African side of the border with Botswana) must bear the same tariff, regardless of whether it is destined for a South African consignee at Ramatlabama or whether it is to be exported to Botswana.

7   The contracting parties agree to consult with each other on the prevention of the spread of animal and plant diseases, parasites and insects. For example, if Botswana were threatened by a swarm of locusts from South Africa, or if South Africa were threatened by foot and mouth disease in Botswana, then there should immediately be discussions among the officials concerned.

8   Each member country has a veto on any other member entering separately into a *concessionary* trade agreement with a country outside the common customs area. For example, South Africa could veto any proposed tariff reductions between Botswana and Zambia; Botswana could veto any new tariff concessions between South Africa and Zimbabwe.

The common revenue pool consists of all collections of customs, excise, additional and surcharge duties collected in any part of the customs union. The pool used also to include collections of sales duty when these were in force. (The new South African retail sales tax is outside the Agreement.) The 1969 Agreement spells out in detail how the pool is to be shared among the four member states.

$$\text{Botswana's share of revenue from} = \frac{\text{Imports into Botswana plus local consumption of locally produced dutiable goods}}{\text{Imports into CCA } plus \text{ CCA consumption of CCA-produced dutiable goods}} \times (\text{total revenue in the pool}) \times 1 \cdot 42 \quad (1)$$

where CCA stands for Common Customs Area.[6] All goods included in the formula are valued on a duty-paid basis, that is, the value of the goods in the formula includes any customs, excise, sales, additional or surcharge duties on the goods. The value of imports also includes the cost of freight up to the Botswana border and the cost of insurance.

For purposes of further discussions, it is convenient to define the rate of revenue as:

$$\text{Rate of revenue} = \frac{(\text{Total revenue in the pool}) \times 1\cdot42}{\text{Imports into CCA plus CCA consumption of CCA-produced dutiable goods}} \quad (2)$$

The member states would all like the rate of revenue to remain reasonably constant. After some initial experience with the new formula, it was noted that over successive years the rate of revenue tended to fluctuate above and below 20 per cent. A revision to the formula which was agreed in 1977, stated that the rate of revenue should be stabilized by means of an averaging formula. This ensures that deviations above and below the target rate of 20 per cent are kept to a minimum, and in any case may not fall below 17 nor exceed 23 per cent. This in turn permits the BLS countries in particular to make more accurate forecasts of the revenue each government will receive from the application of the formula. The stabilization formula was applied to the revenue shares in 1973–4 and subsequent years.

Table 9.2 *Stabilization formula (percentage)*

If originally calculated rate of revenue was	then stabilized rate of revenue is
14 or less	17
15	17·5
16	18
17	18·5
18	19
19	19·5
20	20
21	20·5
22	21
23	21·5
24	22
25	22·5
26 or more	23

If the 'raw' or unadjusted rate of revenue, as originally calculated, is in excess of 20 per cent, then the (downward) stabilizing adjustment to the rate will be in South Africa's favour, since under the revised formula the pool will be paying less revenue to the BLS countries. South Africa will then retain a slightly larger portion of the pool. Conversely, if the raw rate of revenue is less than 20 per cent, then the shares paid to the BLS countries will be slightly enhanced.

Botswana's share of accrued revenue may now be rewritten:

$$\frac{\text{Botswana's share}}{\text{of revenue}} = \frac{\text{imports into Botswana } plus}{\text{dutiable production}} \times \frac{\text{stabilized rate}}{\text{of revenue}} \qquad (3)$$

= 20 per cent of (imports plus dutiable production), approximately.

The local consumption of locally produced dutiable goods means consumption in Botswana of goods which have been produced or manufactured in Botswana and which are liable either to sales duty (now abolished) or excise duty. Excise dutiable goods made in Botswana include beer, soft drinks and jewellery made from semi-precious stones. Sales dutiable goods (when sales duty was in force) which were manufactured in Botswana included paint and furniture. The total value of these dutiable goods has always been small, so formula (3) can be further approximated to read '20 per cent of imports'.

Duty-free goods

It is an interesting feature that the formula includes certain dutiable goods on which the duty is *not* paid. At first sight this seems most odd. The peculiarity arises when certain privileged importers are not required to pay duty that ordinary importers do have to pay. Goods destined for government departments and foreign embassies are included in this category, for example, foreign embassies in Gaborone are allowed to buy liquor and motor cars duty free. The exemption does *not* apply to parastatal bodies such as Escom and the South African Reserve Bank in South Africa, nor to the Botswana Power Corporation and the Bank of Botswana. The exemption *does* apply to South African Railways and to South African Airways, because in South Africa they are government departments and not parastatals. A Boeing 747 aircraft imported for South African Airways increases the denominator of formula (1) above and thereby decreases Botswana's revenue share, since there is no compensating addition to the total revenue in the pool. Similarly, if Botswana imports an expensive American grader for the Roads Department of the government, Botswana's share of revenue from the pool is increased by about 20 per cent of the value of the grader, even though no duty is payable since the Botswana government is itself exempt from paying duty on the grader.

In summary, the 20 per cent average rate of *revenue* derives from the average rate of *duty*, multiplied by 1·42. The average rate of duty is in turn obtained by averaging the rates of duty on all dutiable goods, including those dutiable goods which happen to have a zero rate of duty. The important point is that Botswana receives revenue equal to about 20 per cent of the value of *all* imports, including those consigned to government departments, except for the technical assistance imports mentioned above.

Since the Botswana government does not pay any duties, it is in principle free to buy its imports in the cheapest world market. Unfortunately, it is difficult to measure the extent to which the government has voluntarily taken advantage of this provision. Some contracts with foreign aid donors are tied to products manufactured in the donors' countries, and other contracts may ask Botswana to try not to buy South African goods. Nevertheless, it is interesting to note that the Botswana government pays for only about 56 per cent of its imports in Rand, whereas non-government importers pay for about 89 per cent of their imports in Rand.

The precise definition of 'imports'

For ease of computation and in order to comply with the new Agreement, all values of goods are denominated in Botswana for customs purposes in 'Units of Account', where one UA equals one Rand. No adjustments are made in respect of possible undercoverage due to the failure of importers to complete customs documentation at the official entry points.

For other purposes, such as the presentation of Botswana's balance of payments, the annual value of imports excludes transport, insurance and duties, the values are denominated in Pula, and a reasonable allowance is made for undercoverage. Considerable care should therefore be taken in comparing one set of import statistics with another.

Table 9.3   *The two definitions of 'imports'*

	Customs Union statistics	Balance of payments statistics
Denomination	Units of account	Pula
Transport to border	Included	Excluded
Insurance to border	Included	Excluded
Customs, excise, sales, additional and surcharge duties	Included	Excluded
Adjustment for undercoverage at border posts	Excluded	Included
Technical assistance imports	Excluded	Included
Re-exports	Excluded	Included
Date of importation or exportation	Date goods clear Botswana customs	Date ownership changes hands between importer and exporter

Obtaining the statistics with which to operate the formula

Botswana does indeed contribute certain statistics which are added into the denominator of formula (1). Imports from Zambia into Botswana would be an example of an import into Botswana (and hence into the CCA) from outside the CCA. However, the contribution of South Africa's imports and dutiable production to the denominator of (1) is so huge that we may for convenience regard (2) as almost completely determined by the South African figures. It follows then that, when looking at formula (3) above, Botswana should strive to produce the most accurate statistics of imports and local dutiable production that it can, in order to compute Botswana's share as accurately as possible.

Botswana's Department of Customs and Excise keeps a very close watch on local dutiable production, such as the beer produced at the brewery in Gaborone. Furthermore, the statistics are small in comparison with Botswana's imports. It can thus be seen that Botswana will only receive its fair share of revenue, according to formula (3) above, if imports into Botswana are accurately measured. In particular, considerable effort has to be spent on trying to cover all those imports which enter Botswana from either Namibia or South Africa. Any under-recording of Botswana's imports results in windfall revenue for South Africa.

In the early days of the new Agreement, the BLS countries all experienced difficulty in obtaining precise figures of their imports. Starting in 1969, the Central Statistics Office in Botswana compiled a list of all known importers and sent them a quarterly questionnaire concerning the previous three months' imports. This method was bound to result in undercoverage of Botswana's imports, a fact that was recognized by the other members of the Customs Union.

During the first few years of operating (1) under the new Agreement, the Central Statistics Office increased the recorded import statistics by 11/89ths or 12·4 per cent, on the assumption that only 89 per cent of Botswana's imports were being recorded by the quarterly mail survey. The figure of 89 per cent was probably a generous estimate of the coverage obtained, so even with the 11/89ths enhancement, Botswana was probably not claiming its full entitlement from the pool.

In due course, the Department of Customs and Excise was expanded and took over the vital task of compiling the import statistics. From then on, no enhancement of the recorded statistics was made, that is, the increase of 11/89ths ceased. Unfortunately, some of the more important border posts were not manned by customs officers. The immigration or police officers at these entry points did not always remember to ask importers to fill in customs forms. Some truck drivers were unable to complete the customs forms because they did not know the value of their cargoes. A few of the border posts along the Tuli Block in the east and a few along the Molopo River in the south were for a time not manned on the Botswana side of the border at all. On one occasion, imports were removed from Serule railway station without any customs documentation because the outgoing station master had apparently forgotten to brief the incoming station master on the correct procedure. Mamuno border post with Namibia (West of Ghanzi) once ran out of customs forms. In Gaborone, certain government officials did not always bother to fill in customs forms because they were under the mistaken impression that government imports did not enter the formula, because they are duty free. (See p. 138 above.) A parastatal which imported over P1 million of capital equipment took a year to fill in the customs forms.

Coverage of Botswana's imports cannot be estimated accurately, but was probably only about 85 per cent in 1973–4. Since then coverage has steadily increased. There have occasionally been dramatic improvements, for example when a newly appointed customs officer took over customs formalities at Tlokweng border gate (east of Gaborone) from the immigration officials there. Coverage of imports may now be as high as 97·5 per cent.

The multiplier

Of course, one of the most significant features of the new formula is the 1·42 multiplier in (1) above. The multiplier is an attempt to compensate the BLS countries for certain disadvantages inherent in the Customs Union Agreement. The most significant disadvantages are:

1   The loss of fiscal discretion. The BLS countries can and do set their own rates of direct taxation (mainly income tax and mineral royalties), but have little choice about the amount of revenue raised from indirect taxation (which depends almost entirely on the rates of customs, excise and surcharge duties set by South Africa). As it happens, Botswana has usually not found that the rates of duty are in conflict with any national policy, so the loss of fiscal discretion has probably been more theoretical than real.

2   The price raising effect of buying South African goods with a higher 'factor cost', that is, the basic duty free price, than the factor cost of equivalent overseas goods. As South Africa industrializes, it uses the external tariff to protect more and more South African manufacturers. This factor could now be of greater significance to Botswana than was envisaged when the Agreement was signed.

3   The polarization effect – new industries tend to want to be situated at the economic centre of a customs union, that is, in South Africa, rather than at the periphery, that is, in the BLS countries.

4   The difficulty of protecting infant industries in the BLS countries, even though these countries are permitted to charge an 'additional duty' against South African imports. For example, it is hard for a poultry farmer in Botswana to make a success of his local poultry enterprise when he finds that because of the small size of his business he has to sell live Botswana chickens in Gaborone at a *higher* price than the competing mass-produced frozen chickens imported from South Africa, but on the other hand the Botswana government might be reluctant to place an additional duty on the imported chickens.

The new revenue sharing formula – Part II

It is not possible for South Africa to pay Botswana all the accrued revenue due to Botswana during the year in question, because the statistics on which formula (1) is based are only available some time after the end of the year. For example, the import statistics for the period April 1979–March 1980 were only available in September 1980.

The second part of the formula converts the accrued revenue due to Botswana into the actual cash flow from the common revenue pool, by means of instalment payments. The accrued revenue due to Botswana in respect of any given year is divided into three instalments. These are illustrated below with reference to the revenue accrued by Botswana on account of imports in the 1977–8 fiscal year, that is, between April 1977 and March 1978.

1   During the year in question, a first instalment of what is owing to Botswana is paid to Botswana. This is defined in the Agreement to be equal to the actual accrual two years earlier, and is thus only a rough forecast of what the accrued revenue owed to Botswana will amount to for the current year.

2   Two years later, when the import statistics for the base year are available in draft for all four countries, formula (1) is computed for the base year. Using the answer to the computation, a 'first correction' is made to the forecast paid in the base year. If the forecast in (1) above was too small, the first correction is in Botswana's favour, and vice versa.

3   A year later, when the import statistics for the base year have been finalized,

formula (1) is computed a second time for the same base year and a 'second correction' is made. If the second calculation of (1) yields a bigger share for Botswana than the first calculation, the second correction is in Botswana's favour.

Table 9.4   *Three instalments of total revenue accrued by Botswana on account of imports plus dutiable production in 1977–8*

Instalment	Payable	Based on
First instalment $= g$ (the 'forecast')	In 1977–8	October 1976 estimate of revenue accrued in 1975–6
Second instalment $= i - g$ (the 'first correction')	In 1979–80	October 1978 estimate of revenue accrued in 1977–8 (i) *minus* the first instalment (g)
Third instalment $= i^* - i$ (the 'second correction')	In 1980–81	October 1979 recalculation of revenue accrued in 1977–8 *minus* the two previous instalments (i^*)
TOTAL $= i^*$ (the 'accrued revenue')	Between April 1977 and March 1981	

The cash flow to Botswana

Looked at from the point of view of the Botswana government's budget, the cash flow from the common revenue pool to Botswana in any given year consists of the sum of three items. These are illustrated below with reference to the cash received by Botswana in the 1979–80 fiscal year, that is, April 1979–March 1980.

1   The first component is the forecast of the accrual for that year.
2   The second component is the first correction in respect of the forecast made two years ago of the accrual for that year.
3   The third component is the second correction in respect of the recalculation of formula (1) for the year three years previously.

Comparing accruals with cash flows

The cash flow to Botswana is published each year, but the accruals are not published. The accruals may, however, easily be estimated.

In recent years, the first and second calculations of formula (1) with respect to a given year yielded nearly identical calculations of the revenue shares for that year. This is because the collection of import statistics in Botswana has improved tremendously, and the final set of statistics, item 3, bottom of p. 141, has been nearly identical to the draft set of statistics, item 2, bottom of p. 141. Thus the series of 'second corrections' (item 3, bottom of p. 141) has tended to be small. It is of considerable assistance to a student who wants to compare accruals to Botswana with cash flows to Botswana, if the second correction may be ignored.

Table 9.5 *Three components separately calculated in October 1978 making up total cash flow to Botswana in 1979–80*

Component	Payable	Based on
First component = i	In 1979–80	Forecast for 1979–80, which equals October 1978 estimate of accrual for 1977–8
Second component = $i - g$	In 1979–80	First correction to forecast made in October 1976 of 1977–8 accrual
Third component = $h^* - h$	In 1979–80	Second correction, using recalculation of formula (1), for 1976–7

In table 9.5, for example, we would assume that $h^*{-}h = 0$. Table 9.6 sets out a simplified model whereby the cash flows may be analysed, assuming that the second corrections are small enough to be ignored. Let the accrual in 1969–70 be a, the accrual in 1970–1 be b, etc.

Table 9.6 *Simplified cash flow model*

Year	Accrued revenue	Forecast	First correction	Cash flow Model (R million)	Actual (R million)
1969–70	a	x^1		x	$4 \cdot 8^2$
1970–1	b	y		y	$4 \cdot 6$
1971–2	c	a	$a - x$	$2a - x$	$8 \cdot 3$
1972–3	d	b	$b - y$	$2b - y$	$12 \cdot 5$
1973–4	e	c	$c - a$	$2c - a$	$20 \cdot 9$
1974–5	f	d	$d - b$	$2d - b$	$30 \cdot 4$
1975–6	g	e	$e - c$	$2e - c$	$24 \cdot 6$
1976–7	h	f	$f - d$	$2f - d$	$15 \cdot 4$
1977–8	i	g	$g - e$	$2g - e$	$39 \cdot 1$
1978–9	j	h	$h - f$	$2h - f$	$52 \cdot 4$
1979–80	k	i	$i - g$	$2i - g$	$83 \cdot 0$
1980–1	l	j	$j - h$	$2j - h$	$101 \cdot 8^3$
TOTAL	(T)	$T + x + y$ $- k - l$	$i + j$ $- x - y$	$T + i + j$ $- k - l$	

Notes
[1] The initial forecasts, x and y, for 1969–70 and 1970–1, were negotiated at the same time that the Agreement itself was being negotiated.
[2] The actual cash flow figures for each fiscal year are published firstly in the government's annual estimate of revenue, and secondly in the government's final accounts. Any difference between the estimated revenue and the actual revenue received is due solely to fluctuations between the Pula and the Rand.
[3] The estimated cash flow for 1981–2 was published in March 1981.

It is an interesting arithmetical point to see what would have happened if the accruals $a, b, c, \ldots$ had increased by a constant amount w each year. Suppose that $b = a + w, c = b + w, d = c + w$, etc. In 1973–4, the accrual would have been $e = a + 4w$, and the cash flow would have been $2c - a = a + 4w$. The accrual for 1973–4 would be numerically equal to the cash flow for 1973–4. More generally, in the unlikely event of Botswana's imports growing by an equal amount each year, with a constant rate of revenue each year, the cash flows to Botswana would be numerically equal to the accruals, year by year, from 1973–4 onwards.

The model above has been simplified by the omission of any reference to the small 'second corrections'. On this basis, we may compare the last two columns and solve for the ten unknowns $a, b, c, \ldots, i$ and j. This yields the following results.

Table 9.7   *Rough estimate of accruals to Botswana (R million)*

Year	69–70	70–1	71–2	72–3	73–4
Accruals	$a = 7$	$b = 9$	$c = 14$	$d = 20$	$e = 19$

Year	74–5	75–6	76–7	77–8	78–9
Accruals	$f = 17·5$	$g = 29$	$h = 35$	$i = 56$	$j = 68$ [1]

Note

[1] The estimated accrual for 1979–80 will have been obtained in March 1981, once the estimated revenue for 1981–2 has been published.

We have at last reached the point where we can compare Botswana's accruals with those of the common customs area as a whole. We find that Botswana's share is currently approximately 2·3 per cent of the total revenue in the pool. This may be compared with the 0·3 per cent share that Botswana was receiving under the previous arrangement. The improvement is due partly to the fact that Botswana's recent economic growth rate has been higher than South Africa's, partly because of the improved terms of the new Agreement, and partly because of the continued expansion and increased efficiency of the Department of Customs and Excise.

Effects of the time lag

As mentioned above, part of the revenue accrued in respect of a given year is paid *during* the year; the forecast, and almost all the remainder is paid *two years later*; the first correction. Only a small portion of the remainder is paid three years later; the second correction. During the two years that Botswana is waiting for the first correction to be paid, South Africa has the free use of the money, assuming that the first correction is positive.

It may be seen that the balance owed to Botswana by the common revenue pool has grown considerably in recent years. There is no provision in the Agreement for the payment of interest on the balance.

Table 9.8 *Comparison between accumulated accrual of revenue since start of new Agreement, and accumulated flow of cash to Botswana from common revenue pool*

Year	Accumulated accruals[1]	Accumulated cash flow[2]	Balance owing to Botswana[3]	Estimated value of balance
1	2	3	4	5 (R million)
1969–70	a	x	$a-x$	1·5
1970–1	$a+b$	$x+y$	$a+b-x-y$	5·5
1971–2	$a+b+c$	$2a+b$	$b+c-a-y$	11
1972–3	$a+b+c+d$	$2a+2b$	$c+d-a-b$	18
1973–4	$a+b+c+d+e$	$a+2b+2c$	$d+e-b-c$	16·5
1974–5	$a+b+c+d+e+f$	$a+b+2c+2d$	$e+f-c-d$	3·5
1975–6	$a+b+c+d+e+f+g$	$a+b+c+2d+2e$	$f+g-d-e$	7·5
1976–7	$a+b+c+d+e+f+g+h$	$a+b+c+d+2e+2f$	$g+h-e-f$	27·5
1977–8	$a+b+c+d+e+f+g+h+i$	$a+b+c+d+e+2f+2g$	$h+i-f-g$	44·5
1978–9	$a+b+c+d+e+f+g+h+i+j$	$a+b+c+d+e+f+2g+2h$	$i+j+g-h$	60·3[4]

Notes
[1] = the sum of Botswana's accruals since the start of the new Agreement.
[2] = the sum of all the cash paid to Botswana from the common revenue pool.
[3] = column 1 minus column 2.
[4] It should have been possible to estimate the 1979–80 figure in March 1981.
The arithmetical point made above shows the accruals $(a, b, c, \ldots)$ had increased by a constant amount w each year, that is, if $b = a+w$, $c = b+w$, $d = c+w$, etc, then column 4 would have shown a constant balance of $4w$ owing to Botswana from 1972–3 onwards.

Botswana's departure from the Rand Monetary Area

Botswana left the Rand Monetary Area (RMA) on 23 August 1976. This has in no way affected the basic principles of Botswana's membership of the Customs Union Agreement, but some minor technical effects have been noted.

1 The new Botswana exchange control regulations require a Botswana importer to produce a customs document at his bank before he is allowed to buy the foreign exchange needed to pay for his imports. This has improved the documentation of imports, with a consequent increase in the revenue accrued by Botswana; undercoverage of Botswana's imports may now be as low as 2·5 per cent.

2 Because of the possibility that the Pula and the Rand might not be at par with each other, Botswana's customs tariff had to be rewritten in 'Units of Account' rather than in Pula, where one UA equals one Rand. This particularly affected the so-called 'specific' duties, that is, duties based on mass or volume and not on price; it has also had a slight effect on the non-specific rates of duty on certain goods imported into Botswana from Rhodesia (Zimbabwe).

Some final remarks

The question may be asked, what would be the gains and losses if Botswana were to leave the Customs Union? Obviously, the portion of Botswana's revenue share which derives from the 1·42 multiplier would be lost. Botswana would lose its duty-free access to the South African markets. This would affect the BMC, the clothing industry and possibly the Sua Pan soda ash project. Against this would have to be set the freedom to buy imports in the cheapest foreign market, the freedom to enter into trade agreements with other countries and greater ability to protect infant industries in Botswana by means of a Botswana-oriented tariff. Botswana would have the added cost of an expanded Customs and Excise Department, in both financial and manpower terms, but would not have to wait two years to receive all the accrued revenue. To these kinds of financial arguments must be added both the political and economic benefits of being free to set one's own rates of duty and in particular the freedom to decide what proportion of government taxation should be 'direct' and what should be 'indirect'.

The gross benefit to Botswana of the 1·42 multiplier is probably about P30 million a year at present. It is a matter of debate whether the net benefits to Botswana of leaving the Customs Union could ever equal such a large sum. Even if we leave that aside, we note that Botswana would have to charge about 16 per cent duty on the (duty-free) value of all imports and local dutiable production in order merely to recover the tax element of the present revenue flow. This could cause hardship if it were uniformly applied. Government might instead want to have a lower rate on imports of basic food and clothing, which would imply a higher rate of duty on other items. There could be limited benefits of protection for local markets. Many kinds of products which are available in South Africa would continue not to be manufactured in Botswana, because of the small domestic market. Botswana would continue to buy more expensive South African goods in some instances, because of the convenience of the nearby South African markets.

It is interesting also to look at an alternative to Botswana's membership of the Customs Union, from the point of view of a possible alternative group of African states that might grant each other reciprocal tariff concessions. A hypothetical new trading group might, for example, consist of Botswana, Lesotho, Swaziland, Namibia, Zimbabwe, Malawi, Zaïre, Angola, Mozambique, Kenya, Tanzania and Uganda. But Botswana already has highly effective trade agreements with Lesotho, Swaziland, Namibia, Zimbabwe and Malawi, and Botswana's trade with the other countries above is very small indeed. So the economic advantages, if any, of joining such a new grouping of states would appear to be negligible. The only possible exception might be a small increase in trade with Zambia, which might be able to sell more goods to Botswana if there were no Botswana tariff barriers to overcome, if Zambia had more foreign exchange to spend on imports from Botswana and if the railway from Livingstone to Francistown were freely usable.

In conclusion, one might also argue that all the above points were known to the BLS countries at the time that they negotiated the new Agreement in 1969. There can be no question that the BLS countries have benefited substantially from the new Agreement. Those people who would like to re-examine Botswana's membership in the Southern African Customs Union will have to put in a fair amount of serious study and produce tangible evidence to change the general view that Botswana is better off inside the Customs Union than outside it. Table 9.9 indicates how large the numbers have become in recent years, and how much is at stake for Botswana.

Table 9.9   *The contribution of customs revenue to total recurrent revenue*

Financial year	Customs revenue	Total recurrent revenue	Proportion arising from customs (%)
		(Pula million)	
1899–1900	0·012	0·12	10
1909–10	0·021	0·15	14
1919–20	0·042	0·16	26
1929–30	0·062	0·29	21
1939–40	0·081	0·48	17
1949–50	0·19	1·1	17
1959–60	0·61	3·8	16
1969–70	5·1	17·0	30
1979–80	79·0	210·0	37

Source
Hermans (1974).

Notes

1. Bechuanaland Protectorate became the Republic of Botswana in 1966.
2. Appendix 9.A contains the formal definitions of customs, excise, sales, additional and surcharge duties. Appendix 9.B contains some numerical examples. Appendix 9.C indicates how Botswana's tariff had to be rewritten to permit Botswana to derive the maximum benefit from the Lomé Convention.
3. See Appendix 9.A for a definition of sales duty. The sales duty was to be collected either at the factory in South Africa where the goods were made, or at the point of entry where the goods were imported. It should not be confused with South Africa's recently introduced general sales tax, which is collected by retailers and which applies to services as well as to goods.
4. Sales duty was repealed in 1978, when South Africa introduced a 4 per cent general sales tax on goods and services. The BLS countries did not adopt the general sales tax, which was outside the Customs Union Agreement.
5. In practice, South Africa has negotiated with Botswana a quota on the amount of beef that the Botswana Meat Commission may sell in South Africa, because of an oversupply by South African producers. This is permitted by the Agreement, as long as the restrictions on Botswana producers are similar to the restrictions on South African producers.
6. The CCA consists of Botswana, Lesotho, Namibia, South Africa and Swaziland.

References

Ettinger, S. J., 'South Africa's weight restrictions on cattle exports from Bechuanaland, 1924–41', *Botswana Notes and Records*, Vol. 4 (1972).

Ettinger, S. J., 'The economics of the customs union between Botswana, Lesotho, Swaziland and South Africa', Ph.D. thesis, University of Michigan (1974).

Ettinger, S. J., 'The Bechuanaland Protectorate's participation in pre-1910 customs unions', *Botswana Notes and Records*, Vol. 7 (1975).

Hartland-Thunberg, P., *Botswana: an African Growth Economy*, Boulder, Colorado, Westview Press (1978).

Hailey, Lord William, *The Republic of South Africa and the High Commission Territories*, London, Oxford University Press, (1963).

Hermans, Q., 'Towards budgetary independence – a review of Botswana's financial history, 1900 to 1973', *Botswana Notes and Records*, Vol. 6 (1974).

Iron and Steel Corporation of South Africa, 'Co-operation and lack of co-operation in Southern Africa', Pretoria (1970).

Kowet, D., 'Lesotho and the customs union with the republic of South Africa', in Cervenka, Z. (ed.), *Land-locked Countries of Africa*, Uppsala, The Scandinavian Institute of African Studies (1973).

Kruger, J. P. L., 'Customs unions in South Africa'; M. Bus. Econ. thesis, University of South Africa (1965).

Landell-Mills, P., 'The 1969 Southern African customs union agreement', *Journal of Modern African Studies*, Vol. 9, part 2 (1971).

Mosely, P., 'The Southern African customs union: a reappraisal', roneoed notes, Gaborone (1976).

Robson, P., 'Economic integration in Southern Africa', *Journal of Modern African Studies*, Vol. V, no. 4 (1967).

Selwyn, P., *Industries in the Southern African Periphery*, London, Croom Helm (1975).

Sillery, A., *Founding a Protectorate – a History of Bechuanaland, 1885–1895*, The Hague, Mouton (1965).

Turner, B., 'A fresh start for the Southern African customs union', *African Affairs*, Vol. 70 (1971).

van der Poel, J., *Railway and Customs Policy in South Africa, 1885–1910*, London, Longman (1933).

Vassiliou, N., 'The Southern African customs union: an assessment of its benefits and costs to the BLS countries', roneoed notes, Maseru (1977).

Appendix 9.A
Definitions of the different kinds of duty

A.1 Introduction

Precise definitions of the various kinds of duty are given in the Customs and Excise Duty Act, chapter 50:01. Individual rates of duty are amended from time to time by publication in the *Government Gazette*.

A.2 Customs duty

Customs duty is a tax on those imports into Botswana which originate outside the common customs area.

The rate of duty may be either a percentage of the value of the goods, that is, *ad valorem*, or it may be based on some physical measurement such as the number, mass or volume of the goods, in which case it is called a 'specific' duty. For customs duty purposes only, the value of the goods is measured at the time the goods are loaded on board a ship or aircraft in the country of origin. This is the so-called 'free on board' or f.o.b. value. For purposes of operating the Customs Union revenue sharing formula, goods are valued at the time they cross the Botswana border. This is the 'cost-insurance-freight' or c.i.f. value, which is usually higher than the f.o.b. value.

The rates of duty depend on the country of origin. For example, goods manufactured or produced in Malawi or Zimbabwe are free of customs duty on entry into Botswana.

A.3 Fiscal duty

As explained in Appendixes C2, C3, C4 and C5, a fiscal duty is charged on many goods imported from outside the common customs area. Unlike customs duty, fiscal duty is charged at the same rate regardless of the country of origin.

Examples

These are the combined customs and fiscal duty on a few items:

Live cattle	UA3 each (UA1 = R1)
Live sheep and goats	UA0·50 each
Bananas	5%
Caviar	30%
Tea in bulk	Free of duty
Ready packed tea	UA1·80 per 100 kg
Macaroni and spaghetti	Either 30% or UA4·20 per 100 kg, whichever is greater
Mining equipment	0–5%

A.4 Excise duty

Certain goods are charged an excise duty. This is a kind of luxury tax. It is charged on goods manufactured within the common customs area. A considerable amount of revenue is raised through the application of excise duty.

Examples

Approximate rates of excise duty are:

Lemonade	UA1·76 per 100 litres
Beer	UA25·22 per 100 litres
Wine	UA30 per 100 litres
Spirits (brandy)	UA701·42 per 100 litres
Cigarettes	UA56 per 100 kg *plus* UA0·95 per 100 cigarettes
Cigars	UA140 per 100 kg
Petrol	UA9·34 per 100 litres
Diesel (for private cars)	UA10·16 per 100 litres
Cars	
Less than 1680 kg	UA42 per 100 kg
1681 to 1705 kg	UA47 per 100 kg

| 1706 to 1730 kg | UA52 per 100 kg |
| 1731 to 1755 kg | UA57 per 100 kg |

Certain rates of excise duty were increased at the time that sales duty was abolished.

A.5 *Sales duty* (*now defunct*)

Sales duty was a tax on luxury and semi-luxury goods and was charged both on locally manufactured goods and on imports from outside the common customs area. It was withdrawn early in 1979. Some typical rates were:

Plain white candles	Free of duty
Ornamental candles	20% of the value
Jewellery, sunglasses	20%
Camera film	15%
Carpets	10%
Ball point pens	5%

These rates were applicable in 1975. The rates fluctuated a great deal, depending on the South African government's need to raise funds from this source.

A.6 Import surcharge

In addition to the customs, fiscal and sales duty charged on imports from outside the common customs area, an import surcharge at the rate of 15 per cent was imposed on a long list of commodities in 1977. The object was to make the affected imports into South Africa more expensive and thus reduce the volume of imports, so as to assist South Africa in solving its balance of payments problems. The rate was reduced to 12·5 per cent in 1978 and to 7·5 per cent in 1979.

The import surcharge applied equally to all countries of origin, including Malawi and Rhodesia. The cost of Botswana's imports was increased accordingly. This particularly affected residents in the Chobe, Ngamiland and Northeast Districts, who had up till then paid the same rates of duty on goods coming from either South Africa or Rhodesia, but who now found that Rhodesian goods were charged a higher rate of duty than the equivalent South African products.

Botswana's share of revenue from the common revenue pool was increased in value, on account of the import surcharge. Thus the nation as a whole benefited from the increased revenue, but the increased cost of living fell disproportionately on those living in the north of Botswana who continued to purchase goods from Rhodesia.

A.6 Additional duty

In order to protect infant industries in Botswana, an additional duty may be charged, for up to eight years, on competing goods imported into Botswana from the other parts of the common customs area. Appendix B contains some examples.

Appendix 9.B
Some numerical examples

B.1 Average rate of duty

An interesting comparison is that of annual accruals of revenue with the total value of imports. The comparison yields an approximate average rate of revenue obtained by the Botswana government from Botswana's imports. From this can be derived an approximate average rate of duty paid by Botswana's importers, (see Table 9.B1).

Table 9.B1   *Rates of revenue and rates of duty*

Year	Duty-paid imports[a] (1)	Accrued revenue[b] (2)	Rate of revenue on duty-paid imports[c] (3)	Rate of duty on imports before duty paid[d] (4)
	(UA million)		(percentages)	
1970	40·9	8·5	20	17
1971	59·1	12·7	21	17
1972	84·2	18·5	22	18
1973	115	19·2	16	13
1974	125	17·9	14	11
1975	159	26·1	16	13
1976	181	33·5	18	15
1977	240	50·7	21	17
1978	291			

Notes
[a] The base for the calculation should include local consumption of local dutiable production, but these figures are not published. Total dutiable production is estimated at between P2 million and P3 million per year.
[b] These figures are obtained from Table 9.7 in the text, and therefore are only approximate.
[c] The rate of revenue calculated here is the rate applicable to the *duty-paid* value of Botswana's imports because Botswana's trade statistics are collected on a duty-paid basis. The fluctuations in the rate of revenue are due primarily to changes in the general levels of customs, sales, excise and surcharge duty, as decided on by the South African government from time to time. The size of the fluctuations has been reduced from 1975 onwards, because the revenue stabilization referred to in Table 9.2 was effective from April 1976.
[d] The rate of duty calculated here is the rate applicable to the *duty-free* value of Botswana's imports. The rate of duty is defined as the total of customs, sales, excise, surcharge and additional duty on the duty-free price of all dutiable goods in the customs union, as modified slightly by the stabilization formula. It is derived from column (2) by first dividing by 1·42; and then allowing for the change of base from duty-paid to duty-free imports. There is, of course, an implicit assumption that Botswana's imports bear similar rates of duty to the rates on the imports plus dutiable production of the customs union as a whole. The rate of duty as defined above is the rate that the Botswana government would have to charge, on average, on Botswana's imports if Botswana ever left the customs union and if the government wanted to recover the tax element in the accrued revenue.

B.2 Impact of the Customs Union Agreement on the current account of Botswana's balance of payments

The balance of payments (BOP), of course, shows a large debit each year on account of Botswana's imports. As indicated in Table 9.3 in the main text (p. 140), imports are valued free of duties for BOP purposes. The duties themselves are not shown anywhere in the BOP table, because they are deemed to be taxes paid by Botswana importers to the Botswana government. (The payment of a tax is a transaction between two residents and as such does not appear in the BOP table.)

In practice, however, we know that the taxes are first paid to the common revenue pool in South Africa and then reimbursed to the Botswana government in the form of customs union revenue.

There is no requirement in the Agreement that the revenue received by Botswana on account of a particular import should equal the duty paid by Botswana on that import. On the contrary, there is a built-in assumption that *on average* Botswana will receive 42 per cent more revenue from the pool than the pool has received in taxes from Botswana. What is interesting to look at is the tariff of duties on particular goods and to see whether, *on those goods*, Botswana receives more revenue than has been paid in taxes.

For the purpose of this kind of analysis, one has to compare the cash payment by the importer with the revenue accrual by the Botswana government, as follows:

1   The Botswana importer pays both for his (duty-free) goods and for the duties on them. The total tax paid into the common revenue pool (CRP) is the sum of the customs, excise, sales (now defunct), surcharge and additional duty on the goods.
2   The common revenue pool eventually pays the Botswana government approximately 20 per cent of the duty-free value of the goods plus approximately 20 per cent of the total tax paid on the goods.

If the revenue accrued exceeds the taxes paid, the BOP treats the excess as a contractual obligation from the South African government to the Botswana government, and records the net credit on the current account of the BOP under the heading 'Government transfers, credit'. If the tax paid exceeds the accrued revenue, the difference is a BOP debit.

Examples

The rates of customs and excise duty in the examples below are hypothetical and have been set at certain levels for illustrative purposes only. The rates of additional duty are currently correct; rate of revenue is assumed to be 20 per cent.

Example 1

Suppose a Botswana importer imports a bottle of French wine. The combined customs and excise duty on the wine works out at 25 per cent of the duty-free value of the wine at the Botswana border. The model is:

	%
Value of wine, duty-free	100
Tax paid to CRP	25
Value of wine duty-paid	125
Revenue accrued to Botswana government	25
BOP = revenue − tax	0

The balance of payments is neutral with respect to imports which bear a 25 per cent tax on the duty-free price, if the rate of revenue is 20 per cent.

Example 2

Suppose a Botswana importer imports a bottle of South African wine. The excise duty on the wine works out at 10 per cent of the duty-free price.

	%
Value of wine, duty-free	100
Tax paid to CRP	10
Value of wine, duty-paid	110
Revenue accrued to Botswana government	22
BOP = revenue − tax	+ 12

The balance of payments shows a net credit of 12 per cent of the duty-free value of the wine, when the rate of tax is 10 per cent.

Example 3

Suppose a Botswana importer imports a bottle of Scotch whisky. The combined customs and excise duty on the whisky works out at 100 per cent of the duty-price.

	%
Value of whisky, duty-free	100
Tax paid to CRP	100
Value of whisky, duty-paid	200
Revenue accrued to Botswana government	40
BOP = revenue − tax	− 60

The balance of payments shows a net debit of 60 per cent of the duty-free value of the whisky.

Table 9.B2 summarizes the net effect on the current account of the balance of payments, for different rates of tax on Botswana's imports. A different problem arises when the Botswana government agrees to give infant industry protection to a local manufacturer.

Table 9.B2   *Balance of payments effect of a given rate of tax relative to the duty-free value of imports*[a]

Rate of tax	BOP effect
%	%
0[b]	+ 20 (credit)
5[c]	+ 16 (credit)
10	+ 12 (credit)
15	+ 8 (credit)
20	+ 4 (credit)
25	0 (neutral)
30	− 4 (debit)
35	− 8 (debit)
40	− 12 (debit)
50	− 20 (debit)
70	− 36 (debit)
100	− 60 (debit)
130[d]	− 84 (debit)

Notes
[a] Exactly the same arguments apply to the local consumption of locally produced dutiable goods, as apply to imports.
[b] This is the rate of tax on imports for government departments. Botswana's balance of payments benefits to the extent of 20 per cent of the duty-free value of government imports.
[c] This is the approximate rate of tax that used to be charged on Chibuku traditional sorghum beer. The tax has since been dropped.
[d] This is the approximate rate of tax on a luxury car imported from outside the customs union, when the duty-free value of the car is more than about P10 000 in its country of origin.

Example 4

Suppose a Botswana importer imports a can of Amstel beer from South Africa. Because of the infant industry protection currently given to beer manufactured in Botswana, the importer pays 50 per cent additional duty on the excise-duty-paid value of the Amstel beer. We can follow the flow of the additional duty element of the tax on the Amstel beer. (The tax on the beer includes exactly the same excise duty as is charged on Botswana beer, but we are here looking only at the additional duty on the imported beer.)

The balance of payments shows a net debit of 40 per cent of the excise-duty-paid value of the Amstel, on account of the additional duty. The comparative balance of payments cost, for drinking non-local beer, is approximately the duty-free cost of the imported Amstel plus 40 per cent of the excise-duty-paid price.

	%
Value of Amstel, including excise duty	100
Additional duty paid to South Africa	50
Value of Amstel, duty-paid	150
Revenue accrued to Botswana government on account of total price	30
(of which, revenue accrued on account of additional duty)	10
BOP on account of additional duty	− 40

Example 5

Suppose a Botswana importer imports a bottle of ginger beer from South Africa. In order to protect the local infant industry, there is an additional duty of 100 per cent on all aerated mineral waters. The comparative cost of the imported soft drink is approximately the duty-free cost of the imported ginger beer plus 80 per cent of the excise-duty-paid price.

B.4 Impact on the capital account of the balance of payments

We have noted that any excess of accrued revenue over tax actually paid is recorded as a credit on the current account of the BOP. The process of paying the three instalments to Botswana can, however, result in delays before the accrued revenue is finally paid to Botswana. A careful analysis of column (4) of Table 9.8 in the main text shows that the amount owing to Botswana can go up or down, but usually goes up. If the amount owing to Botswana at the end of a calendar year is greater than the amount owing at the beginning of the year, the difference is shown as a debit on the capital account under the heading 'Government capital'. For example, if the balance in Botswana's favour was R27·5 million at the end of 1976 and R44·5 million at the end of 1977, then the debit (increase in value of a foreign financial asset) is shown as R17 million on the capital account of the BOP.

Appendix 9.C
Relations with the European Economic Community (EEC)

C.1 Introduction

Botswana is a signatory to the Lomé Convention, which is a trade agreement between the EEC and various African, Caribbean and Pacific (ACP) developing countries. A problem arose during the Lomé negotiations in 1975, when it was thought possible that the conditions attached to Botswana's membership in the Southern African Customs Union (SACU) might be incompatible with Botswana's obligations under the proposed Lomé Convention.

The Lomé Convention allows the ACP countries to sell beef to the EEC free of customs duty. Of far greater importance, however, is the question of an abatement, that is, reduction, of a stiff import levy which the EEC charges on beef imports in addition to customs duty. The EEC has granted Botswana, Kenya, Madagascar and Swaziland a 90 per cent abatement of the levy, up to a fixed annual quota of beef for each exporting country. There are two conditions attached by the EEC to the abatement.

C.2 The new export tax

The first condition is that each of the four beef-exporting ACP countries must apply an export tax to their beef exports which is equal to the 90 per cent EEC levy abatement, and, further, each country must use the resulting tax revenue for the general benefit of their cattle industry. In Botswana, the Botswana Meat Commission (BMC) applies an export tax to beef consigned to the EEC, and sends the tax to the government. The government in turn utilizes this tax revenue by making an equal-sized contribution to the running expenses of the BMC.

C.3 Most-favoured-nation status for the EEC

The second condition is that Botswana (and similarly all other ACP beneficiaries under the Lomé Convention) must not charge more customs duty on imports from the EEC than the duty charged on imports from Botswana's 'most favoured nations' (MFN).

The EEC concessions on beef are of great value to Botswana, since the BMC thereby gains access to the high-priced EEC beef market. The prices paid by the BMC to Botswana's cattle producers would probably have to be substantially reduced if access to the EEC were ever lost. It follows that it was most important for Botswana to find some way of satisfying the EEC's second condition. At the same time, Botswana's membership in the SACU is worth millions of Pula per year to Botswana, so any solution to the EEC problem had to be consistent with the rules of the SACU Agreement. The difficulty was to find some way of satisfying both the EEC and South Africa simultaneously.

At first sight, it appeared that Botswana had already:

1   Granted most-favoured-nation treatment to Lesotho, Malawi, Namibia, Rhodesia, South Africa and Swaziland, in terms of existing trade agreements, and
2   Put itself into a position where its membership in the SACU prevented it from granting the EEC's request for MFN treatment.

Botswana told the EEC that the existing duties in the Botswana tariff on imports from the EEC were not used to protect domestic manufacturers in Botswana, but were in fact purely revenue raising or fiscal duties, from Botswana's point of view. It was also pointed out to the EEC that Botswana receives approximately 20 per cent of the value of imports from the countries in (1) above, by means of the working of the SACU formula, and that this should be regarded also as a fiscal duty since it is clearly not a protective customs duty.

C.4 The new format for the Botswana tariff

With the approval of South Africa, the EEC and the other ACP states, the BLS countries then divided the total duty paid on imports into two components, a fiscal duty which applies to imports from all countries and a customs duty which could be higher for countries not on the list of most favoured nations. When the two component duties are applied to a particular import, the total duty charged by BLS equals the duty that South Africa would have charged on the item. The BLS countries thus continue to satisfy one of the key elements of the SACU Agreement, namely that all the members should charge the same rates of duty on goods imported from abroad. Conversely, the newly defined customs duty element in the new BLS tariff provides the EEC with the MFN status for which they were looking.

Considerable credit goes to the Department of Customs and Excise and to the Ministry of Finance and Development Planning for drafting the solution to such a tricky problem.

C.5 Details of the new tariff

The details of the new BLS tariff are as follows:

1   A new most-favoured-nation customs duty has been created for the BLS countries. The MFN duty applies to a long list of countries, basically the signatories to the General Agreement on Tariffs and Trade (GATT). The list includes both the EEC and the countries mentioned above (in C.3). The new MFN customs duty is defined as zero on all goods imported from these countries.
2   Countries which are not on the MFN list are charged a new 'general' customs duty, which can be greater than zero. The rates are set equal to the amount by which the South African non-MFN customs duty exceeds the South African MFN customs duty.
3   All countries are in addition either actually charged a new 'fiscal' duty or else are deemed to have been charged a fiscal duty. A fiscal duty (of about 20 per cent) is deemed to be charged on imports from countries mentioned above (in C.3). This is the revenue that Botswana receives from the common revenue pool of the SACU on account of imports from these countries. All other countries are charged a new fiscal duty by Botswana. This is set at the same level as the rate of customs duty charged by South Africa on MFN imports, including those from the EEC.

The two rates of fiscal duty, one on countries listed in section C.3 and the other on all other countries, are not identical; but since they are not customs duties (as far as Botswana is concerned) they do not enter the argument about the EEC's MFN status.

From Table 9.C1 it is seen that the EEC is not charged more customs duty than Botswana charges any other country. Botswana was thus able to sign the Lomé Convention in 1976 without damaging its relations with South Africa under the SACU Agreement.

Table 9.C1   *Summary of duties charged on imports into Botswana*

Exporting countries	Customs duty		Fiscal duty	Total duty
	MFN rate	General rate		
Lesotho, Malawi, Namibia, Zimbabwe, South Africa, Swaziland	Zero	N/A	Approx. 20%	Approx. 20%
EEC and other most favoured nations	Zero	N/A	South African MFN rates of duty	South African MFN rates of duty
Non-MFN countries	N/A	SA non-MFN rates, *minus* SA MFN rates	SA MFN rates of duty	SA non-MFN rates of duty

C.6 Non-most favoured nations

The general rate of customs duty applies to the following countries:

Asia	Afghanistan, Bhutan, China, India, Iran, Iraq, Japan, Khmer (Cambodia), North Korea, Laos, Lebanon, Mongolia, Oman, Philippines, Saudi Arabia, Sikkim, Syria, Thailand, Vietnam, Yemen Arab Republic
Europe	Albania, Bulgaria, East Germany, USSR (including Ukraine and Byelorussia)
America	Bolivia, Ecuador, El Salvador, Guatemala, Honduras, Mexico, Panama, Paraguay, Venezuela
Africa	Egypt, Ethiopia, Guinea, Libya, Somalia, Sudan

Derek J. Hudson is Director of Research Bank of Botswana, formerly Research Statistician and Government Statistician, Central Statistics Office, Botswana.

10 Aid Management in Botswana: from One to Many Donors

MICHAEL STEVENS

Introduction

The story of Botswana's mobilization of external resources is a remarkable one. At Independence in 1966 aid flows were modest, permitting only a relatively low level of development spending by the government. The bulk of the funds came from a single source, the United Kingdom, and had to be shared between development projects and the continuing need for recurrent budget support. In the next ten years, development spending increased seven and a half times in money terms, and aid agreements had been negotiated with a long list of international agencies and bilateral sources.[1] The country provided an outstanding example of the successful mobilization of aid resources and their deployment. At a time when the efforts of international agencies and developed country governments were under increasing attack for both the low level of transfers and the way in which these transfers were effected, Botswana provided an example of how aid could be made to work.

Although not all of the growth in the government's development spending can be attributed to the growth in external assistance, in 1977–8 some 72 per cent of development spending was externally financed. Clearly, therefore, the impact of aid has been very great. The negotiation and utilization of such a rapidly growing volume and variety of external resources from so many sources greatly strains the administrative machine in Botswana. The aid management lessons that were learned are worth recording for their intrinsic interest and for their wider relevance to the transfer of resources from rich to poor countries.

First, the build-up of aid flows and their utilization is described. Next, some of the reasons for the international community's willingness to continue supporting increasing levels of assistance to Botswana are discussed. Finally, influence of the aid relationships on the country's development strategy is described.

The picture at Independence

On the eve of Independence, the propects for sustained development were, to outside observers, unpromising. A *per capita* income of about $50 per annum placed Botswana firmly in the ranks of the least developed countries. In the middle of the 1960s the country experienced three years of drought that claimed half the national cattle herd. Government revenues covered little more than half recurrent expenditure, and the level of development spending was low. The administrative machinery was weak, handicapped by a virtual absence of trained local manpower, by a lack of sufficient expatriates and by inadequate revenues.

The economic missions which visited Botswana in the last years of the Protectorate had no difficulty in identifying social and physical infrastructure needs, but were cautious about the prospects for sustained development.

Fortunately this view was not shared by the government. A Transitional Plan covering the first two years of independence was quickly put together, to be followed by a succession of five-year National Development Plans, the first covering the period 1968–73. In these documents the government laid out the basic priorities.

One basic priority was to create a sound administrative basis for development. Also fundamental was the need to generate enough domestic revenue to finance the government's recurrent budget in its entirety, and to contribute to development spending. However, there was a paradox. In order to end budgetary support, grant-in-aid had first to be increased, since long overdue investment in administrative, social and physical infrastructure appeared to be an essential precondition of financial self-sufficiency. The Transitional Plan put it as follows:

> However, even on the most optimistic projections and assuming that funds for development are forthcoming as requested, it does not appear possible for Botswana's dependence on grants-in-aid for recurrent expenditure to be ended for a long time to come unless the pace of development is much accelerated.

Financial self-sufficiency was in fact achieved in 1972–3; it was several years earlier than forecast, partly as a result of the renegotiated customs union agreement and mining developments.[2]

At first there was one principal donor, the United Kingdom. In addition to budgetary support, the UK provided the bulk of the capital funds available to the government, in the form of Colonial Development and Welfare Act monies, Intercolonial Loans and Exchequer Loans. These funds were limited and had to cover many needs, ranging from agricultural and educational schemes whose developmental value was self-evident, to equally needed investments in administration and other government infrastructure. In the first five years of independence, 57 per cent of total development spending was financed from the United Kingdom. (See Table 10.3, p. 175).

Other development finance consisted of an IDA (International Development Association) credit, worth P2·6 million, negotiated in 1964, and used for a nationwide programme of road and bridge improvements, an early Swedish grant for teacher training in Francistown, and a series of smaller grants from voluntary agencies such as Oxfam and the UK Freedom from Hunger Campaign, mainly for self-help projects in the rural areas. In addition, the government was able to negotiate a series of modest commercial loans from

Barclays and Standard, the two international banks with branch networks in Botswana.

The build-up of development assistance

In the first four years after 1966 the general level of development spending was low. Then in the early 1970s, development spending rose dramatically (see Table 10.1). There were two reasons for the rise in development spending. First,

Table 10.1   *Development spending 1966–7 to 1977–8 (P million)*

	P m		P m
1966–7	6·8	1972–3	29·9
1967–8	3·8	1973–4	30·3
1968–9	3·3	1974–5	32·8
1969–70	4·9	1975–6	35·4
1970–1	8·5	1976–7	37·6
1971–2	12·3	1977–8	44·4
		1978–9	79·0

Note
1978–9 figure includes write-off of parastatal debt and government's contribution to the new diamond mine at Jwaneng – that is, the large increase over 1977–8 is not all increased development spending by government itself.

Source
Extracted from Table 10.3 at the end of this chapter.

after years of prospecting, negotiation and design, construction of the large copper–nickel complex at Selebi-Phikwe got under way. The project was a joint venture between the government and an international consortium headed by Roan Selection Trust. The latter was responsible for the construction and operation of the mine, and the government undertook to build the infrastructure, the main elements of which were the mining township, a power station and a dam and pipeline to take water from the Shashe river. To meet the government's share of the project, finance was raised from the World Bank (US $32 million), the Canadian government (Can. $30 million), and the United States government (US $6·5 million). These substantial sums of money were far beyond existing levels of project finance. Taken with the mining components of the project, they involved complex multiple financing and interlocking legal responsibilities between the investors, the lenders and the government.[3] Both the size of the project and the complexity of its financing imposed a strain on the slender administrative resources of the government, particularly of high level managers. The government had to put a major effort into the project, including the creation of a special Shashe Project management unit within the administration. The ability of the government to borrow such a disproportionately large amount was partly because the government's debts were guaranteed by the mining companies involved, and partly because of a general belief, shared also by the donors, that Selebi-Phikwe would provide the desired breakthrough to budgetary self-sufficiency. As events transpired, these aspirations were met, but not in the way expected. The costs of the project severely escalated, particularly the mining components. Furthermore, technological troubles delayed start-up and the attainment of full production. Coupled with falling metal prices, this dashed hopes for a profitable return on investment.[4] Although this led to losses and additional capital expenditure for the investors, the project had benefits for the government. First, it added substantially to customs receipts from the Southern Africa Customs Union pool, both during construction and in subsequent operation, leading directly to the attainment of budgetary self-sufficiency. Secondly, it exposed the aid agencies, to an extent that had not happened before, to Botswana and its development prospects, and particularly to the fact that the country had the ability to co-ordinate a project of this complexity and magnitude.

Apart from the Shashe Project itself, the government's additional efforts to diversify aid sources were beginning to be successful. After the United Kingdom, the first major bilateral donor to commit itself to support a programme of projects was Sweden. In 1971, following visits to Stockholm by the Vice-President and senior officials, a major mission comprising members of the Swedish Ministry of Foreign Affairs and the Swedish aid agency, SIDA, arrived in Botswana to establish that Botswana met the criteria for Swedish assistance. This led shortly afterwards to the establishment of a regular annual aid programme. Spending from Swedish aid rose to over P9 million in 1977–8, having started with spending of P0·05 million in 1968–9. Two years later similar arrangements were concluded with the Norwegian government, represented by its aid agency, NORAD.

Although all three aid agencies provided finance for a programme of development projects, chosen in the first instance by the Botswana government, Swedish and Norwegian aid differed operationally from United Kingdom aid. First, the ground rules on spending the money were different. Because the UK Treasury limited spending authority to the year in which funds were voted, the Ministry of Overseas Development could not normally permit a carry-forward of unspent project finance from one year to the next. For an aid recipient, this meant projects that for one reason or another were not completed under one year's funding, lost their unspent allocation and competed with new projects for money in the following year. In other words, aid unspent in one financial year was lost to the recipient, since it could not be added to the following year's allocation. To avoid systematic underspending, since projects are habitually delayed, the British government allowed Botswana to overcommit by up to 40 per cent the total value of projects submitted for approval during the year. This concession was given on the understanding that should it appear in the closing months of the financial year that expenditures were likely to exceed the amount available, projects would be deliberately slowed down, or the excess met with other funds.[5]

Swedish and Norwegian procedures were simpler. Whilst no over-commitment was permitted, funds unspent in one year could be carried forward into the next year. This lessened somewhat the pressure to spend, and in turn pointed Scandinavian assistance towards projects in the rural areas where implementation slippage was traditionally greatest and the rate of project expenditure was harder to predict.

Donor preferences

As Botswana diversified its sources of aid, it became apparent that the new donors had strong preferences about the categories of projects they were prepared to finance. How donor preferences affect the composition of development spending can be difficult initially to tie down. Most donors, for example, stress that the recipient selects the projects and provided there is reasonable economic justification, implementation has been thought through, and the project can be shown to fit the current development strategy, aid money will be forthcoming. Yet behind the apparent willingness to consider all projects, most donors have clear preferences. In the case of Norway and Sweden, there was a strong leaning towards rural projects and projects which were expected to benefit the lower income groups in the population. Fortunately, it was relatively easy for Botswana to assemble programmes that met these criteria. Furthermore, the flexibility with which the aid was administered made these donors the natural funding source for the projects that they were given.

All developing countries suffer from a shortage of administrative capacity in one form or another, and one of the surest ways of wasting precious management talent is to allocate priority projects to the wrong donors. SIDA's and NORAD's procedures were sufficiently flexible for this not to be a problem. But as Botswana's aid sources were further diversified, they were joined by other donors whose procedures were less flexible. Matching donors with suitable projects became critically important if the development programme was not to become bogged down. In most cases, the correct decisions were made, although the procedural difficulties of dealing with one particular donor were underestimated so that several priority projects were delayed.

The interest shown in Botswana by the new donors coincided with the peaking of expenditures on the Shashe Project. Within the country there was concern that the capacity to implement demonstrated by the government should not be lost, but applied in some way to the rest of the development programme. There appeared to be an analogy with the early 1960s, when project implementation capacity had shown a similar sharp rise with the construction of the new capital at Gaborone, only to fall away again in succeeding years through lack of finance and follow-up. In 1973 the situation was different. Not only were new sources of aid becoming available, but substantial surpluses were being projected for the recurrent budget. Buoyant revenues were double edged. Whilst they could finance the recurrent costs arising from capital spending, there was a strong risk that if not applied to development they would find their way into unproductive consumption expenditure. As the construction stage of the Shashe Project wound down, a major effort was mounted to increase implementation capacity for all developmental projects. Agencies that provided expatriate technical assistance were asked to increase their ceilings, and did so. The project management unit concept, used so successfully to co-ordinate the Shashe Project, was applied to some other large projects. Most important of all, a number of existing and planned development projects in the rural areas were brought together in 1973 to form the Accelerated Rural Development Programme (ARDP). When it was wound up three years later, the ARDP's achievements included the construction of 78 miles of tarred road through major villages, 489 primary school classrooms, 425 teachers' houses, 596 latrines, 21 clinics, 43 health posts and 30 nurses' houses – the majority in nearly all cases being in smaller villages.[6]

The ARDP was important not only for giving concrete expression to the government's rural development policies but also for the implications it had on aid programming. Although the heavy concentration on rural projects resulted in delays elsewhere in the development programme (which affected in particular the UK programme), the ARDP was particularly good for the Swedish programme, its major external source of funding. There was also a useful demonstration effect on other donors whose programmes were just beginning. The ARDP showed that a capacity existed for the design and execution of rural projects, not only at central government level, but also in the district councils. Just as in earlier years the country had shown a capacity to make full use of the annual British allocation,[7] and so gain additional sums, so successive years of full expenditure of Swedish monies resulted in a steady raising by SIDA of the country ceiling.

Other donors, too, were showing increased interest in the country. Botswana's first loan from the African Development Bank, for telecommunications, was negotiated in 1972, to be followed by lending for road, health and airport development. Botswana's association with the World Bank group dated back to before Independence, but apart from two road credits, the bank's assistance had been concentrated in the Shashe Project. Following an economic survey mission in 1973, the bank reclassified Botswana as a country eligible for IRBD type loans to replace the IDA credits hitherto available. This meant harder lending terms, but it did hold out promise of a greater volume of resources. In 1974 a five-year rolling programme of projects was agreed between the bank and the government. This implied roughly one project a year, with a cumulative total of $50 million in loan finance over the period. At the same time there was much concern that the country was being promoted directly to hard loan status without enjoying the intermediate status of a combination of soft and hard lending. But the new arrangements did mean both an increased volume of lending and the convenience of being able to plan the preparation of bank projects several years in advance, with reasonable certainty that the requisite finance would be available at the time of implementation.

Another major donor that was keen to expand its assistance was the United States. USAID financing had first been made available for Shashe Project water supplies. The next major project was the construction of the Botswana–Zambia Highway, a project rated highly by the government for its strategic value, but which suffered from delays and cost escalation. This ensured that it absorbed a large amount of US funds; after its completion in 1976, expenditure of AID funds fell back. There were several reasons for this. First, veterinary and other technical reasons caused the indefinite postponement of its successor project, the Northern Abattoir, to the consternation of the United States.[8] Secondly, the strict rules governing where materials purchased under a USAID loan could be obtained limited the projects that were suitable. Thus for several years the bulk of American assistance took the form of technical assistance projects. More recently, USAID has been able to apply more flexible procedures, and the volume of disbursements is increasing.

Another major Western country that has a substantial aid programme is the Federal Republic of Germany. A total of DM22 million (P9·5 million) was available in 1978–9, and the prospects for further assistance are encouraging.

However, the large volume of German assistance is of recent origin. The first major project was the construction of the Francistown–Serule section of the north–south road, but this was slow in getting under way, and it was a long time before co-operation was expanded from a single project to a programme basis, so that only P3·0 million was actually spent in 1977–8.

The final major Western donor was Canada, which had contributed at a critical time in the financing of the Shashe project by providing a low interest loan (later converted into a grant) for the power station, and had broadened its assistance subsequently in the support of the mining sector, the government transport organization, urban development and the university. Initially, the expansion of Canada's role was limited by the requirement that 75 per cent of expenditures had to be on Canadian goods and services, but these requirements were subsequently eased somewhat.

The first efforts of the Botswana government to obtain finance from Arab sources were made in 1974, in the aftermath of the Arab–Israeli war. Approaches were made to several Arab agencies, but despite the solidarity between African and Arab countries at that time, the initiative was premature, and nothing came of it, with the exception of an allocation from the Oil Price Alleviation Fund in 1975 of $4·5 million. More recent approaches are beginning to show results, and in 1978 the first BADEA (Arab Bank for Economic Development in Africa) loan was approved for local vaccine production.

The Lomé Convention between the African, Caribbean and Pacific (ACP) states (including Botswana) and the EEC was signed in February 1975, and within two weeks Botswana had submitted a portfolio of project outlines. Despite this promptness, there was a delay of over a year before the Commission was able to field a programming mission to announce the country ceiling (22 million units of account or US $28·9 million) and agree on a list of projects for financing. These covered a broad range of sectors, but the delay in establishing the programme was an augury of worse to come, for by the beginning of negotiations for the successor to the Lomé Convention in 1978, only 14 per cent of the funds available had been disbursed.

Donor management

By the middle of the 1970s the diversification of Botswana's sources of external assistance was thus well under way. The additional finance, when added to growing local resources, made possible a rapid increase in the level of public sector development spending. It also brought with it a greater complexity to the management of the Development Budget.

In the early days aid administration was simple. With only one major donor, all the implementing departments knew the rules and how to get the most out of them. Two things were important. First, to ensure that the total amount of capital aid available in the year was spent (otherwise it would be lost). Secondly, to follow the rules laid down on procurement. The first gave an immediacy to project implementation. Departments knew that their performance in carrying out their projects on time was the critical factor in deciding whether they would have an increased share of next year's funds, or more immediately, any supplementary finance that might be allocated to Botswana in the last quarter of the financial year. It has been argued that this emphasis on expenditure created bad habits and was at the expense of more carefully thought-out projects, and, worst of all, skewed expenditure in favour of the fast spenders. These tendencies undoubtedly existed but were more than offset by the positive incentives it gave to implementation performance and the focusing of attention on development. Botswana's ability in later years, when aid flows increased, to handle the greater flow of projects is primarily due to the habits learned, and the system of project monitoring developed, in the early days of British aid.

In the early days, procurement rules were quickly learned. Any materials purchased with British aid had to originate either in Botswana or the United Kingdom. There were, however, important exceptions. In the first place, with few building materials produced locally, essentials such as cement, window and door frames, conduit piping, electrical fittings and corrugated roofing sheets had to be imported. It was clearly impractical to ship these supplies from the United Kingdom. Not only would this add to the cost, but delays would occur so that administration of contracts would have become almost impossible. The United Kingdom authorities quickly accepted this point, and a standing waiver for the purchase of general building supplies from South Africa was approved for all projects. Waivers were also granted for certain categories of vehicles that were assembled in South Africa from UK manufactured components, and for equipment items that were substantially more expensive to obtain from the UK, or on which for technical reasons the government had already standardized on a third country source. Aid officials of the Ministry of Overseas Development were under constant pressure, on the one side from the UK Department of Trade to increase the British content of aid spending, and on the other from Botswana to widen the scope of existing waivers. Yet despite these conflicting pressures, the aid programme was operated with commendable flexibility.

As sources were diversified, matters became more complicated. Both Norway and Sweden readily accepted the need to buy essential supplies from South Africa, and were themselves under less balance of payments pressure to maximize domestic procurement. Their aid was therefore completely untied. Other donors, either through a failure to perceive the special position of the BLS countries, or, more frequently, because of restrictions imposed on the aid agency by other arms of government, were not able to take such a pragmatic line, and the usefulness of their aid was thereby diminished. USAID had an elaborate system of codes that listed the third countries eligible for procurement. In practice the ones that could supply were no more accessible than America, and little use could be made of them. Canada for a long while required 75 per cent Canadian procurement which ruled out most projects except consultancy services. The European Development Fund, while appearing in the text of the Lomé Convention to have a flexible approach, ended up applying one of the most impractical waiver systems of all.

The different characteristics of donors clearly influenced the selection of projects and how they were implemented. The policy adopted by the government was to match projects with donors in a way that minimized implementation difficulties, while at the same time trying to retain priorities and to maximize the availability of external resources. How successfully this was done, and some of the unforeseen side effects is discussed below. In the meantime it is worth setting out the main reasons why the international community was so keen to increase aid flows to Botswana.

The attractions of Botswana to aid donors

There were a number of reasons why Botswana in the 1970s was an attractive place for the aid agencies. At the beginning of the period Botswana was unquestionably a poor country, with a *per capita* income level that qualified the country as one of the least developed. Yet unlike other low income countries, once the mineral possibilities were perceived, Botswana offered the prospects of rapid growth. This provided two stimuli: first, the opportunity to participate in the government component of the Shashe Project, seen as critical to that project's success; second, an opportunity to help Botswana with the social, physical and administrative infrastructure that would become even more necessary as mineral-led growth accelerated. The growth potential also meant that Botswana seemed very likely to have the recurrent revenues necessary to maintain the schools, roads, clinics and other schemes that the donor money made possible.

Next, Botswana was quick to establish a routine of planning that led to the production of clear and straightforward development plans in which it was easy to identify the policies of the government and the projects that needed financing. At Independence Botswana issued the *Transitional Plan for Social and Economic Development*, covering the period 1966–8. This was followed by the *National Development Plan 1968–73*, the first of a series of five-year plans, prepared on a rolling basis every two to three years. These plans, moreover, were not prepared in a separate planning commission, detached from the rest of government, but jointly by the planners and the executing departments. Consequently, the resulting sectoral programmes had an operational reality that the donor agencies appreciated.

The ability to prepare effective development plans was matched by a capacity to implement projects that was unusual for a country at such an early stage of development. This advantage was probably more important in the eyes of the donors than the expertise in planning, although both stemmed from the importance given to development by the political leadership. In the clamour for a greater flow of resources from the rich countries to the poor, the point is generally overlooked that poor countries can be inefficient utilizers of the existing flows, inefficient, that is, in the eyes of donor agencies. Aid agencies, irrespective of whether their funds are grudgingly supplied by a government more concerned about domestic priorities, or are striving to disburse a target proportion of a rising GDP, are embarrassed by a failure of developing country governments to spend funds that have been approved. Consequently Botswana's ability not only to spend fully the amounts available under the UK aid programme in the early years, but to absorb at short notice supplementary allocations, resulted in additional aid, an effect that has not been fully appreciated. So not only was Botswana a country that met the normal criteria for aidworthiness, it also appeared able to spend the additional funds agencies provided. This it was able to do in an atmosphere that was remarkably free from corruption and dud projects.

Political factors, too, were important. First, the political philosophy of the country's leadership translated into a real commitment to democratic freedoms and the rule of law that few other developing countries could match. This in turn led to policies for development that were broad based, and (at least in intent) refreshingly free from the modern sector biases found in many comparable countries. Next, the geopolitical position of Botswana, although it added a dimension of vulnerability to the country's future, gave an extra reason for assisting Botswana. If it was not possible for Western countries to alter the apartheid policies of South Africa, then contributing to an independent multiracial and democratic state at its borders was a partly compensating alternative. For some donors this interest in Botswana in a wider setting did influence how they viewed domestic policies, and this is discussed in a later section.

Finally, there was an intangible factor which although perhaps not apparent to new donors, did affect the aid relationship as it matured. This was the ability of Botswana government officials to establish excellent working relationships with those in the agencies that were responsible for determining policies towards Botswana. The result of this was that Botswana became a special case and rules that otherwise would have remained inviolable were bent in Botswana's favour.[9] Some of the best examples come from the early days of the United Kingdom capital assistance. When supplementary loans were made available for spending in the last quarter of the financial year, short cuts were taken in both the preparation and approval of project memoranda based largely on the understanding between the officials of the two sides involved. The same also applied to waiver requests. In part this was due to the long association of the former colonial power and the continuity of individual contact. But it was also due to a genuine identification of agency staff with the development aspirations of the country, shared by other institutions like the World Bank, the Canadian aid agency (CIDA), and the Scandinavian agencies.

Donor influence

The diversification of aid sources and the increase in the total amount available did place a burden on the administrative machinery of the government. At Independence a separate Ministry of Development had been formed, but in 1970 this was fused with the Ministry of Finance to create a powerful Ministry of Finance and Development Planning with the then Vice-President, Dr Masire, as its Minister. For most of the period aid co-ordination was the responsibility of the Division of Economic Affairs (corresponding to the former Ministry of Development), which was also responsible for plan preparation, project preparation and evaluation. Latterly the aid co-ordination role was shared with the budget section of the joint ministry. Aid relations took up a major portion of the time of officials in the division, and it may be asked whether a preoccupation with aid donors was not at the expense of longer term planning and policy activities.

Several answers may be given to this point. First, for much of the period external finance was essential if the development programme was to go ahead, and, as explained below, the co-ordination of donors critically affects the rate of plan implementation. Secondly, there is little evidence to substantiate the claim that long term planning was adversely affected. Inevitably, progress on such policies as equitable income distribution, and industrial development has been less than one might hope. But the lack of progress in these areas is common to almost all developing countries, and it is questionable whether a less heavy aid co-ordination role would have made much difference.

One of the reasons why Botswana throughout the period was able to achieve such a good record of aid utilization was the establishment from the outset of a sound monitoring system. When the United Kingdom was the sole source of programme aid, and the chance of supplementary allocations depended on spending performance, a simple but effective monitoring system was established. At regular intervals throughout the year, increasing to monthly in the final quarter, meetings would be held under the chairmanship of the Vice-President to review the implementation performance of development projects. Ministers accompanied by their officials would be called upon to report progress, and to undertake remedial action if bottlenecks were identified. As the aid programme became diversified and the number of projects both grew and became more complex, it proved impossible to handle the entire development budget in a single plenary session: the review meetings were then handled on an individual ministry basis in more detail, but with longer intervals between reviews.

Such a high inflow of external resources clearly had a major effect on the rate of development in Botswana. Without the amounts made available in the years before and after Independence, the attainment of budgetary self sufficiency would have long been delayed; and if the build-up of aid resources had not continued after the end of grant-in-aid, domestic resources would have been woefully inadequate for the high levels of socal and physical infrastructure investment that Botswana's circumstances required.

What needs to be examined in greater detail is how the diversity of donors, each with their different philosophies of assistance and with different rules and procedures, affected the shape and outcome of the development programme. What was the impact of this massive mobilization of external resources on domestic policy? To what extent did the terms of the aid affect the choice of projects, and how much leverage was applied?

It is easiest to eliminate those aspects of the aid relationship that had little effect on the choice of projects and the outcome of the development programme. Aid funds were offered to Botswana under a range of different financial terms, but all loans had total repayment periods (that is, including the grace periods) of more than twenty-five years. A large proportion of the outstanding external debt consisted of IBRD borrowings (44 per cent in March 1979) which had long repayment periods but commercial rates of interest, and were mostly denominated in the currencies of the surplus countries. Other borrowings, though nominally on concessionary terms, required repayment in hard currencies like the Deutschmark. To what extent did the terms of borrowing affect either the willingness of the government to accept the loans or the uses to which the funds were put?

The short answer is: surprisingly little. With all donor financing on concessional terms, debt service was not normally a significant consideration. Furthermore, as part of a global effort to ease the burden of debt servicing, a number of Western donors retrospectively converted past loans into grants. This was welcomed in Botswana, but with a debt service ratio of about 4 per cent, and debt servicing never more than about 8 per cent of the recurrent budget, it was not a critical problem. Interestingly, as Botswana's *per capita* income rose, the terms of external financing if anything became softer, partly for compositional reasons and partly because of a worldwide trend towards increasing the concessional element in aid. In the early years the emphasis was on increasing the volume of external assistance, and the terms of new aid (seldom onerous) was never a serious factor. And with such a favourable time profile for its borrowings, throughout the period Botswana could afford to take a macro view on its borrowings.

In the future, however, Botswana may have to rely more on near-commercial borrowing such as official export credits, and on fully commercial credit, for example from the eurocurrency markets. The country's first ever large-scale commercial loan, for $45 million from a consortium of banks, was negotiated in 1978, although it had not been drawn on by the end of 1979. The private sector, notably the copper–nickel mining company, has large external debts on commercial terms; although these do not affect the government directly, they do affect it indirectly by postponing the taxation of profits.

A potentially greater influence on poorer countries' development strategies is the aid philosophies of donors and their preferences for projects to support. Most agencies stress that their assistance is guided by the development priorities of the recipient country. The Lomé Convention, for example, talks about the indicative programme being drawn up by 'mutual agreement', with a formal exchange of views between the European Economic Community and the ACP state to 'enable the ACP state to set out its development policy and priorities'. The Scandinavian agencies follow this approach as well, and international institutions like the World Bank are at pains to explain that they exist to respond to, not set, the priorities of the poorer nations. Yet on the other side the agencies themselves have development preferences, which tend to follow the current fashion in development thinking. In the 1950s, when development aid was seen as creating the take-off conditions for sustained growth, agencies liked large infrastructure and industrial projects. There was also a time when investment in education was seen as the key to unleashing the development process; and in the 1960s Botswana found it impossible to gain the interest of one major donor except with regional proposals. In the present decade the emphasis has been on rural development, income distribution and the share of benefits to the poor, with the World Bank in particular being concerned with the plight of the poor both in the rural areas and in the rapidly expanding cities of the Third World.

To workers in the field, with daily contact with these problems, it would be excusable if the successive highlighting of different aspects of underdevelopment by the agencies were greeted with some cynicism. The agencies, of course, have another constituency, the parliaments and taxpayers in the developed countries; and opponents of aid have been quick to criticize the failures of past policies. Nor have developing country governments necessarily followed enlightened policies themselves; for example, they have pressed hard for the financing of wasteful prestige projects.

Yet it must be asked whether donor pressure is productive in the long run. For a start it is questionable whether the approach works, and when it does there can be some harmful side effects. It works something like this. The representatives of a new donor come into town and announce that they would like to assist the development of the country with an annual aid programme of X million dollars. 'Give us your highest priority projects', they say, and the ritual of selling the projects begins. Overlooked are the considerations that, first, while most governments have a general view on what is most urgent, there is no systematic ranking of projects. Theoretically this could be done by calculating internal rates of return, but no developing country government either could or should afford the time for such an exercise. The project evaluation techniques of the textbooks are employed mainly to satisfy donor requirements for individual projects (that are probably going to be financed anyway). Secondly, to the extent that they have been identified, the highest priority projects are in the pipeline for an earlier donor. Finally, even if the highest priority projects were identified and available, it might be better for reasons of procedures and fungibility to finance them with non-donor funds if these are available.

The fungibility argument runs as follows. A donor who wishes to influence the composition of the development programme should not rush for the priority projects. Whether he or someone else does it, they will be financed anyway. Donor finance then simply releases funds for other projects – of which the donor might, or might not, approve. Instead the donor should concentrate on the marginal projects where his influence on what does or does not go ahead might be more effective.

Looking back, then, on Botswana's experience with a multiplicity of donors, the answer is that probably the preferences of individual donors had relatively little effect overall on the composition of the development programme. There were certainly times when a deliberate effort was made to give a donor the type of project he wanted, particularly when the aid relationship was a new one, and the government was keen to build up the programme. But as long as there were other donors who were prepared to accept a different blend of projects, and as long as there were domestic resources available to finance the important but unappealing schemes (such as government infrastructure), the overall composition of the development programme was not really affected. It may, of course, be necessary to exert this sort of leverage in a country that is seriously neglecting important development areas, but in a country that prided itself on having a balanced development programme (on which the donors agreed), the result of such activities is likely to be a waste of many people's time on both sides.

The project preferences of donors are likely, however, to affect the outcome of the development programme in a way that is not generally seen. From the point of view of the people co-ordinating the development programme within the government, the easiest type of money to handle is the one that carries the fewest strings. So the best kind of finance is domestic funds. Approval of the project is an internal process, far faster than a donor's clearance, and there are no restrictions other than the established rules of financial control governing the use of the funds. Donor finance comes with a baggage of procurement, tendering, disbursement, accounting and reporting requirements that can become quite burdensome in a developing country where shortage of administrative skills is one of the greatest bottlenecks. Some of the more advanced donors have realized this and their procedures are commendably simple and adapted to local conditions. British and Scandinavian aid has always been clear on this matter. Most other agencies have made progress with simplifying their procedures and adapting them better to local conditions.

Yet the very priority areas that the donors have been stressing, rural development and the poor, are ones where it is more difficult to design delivery mechanisms and implementation success is less certain. A major highway is designed and supervised by international consultants who can handle most of the special procedures with relatively little administrative cost to the recipient. A village water supply scheme dealing in small units and dependent on local initiatives is a fragile affair by comparison and a lighter touch by the aid agency is essential. Some recognize this but many are still bound by the rigidity of their procedures (sometimes externally imposed); in other cases there is a lack of understanding of conditions on the ground. By insisting on projects which are in any case the most difficult to identify and implement, the donors may, therefore, actually slow down development spending in precisely those areas which both they and the government would like to emphasize.

In some well known cases there was a pronounced cost to using donor money. The implementation of Broadhurst II, a project on which the next stage of Gaborone's expansion depended, became critically delayed by unforeseen evaluation, tendering and procurement delays on the part of the European Development Fund which had agreed to finance the water supply. Two similar village water supply schemes proceeded at different rates because one donor insisted on inspecting each village plant before its installation. The other was content with an annual evaluation after installation was completed.

Yet on balance, Botswana has been remarkably free from this sort of difficulty. There were several reasons for this. First, the largest programme donor during this time, Sweden, arrived quite early on the scene, had incorporated into its programme some large rural development projects, and proved to be the most flexible of all external sources. Secondly, as the programme expanded a policy was evolved in the Ministry of Finance and Development Planning of giving the donors not necessarily the projects that they wanted but the projects that their procedures allowed them best to finance. This is not to suggest that the allocation of projects was tightly controlled and planned; it was a looser arrangement with give and take between the executing departments (who wanted finance for their projects but were not always aware how difficult their life might become if the wrong choice was made), the Ministry of Finance and Development Planning and the aid agencies. Because of the close working relationship, already mentioned, that grew up over the years between government officials and the local representatives of the agencies, much of this was done by mutual agreement.

The impact of technical assistance

Virtually all of the bilateral donors, and the United Nations Development Programme (UNDP), provided Botswana with large amounts of technical assistance, in the form of consultants, advisers and executive personnel holding established posts at the technical or administrative level. Some programmes were fully funded. Others like the United Kingdom's OSAS (Overseas Service Aid Scheme) programme supplemented the salaries of expatriate staff on government of Botswana contracts. In addition there were a large number of third country nationals occupying mainly middle level positions, directly recruited by the government. One donor, with unusual flexibility, even provided funds to finance key people in the latter category. Just as capital aid was being diversified the same process was happening with technical assistance personnel, although the numbers provided by the United Kingdom were so much in excess of other nationalities that the relative shift was much less. The need for such large numbers of foreign personnel was clear. Because of the lack of investment in education in colonial times, at Independence Botswana was in critical need of

Table 10.2 *Non-citizen employment*

1972	1973	1974	1975	1976	1977
3708	3940	3962	4027	—	4230
(8%)	(7%)	(7%)	(6%)	—	(7%)

Sources
National Development Plan 1976–81 and *Employment Survey 1977.*

the skills to manage development. And as the pace of change accelerated, the manpower gap grew. Although manpower projections showed that investments in education and training would close the gap in the 1980s, Botswana in the first decade of Independence had no alternative but to expand considerably the numbers of expatriate staff in the public sector.

There was, of course, an implicit trade-off between the pace at which the government could tackle the challenges of development and the rate at which localization could be achieved. In 1966 there was no doubt in the minds of ministers that to tackle the agenda that the development plan set forth required an expansion for a period in the numbers of expatriate personnel. The long-run plan for localization laid down in the first National Development Plan was self-sufficiency in higher level manpower for the whole economy by 1990, and the localization of all posts of a non-specialized administrative nature by 1972, with full localization for the public sector by the early 1980s. Such was the determination to break out of the stagnancy of the colonial period that considerations of localization were secondary. For the latter to be achieved, there needed to be substantial investment in education, and in other sectors to generate the revenues that would pay for the teachers and extension workers that were the front rank of the government's development strategy. No other route existed. In the early days a trade-off between alternative rates of growth and localization was never seriously debated: the key objective was to get the growth process started.

However, in 1973, when the country broke free from grant-in-aid and faced the prospects of larger surpluses in the future, a clear choice faced policy makers. Implementation capacity rather than finance was the new bottleneck. There was a risk that with the running down of construction activity on the Shashe project, the overall level of development spending would fall, resulting in a partially completed third National Development Plan and the temptation to use the new domestic revenues for public sector consumption, not investment. Accordingly, approaches were made to the agencies that provided technical assistance to raise the ceilings on their technical assistance, a request that was generally met.

Thus a further growth in the numbers of technical assistance personnel took place, so that by 1978 there were more expatriate personnel serving in the public sector than at any time previously. At the same time, of course, the public sector was both growing very rapidly and making solid progress with localization, although it was increasingly clear that the targets of the first National Development Plan were unachievable.

For most of this period there was little doubt in the mind of the government that the course that was followed was the right one. Outside commentators have generally failed to grasp the depth of feeling Botswana policy makers had about the lack of progress during the colonial period. Given, then, that Botswana's strategy for development did result in a large number of expatriates in the public sector, what were the particular consequences on the pattern of development that followed? The obvious one is that the expatriates brought with them technical and managerial skills that made the devising of key policies and the implementation of the government's development programme possible. The government could not have launched the Tribal Grazing Land Programme in the form it took without substantial additional expatriates in land-use planning and other planning capacities, and the same will be true for the new initiatives in dryland farming. The launching of the currency and the operation of the central bank would have been delayed, and it is hard to see how district planning and the channelling of funds for council projects could have been set up without the key role played by the volunteer agencies. Perhaps most important of all, the government would not have been able to play such a calculated hand in its dealings with the mining companies, and the level of revenues would have been less.

But there were costs associated with such a large inflow of foreign personnel, with different living standards and many without experience of developing countries. Undoubtedly there was a powerful demonstration effect that showed through in wage demands and other areas. There were also costs in accommodating expatriates: houses had to be built and places found in English language primary schools. Some of the capital costs were met through aid funds, but a large part devolved on domestic revenues. However, the latter were costs that the growing revenues could accommodate.

More difficult to assess is the effect the expatriates had on the style of the government. Such an assessment has a high degree of subjectivity, but I think the following conclusions can be fairly drawn. First, although the personnel provided by the agencies were on the whole well qualified and able, the short period many of them served limited their contribution and made the job of training and localization more difficult. There was less time to find the best mode of operation and understand the wider setting into which their activities fitted. In turn this led to a second effect. In any job people tend to bring to it the standards and methods learned in their previous employment. In the early days the bulk of expatriates could show a continuity of service within the country, or in a similar territory where resources were limited and means had to be found for building roads, housing teachers and training farmers within a very tight budget. By later plan periods this continuity had been lost. At the same time projects and policies had become more complex, requiring longer time and more resources to carry them out. They also imposed a greater load on the largely local managerial cadre.

In part this was a natural consequence of Botswana's economic growth, and the increased range of government involvement. Early plans were comprised of the simple and obvious projects that departmental heads had considered for years, in the absence of financial resources to put them into effect. Once the first generation of programmes was completed, the next rank was harder. Most of the key government policies, for example, grazing policy, dryland farming, mineral policy, employment, etc., were mentioned as objectives in the early plans, but it was left to the later period for comprehensive policies to be worked out. Yet while the technical expertise the donors provided made these new approaches possible, there is no doubt that the loss of continuity meant that in many cases technical and administrative approaches were devised that were fundamentally out of scale with the supply of indigenous technical and administrative resources.

One example is the consultant who recommends a solution that can only be implemented if further consultants are employed. The history of regulations provides further examples. It will never be possible to more than guess at the cost of this phenomenon.[10] As the economy has grown, it has also become more complex, which in turn has been reflected in the complexity of regulations emanating from the public sector. This process must have been worsened by the use of technical assistance personnel, although the impact cannot be quantified.

Conclusions

There can be little questioning that the overall impact of foreign assistance in Botswana has been a beneficial one. Initially, the role played by British aid from the early 1960s until 1972–3, with both capital, recurrent and technical assistance support, when little other assistance was available, was vitally

Table 10.3 *Sources of external development finance (P million)*

Year ending March	1967	1968	1969	1970	1971	1972	1973	1974	1975	1976	1977	1978	1979
Canada	—	—	—	—	—	—	10·4	5·3	1·6	2·7	1·5	1·3	1·4
Denmark	—	—	0·1	0·2	0·2	0·2	0·1	0·6	0·9	1·0	0·9	3·1	0·8
West Germany	—	—	—	—	—	—	—	—	0·1	0·1	0·1	2·9	3·7
Norway	—	—	—	—	—	—	—	0·3	1·2	1·7	6·4	5·3	2·4
Sweden	—	—	0·1	—	neg.	0·2	0·8	2·6	4·2	4·9	7·1	9·3	6·1
UK	3·2	2·9	2·6	3·0	4·1	4·6	3·7	3·2	2·8	5·2	3·4	2·7	5·4
USA	—	—	—	—	—	—	3·1	2·5	2·8	3·4	4·4	0·4	6·1
ADB^a/ADF^b	—	—	—	—	—	—	—	—	0·2	0·1	0·2	2·0	2·9
EDF^c	—	—	—	—	—	—	—	—	—	—	—	0·1	3·2
IBRD^d/IDA^e	—	—	neg.	—	1·4	6·2	8·7	9·9	4·4	2·0	4·5	3·5	7·5
Other	—	—	0·2	1·7	0·9	0·2	2·2	2·0	0·7	1·2	0·9	1·4	5·6
TOTAL External	3·2	2·9	2·9	4·8	6·5	11·2	29·1	26·3	18·9	22·2	29·3	32·0	45·1
Internal funds	3·4	0·9	0·4	0·1	2·0	1·0	0·8	4·0	13·9	13·2	8·3	12·4	33·9
TOTAL Development spending	6·8	3·8	3·3	4·9	8·5	12·3	29·9	30·3	32·8	35·4	37·6	44·4	79·0

Notes
^{a} ADB – African Development Bank.
^{b} ADF – African Development Fund (soft loans from the ADB).
^{c} EDF – European Development Fund (multilateral aid agency of the EEC).
^{d} IBRD – International Bank for Reconstruction and Development (World Bank).
^{e} IDA – International Development Agency (soft loans from IBRD).

Table 10.4   *Breakdown of external finance (P million)*

	1969	1970	1971	1972	1973	1974	1975	1976	1977	1978	1979
Hard loans	—	1·5	0·7	5·9	8·3	8·7	3·5	1·4	3·4	4·7	11·5
Soft loans	neg.	—	5·5	4·9	17·9	12·3	8·2	11·2	9·9	6·6	8·4
Grants	2·9	3·3	0·4	0·4	2·9	5·3	7·1	9·6	16·0	20·7	25·2

Notes to Tables 10.3 and 10.4
1   Figures are derived from expenditure of development funds. These may differ slightly from development revenue, that is, accruals to the Development Fund.
2   The criterion for dividing loans into hard or soft is the rate of interest (virtually all loans had extended repayment periods). 'Hard' loans are those with a commercial or near-commercial rate of interest (for example, IBRD); 'soft' loans are interest free (for example, UK for most of the period) or have a concessionary rate (for example, IDA, USAID). Some loans have subsequently been converted into grants (for example, CIDA, SIDA, UK); this is not taken into account in the table.

important, since it enabled Botswana to lay the foundations for future development. Many of the features that attracted later donors are directly traceable to this period. Secondly, the financing of the copper–nickel complex at Selebi-Phikwe by a consortium of donors under the co-ordination of the World Bank was also crucial. Although the profitability of the mine itself has proved a disappointment, its scale both in terms of construction and operation had major indirect effects on government revenues and economic activity as a whole. It established the ability of the government to co-ordinate such a large project, and in turn a determination to apply those management skills in other sectors.

The subsequent diversification to many donors has made management of the development programme more complex, but that complexity has proved in some real sense to be manageable; meanwhile there are other (mainly strategic) advantages to diversity, so that the flow of development finance is now more secure than it was when there was only one donor.

Notes

1. Development spending in current terms increased from a P5·2 million average in the three years to 1967–8 to an average of P39·1 million ten years later. See Table 10.1.
2. See Chapter 1 by Hans-Erik Dahl, pp. 1–13.
3. 'Sixty-five men sat down in Gaborone to sign or act upon the forty-three interrelated legal agreements that became effective simultaneously at 12:15 on 7 March 1972.' F. Taylor Ostrander, 'Botswana nickel–copper: a case study in private investment's contribution to economic development', in John Barratt *et al.* (eds), *Accelerated Development in Southern Africa*, New York, St Martin's Press, for the South African Institute of International Affairs (1974).
4. See Chapter 7 by Stephen R. Lewis, Jr, 'The impact of the Shashe Project on Botswana's economy', pp. 104–14.
5. On overcommitment, and other details of aid negotiations with the UK, see David Jones, *Aid and Development in Southern Africa*, London, Croom Helm (1977), Chapters 3 and 8. UK aid to Botswana is compared to other sources in Chapter 9.
6. Chambers, *Botswana's Accelerated Rural Development Programme 1973–6: Experience*

and Lessons, Gaborone (1977), p. 10. This report also discusses the costs of deliberately speeding up rural development.

7. Jones, op. cit., pp. 123–5.

8. See Chapter 4 by Michael Hubbard, pp. 44–65.

9. For the working relationship with UK aid administrators and the role of the UK High Commission, see Jones, op. cit., pp. 141–2.

10. For a detailed attack on licensing and regulation, see Appendices 8.3 and 8.4 in Lipton, *Botswana: Employment and Labour Use in Botswana*, Vol. II, Gaborone (1978).

Michael Stevens OBE (for services to the Botswana Government) is with the World Bank; formerly Director of Economic Affairs, Government of Botswana.

11 Economic Co-ordination, Liberation and Development: Botswana–Namibia Perspectives[1]

REGINALD HERBOLD GREEN

We need to gain mastery of our own destiny in this turbulent region of our continent and we can only succeed ... within the framework of a united Southern African community. I am not calling for the dismantlement of our independent states ... I am calling for co-operation and unity of purpose so that we can together plan for our future and the future of our children ...

A Trans-Kgalagadi [Kalahari] railway line and a road from Francistown in the north of Botswana to Angola and Namibia would encourage trade and communications among the three countries, as well as enabling us to have access to the seaports of Namibia ...

The full exploitation of our natural resources and the development of our productive sectors are constrained by the small markets in our economies, but taken as a whole, Southern Africa forms a sizeable market. Economic regional co-operation would of necessity lead to co-ordinated production expansion which would in turn encourage the expansion of markets for intra-Southern African trade.

South Africa in particular would be only too happy to continue to exploit us individually in the hope that we would in time be lured by the economic power to join the so-called constellation of Southern African states in which we would be bundled together with the so-called independent Bantustans and UDI regimes in Zimbabwe and Namibia. These manoeuvres must be frustrated ... we must ensure that the struggle for political independence in Namibia and Zimbabwe continues to advance.

President Seretse Khama,
opening address, Southern African Development
Co-ordination Conference, Arusha, 3 July 1979[2]

Toward economic liberation or constellation?

Economic co-ordination in Southern Africa has a surprisingly wide range of backers. Prime Minister P. W. Botha in June re-advanced the contention that by economic co-ordination the Republic of South Africa could build a stable, mutually beneficial Southern African economic constellation.[3] In September the Chief of Defence Forces, Malan, emphasized the same theme in an address in Windhoek.[4]

The same dual strands appear on the customs union front. The South African Customs Union (SACU) links the Republic of South Africa (RSA) with Botswana, Lesotho, Swaziland (BLS) and *de facto* Namibia. Its free trade provisions have clearly played a role in South African domination of BLS and Namibian markets. Its customs union element has excluded outsiders. Its fiscal provisions have benefited BLS, at least in the medium term, but at the price of reinforcing dependence on Pretoria. In 1978 the UN Economic Commission for Africa (ECA) completed a series of conferences toward an East and Central African Preferential area, which would reduce barriers (tariff and non-tariff) to trade among the seventeen states of its Eastern and Central African Region (including BLS and, on its genuine independence, Namibia). Most of the potential members have agreed, albeit in the BLS case with major reservations flowing from their SACU status, while Angola, Mozambique and Tanzania have expressed doubts that a classic *laissez faire* trade promotion approach is either necessary or sufficient as a means to promote economic co-ordination, liberation and development in Southern Africa.[5]

The Trans-Kalahari (Kgalagadi) Railway (Botnam) has an equally mixed history. In the late 1950s and 1960s it was mooted as a Wankie-to-the-sea line for Federation of Rhodesia and Nyasaland coal exports. Some survey and port design work was carried out by South Africa. Today South African Railways and Harbours remain interested and commercial consulting bodies[6] are busily conducting studies to be peddled to South Africa, Botswana, a 'UDI' Namibia or a genuinely independent Namibia.

At the same time – as evidenced by President Khama's address – Botswana sees the Trans-Kalahari as part of a strategy for breaking out of dependence on South Africa and for developing Botswana resources. SWAPO (the Namibian Liberation Movement) also sees it as an integral part of regional co-ordination toward achieving political economic independence.

What meaning can be put on these apparently contradictory strands of support for what appear to be the same means but posited as serving very different ends? What is economic integration about? Is there any real scope for it between Botswana and Namibia?

The customs union model and its children

The original work on free trade areas (no tariffs within the region), customs unions (common external tariff) and economic unions (common economic policies) was done within the neo-classical free trade theory model.[7] Regional free trade areas were perceived as second best alternatives to global free trade. The case for them was that diversity of resources (different natural comparative advantage) and economies of scale in a larger economic area (leading to acquired comparative advantage through specialization) would lower costs and increase output.

In the short term, benefits would come from competition and concentration of output in the most efficient firms: the implications include output cutbacks and closures in less efficient units. Over the long term, benefits would come from economies of scale and of specialization in new production units.

A distinction is drawn in the basic classical customs union model between trade creation (among member economies) and trade diversion (away from outside economies). The former is endorsed and the latter criticized on standard global allocational efficiency grounds.

Several problems arose in applied analysis as well as application.

1   There is no automatic mechanism to ensure equal, equitable or even positive gains for each member. Therefore, either fiscal transfers (as in SACU), regional development banking (as in the former East African Community), or/and industrial allocation (as in the Andean Pact and Association of South East Asian Nations) tend to be needed to buy the weaker partners' acceptance of higher cost imports from the stronger.

2   The allocational efficiency losses on trade diversion are basically costs to outsiders unless one assumes full employment in the regional economies. Therefore, a 'some production is better than no production' approach tends to be adopted especially in respect to manufacturing, usually with an infant economy plus economies of scale justification.

3   Trade diversion is a slightly unreal concept if the regional economies face either *de facto*, for example, limits to exploitable resources or/and total inability to break through to manufactured exports, or *de jure* export ceilings, for example, EEC quotas on Botswana beef, Central Selling Organization quotas on Botswana diamonds – both negotiated but neither totally flexible nor open to unilateral amendment by Botswana. In that case imports from outside the region are basically constrained by the export ceiling and all intra-regional trade can be viewed as trade creation.[8]

4   Trade does not automatically flow from absence of customs barriers – for example, Botswana–Angola trade is blocked by lack of transport links even more effectively than by SACU. Therefore, to function, an economic co-ordination programme may need to include areas of policy well beyond common market creation.

Most orthodox economic integration literature and most efforts toward Third World regional schemes have taken these points on board to a greater or lesser degree.[9] However, the record suggests that even these modifications may not be sufficient – or that the theory is largely irrelevant to the actual purposes, processes and problems of Third World economic co-ordination.

SACU[10] is a common market plus a fiscal redistribution mechanism. Because the RSA is larger, more technologically advanced, characterized by powerful private cartels and in full command of the 'fine print', for example, what rebates are allowable on what items, there is little doubt that SACU diverts both imports (from outside the union area) and production; that is, BLS/Namibia produce less, import more and import from South Africa rather than from lowest cost sources. The offset is a large fiscal transfer, which in the short run more than offsets the losses from production and higher cost imports. However, it tends to limit consideration of – and raises the cost of shifting to – alternative policies to protect Botswana rather than South African production.

The former East African Community was in form a common market, plus joint services, plus a regional development bank, plus an interim intraregional preference (Transfer Tax) scheme.[11] In practice it was intended to include a production co-ordination (industrial allocation) side but this failed to come into being before the Amin coup halted progress. The loss of momentum, very bad management of the joint railway enterprise, arguments about trade and gains division and the shock of the 1974–7 balance of payments crisis greatly weakened EAC. Attempts either to return it to a pure *laissez-faire* model, or to transform it into a system based on the co-ordination of production, failed and it collapsed in 1977.[12]

The Economic Community of West African States (ECOWAS) has the most elaborate provisions of any traditional economic community ever floated. Fiscal transfers, regional bank, joint projects, agricultural co-ordination, functional and technical co-operation – name it and an ECOWAS article can be found covering it. In fact the key goals are a sequence of preferential area to free trade area to customs union, plus a large regional bank/aid agency. All articles and timetables are very vague and ECOWAS has experienced great difficulties in actually beginning operations in any serious way, either in trade preferences or on regional financial transfers.[13]

Toward a different model

Much of the criticism of the standard customs union model flows from general critiques of neo-classical, free trade development models.[14] It is, in fact, not readily incorporated in the Vinerian mould except in a purely formal sense because it posits a transition away from purely north–south axes of exchange/control and, in the case of some writers, a transition towards socialism. Initially much of this critique was cast in fairly standard customs union terms[15] – over time that has become less typical.[16]

Five main themes have emerged.

1 Economic co-ordination as a means to economic liberation (or in milder variants 'room to manoeuvre') by extending the range of practicable economic activities, broadening the range of relevant partners, reducing the leverage of (degree of dependence on) any one external partner (TNC or State).[17,18]

2 Primacy of active new production-oriented measures, over passive, new trade-facilitating measures[19] (for example, industrial co-ordination, multinational ventures, financial institutions among Third World states seen as ultimately more critical than tariff preferences or clearing arrangements).

3 The importance of using regionalism to co-ordinate policies *vis-à-vis* foreign firms, in order to shift the balance of power and the pattern of bargaining in favour of the states and against the TNCs (as in OPEC and the Andean Pact).[20]

4 Doubts about the positive contribution of 'free trade', because it may create more losers and frictions than gainers and co-ordination advances[21] and thus violate the principle of the primacy of prompt, perceived gains for each participant.[22]

5   The necessity of examining, operating and analysing co-ordination as an ongoing political economic process with multiple actors, not a comparative static technical economic exercise carried out by neo-academic analysts or consultants.[23]

The logic of this critique has not been fully explored – let alone agreed. There is no presently functioning African regional exercise built on it; bilaterally the Mozambique–Tanzania arrangements probably qualify but are quite explicitly interim, experimental and somewhat limited in scope and time so far as present operations are concerned.

However, several implications do emerge.

1   The appropriate strategy and tactics for any particular co-ordination scheme (bilateral, regional or sectoral, for example, Botswana–Namibia, Southern Africa, Independent African Diamond Producing States) cannot be deduced directly from pure theory; they must also be built up from state needs, constraints, goals and resources.
2   It cannot be automatically assumed that trade is the key or the initial sector for co-ordination.
3   Common interests perceived as pursued more effectively together than separately, leading to visible and adequate gains, are critical to viability and stability. Neo-classical gains are usually rather beside the point, even when they exist and can be computed.

Southern Africa development co-ordination[24]

At the Southern Africa Development Co-ordination Conference (SADCC) at Arusha in July 1979, dialogue and pre-planning proceeded along the lines of the critique, not of the classic Vinerian model. SADCC also marked the first major development co-ordination initiative run by the would-be core regional states (in this case, Angola, Botswana, Mozambique, Tanzania, Zambia, the Front Line States) rather than a group inherited from the colonial past, or stage managed by European sponsors or the Economic Commission for Africa.[25]

SADCC – following a good deal of technical background work – was put to the Front Line States (FLS) by President Khama early in 1979 and approved by a Foreign Ministers meeting in Gaborone in April. An official meeting (of FLS economic ministry personnel and associated consultants) followed in June also in Gaborone. The Arusha meeting in fact had two halves – the first a meeting of FLS Finance Ministers and the second a presentation to invited participants from international organizations and potential multilateral and bilateral sources of finance. The emphasis was on Southern African directed co-ordination, as illustrated in a speech by Mozambique's Finance Minister, Rui Baltazar Santos:

The establishment of co-operation in new moulds requires, on the part of the developed countries, a deeper knowledge of the African reality and, in particular of Southern Africa. It equally requires the recognition that the African peoples have the capacity to manage their own interests, without disagreeable pressures or interferences made against their dignity, freedom and independence.[26]

The central theme was economic liberation. In the Southern Africa context the first requirement was seen to be reduction of dependence on the Republic of South Africa. Chairman Quett Masire stressed:

Precisely because of our progress on the political front of the liberation struggle, it is now both possible and necessary to include economic liberation in the programmes and priorities of the Front Line States. We must free our economies from their dependence on the Republic of South Africa, overcome their imposed economic fragmentation and co-ordinate our regional and national development.[27]

This was perceived as a developmental strategy linked to increasing levels of productive forces as stressed by the Chairman:

The Front Line States will identify areas in which, working in harmony, we can gear national development to provide goods and services presently coming from the Republic of South Africa and thereby weave a fabric of regional co-operation and development.[28]

The first priority was seen to be transport and communications:

Key to this strategy are transport and communications. The dominance of the Republic of South Africa has been reinforced and strengthened by its transport system. Without the establishment of an adequate regional transport and communications system, other areas of co-operation are impractical.[29]

Other areas stressed included:

1   Finance – particularly mobilization of regional and external finance for joint or co-ordinated projects, initially largely in the transport field.
2   Mineral prospecting and negotiations, to speed the build-up of knowledge and to create a situation in which companies bid for access to national resources not states for access to company finance/expertise.
3   Food security – regional co-ordination of and emergency loans among national food reserves (as carried out between Mozambique and Tanzania in 1978).
4   Knowledge and training – co-ordination of research and exchange of results, development of procedures for agreeing on medium term use of specialized training institutions.
5   Trade flowing from production co-ordination and probably modelled more on the draft levels of exchange and goods list target system of the Tanzania–Mozambique arrangements than on a standard market preference approach.

SADCC sought to minimize new institutions. National co-ordinating committees, small regional units servicing meetings and facilitating information flows, and working groups in particular projects were seen as both more practicable (given senior personnel shortages) and more desirable than large supranational bodies.

Southern Africa Development Co-ordination was perceived as open in three senses:

1   Any genuinely independent Southern African state and – to the extent practicable – any recognized liberation movement was welcome to participate.
2   Any project or programme of interest to two or more states could be seen as regional and no state was to be under pressure to participate in each and every project/programme.
3   SADCC membership would not preclude participation in other bilateral (for example, Angola–Zaire) or subregional (for example, Tanzania–Rwanda–Burundi–Uganda in Kagera Basin Authority) memberships.

Summing up, the Chairman declared:

Until our economies are free from the domination of the Republic of South Africa and linked regionally with one another we cannot go forward with assurance or in safety. We must ensure that the efforts of our people to achieve development, to meet their basic human needs, are in a setting which gives them the greatest chance of success. That setting is Southern African regional development co-ordination.[30]

What meaning can Botswana–Namibia co-operation have?

The logic of the SADCC positions does not, by itself, demonstrate either that they can be implemented nor that Botswana–Namibia is self-evidently a key axis of co-operation. Both require further examination of Botswana's requirements and of the means toward fulfilling them which might be secured by economic co-ordination with a genuinely independent Namibia.

Botswana's potentially relevant requirements are fairly easy to sketch:

1   Reduction in dependence, with particular reference to external transport and to food supply.
2   Expansion of productive forces, with special reference to minerals, agriculture and livestock.
3   National integration with special reference to linking the north and west to the east and south both in terms of transport and of economic participation.

In respect of providing direct access to the sea (in this case the Atlantic) Namibia evidently qualifies. Walvis Bay is the closest major port to Gaborone. However, with Zimbabwe genuinely independent, direct access to the Indian Ocean is open via Bulawayo and Beira. While longer, that route is already in existence – the Trans-Kalahari is not.

Co-operation with Namibia can hardly provide food from Namibia to replace present imports from South Africa (tinned fish are Namibian but hardly need a new road, let alone railway, to move them – butter is a trivial item). Namibia will have grave problems itself in securing imports to replace those from South Africa and in raising its domestic grain, vegetable, fruit and milk production.[31] The Trans-Kalahari could be useful to Namibia in respect of grain imports if Zimbabwe and/or Zambia regain surplus levels. However, the potential contribution to Botswana is different. The most promising arable area in Botswana lies to the south of the Okavango Delta around Maun. The greatest single barrier to its development to date has been the high cost and limited physical availability of transport. A rail line through Maun would alter cost and availability of transport parameters quite radically.

Productive forces in Botswana are, and are likely to remain, rather specialized as to function. Minerals – with coal, soda ash, copper and uranium next in the list – can provide some employment, high export earnings, substantial investible surplus and major contributions to government revenue. Livestock can provide substantial employment and rural income generation, a good deal of foreign exchange and some potential for manufacturing, for example, leather, leather products. Crops can provide employment, rural incomes and domestic food sufficiency.

The coal and soda ash deposits could probably be linked to the existing rail line for export via Richards Bay or Beira. The first, of course, would increase dependency on the Republic. However, the Ngami Ridge (Xeta-Theta) copper and some uranium prospects cannot be handled in that way. Nor would such routes help build up either northern and western livestock offtake or Maun area agriculture.

National integration clearly requires east–west links. It is doubtful whether these can be economically viable on domestic traffic alone if they are built to a standard above that of mere tracks. Further national integration requires more focal points or zones of economic activity west of the Lobatse–Gaborone–Selebi–Phikwe–Francistown line.

The two requirements interact: without low or at least lower than present cost transport, the viability of enhanced production is dubious; unless production is linked to new transport facilities their viability is also dubious. A heavy duty Botswana–Namibia link might be able to cut through this Gordian knot by diverting existing external trade now routed by South African ports and railways, and making enough new foci of Botswana production viable at relatively low charges.

The Trans-Kalahari is not the only area for potential co-ordination. The Okavango is Botswana's potential key source of water. It is also an international river with no present agreement on water rights among the riparian states. A variety of knowledge and personnel development challenges facing Botswana and future independent Namibia[32] seem to be similar. This suggests the possibility of research and training co-ordination. Both economies are mineral centred – and will remain so for some decades in respect to exports, state revenue and investible surplus. Diamonds, copper and perhaps uranium figure prominently in each case, which might suggest opportunities for co-ordination. There could even be opportunities for more trade than seems possible at first glance, for example, Botswana vaccine, coal, Namibian cement. A joint petroleum refinery at Walvis Bay could be considered. But the pivotal question concerns the Trans-Kalahari.

The Trans-Kalahari: Botswana's liberation line?

Proposals for an east–west link in Botswana are varied as to mode and route.[33] There are three conceivable modes – pipeline, road and rail – and five conceivable routes.

Pipelines are – just – plausible for coal (to Walvis Bay) and soda ash (to Walvis Bay or Francistown). They would drain a substantial share of water resources (presumably from dams on the Zambezi) and would, by definition, do nothing for general development. Apparently nobody – including Shell, the main potential coal producer – looks on them with much enthusiasm.

Highways are practicable on any of the five routes – on the southern one, running roughly from Lobatse through Jwaneng to Ghanzi to the border, no other mode is plausible. They are totally unsuitable for coal or soda ash and not very suitable for copper, copper concentrate or uranium concentrate. For cattle, road transport costs about three times as much per tonne/kilometre as rail.

A railway is suitable for coal, other minerals, cattle and agricultural products. It has the disadvantage of the highest fixed cost and, therefore, the highest required volume of traffic. Thus the southern route is implausible for a railway as it would generate no mineral traffic. On the other hand, with a high volume and long hauls (over 250 km/87 mi) or bulk cargo (over 200 000 tonnes a year of homogenous cargo on a single route) railway cost per tonne/kilometre is lower than highway.

The southern route (see Figure 11.1) has the major disadvantage that it cannot serve new cargo except from Ghanzi. Indeed it looks more like a South African Rand–Botswana–Namibia penetration route than a liberation line.

Two routes direct from the coal fields to Ghanzi (Routes 3 and 4 on Figure 11.1) would meet the needs of the haulage of coal, western copper, uranium and livestock. One has a difficult alignment (Central Kalahari sands) and both miss the soda ash and Okavango delta agricultural areas. The same general comments apply to a line from Francistown south of the Makgadikgadi Pans (Route 2).

The rail route Palapye–Francistown–Nata–Maun–Ghanzi–Border–Gobabis (Route 1) is the only one which could, in principle, serve general import/export, coal, soda ash, eastern and western copper, uranium, livestock and Okavango delta irrigated agricultural traffic. The total length (Francistown–Gobabis) is almost 1000 km (620 mi) and to Walvis Bay about 1700 (1050). The shortest route which could serve the coal mine – Route 4 – would be about 925 km (575 mi) to Gobabis and 1525 (946 mi) to Walvis Bay.

The case for the Trans-Kalahari (or Botnam) – viewed from Botswana

The Trans-Kalahari would provide a relatively low cost general import/export route. Thereby it would break dependence on the Mafeking–Cape Town connection. It could also be a major factor in making several new productive units and areas viable, by lowering the transport costs to each through the provision of a common carrier.

1   *Coal* – at least 1000 million tonnes reserves. Suitable for European furnace coal use; probably viable late 1980s. Shell and Anglo American concessions/mines. Shell envisages a mine of up to 5 million tonnes initial

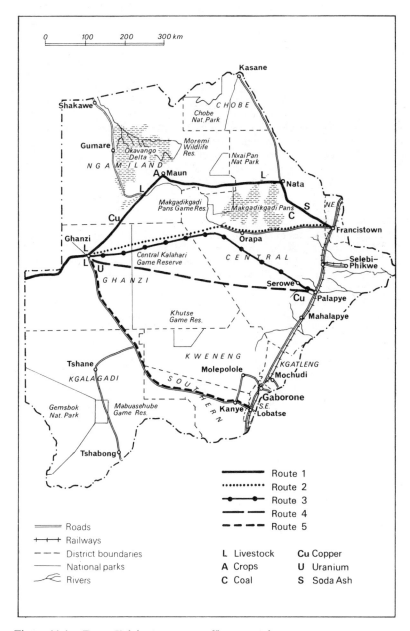

Figure 11.1   *Trans-Kalahari routes: traffic potential*

output. A Richards Bay route would be feasible – if South Africa would allocate further development there – as probably would a Beira one – both are less suitable for shipment to North Europe than an Atlantic one.

2   *Soda ash* – like coal a probable boom sector of the late 1980s. The artificial caustic soda technology has been rendered obsolete by a 1970s natural (soda ash) based one. The only present producers of the raw material are the USA and Kenya. Japan and the EEC by the late 1980s must either import the raw material, for example, from Sua Pan, or the finished product from the USA.

3   *Copper* – minor deposits near Sua Pan could use the railway for enriched ore shipment to Selebi-Phikwe smelters and minor Ngami Ridge deposits could send concentrate to Tsumeb smelters in Namibia. Most projections (and major company money allocations) suggest a mid-to-late 1980s copper boom which would make both areas viable.

4   *Uranium* – the known ore is near Ghanzi; more may be discovered. If only the present deposit is exploited, a route for concentrate to the Rossing concentration plant is needed as projected output seems to be below the 1500–2000 tonnes of concentrate a year needed for a plant.

5   *Livestock* – offtake rates could be raised and transport costs lowered if Ghanzi–Maun–Ngamiland were linked by rail to Lobatse (or a new northern abattoir). Perhaps 1000 000 head a year (50 000 tonnes) would be carried.

6   *Crops* – under irrigation near Maun crops could be grown on a large scale, that is, 150–300 000 tonnes.[34] The isolation of the area at present deters serious attention to answering ecological, agronomic and agro-economic questions and would render grain production uneconomic.

The particular location of many of the production possibilities and the fact of a Francistown–Nata–Maun–Ghanzi–Border link would have major national integration implications. These are distinct from, and additional to, the reduction of dependence on RSA and the potential major revenue impact from coal.

The case for the Botnam – viewed from Namibia

The Botnam would require relaying the light line from Gobabis to the main route to Walvis Bay (whether via Windhoek or on a new alignment direct to Okahandja), some additions to planned upgrading of the Okahandja–Walvis Bay line, bulk loading facilities (and dredging) at Walvis Bay Harbour. These will be expensive in terms of attention and institutional capacity as well as funds. Why would Namibia see the Trans-Kalahari as a priority?

First, a genuinely independent Namibia is likely to place a significant value on building up relations with its three African neighbours (Angola, Zambia, Botswana). Second, Namibian metal smelting requires coal – about 100 000 tonnes a year at present. Botswana is the logical alternative source to South Africa if a transport route exists. Third, Namibia is interested in diversification of production and further use of national assets. Transit traffic would meet that test. So – if on detailed study they proved viable – would a joint Botswana–Namibia oil refinery (joint demand perhaps 600 000 tonnes by 1986 requiring 850 000 tonnes refined and 250 000 in re-exports of furnace oil) and a joint cement plant (joint demand perhaps 200 000 tonnes).

Regionally, the Trans-Kalahari would have broader uses. Zimbabwean coal exports would normally pass via Beira but those for north Europe might well use Walvis Bay. Similarly, a division between Atlantic and Indian Ocean ports for general Zimbabwean imports and exports would appear to have technical, cost and political economic logic.

Zambia and Zaire would not normally use Walvis Bay. But neither would they normally use Durban or Port Elizabeth, as they do now. Once built, the Trans-Kalahari would become an export/import route of last resort for them, albeit not one much utilized under normal conditions.

Financial and temporal considerations

Is the Trans-Kalahari viable? The data in Table 11.1 do not answer that question. They are far too approximate. However, they suggest a positive answer.

The total capital cost – including work in Namibia – would be P250–300 million. The total operating cost might be of the order of P60–72 million. Revenue (assuming use of Walvis Bay as the main port for all Botswana's external trade) could be in the region of P62–101 million for Botswana and P80–120 million for Botswana–Zimbabwe traffic. These data may be too optimistic, but they do suggest that full scale studies of Trans-Kalahari (railway, northern route) costs, and of associated production projects (recosted to allow for use of a common carrier) revenues are amply justified. On the face of it breaking transport dependence, raising output, increasing food self-sufficiency and bolstering national economic integration can be achieved through a highly profitable infrastructure project – a most unusually favourable perspective.

The earliest the Trans-Kalahari can come into use is 1986. The mineral development timing probably requires that in any event, but there are ineluctable time constraints. Engineering studies would require one year, financial and institutional mobilization a second year, construction three or four years. Assuming an independence date for Namibia in the near future, that takes one to at least 1986. Further, the peak of the manpower and institutional development requirements of the takeover of the existing Botswana rail system should be passed before 1986, allowing a relatively smooth continuation of capacity buildup if the Botnam is completed then.

Okavango water allocation and management

Potentially Okavango Delta waters – and boreholes and pump schemes drawing on groundwater related to them – are central to the development of Ngamiland, to arable agricultural output in Botswana and to national food self-sufficiency. To serve any of these purposes they must be made secure.

One side of security is hydrological/ecological. Co-ordination with Namibia – whose Caprivi swamp and Etosha Pan perimeter areas have some aspects in common with the Okavango Delta – might be useful in research planning and data exchange. However, it can hardly be perceived as critical, much less essential.

Another side of security, however, is assured water flow. The Okavango is an international river. It rises in Angola, runs along the Angolan–Namibian border, crosses Namibia and reaches its deltaic mouth in Botswana. The

Table 11.1   *Trans-Kalahari estimates (nominal year 1986)*[a]

A. Distance (km/mi)

Francistown/Nata	190 (118)
Nata/Maun	300 (186)
Maun/Ghanzi	290 (180)
Ghanzi/Border	210 (130)
Border/Gobabis	120 (75)
TOTAL	1110 (689)

B. Possible capital cost[b] (P million)

Francistown/Gobabis	175–200
Gobabis/Okahandja[c]	25–35
Share Okahandja/Walvis Bay[d]	25–35
Port facilities[e]	25–30
TOTAL	250–300

C Rough operating costs[f] (P million)

Depreciation	(5%)	12·5–15
Maintenance	(3%)	7·5–9
Other operating	(6%)	15–18
Interest	(10%)	25–30
TOTAL		60–72

D Traffic/revenue potential[g] (quantities in tonnes) P million

Rerouted exports[h]	12 – 12·5
Rerouted imports[h]	13·5 – 20·5
Coal 4–7 500 000 + @ P6	24 – 45
Copper 50 000 + @ P30[i]	·· – 1·5
Copper concentrate 100 000 + @ P20[j]	·· – 2
Uranium concentrate 20–50 000 + @ P40	0·75– 2
Soda ash 500 000/1 000 000 + @ P10/12·5	5 – 12·5
Cattle 20–40 000 + @ P20	0·5 – 0·75
Crops 75–150 000 + @ P12·5	1 – 2
Miscellaneous internal[k]	1·5 – 2·5
TOTAL BOTSWANA TRAFFIC	61·75–101·25
Zimbabwe traffic[l]	
Coal to Europe 1 500 000 @ P6	9
General imports/exports 200 000 @ P40	8
Zambia/Zaire traffic[m]	1
TOTAL REVENUE POTENTIAL	79·75–119·25

Notes

[a] 1986 prices for Operations/Revenues.
[b] Assumes 1981–6 construction.
[c] Windhoek–Gobabis is a very light line. If rebuilt a new alignment to Okahandja avoiding hills around Windhoek would appear logical.
[d] Okahandja–Walvis Bay is scheduled for upgrading. To raise it to 10 million tonnes a year Botswana–Zimbabwe traffic would raise upgrading cost.
[e] Rough guess specialized loading facilities plus dredging.
[f] Computed on whole operation to Gobabis plus costs through to Walvis Bay for new project goods.
[g] Revenues through to Walvis Bay on new project goods, only revenue to Gobabis on rerouted goods. Very approximate.
[h] From Bank of Botswana 1985–6 projections of imports/exports. Assumes about 3 per cent of shiftable import value and 3 per cent of shiftable export value can be allocated to present rail/Gobabis freights share of transport costs.
[i] Dukwe area – refined at Selebi-Phikwe.
[j] Ngami Ridge – refined at Tsumeb.
[k] Passenger, local produce, distribution of imports from wholesale, etc.
[l] Coal to North Europe cheaper via Walvis Bay than Beira. Some general cargo assumed to be routed via Atlantic.
[m] Nominal. Francistown–Windhoek would be a 'last resort' not a 'normal choice' route – replacing Durban and Port Elizabeth in that role.

Namibian Okavango valley is among the best of her arable areas – some irrigation is already practised. With the use of pumps more irrigation might be practised. Southern and southern plateau agrarian development in Angola might use Okavango water for irrigation; some old Portuguese plans reportedly envisaged quite heavy drawings.

At present there are no water rights agreements. Since Botswana does not now use the delta water directly, it would have difficulty pleading established downstream user's status (as Egypt did when Kenya and Tanzania pointed out that the colonial Nile Waters Convention did not, in fact, bind them). To safeguard the flow into Botswana requires a convention with Namibia and Angola.

There is no reason to suppose such a convention would prove unattainable. Namibia's portion of the Okavango is largely in a rather narrow and steep valley so that its probable offtake is limited. Southern Angola has few immediate major water demands and more alternatives than Botswana. A related issue is drainage in the mid-Caprivi area of Namibia which might augment Okavango flow or might create problems in Ngamiland depending on the exact local drainage patterns.

This appears to be an area in which co-ordination can lead to guaranteed water rights to Botswana, fixed offtake rights for the upriver states and Namibia–Botswana liaison and consultation in Caprivi swamp drainage. The danger is to let the issue lie dormant and raise it only when Namibian Okavango offtake or swamp drainage creates problems for Botswana, after it has also created a vested interest in continuation for Namibia.

Additional areas of common interest

No other areas of Botswana–Namibia economic co-ordination are likely to be of the same magnitude or breadth of impact as a Trans-Kalahari Railway and an Okavango Waters agreement. Indeed, the scope of the other possible sectors for co-ordination is rather hard to discern because they appear to comprise a number of relatively small items.

Trade and production co-ordination – beyond the coal/cement/petroleum refining possibilities related to the Trans-Kalahari – is not likely to be large for some years. Botswana vaccine is one evident product as is Namibian tinned fish. Beyond that, expanded trade is likely to require some co-ordination of forward investment and production plans leading to joint planning of annual trade target agreements. These may need state trading ventures to administer, but are rather more production-based, certain of implementation and compatible with a phased withdrawal from SACU than a standard preferential or free trade area.

Mining may offer more scope for co-ordination involving Namibia. Exchange of geological survey results and joint formulation of basic bargaining positions *vis-à-vis* foreign firms would seem useful. More active efforts in respect to uranium and diamonds (both products with fairly effective producers' cartels but ones with limited African participation) would need to go beyond – but could be based on – Botswana–Namibia bilateral action.

Research co-ordination is likely initially to be relatively one way – Namibia seeking advice (particularly in respect to crops and livestock) from Botswana. However, once the initial transition is past, a more balanced exchange should be practical. A number of livestock, pasture, crop, pest, water, soils, construction and related issues seem to be common to Botswana and Namibia. Exchange of information and discussion from the programme design phase through the results dissemination phase are likely to speed and to lower the cost of acquiring more relevant knowledge.

Education again would appear likely to afford opportunities only for one way co-ordination initially. However, over time opportunities may exist for regular cross placements in certain specialized secondary and tertiary level vocational, artisan and technical training institutions. Joint educational institutions have a history of failure in Africa; multi-year placement arrangements have a somewhat better record and, indeed, are *de facto* used by Botswana in respect to at least three or four other African states.

In retrospect and prospect

Economic co-ordination is not an end in itself. Nor is it an all purpose means to costless achievement of any and all ends. The standard customs union approach to economic co-ordination is well known – too well known – to Botswana and has produced – via SACU – losses of economic degrees of freedom and of local production in return for negotiated fiscal gains. A standard trade-centred agreement with Namibia – apart from inconsistency with SACU – would be irrelevant. The Botswana and Namibia economies are today neither complementary nor directly competitive – they are competitive in respect to third country markets but not in goods that either could readily utilize at home.

However, more broadly perceived Botswana–Namibia economic co-ordination could contribute substantially toward achievement of several major Botswana political economic goals.

1   Reduced dependence on South African transport routes (access to Walvis Bay).
2   Reduced dependence on South African or other external food supplies (encouragement of Okavango Delta area production).
3   Increased production opportunities capable of generating substantial state revenue, investible surplus, foreign exchange earnings and medium to high wage employment (minerals including coal and soda ash).
4   Increased production and marketing opportunities, generating rural incomes and self-employment particularly in the north and west (Ngami–Maun–Ghanzi livestock, Okavango Delta crop growing).
5   Strengthened Botswana national integration, through improved transport, broader distribution of economic activity and more intra-regional transactions.

The critical programmes, if these goals are to be furthered by Botswana–Namibia economic co-ordination, centre on the Trans-Kalahari railway and the major production units (coal, copper, soda ash, irrigated agriculture, livestock, uranium oxide, copper concentrate) which the railway should make economically viable and which should, in turn, provide the traffic to make the railway profitable. The Trans-Kalahari cannot proceed on the ground until Namibia is genuinely independent – and has control over a useable deepwater port – but the pre-feasibility, feasibility and design work on the railway and the associated projects can be carried out prior to the independence of Namibia.

The comments of President Khama on regional co-ordination are equally applicable to its Botswana–Namibia aspects:

> to ensure that regional economic co-operation does not remain a mere wish, it is vital that we should begin now to think seriously about the sort of institutions that would be required for the promotion of multi-state projects. . . . I harbour no delusions of grandeur; nevertheless I am convinced that with the will and the determination which have sustained us through the years of turbulence, conflict and chaos by which our region has always been characterized we can begin now to forge a united Southern African community wherein lies our strength for survival in the future.[35]

Notes

1. The author, R. H. Green, has served as a consultant to Botswana under the auspices of the Commonwealth Secretariat, and to the United Nations Institute for Namibia. He served on the Steering Committee for the Southern Africa Development Co-ordination Conference and is a member of the Southern Africa Development Co-ordination London Liaison Committee and a consultant to the economic secretariat of SWAPO. However, the analysis and conclusions of this paper are his personal responsibility and are not necessarily those of Botswana, SWAPO, the Front Line States or the Commonwealth Secretariat.

2. SADCC, Arusha (3 July 1979) mimeo, pp. 2–4.

3. Reported in *New African*, July 1979.

4. Reported in *Windhoek Observer* (8 September 1979).

5. See *Africa* (August 1979); *New African* (September 1979); Green, R. H., 'Southern African development co-ordination: toward a functioning dynamic?', *IDS Bulletin* (10 April 1980), for fuller discussion of the Conference, and Green, R. H., 'Toward Southern African regionalism: the emergence of dialogue', *Africa Contemporary Record, 1978–9*, London, Africana (1979), for an exploration of its broader background.

6. See 'Namibia', *Africa Contemporary Record*, 1978–9, loc. cit.

7. The basic early works are Viner, J., *The Customs Union Issue*, New York, Carnegie Endowment (1950); Meade, J., *The Theory of Customs Unions*, North Holland, Amsterdam (1955); Balassa, B., *The Theory of Economic Integration*, Homewood, Illinois, Irwin (1961).

8. See Linder, S. B., *Trade and Trade Policy for Development*, New York, Praeger (1967).

9. See for example Krishna, K. G. V., and Green, R. H., *Economic Co-operation in Africa: Retrospect and Prospect*, Nairobi, Oxford (1967); Ewing, A. F., 'Prospects for economic integration in Africa', *Journal of Modern African Studies* (5 May 1967); Robson, P., *Economic Integration in Africa*, London, Allen & Unwin (1968).

10. For a fuller description of SACU especially as it affects Botswana see Chapter 9 by Derek Hudson in this book, pp. 131–58.

11. See Hazlewood, A., *Economic Integration: The East African Experience*, London, Heinemann Educational Books (1975).

12. See Green, R. H., 'The East African Community: 1975 and after', 'The East African community: the end of the road', 'The East African Community: death, funeral, inheritance' in *ACR*, 1975–6, 1976–7, 1977–8, London, Africana.

13. See Renninger, J. P., *Multinational Co-operation for Development in West Africa*, New York, Pergamon (1979) especially Chapters 3–4.

14. See Demas, W., *The Economics of Development in Small Countries*, Montreal, McGill (1965); Green, R. H. and Seidman, A., *Unity or Poverty: the Economics of Pan Africanism*, London/Baltimore, Penguin (1967–8); Brewster, M. and Thomas, C. Y. 'Aspects of the theory of economic integration', *Journal of Common Market Studies*, VIII (December 1969).

15. Both Demas, op. cit., and Seidman and Green, op. cit., are examples.

16. For example Brewster and Thomas, op. cit.; Vaitsos, C. V., 'Crisis in regional economic co-operation (integration) among developing countries', *World Development* (1979).

17. See for example Ghai, D. P. (ed.), *Economic Independence in Africa*, Nairobi, East African Literature Bureau (1973) especially chapters by Ghai, Onitiri, Green, Harvey.

18. See Brewster and Thomas, op. cit., and Seidman and Green, op. cit., and more recently *Economic Co-operation Among Developing Countries* (Report of a Group of Experts), Geneva, UNCTAD (1976).

19. ibid.

20. See Vaitsos, C. V., *The Role of Transnational Enterprises in Latin American Economic Integration Efforts*, Geneva, UNCTAD (1978).

21. See Vaitsos, 'Crisis in co-operation', op. cit.

22. See Mytelka, L. K., 'The salience of gains in Third World integrative systems', *World Politics*, XXV (January 1978).

23. See Axline, W. A., *Caribbean Integration: The Politics of Regionalism*, London/New York, Pinter/Nichols (1979), especially Chapters I, II, III, VIII.

24. This section draws on SADCC speeches and consultants' papers – especially *First Steps Toward Economic Integration and Economic Dependence and Regional Co-operation*, London, SADCC (1979). These were to be edited with a summary by the Conference Secretary-General, A. J. Nsekela, and published around 1981.

25. Indeed the ECA has been overtly hostile to the SADCC initiatives. Most Western states have been cautiously positive, the EEC has been somewhat more enthusiastic, but as a gambit to urge Angola, Mozambique and – on independence – Namibia and Zimbabwe to sign the second coming of the Lomé ACP/EEC Convention.

26. Speech to SADCC introducing discussion on 'External Co-operation', SADCC (4 July 1979).
27. Chairman's 'Opening Statement', SADCC (3 July 1979).
28. ibid.
29. ibid.
30. Chairman's 'Closing Statement', SADCC (4 July 1979).
31. For data on Namibia see Green, R. H., *Namibia: A Political Economic Survey*, IDS Discussion Paper No. 144, Institute of Development Studies, Sussex (1979); Chambers, R., and Green, R. H., 'Agrarian transition in Namibia', in Green, R. H., Kiljunen, M. L., and K. K. (eds), *Namibia: The Last Colony*, London, Longman (forthcoming).
32. See United Nations Institute for Namibia, *Manpower Projections and Development Implications* (R. H. Green, Consultant), Namibia Studies Series No. 1 (N. K. Duggal, ed.), Lusaka (1978).
33. This section is based on discussions with many individuals in several countries and on SADCC documentation sources and does not purport to present an official Botswana viewpoint.
34. The best discussions of the Okavango delta area potential are: Botswana Society, *Symposium on the Okavango Delta*, Gaborone (1976); SWECO, *Study of the Use, Extraction and Transfer of Okavango Water for Development of the Okavango Corridor*, Gaborone/Stockholm (1976), 4 vols.
35. 'Opening Address', SADCC, op. cit., pp. 3, 5.

Reginald Herbold Green is Fellow, Institute of Development Studies, Sussex, consultant to the economic directorate of SWAPO; formerly Economic Adviser to the Treasury, Tanzania and Professor of Economics, University of Dar es Salaam.

12 The Application of Incomes Policy in the Private Sector, with Reference to the Strike of Bank Employees in 1974

NELSON MOYO

Botswana's incomes policy dates from 1972. The policy is set out in a White Paper, Government Paper no. 2 of 1972 (Revised May, 1976) entitled *National Policy on Incomes, Employment, Prices and Profits*. It has been suggested that 'the proper aim of incomes policy is to keep incomes and value-productivity roughly in line among sectors, and growing at similar rates'.[1] This sounds like an extremely simple rationale. But great problems begin to emerge as soon as we try to map out some of its implications. To begin with, linking wage increases to productivity increases requires an estimate of the rate of productivity increase throughout the economy which in turn requires some degree of forward planning of the economy. Thus planning incomes must necessarily involve other sorts of planning.

Even if it is agreed that national wage increases must be kept in line with increases in national productivity the question remains of distributing the permitted total among particular industries and wage and salary earners. Here there are a number of possibilities. One possibility is that wages could be related to productivity increases in each industry or sector. But would such a policy be fair? Is it just? What about sectors such as the service industries and the government service where it is not easy to increase productivity or, even if it is increasing, it is not easy to measure? How would government servants, teachers and nurses, for example, be treated under such a system? Another possibility would be to say the benefits of growth should be equally distributed regardless of variations in productivity increases.

But fundamentally, the requirement that wages rise in line with productivity increases is not simply an old-fashioned piece of economics, it is in fact a highly political proposition for it takes for granted the present distribution of wealth, incomes and life chances.[2] Some economists argue that a fairer distribution of income is the proper goal of taxation and public expenditure. But a major feature of the tax systems of less developed countries – indeed of the advanced countries as well – is their inability to 'look after' equity. Hence the insistence of trade unionists that incomes policy be accompanied by a visible programme of social reform. The two cannot or should not be separated.

One basic requirement is that an incomes policy must be an incomes policy. Very often *incomes* policies degenerate into *wages* policies and this almost invariably leads to their being rejected by trade unions. Botswana is lucky in that, despite official sponsorship, the trade union movement is still weak and poorly led. It poses no real challenge to the government or the employing class.

On paper, Botswana's incomes policy aims to control *all* incomes not just wages. Thus profits, prices and, 'if it becomes necessary', rents were to be controlled. A National Employment, Manpower and Incomes Council (NEMIC) was established to advise government on the measures required for the effective implementation of the policies on incomes, employment, prices and profits. NEMIC was composed of representatives of employers, employees, the parastatal organizations and government. In 1974 a sub-committee of NEMIC, the Wages Policy Committee, was established to review the wages and salaries paid by employers outside the public sector. The committee comprises representatives of the Office of the President, the Directorate of Personnel, the Ministry of Home Affairs, the Labour Department, and the Ministry of Finance and Development Planning. It is chaired by the Assistant Minister of Finance and Development Planning. The work of this committee will be discussed fully later. Suffice it to say that government's tough wages policy has not been matched by an equally severe attitude towards prices, rents, profits and managerial incomes. So far, the Wages Policy Committee is the only sub-committee of NEMIC which shows any sign of life. NEMIC itself has not met for more than two years. It met only irregularly before then.

The greatest failure of government incomes policy has been in the area of prices, rents and profits control. It is an old trade union argument that stable prices make the best environment for wage restraint. And governments embarking on an incomes policy normally undertake to stabilize the cost of living by means of subsidies and other measures. In Botswana the government is not able to give such a *quid pro quo* for its incomes policy. Stable prices, in other words, are not a pre-condition of reasonable pay restraint. Instead, it is considered that strict wage restraint is the pre-condition of stable prices. The government's powerlessness to ensure stable prices is revealed clearly in the white paper which states that, 'a major part of consumption consists of imports; thus the main cause of inflation in Botswana is increases in the prices of imports, over which the Government has no control'.[3] All that the government tries to do is 'to ensure that traders' profit margins do not become excessive, and that situations do not arise where individual traders exploit a monopoly position' (para. 22). This objective was going to be achieved 'by ensuring wherever possible that healthy competition exists in the retail and wholesale trade'. Lipton has suggested that the government's present policy of attempting to control traders' mark-ups has little effect and diverts the Ministry of Commerce and Industry (MCI) from its job of assisting industrialization.[4]

The government's Price Control Unit, which is charged with keeping a check on traders' profit margins, is terribly understaffed. The Unit, which is located in the MCI, is headed by a Commercial Officer with a staff of about eleven, most of whom are based in Gaborone. They have to perform an almost impossible task.

The government, moreover, does not believe in subsidizing basic commodities. At the present time the government fixes the prices of only two commodities: sugar and petrol. The prices of such basic commodities as milk, bread, mealie meal, etc., are not fixed.

The government's policy on rents is also in bad shape. It has simply not been possible to keep rents down to realistic levels. And the government's noises in the white paper about keeping a check on property owners in the private sector so that they 'do not exploit temporary housing shortages in the urban area' (para. 24) have come to nothing. In big towns like Gaborone there is a thriving rent racket. For anyone who owns a decent house it pays to vacate the house and rent it to some embassy, business executive or other desperate customer (of whom there are plenty). The owner of the house then joins the queue for a BHC (Botswana Housing Corporation) or local authority house. It is widely believed that such persons are very often able to jump the queue at the expense of the 'small man'. The rent obtained is often so high that it is able to cover the mortgage, the rent due for the new dwelling and still leave a handsome profit for the owner. A lot of people, including those renting BHC houses, also make money by sub-letting, at very high rents, their servants' quarters. This kind of profiteering is not only confined to the richer areas of towns but is also prevalent in the less endowed parts such as Bontleng in Gaborone.

The scope for controlling profits is also very limited because of the government's desperate desire to attract private foreign investment to Botswana. The white paper says, 'Botswana depends heavily on foreign private investment to develop the industrial and commercial sectors. . . . It is clearly recognised that such investment will only be attracted to Botswana if it is permitted a rate of return not less favourable than that normally obtainable elsewhere' (paras 26–7). But it will be extremely difficult to persuade wage earners to accept restraint unless other incomes are also controlled. The least that should be done is to ensure that profits do not rise faster than wages. In certain circumstances equity considerations may demand that the share of profits in national income is actually reduced. There could be problems, though, including the possibility that profits tax might be passed on to consumers in the form of higher prices. But there can be no running away from the requirement that an incomes policy must not only be fair, it must be seen to be fair.

Salary reviews in the public service

Salary reviews in the public service have formed the basis of government wages policy. There have been four such reviews since Independence. The first was in 1970, four years after Independence (the Okoh Report). The other three came after the introduction of the incomes policy in 1972. They were:

1   the Makgekgenene Commission Report 1974,
2   the Chiepe Commission Report 1976, and
3   the Mmusi Commission Report 1978.

The Okoh Report came at a time when Botswana was still heavily dependent on aid from Britain, both to balance its recurrent budget, as well as to finance development expenditure. Also, the rise in the cost of living was still within tolerable bounds.[5] This was before the unprecedented rise in the price of oil. The Okoh Report argued strongly that, 'any wage proposals must depend on the burden of their financial implications; on the extent to which savings can be generated by measures to increase efficiency and productivity in the Service, and ultimately on the Government's ability to meet the costs involved, having regard to its other commitments and responsibilities.'[6] The commission's particular concern was that the annual costs of administration, the government's wages and salaries bill, should not be allowed to exceed 40 per cent of the total annual recurrent expenditure.[7] Taking all these considerations into account the commission concluded that 'there can be no case, in spite of the rise in the cost of living since the last Salaries Review, for a general increase in the present levels of wages and salaries in the Civil Service' (para. 37). There were, therefore, only modest rises in some salary scales, others stayed the same, while most, especially at the top, were actually revised downwards.

The Okoh Report actually laid the foundations for the government's incomes policy. In accepting the report, government reaffirmed that it 'would not create a society in which there was a great contrast in the living standards of farmers and those of miners, industrial workers, and Government servants, and that Government's efforts would be directed to ensuring that as many Batswana as possible share the benefits of the expanding economy'.[8]

At the same time government accepted the view that competition with the private sector for the limited skilled manpower could be harmful to the economy. Government, therefore, decided that 'the more realistic approach would be to establish a public sector salary structure which should be followed by the private sector'.[9] This formed the basis for the government's present incomes policy which called for restraint all round. The hope of keeping wages and salaries down and of minimizing differentials seems to have been severely undermined by subsequent Salary Reviews.

The Makgekgenene Commission 1974

This was the first commission to recommend very large increases in the pay of civil servants. The commission's recommendations for sizeable pay increases all round rested in part on cost of living considerations. Evidence produced at the time suggested that the cost of living had risen sharply in 1970–3. Moreover, the indications were that the rate of rise in the cost of living was accelerating. As a result, all income groups were experiencing a fall in living standards.

The commission's other main consideration was what was described as the 'market scarcity value' of certain personnel who, because of their training or skill, had to be rewarded by improved pay. These persons were said to be highly conscious of their qualifications. There was also the need to attract and retain expatriate personnel by internationally competititive salary scales. The whole argument consists in saying that the government should pay its employees in accordance with their market values. One serious omission in the report was any discussion of productivity considerations. This is, of course, a difficult concept in the case of civil servants since they do not produce a marketable product.

The actual pay increases ranged from 17 per cent at the bottom of the superscale grade to 150 per cent at the bottom of the industrial class. A particularly important change in the superscale grade was the introduction of incremental steps into the salary structure to provide some protection against rising costs of living. Previously, this grade was on fixed scales. The commission noted that superscale officers and others who had reached the top of their scales were 'singularly vulnerable to the impact of inflation'.[10] On the whole, it would appear there was some slight narrowing of wage differentials within the public service as the lower grades got relatively higher pay increases than the top grades. The provision of 'fringe' benefits to higher civil servants meant, however, that the income gap remained large.

'Fringe' benefits
Apart from their basic pay public officers also received 'fringe' benefits of various kinds. Perhaps by far the most important in terms of actually increasing the pay packet was the housing allowance. Table 12.1 shows the relevant rates. The lowest paid superscale officer received an additional R1140 per annum in housing allowance whereas the lowest paid teacher received R108 per annum. A husband and wife qualified for housing allowance if both were working for government. Industrial class employees did not receive housing allowance.

Table 12.1   *Housing allowances (Rand per annum)*

Basic salary	Housing allowance
480– 624	108
672–1116	168
1188–1572	240
1656–2268	360
2412–3276	540
3420–4428	780
4572–5436	984
5496–7452	1140

Source
Personnel Directive No. 12 of 1974.

The Chiepe Commission 1976

The Chiepe Commission raised wages and salaries by roughly 20 per cent across the board. So it did not tamper with differentials. The main consideration was to compensate for the rise in the cost of living since the 1974 Commission.

The Mmusi Commission 1978

The commission which seemed to destroy all canons of equity and social justice was the Mmusi Commission. For example it recommended massive salary increases for the superscale posts ranging from 44 per cent at the *bottom* of the scale to 66 per cent at the top. (But the increases were 2·5–28 per cent if allowance is made for including grossed up housing allowances in salary.) For the industrial class, however, the increases ranged from 13 per cent at the bottom to as low as 2 per cent at the top. Thus the income gap between superscale posts and the industrial class was considerably widened. The commission apparently rejected requests to award higher increases to officers in the lower part of the salary scales on the grounds that 'due to the effect of income tax, a fixed sum or fixed percentage award automatically provided greatest relative benefits to the more lowly paid in terms of take home pay' (p. 8).

It would seem that an overriding theme in the commission's report was the notion of paying officers according to their 'responsibility'. The commission's views on social justice are revealing. The report says about social justice,

> the Commission was of the opinion that the concept is misunderstood; social justice does not mean paying everyone the same salary irrespective of his responsibilities, but rather paying fair salaries that reasonably reflect the different levels of responsibility.

The report went on,

> In this regard it was felt that this was no longer the position in the very senior levels of the civil service and that unless action was taken to restore reasonable differentials the possible loss of senior civil servants could become critical. (p. 7).

The result was that not only was a severe burden placed upon the government budget but serious distortions and anomalies were introduced in the salary structure. The report represented a major violation of government policy on differentials. The 1969 election manifesto of the ruling party, of the Botswana Democratic Party (BDP), declared in part,

> the legacy of colonialism has meant that certain sections of the civil service have been enjoying pay, conditions and privileges, designed for expatriates. An important contribution to achieving self-reliance would be to induce restraint and austerity in civil service salaries, *especially at the highest level.* (p. 42).

The Mmusi Report went directly against this.

Incomes policy and the private sector

A major source of difficulty in applying incomes policy to the private sector has been the insistence that wage and salary increases in the private and parastatal sectors must be kept, not so much in line with the rise in productivity in those sectors, but in line with increases in wages and salaries in the public service. That is to say, wages and salaries paid by government were to be regarded as firm guidelines by employers in the private and parastatal sectors. The government, in other words, assumed the role of 'wage leader'. Paragraph 18 of the white paper states,

> basic local wage and salary levels in the private and parastatal sectors should generally conform to and on no account significantly exceed, those paid by Government to comparable grades of public employees, taking all factors into consideration (e.g. benefits in kind, pensions, gratuities, etc.).

The crux of the matter is: can jobs in the civil service be precisely or even roughly compared with jobs in the private sector? The Okoh Commission Report had this to say about comparisons between 'public' and 'private' sector jobs:

the permanent civil servant, unless he is downright inefficient, has considerable – many would say excessive – security of tenure, opportunities for training and regular promotions during his career, and a gratuity and pension when he retires. Moreover, he has a generally well respected position in society. By and large the few clerical, executive and managerial employees in the private sector, although sometimes well paid, are remunerated more strictly according to their immediate qualifications, efficiency and ability. They are more likely to be sacked if, in the eyes of the employer, they fail to measure up quickly to reasonable expectations. In any event their advancement and promotion prospects depend much more than in the Civil Service on their personal output, and sometimes on the success and prosperity or otherwise of the enterprise in which they are employed. In other words, the private sector does not uniformly offer the same kind of career and security associated with the Civil Service. Because there are at present few large employers in Botswana, and many small owner-managed businesses, the promotion prospects for Batswana in the private sector are very limited indeed. (para. 50).

The Wages Policy Committee (WPC)

The task of the WPC is to ensure that wage and salary increases in the private and parastatal sectors are in line with those in the public service. Until recently the procedure was that *employers* presented their detailed proposals for consideration by the committee. The committee subsequently advised whether the proposals were in line with government policy or whether modifications were required before implementation. Once agreement was reached with the WPC the employer then began negotiations with the trade union where one existed. This has created problems in that some employers conveniently hid behind the government, claiming that they were willing to pay more but that the WPC would not permit a larger increase. The procedure clearly undermined the position of trade unions and made wage negotiations a farce.

Now, however, employers are required to negotiate and if possible reach agreement with trade unions *before* approaching the WPC. But the WPC ultimately produces a maximum scale beyond which the negotiators cannot go.

Initially, and for administrative reasons, the work of the Committee was to be limited to considering the wage structures of the larger private and parastatal concerns in the economy, that is, those employing 200 or more workers.

The bank dispute

The banks

There are only two commercial banks in Botswana: Barclays Bank of Botswana Ltd and Standard Bank Botswana Ltd. They employ roughly seven hundred workers. In the past, the two banks were administered from South Africa and their policies were largely determined in that country. Moreover, most senior employees were South African. The ties with South Africa meant that bank employees in Botswana were on similar pay and conditions of service as their counterparts in South Africa. In the early 1970s the ties with South Africa were gradually loosened in favour of direct ties with London. The local incorporation of the two banks in 1976 gave them some measure of local autonomy. They now have local boards which take most decisions locally. In wage negotiations the two banks work together.

The union

The banks recognize the Botswana Bank Employees Union as the sole bargaining or negotiating body for all employees except those in the supervisory grades. The union was first registered in October 1971. It does not appear to be a particularly strong union. The late Minister of Home Affairs, B. K. Kgari, was particularly scathing in his speech to the 1977 Annual Convention of the Union. He noted the following advantages of the union compared to other unions in the country:

1 the compactness of the banking industry and the fact that the union membership is located in the major towns, making communications between members and between branches relatively easy;
2 the bank workers are better educated and more articulate.

But the late minister noted, with regret that:

> You are no better organized than a number of our Unions which have the difficult task of organizing uneducated workers spread in small groups throughout the country. They have none of your advantages. You should be a model for other Trade Unions. But are you? Do you hold branch meetings regularly? No. Do you run courses for your members? No. Does your national executive meet regularly? No. Are you actively recruiting? No. Have you extended trade union benefits to areas such as savings and loan schemes, bursaries and other co-operative efforts? No. Just what are you doing? How do you justify calling yourself a Union?[11]

The wages of bank employees and the 1974 strike

In 1974 it was commonly held that banks paid about 40 per cent above government for comparable posts. In 1970, the Okoh Commission Report said about the banks, 'with the exception of Banks there would not appear to be divergencies of much magnitude between the Civil Service and private sector salaries in Botswana' (para. 49). The Report of the Committee of Investigation into the Dispute between the Banks and the Bank Employees Union (The Matthews Report of January 1974) said, while noting that the salaries paid to the bank employees were high,

> On the other hand, it was noted that the Banks were financial institutions whose employees handle large sums of public money. Obviously, people who were in daily contact with large sums of money as part of their employment had to be placed beyond normal temptation by being paid adequate salaries.[12]

The banks themselves believed they paid above average wages for comparable jobs in other sectors.[13] In government circles, therefore, there was a feeling that bank employees must somehow 'mark time' in keeping with government incomes policy. But the strike was not caused solely by the demands of government incomes policy. The real problem began as far back as 1970. As we indicated earlier, the banks were then administered from South Africa. The issue was that, in 1970, an agreement on basic salary scales was reached between the South African Society of Bank Officials (SASBO) and the banks in South Africa. By tradition, the agreed salaries were automatically extended to all bank staff everywhere in southern Africa. In 1970, however, the banks in Botswana decided not to increase the basic salaries of all bank employees but only those of expatriate employees. Such an increase was to be in the form of a 'Special Allowance'. Local employees immediately felt they were being discriminated against. The older local employees, who had benefited from previous agreements negotiated by SASBO, were particularly annoyed by the management decision.

In 1971, the Botswana Bank Employees Union took up the matter with the management. The dispute led to the appointment in July 1973 of a Committee of Investigation headed by Mr V. J. G. Matthews.

After studying the issue and related matters the Committee recommended that:

1 the differential introduced in October 1970 between local and expatriate employees should be removed by the payment to each local of a lump sum covering the period 1970 to date;
2 a new basic salary structure be considered for all bank employees and a supplementary allowance for expatriates introduced;
3 all bank employees in Botswana should enter into new contracts drawn up to accord with present day conditions in Botswana as a state independent of any regional grouping.[14]

The above recommendations were accepted by the government and the banks were expected to act upon them.

The 1974 negotiations were soured, in the view of the union, by the banks' failure to implement fully the Committee of Investigation's recommendations. In particular the union complained that the banks had removed only the 1970 differential but that meanwhile other increases in 1972, 1973 and two in 1974, had been paid only to expatriates in the same disguised manner of 'special allowances' thus widening the differential between locals and expatriates.[15] So the issue of differentials between locals and expatriates was a burning issue in the 1974 wage negotiations. There were other issues as well. The union argued, among other things, that comparison with government was unfair for the following reasons:

1 government scales were designed to ensure comparatively short periods on one grade before promotion whereas bank scales permitted very long periods on one grade;
2 government paid housing allowance which effectively gave its employees an additional 20 per cent on basic salaries. Moreover, government had housing schemes which enabled government officers to purchase houses at subsidized prices. Banks had none of these advantages;
3 bank employees worked on Saturdays and had longer hours than government;

4   pension and retirement schemes were better in government;
5   in government, unlike in the banks, the dependants of an officer who died after completion of his probation period were entitled to his annual salary as gratuity;
6   banks provided little training and there were fewer chances for promotion.[16]

When all the benefits were converted into cash government scales were far more generous than those of the banks. The negotiations were held against the background of massive wage and salary increases in the public service following the Makgekgenene Commission Report. After numerous, apparently fruitless meetings with the management, the union became convinced that further negotiations would achieve nothing.

The strike

In a letter to the Commissioner of Labour dated 4 November 1974, the union gave notice that following a meeting of all branches of the union 'it was agreed that on 25th November, 1974, the Union should go on strike . . . The main reason for striking being disagreement on salary structures . . .' The union called upon the Labour Department to come and supervise secret ballots at its branches in Francistown, Selebi-Phikwe, Mahalapye, Gaborone and Lobatse on Wednesday, 13 November 1974. The Commissioner of Labour replied on 11 November saying that before secret ballots could be conducted the matter should be referred to his Department as a trade dispute under the Trade Dispute Act, 1969.

On 20 November the union gave formal notice that its members were to go on strike as from 25 November. This was contained in separate letters addressed to both banks and copied to the Office of the President. On 22 November, in a Government Gazette Extraordinary, the Minister for Home Affairs declared the threatened strike to be unlawful until such time as a secret ballot of the members of the union employed in the banks had determined a two-thirds majority in favour of such a strike. But the strike did indeed begin on Monday, 25 November and lasted the whole week. The strikers returned to work on Monday, 2 December. This followed a statement by the banks that those not resuming work by that date would have their employment terminated.

The issues surrounding the strike would appear to fall into two separate but related categories. The first, and perhaps most sensitive, issue concerned pay disparities between local and white expatriate employees. This issue began as far back as 1970 and had become cumulative as we indicated earlier. The union claimed that expatriates earned as much as 67 per cent more than locals.[17] But the issue went beyond pay disparities between expatriates and locals. The question of training and promotion prospects for locals was also a burning issue. The union's letter dated 20 November addressed to both banks is most revealing. It referred to 'pathetic, inhuman and despicable injustices' in the two banks and to 'continued and unjustified ostracism of Africans from positions of responsibility'. It called for disparities between black and white to be removed forthwith. In a memorandum dated 6 December 1973, addressed to the Minister of Health, Labour and Home Affairs, the union had the following to say about training and localization in the banks:

It is the Union's wish to know if the Banks have already submitted their training programmes as required by law. If such training programmes have already been submitted, it will please the Union to know if there are any locals understudying the present expatriates and the stipulated period of takeover. In a majority of cases, the local members of staff train these expatriates who, as we are made to understand, are recruited solely to come and train the local staff. . . . The Union has come to conclude that Botswana will always remain a training depot. The aspirations of our members are used to promote the expatriates who come to work and get trained by us rather than give us the training.

Feeling was particularly strong against white South African expatriates. The same memorandum asked,

Why do we get recruits from South Africa and not from London which is our Headquarters? The inhuman practices of South Africa are widely known. The white South Africans are indoctrinated in discriminatory policies of apartheid and can never work with the Batswana without practising discrimination.

It is clear from the above that the union and its membership strongly believed that the banks were practising racial discrimination in a democratic and non-racial country.

The second major issue concerned pay differentials between bank employees and public servants following the Makgekgenene Commission Report. The union's demand for a 40 per cent pay rise was, as they put it, intended to bring them up to par with civil servants. Three days before the strike began management made a final offer which they said was the maximum permitted under the government's wages policy. This offer had actually been approved by the Wages Policy Committee (see Table 12.2). The new wage rates were to be back-dated to 1 April 1974 and were to apply equally to male and female employees, thus removing long standing discrimination against women. The union rejected the offer as being totally inadequate and derisory. But management's offer was never in fact changed and the strikers were forced to return to work under the threat of dismissal. The union subsequently lodged the

Table 12.2   *Management's final offer*

Grade	Existing wage rates (Pula)	New wage rates offered in 1974 (Pula)	% changes
Junior Clerical	1032–1512	1308–2400	27–59
Senior Clerical	1572–3072	2124–3600	35–17
Senior Grade 1	1668–3480	3000–4500	80–29
Senior Grade 2	2760–3804	3600–5208	30–37
Senior Grade 3	3420–4620	4500–6012	32–30
Senior Grade 4	4212–5460	5160–6888	22–26

Note
The wage rates offered in 1976 and 1978 are shown in Appendix 12.A.
Source
Botswana Daily News, Friday, 29 November 1974.

dispute formally with the Labour Department but nothing had happened six months later when the union wrote to complain.[18] It should be said, however, that since 1975 there have been important changes in conditions of service for bank employees including the introduction by the banks of pension schemes and training programmes for locals.

Conclusions

It is difficult to single out one cause of the strike. There were many causes. On the one hand were the restrictions imposed by the requirements of government incomes policy and the question of the pay differential between bank employees and government servants. On the other were the long standing and perhaps more basic grievances involving the differences in pay between expatriate officers and locals and the lack of training and promotion opportunities for locals in the banks. Although there is no evidence to suggest that the strike was also directed against the structure of managerial control, we cannot escape the conclusion by Lane and Roberts that 'any strike amounts amongst other things to a crisis in an established system of authority'.[19]

What are the implications for government incomes policy? The first is that to gain wide acceptance government policy must be seen as an incomes policy not just a policy on wages. In this connection, it is particularly important to ensure that the other sub-committees of NEMIC do work and are seen to work. This point is stressed in the Lipton Report.

Secondly, the Wages Policy Committee, in my view, must have tripartite representation, not just government representatives as at present. Furthermore, the Wages Policy Committee must have ground staff to facilitate its work – people who can make meaningful studies on wage trends and wage levels in various sectors of the economy.

Thirdly, a job analyst has already been appointed and hopefully his work will help in the very difficult task of comparing jobs. This is a particularly thorny problem.

But perhaps the most fundamental problem of incomes policy, at least from the point of view of trade unionists, is as Hyman and Brough have observed, that, 'no procedure exists whereby restraint on higher paid employees might lead to the transfer of resources to the lower-paid, rather than simply to their own employers'.[20]

Notes

1. Lipton, M., *Employment and Labour Use in Botswana*, Final Report, Vol. 1 (December, 1978), p. 43.

2. Hyman, R. and Brough, I., *Social Values and Industrial Relations: A Study of Fairness and Inequality*, Oxford, Basil Blackwell (1975), p. 106.

3. Government Paper No. 2, March 1972 (revised May 1976) p. 7, para 22.

4. Lipton Report, Vol. 1, p. 48.

5. The report estimated that the cost of living had risen 'by some 18 per cent measured by the South African index – over the period since the last salaries revision in 1964' (para. 46).

6. Report of the Commission on the Salaries and Conditions of Service of the Public Service and the Teaching Service (The Okoh Report) (July 1970), para. 28.
7. ibid, paras. 32 and 33.
8. Report of the Salaries Review Commission (1974), p. 3.
9. ibid, pp. 4–5.
10. ibid, p. 12.
11. 'The Role of Workers and Trade Unions in Botswana', speech by the late B. K. Kgari, MP, Minister of Home Affairs to the 1977 Annual Convention of the Botswana Bank Employees Union, BTUEC, Gaborone (27 February 1977), p. 26.
12. Report of the Committee of Investigation into the Dispute between the Banks and the Bank Employees Union (The Matthews Report) (1974), para. 14, p. 3.
13. The Matthews Report, para. 8, p. 2.
14. ibid, pp. 4–5.
15. Letter by the Botswana Bank Employees Union dated 18 December 1974, addressed to the Commissioner of Labour.
16. Union's letter as above.
17. *Botswana Daily News* (Tuesday 26 November 1974).
18. Botswana Bank Employees Union letter dated 25 June 1975, addressed to the Commissioner of Labour.
19. Lane, T. and Roberts, K., *Strike at Pilkingtons*, London, Fontana (1971), p. 16.
20. Hyman, R. and Brough, I., op. cit., p. 104.

Appendix 12.A
Botswana bank employees' salary scales 1976–8

Grade of employee	1976 Wage rates (Pula)	1978 Wage rates (Pula)	% changes
Junior Clerical	1548–2964	1944–3672	26–24
Senior Clerical	2772–4500	3480–5208	26–16
Senior Grade 1	4080–6024	4632–6312	14– 5
Senior Grade 2	4896–6840	5592–7356	14– 8
Senior Grade 3	5700–7644	6600–8532	16–12
Senior Grade 4	6960–9120	7704–9720	18– 7

Source
Standard Bank Botswana Ltd.

Nelson Moyo is a member of the Economics Department, University of Zimbabwe; formerly Senior Lecturer in Economics, University of Botswana and Swaziland.

13 Foreign Investment in Manufacturing: the Case of Botswana's Brewery

CHARLES HARVEY

Investment decisions: the relevance of theory

In the hope of attracting investment from abroad, with its accompanying technology and management, the governments of African countries, in common with the governments of most developing countries, have offered at various times all sorts of investment incentives. The details vary, but they frequently include tax holidays, accelerated depreciation of fixed assets, the provision of low-cost industrial sites and other measures aimed at reducing costs.

There is a theory behind such cost-reducing incentives, even though the civil servants and politicians involved may not perceive the matter in those terms. The theory in this case is an attractively simple one, namely that if a profitable investment opportunity exists then someone will take advantage of it.

In countries with an adequate local supply of savings, financial intermediaries, technology and skilled manpower (including managers) the theory is quite likely to hold true. African governments are obviously aware that these conditions do not apply to their own economies – indeed, if they did, then the problem of underdevelopment would scarcely exist. So investment incentives are aimed at foreign companies, as the only likely source of investment in a large range of modern manufacturing industry. But it is a serious mistake to assume that the same theory applies to foreign investors, that is, to companies already established in another (almost certainly developed) economy and considering setting up a subsidiary manufacturing plant in a developing country.

All investors are interested in making a profit; but there is a big difference between companies operating entirely within a country, and companies operating across national borders. The latter have a choice as to where they make profits and will normally try and do so where taxes are lowest, where risks are thought to be least and where there is as little danger as possible of not being able to transfer profits – to shareholders or for investment, wherever in the world it seems most profitable. If, therefore, foreign companies can make profits by exporting to African countries, they will normally prefer to do so. That way they will continue to make a profit out of selling to an African country without having to invest in what appears to them to be a remote, risky, difficult environment.

Normally, a manufacturer who is already supplying a foreign market will only consider investing in manufacturing capacity (as opposed to distribution facilities) if he is threatened with a loss of that market. Such a threat comes either from rival manufacturers or from governments. A rival manufacturer can threaten a competitor's market in any given country by offering to manufacture locally behind tariff protection provided by the government. In that way, one exporter can attempt to capture a larger share of the market by excluding his rivals. Alternatively, a government interested in forcing its import suppliers into manufacturing locally, can itself take the initiative by threatening to exclude those suppliers who continue to supply the market from factories abroad.

There are, of course, other reasons why foreigners may be reluctant to invest in African countries. Wages, although low, may reflect low levels of skill, experience and therefore productivity. Governments, from a distance, appear unstable. Skilled labour is scarce and expensive. There are also the risks of nationalization and exchange controls on the remission of profits. Meanwhile, for most African countries, markets are small, so that the economies of large-scale production are not usually available and the foreign investor may have to change his production methods from those with which he is most familiar.

However, it seems that the desire to supply the market from abroad, for as long as conceivably possible, is the dominant factor. This is neatly illustrated by Kilby's work on Nigeria, because it related mainly to the colonial period when political risks were minimal, and because Nigeria has by African standards an exceptionally large market, with a population some hundred times larger than that of Botswana.

Kilby has shown that, for a whole range of products, the local market had grown large enough to make local manufacture profitable, while the market continued to be supplied from abroad. This situation continued for many years – in some cases for more than 50 years. Then within a very short period, several manufacturers set up in Nigeria, each protecting his share of the market from the others – hence Kilby's name 'market-protector' for this type of investment.[1]

From the point of view of the foreign investor, this pattern of market-protecting investment is wholly rational. In most cases, that is, where the export market is fairly small, production facilities in the investor's home country will have adequate capacity to supply the export market, in which case building additional capacity abroad is completely unnecessary and indeed will reduce the profitability of existing factories. Where additional production capacity is needed, the risks and problems of investing abroad are unlikely to seem worthwhile, even when such costs as unskilled wages may appear lower. So the manufacturer will prefer to expand his production capacity at home, for continued export.

Furthermore, even when investment abroad becomes necessary in order to protect a company's market share, or desirable in order to try and capture a larger market share, the foreign investor will normally build only last-stage assembly and packaging facilities. There are two reasons for this: first, it minimizes the investment and therefore the risk; secondly, it maximizes the sale of intermediate inputs by the parent company. At its best (from the investor's point of view) or its worst (from the host country's point of view) a company can protect or increase its share of the market, behind tariff barriers and at a higher selling price, with a minimal investment in bottling, packaging, assembling and labelling, while continuing to supply the greater part of value added from abroad.

Examples of this type of investment are very numerous, although so far, not in Botswana, where the brewery was the first manufacturing investment to be given protection. In Zambia, the Italian Fiat Motor Company set up an assembly plant to put together complete kits imported from Italy, refusing at first to buy even those components which were already being manufactured in Zambia, such as batteries and tyres. Machinery for the factory was also, of course, imported. Another, almost comical example in Zambia was a factory which imported machinery, bottles, labels, and essence of whisky, gin and brandy in order to assemble them and add the only local component – water. There was even talk at one stage of importing Scottish water in order to improve the taste of the whisky, although this was never done.

It is also worth noting that if a company supplies inputs to a local assembly and packaging operation, where it used previously to supply finished products, then it is in a very strong position to supply those inputs at a higher price than if it were selling to a third party. This higher price can then be passed on in higher prices, made possible by protection and (very often) the monopoly position given to new industries by governments. Although 'transfer pricing' is a problem wherever associated companies trade across national frontiers, it is obviously a much greater risk in the sort of manufacturing investment, in last stage assembly, being described here.

It remains to be asked what motive an investor can have for investing (in manufacturing) if he is not already exporting to a market, and is not therefore protecting or expanding an existing market. Why, in other words, would a foreign company launch itself in an unknown country, of which it has no previous knowledge, and with (usually) a small market? The answer in most cases has been in order to make a profit out of selling its own, or other people's machines. This strategy requires, however, that the profit or commission realized from the sale of machines is greater than the investor's share of the investment. So the investor seeks some form of partnership with government, or with a government owned development corporation, or he seeks to be financed out of money borrowed from local banks – since otherwise the investor would also have to make a profit out of *production* in order to recover his money. Thus 'the actual investments made by these firms (machinery merchants) has been very small – typically 10 per cent of the equity, which represents 3–4 per cent of the combined equity – debenture capital commitment'. Clearly it is possible to recover 3–4 per cent of the total capital cost of a project out of the profit margin on machinery sales, and make a large return on the investment as well, especially if capital costs are inflated 'by 100 per cent or more'.[2] This sort of investment tends to be very unsuccessful from the host country's point of view, since the primary objective of the foreign 'investor' is to make a profit on the sale of machinery rather than from successful production. Alternatively, a management contract based on sales (rather than profits) can be used as a supplement to profits on the sale of machinery, while relieving the investor of responsibility for making a success of the investment.

There are many other types of investment, each with its own rationale.[3] For example, mining investment needs to be analysed quite differently, since it usually involves a large fixed investment and depends, apart from the obvious requirement of identifying something to mine, mainly on estimates of future mineral prices and the need to secure sources of supply.

The main point in the present context is to ask the question, why should any manufacturing company think of investing in a small, remote country in Africa, of which it has no previous experience, if it is not threatened with the loss of a market? The answer is, of course, in order to make a profit. But the crucial subsidiary question is then whether its profit is expected from selling machinery, from selling intermediate inputs, or from the local manufacturing process. Only if the host country can be fairly sure of the answer to these questions will there be a proper understanding of the investor's motives, and therefore a reasonable chance of successful negotiation. While it is difficult to make a success of a factory set up by a machinery salesman or machinery merchant, there can be considerable advantages to be derived by host countries from market-protecting investments. Those advantages have to be actively sought, though, by monitoring of transfer pricing, by insistence on the use of local inputs where they exist and by many other means. The danger lies in assuming that the building of a factory will automatically result in a positive net flow of benefits.

The negotiating position of a government is quite considerable. Although the foreign firm has control of know-how and management, the host government has in its power the right to give protection and exclusive licence – in other words the local market. Both lose negotiating power once the factory is built: the investor has, if the bargain is a fair one, committed some resources and begun to transfer some of its know-how; the government has granted the market and is usually most unwilling to throw people out of work by closing an unsuccessful factory.

The Botswana brewery: investment motives

By 1973 the market for beer in Botswana had reached the minimum size, approximately 30 000 hectolitres (hl) (650 000 imp. gal–790 000 US gal) per annum, for the establishment of a modern brewery. Most of this market, probably as much as 90 per cent, was being supplied by South African Breweries (SAB) which had a similarly dominant share of the South African market. Clearly SAB was not interested in setting up a brewery in Botswana unless threatened with the loss of the Botswana market. Equally clearly, no other brewer would be able to compete initially with the long established SAB products, without a fairly high level of protection. Swaziland had succeeded in capturing only 10 per cent of the Swazi market for beer with an unprotected brewery, which as a result lost more than R1 million in two years.

The choice for Botswana, therefore, lay between a SAB brewery which would supply the same brands of beer as before, or a brewery from much further afield, probably Europe. One unusual feature of the Botswana situation was that SAB might have been prepared to manufacture beer in Botswana without any tariff protection, since it would have been in a position to 'protect' an SAB Botswana brewery simply by withholding supplies of competing products. SAB would have been prepared to supply some of the nearest points in South Africa from a Botswana brewery.

The Botswana Development Corporation (BDC), having identified the possibility of what was thought to be a highly profitable beer manufacturing investment, approached three European brewers as well as SAB. The choice lay in the end between a member of the Oetker group called Brau Finanz, from Germany, and SAB.

Both potential partners agreed to a majority BDC shareholding, for which BDC would have to pay. On the projections produced at the time there was little to choose between the two on financial grounds. It was pointed out that there was almost no risk of failure in an SAB investment; the risk of failure with a Brau Finanz investment was thought to be 'slight', although Brau Finanz would require protection. Although with hindsight it is easy to see that the risk of failure was underestimated, the sheer size of the brewing division of Oetker, approximately twice as big as SAB, must have made it seem unlikely that Oetker would not have the resources to make a success of the Botswana brewery.

On broader strategic grounds there was a powerful argument for avoiding another large South African investment. Botswana's prosperity since 1970 has been created by two major mining investments: the copper–nickel mine at Selebi-Phikwe and the diamond mine at Orapa. These two investments, large in absolute terms and enormous relative to Botswana's economy, combined with the renegotiation of the Customs Union revenue formula and favourable rainfall, generated a 10–15 per cent growth rate in real GDP over a number of years. But both the big mining investments have a major South African component. The diamond mining operation iš owned 50 per cent by De Beers, a South African company, and 50 per cent by government; and the copper–nickel mining operation is owned 15 per cent by the government and 85 per cent by Botswana RST which in turn is owned 30 per cent each by Anglo American, a South African company, and AMAX, an American company, with the remainder owned through foreign stock exchanges by the general public.[4] The government was keen, therefore, to diversify both the ownership and the sources of management and technology in major foreign investments in the economy. The brewery fell into this category, being by some margin the largest manufacturing investment in Botswana, with the exception of the Botswana Meat Commission (BMC) which converts cattle into deboned chilled beef (and by-products) for export. Brau Finanz was chosen, and at the same time BDC reached an agreement with a firm of consultants called Brewery Executive Services (BES) who would provide advice and would have 5 per cent of the equity. The Oetker group is the third largest manufacturer of beer in Germany. Germans drink more beer per head than the people of any other country in Europe (151 litres/265·7 pts a year for every man, woman and child, in 1976, compared with 135 litres/233 pts for every Belgian, the next highest)[5] and there are a lot of Germans (more than 60 million, or about 85 times as many Germans as Batswana). In fact, the Oetker group sold at that time about 8·5 million hl a year, which made the proposed Botswana brewery about 0·35 per cent of the group's total production. The question that remains is why the Oetker group should have been interested in building and operating a 30 000 hl brewery in a remote corner of Africa.

At the time the Oetker group was definitely interested in foreign expansion: a brewery had already been built in Libya and breweries were being planned for Alaska, Nigeria and Zaïre. Furthermore, the head of Brau Finanz, who took a personal interest in the Botswana project and came to Botswana several times, had himself been promoted to chief executive as a result of making a success of a brewery in Italy. There may, therefore, have been a personal commitment to try and repeat that success, and Botswana could have been a very small and to some extent experimental component in a broad policy of expansion in Africa. It is also true that all of Botswana's neighbouring countries already had well established breweries, so that the Oetker group may well have responded to BDC's approach because it was a way of getting itself established in this region of Africa, without having to compete initially with other breweries. This supposition is supported by the fact that Brau Finanz personnel visited several South African 'homelands' to investigate the possibility of setting up more breweries.

The second possibility is that Brau Finanz expected to make sufficient profit on the sale of machinery to recover its own investment plus a profit, even if the project failed to brew beer successfully. There are two reasons for rejecting this theory in this case. First, the cost of machinery was about twice the equity investment put into the brewery by Brau Finanz; so in order to make money out of the project simply through machinery sales, Brau Finanz would have had to make a profit of more than 50 per cent on the value of machinery supplied to the factory. Such a degree of overpricing would have been difficult to impose undetected by BDC, even if the machinery had been manufactured and supplied by Brau Finanz itself. In the event, Brau Finanz ordered machinery and equipment from a wide variety of suppliers, mostly German, including a German company in Spain and one South African company. BDC did not know whether Brau Finanz or associated companies were shareholders in these suppliers, or whether Brau Finanz received sales commissions or kickbacks from them. But it seems inherently unlikely that such hidden revenue could have amounted to more than 50 per cent of the stated price.

There was a great deal of trouble with some of the machinery, particularly that bought from the German company based in Spain. It seems that this equipment was of relatively poor quality. The problem may have been caused by BDC's insistence on 'limited cost over-runs', that is, a cash limit on the cost of the factory. BDC's concern was to avoid choosing an apparently low-cost bid to build and supply the factory, only to be faced later with higher costs when it would be too late to change partners. The big increase in inflation that occurred throughout the world in 1973 and 1974 rapidly made these cash limits out of date, and may have encouraged Brau Finanz to buy cheaper equipment than they would otherwise have chosen. However, Brau Finanz accepted the original limits and never asked for them to be changed, although free to do so. Equipment from the Spanish-based supplier in question had been used successfully in Europe, but conditions in Africa proved to be damagingly different – in the quality of installation, use and maintenance. There is no simple solution to this dilemma of wanting to prevent both cost escalation and equipment problems as a result of penny-pinching; but it does seem on this evidence that the Botswana brewery was not a victim of a machinery merchant with no interest in successful production.

The position of Brewery Executive Services also requires explanation. With only 5 per cent of the equity it was clearly possible for BES to make a profit out of commission on equipment sales. Through the BES director on the brewery board, BES did in fact recommend some purchases, and not all of the BES-recommended equipment performed satisfactorily. Again with hindsight, the policy of bringing in a consultancy firm was unlikely to be successful. BDC would have found it difficult to take the consultant's advice if it had differed from that of the main technical partner, Brau Finanz. The success of the whole project depended utterly on being able to trust Brau Finanz and good relations were essential. Furthermore, BES was inherently more likely to want to keep in with Brau Finanz than with BDC, since BDC would not be building any more breweries – Brau Finanz almost certainly would. On one crucial point, BES expressed confidence initially in the Spanish-built equipment.

In any case, when the brewery ran into financial difficulties a year after production started, Brau Finanz was prepared to put more of its own money into the project, in order to keep the brewery going until the hoped-for moment when it would become profitable. Brau Finanz would presumably not have been willing to put up more of its own money if its primary objective had been to make a quick profit out of machinery sales. It must, on this evidence, have been committed to making a success of production, although it may also have made something on equipment sales, and probably did.

The most likely explanations, therefore, are the personal commitment of the Brau Finanz chief executive to foreign expansion in general, and the opportunity of establishing a protected brewery in Southern Africa, with the long-term objective of marketing the company's beer more widely, once the name and quality had been established with the help of a protective tariff. Certainly the South African beer market might have seemed big enough to attract even a large brewing firm; while the Swaziland experience referred to already showed the extreme difficulty of competing with the established breweries, without some form of protection.

A further point is that everyone concerned with planning the project seems to have assumed without question that a protected brewery would be extremely profitable; indeed, BDC insisted on a majority shareholding from the beginning in order to have a majority share of the expected profits. So the foreign partner was apparently in the position of being able to establish itself in Botswana for a quite small sum of money, with the prospect of handsome profits on the investment, and the attractive additional possibility of making inroads into the very much larger South African market. From Botswana's point of view it did not really matter whether Brau Finanz had a realistic prospect of competing in South Africa, since Botswana would definitely get what was expected to be a highly profitable brewery, with the resulting creation of employment, tax revenues and share of profit for BDC. Exports to South Africa would be a bonus.

BDC announced the new project in a press release dated 14 February 1974, referring to the new brand name Prinz Brau, 'a brand which is already popular in some other African countries and in Europe'. The release also referred to a lengthy period of planning and negotiation: 'The best offer was eventually made by Brau Finanz, a company based in West Germany . . . Their offer also has the advantage of diversifying Botswana's economic links, in line with Government policy.' This was not strictly true, since the Brau Finanz offer could only be described as the best offer if diversification of economic links was included in the calculation, rather than described as an additional benefit, especially if loss of consumer choice and increased costs of imported beer (and soft drinks since the factory was to include a soft drink bottling plant) were to be included in the calculation. However, the decision having been taken, it was perhaps reasonable to present it in the best light.

Operational failure

The brewery was ready to start production in the first half of 1976. A four year *exclusive* licence had already been granted, that is, the government promised not to allow anyone else to set up a brewery for four years, and there was a promise to extend this if necessary for a further four years. Eight years is the maximum period allowed for the protection of a new industry under the Southern African Customs Union Agreement. Meanwhile the brewery was pressed by the government for its plans to supply the whole of Botswana, since the government was reluctant to force people to pay extra for imported beer if they could not get supplies of locally produced beer.[6]

Token sales began in June 1976, even though protection had not then been established; the new 50 per cent tariff on imported beer was eventually gazetted on 27 August. The first brews were excellent; but already in the early months of production the brewery management seemed to have difficulty with producing timely and accurate information about how things were going, so that although losses were expected at first, it was difficult to find out how big they were. In addition, there were problems in getting beer distributed all over Botswana – admittedly an appalling task because of huge distances and bad roads. Meanwhile the canning line broke down in September, was out of action for six months, and never thereafter worked satisfactorily. Thus Prinz Brau was forced to supply the whole market with bottled beer, although originally the plan had been to supply roughly half the market with canned beer. (Before the brewery was established, nearly all beer in Botswana was supplied in cans; the decision to use bottles was based partly on costings, but was also influenced by public health and environmental arguments, that is, the tendency for Botswana's towns and villages to become littered with used beer and soft drink cans.)

Production began to go badly wrong early in 1977. Simultaneously, the brewery produced a foul tasting brew; and the bottle washing plant proved unable to clean returned bottles that had been standing in the sun in remote parts of Botswana, and used in all sorts of unlikely ways before finding their way back to the brewery.[7] As a result, the very respectable market share won by the brewery by the end of 1976, thought to be of the order of 70 per cent, fell disastrously to 20 per cent, as bad beer in dirty bottles flooded the market. For a great many beer-drinkers, this new development confirmed their worst fears. Having been more or less forced to give up drinking their long-established favourite brands, or pay substantially more for them, the alternative now proved undrinkable. Although Prinz Brau did later brew drinkable beer, the brand name never recovered from this disaster.

Throughout 1977 Prinz Brau made strenuous efforts to retrieve the situation. An approach was made to BDC and the Botswana government for more money; BDC refused until Brau Finanz could show at least a 50 per cent market share; so Brau Finanz put in some more of its own money. In the second half of the year, the brewery introduced a new product, Prinz Lager, in non-returnable bottles, as much like a rival (imported) product as could be devised. The new brand met with some success, but by then it was really too late. Lack of finance, as a result of past accumulated losses, was hindering the marketing effort, and the overall shortage of experienced managers throughout the period since the project started had produced a near-chaotic situation in the brewery's accounts, stock control, in fact, in every area of activity. Finally, towards the end of 1977 the brewery came to BDC for more money again, this time for a much larger sum. BDC refused, having by this time lost all confidence in the ability of Brau Finanz to make a success of the brewery. Any further injection of capital would have to come from Brau Finanz.

Takeover

At this point the company obtained government permission to approach SAB, to see if SAB would be willing to take over the whole operation. Agreement was reached quite quickly, and SAB bought the Brau Finanz share in the brewery in March 1978. (Strictly speaking, SAB, through a foreign subsidiary, bought a 75 per cent stake in the company which bought the 40 per cent of the brewery originally held by Brau Finanz and BES.)

The price paid by SAB to Brau Finanz and BES for its shares is not known, as these were private deals between the three companies. With SAB as its new partner, BDC agreed to put in another P360 000 in payment for shares which had not at that time been paid. In addition, BDC and SAB have together guaranteed additional bank loans. Without knowing how much Brau Finanz and BES got for their shares it is difficult to comment on their position. But it would seem they were lucky to get anything considering that the brewery company had accumulated P1·8 million of losses against original paid-up share capital of P0·9 million.

Presumably, SAB was happy enough to prevent any potential rival from getting in first, in particular its South African rival Intercontinental Breweries with whom it was (and still is at the time of writing) engaged in a major marketing war. SAB can hardly have felt threatened by Prinz Brau at that stage, since Prinz Brau had thoroughly ruined the reputation of its own brand name, and thus spoilt any chance it may have had of penetrating the South African market.

Conclusion

Botswana thus ended up with the partner it had originally chosen to avoid, *with* protection against other products; whereas originally SAB was willing to set up a brewery without protection. On the other hand, having chosen a partner who, as it happened, made a thorough mess of what should have been a profitable opportunity, BDC got out of the whole mess relatively lightly. BDC's main loss was the postponement of profits on its original investment for some four years, plus the need to put up additional capital; although it is likely that some of this money would have had to be invested anyway. The project also absorbed a disproportionate amount of senior management time and energy.

Botswana did rather less well. For a period consumers had a choice between a cheaper beer that they did not want, and which was at times undrinkable, and more expensive imported beers. Not surprisingly, those who could afford it chose to drink imported beer in spite of higher prices. Meanwhile, the 50 per cent tax paid on imported beer was paid into the customs pool and only (approximately) 20 per cent will be recovered by the government under the Customs Union revenue formula.[8] On the other hand, BDC, and the government which is the owner of BDC, were saved from having to scrap the whole investment by the willingness of SAB to buy out Brau Finanz and manage the brewery. It is now running profitably and in due course the losses should be paid off and dividends paid.

The question that remains to be asked is whether any general lessons can be learnt from the failure of the partnership with Brau Finanz. In order to answer the question, it is really necessary to know what caused the failure, and that is extremely difficult. Brau Finanz seemed to have been fundamentally wrong on one crucial point, namely the amount of management that would be required, on the spot, to get the brewery going successfully. At the beginning the brewery employed five expatriate staff (two from Germany) for the whole operation – production, finance, accounting, sales, distribution, marketing, stock control, etc. This was not enough. By late 1977, when the company was trying desperately to recover from earlier mistakes, there were fourteen; but by then it was too late. Underlying this underestimation of the number of high-level staff needed was probably a serious ignorance of the tremendous shortages of skilled labour in Botswana and of the amount of training and experience that would be needed to weld the relatively unskilled labour into a productive work-force.

BDC had advised from the first that a much larger number of expatriate staff would be needed; the number suggested was 10 or 12, and even this may have been an underestimate. But Brau Finanz refused to accept that a tiny 30 000hl a year brewery (actually this proved an underestimate of the market and the brewery was in the process of having its capacity doubled at the time production was starting) could possibly need more than five experienced senior staff. Indeed the first senior executive was a management trainee, quickly withdrawn after BDC protests. The problem was compounded by the refusal of his successor to ask for help from Germany for a long time after it had become necessary. The inadequacy of the high-level management input became clear *before* the crisis of bad beer in dirty bottles; BDC was already protesting in the strongest possible terms in December 1976.

Although the Oetker Group was investing elsewhere in Africa at the time, it had not yet successfully established a brewery in Africa; and in fact the breweries in Libya and Zaire failed as well. Setting up breweries in Germany and Italy is inevitably a very different proposition from setting up breweries in Africa. The Oetker management probably had no idea of how much more difficult it is to set up a new operation in a country where the labour force, through no fault of its own, has a much lower level of education and industrial experience than the workforce in Europe. The problems are especially acute in Botswana because of neglect during the pre-independence period, and because of the lack of industry.

In addition, Botswana is short of supporting services and the roads are bad, thus increasing the problems of distribution. In addition the brewery was faced with a number of demands from the various government departments which seem, in combination, to constitute a formidable barrier to productive investment; but with the government-owned BDC as a partner, these problems were not nearly as serious as they are for smaller private businesses. Indeed the government went out of its way to help the brewery on numerous occasions, for example when a majority of bottles were found to contain short measure. There were other minor problems: of the expatriate staff, three out of five did not speak English as their first language; the brewery should have started selling earlier during the cold season when the demand for beer is lower and it would have been easier to supply the market and build production up gradually towards peak summer demand.

These latter problems would probably not have been crucial on their own in causing the brewery to fail. It is doubtful whether so few managers could have coped successfully with an *ongoing* operation, even with technical and other support near at hand; the fundamental error was in believing that such a small number of skilled men with previous experience of managing a brewery operation could really have got it going successfully, so far from the parent company. By the time the error became apparent, the damage had been done.

Unfortunately it is not enough to say that technical partners should be sought from companies with previous experience of investing in Africa and with large-scale operations sufficiently close to enable mistakes to be corrected quickly. That may be a necessary condition. But it is not sufficient, in all cases: Anglo American and AMAX, two of the world's really large and experienced mining groups, managed to make an expensive technical error in developing Botswana's copper–nickel mine at Selebi-Phikwe, leading to huge losses and a horrendous accumulation of debt. Nevertheless, an experienced and conveniently placed technical partner must surely reduce the risk of failure. This is a rather depressing conclusion if Botswana is to succeed in diversifying away from South Africa as a source of technology and investment, since there is no other likely source which is so convenient. The ability to have a technician or a senior executive on the spot at half a day's notice is, if not vital in all cases, very valuable. However, there *are* companies from other countries, including some African ones such as Kenya, with plenty of successful African experience; so Botswana should no doubt continue the strategy of diversification whenever the risk seems reasonable, and with care to avoid partners whose objectives are likely to be irreconcilable with those of Botswana.

Notes

1. Kilby, P., *Industrialisation in an Open Economy: Nigeria 1945–66*, Cambridge, Cambridge University Press (1969), Chapter 3, especially Table 16, p. 54.
2. ibid., pp. 77, 78.
3. An attempt to provide a brief overview is in Chapter 7 of my textbook *Macroeconomics for Africa*, London, Heinemann Educational Books (1978).
4. For a more detailed description of the financing of the copper–nickel mine, see Chapter 7 by S. R. Lewis, Jr in this book, pp. 104–14.
5. *Financial Times* (22 February 1979), p. 15.
6. It is widely believed in Botswana that the Customs Union Agreement forbids protection, unless a certain percentage of the market can be supplied by the protected industry. This is not so, the decision rests with the Botswana government; see also Chapter 9.
7. Interestingly, a high proportion of bottles from the early production were never returned. Botswana appeared to have a large unsatisfied demand for bottles.
8. See Hudson, op. cit., pp. 154–5.

Charles Harvey is Fellow, Institute of Development Studies, Sussex and visiting lecturer at Williams College, USA; formerly Assistant Director of Research, Bank of Botswana and part-time lecturer in Economics, University of Botswana and Swaziland.

14 Railways, Immigrants, Mining and Cattle: Problems of Measurement in Botswana's National Income Accounts[1]

RAY WEEDON and ODD YSTGAARD

Introduction

An understanding of Botswana's national income and balance of payments statistics is made difficult by some rather unusual features of the Botswana economy. These features are connected with the need to impute certain flows in order that the accounts reflect better the economic reality of the production, income-generating and expenditure processes. Such imputations and adjustments are carried out in all countries when compiling their national accounts. But the difference in Botswana's case is the relative scale of the imputations, combined with the importance to Botswana of the sectors involved.

Thus Botswana's only railway is at present owned and run by Rhodesia Railways as an integral part of a foreign railway system. Consequently much of the contribution of the Botswana section of the railway to Botswana's total production of goods and services has to be imputed. What is more, the Botswana section of the railway runs at a loss, so that the financing of the operating loss has also to be imputed, even though the capital flow is a purely notional one.

Migrant workers also play a major role in Botswana. Large numbers of Batswana work abroad. Although precise statistics are available only for certain mineworkers, it is thought that there are almost as many Batswana with jobs abroad as there are with formal sector jobs in the private sector inside Botswana. Botswana also remains very dependent on foreign skilled labour, so that the treatment of such matters as expatriate remittances and technical assistance payments are unusually important.

Botswana's membership of the Southern African Customs Union creates an unusual statistical problem. Whereas in most countries the amount of tax paid on imports is known and certain, in Botswana it must be estimated; and in most recent years some of that estimated tax has been notionally 'lent' to South Africa, because of the way that the revenue formula works to delay its transfer to the Botswana government (see Chapter 9, pp. 131–58).

Botswana's agricultural production is dominated by the cattle industry. Whereas in most types of commercial agriculture the calculation of production is relatively easy, in the cattle sector production, and therefore income, accrues in the form of cattle growing heavier, and cattle having calves, even if no sales for cash take place at all. Putting a value on this part of production is much more difficult than estimating production of an annual cash crop.

BCL, the copper–nickel mine at Selebi-Phikwe, produces about one third of Botswana's exports. Because of prolonged problems with the smelter, BCL was late in reaching full production and has, as a result, enormous debts. The payment of interest on those debts has resulted in huge losses at BCL, losses which have had to be financed by the company's main foreign shareholders. As a result, large payments in and out of Botswana must be shown in the accounts even though no actual payments are made; and BCL's losses affect national income even though variations in those losses have almost no current impact on Botswana.

Botswana is not, of course, the only country with migrant workers, a cattle industry and some loss-making foreign investors. However, the size of the numbers involved make it important for any student of Botswana's economy to understand how these matters are treated in the statistics.

A basic national income accounts model

In order to deal with the various problems outlined above, it will be helpful to review briefly the different ways of estimating what a country has produced while developing a model which will show the relationship between the flows arising from the productive, income-generating and expenditure processes. In order to facilitate the presentation abbreviations will be used wherever possible and a key to these abbreviations is set out in Appendix 14.A. Also all figures throughout the text will represent P million unless otherwise specified.

Supply and disposition

Basic to the economic process is, first, the 'supply' of goods and services and secondly the 'disposition' of these same goods and services, that is, the manner in which they are used. As regards the supply of goods and services there are only two sources available to a country: namely,

1 domestic production or GDM at market prices (GDP million): and
2 imports from abroad (M).

On the other hand, the way in which this supply is disposed of, is normally divided into four categories; namely that which is:

1 consumed by private households (C_p);
2 consumed by government (C_g);
3 invested (I); and
4 exported (X).

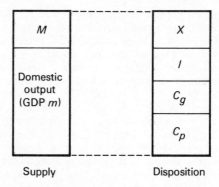

Figure 14.1 *Supply and disposition of goods and services*

It is important from a national accounting point of view to note that Supply always equals Disposition as shown in Figure 14.1. This is because for accounting purposes, any goods not disposed of in the ordinary every-day sense of the word, for example, by an involuntary build-up of stocks by producers and suppliers, are, by definition, considered as invested, that is, put aside for future use.

The circular flow model

The equality of Supply and Disposition leads on to a vital aspect of the national income accounting model: the circular flow nature of the processes being measured. On the one hand producers sell output and purchase factor services; on the other hand the owners of factors of production receive income and spend it on available supply. The model is shown in Figure 14.2. At the top of the diagram is the production account which reflects the income-generating processes of the domestic production sector. The production sector is shown as paying out incomes to the factors of production, and as receiving payments for final goods and services from the recipients of income. The latter are embodied in the sectoral or institutional accounts at the bottom of the diagram. Four of the institutional accounts reflect the activities of domestic institutions (namely, households, government, private enterprises and capital finance), while the fifth depicts the activities of the rest of the world which as far as the circular flow is concerned receives payment for imports and purchases exports.

This is the simplified framework of the accounts. Additional complications will be brought in as the various components of the circular flow are analysed in more detail below.

The production account

In analysing the basic framework presented above, the figures for Botswana's set of national accounts 1976–7 will be used. However, the structure of the economy will be simplified to show only three industries within the productive sector; agriculture, mining and other. This reflects the dominant position of agriculture and mining in the Botswana economy. 'Other' includes government, Rhodesia Railways and BMC (which according to conventional definition is

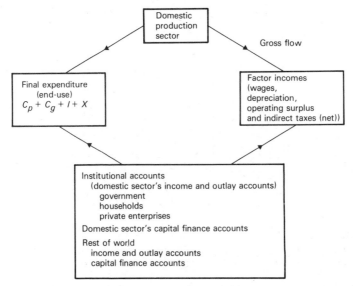

Figure 14.2 *Simplified circular flow model*

included in manufacturing rather than agriculture), plus the relatively unimportant sectors such as manufacturing (excluding BMC) and services.

In producing the Gross Domestic Product (GDP)[2] of a country, the various industrial sectors of an economy:

1   purchase inputs (called intermediate consumption):

    a   from each other;
    b   from abroad (in which case the inputs are part of imports);

2   pay out incomes to the factors of production which are required to transform inputs into outputs. These incomes are broadly categorized into:

    a W – wages and salaries (payment to labour);
    b D – depreciation (a charge to capital for, as it were, 'wearing itself out' during the productive process) – depreciation is included because output is calculated 'gross', hence the 'gross' in GDP;
    c O – operating surplus (which includes payments to capital and land).

3   pay to government indirect taxes (T) less subsidies (U) which they have collected when selling output (or when buying inputs – for example tariffs on imports); and finally

4   dispose of their output (which can include adding to their stocks or work-in-progress) in two forms:

    a   as intermediate consumption by other industries;
    b   as final expenditure by:
        i   households

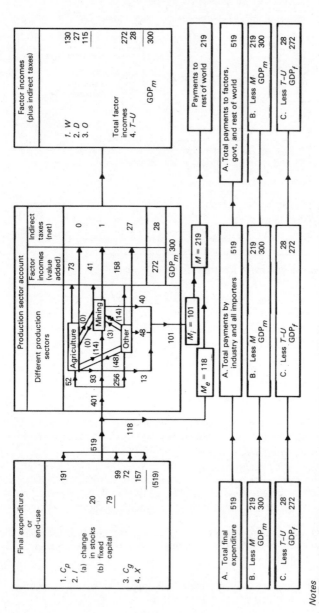

Notes

1. This model reflects the structure and monetary flows of the Botswana economy in 1976–7.
2. Arrows show direction of monetary flows.
3. Figures in brackets represent intermediate consumption (INT).

Source

Botswana National Accounts 1976–7.

Figure 14.3　*National accounts model production sector*

    ii   government
    iii   investors
    iv   rest of the world

The relationship between the various payments and receipts listed in the above paragraph is such that

    factor payments (2) = sale of output (4)
                   minus payment of indirect taxes (3)
                   minus purchase of inputs   (1)

These factor payments or factor incomes are also given the technical name of 'value added at factor cost'. This term conveys the idea that factors of production are required to transform inputs into outputs and that the added value (adjusted for indirect taxes) is equivalent to the incomes paid to these factors.

    Figure 14.3 shows, amongst other things, this process for the Botswana economy in 1976–7. The middle box of this figure shows diagrammatically the payments and receipts of the production account. For example, all the income flows shown entering and leaving the agricultural industry can be organized into a table, such as Table 14.1.

Table 14.1   *Production account for agriculture (P million)*

Inputs			Outputs		
1. Intermediate consumption			4. Sale of output		
(a) inputs from other			(a) as final expenditure		52
domestic industries	14		(b) as inputs to other		
(b) imports	13	27	domestic industries		48
2. Indirect taxes (net)		0			
3. Factor incomes					
$(W+D+O)$		73			
TOTAL		100	TOTAL		100

Notes

Value added at factor cost in agricultural sector

                = Sale of output (item 4) − intermediate
                   consumption (item 1) − indirect taxes
                   (item 2)
                = 100 − 27 − 0   =   73
                = Factor incomes paid out (item 3)

Source

Botswana National Accounts 1976–7.

    When the production accounts of all the productive sectors shown in Figure 14.3 are combined, an aggregate production account is obtained. The elements of such an account are of less direct relevance in describing the problems which are the main subject matter of this paper. However, for the sake of completeness, they are set out in Appendix 14.B.

Final expenditure or end-use

The box entitled 'Final expenditure or end-use' in Figure 14.3 shows how the total supply of goods and services available to the economy (imports, plus the sum of value added by domestic factors, plus indirect taxes) is used, that is whether it is:

1 consumed by households (C_p);
2 consumed by government (C_g);
3 invested (I); or
4 exported (X).

If imports are subtracted from $C_p + I + C_g + X$ we arrive at a market price valuation of Gross Domestic Product (GDP$_m$). This includes indirect taxes (net $- T - U$), since these are naturally included in the market price.

The item 'Change in stocks' which is listed under Investment (I) in the 'Final expenditure' box needs to be highlighted because of its relevance to the increase in Botswana's cattle herd, a topic to be discussed below, (pp. 242–5). Paradoxically, it represents the value of unfinished and finished goods which have *not* been sold as final expenditure and yet appear as part of final investment expenditure. The explanation for this seeming contradiction is that, although firms do not technically sell their stocks or work-in-progress, they still have to find the funds necessary to pay for the inputs and, in addition, reimburse the factors which have been responsible for transforming these inputs into partly or completely finished output. An increase in stocks is part of *investment*, because it is part of production which is not consumed, but available for consumption, etc., in the future.

It should be noted that a part of total final expenditure, that is, total supply of goods and services, does not originate in the domestic productive sector but is imported (M_e) directly from the rest of the world. Consequently the total value of output produced domestically for end-use (401 from Figure 14.3) is less than total end-use value (519) by the value of these direct imports ($M_e = 118$).

Factor incomes

The box headed 'Factor incomes' in Figure 14.3 shows the aggregate breakdown of factor incomes (value added) into: wages and salaries (W), depreciation (D) and operating surplus (O). By convention it also includes indirect taxes (net $-$ $T - U$) which although not income in the sense of factor incomes (and hence value added) are nevertheless a form of income paid to government. Consequently the total of this column also sums to GDP$_m$.

It may surprise the reader that the items listed under factor incomes in the above paragraph do not include profits, interest and rent. The latter, however, are all incorporated in the item, 'operating surplus'. Consequently, as will be seen below when dealing with BCL losses, a firm's operating surplus can be positive even though its profits are negative.

Institutional accounts

Finally, to complete the analysis of the circular flow diagram presented above an outline of the institutional (or sectoral) accounts must be given. These accounts play a similar role in the formal national accounts framework to that played by the sector owning the factors of production in the simple macro-economics circular flow model. In other words the institutional accounts are receivers of

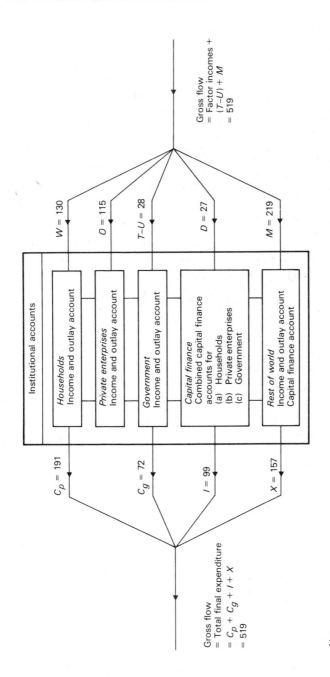

Note
All figures derived from Figure 14.3.

Figure 14.4 *Institutional accounts and the gross circular flow (1976–7)*

income (in this case the gross flow of 519 referred to above) and purchasers of the total available supply of goods and services (also equal to 519).

It has been found useful to divide the institutional accounts into five institutional sectors. These reflect broadly:

1   the lines along which factors of production are owned and controlled, as well as,

2   which sectors are responsible for the particular end-use to which the total supply of goods and services will be put.

Figure 14.4 shows the divisions in question and how each institution is both a receiver of income and an agent of final expenditure.

It is not intended to describe the workings of these accounts in detail. Suffice it to note that:

1   two types of account are incorporated into the sectoral accounts, namely,

   a   a current (or income and outlay account); and
   b   a capital finance account.

   This reflects the economic importance of distinguishing between the consumption and investment of the supply of goods and services. As will be seen from Figure 14.4, three of the domestic sectoral accounts reflect only their current activities while the fourth account is an aggregate of their capital transactions.

2   transfer flows as well as borrowing and lending do of course take place between the various accounts. This accounts for the fact that the flows into the individual accounts from the right do not match the flows out of the same accounts on the left.

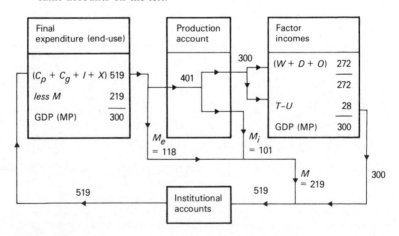

Notes
All figures derived from Figures 14.3 and 14.4.
MP = at market prices.

Figure 14.5   *Completed model*

The rest of the world account and the balance of payments
Since it incorporates both current and capital transactions with the domestic economy, the rest of the world account, in the sectoral accounts, is, in fact, equivalent to the domestic balance of payments account with the one difference that what is a debit to the rest of the world, for example, the purchase of domestic exports, is a credit to the domestic balance of payments.

Completed model
Having analysed and shown the relationships existing between various components of the national accounts which will aid the exposition to be undertaken in the next section, a completed model of the circular flow diagram shown in Figure 14.2 is set out in Figure 14.5.

Finally, some important identities associated with the national accounts are included in Appendix 14.C.

Customs revenue

As a member of the Southern African Customs Union (SACU), Botswana receives a certain share of the common revenue pool. The overall formula for this (see Chapter 9 by Hudson pp. 131–58 is:

$$R_t = (BM_{t-2} \times \frac{TR_{t-2}}{CM_{t-2}} \times 1.42) + (\Sigma A_{t-m})$$

$$= \text{part A} \qquad\qquad + \text{part B}$$

where R_t = Botswana's customs revenue in year t

BM_{t-2} = Botswana's imports and production of dutiable goods in year $t-2$

CM_{t-2} = Imports into and production of dutiable goods in the whole customs union in year $t-2$

TR_{t-2} = total import, excise and sales duty collected in the customs union in year $t-2$

ΣA_{t-m} = sum of all the adjustments made in respect of the revenue which should have been received in previous years

1.42 = a multiplier meant to compensate the BLS countries for certain disadvantages arising from being in a customs union with a larger and very much more developed partner.

In other words the customs revenue to Botswana in 1976–7, for example, was composed of two parts:

1   revenue as calculated from part A of the formula using imports and dutiable goods (hereafter simply referred to as imports) for 1974–5.
2   adjustments to the revenue received in previous years (part B of the formula). For example revenue in 1975–6 as calculated using part A of the formula was based on actual imports and customs revenue in 1973–4. By 1976–7 estimates of the actual imports etc for 1975–6 were available and this necessitated an adjustment for what the actual revenue should have been.

Taking 1976–7 as an example, the total revenue from the pool was 24 of which 20 derived from part A of the formula using figures for 1974–5 and 4 from part B of the formula, namely, adjustments to previous years' revenue. The total expenditure on imports during 1976–7 was 247 (the reason why 219 is the amount shown in Figure 14.3 will become clear from what is said below). A straightforward representation of the resulting flows in terms of the model developed earlier is shown in Figure 14.6(a).[3] This shows that Botswana paid 247 to the rest of the world for its imports including duty. The rest of the world in turn paid 24 back to the Botswana government from the customs pool.

The first complication to this simple picture is the fact that for national income purposes the accounts should, according to the UN System of National Accounts (SNA),[4] be drawn up on an accrued basis in the case of taxes. In other words the accounts must reflect what Botswana was really owed from the customs pool in 1976–7 on the basis of import figures for 1976–7 and not 1974–5. This, of course, will conflict with the actual flows as depicted in Figure 14.6(a) and therefore compensating adjustments must be made in the manner described below and shown in Figure 14.6(b).

Secondly, the accrued revenue from the pool is notionally split into 2 parts: one part which is considered as reflecting the duty content of imports and dutiable goods; and the other part considered as a transfer from South Africa to compensate Botswana for the various disadvantages of being in a customs union with a more developed country. The latter element is estimated as the 0·42 factor included in the 1·42 multiplier of the formula (see above). In other words,

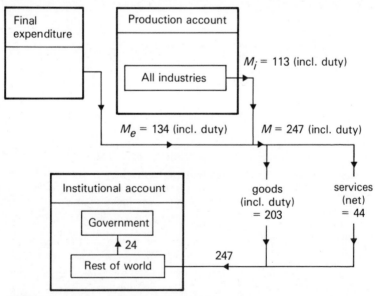

Source
Botswana National Accounts 1976–7.

Figure 14.6(a)   *Customs revenue and imports: actual flows (1976–7)*
(P million)

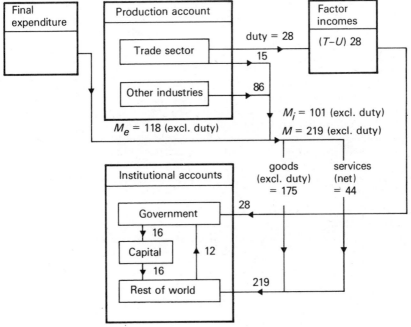

Note
The duty $(T-U)$ of 28 is calculated by multiplying the *accrued* revenue for 1976–7, 40, by $1/1 \cdot 42$. The remainder of this accrued revenue, namely, 12 (= $0 \cdot 42/1 \cdot 42 \times 40$) is considered as a transfer payment from rest of world to government.

Source
Botswana National Accounts 1976–7.

Figure 14.6 (b)   *Customs revenue and imports: notional flows (1976–7) (P million)*

only this 0·42 element is considered as being a transfer from South Africa. The remaining part of the accrued revenue, that is, the estimated duty content of Botswana's imports is subtracted from the actual value of imports (which, as mentioned above, come into Botswana inclusive of duty). In other words the value of imports entering Botswana is regarded for national accounts purposes as being free of all tax. The fact that Botswana's imports are now cheaper by the amount of the duty is compensated for by the elimination of the equivalent transfer payment from South Africa to the Botswana government.

The third and final complication is that the Botswana trade sector (under the production account) is regarded as having to reimburse government for the total accrued duty content of all imported goods in the form of indirect taxes even though all imports do not pass through the trade sector. This sector in turn is regarded as recovering the value of this duty in its sales to final end use and intermediate consumption.

Accrued revenue on the basis of imports for 1976–7 was calculated at 40 of which 28, that is, $(1/1\cdot42) \times 40$, was considered as the duty content of imports and 12, that is, $(0\cdot42/1\cdot42) \times 40$, as a transfer from South Africa. Consequently, taking into account all the adjustments described above, the imputed flows appear in the national accounts as shown in Figure 14.6(b). Since accrued revenue equals 40, as opposed to actual revenue of 24, in the final analysis it is considered that Botswana lent SA the 16 necessary to make accrued flows equivalent to actual flows. It could, of course, turn out that accrued flows are less than actual flows in which case SA would be considered to be lending Botswana the difference. It is easily shown that in terms of the net receipts and payments of each account, Figure 14.6(a) is equivalent to Figure 14.6(b).

Finally to complete this section it is instructive to show in Table 14.2 the effects on the balance of payments of the adjustments described above. It will be seen that although the balances of certain accounts are changed the overall net balance is unaltered.

Table 14.2 *Customs revenue imports and the balance of payments (P million)*

	Actual flows		Imputed flows	
	debit	credit	debit	credit
Goods and services				
(i) import of goods	203	—	175	—
(ii) Import of services	44	—	44	—
Unilateral transfers				
from SA to Botswana	—	24	—	12
Long term capital				
net loan from Botswana to SA	—	—	16	—
NET BALANCE	223		223	

Source
Botswana National Accounts 1976–7.

Rhodesia Railways (RR)

RR owns and operates the 672 km (418 mi) railway line running along the eastern part of the country between South Africa and Rhodesia. In addition it also operates the government owned spurs linking Selebi-Phikwe and the Morupule coal mine with the main line.

From a national income accounts point of view, it is desirable that an estimate be made of the total output produced by the railways within Botswana including all the inputs necessary to produce this output. The computations are made difficult for two reasons. First on the output side, no revenue is received by the RR in Botswana for through-traffic between South Africa and Rhodesia even though, economically speaking, the Botswana portion contributes to the production of such (exported) output. However, from the figures which RR supply to the Botswana government it is relatively easy to calculate this revenue.

Secondly, RR in Botswana incurs few of the input expenditures which are necessary for its operations. These include:

1 imports of:
   a goods,
   b services such as maintenance of locos, administrative overheads, freight handling, etc.,
2 interest on the finance associated with the assets used on the Botswana branch,
3 depreciation on these assets.

Unfortunately these costs are more difficult to estimate than those for through-traffic, since RR's annual accounts do not apportion costs to the Botswana branch. The solution adopted has been to apportion these costs to the Botswana line according to the ratio which total revenue earned on the Botswana section (including revenue on through traffic) bears to total RR revenue. In other words as the relative use of the Botswana branch increases (and hence revenue increases), so do the costs allocated to the Botswana branch.[5] This might give a correct picture for the variable portion of the costs

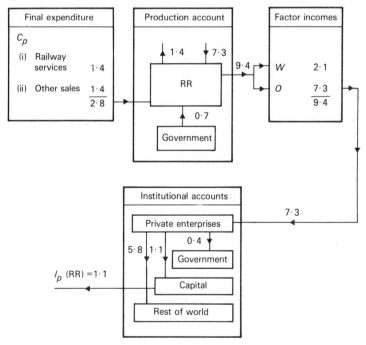

Source
Botswana National Accounts 1976–7.

Figure 14.7 (a)   *Rhodesia Railways operations in Botswana: actual flows (1976–7)*

but is unlikely to give a realistic estimate of overhead and other fixed costs. However, it is not easy to overcome this problem given available statistics.

Before translating the above into figures it is interesting to note one minor complication in the RR production account. This is connected with the fact that the Botswana government owns two spurs as mentioned above. RR is paid a fee for maintaining these spurs. This fee, plus an amount to cover the capital cost of the line is recovered by the Botswana government by means of a surcharge levied on the spur-line traffic. In other words, government purchases an input from RR and in turn sells part of its output as intermediate consumption to the users of the line.

Figure 14.7(a) shows diagrammatically the flows as they appeared in 1976–7 based on *actual* receipts and expenditure of RR in Botswana. It will be seen from this diagram that the apparent operating surplus of RR in Botswana equalled 7·3. After meeting the cost of way-leave payments to government and capital expenditures on the facilities in Botswana, 5·8 remained to be transferred back to RR headquarters in Rhodesia, creating a debit of this amount on the balance of payments.

However, when all the adjustments referred to above are made Figure 14.7(a) changes into Figure 14.7(b). It can be shown that every account is left in

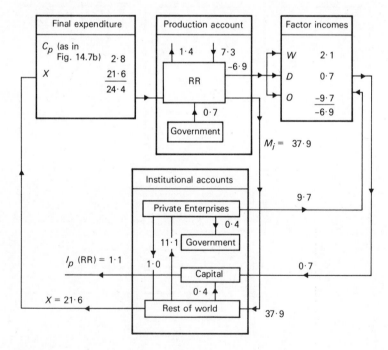

Source
Botswana National Accounts 1976–7.

Figure 14.7(b)   *Rhodesia Railways in Botswana: imputed flows (1976–7)*

Table 14.3   *Rhodesia Railways and the balance of payments (P million)*

	Actual flows		Imputed flows	
	Debit	Credit	Debit	Credit
Goods and services				
(i) goods (imported)	—	—	2·0	—
(ii) services				
– imported	—	—	35·9	—
– exported	—	—	—	21·6
– profits/dividends/interest	5·8	—	1·0	—
Unilateral transfers				
Transfer to cover operating deficit, way-leave payment and interest	—	—	—	11·1
Long term capital				
Loan for capital construction	—	—	—	0·4
NET BALANCE	5·8		5·8	

Source
Botswana National Accounts 1976–7.

precisely the same net state in both figures. For example, the rest of the world account is again in net receipt of 5·8 in Figure 14.7(b). Likewise, receipts and expenditures balance each other in the Production Account but in a rather more complex way. The new notional flows namely, 37·9 for imports (expenditure), 0·7 for depreciation (expenditure), 21·6 from exports (revenue), that is a net expenditure of 17, result in the operating surplus changing from +7·3 to −9·7. This necessitates a compensating payment through the private enterprises account of 6·9 in order that the revenue and expenditure of the production account should balance.

Finally to round off this section it is shown in Table 14.3 that the effects of the notional adjustments on the balance of payments have no effect on the net balance due to RR operations in Botswana.

BCL losses

Since coming into production the copper–nickel mine owned by BCL in Selebi-Phikwe has been bedevilled by problems and to date it has incurred heavy annual losses. To enable the firm to keep operating these losses have to be financed. BCL is largely foreign-owned and this financing is for the most part obtained from abroad and hence reflected in the rest of the world, that is, balance of payments accounts.

To preserve the confidential nature of the statistics gathered for national

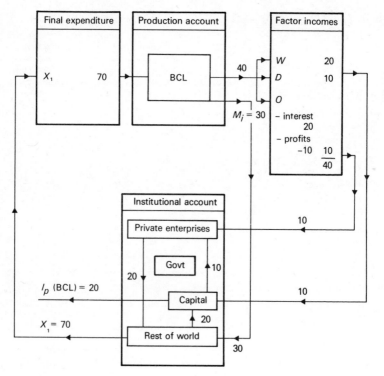

Figure 14.8 (a) *BCL operations: example showing loss*

accounts purposes imaginary flows must be used to illustrate the effects which the BCL loss has on the accounts. Two situations are shown:

1   how the actual flows would appear in the accounts, Figure 14.8(a); and
2   a hypothetical case showing BCL making a profit, Figure 14.8(b).

The only differences between (1) and (2) are that revenue from sales in (2) is increased in order to yield a profit instead of a loss and direct taxes must then, of course, be paid to government.

A number of points should be noted in connection with the diagrams in Figures 14.8(a) and (b).

1   As mentioned in the first part of this paper, the item 'operating surplus' is what remains to a firm after paying out wages and salaries and depreciation. Hence it is not necessarily equivalent to profits since in addition it includes fixed interest payments and rent (if any). In the imaginary figures for operating surplus in Figures 14.8(a) and (b) only interest payments have been included and these are assumed to accrue to foreign creditors.
2   Figure 14.8(a) shows that the BCL loss is financed by borrowing from abroad through the capital account.

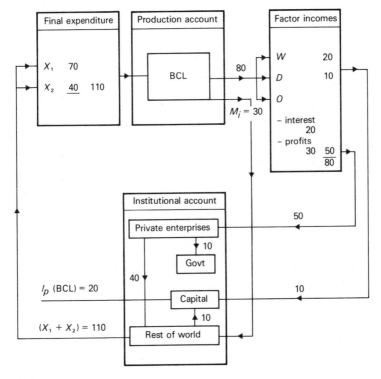

Notes

1. All flows in Figs 14.8(a) and (b) are based on imaginary figures.
2. The payment of 40 to the Rest of world account in Fig. 14.8(b) includes undistributed profits of 10 (see text).
3. X_2 means the change in exports due to improved operations of BCL.
4. Payment of 10 to government represents tax on profits.

Source
Botswana National Accounts 1976–7.

Figure 14.8 (b)   *BCL operations: example showing profit*

3   in the case of Figure 14.8(b) the post-tax profits are sent out of the country as dividends. It is important to note that undistributed profits of 10 are also assumed to go out even though they are actually used for domestic investment. Borrowing them back from the rest of the world account for this purpose reflects better the change in foreign-owned domestic assets which actually takes place through such investment.

Finally, the relevant flows of Figures 14.8(a) and (b) are shown in Table 14.4 as they would appear in the balance of payments accounts. It will be seen that given the figures chosen the balance of payments suffers as a result of a BCL profit. This is to be expected since, with a loss, compensating payments flow in while, with a profit, dividends (distributed profits) flow out.

Table 14.4   *BCL operations and the balance of payments*

	Loss		Profit	
	Debit	Credit	Debit	Credit
Goods and services				
(i) goods – imports	30	—	30	—
– exports	—	70	—	110
(ii) services				
– profits/dividends/interest	20	—	40	—
Long-term capital				
– loan to cover loss	—	10	—	—
– loan to cover capital expenditure	—	10	—	10
NET BALANCE		40		50

Source
Botswana National Accounts 1976–7.

Migrant and expatriate incomes

Migrant labourers are defined as foreigners who although working in a particular country are not considered as residents of that country.[6] Apart from affecting their legal status in their country of work, for example, tax liability, etc., the non-residential status of migrants also affects the treatment accorded them in the national accounts of both their country of work and country of permanent residence. Since Botswana relies heavily on its migrant workers finding work in South Africa (40 000 compared with formal sector employment inside Botswana of 50 000 in 1976–7) their impact on the national accounts is significant.

Basically there are two major ways in which migrants affect the accounts. First, their incomes constitute one of the factors contributing to the difference between Gross Domestic Product (GDP) and Gross National Product (GNP) (see note 2 p. 245 and Appendix 14.C, item 6, p. 249. In other words, since Botswana's migrants work in another country, their income is not considered as part of Botswana's GDP. On the other hand since they are permanently resident in Botswana, their income is included in the country's GNP.

Secondly, there is the problem of how to assess migrant incomes. Ideally, their *gross* income is the most appropriate figure to use. In other words, it should be assumed that the total income of migrants is repatriated to their home country. In practice the most readily available figure for Botswana migrants is the amount which they remit home, defined as their net income. This excludes all purchases of goods and services made during their sojourn in South Africa which are equivalent to imports since they are purchased by permanent residents of Botswana. In other words such purchases should in theory be considered as part of Botswana's household consumption (C_p), and also included in imports (M_e).

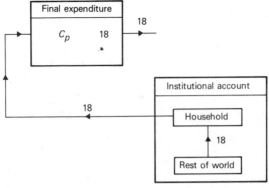

Source
Botswana National Accounts 1976-7.

Figure 14.9(a)   *Migrant incomes: net flows (1976–7)*

However if C_p and M_e were to be adjusted in this way it would be necessary in the accounts to record migrant remittances on a gross basis, that is, total income earned abroad, rather than on a net basis. Unless such an adjustment were made, the balance of payments accounts would not reflect, overall, the actual flows taking place between the two countries.

Unfortunately, at present there is not sufficient data to enable gross migrant incomes to be calculated and therefore in the Botswana national accounts a net figure is used, that is, actual remittances transferred to Botswana with purchases of goods and services in SA excluded from domestic consumption and imports.

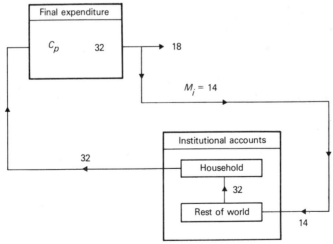

Source
Botswana National Accounts 1976-7.

Figure 14.9(b)   *Migrant incomes: net flows (1976–7)*

Appendix 14.D shows income and expenditure statistics that are available for Batswana mineworkers in SA (not all migrants are mineworkers since some work in SA farms, or as household helpers, etc.). Figure 14.9 (a) goes on to show the treatment in the accounts of actual migrant remittances (net income) in 1976–7 while 14.9 (b) shows imputed flows using approximate figures for gross income, and the amount spent on goods and services while staying in South Africa.

Finally a comparison of gross and net income as they affect the balance of payments accounts is shown in Table 14.5. As expected the net effect of the two cases is the same.

Expatriate personnel working on contract in Botswana are for the most part not considered as migrants since they stay longer than six months (see note 6). However, a complication arises because the gross incomes of many government expatriates take one of the following forms:

1   salary, gratuity, etc., paid by local (Botswana) employer *plus* a 'topping-up' paid by an aid agency or donor into a foreign account, or
2   total salary, etc., paid by aid agency or donor into a foreign account.

In other words except for remittances to Botswana to cover living expenses part of the income received by certain expatriates never enters Botswana. For example in 1976–7, P12·5 million was paid outside Botswana to expatriate personnel. Of this amount P8·5 million was remitted to Botswana (which amount would of course show up in the balance of payments as a current transfer to the household account) and P4·7 million was left abroad.

Table 14.5   *Migrant incomes and the balance of payments*

	Actual flows (net basis)		Imputed flows (gross basis)	
	Debit	Credit	Debit	Credit
Goods and services				
(i) goods – imports	—	—	14	—
(ii) services –				
– mineworkers' remittances	—	18	—	32
NET BALANCE		18		18

Source
Botswana National Accounts 1976–7.

Now clearly these 'overseas' salaries paid to expatriates form an important part of their income and such income should be reflected in Botswana's national accounts if an accurate assessment of goods and services produced in the country is to be made. In order to do this the P12·5 million in 1976–7 was assumed to be transferred from abroad to government which in turn used this amount to employ expatriates and so generate income. In national accounts terms this would in addition involve crediting the P12·5 to the household institutional account, and from there, in order to make the notional flows equivalent to actual ones, imputing a current transfer of P4 from the household to the rest of the world account.

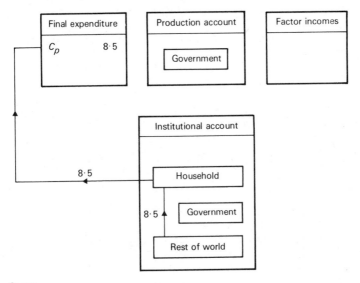

Source
Botswana National Accounts 1976–7.

Figure 14.10 (a)   *Expatriate salaries paid abroad: actual flows (1976–7)*

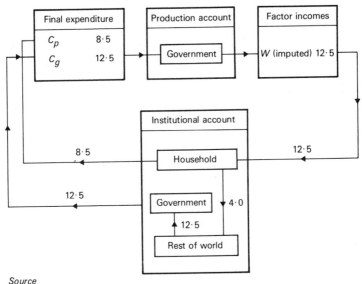

Source
Botswana National Accounts 1976–7.

Figure 14.10 (b)   *Expatriate salaries paid abroad: imputed flows (1976–7)*

Table 14.6   *Expatriate incomes and the balance of payments*

	Actual flows		Imputed flows	
	Debit	Credit	Debit	Credit
Unilateral transfers				
– transfer to expatriates	—	8·5	—	—
– transfer to government	—	—	—	12·2
– transfer to abroad	—	—	4·7	—
NET BALANCE		8·5		8·5

Source
Botswana National Accounts 1976–7.

Figures 14.10(a) and (b) show actual and imputed flows respectively, while Table 14.6 shows the effect on the balance of payments of each case. It will be seen that the net effect on all the accounts is, as expected, identical.

Imputed income in agriculture: increase in the cattle herd and the subsistence sector

In any set of national income accounts one encounters the problem of having to impute figures because of lack of statistics. It was seen above, for example, how, in order to assess more realistically the contribution made to the economy by Rhodesia Railways and migrant workers, it was necessary to use certain imputed values. Even more important, however, are the imputations made necessary in calculating production in the traditional agricultural sector[7] which contributes 19 per cent to the value added in the economy. Of the 19 per cent, some two thirds (13 per cent) was imputed since the output concerned was not marketed.

The components of production in this sector (traditional agriculture) are as follows:

1   Cattle production, including the production of
    a   milk   – production for own use
    b   meat   – marketed offtake
                   – off-take for own use (non-marketed)[8]
                   – increase in the herd (non-marketed)
2   Crop production– marketed production
                            – production for own use (non-marketed)

From this it will be seen that imputed production covers:
– milk production
– offtake for own use
– increase in the herd
– crop production for own use
Of these four items the increase in the herd poses the most serious problem of

estimation. The other three items on the other hand are thought to have been estimated relatively satisfactorily in recent years using data from the 1974 Rural Income Distribution Survey and the annual Agricultural Surveys. In 1976–7 total imputed production for these three items was estimated at 25·4.

The increase in the herd has to date been estimated on the basis of sales and own consumption (offtake) and of the net increase (births minus deaths) in calves during the year in question using available information on the cattle herd and fertility rates (see Appendix 14.E for estimated figures relating to the growth in the herd). In putting a value on this increase, each calf was valued at P25 for 1976–7 yielding a figure of 12·5 in 1976–7 for the traditional agricultural sector alone. However, calculating the value of the increase in the herd in this way can only be accurate given a rather restrictive assumption. Conceptually the total production from the Botswana herd (excluding milk) is equal to the value of the weight gained by the herd during the year in question plus the net value of the increase in calves. In other words:

$$P_t = \Delta W_t + \Delta C_t \tag{1}$$

(where P_t = value of cattle production in year t

ΔW_t = value of weight gained by existing herd during year t

ΔC_t = value of net increase in calves during year t.)

Ideally some sort of reliable population model along the lines of the one set out in Appendix 14.F should be used as a basis for estimating P_t. Unfortunately such a model has not yet been fully developed for Botswana although the Central Statistics Office is presently doing work in this area.

It should also be noted that total value of cattle production (P_t) is equivalent to annual offtake (OT_t) plus increase in the herd (ΔH_t). In other words

$$P_t = OT_t + \Delta H_t \tag{2}$$

The method presently used to obtain an estimate of P_t is to add the value of the annual offtake (marketed plus non-marketed) to the value of the net increase in calves (ΔC_t). In other words it is assumed that:

$$\Delta W_t + \Delta C_t = OT_t + \Delta H_t = OT_t + \Delta C_t \tag{3}$$

and therefore that

$$OT_t = \Delta W_t \tag{4}$$

$$\text{and} \quad \Delta C_t = \Delta H_t \tag{5}$$

This means that for the present method to work OT_t must be a reasonable approximation to ΔW_t. If it is not then ΔC_t does not give an accurate estimate of increase in the herd (ΔH_t). For example, if $OT_t = 0$ (during the recent foot and mouth outbreak offtake dropped dramatically) then our method grossly undervalues output of the herd since we will not pick up the increase in weight of mature cattle, that is, cattle other than calves. However, even ignoring extreme cases such as assuming $OT_t = 0$, it is considered that the existing method $(OT_t + \Delta C_t)$ underestimates the 'true' value of cattle production $(\Delta W_t + \Delta C_t)$ and hence under-estimates increase in the herd. This is because it is considered that:

1   actual herd size is underestimated;
2   actual offtake (OT_t) over recent years has been less than ΔW_t because of favourable weather conditions, because of the traditional attitude of holding cattle as a security rather than a productive asset and because investment in cattle is expected to be more profitable than available financial assets or alternative direct investments.

In other words, over time, a steady growth in the herd tends to be underestimated.

Thus imputed values in traditional agriculture are treated as follows in the national accounts. First, the imputed values in question for 1976–7 are as follows:

1	Production for own use (including milk, cattle offtake and crop production)	25·4
2	Increase in the herd	12·5
		37·9

Secondly, in terms of the model developed, 1 and 2 above are included as part of the final expenditure (end-use) as follows:

1	Consumption expenditure		26·1
2	Investment (I_p):		
	– Increase in the herd	12·5	
	– Increase in stocks	−0·7	11·8
			37·9

Finally, it is assumed that traditional agriculture pays out an equivalent amount of factor incomes. The breakdown of these imputed incomes was reflected in the 1976–7 accounts as follows:

1	Wages and salaries (W) (Wages in kind to herd boys)	11·6
2	Operating surplus (O): (i.e. surplus in kind)	26·3
		37·9

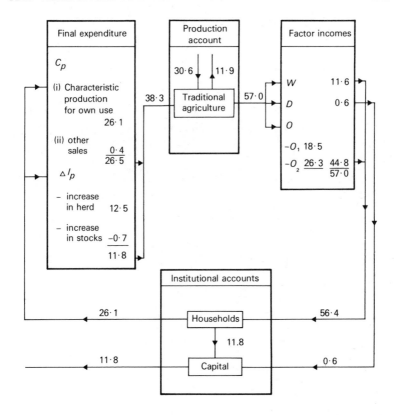

Note
Operating surplus (O) is divided into two components:
    O_1, Operating surplus due to marketed flows;
    O_2, Operating surplus due to non-marketed flows.

Source
Botswana National Accounts 1976–7.

Figure 14.11 (a)   *Traditional agriculture: marketed and imputed flows*

Figures 14.11(a) and (b) demonstrate the effects of including in the national accounts model the imputed values as described above. Figure 14.11 (a) includes the imputed non-marketed flows, while Figure 14.11 (b) shows the flows of marketed output only. The net effect on all accounts is the same for both cases. It should also be noted that a transfer between institutional accounts is made necessary by the fact that the capital account must obtain sufficient of the imputed income in order to 'purchase' that part of the imputed production which is invested.

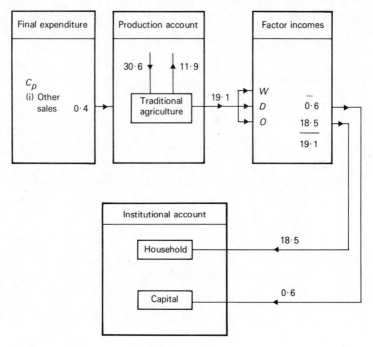

Note
Intermediate consumption is as follows:
30·6, sale of cattle to BMC
11·9, purchase of inputs (imports are not shown separately).

Source
Botswana National Accounts 1976–7.

Figure 14.11 (b)   *Traditional agriculture: marketed flows*

Notes

1. As this article is based on Botswana's 1976–7 national accounts, Rhodesia and Rhodesia Railways are referred to by their old names.
2. Gross Domestic Product (GDP) is defined as the total value of output produced within the borders of a country and
   (a) includes income paid to foreign-owned factors of production, and remittances to non-resident migrant workers: but
   (b) excludes income accruing to residents from owning factors of production abroad.
To calculate Gross National Product (GNP) which is intended to give an estimate of output produced and income generated by the factors of production owned by a country's own residents, GDP must be adjusted as follows:

$$GNP = GDP - (a + b)$$

3. In this section, all the diagrams and tables dealing with the circular flow model show only those parts of the flow which are relevant to the problem being discussed.

4. UN Series F No. 2 Rev. 3 (1968).
5. Also, if revenue on the system's Rhodesian portion of the system falls (as it did when Zambia ceased using it in the early 1970s), imputed costs on the Botswana section go up and vice versa.
6. Foreigners working in Botswana for longer than six months are considered residents.
7. The imputations necessary in the Freehold Farming section are minor and therefore ignored in this presentation.
8. Offtake for own consumption, that is, from dead cattle or killed for the purpose, is often referred to as 'dead meat'.

Appendix 14.A
Key to abbreviations used

Aggregated measures
1.	GDP_m	Gross Domestic Product at market prices
2.	NDP_m	Net Domestic Product at market prices
3.	GDP_f	Gross Domestic Product at factor cost
4.	GNP_m	Gross national Product at market prices
5.	NDI	National Disposable Income

Production account
6.	GO	Gross output (at producers' prices)
7.	INT	Intermediate consumption (at purchasers' prices)

End-use
8.	C_p	Private final consumption expenditure
9.	I_p	Private gross capital formation (stocks plus fixed capital)
10.	C_g	Government final consumption expenditure
11.	I_g	Government gross capital formation
12.	I	Total gross capital formation $(I_p + I_g)$
13.	G	Total government expenditure $(C_g + I_g)$
14.	X	Exports of goods and services (excluding factor services) (recorded f.o.b.)
15.	M_e	Imports purchased directly for end-use (recorded c.i.f.)
16.	M_i	Imports purchased by the production section as intermediate consumption (also recorded c.i.f.)
17.	M	Total imports of goods and services (excluding factor services) (recorded c.i.f.) $(= M_e + M_i)$

Factor incomes
18.	W	Compensation of employees (wages and salaries)
19.	D	Consumption of fixed capital
20.	O	Operating surplus
21.	T	Indirect taxes
22.	U	Subsidies

Sectoral accounts
23.	S	Savings (all domestic sectors)

Balance of payments
24.	BOP^c	Balance of payments on current account

25. FC_{RD} Net foreign claims (i.e. increase in foreign financial assets excluding reserve items, less increase in foreign liabilities)
(RD indicates that the direction of net payments is from the rest of the world (R) to the domestic (D) economy)

26. DR_{es} Change in foreign reserves (exclusive of exchange rate adjustments)

27. W_{RD} (net)   Net wages from the rest of the world (i.e. wages received by residents working abroad less wages paid to non-residents working in domestic activities)

28. R_{RD} (net)   Net property income (interests, dividends, rent and royalties) from the rest of the world

29. FS_{RD} (net)   Net factor services from abroad ($= W_{RD}(net) + R_{RD}(net)$)

30. CT_{RD} (net)   Net current transfers from the rest of the world

Appendix 14.B
Aggregate production account for all three production sectors

Inputs			Outputs		
1. Intermediate consumption			4. Disposition of gross output		
(a) as inputs from other domestic industries	79		(a) as inputs to other domestic industries		79
(b) as imports (to industry) (M_i)	101	180	(b) as final expenditure		401
2. Indirect taxes		28			
3. Factor incomes		272^b			
Total payments by producers		480	Gross output		480^a
Less intermediate consumption (item 1 above)		180	Less inputs (item 4(a) above)	79	
			Less imports (item 1(b) above)	101	180
Net output = GDP_m		300	Net output = GDP_m		300

Notes
1. The total of the output column yields a figure which is termed the gross output of the economy. This includes all intermediate consumption (i.e. inputs flowing between domestic industries and inputs from abroad). Consequently to arrive at an estimate of the domestically produced output delivered for final expenditure (end-use), total intermediate consumption must be subtracted from gross output. This yields the Gross Domestic Product at market prices (GDP_m).
2. By subtracting indirect taxes (net) from GDP_m, the GDP at factor cost (GDP_f) is

obtained. This is equivalent to the total of all the values added by individual industrial sectors as shown in Table 14.1.

Source
Botswana National Accounts 1976–7.

Appendix 14.C
Identities in the national accounts

1. GDP_m $= GO - INT$ (Output side of GDP)
2. GDP_m $= C_p + I_p + G + (X - M)$ (End-use side of GDP)
3. GDP_m $= W + D + O + (T - U)$ (Cost structure of GDP)
4. NDP_m $= GDP_m - D$
5. GDP_f $= GDP_m - (T - U)$
6. GNP_m $= GDP_m + FS_{RD}$ (net)
7. NDI $= GDP_m + FS_{RD}$ (net) $+ CT_{RD}$ (net)
    $= GNP_m + CT_{RD}$ (net)
8. S $= NDI - C$
9. BOP^c $= X - M + FS_{RD}$ (net) $+ CT_{RD}$ (net)
10. DRes $= BOP^c - FC_{RD}$ (net)

Appendix 14.D
Migrant and expatriate incomes

1 Disposition of mineworkers' earnings

	Total earnings	Deferred pay earned	Remittances	Imports of returning mineworkers	Cash holdings of returning mineworkers	Cash spent on consumption in South Africa
1974	11·20	4·18	0·63	1·02	0·60	4·77
1975	21·89	7·08	1·09	3·40	1·20	9·12
1976	32·17	11·52	1·84	4·50	1·70	13·71
1977	—	10·53	2·57	5·54	2·12	—
1978	—	7·67	2·86	5·66	1·65	—

Source
Central Statistics Office.

2 Payments by foreign agencies to expatriate personnel (P million)

1973–4	1974–5	1975–6	1976–7
4·3	5·2	8·7	12·5

Source
Central Statistics Office.

Appendix 14.E
National herd of cattle 1965–77[a] ('000)

			Offtake			
At 1 July	Opening no.	Natural increase[b]	BMC	Other	Closing no.	At 30 June
1965	1481	−83	138	23	1237	1966
1966	1237	408[c]	136	17	1492	1967
1967	1492	336	122	18	1688	1968
1968	1688	376	99	20	1945	1969
1969	1945	205	110	23	2017	1970
1970	2017	248	147	26	2092	1971
1971	2092	178	162	31	2177	1972
1972	2177	163[d]	183	40	2117	1973
1973	2117	431	198	34	2316	1974
1974	2316	473	187	38	2564	1975
1975	2564	522	212	42	2832	1976
1976	2832	576	221	45	3124	1977

Notes
[a] The series up to 1971 is not quite comparable with the 1972–7 series. The former is based on veterinary counts, while the latter is based on three CSO baseline sample surveys conducted during 1972, 1973 and 1976. For later years the cattle levels have been estimated through a simple recursive model, based on information on offtake, births, deaths and on age composition of the herd. The 1976 survey estimates the stock in the traditional sector to be 2 518 600 cattle. The freehold farmers' stocks of roughly 350 000 has to be added to give the total national herd estimate in September 1976 of 2 968 600 cattle. This tallies remarkably well with the estimate in the table above of 2 832 000 end June 1976.

Even though the model-estimates tally remarkably well with the point estimate from the cattle survey in 1976, the estimates on cattle as presented in the above time series are still viewed with some uncertainty. The figures should be regarded as approximations rather than exact, the error in estimates ranges around a maximum of ± 300 000.

[b] Births less (natural) deaths. For the years 1965 to 1971 the increase is implied by the annual cattle counts and the offtake. For the years 1972–7, the natural increase has been estimated and annual levels implied.

[c] The 1966–7 weighted average rainfall for cattle areas was about 57 per cent above the weighted long-term seasonal norm.

[d] The 1972–3 weighted average rainfall for cattle areas was about 44 per cent below the weighted long-term seasonal norm. The low natural increase is implied by the known cattle numbers in 1972 and 1973, as estimated by the CSO cattle sample censuses of August 1972 and 1973, the 1971–2 Freehold Farm Survey, etc.; and by the known BMC offtake and the estimated 'other' offtake.

Source
Central Statistics Office and Ministry of Agriculture.

Appendix 14.F
Model showing changes in cattle stock

The following simple model has been developed by the CSO to try to check (and give consistency to) the time series on cattle stock.

Equation I $S_{t+1} = S_t + Y_t - O_t$

Equation II $Y_t = S_t \cdot C_t \cdot f(r_t) \cdot [1 - m_1(r_t)] - S_t \cdot m_2(r_t)$

where S_t = total stock of cattle at beginning of period t

O_t = offtake during period t (given exogenously)

Y_t = net increase in period t (born – dead)

C_t = fraction of fertile cows out of total herd for period t

r_t = weighted rainfall in cattle areas in period t

$f(r_t)$ = fertility of fertile cows as a function of rainfall in period t

$m_1(r_t)$ = mortality of calves (less than 1 year) as a function of rainfall in period t

$m_2(r_2)$ = mortality of mature cattle (greater than 1 year) as a function of rainfall.

Ray Weedon is Lecturer in Economics, University of Botswana and Swaziland; formerly Senior Planning Officer, Government of Botswana.
Odd Ystgaard is with the Research Division, Central Bureau of Statistics, Norway; formerly head of National Accounts Unit, Central Statistics Office, Botswana.

15 The Botswana Social Accounts Matrix in the Analysis of the Impact of the Foot and Mouth Epidemic

CAROL HAYDEN and TONY WILLIAMS

Introduction

This paper draws heavily on the work of the two SAM missions to Botswana. The description draws upon papers by C. C. Greenfield, Chief Statistician, Ministry of Overseas Development and the analysis of the foot and mouth epidemic is extracted from a paper by Carol Hayden. These and other sources are detailed at the end of this paper.

Planning in Botswana, as is common in developing countries, is hampered by a shortage of pertinent and up-to-date statistics. Efforts to provide a comprehensive statistical base are hindered by shortages of skilled manpower and financial resources that may be directed towards that end. It is important, therefore, that the limited resources available be directed towards satisfying priority data needs, and that data collected are presented in the form most suitable for planning. This requires continuous consultation and co-operation between the Central Statistics Office and the relevant planning offices. The development of a Social Accounts Matrix (SAM) in Botswana is presented as an example of use being made of a limited statistical base to provide a valuable tool to planners for the consideration of the likely effects of policy decisions.

The 1974–5 SAM discussed in this paper was prepared following a mission to Botswana in 1977 by a team comprising UK Ministry of Overseas Development (ODM) and university personnel. The mission was financed by ODM and by the Norwegian Agency for International Development. The intention was to produce a SAM which was both useful and easily understood. A second mission in 1978 worked on 1976–7 data, but the results were not available at the time of writing and the analysis of the foot and mouth epidemic is based on 1974–5 data.

What is a SAM?

A SAM is a comprehensive model of the economy showing the interrelationship between real and financial transactions. It shows the channelling of income from domestic production activities to various categories of factors of production and

(MILLION PULA)

Expenditure by: CURRENT — FACTORS (01–08), INSTITUTIONS (09–22), PRODUCTION ACTIVITIES (23–37), PRICE EFFECTS (38–39), ROW (40–41); CAPITAL — ROW (42), INSTITUTIONS (43–49), FINANCIAL CLAIMS (LIABILITIES) (50–61); UNALLOCATED (62); TOTAL (63)

Columns 01–22 (Current: Factors; Institutions)

Code	Income to	01	02	03	04	05	06	07	08	09	10	11	12	13	14	15	16	17	18	19	20	21	22
01	Factors: Admin & prof employ's - local																					1.7	3.1
02	" " " - expat																					1.0	3.8
03	Skilled, manual and clerical employees - local																					2.2	11.0
04	- expat																					0.2	1.9
05	Unskilled employees																					1.7	1.4
06	Self-employed																						
07	Operating surplus																					0.1	
08	Depreciation																					0.4	0.7
09	Households: Peri-urban households	0.1		0.5		9.7	0.2									0.2	0.2						
10	Urban h'holds: High density	0.2		8.2		13.5	0.9									0.2	0.2	0.1	0.3					
11	Servants quarters			0.3		3.6											0.1							
12	Med density	0.5	0.9	4.2	3.5	-.1																0.1		
13	Low density	0.3	11.7	1.3	5.4	0.4																0.6		
14	Rural h'holds: < 10 cattle	2.5	0.1	5.7	0.4	3.1	16.3	0.3	2.4	0.8	1.5	0.3	1.0	0.2				1.5					
15	10–80 cattle	2.0		3.2		0.7	29.5	2.2	2.5	0.7	1.2	0.3	1.0	0.2				1.0					
16	> 80 cattle	0.6		0.9			6.6	9.0	1.0		0.2									8.6			
17	Migrant workers abroad			18.6		4.4																	
18	Enterprises: Major mining enterprises							2.1	7.8											0.1			
19	Other private ents							11.8	5.9	0.1			0.3	0.1			0.3		0.8	5.9	0.3		1.2
20	Parastatal enterprises							7.7	1.4											0.8	0.2		
21	Priv non profit & local gov't							0.3	0.4	0.1	0.4		0.6	0.5	1.6	0.6	0.6						5.3
22a	Central government: Transfers							0.1	1.7	0.1	0.2		0.6	2.0	0.1	0.1	0.1		12.9	4.3	7.4		
22b	Sales										0.3		0.9	0.7		0.4	0.4						
22c	Indirect taxes												0.1	0.1		0.1	0.2						
23	Production: Freehold farms																0.3						
24	Traditional farmers - l'stock														4.0	9.0	2.1						
25	" " - crops										0.1				2.3	3.4	0.5						
26	" " - other acts										0.2		0.2		3.5	1.6	0.5						
27	Mining and prospecting																						
28	Botswana Meat Commission																						
29	Other manufacturing									0.4	1.2	0.2	0.4	0.1	3.1	2.3	0.8						0.4
30	Water & electricity supply									0.1	0.2		0.1	0.3		0.1	0.5						0.9
31	Construction																						
32	Wholesale & retail trade									1.5	3.3	0.6	0.8	1.0	3.4	2.0	1.0					0.1	0.3
33	Hotels, bars & restaurants												0.2	0.2		0.1	0.3					0.2	0.7
34	Rail transport									0.1	0.1		0.1		0.1	0.1							0.2
35	Other transport & comm's									0.1	0.1		0.1	0.2	0.1	0.2	0.2					0.2	7.0
36	Services nes (incl. dwellings)										0.6		0.9	1.3	2.9	2.2	0.9					0.1	0.5
37	Personal & h'hold services									0.1	0.4		0.1	0.5	0.3	0.7	1.2						
38	Price effects									0.9	1.9	0.4	0.6	0.9	1.8	1.8	1.6						
39	Price effects									0.1	0.1		0.2	0.2	0.2	0.4	0.3						0.2
40	ROW: Goods & non factor services									5.7	11.1	2.1	3.7	4.5	10.7	10.9	9.6	16.6	0.7	1.2	0.5	0.9	5.6
41	Factor services & transfers		0.7		3.1								0.6	5.4					-9.3	6.1	0.2		1.4
42	ROW capital transactions																						
43	Capital institutions: Households									0.2	0.4	0.1	0.8	1.3	2.2	8.0	5.5	4.6					
44	Major mining enterprises																		5.9				
45	Other priv (non-fin) & loc. gov.																			1.6		2.7	
46	Parastatals (non-financial)																				1.5		
47	Banks																			1.0			
48	Other fin. ents. incl. B.D.C.																			0.3	0.2		
49	Central government																						19.1
50	Financial claims (assets): Domestic currency																						
51	Bank deposits																						
52	Other domestic deposits																						
53	Treasury bills																						
54	Bank advances																						
55	Other domestic lending/borrowing: S. term																						
56	L. term																						
57	Comm. cust. area account																						
58	Other: Short term																						
59	Foreign lending/borro'ing: L.T. from govts																						
60	L.T. from orgs																						
61	L.T. from private																						
62	Unallocated / errors & omissions																						
63	TOTAL	6.2	13.3	42.6	12.5	39.5	53.6	33.4	23.2	10.9	23.6	4.0	13.4	19.8	36.3	44.6	27.1	23.0	11.0	30.5	10.3	11.6	64.6

Columns 23–41 (Current: Production activities; Price effects; ROW)

Code	Income to	23	24	25	26	27	28	29	30	31	32	33	34	35	36	37	38	39	40	41
01	Admin & prof employ's - local	0.1				0.1	0.1	0.1		0.1	0.3			0.1		0.5				
02	" " " - expat	0.1				1.2	0.4	0.4	0.9	0.9	0.5	0.1		1.8	1.8	0.4				
03	Skilled, manual and clerical - local	0.7	1.6	0.1		1.4	0.3	0.8	0.8	1.0	1.8	0.2		0.4	1.7	0.1				18.6
04	- expat	0.4				2.7	0.1	1.1	0.3	3.1	0.9	0.1	0.8	0.5	0.4	0.2				
05	Unskilled employees	1.3	1.8	0.1		3.6	1.4	3.4	0.4	9.4	4.3	0.5	0.8	0.4	0.8	3.6				4.4
06	Self-employed	1.3	26.9	5.2	6.1			2.9		0.8	7.9	0.3		0.1		2.0				
07	Operating surplus	3.7	9.8			0.4	3.4	0.2	3.4	4.6	4.7	0.1	-1.9	0.6	4.1					
08	Depreciation	0.7	1.2	0.1		7.9	0.5	0.7	1.0	2.0	1.0	0.2	0.5	1.4	4.4	0.4				
09	Peri-urban households																			
10	Urban: High density																			
11	Servants quarters																			
12	Med density																			
13	Low density																			
14	Rural: < 10 cattle																			
15	10–80 cattle																			
16	> 80 cattle																			
17	Migrant workers abroad																			
18	Major mining enterprises																		0.9
19	Other private ents																		3.6
20	Parastatal enterprises																		0.2
21	Priv non profit & local gov't						0.1				0.2					0.1				0.7
22a	Central government: Transfers																		12.9
22b	Sales		0.1			0.2						0.1		0.1						
22c	Indirect taxes	0.1	0.1			0.1	0.5				0.5			0.1	0.2	0.2	16.4			
23	Freehold farms						10.5	0.4									0.3	0.1	
24	Traditional farmers - l'stock						15.7	0.3										0.1		
25	" " - crops							0.7											1.0	
26	" " - other acts																			
27	Mining and prospecting					1.2			0.5	0.6							0.9	51.0	
28	Botswana Meat Commission	0.2	0.2														1.1	32.1	
29	Other manufacturing					5.5				0.1		0.2					0.3	9.9	
30	Water & electricity supply					5.8	0.6	0.1		0.5	0.2	0.2	0.1	0.2	0.2	0.1		0.1		
31	Construction					6.2											0.6		
32	Wholesale & retail trade	0.5	0.3			1.3	1.1	2.6	0.8	4.8		0.3	0.4	0.9	0.3	0.5		1.3	0.7	
33	Hotels, bars & restaurants														0.3				1.3	
34	Rail transport	0.2	0.3	0.1		0.9		0.6	0.1	0.1	1.1			0.5	0.1			0.2	14.9	
35	Other transport & comm's	0.1	0.2	0.1		0.6				0.1	0.5				1.4			0.3	1.1	
36	Services nes (incl. dwellings)	0.1	0.3	0.1		1.1		0.4	0.1	1.5	1.9	0.1		0.1				0.5	1.8	
37	Personal & h'hold services	0.4	0.6	0.2		0.5		0.6		1.1	0.7	0.1		0.7				0.3	2.0	
38	Price effects	0.2				0.5	0.1	0.2	0.1	0.4	0.1		0.2	0.1	0.1					
39	Price effects					0.3	0.4	0.1		0.2	0.1			0.1						2.2	
40	Goods & non factor services	2.7	1.1	0.2		16.2	1.4	10.1	3.0	19.9	7.1	1.3	19.7	4.7	1.7	2.3				
41	Factor services & transfers																			
42	ROW capital transactions																			-11.5
43	Households																			
44	Major mining enterprises																			
45	Other priv (non-fin) & loc. gov.																			
46	Parastatals (non-financial)																			
47	Banks																			
48	Other fin. ents. incl. B.D.C.																			
49	Central government																			
50	Domestic currency																			
51	Bank deposits																			
52	Other domestic deposits																			
53	Treasury bills																			
54	Bank advances																			
55	Other domestic lending/borrowing S. term																			
56	L. term																			
57	Comm. cust. area account																			
58	Other short term																			
59	L.T. from govts																			
60	L.T. from orgs																			
61	L.T. from private																			
62	Unallocated / errors & omissions																			
63	TOTAL	12.9	44.4	6.2	6.1	57.4	36.5	25.5	11.1	51.2	33.6	3.6	20.5	12.6	17.6	10.6	16.4	6.2	147.7	

Columns 42–63 (Capital: ROW; Institutions; Financial claims (liabilities); Unallocated; Total)

Code	Income to	42	43	44	45	46	47	48	49	50	51	52	53	54	55	56	57	58	59	60	61	62	63
01	Admin & prof employ's - local																					6.2
02	" " " - expat																					13.3
03	Skilled, manual and clerical - local																					42.6
04	- expat																					12.5
05	Unskilled employees																					39.5
06	Self-employed																					53.6
07	Operating surplus																					33.4
08	Depreciation																					23.2
09	Peri-urban households																					10.9
10	Urban: High density																					23.6
11	Servants quarters																					4.0
12	Med density																					13.4
13	Low density																					19.8
14	Rural: < 10 cattle																					36.3
15	10–80 cattle																					44.6
16	> 80 cattle																					27.1
17	Migrant workers abroad																					23.0
18	Major mining enterprises																					11.0
19	Other private ents																					30.5
20	Parastatal enterprises																					10.3
21	Priv non profit & local gov't																					11.6
22a	Central government: Transfers																					
22b	Sales																					64.6
22c	Indirect taxes																					
23	Freehold farms		0.9			0.3																	12.9
24	Traditional farmers - l'stock		13.0																			44.4
25	" " - crops		-1.9																			6.2
26	" " - other acts																					6.1
27	Mining and prospecting			3.0																		57.4
28	Botswana Meat Commission					2.7																	36.5
29	Other manufacturing				0.5																	25.5
30	Water & electricity supply								0.5														11.1
31	Construction		1.8	5.5	8.9	7.4	0.8	0.1	19.7														51.2
32	Wholesale & retail trade		0.2	0.8	1.7	0.2			0.4														33.6
33	Hotels, bars & restaurants				0.1																	3.6
34	Rail transport				0.5																	20.5
35	Other transport & comm's																					12.6
36	Services nes (incl. dwellings)				0.3																	17.6
37	Personal & h'hold services				0.2																	10.6
38	Price effects		0.2	1.1	2.5	0.3			0.5														16.4
39	Price effects		0.1	0.2	0.2	0.2			0.3														6.2
40	Goods & non factor services	-80.9	1.4	15.2	14.1	2.0	0.1	0.4	3.8													9.1	147.7
41	Factor services & transfers																					
42	ROW capital transactions			6.5						5.4							-6.2	5.6						-
43	Households				0.1									0.2	1.0	0.5								25.1
44	Major mining enterprises													-1.1		1.5		3.1			21.8		41.4
45	Other priv (non-fin) & loc. gov.													8.4	2.0	0.9		5.1			11.2		32.0
46	Parastatals (non-financial)													2.2	1.5	9.9						1.4	16.5
47	Banks										20.0							3.5			2.2	-9.6	17.2
48	Other fin. ents. incl. B.D.C.											2.9		0.1	1.4	1.7						-0.1	6.5
49	Central government	23.5	0.1			0.1							0.6	1.2	·				6.0	4.6	0.1	-1.7	53.9
50	Domestic currency		4.5	0.1	0.4		0.4																5.4
51	Bank deposits		3.5	1.9	1.0	0.1		0.5	12.9														20.0
52	Other domestic deposits		2.8																			2.9
53	Treasury bills						0.6																0.6
54	Bank advances						10.9																11.0
55	Other domestic lending/borrowing S. term		0.4	2.1	0.9	2.5																	5.9
56	L. term			-0.1	0.6	0.2		3.1	20.6														24.5
57	Comm. cust. area account								-6.2														-6.2
58	Other short term	11.7	-1.7	5.2		0.5			1.5														17.3
59	L.T. from govts	6.0																				6.0
60	L.T. from orgs	4.6																				4.6
61	L.T. from private	35.2																				35.2
62	Unallocated / errors & omissions						4.4	2.4															6.8
63	TOTAL	-	25.1	41.4	32.0	16.5	17.2	6.5	53.9	5.4	20.0	2.9	0.6	11.0	5.9	24.5	-6.2	17.3	6.0	4.6	35.2	-0.9	

Figure 15.1 *1974–5 Social Accounts Matrix at basic prices*

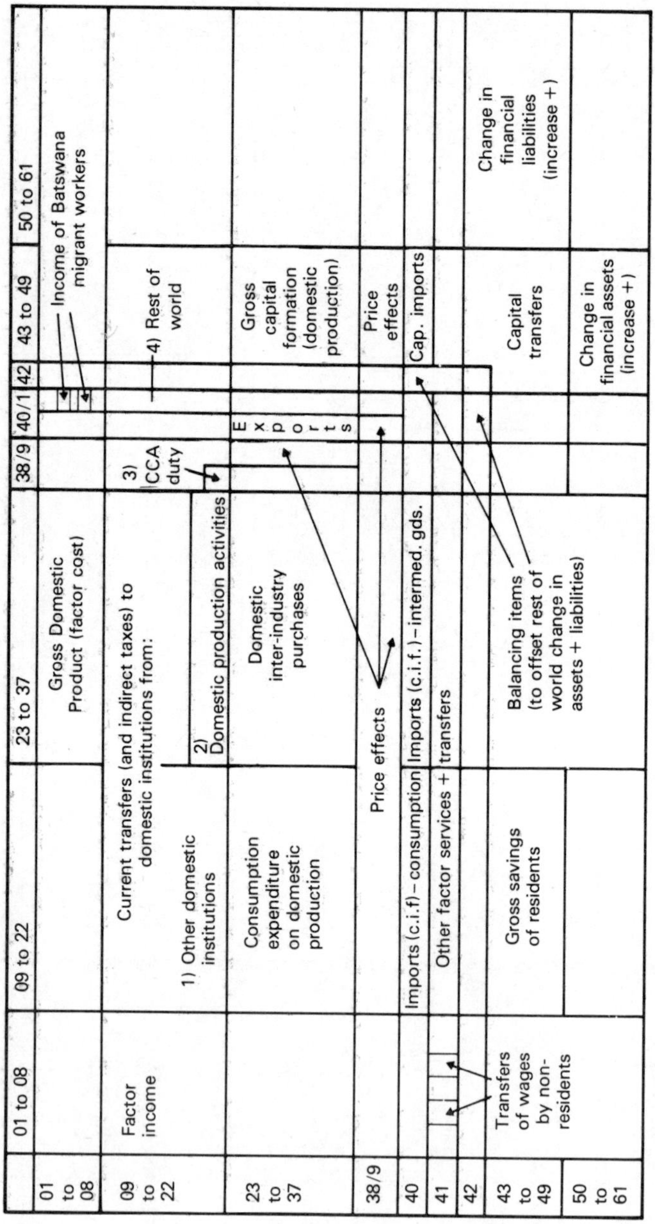

Figure 15.2 *1974–5 SAM: sub-matrix identifications*

thence to households, enterprises and government; transfers of income between households, enterprises, government and the rest of the world; consumption and intermediate expenditure on domestically produced and imported goods and services; exports; capital formation; savings; and external and domestic financial transactions. As such, the SAM is an extension of the national accounts, but with major emphasis placed upon households in respect of sources of income, income distribution, expenditure, savings and change in assets and liabilities. The row and column headings are selected to highlight features of the economy relevant for policy evaluation purposes.

Figure 15.1 represents the 1974–5 Botswana SAM at basic prices and Figure 15.2 illustrates the content of each sub-matrix. Only the rows are identified because the corresponding column would bear the same description. Rows represent receipts, that is, income, whilst columns represent payments, that is, expenditure, by each particular factor, institution, etc. For instance, the intersection of row 14 and column 10 represents payments of P1·5 million by urban high density households to rural households owning less than 10 cattle. The sum of all payments attributed to each column includes savings and so, by definition, equals the incomings (row total) for the same factor, institution, etc.

The matrix is divided into current account and capital account transactions. The current account transactions are classified into accounts for factors of production (labour, capital and entrepreneurship), production activities (agriculture, mining, manufacturing, etc.), institutions (households, enterprises and government), the rest of the world (current account balance of payments) and price effects (the price raising effects of indirect taxes). Capital account transactions are classified into accounts for institutions, the rest of the world (which can be regarded as a further institution), and financial assets and liabilities.

Classifications

The classifications for the matrix – that is, the row/column content, were determined through discussions between the SAM team and government representatives who constituted a SAM Reference Group. For any particular item to be identified it had to be both useful for policy and analytical purposes and to be quantifiable on the basis of data already available. A major interest of the government is income distribution – to understand, monitor and influence it; hence, nine household groupings were identified as shown in rows/columns 09–17 in the matrices.

A classification of households simply by income level might appear to be the most relevant in order to assess the effect of various policies directed at income distribution. However, such a classification would not be very useful. Households would cross continually between the arbitrary income bands for many different reasons, thus complicating the monitoring of policies. It is also extremely difficult to define policies in relation to particular deciles of the income distribution alone as different households in any given part of the income distribution are likely to have disparate characteristics and so may not be affected equally and predictably by given policy interventions. In selecting households by housing type in the urban areas, and by ownership of cattle in the rural areas, the SAM utilizes a classification for which data are available and can be updated; also, the groups of households are fairly homogenous from the income/wealth and source of income point of view.

Some clarification is perhaps required on the classification of households. Peri-urban households are essentially squatters. Households owning less than 10 cattle were taken to represent the rural poor, whilst those owning between 10 to 80 cattle would require some other source of income besides cattle. The group designated as owning more than 80 cattle included Barolong farmers who are engaged in large-scale arable agriculture. Over 80 per cent of households lived in the rural areas. Of these 60 000 owned less than 10 cattle, whilst 30 000 and 3000 owned 10–80 cattle and more than 80 cattle respectively.

Income and expenditure of institutions

Factor incomes

Factors of production (labour, capital and entrepreneurship) are shown to derive income from production activities including those of general government and the rest of the world (rows 01–08). These factors of production are owned by households, enterprises, government and the rest of the world and income is channelled to the appropriate institution in columns 01–08. In general, labour income, including self-employment income, is shown as a receipt by households (wage and salary earning members of households being the factor of production) whilst operating surplus and depreciation, the returns to capital and entrepreneurship, are channelled mainly to enterprises and government.[1] The income of Batswana migrant workers is shown as being earned overseas by skilled and unskilled employees in column 41, rows 03 and 05, and is channelled to the appropriate households in row 17, columns 03 and 05. The wage earnings in Botswana of temporary residents, that is, persons remaining for less than six months, are transferred to households in the rest of the world in row 41, columns 02 and 04. The sum of rows 01–08 (less the income earned abroad by migrant workers) represents Gross Domestic Product at factor cost (P201·3 million). This is made up of P91·1 million of wages and salaries, P53·6 million of self-employed income and P23·2 million of gross 'profits' (operating surplus and depreciation). Adding indirect taxes (row 22c) gives GDP at market prices (P220 million). The sub-matrix row 01–08 at intersection with columns 21–37 shows the importance of certain production activities in the generation of different types of income. For example, 30 per cent of wage and salary income comes from direct employment in government (excluding the parastatal industries) and over 70 per cent of self-employed income comes from agricultural activities.

The sub-matrix rows 09–22 at intersection with columns 01–08 show the dependence of each household group on the different types of factor income. The lower income rural households are shown to depend very heavily on income from self employment, an important point to consider when determining policies aimed at the redistribution of income.

Current transfers

The remaining entries in rows 09–22 represent current transfers. Rows 09–22, columns 09–22 show transfer payments between domestic institutions (including Batswana migrant workers). Transfers from rural to urban households of P1·3 million are given in rows 09–13 (and intersection with columns 14–16) and from urban to rural households totalling P7·4 million in rows 14–16 (at intersection with columns 09–13). Remittances from migrant workers abroad to rural and urban households are shown in rows 09–16, column 17. It can be seen from the SAM that these transfers from friends and relatives working in urban areas, or as migrant workers abroad, are an important supplementary source of income for the poorer rural households. Direct and indirect taxes paid to government from households appear in rows 22a and 22c respectively at the intersection with columns 09–16. The burden of direct taxation on households is relatively small. The majority of the central government's current income from domestic transfer payments comes from enterprises. Row 22a at the intersection with columns 18–20 show the income received by the central government in the form of taxes, royalties and dividends from the major mining enterprises and in taxes and interest payments from the parastatal and private enterprises. These transfers total P24·6 million, approximately 40 per cent of *all* current central government income. Other transfers between institutions in the form of interest, dividends, grants and direct taxes are shown in the remaining cells of this sub-matrix.

Payments received by government from domestic production activities appear in rows 21, 22b and 22c against columns 23–37. These comprise indirect taxes paid to central and local government and sales by central government. The figure of P16·4 million shown in row 22c, column 38 is an estimate for the duty content of Botswana's imports, that is, part of Botswana's receipts from the Common Customs Area. Finally, receipts of interest, dividends, profits, etc., by domestic enterprises and central government from the rest of the world are given in rows 18–22a, column 41.

Expenditure by institutions

The gross income of institutions is given in the totals of rows 09–22. The disposal of this income is shown in the corresponding columns. We have already discussed transfer payments (rows 09–22, columns 09–22) and the next sub-matrix (rows 23–37 by columns 09–22) shows the consumption expenditure by households and government on domestic production activities categorized by our seventeen production activities.[2] Imports (c.i.f.) for consumption by institutions are shown in row 40 against the same column. The entries in the cells in rows 23–6 at the intersection with columns 14–16 represent mainly imputed expenditure by rural households on own produced goods, for example, food, hut building materials. This accounts for 20 per cent of total household expenditure on goods and services. Direct imports account for a further 50 per cent.

The data used to derive household consumption expenditure by domestic producing industry and the rest of the world are based on the 1968–70 Household Expenditure Survey and, as such, are tentative extimates. The data are being updated through a 1978–9 survey for inclusion in a SAM for those years. Row 41 shows payments of interest, dividends and profits abroad, whilst the gross savings of Botswana resident institutions (including depreciation) are given in rows 43–9.

One figure requiring some explanation appears in row 40, column 17. This P15·6 million is an estimate for the expenditure by Botswana migrant workers abroad, plus the value of goods that they bring back with them to Botswana. The remaining income of these migrant workers is channelled to urban and rural households (P2·8 million) or saved (P4·6 million) as shown in rows 09–16 and row 43 respectively against column 17.

Income and expenditure of production activities

Production activities obtain income (rows 23–37) though selling their output to domestic institutions for current consumption expenditure (intersection with columns 09–22) to other domestic production activities (the input-output matrix, rows × columns 23–37); to the rest of the world (exports, column 40); and to domestic institutions for capital formation (rows 23–37, columns 43–9). Column 40 (exports) clearly shows the reliance of the economy on beef and mining for foreign currency earnings. These two industries account for over 70 per cent of total exports.

The expenditure of production activities appears in columns 23–37, namely, payments to factors (intersection with rows 01–08), purchases from government and indirect taxes (rows 21–2), purchases from other domestic producers (rows × columns 23–37) and purchases of imported goods and services (row 40). The input-output sub-matrix shows the degree of inter-industry dependence within the economy to be relatively slight, but one would expect the degree of interdependence to increase as the economy expands. Conversely, the import content of domestic production is relatively high particularly in the 'heavier industries' such as mining, manufacturing and construction.

Capital formation

Gross capital formation comprises investment by domestic institutions in locally produced equipment and new construction work (rows 23–37, columns 43–9) and imported capital goods (row 40, columns 43–9). This investment includes changes in stocks. Capital investment goods produced domestically are categorized according to the production activity which supplies these goods.

Price effects

Indirect taxes levied by the government and by the Common Customs Area (CCA) increase the costs of producers and distributors who pay them. It is assumed that the entire additional costs are recouped through higher prices to purchasers. Where the purchasers are also producers, the increased costs of these inputs are in turn recouped through higher prices, thus inducing further price raising effects. The appended SAM is given at basic prices – that is, the price-raising effects of indirect taxes have been excluded from the valuation of inter-industry and industry-institution transactions. These effects are shown separately in the row and columns headed 'Price Effects'. Row 38 presents estimates for the allocation of the estimated P16·4 million of CCA duties shown in column 38 between institutions and production activities. Row 39 gives estimates of locally-levied indirect taxes plus the additional price increases caused through inter-industry transactions. Column 39 represents the indirect taxes recouped by production activities through sales.

Flow of funds

The remaining entries in the matrix are financial transactions, both domestic and foreign. Rows 43–9 by columns 43–9 show interinstitutional capital transfers, largely on account of the sale and purchase of land. Rows 43–9 by columns 50–61 present the change in financial liabilities (increase positive) of domestic institutions, whilst their change in financial assets (increase also positive) are given in rows 50–61 by columns 43–9. For example, the cell at the intersection of row 46 and column 54 contains the figure P2·2 million. This represents an increase of P2·2 million in borrowing by the non-financial parastatals in the form of bank advances.

For each institution, gross savings plus the net increase in financial liabilities is equal to gross capital formation plus the net increase in financial assets. Financial claims must balance, because any increase in financial assets held by a particular sector will be matched by corresponding liabilities of another sector, either domestic or external.

Balance of payments entries

The matrix shows a current account balance of payments deficit of P69·4 million. Imports of goods and services and transfers of wages, interest, dividends, etc., abroad of P228·6 million were partly offset by exports of P159·2 million. The deficit was financed by increased financial liabilities to the rest of the world of P80·9 million (rows 40, 41, column 42) less an increase in assets held abroad of P11·5 million (row 42, columns 40, 41). The rest of the world increase in financial assets held in Botswana, equalling Botswana's increased financial liabilities abroad, comprise the remaining entries in column 42; the rest of the world's increase in liabilities in Botswana balance Botswana's increase in external assets in row 42.

Use of a SAM

Before turning to the specific application of the SAM to be considered in this paper, we should first consider its usefulness in more general terms. Probably the most valuable, immediate use of the matrix arises from the fact that it presents a summarized but comprehensive picture of the economy, showing the interrelationship between different aspects of economic transactions in production, consumption, investment and other real and financial flows. The effects of changes in key variables – either through planned policy decisions, for example, relating to wage changes, tax rates, etc., or as a result of events beyond the control of policy makers, for example, drought, foot and mouth epidemic, etc.–can be traced through the matrix. Provided that one operates within the framework of the matrix, the major and minor implications of these various exogenous changes are unlikely to be overlooked although it may remain difficult to calculate their precise numerical magnitude.

Once we start to consider the use of the matrix in this way we are moving to regarding the SAM not just as a set of accounting identities but as a basis for a model of the economy which can be manipulated alone or in conjunction with other types of models. Other data are available to planners to be used in conjunction with the SAM, for example, numbers of households/persons within each household group, numbers of employees within each category of employee, physical output levels, etc. The matrix could be regarded as supplying estimates of fixed coefficients for relationships throughout the economy. However, such an assumption could be unrealistic in many cases. There are a variety of ways to manipulate the matrix to avoid making such assumptions, such as making direct use of existing projections of future income and expenditure patterns, or employing econometric estimation techniques outside of the matrix such as the estimation of consumption functions for different types of households, and feeding the results back into the matrix. In this context the SAM forms a major input into a macro-economic model being developed by Botswana's Ministry of Finance and Development Planning.

A third, but important use of the SAM relates to statistical development. On the one hand, it provides a complete framework as a guide to the development of economic and various types of social statistics. In turn this should help to ensure that the surveys, and analyses of surveys undertaken by statisticians are of the types required and are used by economists and other planners. It also provides a powerful consistency check on data obtained from different sources which, at the minimum, identifies gaps in existing data and pinpoints areas where major errors apparently exist.

Analysis of the impact of the foot and mouth epidemic

This section is taken from a paper by Carol Hayden, 'The Botswana Economy: Some Analyses of the Impact of Foot and Mouth Epidemic', Warwick University, July 1978. A number of analyses based on the SAM, pertinent to policy decisions, are being undertaken at Warwick University at the request of the Botswana government. At present Botswana does not have the resources either to produce SAMs or to undertake sophisticated analyses, although it is intended that this capability will be developed following a final mission by ODM and university personnel to Botswana to produce a 1978–9 SAM. Subsequent SAMs will be developed by locally based CSO staff.

An outline of the effects of the epidemic

Figure 15.3 shows by means of a flow diagram the various sectors in the economy that would be affected by the epidemic, through the interrelationship of the different accounts of the SAM. The immediate effect of the epidemic is to reduce the throughput of cattle slaughtered by BMC. This obviously affects exports of cattle and reduces BMC's purchases of cattle from the agricultural sector. The stocks of meat held by BMC will fall and the physical stocks of live cattle will rise although the value of live cattle stocks will fall due to the disease.[3] Intermediate demand by BMC for inputs in the production process will fall, affecting both domestic industries and imports.

The reduction in sales of BMC and of the agricultural and other domestic production activities, will result in a fall in their value added thereby reducing factor incomes (wages, salaries, operating surplus). This will in turn mean a fall in institutional incomes, that is, current income of households, enterprises and government, due to both the reduction in factor incomes and any associated transfers, etc. A fall in institutional income will affect savings and consumption expenditure of households and, in turn, changes in consumption expenditure will affect both domestic final demand and imports.

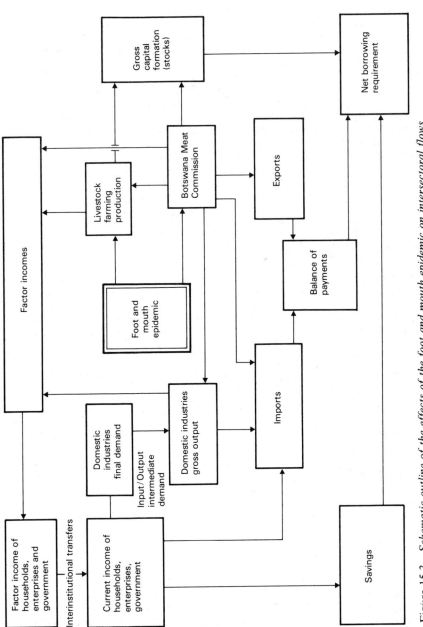

Figure 15.3 Schematic outline of the effects of the foot and mouth epidemic on intersectoral flows

The gross output of domestic production activities will be decreased due to both reductions in final demands of households and changes in intermediate demand due to the interdependence of certain domestic activities shown in the SAM Input/Output Matrix. The decrease in output of each domestic industry will in turn decrease factor incomes and the intermediate demand for imports. This decrease in factor incomes generates (second round) income effects on households and enterprises, all of which have consequential effects on taxes, transfers, expenditures and savings as were witnessed from the initial factor income decreases. This process continues indefinitely, but each reduction in income and spending is smaller than the previous one, until eventually the changes are too small to be significant.[4]

TABLE 15.1   *BMC throughput as percentage of normal (1974–5) levels*[5]

	Pessimistic scenario	Medium scenario	Optimistic scenario
Year 1 Nov. '77–Oct. '78	7	26	40
Year 2 Nov. '78–Oct. '79	0	78	79
Year 3 Nov. '79–Oct. '80	96	99	99

Methodology and assumptions

In any analysis of this type the conclusions are dependent upon various assumptions relating to affected variables. In respect of the foot and mouth epidemic major assumptions were required regarding the length and seriousness of the epidemic. To this end the Warwick University group was asked to analyse three scenarios with the following impact on the BMC's throughput of cattle. The proposed scenarios are shown below. At the time of writing the optimistic scenario seems the most appropriate approximation to reality and this paper draws upon the results for that scenario only. However, this does not devalue the importance of analysing effects under the alternative scenarios as these analyses demonstrate the likely range of effects of an epidemic, and are also relevant in considering alternative situations, for example, the effect of drought, a fall in beef prices, etc.

Other necessary assumptions related to prices and costs, BMC employment, livestock farming production functions, the value of BMC's and cattle owners' stocks and household behaviour relating to expenditure, transfers and savings in response to a fall in income during the epidemic. Details of the rationale behind, and the precise nature of these assumptions are to be found in the appendix of the original paper from which the extract is taken. The main assumptions will, however, be briefly outlined as notes to this extract where they are necessary to the understanding of the text.

Revised results could be produced by varying many of the assumptions, but the assumptions made were considered to be realistic and minor changes should only affect the results marginally, in comparison with the magnitude of differences in the impact of the epidemic according to the three scenarios relating to its length and seriousness.

The analysis covers three complete years starting with the initial closure of BMC on 1 November 1977. The results will be of the comparative equilibrium variety. That is we shall show what we consider to be the eventual overall effects of the epidemic for each complete year of duration, without alluding in any way to the length of each adjustment process within the year, since we have no basis for specifying the time it might take for the various stages to work themselves out.

It should also be noted that the current account results are shown separately for each year. The third year (Nov. '79–Oct. '80) contains eleven months when the epidemic is assumed to have been eradicated, with a return to normal throughput by BMC. However, although by the end of the third year the current account flows will be restored to near their pre-epidemic levels, the cumulative effects of the epidemic over the three years will be shown through the capital accounts of the institutions – the total borrowing requirement at this stage being the cumulative net change in liabilities over the three years. In other words, if the BMC, for example, were to run at a loss during the first two years, it would have to run down its reserves and increase its borrowing to cover those losses. So even if the BMC were back to 'normal' in the third year, it would still have an accumulated debt, on which interest and capital repayments would have to be made. Similarly, farmers who borrowed to help them through the crisis would also have debts to service, or reduced savings, when the crisis was over.

The results of the analysis

The immediate effects on BMC and the livestock farming industries

The immediate outcome of the foot and mouth epidemic is the reduction in exports of slaughtered beef due to the closedown or reduced throughput of the BMC. The fall in BMC's gross output has the consequence of reducing intermediate sales of cattle from the livestock farming industry to BMC,[6] along with other intermediate inputs into BMC's production process, namely, those of water and electricity and the wholesale and retail services.

The value added by all these production sectors is thus reduced, the estimated effects being shown in Table 15.2. The table shows that both the wages and salaries bill and the operating surplus of BMC would fall, the fall in the wage bill being mainly due to the assumed layoff of unskilled labour. Operating surpluses of the water and electricity and the wholesale and retail industries fall due to the reduction of their sales to BMC. The livestock farming industry's decrease in income from sales to BMC results wholly in a reduction in operating surplus for the freehold farms and in operating surplus and self-employed income for traditional farms. This is because farmers cannot reduce their production costs in the face of falling sales caused by the epidemic; on the contrary, their physical stocks of cattle are increasing because of this.

The effects on household income and domestic gross output

The changes in wages and salaries from BMC, together with the decrease in self-employed income and operating surplus from the traditional farms, and part of

Table 15.2 *Total changes in value added directly due to the foot and mouth epidemic (P million)*

Production activity factor payments	Pre-foot and mouth levels of value added	Year 1		Year 2		Year 3	
		Change	Total	Change	Total	Change	Total
BMC wages and salaries (01–05)	2·3	−0·8	1·5	−0·3	2·0	—	2·3
BMC operating surplus (inc. Dep.) 07–80	3·9	−1·9	2·0	+0·8[a]	4·7	+0·2	4·1
Freehold farms operating surplus (07)	3·7	−6·9	−3·2	−3·1	0·6	−0·2	3·5
Traditional farms – livestock self-employed (06)	26·9	−7·4	19·5	−3·4	23·5	−0·2	26·7
Traditional farms – livestock operating surplus (07)	9·8	−2·7	7·1	−1·2	8·6	−0·1	9·7
Water and electricity operating surplus	3·4	−0·4	3·0	−0·1	3·3	—	3·4
Wholesale and retail operating surplus	4·7	−0·7	4·0	−0·2	4·5	—	4·7

Note
[a] The positive change is due to the 10 per cent reduction in prices paid by BMC to cattle farmers outweighing the reduction in export earnings.

the operating surplus from freehold farms, result in decreases in household income.

This decrease is shown as '1st round change in factor income' in Table 15.4 and mainly affects rural households as would be expected, for the reduction in urban wages (from BMC) is very small when compared to the reduction in factor incomes from the livestock farming industries. However, during the epidemic, transfers from urban and migrant worker households to rural households are assumed to increase. The rural households that benefit from these are the 'less than 10 cattle', and the '10–80 cattle' households. The 'more than 80 cattle' households suffer a fall in transfer income, a large proportion of which is in the form of incorporated freehold farms' operating surplus that is attributable to 'other private' enterprises and subsequently transferred to these households. The above changes in factor and transfer income result in a new income level after the 1st round effect shown as 'Total 1st round change in income' (Rows 4, 10, 16) in Table 15.4. These lower income levels then result in a fall in both household savings[7] and consumption expenditure[8] which in turn affects both final demand for domestically produced goods (excluding agricultural produce)[9] and for imports. The fall in demand for imports is shown in Table 15.5. The effect on the gross output of domestic industries is shown in Table 15.4.

A direct consequence of the decreases in gross output is a decrease in the demand for both imports and factor services by domestic industries. The latter results in a further reduction in factor incomes, and therefore household incomes which is shown under '2nd round change in factor income' in Table 15.4. The income/expenditure loop repeats itself as above leading to 2nd round demand/gross output effects shown in Table 15.4.[10] These are added to the 1st round effects giving the total changes in household income and domestic gross output.

By looking at the household income results it can be seen that 'rural households with over 80 cattle' is by far the worse affected household group. This should be expected since virtually all their factor income is derived from cattle farming for export, unlike the other rural groups which also receive income from other agricultural (mainly crop farming) and non-agricultural production. However, for the same reason they are the group least hit by the second round factor income effects, these income reductions falling heaviest on the households of employees in the manufacturing, wholesale and retail and service industries. The fall in gross output of these industries accounts for approximately 88 per cent of the total fall in gross output due to changes in household demand.

Table 15.3   *Changes in gross output of domestic industries due to household demand effects*

	Year 1		Year 2	
Output changes	Δf	Δg	Δf	Δg
Round 1	−4·6	−5·1	−1·8	−1·8
Round 2	−0·2	−0·2	—	—
TOTAL CHANGE	−4·8	−5·3	−1·8	−1·8

Notes
1. There are no demand effects in Year 3 of the epidemic. Reductions in household income during this period are absorbed wholly by reduced savings or reduced imports.
2. We assume that prices do not change in response to changes in demand.
3. Δf – change in final (household) demand
   Δg – change in gross output.

The effects on the balance of payments current account

The balance of payments deficit is affected by a decrease in both exports (from BMC) and imports. Imports decrease due to reduced consumption expenditure by households (final demand) and to a fall in intermediate demand from both BMC and the domestic industries that experience a reduction in gross output due to a fall in household demand. These effects and the total effect on the balance of payments deficit can be seen from Table 15.5. During the first year,

Table 15.3 *Effects on total current household income (P million)*

Household Income	(09) Peri-urban	(10) High density housing	(11) servants quarters	(12) Medium density housing	(13) Low density housing	(14) Rural <10 cattle	(15) Rural 10–90 cattle	(16) Rural >80 cattle	TOTAL
Pre-foot and mouth income	10·9	23·6	4·0	13·4	19·8	36·3	44·6	27·1	202·7
Year 1									
1st round change in factor income	−0·2	−0·3	−0·1	−0·1	—	−2·2	−5·5	−5·7	−14·1
1st round change in transfer income	—	—	—	—	—	+1·7	+1·4	−3·7	−0·6
TOTAL 1st round change in income	10·7	2·3	3·9	13·3	19·8	35·8	40·5	17·7	188·0
2nd round change in factor income	−0·1	−0·3	−0·1	−0·1	−0·2	−0·3	−0·3	−0·1	−1·5
TOTAL year 1 income	10·6	23·0	3·8	13·2	19·6	35·5	40·2	17·6	186·5
Percentage of original	97·2	97·5	95·0	98·5	99·0	97·8	90·1	64·9	92·0
Year 2									
1st round change in factor income	−0·1	−0·1	—	—	—	−0·9	−2·6	−2·5	−6·2

1st round change in transfer income	—	—	—	—	—	+1·7	+1·4	-1·7	+1·4
TOTAL 1st round change in income	10·8	23·5	4·0	13·4	19·8	37·1	43·4	22·9	-97·9
2nd round change in factor income	-0·1	-0·1	—	—	—	-0·1	-0·2	—	-0·5
TOTAL year 2 income	10·7	23·4	4·0	13·4	19·8	37·0	43·2	22·9	197·4
percentage of original	99·1	99·2	100·0	100·0	100·0	101·9	96·9	84·5	97·4
Year 3 / 1st round change in factor income	—	—	—	—	—	-0·1	-0·1	-0·2	-0·4
1st round change in transfer income	—	—	—	—	—	—	—	-0·1	-0·1
TOTAL year 3 income	10·9	23·6	4·0	13·4	19·8	36·2	44·5	26·8	202·2
Percentage of original	100·0	100·0	100·0	100·0	100·0	97·7	99·8	98·9	99·8

the epidemic has the effect of considerably worsening the current balance of payments deficit. The pre-foot and mouth deficit was P69·4 million (1974–5) and this would be increased by P7·3 million (10·5 per cent) above what it otherwise would have been in year 1. This represents 4·6 per cent of pre-epidemic exports. It is worth noting that although the urban households have a far greater propensity to import, 75–80 per cent of the fall in direct imports by households is attributable to decreased demand by rural households. This is primarily because the income of the latter is much more heavily affected by the epidemic but also because we assume that consumption of domestic agricultural produce by rural households does not change.

Table 15.5   *Net changes in the balance of payments – current account (P million)*

Imports/exports	Year 1	Year 2	Year 3
Changes in exports			
BMC exports	−19·9	−7·0	−0·3
Changes in imports			
BMC intermediate demand	−0·7	10·3	—
Household (Hh) demand			
Round 1	−9·2	−4·9	−0·3
Round 2	−1·3	−0·4	—
Round 3	—	—	—
TOTAL Hh demand	−10·5	−5·3	−0·3
Intermediate demand (production activities)			
Round 1	−1·4	−0·6	—
Round 2	—	—	—
TOTAL intermediate demand (exc BMC)	−1·4	−0·6	—
TOTAL change in imports	−12·6	−6·1	−0·3
Net change in balance of payments deficit (exports-imports)	−7·3	−0·9	—

The government net revenue effects

The initial effects on the central government (current) account will arise out of the reduction in income from direct and indirect taxes. These are shown in Table 15.6. The majority of the reduction is due to the decrease in direct and indirect taxes from BMC, the remainder being attributable to direct taxes from other domestic enterprises which stem from the overall reduction in gross output/operating surplus.

Although central government receives direct taxes from households the majority of this revenue is from the 'medium and low density housing' urban groups. As these households suffer only a minimal drop in income this taxation is not much affected. Local authorities receive direct taxes mainly from rural households although at a fairly low rate.

The central government will also experience an eventual decrease in receipts under the Customs Union Agreement arising out of the decrease in imports. Our estimates of this area are also shown in Table 15.6. However, this effect would probably not be felt within the period of the foot and mouth epidemic, leaving central government 'savings', as shown in Table 15.7, to fall by the change in taxation receipts.

This 'savings' estimate can only be taken as representing the reduction in government current income. It does not allow for any changes in government current expenditure as these will be dependent on policy decisions and therefore cannot be quantitatively estimated at this stage. Increased expenditure by both central and local government under a number of categories such as veterinary measures, emergency cash grants to households, etc., would lead to a further fall in government savings.

It should be stressed that the above paragraphs only refer to the effects of the epidemic on the government's current account. Central government also has a major role to play in the management of the financing of the epidemic particularly in relation to the increased balance of payments deficit and the possible need for loan capital by BMC and the cattle farmers.

Table 15.6 *Changes in central government tax revenue and Customs Union Agreement receipts (P million)*

Govt. current account	Year 1	Year 2	Year 3
Change in indirect taxes (BMC)	−0·3	−0·1	—
Change in direct taxes			
BMC	−1·3	—	—
Other	0·2	0·1	—
TOTAL	−1·5	−0·2	—
Change in Customs Union Agreement receipts relating to year	−1·2	−0·6	—

Effects on savings of domestic institutions

Finally we can turn to the effect on the savings of households, enterprises and government. Estimates of such changes are shown in Table 15.7. It should be noted that there is likely to be no change in the savings of urban households, due to the relatively small reduction in their current income. Parastatal enterprises savings are affected owing to the reduction in BMC's operating surplus and, though to a far lesser extent, by the change in operating surplus of the water and electricity industry. The savings (retained profits) of 'Other private enterprises' fall due to the decrease in gross output of the relevant production activities. Central and local government savings fall due to the reduction in revenue from taxation.

The reduction in savings can now be used to determine the magnitude of the borrowing requirement of the various institutions during the epidemic.

Table 15.7 *Changes in savings and net profits of domestic institutions*

Institution	Pre-foot and mouth savings	Year 1 change	Year 2 change	Year 3 change	Accumulated total change
Households					
Rural <10	2·2	—	+0·8[a]	—	+0·8
Rural 10–80	8·0	−0·7	−0·2	—	−0·9
Rural >80	5·5	−1·9	−0·9	−0·1	−2·9
Total rural households	15·7	−2·6	−0·3	−0·1	−3·0
Other private enterprises	2·9	−1·5	−0·4	—	−1·9
Parastatal enterprises	1·7	−1·1	+0·7[b]	+0·2	−0·2
Local government	2·7	−0·1	—	—	0·1
Central government (ex CUA changes)	19·1	−1·8	−0·2	—	−2·0
TOTAL change in savings for all domestic insts.		−7·1	−0·2	+0·1	−7·2

Notes

[a]Savings increase as the transfer payments from urban households were assumed to be greater than the decrease in factor income.

[b]Savings increase as prices paid for cattle by BMC are assumed to remain at 10 per cent below pre-epidemic levels.

The financing of the epidemic

Our analysis has so far been concerned with the effects of the epidemic on the current accounts of the sectors of the economy. We have not considered any change in real capital flows and therefore have implicitly assumed that monetary finance has been forthcoming to meet the fall in savings and hence maintain unchanged the level of investment. Moreover, we have assumed that loans secured for this purpose will not be repaid[11] until after the full recovery period of the epidemic.[12] On such assumptions the monetary capital required to finance the epidemic would be equal to the decrease in savings over the three-year period as shown in Table 15.7.

The actual availability and nature of the necessary monetary finance cannot be estimated solely by this type of analysis. While part of the programme of financial relief may be met by the draw down of foreign exchange reserves[13] and increase of liabilities to the rest of the world, the Central Government and domestic financial institutions, for example, National Development Bank, commercial banks, will have a crucial role to play in the provision of financial credit to the affected sectors of the economy. The specific measures for credit expansion and diversion will necessarily depend upon the behaviour of financial markets in Botswana and on government policy decisions.

Conclusion

The Botswana SAM has been produced specifically for practical planning purposes and the justification for diverting scarce manpower resources into its preparation should be sought in terms of its usefulness. The analysis of the foot and mouth epidemic illustrates just one use to which it has been put. However, its full potential will only be realized after a time series of SAMs is developed, and after the reliability of certain estimates is improved. Little, if any, information is required for the SAM that is not needed for other purposes, although it does indicate current weaknesses in data and as such provides a good guide for statistical development. The most serious deficiency of the 1974–5 and 1976–7 SAM relates to household data (expenditure and, for urban households, income by source by household type) and this was to be remedied through surveys. The expenditure of manpower and other resources on producing the SAM is quite small (about 40 man-weeks for 1974–5 and only 15 for 1976–7), particularly when considered against the usefulness of the tool provided for planners.

Notes

1. The operating surplus of unincorporated traditional farms is transferred to rural households (only incorporated operating surplus goes to enterprise).
2. Household expenditure on sales of government goods and services, for example, education, veterinary fees and requisites, is shown in row 22b at intersection with columns 09–16.
3. It is difficult to estimate precisely the effect on livestock. The physical level will probably increase by the change in sales to BMC minus the cattle that die due to the disease. However, the *value* of this stock will decrease due to overgrazing, over-reaching peak time for slaughter, etc. We therefore assume no change in the yearly *change* in the level of stocks.
4. Until changes caused are too small to affect matrix entries, that is, changes of less than P0·5 million.
5. The yearly levels of throughput have been weighted for seasonal variations in BMC's throughput.
6. In addition to the physical reduction of sales, the price of intermediate sales of cattle from cattle farmers to BMC is assumed to be reduced by 10 per cent during the periods of reduced throughput.
7. Household savings are assumed to be maintained at a constant proportion to income for each household group.
8. Consumption expenditure of urban and migrant worker households also falls to balance the increases in transfer payments to rural households totalling P2·1 million.
9. We assume that expenditure for rural households on agricultural produce is constant.
10. The loop converges after the 2nd round, that is, changes are less than P0·05 million.
11. Including interest payments on such loans.
12. The end of year 3 (31 October 1980).
13. Due to the increased balance of payments deficit.

References

Greenfield, C. C., *Social Accounting Matrices and Developing Countries*, Ministry of Overseas Development, UK.

Greenfield, C. C., *The 1974–5 Social Accounting Matrix for Botswana*, Ministry of Overseas Development, UK.

Hayden, C. G., 'The Botswana economy: some analyses of the impact of foot and mouth epidemic', Department of Economics, University of Warwick, UK.

Hayden, C. G., 'Social Accounting Matrix, Botswana 1976/7 – report on the updating of the Botswana SAM', University of Warwick, UK.

For further reading:

Ministry of Finance and Development Planning, *Social Accounts Matrix, 1974/5*, Central Statistics Office, Gaborone.

Pyatt, F. G. and Roe, A. R., *Social Accounting for Development Planning*, ILO (1976).

Pyatt, F. G. and Thornbeck, E., *Planning Techniques for a Better Future*, ILO (1976).

Carol Hayden is a member of the Economics Department, University of Warwick; member of the Social Accounts Matrix Mission to Botswana.

Tony Williams is a statistician with the UK Ministry of Overseas Development. He was seconded to Botswana as a Research Statistician in the Central Statistics Office, Gaborone, between 1976 and 1977.

Index

STUDIES IN THE ECONOMICS OF AFRICA